Dreamweaver® CC

FOR

DUMMIES®

A Wiley Brand

Dreamweaver® CC

FOR DUMMIES®
A Wiley Brand

by Janine Warner

FOR DUMMIES®
A Wiley Brand

Dreamweaver® CC For Dummies®

Published by
John Wiley & Sons, Inc.
111 River Street
Hoboken, NJ 07030-5774
www.wiley.com

Copyright © 2013 by John Wiley & Sons, Inc., Hoboken, New Jersey

Published simultaneously in Canada

For general information on our other products and services, please contact our Customer Care Department within the U.S. at 877-762-2974, outside the U.S. at 317-572-3993, or fax 317-572-4002.

For technical support, please visit www.wiley.com/techsupport.

Wiley publishes in a variety of print and electronic formats and by print-on-demand. Some material included with standard print versions of this book may not be included in e-books or in print-on-demand. If this book refers to media such as a CD or DVD that is not included in the version you purchased, you may download this material at http://booksupport.wiley.com. For more information about Wiley products, visit www.wiley.com.

Library of Congress Control Number: 2013934756

ISBN 978-1-118-64614-4 (pbk); ISBN 978-1-118-65879-6 (ebk);
ISBN 978-1-118-65890-1 (ebk); ISBN 978-1-118-65894-9 (ebk)

Manufactured in the United States of America

10 9 8 7 6 5 4 3 2 1

About the Author

Janine Warner's best-selling books and videos about the Internet have won her an international following and earned her speaking and consulting engagements around the world.

She is also the founder and managing director of DigitalFamily.com, a full-service interactive design and training agency that offers web and mobile design, content strategy, and Internet marketing services.

Janine's skills as a "techy translator" helped her land the deal for her first book in 1996. Since then, she's written or coauthored more than 25 books, including *Web Sites For Dummies*, *Mobile Web Design For Dummies*, and every edition of *Dreamweaver For Dummies*. She has also created more than 50 hours of training videos about web design and content strategy for Lynda.com and Kelby Training.com.

Janine has taught courses at the University of Miami and the University of Southern California. She's also been a guest lecturer at more than 20 other universities in the United States and Latin America, and she helped create an Internet Literacy program for high school students in Central America.

She is a member of the TV Academy's Interactive Media Peer Group and has served as a judge in the Interactive Emmy Awards, the Knight News Challenge, and the Arroba de Oro Latin American Internet Awards.

In 1998, Janine's experience as a journalist and Internet consultant, combined with her fluency in Spanish, took her to *The Miami Herald* as Online Managing Editor. A year later, she was promoted to Director of New Media. She left that position to serve as Director of Latin American Operations for CNET Networks.

Since 2001, Janine has run her own business as an author, a consultant, and a speaker. Over the years, she's worked with one of Russia's largest publishing companies in Moscow; traveled to New Delhi to speak at Internet World India; and worked with media companies and other businesses in Colombia, Chile, Brazil, Panama, Costa Rica, Nicaragua, El Salvador, Mexico, and Spain.

When she's not traveling, she is based in Southern California, where she lives with her husband, David LaFontaine, manages DigitalFamily.com and occasionally takes a break to run on the beach.

Dedication

To all those who aspire to share their stories and passions on the web: May all your dreams come true.

Author's Acknowledgments

More than anything, I want to thank all the people who have read my books or watched my videos over the years. You are my greatest inspiration, and I sincerely enjoy it when you send me links to your websites. You'll find my e-mail address on my site at www.DigitalFamily.com.

Special thanks to David LaFontaine, my partner in all things digital and analog, whose patience and support keep me fed, loved, and (mostly) sane, even when I'm up against impossible deadlines.

For letting me feature their websites in this book, a heartfelt thanks to my friends and clients Laurie Ann Schag and Casey Stoll (www.Cinembargo.com), and James Kober (www.AssetShield.com).

Thanks to the entire editorial team on this book: Susan Pink for her attention to detail and quick turnaround on the editing, Jon McFarland for reviewing all the technical details, and Bob Woerner for shepherding this book through the development and publishing process (again and again and again).

Over the years, I've thanked many people in my books — family, friends, teachers, and mentors — but I have been graced by so many wonderful people now that no publisher will give me enough pages to thank them all. So let me conclude by thanking everyone who has ever helped me with a website, book, video, or any other aspect of the writing and research that goes into these pages. Okay, now I think I can go to sleep tonight without fearing that I've forgotten anyone. Thank you, thank you, thank you.

Publisher's Acknowledgments

We're proud of this book; please send us your comments at http://dummies.custhelp.com. For other comments, please contact our Customer Care Department within the U.S. at 877-762-2974, outside the U.S. at 317-572-3993, or fax 317-572-4002.

Some of the people who helped bring this book to market include the following:

Acquisitions and Editorial

Project Editor: Susan Pink

Acquisitions Editor: Bob Woerner

Copy Editor: Susan Pink

Technical Editor: Jon McFarland

Editorial Manager: Jodi Jensen

Editorial Assistant: Annie Sullivan

Sr. Editorial Assistant: Cherie Case

Cover Photos: Front cover image courtesy of Janine Warner; computer monitor © iStock-photo.com/MorganLeFaye; back cover images courtesy of Janine Warner

Composition Services

Project Coordinator: Sheree Montgomery

Layout and Graphics: Carrie A. Cesavice, Jennifer Goldsmith, Amy Hassos, Joyce Haughey

Proofreaders: Melissa Cossell, Lisa Young Stiers

Indexer: BIM Indexing & Proofreading Services

Publishing and Editorial for Technology Dummies

    Richard Swadley, Vice President and Executive Group Publisher

    Andy Cummings, Vice President and Publisher

    Mary Bednarek, Executive Acquisitions Director

    Mary C. Corder, Editorial Director

Publishing for Consumer Dummies

    Kathleen Nebenhaus, Vice President and Executive Publisher

Composition Services

    Debbie Stailey, Director of Composition Services

Contents at a Glance

Table of Contents

Introduction

*I*n the last few years, the Internet has experienced extraordinary growth and has gone through incredible changes. As more and more users access the web with smartphones, tablets, Apple TVs, dashboard-mounted touch-screens in cars, and even tiny head-mounted displays on Google Glass, web designers have been forced to design sites that work on devices from tiny mobile screens to giant television sets.

Simultaneously, the technologies that work best on the web are changing. The once popular design tool Adobe Flash is losing its audience because videos and animations created in Flash don't work on the iPad or iPhone. Fortunately, HTML5 and CSS3 (the latest flavors of the Hypertext Markup Language and Cascading Style Sheets, respectively), make it possible to add new design features and greater interactivity without the need for Flash.

I can't cover every detail of all these technologies in this book, but I do give you a solid introduction to modern web design. You discover how the newest features in Dreamweaver CC make it easier to create web pages that meet modern standards and adapt to all the screens used to view websites today.

In this fully updated version of *Dreamweaver For Dummies,* I added a new chapter to show you how to create responsive web page designs that adjust to fit different screen sizes, using Dreamweaver's fluid grid layout features.

Over the years, web design has evolved into an increasingly complex field, and Dreamweaver has evolved with it, adding features that go way beyond the basics of combining a few words and images. Adobe's dedication to keeping up with changing standards and adding new features with each new version is why Dreamweaver is such a popular program among professional web designers, as well as among a growing number of people who want to build sites for their hobbies, clubs, families, and small businesses.

In the 15-plus years that I've been writing about web design, I've seen many changes — from the early days (before Dreamweaver even existed) when you could create only simple pages with HTML 1.0, to the elaborate designs you can create with Dreamweaver today using HTML5, CSS3, jQuery, multi-media, and more.

If you're not sure what those acronyms mean yet, don't worry. I remember what it was like to figure out all this stuff, so I designed this book to introduce you to the basic concepts before you get into the more advanced features. To prepare you for the ever-changing world of web design, I show you how to use Dreamweaver to create websites that take advantage of the latest advances in web technology — including CSS3, covered in the Chapter 7, and responsive design, covered in the brand-new Chapter 8.

One of the challenges of web design today is that web pages are not only displayed on different kinds of computers but also downloaded to computers with monitors as big as widescreen televisions — or as small as the little screens on cell phones. As a result, creating websites that look good to *all* visitors is a lot more complex than it used to be — and standards have become a lot more important. This book shows you not only how to use all the great features in Dreamweaver but also how to determine which of those features best serve your goals and your audience.

About This Book

I designed *Dreamweaver CC For Dummies* to help you find the answers you need when you need them. You don't have to read through this book cover to cover, and you certainly don't have to memorize it. Consider this a quick study guide and a reference you can return to. Each section stands alone, giving you easy answers to specific questions and step-by-step instructions for common tasks.

Want to find out how to change the background color in page properties, design CSS style rules to align images, or add an interactive photo gallery with the Swap Image behavior? Jump right to the pages that cover those features. (Hint: the Table of Contents and index can help you find the sections that interest you most.) Don't worry about getting sand on this book at the beach or coffee spilled on the pages at breakfast. I promise it won't complain!

You find templates, artwork, and other goodies to use with this book at `www.DigitalFamily.com/bonus`.

Using Dreamweaver on a Mac or PC

Dreamweaver works almost identically on Macintosh or Windows computers. To keep screenshots consistent throughout this book, I've used a computer running Windows 7. However, I've tested the program on both platforms, and whenever I find a difference in how a feature works, I indicate that difference in the instructions.

Conventions Used in This Book

Keeping things consistent makes them easier to understand. In this book, those consistent elements are *conventions*. Notice how the word *conventions* is in italics? I frequently put new terms in italics and then define them so you know what they mean. It just makes reading so much nicer.

When I type actual *URLs* (web addresses) in regular paragraph text, they look like this: `www.digitalfamily.com`.

I also assume that your web browser doesn't require the introductory `http://` for web addresses. If you use an older browser, remember to type that quaint prefix before the address (also make sure you include that part of the address when you're creating links in Dreamweaver).

Even though Dreamweaver makes understanding HTML pages easier, you may want to wade into HTML waters occasionally. I include HTML code in this book when I think it can help you better understand how things work in Design view. Sometimes it's easier to remove or edit a tag in Code view than Design view. When I do provide examples — including filenames, file extensions, attributes, and tags, such as the following code that links a URL to a web page — I set off the HTML in monospaced type:

```
<a href="http://www.digitalfamily.com">Learn more about
        Dreamweaver at Janine's DigitalFamily website</a>
```

When I introduce you to a new set of features, such as options in a dialog box, I set those items apart with bullet lists so you can see that they're all related. When I want you to follow instructions, I use numbered step lists to walk you through the process.

What You're Not to Read

If you're like most of the web designers I know, you don't have time to wade through a thick book before you start working on your website. That's why I wrote *Dreamweaver CC For Dummies* in a way that makes it easy for you to find the answers you need quickly. You don't have to read this book cover to cover. If you're in a hurry, go right to the information you need most and then get back to work. If you're new to web design or you want to know the intricacies of Dreamweaver, skim through the chapters to get an overview — and then go back and read what's most relevant to your project in greater detail. Whether you're building a simple site for the first time or working to redesign a complex site for the umpteenth time, you find everything you need in these pages.

Foolish Assumptions

Although Dreamweaver is designed for *professional* developers, I don't assume you're a pro — at least not yet. In keeping with the philosophy behind the *For Dummies* series, this book is an easy-to-use guide designed for readers with a wide range of experience. If you're interested in web design and want to create a website, that's all I expect from you.

If you're an experienced web designer, *Dreamweaver CC For Dummies* is an ideal reference for you because it gets you working quickly with the program — starting with basic web-page design features and progressing to more advanced options. If you're new to web design, this book walks you through all you need to know to create a website, from creating a new page to publishing your finished project on the web.

How This Book Is Organized

To ease you through the learning curve associated with any new program, I organized *Dreamweaver CC For Dummies* as a reference. This section provides a breakdown of the four parts of the book and what you can find in each one. Each chapter walks you through the features of Dreamweaver step by step, providing tips and helping you understand the vocabulary of web design as you go along.

Part I: Getting Started with Dreamweaver CC

Part I introduces you to the basic concepts of web design as well as the main features of Dreamweaver. In Chapter 1, I give you an overview of the many approaches to web design, so you can best determine how you want to build your website before you get into the details of which features in Dreamweaver are best suited to any particular design approach. In Chapter 2, I start you on the road to your first website — including creating a new site, importing an existing site, creating new web pages, applying basic formatting, and setting links. To make this chapter more interesting and help you see how all these features come together, I walk you through creating a real web page as I show you how the features work.

In Chapter 3, I move on to graphics, with an introduction to creating graphics for the web, an overview of the differences in formats (GIFs, JPEGs, and PNG files), and detailed instructions for adding and positioning graphics in your pages. In Chapter 4, you discover Dreamweaver's testing and publishing features, so you can make sure that all your links work and that your website will look good in the most important web browsers. You also find everything you need to start uploading pages to the Internet.

Part II: Creating Page Designs with Style

Chapter 5 provides an overview of how Cascading Style Sheets work and how they can save you time. CSS has become *the* way to create page designs and manage formatting on web pages, and these features have been dramatically improved in Dreamweaver CC. In this chapter, you find descriptions of the style definition options available in Dreamweaver as well as instructions for creating and applying styles. In Chapter 6, I take you further into CSS, introducing you to the power of `<div>` tags, how to create CSS layouts, how to create centered CSS designs, and how to use Dreamweaver's newest CSS testing features. In Chapter 7, I show how Dreamweaver CC has more fully integrated some of the hot new design options, such as drop shadows and gradients, which were made possible by CSS3.

In Chapter 8, I introduce fluid grid layouts, which make it easier to create websites using a new technique called *responsive design*. The advantage of responsive design, sometimes called adaptive design, is that it enables you to create page layouts that adjust to different screen sizes so that they look as good on tiny smartphone screens as they do on giant desktop monitors. In Chapter 9, I cover the use of templates and Dreamweaver's Library items, which come in handy for commonly used elements, such as the copyright on all your web pages. In Chapter 10, I take a look at HTML Tables, and show where and how this time-honored technique is still relevant with modern web design.

Part III: Making Your Site Cool with Advanced Features

In Part III, you discover how cool your site can look when you add interactive images, audio, video, and drop-down menus. In Chapter 11, you find instructions for creating an interactive photo gallery with the Swap Image behavior, as well as how to use other features in Dreamweaver's Behaviors panel — including the Open New Browser behavior. In Chapter 12, you discover how great the Spry features are for adding AJAX interactivity to your site. You find instructions for creating and customizing drop-down lists, collapsible panels, and more. In Chapter 13, you find out what it takes to add multimedia to your web pages, including how to insert and create links to a variety of file types — from Flash to HTML5 animations, and video and audio files.

Part IV: The Part of Tens

Part IV features two quick references to help you develop the best websites possible. Chapter 14 provides a collection of online resources where you can register domain names and find hosting services, as well as a few services that can help you take care of more advanced challenges (such as setting up interactive forms and e-commerce shopping carts). In Chapter 15, you find ten ways to promote your website, from search engine optimization to social media and beyond.

Icons Used in This Book

This icon points you toward valuable resources on the web.

This icon reminds you of an important concept or procedure that you'll want to store away in your own memory banks for future use.

This icon signals technical stuff that you may find informative and interesting, though it isn't essential for using Dreamweaver. Feel free to skip over this information.

This icon indicates a tip or technique that can save you time and money — and a headache — later.

This icon warns you of any potential pitfalls — and gives you the all-important information on how to avoid them.

Where to Go from Here

To familiarize yourself with the latest in web design strategies and options, don't skip Chapter 1, which guides you through the many ways to create websites that you have to choose from today. If you're ready to dive in and build a basic website right away, jump ahead to Chapter 2. If you want to find out about a specific trick or technique, consult the Table of Contents or the index; you won't miss a beat as you work to make those impossible web design deadlines. Most of all, I wish you great success in all your web projects!

Occasionally, we have updates to our technology books. If this book does have technical updates, they will be posted at

dummies.com/go/dreamweaverccfdupdates

Part I
Getting started with Dreamweaver CC

For Dummies can help you get started with lots of subjects. Visit http://www.dummies.com/extras/dreamweavercc to learn more and do more with *For Dummies*.

In this part . . .

- ✔ Compare different layout techniques you can use in Dreamweaver.

- ✔ Explore the toolbars, menus, and panels that make up Dreamweaver's interface.

- ✔ Set up a website, create web pages, and add text, links, and meta data for search engines.

- ✔ Optimize web graphics, with instructions for using Photoshop (or Photoshop Elements) to covert images to GIF, PNG, and JPEG formats.

The Many Ways to Design a Web Page

1

*I*n the mid-1990s, learning to create websites — and teaching others how to do it — was easy. Almost 20 years and as many books later, the process has become much more complex. I've come to realize that one of the first things to understand about web design is that there isn't just one way to create a website anymore.

In this chapter, I being with an introduction to the many ways you can create a website and the tools Dreamweaver offers to make those designs possible. I also introduce you to the basics of HTML and how websites and browsers work. At the end of this chapter, you find a quick tour of the Dreamweaver CC interface to help you get comfortable with the workspace.

Comparing Static and Dynamic Sites

Websites fall into two very broad categories: static sites, which are generally built with a program such as Adobe Dreamweaver, and dynamic sites, which combine advanced programming with a database to generate web pages dynamically.

A *static site* is like a unique book, where each page has been created by hand. The process can be compared to illuminated manuscripts, where monks toiled for years and each page was an individual work of art. Static websites are made up of a collection of individual pages with the `.html` or `.htm` extension. You might think that all websites are made up of individual pages (and in a way they are), but with a static site, each page is saved as a separate file.

In contrast, a *dynamic site* works more like a warehouse full of words, images, videos, and colors with a super-fast clerk who can run at light speed through the aisles, grabbing items and assembling them into pages as you read them. With a dynamic site, the pages you view in a web browser are created as they are delivered to the browser, so they're not saved as individual pages but as pieces of pages that can be mixed and matched. That gives dynamic sites many advantages, but it also makes them a lot more complicated to create. On a large website such as Amazon.com, for example, this dynamic process makes it possible for Amazon to create a page with recommended books for you that looks different from the page it recommends to me, even though we're both entering the same URL into a web browser.

If you're just creating a simple profile or small business site, go with a static site. Dynamic websites are often not worth the extra effort, unless you're creating a site that you expect to grow to 100 pages or more.

Although you can create custom dynamic websites in Dreamweaver using popular technologies such as PHP or ASP.NET, most programmers who are creating sites with Amazon.com levels of complexity use more advanced programming tools, such as Eclipse or Microsoft Visual Studio.

I used to teach the basics of dynamic site creation in Dreamweaver, but today better options exist. Instead of reinventing the wheel by creating their own dynamic site system with Dreamweaver, many web designers are using a content management system (CMS), such as WordPress and Drupal.

Following are some of the most popular content management systems:

- ✔ **WordPress** (`www.wordpress.org` or `www.wordpress.com`): One of the most popular and powerful blogging tools, WordPress is increasingly used as a CMS for more complex sites. You'll find many great extensions for WordPress. After a site is built, teaching people to use the administrative tools to update the site (even if they don't know HTML) is relatively easy, making this an especially popular tool among web designers who are creating sites that they want their clients to be able to update themselves.

- ✓ **Joomla!** (www.Joomla.org): Joomla! offers many of the features of WordPress. Joomla! is a good choice for magazine-style sites and directories because it enables you to create categories and subcategories far more easily than in WordPress.

- ✓ **Drupal** (www.drupal.org): Designed by programmers for programmers, Drupal offers more advanced functionality for creating highly complex, interactive websites. Sites where security is a concern (such as the sites for the U.S. State Department, Congress, or many universities) often use Drupal. Drupal is a powerful CMS, but the learning curve is steeper than for WordPress or Joomla!.

You can use Dreamweaver to create and edit templates for any of the content management systems listed here. Before you do, however, you have to set up a web server on your local computer. You learn more about how to work with these programs in the section, "Working with Templates in Dreamweaver," later in this chapter.

If you're interested in learning more about WordPress, check out *WordPress For Dummies,* 5th Edition, by Lisa Sabin-Wilson (Wiley).

Most of this book is dedicated to helping you create static websites — but that doesn't mean you can't get many of the same benefits of dynamic sites, including the capability to update pages quickly. As you find in this book, you can combine Cascading Style Sheets, or CSS (covered in Chapters 5–8), with Dreamweaver's .dwt template features (covered in detail in Chapter 9) and get many features of a big-budget website without all the complicated programming skills. (You find a general description of Dreamweaver's template features, as well as a look at the differences among templates, later in this chapter.)

Static pages work well for small- and medium-sized websites, such as a professional profile or online gallery. Because static web pages are written in plain text, you can create them in a program as simple as Notepad or SimpleText, although tools such as Dreamweaver make designing pages a lot easier because you don't have to remember all the cryptic HTML tags.

A static website offers a few advantages, especially if you're just starting out. A static website

- ✓ **Is easy to learn to develop:** Anyone who can resize a photo has a head start on the skills needed to create and arrange graphic elements on a static page.

- ↙ **Gives you complete control over the design of each page:** You can tweak the size, colors, fonts, and arrangement of the elements on each page individually, and you can edit templates for these kinds of sites more easily than the templates for dynamic sites.

- ↙ **Is easy to build, test, and publish to a web server:** You can create and test static web pages on any personal computer and then host them on any commercial web server — and you need only FTP access (built in to programs such as Dreamweaver) to publish pages to the Internet.

Working with Templates in Dreamweaver

The term *template* is used in different ways for different kinds of design work (on and off the web), but essentially a template is a shortcut in the design process. By working with Dreamweaver templates, you can set or adjust almost any aspect of a site's design or functionality, including a header, logo, navigation bar, or sidebar. Whatever you include in a Dreamweaver template, you can then apply to any new page based on the template, which automatically applies the settings you want to appear throughout your site. Moreover, if you want to adjust the overall settings in your site, you can make those updates once in the template, update your pages, and — voila — all pages based on the template are updated automatically.

But not all templates are created equally. Although they all share those basic characteristics, many kinds of templates are in use on the web today. For example, templates for static websites (which you find instructions for creating in Chapter 9) are quite different from the kinds of templates you would use if you were creating a blog with WordPress.

You can download many kinds of templates from the web, but they don't all work in all programs. For example, if you download templates designed for Adobe Flash, you won't be able to use them in Dreamweaver (although you can insert Flash files in Dreamweaver, as you discover in Chapter 13).

You can edit many kinds of templates in Dreamweaver. Before you start using Dreamweaver to create or edit templates, however, it's helpful to better understand how they are different. The following sections cover two of the most common types of templates in use on the web today (and what you should know about how they differ). See the nearby sidebar, "So many Dreamweaver template options," for a complete list of template options.

Creating and editing Dreamweaver templates

Dreamweaver templates (extension .dwt) offer many advantages without requiring advanced programming skills. When you create Dreamweaver templates with the .dwt extension, you can use HTML and CSS to create static websites that include many of the high-end features found on dynamic sites — such as the capability to create new pages quickly and to update every page in your site with the click of a button.

Although you can use Dreamweaver to create templates that use advanced programming (such as PHP or Java), the .dwt Dreamweaver template is a much simpler option that's ideal for small- to medium-size websites — which is why I've dedicated much of Chapter 9 to making the most of Dreamweaver templates.

Editing WordPress, Joomla!, and Drupal templates

Templates like the ones you get with a blogging program such as WordPress use the extension .php because they're written in the PHP (Hypertext Preprocessor) programming language. Although you can create PHP pages and templates in Dreamweaver and use them for more than just WordPress, these types of files are far more complex to create than .dwt Dreamweaver templates.

Because so many people use WordPress (such as the blog shown in Figure 1-1) and so many sites offer WordPress template downloads, many people are confused about why WordPress templates don't work in Dreamweaver in the same way that .dwt Dreamweaver templates work.

So many Dreamweaver template options

Dreamweaver supports many kinds of technologies, as well as the templates that go with each. When you create new pages in Dreamweaver by choosing File➪New, you have the option of creating a blank page or a blank template. When you create a simple HTML template, Dreamweaver uses the .dwt extension. Dreamweaver also supports Microsoft ASP and ASP.NET, and you can create templates using either ASP JavaScript or ASP VBScript (both of which use the .asp extension) — or you can use ASP.NET C# or VB (which use the .aspx extension). The templates for a site created using Java end in .jsp. And if you use Adobe's ColdFusion technology, your templates end in .cfm.

The big lesson is this: Make sure you have the right kind of template for the kind of site you're creating — and rest assured that Dreamweaver supports just about any kind of technology you can use to create a website.

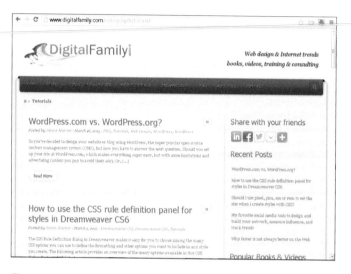

Figure 1-1: I used WordPress to create this blog on my DigitalFamily.com site.

WordPress templates offer many of the same benefits as Dreamweaver templates — except that templates for blogs such as WordPress draw their content from a database. As a result, they include HTML and CSS (as do the Dreamweaver templates), plus much more complicated code in the PHP programming language, which describes how content from the database should be displayed in a web page.

As a result, to make WordPress, Joomla!, or Drupal templates work in Dreamweaver, you must first set up your computer as a web server and install MySQL and WordPress. Because so many people are using these programs, you can get all the software you need in one nifty package from MAMP.com (for Mac) and XAMP.com (for Windows). You will find links to these tools, as well as instructions for using them to set up your computer as a web server, at www.digitalfamily.com/tutorials/set-up-a-testing-server-on-your-computer/.

Assessing Other Web Design Tools

People who just want to set up a web page as quickly and simply as possible can turn to services that offer what designers call a "website in a box." Web-based services such as SquareSpace, Sitegrinder, and Zenfolio provide templates you can use to design your site and as well as basic customization, usually for a monthly fee.

Although this approach works for simple sites, these services often promise more than they deliver, especially when it comes to customization or adding new features. Your site may also be vulnerable: If the service ever changes their business model or goes out of business, you can be left at their mercy.

In contrast, Dreamweaver enables you to create a completely custom website and host it on your choice of hundreds of hosting services. If your hosting service raises rates or goes out of business, you can simply move your site to a new host.

Understanding How to Build a Website in Dreamweaver

In a nutshell, building a website involves creating individual pages and linking them to other pages. You need to have a *home page,* the first page visitors see when they arrive at your web address (also known as your URL), and that page needs to bring them into the rest of the pages of the site, usually with links to each of the main sections of the site. Those pages, in turn, link to subsections that can then lead to deeper subsections.

After you create a website, you can test all the links on your own hard drive and then upload the pages to a web server when everything is ready and working well. You can read more about setting up a site and using Dreamweaver to create pages on your local computer in Chapter 2. In Chapter 4, you discover how to upload your pages to a web server when you're ready to publish your site on the Internet.

The most important thing to remember is that you need to create a folder on your local computer that will mirror your website on your web server when you publish your site. The site setup process in Chapter 2 is so important because it sets up Dreamweaver to help you create these two versions of your site: the version you create and edit on your computer and the copy you need to maintain on the web server.

Although you have to save all the files in your site in one main folder, you can create subfolders to organize the site. Thus, a key part of planning a website is determining how to organize the pages of your site into sections and how those sections should link to one another. Dreamweaver makes creating pages and setting links easy, but how you arrange the pages and links is up to you.

 If you're just planning to create a small website, you may think you don't need to worry about how your site will grow and develop. Think again. All good websites grow, and the bigger they get, the harder they are to manage. Planning the path of growth for your website before you begin can make a tremendous difference later. Neglecting to think about growth is probably one of the most common mistakes among new designers. This oversight becomes even more serious when more than one person is working on the same site. Taking a little time to organize the structure of your site, and developing a few consistent conventions for tasks such as naming files, can make everything else go more smoothly.

Managing your site's structure

Managing the structure of a website has two sides: the side that users see, which depends on how you set up links, and the side that's behind the scenes, which depends on how you organize files and folders.

What the user sees

The side that the user sees is all about design and navigation. When users arrive at your home page, where do you direct them? How do they move from one page to another in your site? A good website is designed so that users navigate easily and intuitively and can make a beeline to the information most relevant to them. As you plan, make sure that users can

- Access key information easily from more than one place in the site
- Move easily between pages and sections
- Return to main pages and subsections in one step

Setting links is easy in Dreamweaver; the challenge is to make sure that those links are easy for visitors to follow. One of the best ways to ensure that visitors can easily move around your site is to create on every page of your site a navigation or menu bar that includes links to the main pages of your site. You find instructions in Chapter 6 for creating a menu bar with CSS. In Chapter 12, you find out how to use Dreamweaver's jQuery UI features to create interactive menus with tab groups and collapsible panels. And in Chapter 9, you find instructions for using Dreamweaver's template and library features, which make menus easier to include on your pages — as well as faster to update if you add or change a menu link later.

What's behind the scenes

The second side to managing your website structure happens behind the scenes (where your users can't see the information, but you want some kind of organizational system to remember what's what). Before you begin designing and linking the pages in your site, think about how to keep track of all the text, images, animations, and other files that make up your site. At minimum, consider the following:

✔ **A file-naming system:** For example, naming image files consistently can make them easier to find if you need to edit them later. For example, if you use thumbnail images as well as bigger versions, give both files similar names to make it easier to match them later. An easy way to do that is to add *th* to the thumbnail versions, like this: `bird.jpg` and `bird-th.jpg`. Similarly, giving the main section pages in your site names that match the text of the links on your pages can make setting the links easier. For example, if the navigation bar on your home page includes an About Us page and a Contact page, you can easily figure out what page a link should point to if your pages are named `aboutus.html` and `contact.html`.

✔ **A folder structure:** When your website grows past a handful of pages, organizing them in separate folders or directories can help you keep track. Fortunately, Dreamweaver makes this easy by providing a Files panel where you can see all the files of your site — and even move and rename files and folders (see Chapter 2 for more on how to use Dreamweaver's Files panel).

Exploring HTML, XHTML, and HTML5

Contrary to popular belief, HTML isn't a programming language. Rather, it's a *markup* language: That is, HTML is designed to mark up a page, or to provide instructions for how a web page should look. HTML is written by using *tags*, which are markup instructions that tell a web browser how to display the page. For example, to apply italic formatting to text, you (or Dreamweaver) insert the HTML tag <em>, which stands for emphasis, where you want the italics to begin and end. Most tags in HTML include both an open tag and a close tag, indicated by the forward slash /. Thus, to make the name of this book appear in italics, I would write the code like this:

```
<em>Dreamweaver CC For Dummies</em>
```

Another challenge of HTML is that the tags have changed over time, and so has the acronym. When I'm referring to the code in a general way, I use the acronym HTML, but the two most popular versions of HTML today are really called XHTML and HTML5.

XHTML, a stricter version of HTML, is still in use on a majority of websites. HTML5, which has garnered lots of hype, is the newest version, and most forward-thinking designers or people who are redesigning older sites are moving to HTML5. Although HTML5 hasn't been officially approved as a standard, most of the new tags introduced in this latest version are already supported by the latest versions of all major web browsers.

You have two ways to see what the code behind a web page looks like:

- In most browsers, choose View⇒Source.

- If you're using Dreamweaver (as shown in Figure 1-2), you can click the Split button (upper-left corner of the workspace) to see the code and the design areas of the program at the same time in *Split view*.

If you want to see only the code, click the Code button. However, while I'm working on the site design, I find Split view is a useful way to keep an eye on what's going on behind the scenes — and, as a bonus, you can learn a lot of HTML as you go along. Split view also makes it easy to find code related to a specific element or section of text. In Figure 1-2, for example, I've selected the headline in Design view, and Dreamweaver automatically highlighted the same text in Code view, making it easy to see that the headline is formatted with the <h1> tag.

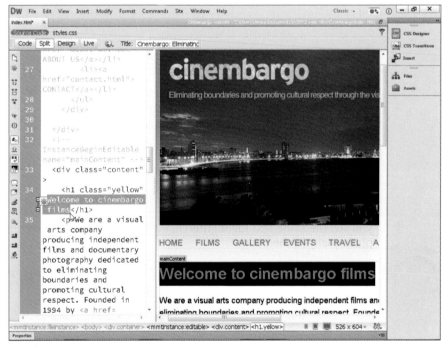

Photos by Casey Stoll

Figure 1-2: Use Split view in Dreamweaver to display the page design and the code behind the page.

How web browsers work

Web browsers such as Internet Explorer, Firefox, Chrome, and Safari are designed to decipher HTML, CSS, JavaScript, and other code — and display the corresponding text, images, and multimedia on a computer screen. Essentially, browsers read the code in a web page and interpret how to display the page to visitors. Unfortunately, because web browsers are created by different companies and the code they display has evolved dramatically over the years, not all web browsers display web pages the same way. Differences in browser display can lead to unpredictable (and often frustrating) results because a page that looks good in one browser may be unreadable in another. For more information on browser differences and testing your pages to make sure they look good to all your visitors, see Chapter 4.

Dreamweaver offers four view options:

- **Code view:** In Code view, you see only the HTML and other code.
- **Split view:** In Split view, the page is divided so you can see the code in one part of the workspace and a view of how the page should be displayed in a web browser in the other part.
- **Design view:** In Design view, you see only the page as it should be displayed in older web browsers.
- **Live view:** In Live view, you get a more accurate preview of how your pages will look in the latest web browsers, and you get an interactive view, where you can test rollovers and other interactive features without having to leave Dreamweaver and launch another program.

In Dreamweaver's Split view, the Code and Design views are integrated. If you select something in Design view — say, the headline shown in Figure 1-2 — you see the same text highlighted in Code view, enabling you to find your place easily in the code.

Here are a few points to help you better understand the similarities and differences among older versions of HTML as well as XHTML and HTML5:

- **All versions of HTML include tags that are designed to be hierarchical.** Examples are the <h1> (heading 1) through <h6> (heading 6) tags, which are ideally suited to formatting text according to its importance on a web page. Reserve the <h1> tag for the most important text on the page, such as the top headline. The <h2> tag is ideal for subheads or secondary headings, <h3> for the third level of headings, and so on. A headline formatted with the <h1> tag looks like this:

```
<h1>This is a headline</h1>
```

⮑ **HTML5 adds new tags.** HTML5 adds a collection of tags designed to make webpages more *semantic*, or more meaningful. New tags, including `<header>` and `<footer>`, can be used to identify the type of content in a webpage.

⮑ **XHTML tags must be written in lowercase.** HTML5 and older versions of HTML are not case sensitive.

⮑ **In XHTML, all tags must include the closing slash.** A few tags can stand alone, such as the `<br />` tag, which adds a line break. As a rule, XHTML tags must have a close tag, even if there's only one tag, and the close tag must always contain a forward slash (/). Thus the line break tag is `<br>` in HTML and `<br />` in XHTML.

⮑ **Some tags are more complex, and the open and close tags don't always match.** More complicated tags, such as the tags used to create links or insert images into pages, are more challenging to use because they include link information, and the close tag doesn't always match the open tag. For example, the code to create a link to another website looks like this:

```
<a href="http://www.digitalfamily.com">This is a link to
        DigitalFamily.com</a>
```

At their heart, all versions of HTML are just text — and believe it or not, you can write HTML in a plain-text editor as simple as Notepad, SimpleText, or TextEdit. However, you have to be careful to type all the code perfectly because there is no room for error or typos in HTML. After writing code yourself, even to create a simple page, you're sure to appreciate how wonderful it is to let Dreamweaver write the code for you.

If (at first glance) you think that HTML code looks like hieroglyphics, don't give up too quickly. With just a little practice, you can start to recognize at least the most common tags, such as `<h1>` (heading 1) tag used to format the headline shown in Figure 1-3.

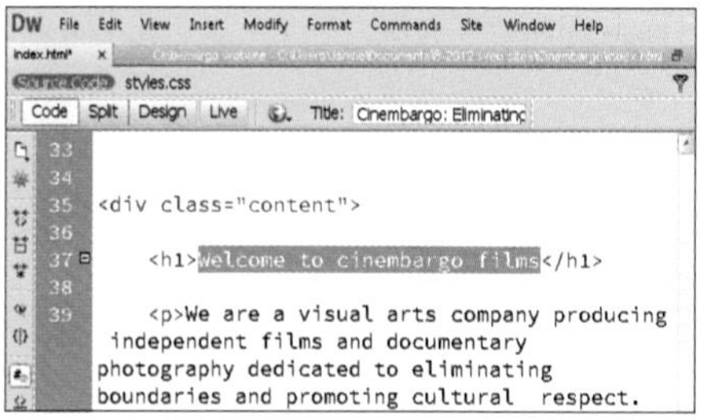

Figure 1-3: A heading 1 tag highlighted in Code view.

Comparing Tables, Frames, and Layers

If you've already done a little web design, you may be wondering what happened to some of the old ways of creating web page layouts. For years, web designers used the HTML feature called tables to create page layouts. Then frames came along, and many people were excited by the capability to display multiple pages in one browser window (which frames and iFrames make possible). Then came layers, which were especially popular among designers because they seemed to offer precise design control.

Today, most professional designers agree that the best way to create a web page design is to use HTML with Cascading Style Sheets, which are covered in detail in Chapters 5–7. In Chapter 8, you find out how to use Dreamweaver's new fluid grid layouts to combine one HTML file with multiple sets of style sheets to create responsive designs that work well on both small mobile screens and large monitors.

Over the years, all these other options have become less desirable except in a few special cases. In this section, you find a quick review of when tables, frames, and layers may still be useful.

Creating page designs with HTML tables

In the early days of web design, most page layouts on the web were created with tables. By merging and splitting table cells and even adding background images, designers created complex web designs. CSS expands upon this concept by adding many new design options — including the capability to add precise margins and padding around elements, which offers better control of how and where background images appear.

Figure 1-4 provides an example of an old-school site created with the HTML table tag. Most designers turn off table borders by setting the table border to 0 to create cleaner layouts, but in Figure 1-4, I've set the borders to 2 pixels so you can see the outline of the table. Table cells surround each of the photos and captions in this two-column layout; I've merged the columns at the top of the design to make room for the banner image, which spans the full width of the page.

Photos by Janine Warner

Figure 1-4: In the old days, complex web page designs used HTML tables to control text and image placement.

Although tables are no longer recommended for creating page layouts, they're still considered the best way to format tabular data like that you'd find in a spreadsheet program. You can use tables to format a consistent collection of information — such as the table listing the winners of the chocolate game, as shown in Figure 1-5. (You find out how to create tables to format tabular data, like the table shown in Figure 1-5, in Chapter 10.)

Although I recommend that you redesign sites like the one shown in Figure 1-4 with CSS and <div> tags, I do understand that some designers still find it easier to create layouts with tables, and not everyone has time to redesign their websites right away. I have to admit, I've been guilty of leaving online a few sites designed with tables long after I knew better. I recommend using only CSS today for all your web page layouts — except when you're creating a layout for tabular data. Even then, I still urge you to use CSS to add any styling (such as background colors or padding) that you might want in your tables.

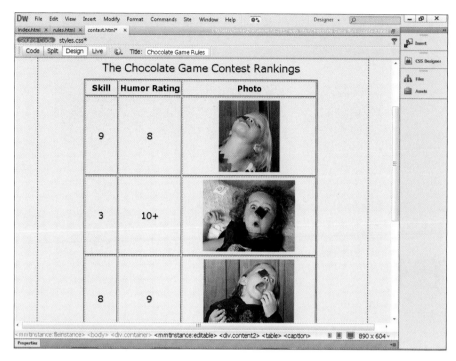

Photos by Janine Warner

Figure 1-5: Tables are still the best way to display tabular data in columns and rows.

Considering design options with HTML frames

You won't find any instructions in this book for creating websites that use frames, such as the website about flamingos shown in Figure 1-6. Frames enable you to display multiple web pages in one browser window. Although frames are still used on a few sites on the web, most designers don't like them because they can make navigation confusing to site visitors.

Frames are also problematic because when you use frames, the URL at the top of a web browser does not change, even when you click links and change the pages displayed within the frames. As a result, you can only *bookmark* (create a link to) the first page of a site that uses frames. Worse yet, search engines have a hard time properly indexing a site designed with frames — which can diminish your site's search engine ranking.

Figure 1-6: Frames enable you to display multiple web pages in one browser window.

For all these reasons, Adobe removed the features that supported frames in Dreamweaver CC. If you discover that a website you're redesigning was created with multiple pages displayed in one browser window, I suggest that you redesign the site to remove the use of frames. Using CSS is a far better way to create page layouts today.

Appreciating the Benefits of Cascading Style Sheets

The concept of creating styles has been around since well before the web. Desktop publishing programs (such as Adobe InDesign) and even word processing programs (such as Microsoft Word) have long used styles to manage the formatting and editing of text on printed pages. In a word processor, you can create and save styles for common features, such as headlines and captions. In print design, styles are great timesavers because they enable you to combine a collection of formatting options (such as Arial and bold and italic) into one style — and then apply all those options at once to any selected text in your document, using only a single style. The advantage is that if you change a style, you can automatically apply the change everywhere you've used that style in a document.

On the web, you can do all that and more with CSS — because you can use style sheets for more than just text formatting. For example, you can use CSS to create styles that align images to the left or right side of a page, add padding around text or images, and change background and link colors. You can even create more than one style sheet for the same page — say, one that makes your design look good on computers, another for cell phones, and a third for a printed page.

For all these reasons (and more), CSS has quickly become the preferred method of designing web pages among professional web designers. One of the most powerful aspects of CSS is that it enables you to make global style changes across an entire website. Suppose, for example, that you create a style for your headlines by redefining the <h1> tag to create large, blue, bold headlines. Then, one fine day, you decide that all your headlines should be red instead of blue. If you aren't using CSS, changing all your headlines could be a huge undertaking — a matter of opening every web page in your site to make changes to the font tags around every headline. But if you're using CSS in an external style sheet, you can simply change the style that contains for-matting information for the <h1> tag in the style sheet and all your headlines turn red automatically. If you ever have to redesign your site (and believe me, every good site goes through periodic redesigns), you can save hours (or even days) of work if you created your design with CSS in the first place.

A website designed with CSS separates content from design. Keeping the con-tent of your site (such as the text and headings) separate from the instruc-tions that tell a browser how the content should look benefits both you as a designer and your site visitors. Here are some of the advantages:

  ✔ **CSS simplifies design changes.** CSS styles can be saved in the header section at the very top of an HTML page, or they can be saved in a sepa-rate file that can be attached to multiple HTML pages. Either way, if you use a style to format many headlines, you can make formatting changes by simply editing the style.

  ✔ **Separating content from design enables you to create different style sheets for different audiences and devices.** Today's websites are as likely to be viewed on giant, wall-size screens as they are to be seen on screens small enough to hide in the palm of your hand during a lunch date. CSS enables you to create web page designs that are more adapt-able so they look good on big *and* small screens, as well as everything in between.

    As you get more advanced with CSS, you can even create multiple style sheets for the same web page. For example, you can create one that's ideally suited to a big computer monitor, another that's designed to get the best results when the page is printed, and yet another designed with a larger font size for anyone who may have trouble reading the small print that's so common on web pages.

 ✓ **Using CSS makes your site comply with the current standards.** Today, the W3C, which sets standards for the Internet, recommends using CSS for nearly every aspect of web design because the best CSS designs are accessible, flexible, and adaptable.

 ✓ **Websites designed in CSS are accessible to more visitors.** Today, a movement is growing among some of the best designers in the world to get everyone to follow the same standards, create websites with CSS, and make sure sites are accessible to everyone.

 When web designers talk about *accessibility,* they mean creating a site that anyone who might ever visit your pages can access — including people with limited vision who use special browsers (often called *screen readers*) that read web pages aloud, as well as many others who use specialized browsers for a variety of other reasons.

 If you work for a university, a nonprofit, a government agency, or a similar organization, you may be required to create accessible designs. Even if you're not required to design for accessibility, know that pages that meet accessibility standards also tend to score better in search engine rankings because accessible designs also enable search engines to access and interpret site content more easily.

In Chapters 5 and 6, you find an introduction to creating styles and page designs with CSS. In Chapter 7, you find an introduction to some of the new features introduced in CSS3. In Chapter 8, you find out how to use the latest web design techniques to create responsive designs that work on small mobile screens as well as large monitors by targeting multiple style sheets based on the size of the browser window.

Understanding Browser Differences

HTML was created to share information in a way that could be displayed on every computer on the planet — one of the greatest advantages of the web. However, for web designers, this advantage is also a challenge because not all those computers use the same browsers, the same fonts, or the same monitor size. On top of that, a lot of older web browsers that can't display the latest web features are still in use and even newer browsers don't all display pages that use those features in the same way. So before you start creating web pages, know that no matter how carefully you create your designs, your pages will never look exactly the same to every possible visitor to your site.

If you want to create page designs using the latest technology and reach the broadest possible audience, pay special attention to Dreamweaver's Live view, browser preview, and compatibility features — and be prepared to move on to training that's more advanced than this book. Entire books and websites are dedicated to teaching you how to create highly complex CSS layouts that are displayed well on various computers and browsers — and to combining CSS and other special code to make complex pages look good in older and newer web browsers.

In Chapter 4, you find more information about browser differences, as well as Dreamweaver's testing and compatibility features, which can help ensure that your pages work well for a broad audience.

Introducing the Dreamweaver CC Workspace

Dreamweaver can seem a bit overwhelming at first. You can easily get lost with so many features spread among so many panels, toolbars, and dialog boxes. If you prefer to build an understanding by poking around, have at it (and feel free to skip to Chapter 2, where you start building your first web page). If you want a tour before you get started, read this last section, which introduces you to the interface and gives you a quick overview of the features in this powerful program.

When you launch Dreamweaver, the Welcome screen, shown in Figure 1-7, appears in the main area of the program (and reappears anytime you don't have a file open, unless you close the Welcome screen by selecting the Don't Show Again option). After you select an option on the Welcome screen (these options are explained in Chapter 2), Dreamweaver creates a new blank HTML page in the main workspace, the main area of the program where you design your page. The *workspace* consists mainly of a Document window, which displays the page you're working on and is where you add text, images, and other elements that will appear on your web pages. The *Document window* is surrounded by a collection of panels, toolbars, and menus that provide easy access to Dreamweaver's many features. Details of these controls follow.

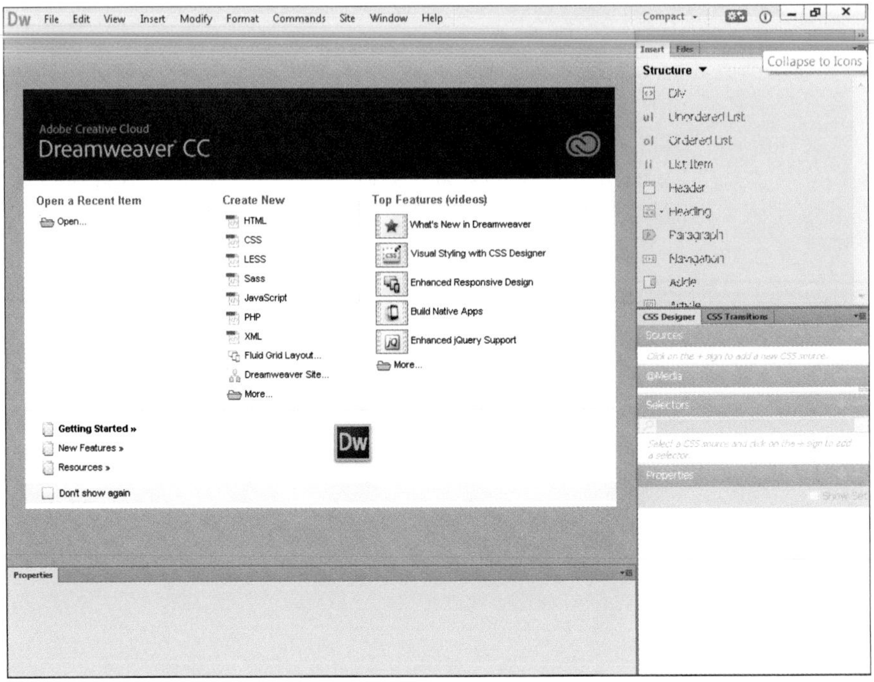

Figure 1-7: When Dreamweaver opens, the Welcome screen provides easy access to commonly used items, such as recently opened files.

Changing workspace layouts

One of the bigger changes in Dreamweaver CC is the simplification of the various workspace layout choices. In the past, many choices were available from the layout drop-down list (located in the top right of the workspace). In Dreamweaver CC, most of the layouts, which were designed to meet the different work styles of programmers and designers, were removed. The layout drop-down list has been reduced to just two workspace layouts: Classic and Expanded. However, you're not limited to these two ways of using Dreamweaver. Almost every panel and toolbar in Dreamweaver CC is highly customizable, making it easy to change the workspace to best match the way you work. And because you can save your own workspace layouts, many designers create multiple layouts, each optimized for different tasks.

You can create your own custom layout by following these steps:

1. **Open, close, move, or resize any of the panels, toolbars, inspectors, and other features in Dreamweaver's workspace.**

2. Choose Window⇨Workspace Layout⇨New Workspace.

The Manage Workspaces dialog box opens.

3. In the Manage Workspaces dialog box, give your new workspace a name and click OK.

Your custom workspace is added to the layout drop-down list, so you can easily reset the program to match your favorite settings.

The name that the layout drop-down list displays matches the last layout you chose and used. If your last choice was Classic, it says Classic; if your last choice was a custom layout you named My Layout, it says My Layout.

If you move a panel or an inspector and then want to return it to the location you saved in the layout, click Reset [layout name] in the layout drop-down list. Dreamweaver will restore the workspace to match the layout you saved.

Create a collection of workspace layouts optimized for common tasks, such as creating and applying CSS, or working with database content, and save them so you can easily arrange the program to best suit your preferences.

The menu bar

As with most programs you've used, the menu at the top of the screen provides easy access to most program features, including the options you find in the Insert bar, Property inspector, and panels, as well as a few others that are available only from the menu.

The Document toolbar

Across the top of the workspace — just under the menu bar and document tabs, and just above the workspace — is the Document toolbar. Here you find the following options:

✓ **Code, Split, Design, and Live views:** This series of options controls how Dreamweaver displays a document that's open in the Document window. Code view displays only the code editor, Design view displays only the visual editor (which hides the code), Split view cuts the page in half and displays both the Code and Design views. *Note:* In Split view, you can drag the edge of the Document window to reveal more or less of the code.

Live view, the newest view option, displays a preview of how the page will appear in the latest versions of the Safari and Chrome web browsers, which display most of the new CSS3 and HTML5 options not supported by many older web browsers. The Safari and Chrome web browsers and the Dreamweaver Live view feature are built on webkit, the open-source browser engine. When Live view is selected, a Refresh button is added to the toolbar that looks like a circle with an arrow in it. The Refresh button works like the refresh button in a web browser and can be used to reload the contents of the Document window.

✔ **Live Code:** Available only when Live view is activated, the Live Code option displays both Code and Design views with the Live preview activated.

✔ **Inspect button:** Available only when Live view is activated, the Inspect option helps you identify and troubleshoot CSS by highlighting the styles that apply to any element you select in the page.

✔ **Preview/Debut in Browser:** Provides quick access to a drop-down list of all the web browsers you can use to preview a page open in the Document window. Choose Edit Browser List, at the bottom of the drop-down list, to add more browsers (see Chapter 4 for detailed instructions).

✔ **Title field:** Displays the *page title,* which is the text that appears at the top of a browser window when a page is displayed. The title page text also identifies the page when bookmarked.

The Document window

The big, open section in the main area of the workspace is the Document window, which is where you work on new and existing pages.

If you use the Classic workspace layout, the Document window is displayed in Split view, showing the code on the left and the Design view on the right. To change the Split view from left-right to top-bottom, choose View➪Split Vertically to deselect the Split Vertically option (which is selected by default in version CC). If you want to hide the code to focus only on your design, click the Design view button in the Document toolbar.

The docking panels

The docking panels are located to the right of the work area .The docking panels display a variety of features, including the following:

✔ **The CSS Designer panel** displays the style sheets, media queries, selectors, and properties associated with any page open in the Document window.

✔ **The Insert panel** is described in detail in the following section.

✔ **The Files panel** displays all the files and folders in a site.

✔ **The CSS Transitions panel** displays a list of all transitions as well as the New Transition panel, to allow you to animate elements on your page using CSS3.

You work with the panels in the following ways:

✔ **To open and close panels,** double-click the gray bar. Or single-click a specific tab in a panel to open or close it.

✔ **To move panels anywhere on the screen,** click the dark gray bar at the top of the panel and drag it to the desired location.

✔ **To display more panels,** select the panel name from the Window menu.

✔ **To expand or collapse all the visible panels at once,** click the double arrow just above the top-right corner of the topmost panel, as shown in Figure 1-8.

✔ **To expand or collapse a single panel when the panel collection is collapsed,** click the name of the panel.

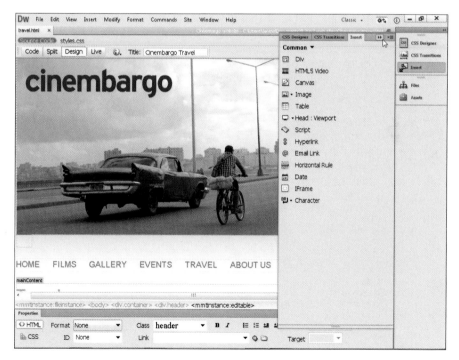

Photos by Casey Stoll

Figure 1-8: Expand or collapse all the panels at once by clicking the double arrow at the top-right corner of the topmost panel.

The Insert panel

The Insert panel, located at the top of the panel section, includes eight *subcategories,* each with a different set of icons representing common features. Click the small arrow to the right of the name to access the drop-down list and switch from the buttons of one subcategory to the buttons for another. The options are

- **Common Insert panel:** Displays icons for many of the most common features, including links, tables, and images

- **Structure Insert panel:** Displays Div, List, Paragraph, and Navigation options (essential for creating page layouts)

- **Media Insert panel:** Allows you to simply and quickly insert Edge animations, HTML5 video, or multimedia plug-ins

- **Forms Insert panel:** Features the most common form elements, such as radio buttons and boxes

- **jQuery Mobile panel:** Displays options for adding jQuery functionality to web pages that are intended to be viewed on mobile devices

- **jQuery UI panel:** Allows you to insert common jQuery functions, such as a progress bar, a slider, or an accordion menu that expands or collapses

- **Templates Insert panel:** Displays common functions that allow you to create or edit templates

- **Favorites Insert panel:** Enables you to right-click (Windows) or Control-click (Mac) to add any icons from the other Insert bar options as a favorite, so you can create your own collection of favorite features, such as symbols for foreign currency or even ASP functions

At the end of the drop-down list is the option that controls the display of the list of options in the Insert panels:

- **Hide Labels/Show Labels:** Enables you to display the names of the Insert panel features next to each icon, or to remove the names

The Property inspector

The Property inspector is docked at the bottom of the workspace in Dreamweaver. If you prefer, you can click the gray bar at the top of the inspector and drag it to detach it so it floats in the workspace. You can move the inspector anywhere on the screen or you can drag and dock it in the panel group. When you dock the Property inspector with the other panels, you can expand and collapse it just as you would any other panels.

To restore the inspector to its location in the saved workspace, choose Window⇨Workspace Layout⇨Reset [layout name]. (I rather like that the Property inspector is handy but out of the way, at the bottom of the screen.)

The Property inspector displays the *properties,* or options, for any selected element on a page, and it changes based on what's selected. For example, if you click an image, the Property inspector displays image properties. If you click a Flash file, the Property inspector displays Flash properties.

For many elements, the Property inspector is split into two sections, one for HTML features and the other for CSS. Use the CSS and HTML buttons on the left side of the Property inspector (as shown in Figure 1-9) to switch from one to the other. (You find detailed instructions for how to use these two modes of the Property inspector in Chapters 5–7.)

Figure 1-9: The status bar and the Property inspector in CSS mode.

The Property inspector is divided into top and bottom parts. If the bottom part is not open, as shown in Figure 1-9, double-click in the bottom-right corner of the inspector to reveal additional attributes, such as the image map options when a graphic is selected. Double-click the gray bar at the top of the inspector to close and open the entire inspector.

The status bar

The status bar is located at the bottom of the Document window and just above the Property inspector, as shown in Figure 1-9. As with the workspace layout list, the status bar has been simplified, and some features that users of previous versions of Dreamweaver may have grown accustomed to, have been removed. The status bar includes access to a number of features that control the display of a page in Dreamweaver's workspace:

✔ **Tag selector:** On the far left of the status bar, as shown in the top of Figure 1-9, you find the tag selector, which displays the HTML tags and CSS rules that apply to any selected element on the page. In Figure 1-9, the cursor is inside a text block that's formatted with the <h1> tag, which is inside a `<div>` tag with a `#container` ID, which is inside the `<body>` tag.

- *Clicking* any tag in the tag selector selects the tag and its contents in the workspace.

- *Right-clicking (Control-clicking on a Mac)* a tag opens a pop-up menu with options to add, edit, or remove tags and CSS rules.

✓ **Mobile, Tablet, and Desktop Size buttons:** These buttons provide a quick view of what your web design might look like when viewed using one of these three platforms. The results are not exact: So many possible screen resolutions exist that your computer screen couldn't hold buttons for them all.

Changing preference settings

The more you use Dreamweaver, the more you're likely to appreciate how readily you can customize its features. Remember that you can always change the workspace to better suit the way you like to work, and you can easily alter Dreamweaver's preference settings using the Preferences dialog box.

To open the Preferences dialog box, choose Edit➪Preferences on a Windows computer, or Dreamweaver➪Preferences on a Mac. Dreamweaver includes 19 categories in the Preferences dialog box and makes it possible to change the appearance, default settings, and many other options throughout the program.

Opening and Creating Sites

In This Chapter

▷ Starting with the site setup process

▷ Creating new web pages

▷ Inserting and formatting text

▷ Creating links

▷ Adding search engine keywords to meta tags

*W*hether you're building a new site or need to make changes to an existing site, this chapter is the place to start. Here you discover an important preliminary step: the *site setup process* that enables Dreamweaver to keep track of the images and links in your site. After you set up your website in Dreamweaver, you're ready to create web pages. (You find instructions for creating a page, inserting text and images, and setting links in this chapter, too.) But whatever you do, don't skip the first step of defining a site — the process takes only a minute or two.

Although you can use Dreamweaver without doing this initial site setup, you run the risk of breaking links when you publish your site using the built-in FTP features. Other features, such as templates, automated link checking, and the library, won't work at all if you don't first define each site in the Site Setup dialog box, covered in this chapter.

The best approach to web design with Dreamweaver is to first create a website on your computer's hard drive. If you're working on an existing site, start by copying it to your computer's hard drive. (In Chapter 4, you find detailed instructions for downloading an existing website from a web server.) Then you can edit your site, add pages, and set links, in the privacy of your own computer and use Dreamweaver's preview options to test your work before you publish it on the Internet. When you're ready, you can use Dreamweaver's built-in publishing features to transfer your site (or individual pages of your site) to a web server.

A *web server* is a computer with a permanent connection to the Internet and special software that enables it to communicate with web browsers, such as Internet Explorer and Firefox. Find detailed instructions for previewing and publishing a website in Chapter 4.

Setting Up a New or Existing Site

To set up a site in Dreamweaver, you need to store all your site's resources in one main folder or directory on your hard drive. Dreamweaver calls this folder the *local site folder,* and when you set up a new site, you essentially just identify that folder in Dreamweaver. The site setup process is a crucial first step because all the elements of your site must remain in the same relative location on your web server as they are on your hard drive for your links, images, and other elements to work properly. Identifying the local site folder on your computer and keeping all images, text, and other files in your website in that one main folder help Dreamweaver set all your links properly and ensure that they still work when you publish your site to a web server (which you find out how to do in Chapter 4).

In earlier versions of Dreamweaver, the local site folder was called the local root folder and the site setup process was called the site definition process.

The Site Setup dialog box also contains a category called Servers (accessible by a link on the left side) where you can set up your site to use Dreamweaver's file transfer features, including its FTP (File Transfer Protocol) capabilities to transfer files from your computer to a web server (and vice versa). FTP is a common method of copying files to and from computers connected across a network, such as the Internet, and one of the most popular options for publishing a website online. To keep things simple for now, you can skip all the categories except the Site category covered in the section that follows. In Chapter 4, you find detailed instructions for using Dreamweaver's FTP and other publishing features, as well as instructions for downloading an existing website hosted on a remote web server.

If the site setup process seems a little confusing at first, don't worry. Site setup is a quick, relatively painless process that you must do only once for each site. After you've set up a site in Dreamweaver, the site is stored in the Files panel, where you can easily load the site into Dreamweaver whenever you want to work on it. You can set up one site or many sites in Dreamweaver.

Whether you're creating a site or working on an existing site for the first time, the following steps walk you through the process of defining the *local site folder,* a folder where you store all the images, text, and other files in your site:

1. **Choose Site⇨New Site.**

   The Site Setup dialog box appears.

2. **On the left side of the dialog box, click the Site category.**

   When you open the Site Setup dialog box, the Site category should be selected by default. This dialog box contains three other categories (shown in Figure 2-1), where you can manage server connections and other options, but you don't need to open these categories to complete the basic site setup process.

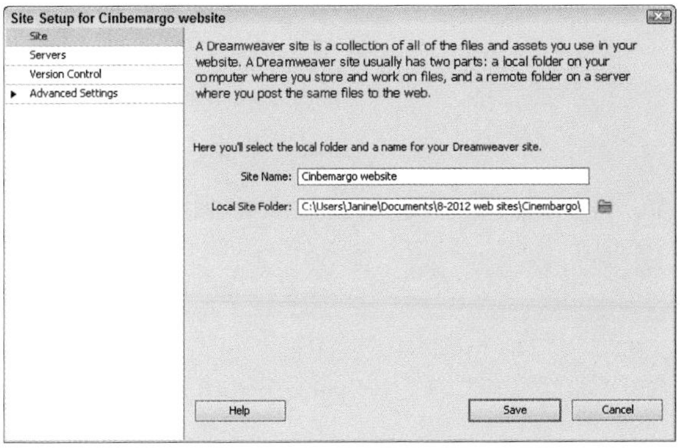

Figure 2-1: Use the Site Setup dialog box to identify the local site folder for any new or existing website.

3. **In the Site Name text box, type a name for your site.**

   You can call your site whatever you like; this name is used only to help you keep track of your sites in Dreamweaver. Many people work on more than one website. The name you enter here is listed in the Files panel, where you select which site you want to work on in Dreamweaver. (The next section discusses moving among sites using the Files panel in more detail.)

4. **Click the Browse (file folder) icon, which is next to the Local Site Folder text box, and browse your hard drive to locate the folder you want to serve as the main folder for all the files in your website.**

If you're working on an existing site, select the folder that already contains the files for that site. If you're creating a site, you can create a new folder as follows:

- **In Windows:** Click the Create New Folder icon at the top of the Choose Root Folder dialog box.

- **In Mac OS X:** Click the New Folder icon at the bottom of the Choose Root Folder dialog box.

The goal is to simply select the folder so that Dreamweaver can identify where all the files and folders for your site will be stored. When you've completed this step, the name of the folder and the path to that folder's location on your hard drive appear in the Local Site Folder field.

5. **Click Save to close the Site Setup dialog box and save your settings.**

If the folder you selected as your local site folder already contains files or folders, all the files and folders in your site are displayed in the Files panel. As you see in Figure 2-2, I already had many files in my personal profile site, which I'm using as the example in this chapter, so they're listed in the Files panel. If I were creating a new site with a new empty folder, the Files panel would contain only the main site folder.

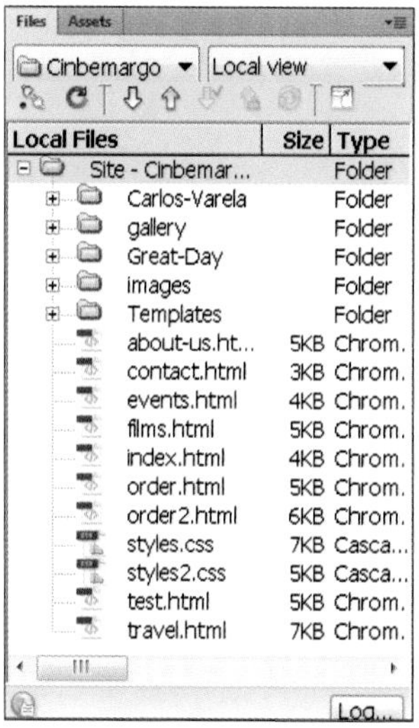

Figure 2-2: When site setup is complete, the files and folders are displayed in the Files panel.

Switching among Sites

You can set up as many sites as you like in Dreamweaver and change from one site to another by selecting the site name in the Files panel. To load a different site into the Files panel, use the drop-down arrow next to the site name and choose the name of the site you want to display. If you're editing more than one website in Dreamweaver, make sure you switch to the site you want so that it's displayed in the Files panel.

In Figure 2-3, I'm selecting the Cinbemargo website from a list of sites I've defined in Dreamweaver. When you select a site, the files in that site replace the ones of any currently open site in the Files panel.

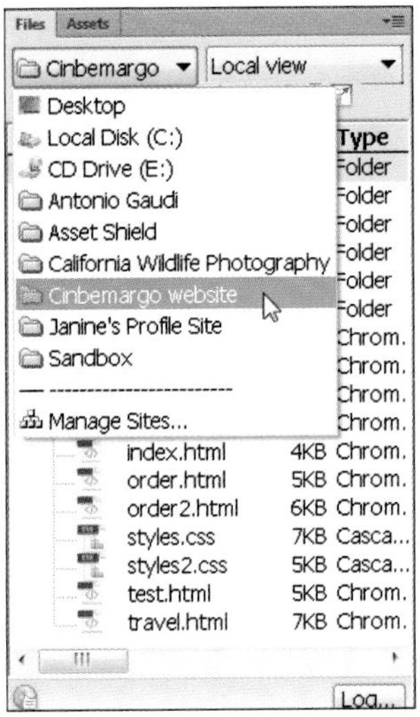

Figure 2-3: Use the drop-down list in the Files panel to choose among defined sites.

Managing Sites in Dreamweaver

After you complete the site setup process covered in the preceding exercise, you can make changes and additions to the site setup by choosing Site⇨Manage Sites to open the Manage Sites dialog box, as shown in Figure 2-4.

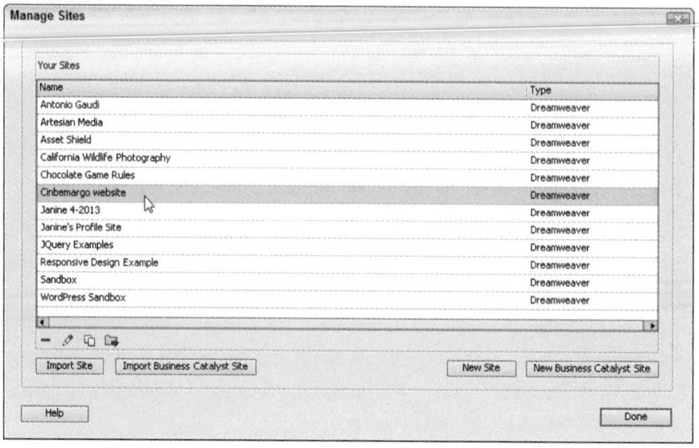

Figure 2-4: You can edit any site setup by selecting it from the Manage Sites dialog box.

To edit a site that you've already set up, select the name of the site in the Manage Sites dialog box, and then click an icon at the bottom left of the dialog box to make changes. Your options using the icons, from left to right, are as follows:

- ✔ **The minus sign icon** deletes a site from the Manage Sites dialog box. When you delete a site from the list, you don't delete the site's files or folders from your hard drive; you simply remove the site setup in Dreamweaver.

- ✔ **The Edit icon** looks like a pencil and opens the site in the Site Setup dialog box, where you can change the name by replacing the text in the Site Name field and change the local site folder by clicking the Browse icon (which looks like a file folder) and selecting a different folder. In Figure 2-4, I selected the Cinbemargo site.

- ✔ **The Duplicate icon** (the third icon from the left) makes a copy of the site setup but does not make a new copy of the files and folders of the site on your hard drive. To make a copy of all files in a website, duplicate the site folder on your hard drive (outside Dreamweaver), just as you'd make a copy of any other folder or file on your computer.

- ✔ **The Export icon** (the fourth icon from the left) exports the site setup definition. Similar to the duplicate option, the option does not create a copy of the files in the site. Instead, the Export icon exports the .ste file, which can be used to share site setup information from one computer to another. This feature is especially useful if you've set up the web server information as part of your site setup, which is covered in Chapter 4.

At the bottom of the Manage Sites dialog box, you find four buttons:

- **Import Site:** The Import Site button lets you import a `.ste` file to add site setup information to Dreamweaver.

- **New Site:** Click this button to define a new site. (The process is the same as choosing Site⇨New Site, as explained in "Setting Up a New or Existing Site," earlier in this chapter.)

- **Business Catalyst buttons:** You also find two buttons specifically for importing and creating new sites using Adobe's Business Catalyst service. Business Catalyst is a hosted web service that extends the features of Dreamweaver to include advanced features, such as a shopping cart e-commerce service. You can learn more about this optional service at `www.BusinessCatalyst.com`.

Creating Pages

Every website begins with a single page. Visitors are first greeted by the front page — or *home page* — of your site, and that page is usually a good place to start building.

Dreamweaver makes creating pages easy: You can work from the Welcome screen or use the New Document window, which provides more options. The following sections explain both methods, and you find details about the best names to use for new pages so that they'll work well when you publish your site to the web.

Starting from the Welcome screen

When you open Dreamweaver, a Welcome screen greets you with shortcuts to many handy features for creating pages in a variety of formats:

- The left column provides a list of shortcut links to recently opened files. Click the name of any file in the list to open the file in Dreamweaver.

- If you want to create a simple, blank web page, choose HTML from the Create New list in the middle column (see Figure 2-5). Remember that choosing HTML doesn't mean that you have to write the HTML code yourself. Rather, you're just telling Dreamweaver that you want to create a page written only with HTML, not with one of the more complex technologies, such as PHP. You still have the option to work in the code editor or the design editor and let Dreamweaver write the underlying HTML for you.

- Choose one of the other page format options under New to create a CSS, JavaScript, PHP, XML, or other more complex file type.

- The Top Features (videos) list on the right side of the dialog box includes links to a collection of video tutorials where you can learn more about Dreamweaver's most popular features.

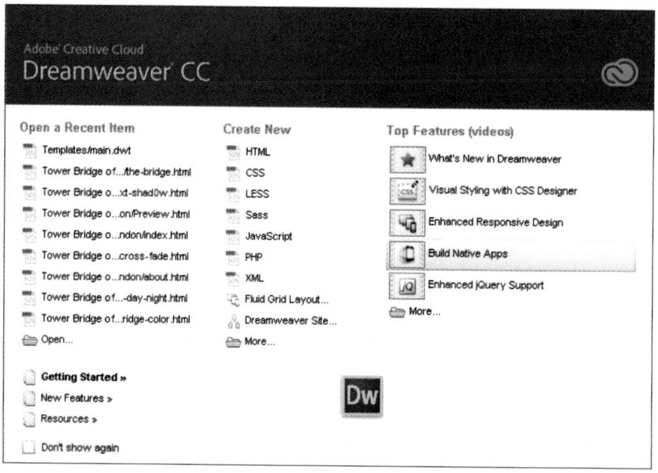

Figure 2-5: View a list of shortcuts for creating files or opening pages.

 If you prefer not to use the Welcome screen, you can turn it off by selecting the Don't Show Again check box in the bottom-left corner. If the Welcome screen is not visible, you can turn it back on by choosing Edit⇨Preferences (Windows) or Dreamweaver⇨Preferences (Mac), and then selecting the first check box in the General settings next to Show Welcome Screen.

Creating an HTML page with the New Document window

You can also create a new HTML page by using the New Document window, which offers more options than the Welcome screen, including access to any templates you've created with Dreamweaver (covered in Chapter 9) as well as a collection of predesigned layouts, which can give you a head start on your designs.

You can create many kinds of files using the New Document window, and you can mix and match the options. This versatility can be confusing at first because you have so many choices. In Dreamweaver CC, this dialog box was simplified so that you need to choose only one option from each of the three sections.

To create a new HTML page, follow these steps:

1. **Choose File⇨New.**

   The New Document window opens, as shown in Figure 2-6. In the first section, on the far left, you choose the type of page you want to create:

   - **Blank Page:** Choose this option to create HTML pages, as well as pages in the more complex PHP or JSP format.

   - **Fluid Grid Layout:** This option opens the fluid grid layout features, which you can use to create responsive web designs that adjust to different screen sizes automatically. These features are covered in Chapter 8.

   - **Starter Templates:** If you create templates using Dreamweaver's `.dwt` template format, you can create pages based on those templates using this option. Templates are covered in Chapter 9.

   - **Site Templates:** Choose this option to create customizable mobile web app designs using jQuery Mobile. To learn more about creating mobile web apps with jQuery, read *jQuery For Dummies* by Lynn Beighley.

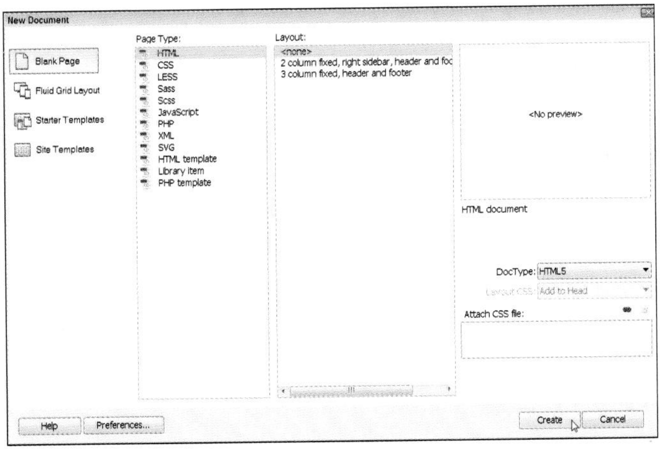

Figure 2-6: The New Document window offers many options when you are creating a file.

2. **From the left side of the screen, select Blank Page.**

3. **In the Page Type list, select HTML.**

4. **In the Layout section, choose <none>.**

   The layouts are included to provide a head start on designing HTML pages with CSS. How to create pages using these layouts is covered in Chapter 6.

5. **If you want to change the document type, use the drop-down list next to DocType.**

   By default, Dreamweaver CC creates pages using HTML 5, which most designers consider the best option for web pages today. If you're working on a site that uses an earlier version of HTML, such as XHTML 1.0 Transitional, make sure to change this setting.

6. **Click Create, in the bottom right of the window.**

   The New Document window closes, and a new blank page is created and opened in the workspace.

   Note: If you're using a Macintosh, the Create and Cancel buttons are swapped.

7. **Choose File⇨Save to save your page and give it a filename.**

   Dreamweaver automatically names all new files Untitled, followed by 1, 2, and so on in the order created. I *highly* recommend that you get in the habit of giving your files names that have more meaning to you. Also note that filenames in websites should not include spaces or special characters (although the hyphen and underscore are okay). For more on how best to name files and folders in your website, see the upcoming sections "Naming new page files" and "Naming the first page index.html."

   Get in the habit of saving new web pages in your local site folder as soon as you create them, even though the pages are still blank. As you create links or add images to your pages, Dreamweaver needs to be able to identify the location of your page within your site folder. Although Dreamweaver sets temporary links until your page is saved (and will give you a warning about this when it does), saving a page first is best because many Dreamweaver features won't work until a page is saved.

Naming new page files

Over the years, I've received many e-mail messages from panicked web designers because of broken links caused by filename conflicts. These problems usually don't occur until after a website is published on a server, so they can be especially confusing and difficult to understand. If you're publishing your website to a web server that runs on a Mac or under Windows, the following may not apply to you. But if you're using a web server that runs Unix or Linux (used by many commercial web-hosting companies), the following instructions are especially important. If you're not sure, be safe and follow these rules when you save web pages, images, and other files on your site:

✔ **Include an extension at the end to identify the file type.** Examples include `.html` for HTML files and `.gif` for GIF images. Dreamweaver automatically adds the `.html` file extension to the end of HTML files, which works for most web servers. However, in the rare case that you need to change the extension to `.htm` for your web server, you can do so in Dreamweaver's Preferences dialog box by choosing Edit➪Preferences (Windows) or Dreamweaver➪Preferences (Mac). See the "Displaying file extensions in Windows" sidebar for tips on how to view file extensions, which are hidden in Windows.

✔ **Don't use spaces or special characters in filenames.** For example, don't name a web page with an apostrophe or spaces, such as `cat's meow page.html`. If you want to separate words, you can use the underscore (_) or the hyphen (-). For example, `meow-page.html` is a fine filename. Numbers are okay in most cases, although it's best not to start a file name with a number. Capital letters generally don't matter, but most designers stick with lowercase. Doing so keeps filenames consistent and makes setting and checking links easier because the name of the file and its reference in any links must match.

Displaying file extensions in Windows

When you view pages in Windows Explorer, you won't see the file extension of your GIFs, JPEGs, or HTML pages (although these extensions will be displayed in the Files panel in Dreamweaver) unless you change the settings on a Windows computer. To change the settings so that you can see extensions in Windows Explorer, open the Folder Options dialog box, as shown in the figure, choose the View tab, and then look through the long list of options and deselect Hide Extensions for Known File Types. How you open the Folder Options dialog box depends on which version of Windows you're using. You should be able to find the dialog box easily if you search for Folder Options in the Help section.

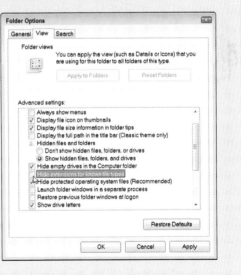

The reason for all this fuss? Filenames are especially important in websites because they're included in the HTML code when you set links. A link from one page to another, as you discover later in this chapter, is essentially made up of the name of the file. Links with names that include spaces and special characters work just fine in most browsers when you test pages on a Mac or a PC computer, but many web servers on the Internet use software that doesn't accept spaces or special characters in links. Thus, links that don't follow these rules may get broken when you publish the site to a web server. By following these three simple rules — no spaces, no special characters, and keep everything lowercase — you ensure that your links will work on any system.

Naming the first page index.html

Another confusing rule — and one of the most important — is that the main page (or the front page) of your website must be called `index.html` (on some Windows-based servers, the first page should be named `default.html`). Most servers on the Internet are set up to serve the `index.html` or `default.html` page first, but you should check with your web-hosting service or the administrator who managers your web server to confirm the name required for your server.

Essentially, when a web browser comes to a domain name, such as DigitalFamily.com, the first page that opens is `index.html`. Similarly, when a web browser is directed to a subfolder within a site, it also displays the `index` page first. As a result, if you create a subfolder with the name `books`, for example, and inside that subfolder you create a page named `index.html` as the main page, you can tell visitors to your site to simply enter **www.DigitalFamily.com/books** to arrive at the books page within your site. If you name the first page anything else, such as `books.html`, visitors have to type **www.DigitalFamily.com/books/books.html** to open the page. The rest of the pages in your site (or any subfolder) can be named anything you like. Just remember: Don't include spaces or special characters (except the hyphen or underscore).

It doesn't matter if you use uppercase or lowercase letters when typing a domain name, but everything that comes after the `.com` (or `.net`, or whatever the ending of your domain name) must match the case of the file and folder names. Thus, `www.DigitalFamily.com` and `www.digitalfamily.com` are the same, but if you create a folder named `books`, the address typed into a browser must use a lowercase *b*, as in `www.DigitalFamily.com/books`. If someone enters `www.DigitalFamily.com/Books` in a browser, he or she will get a 404 error, indicating that the link is not valid.

Bestowing a page title

When you create new pages, adding a page title right away is also good practice. A *page title* is the text that appears in the title bar when a visitor opens your site in a browser window.

In Dreamweaver, you can add a page title by changing the text in the Title box at the top of the workspace. This detail is easy to forget, but page titles play an important role in your site's appearance as well as behind the scenes:

- ✓ The title won't appear in the main part of your web page, but it does appear at the top of a browser window, usually just to the right or left of the name of the browser. Pages on the web look unfinished when the words *untitled document* appear at the top of the browser window.

- ✓ The page title is also the text that appears in a user's Favorites or Bookmarks list.

- ✓ Many search engines give special priority to the words that appear in the title of a web page and display title text in the list of search results, so including the name of your site and a few keywords can help you score better in search results.

Changing Page-Wide Styles with the Page Properties Dialog Box

You can change many individual elements on a page in the Property inspector. If you want to make changes that affect the entire page — such as changing the background color of the entire page or changing the way links and text are formatted — use the Page Properties dialog box.

As shown in Figure 2-7, the Page Properties dialog box includes a list of categories on the left. Each of these reveals different options for specifying page settings. Some of these options are covered in other parts of the book, such as the Background Image feature, covered in Chapter 3.

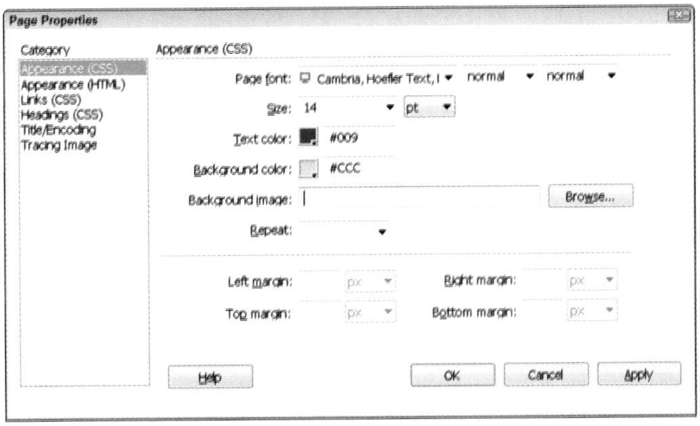

Figure 2-7: Use the Page Properties dialog box to change text color, font face, font size, background, and margins for the entire page.

Changing background and text colors

This section focuses on changing the background and the text colors available from the Appearance categories, as shown in Figure 2-7. Note that the CSS options are recommended over HTML options. When you use the Appearance (CSS) options, Dreamweaver creates corresponding styles for the body tag automatically. When you use any CSS options in the Page Properties dialog box, Dreamweaver creates corresponding styles automatically and lists them in the CSS Styles panel. You find more about editing CSS in Chapters 5–7.

Although you can apply global settings, such as text size and color, in the Page Properties dialog box, you can override those settings with other formatting options in specific instances. For example, you could set all your text to Helvetica in Page Properties and then change the font for headlines to Arial using CSS (covered in Chapter 5).

To change the font settings, background color, text color, and page margins for an entire page, follow these steps:

1. **Choose Modify⇨Page Properties.**

   The Appearance (CSS) category of the Page Properties dialog box appears (refer to Figure 2-7).

2. **In the Page Font drop-down list, specify the fonts you want for the text on your page.**

   In this example, I set the font face to the collection that begins with the Cambria font. If you don't specify a font, your text appears in the font specified in your user's browser, which is usually Times. (You find instructions for using custom fonts in Chapter 7.)

3. **If you want all the text on your page to appear bold or italic, choose the corresponding font options in the drop-down lists to the right of the Page Font options.**

   If you select one of these options, all your text appears bold or italic in the page. Most designers leave these two fields blank because they want to limit the use of bold or italics to drawing special attention to a word or words.

4. **In the Size drop-down list, specify the font size you want for the text on your page.**

   Again, you can override these settings for specific text on the page, such as headlines. In Chapter 5, you find more information about the many size options you can use when formatting text with CSS.

5. **Click the Text Color swatch box to reveal the color palette. Choose any color you like.**

   The color you select fills the color swatch box but won't change the text color on your page until you click the Apply or OK button.

6. **Click the Background Color swatch box to reveal the color palette. Choose any color you like.**

   The color you select fills the color swatch box, but the color doesn't fill the background until you click the Apply or OK button.

7. **If you want to insert a graphic or photograph into the background of your page, click the Browse button next to the Background Image box and select the image in the Select Image Source dialog box.**

   When you insert a background image, it automatically repeats, or *tiles,* across and down the page unless you choose an option from the Repeat drop-down list. No-Repeat prevents the background image from repeating at all. Repeat-X and Repeat-Y repeat the image vertically (x axis) or horizontally (y axis), respectively, across the page.

8. **Use the margin options at the bottom of the dialog box to change the left, right, top, or bottom margins of your page.**

   Most web browsers add a little space to the top and left sides of the browser window around any web page. Entering **0** in all four of these fields removes any default margin space, enabling you to create designs that begin flush with the edge of a browser.

9. **Click the Apply button to see how the colors look on your page.**

10. **Click OK to finish and close the Page Properties dialog box.**

Changing link styles with Page Properties

If you're like many designers, you probably don't like the underline that automatically appears under all the linked text in a web page. In this section, you discover how easy it is to remove that underline and change the color, font, and size of your links with Dreamweaver's Page Properties dialog box. You can also change other page-wide settings, such as the background color and page margins, from the Page Properties dialog box.

The easiest way to alter all your link styles at once is to change them in the Page Properties dialog box. When you use this option, Dreamweaver creates the corresponding tag selector styles automatically and lists them in the CSS Styles panel. Other page-wide settings in this dialog box work similarly, and you can edit all these options by using the CSS tools covered in Chapters 5–7.

To change hyperlink and other styles with the Page Properties dialog box, open an existing page or create a new one and follow these steps:

1. **Choose Modify**➪**Page Properties.**

   Alternatively, you can click the Page Properties button in the Property inspector. The Page Properties dialog box appears.

2. **On the left of the Page Properties dialog box, select the Links (CSS) category, as shown in Figure 2-8.**

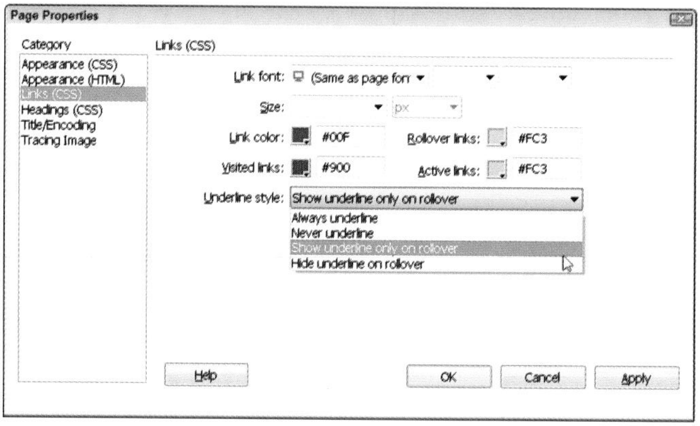

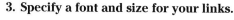

Figure 2-8: Change the style definitions for all four hyperlink states.

3. **Specify a font and size for your links.**

   If you want to use the same font size and face for your links as you use in the rest of the text on your page, it's best to leave these options blank. Then, if you change the text settings for the page, you won't have to remember to change them for your links as well.

4. **Specify colors for each hyperlink state by clicking the corresponding color well and selecting a color from the Color dialog box.**

   You can change any or all link color settings. If you don't specify a link color, the browser uses the default link color. Here's an explanation of each of the four link states:

   • **Link Color:** The color in which your links appear when the page is first loaded and the linked page hasn't yet been visited by the browser. The corresponding HTML tag is `<a:link>`.

   • **Visited Links:** The color your links change to after a browser has already viewed the linked page. The corresponding HTML tag is `<a:visited>`.

- **Rollover Links:** The color a link changes to as a user rolls a cursor over a link. The corresponding HTML tag is `<a:hover>`.

- **Active Links:** The color a link changes to as a user is actively clicking a link. The corresponding HTML tag is `<a:active>`.

5. **Select a style from the Underline Style drop-down list.**

By default, links displayed in a web browser are underlined. Many designers prefer to remove the underline that automatically appears under linked text by choosing Never Underline. I like to give visitors the visual cue of the underline, but only as they roll a cursor over a link, so I generally prefer the option Show Underline Only on Rollover option (refer to Figure 2-8).

6. **Click OK.**

The Page Properties dialog box closes, the style settings are applied automatically to any links on the page, and the corresponding styles are added to the CSS Styles panel.

To fully test link styles, preview your page in a web browser or click the Live View button at the top of the workspace. It's good practice to test link settings in a browser when you make changes like the ones in the preceding exercise. Take a look at how your links appear. For example, check whether the active and visited link colors look good against the background color of the page. Remember that any styles you create using the Page Properties dialog box affect *all* links on your page unless you specifically apply a different style to an individual link that overrides the redefined tag style. If you want to use different link styles in different parts of the same page, you can create compound styles to create different link styles (see Chapter 6 for instructions on creating compound styles).

Adding and Formatting Text

Many people are pleasantly surprised by how easily they can create a basic web page with text and images in Dreamweaver. This section focuses on text and the next section describes images.

In this chapter, I do basic text formatting by using Dreamweaver's HTML formatting options, including the heading and paragraph tags. I start with these basic HTML tags to keep things simple at this stage and to introduce you to what many designers consider the fundamental building blocks of a good web page. In Chapters 5–7, you find detailed instructions for using CSS to change the size, color, font, and other style options of text formatted with these HTML tags.

Adding text to a web page

To add text to a page, you can simply click to insert your cursor at the top of a page and type. If you want to add text that you have somewhere else, such as in a file created in Microsoft Word, you can copy and paste the text into Dreamweaver instead of retyping it.

Dreamweaver offers many ways to maintain formatting when you copy and paste text from another program. This feature is especially important when you copy text from Microsoft Word because if you just paste text as is, you risk including a lot of extra code that is unique to Microsoft Word and can cause problems in your web page.

You can change the default for how Dreamweaver handles formatting when you choose Edit⟳Paste by altering the Preferences in the Copy/Paste category. You can also choose Edit⟳Paste Special to display these options any time you paste new content.

Following are your four main options for inserting text when you choose Edit⟳Paste Special as well as three ways to refine your choice:

- ✓ **Text Only:** Dreamweaver strips any formatting and inserts plain text.

- ✓ **Text with Structure:** Dreamweaver includes paragraphs, lists, tables, and other structural formatting options. (This choice is my favorite because it removes any code specific to a program such as Word if you use the Clean Up Word Paragraph Spacing check box, described a little later, while preserving basic formatting.)

- ✓ **Text with Structure Plus Basic Formatting:** Dreamweaver includes structural formatting as well as basic formatting, such as bold and italic.

- ✓ **Text with Structure Plus Full Formatting:** In addition to the previous options, Dreamweaver includes formatting created by style sheets in programs such as Microsoft Word.

- ✓ **Retain Line Breaks:** Line breaks are preserved, even if you don't keep other formatting options. This option is not available if you choose Text Only.

- ✓ **Clean Up Word Paragraph Spacing:** This option removes special formatting code unique to Microsoft Word and is unnecessary (and not recommended) for text on the web.

- ✓ **Convert Smart Quotes to Straight Quotes:** Smart quotes — the common name for those fancy curly quotes that designers love to use in print documents — require a special character to be displayed properly on the web, and that special character does not work in all web browsers. As a result, smart quotes are often displayed as strange characters in documents and look terrible. To avoid this potential problem, select this box and convert all your smart quotes to straight ones.

I describe many more text formatting options in Chapter 5, which covers CSS, because formatting on the web is best done with CSS and you need to understand the basics of CSS before you start using styles to format text beyond the basic HTML tags covered in the next section.

Formatting text with the heading tags

One of the best formatting options for headlines is the collection of heading tags. In HTML, using heading tags (<h1>, <h2>, and so forth) to format text that serves as a title or headline offers many advantages. Heading tags are designed to be displayed in relative sizes, with <h1> the largest, <h2> smaller, <h3> smaller still, and so on through <h6>. So no matter what a web page's default text size is (and text sizes can vary due to browser settings and computer platform), any text formatted with an <h1> tag is always larger than text formatted with <h2>.

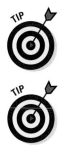

In Chapter 5, you find instructions for creating styles that can change the appearance of heading tags while preserving these benefits. So even if you're using CSS, you'll still want to start by formatting your headlines using the heading tags.

Popular belief is that many search engines give priority to keywords in text formatted with an <h1> tag because the most important text on a page is generally included in the largest size headline. Similarly, search engine experts will tell you that you should use the <h1> tag only once per page.

To format text with a heading tag, follow these steps:

1. **Highlight the text you want to format.**

2. **In the Property inspector, at the bottom of the workspace, make sure the HTML button on the left side of the inspector is selected.**

3. **Use the Format drop-down list to select a heading option.**

   In Figure 2-9, I'm applying the <h1> tag to a headline. When heading tags are applied, the text automatically changes to become big and bold in Design view.

In general, I find the Property inspector the easiest way to apply basic formatting, but you can find these HTML formatting options also by choosing Format⇨Paragraph Format and then selecting a heading option from the submenu that appears.

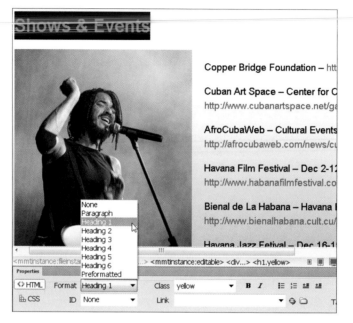

Photo by Casey Stoll

Figure 2-9: The Property inspector provides easy access to common HTML formatting features, such as the Heading 1 tag.

Adding paragraphs and line breaks

When you create page designs for the web, you must work within many limitations that may seem confusing at first. Web design and print design are fundamentally different, and that can make even seemingly simple tasks more complicated than you might expect. How you create paragraph and line breaks is a good example.

If you're working in Design view in Dreamweaver and press the Enter key (Windows) or the Return key (Mac), Dreamweaver inserts a paragraph tag, or <p>, in the code, which creates a line break followed by a blank line. If you want a line break without the extra blank line, hold down the Shift key while you press Enter (or Return) to tell Dreamweaver to insert the <br /> tag into the code, creating a single line break.

Best practice is to avoid using multiple paragraph or break tags to create extra space in a web page (and not all browsers will maintain the blank space if you create it that way). If you want to add a lot of space between paragraphs or other elements on a page, your best option is to use CSS, which I cover in Chapters 5–7.

If you're working in Code view and add space using the Enter or Return key, you add blank space within the code. Extra space in HTML code can be useful because extra space can make code easier to read, but in general, it doesn't affect the way a page is displayed in Design view or in a web browser.

Setting Links in Dreamweaver

Dreamweaver is truly a dream when it comes to setting links. As you set links, remember that a link is essentially an address on the Internet (a URL, or Universal Resource Locator) that tells a viewer's browser what page to open and where it is located when a viewer clicks the text or image containing the link.

To link to a page within your website, you can create a *relative link* that includes a path describing how to get from the current page to the linked page within your local site folder. A relative link doesn't need to include the domain name of your site; this type of link just has instructions for a browser to get from one page within your site to another.

Linking to a page on another website — called an *external link* — is even easier than linking to an internal link. All you need is the URL of the page to which you want to link, and you're most of the way there.

In the following sections, you find step-by-step instructions for creating internal and external links, and e-mail links.

Linking pages within your website

Linking from one page to another page in your website is easy. Just make sure to save your pages in your local site folder (as described in the "Setting Up a New or Existing Site" section, at the beginning of this chapter) before you start setting links.

Here's how you create a link from one page in a website to another:

1. **In Dreamweaver, open the page where you want to create a link.**

2. **Select the text or image that you want to serve as the link (meaning the text or image that a user clicks to trigger the link).**

   Click and drag to highlight a section of text or click once to select an image.

Creating multiple pages to set links

Creating a new page to start a website may seem obvious, but consider this: Before you get too far in your development, you may want to create a few new pages and start organizing the new pages in subdirectories, even if you don't add text or images to them. Doing so enables you to organize the structure of your site before you start setting links. After all, you can't use Dreamweaver's link features to link to a page that doesn't exist. If you plan to have three links on your front page that link to the three main sections of your site, go ahead and create those three main pages, even if you don't put anything but a little text on each page as you create it. (You can always edit or replace those pages later and add more pages to each section, but setting up the main links to the main sections is a great way to start designing the structure of your site.)

For example, say you're creating a site for your small business. You likely want a few main pages, such as a page about your staff, another page about your products or services, and a third page with general information and resources. At this initial stage, you could create four pages — one for the front page of the site and one for each subsection. Name the front page `index.html`

and the other pages `staff.html, about. html,` and `general.html`.

If you expect to create many related pages in each section, consider creating subfolders for each, with a main page in the subfolder. For example, you could create a main `index. html` page inside a `services` subfolder and another `index.html` page inside a `staff` subfolder. Remember, naming the main page within a subfolder `index.html` enables you to use addresses to subpages that include the folder name, such as `www.domain.com/ services`. Your site can include as many `index.html` pages as you like, as long as each is in a separate subfolder.

As you start creating your site, setting up all these main section pages helps you to organize your site and makes setting up the main links on all the site pages easier.

Note: If you're adding more than a few pages to a website, creating a template and then using it to create the rest of your pages can save you time and make updating your site much faster. You find instructions for using Dreamweaver's template features in Chapter 9.

3. **Click the Hyperlink icon in the Common Insert panel (see Figure 2-10), at the top right of the workspace.**

    Alternatively, you can set a link by clicking the Browse icon (which looks like a file folder) just to the right of the Link field in the Property inspector, or choose Insert ⇨>Hyperlink.

4. **In the Hyperlink dialog box, shown in Figure 2-11, click the Browse (file folder) icon to the right of the Link drop-down list.**

    The Select File dialog box opens.

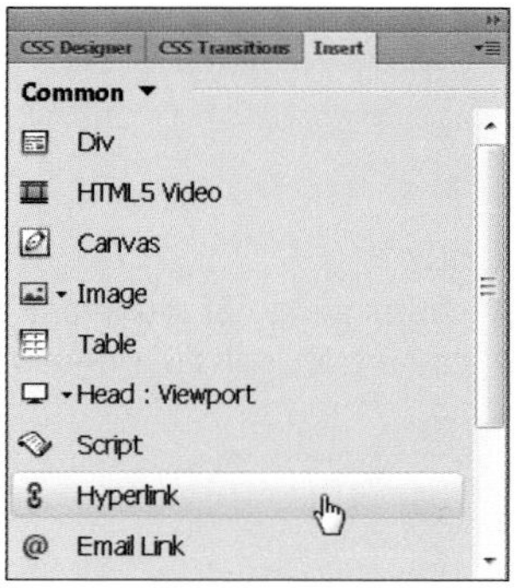

Figure 2-10: Click the Hyperlink
option to create a link.

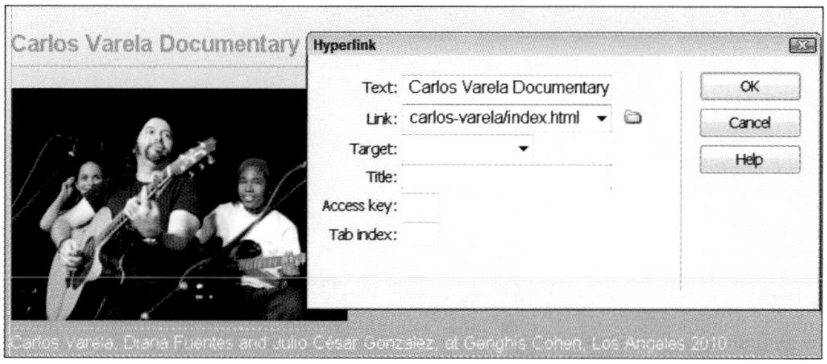

Figure 2-11: The Hyperlink dialog box has several link settings not
available when setting a link from the Property inspector.

Photo by Casey Stoll

5. Click the filename to select the page that you want your image or text to link to, and then click OK (Windows) or Choose (Mac).

When you click OK, the Select File dialog box closes, but the Hyperlink dialog box remains open.

6. (Optional) Use the Target field in the Hyperlink dialog box to define where your linked page opens.

To open the linked page in a new browser window or in a new tab within a browser, choose the _blank option. The New option is not recommended because it is not standard. Choose _self to open the linked page in the same window (the default). Choose _top to force the page to open in a fresh browser window, even if the page is displayed within a frame. The _parent option is almost never used anymore, but if you page is

within a frameset, you can select this option to open the linked page a
level above the current page in the frame structure.

7. Click OK.

The Hyperlink dialog box closes and the link is set automatically. Note
that to test your links, you have to view your page in a web browser,
such as Google Chrome or Apple Safari. Dreamweaver makes it easy to
preview pages in multiple web browsers, a process I cover in Chapter 4.

Setting links to many pages at once

After you become used to setting links, here's a great shortcut that is especially useful if you're setting many links to many pages at the same time:

1. Select the image or text that you want to serve as the link.

2. Click the Point to File icon in the Property inspector.

The icon is a crosshair (a circle with a dot in the middle) and is located
just to right of the Link field and to the left of the Browse icon (which
looks like a folder).

**3. Drag your cursor across the page (without taking your finger off the
left mouse button) and rest it on the name of any file in the Files
panel.**

When you click and drag from the Point to File icon to a filename in this
way, Dreamweaver extends a line to help you visualize that you're setting the link properly, as shown in Figure 2-12.

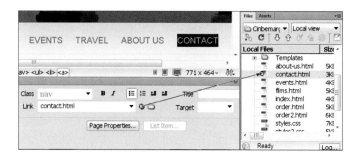

Figure 2-12: Drag from the Point to File icon to any file in the Files panel
to set a link.

The file must be visible in the Files panel, so you may need to open a
subfolder to reveal the file before you can set a link this way.

Linking to another website

To link to a page on another website — sometimes called an *external link* — all you need is the URL of the page to which you want to link, and you're most of the way there.

To create an external link, follow these steps:

1. **In Dreamweaver, open the page where you want to create the link.**

2. **Select the text or image that you want to act as the link.**

3. **In the Link text box in the Property inspector, type the URL of the page to which you want your text or image to link.**

   The link is set automatically. In the example in Figure 2-13, I created a link using the text *Wikipedia* to link to `http://wikitravel.org/en/Cuba`, the specific section of the Wikipedia website that covers Cuba.

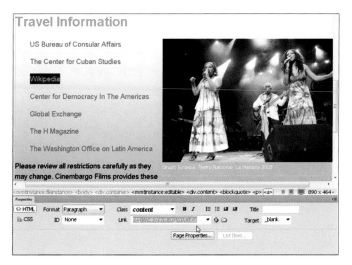

Photo by Casey Stoll

Figure 2-13: In the Link text box, enter the URL of any website to which you want to link.

Although you don't have to type the `http://` or even the `www.` at the beginning of a website address to get to a site in most web browsers, you must always use the full URL, including the `http://`, when you create a link to another website in HTML. Otherwise, the browser can't find the correct external site address, and the visitor will probably end up on an error page.

Setting a link to an e-mail address

Another common link option goes to an e-mail address. Visitors can send you messages easily with e-mail links. I always recommend that you invite visitors to contact you because including contact information helps establish credibility on the web and because visitors to your site can point out mistakes and give you valuable feedback about how you can improve your site. Setting a link to an e-mail address is just as easy as setting a link to another web page. All you need to know is the e-mail address you want to link to and what text or image you want to use when you set the link.

To create an e-mail link, select the text you want to link and then click the Email Link icon in the Common Insert panel. In the Email Link dialog box, enter the e-mail address in the Email field and then click OK. If you want to use an image as an e-mail link, select an image in Dreamweaver's main work area, click the Email Link icon in the Common Insert panel, and then type the e-mail link into the Email field.

You can also set e-mail links using the Link field in the Property inspector, but you must enter the code `mailto:` (no `//`) before the e-mail address. For example, if you typed a link to my e-mail address into the Property inspector, you'd need to type **mailto:janine@digitalfamily.com**. Here's what the full line of code behind that e-mail link would look like:

```
<a href="mailto:janine@digitalfamily.com">Send a message to
        Janine</a>
```

When visitors to your website click an e-mail link, their computer systems automatically launch their e-mail program and create a blank e-mail message to the specified e-mail address. Although this trick is cool, your users may find an e-mail's sudden appearance disconcerting if they don't expect it to happen, and the e-mail link won't work if your users don't have e-mail programs on their computers. That's why I always try to let users know when I use an e-mail link. For example, instead of just linking the words *Contact Janine,* I link the words *E-mail Janine.* Even better, I often link the actual e-mail address.

Linking to PDFs

Adobe's Portable Document Format (PDF) is popular on the Internet, and with good reason. Now that Adobe's Acrobat Reader is widely distributed and even built into more recent browser versions, you can assume that most of your audience can read files in PDF.

PDF is a great option for files that you want to make easy to download in their entirety to be saved on a hard drive, as well as documents that you want printed exactly as they're designed. Because the PDF viewer is free, your users don't need expensive software, such as Microsoft Word or Lotus Notes, to view your documents.

In the early days, PDFs were limited to text and images, but the most recent versions support audio, video, and even Flash files, so you can now create complex multimedia presentations in PDF format.

To add a PDF file to your website, simply copy the file into your local site folder and link to it as you'd link to any other web page on your site. When you upload the page with the link to your PDF file, make sure to upload the PDF as well.

Adding Meta Tags for Search Engines

If you've heard of meta tags, you probably associate them with search engines, and you'd be right. Meta tags are used for a variety of things, but one of the most common uses is to provide special text in the code at the top of the page. This code doesn't appear in a web browser when your page is viewed but can be read by crawlers, bots, and other programs that scour the web cataloging and ranking web pages for Bing, Google, and a long list of other search-related sites.

In Dreamweaver you find features that help you add meta tags for keywords and descriptions. Here's a brief explanation of each tag; the steps for filling each tag with text are coming up:

- **Meta keyword tag:** A meta keyword tag enables you to include a list of keywords you would like search engines to match if someone searches for those words. Unfortunately, meta keywords have been so abused by web designers attempting to mislead visitors about the true content of their web pages that most search engines ignore the meta keyword tag and its contents. That said, using this meta tag won't hurt your ranking with any search engines and many search engine experts still include them.

- **Meta description tag:** This tag is important and should be included in every page in your website. The meta description tag is designed to let you include a written description of each page — a worthwhile endeavor because most search engines, including Google, use the meta description as the brief description that appears in search results pages. Make the description a call to action, almost like a short advertisement, for the page that will get potential visitors to click your link when they are reading through a list of matches to a search. If you don't include your own text in a meta description tag, many search engines use the first several words that appear on your page as the description. Depending on your design, the first few words may not be the best description of your site.

The advent of social media has made the meta description tag even more important. When someone posts your web page by entering the URL into a social media site, the text you include in the meta description tag is included automatically with their post. Similarly, the meta description is included when someone shares a page on your site using a social media icon. (See Chapter 15 for tips on adding social media icons to your website.)

You can include the same meta description on every page of your site, but the best strategy is to include a description specific to the contents of each page on your site.

Follow these steps to add a meta description tag to your page:

1. **Open the page where you want to add a meta description.**

2. **Choose Insert➪Head➪Description.**

   (Alternatively, you can use the Head option from the Common Insert panel.) The Description dialog box appears.

3. **In the Description text box, enter the text you want for your page description.**

   Don't add any HTML to the text in this box. Most search engine experts recommend that you limit this text to no more than 160 characters because that is all that will be included in the search results page on sites such as Google.

4. **Click OK.**

   The description text you entered is inserted between the <head> tags area at the top of the page in the HTML code. Meta content doesn't appear in the body of the page, but you can find it just below the <title> tag if you look at the code behind the page.

If you want to add keywords, repeat Steps 1–4, choosing Insert Head ➪ Keywords in Step 2. Type a list of keywords, separated by commas, in place of a description in Step 3.

Dreamweaver's meta tag tools are somewhat limited. You can use them to add these tags but not to edit them. To edit the text in meta description or keyword tags after you've inserted them, you have to view the code in Dreamweaver and edit the text in Code view. You'll find this text near the top of the HTML code, just below the <title> tag in the area surrounded by the <head> tags.

Creating Web Graphics

*N*o matter how great the writing on your website may be, the graphics always get people's attention first. The key to making a good first impression is to use images that look great and download quickly.

If you're familiar with using a graphics-editing program, such as Adobe Photoshop or Fireworks, to create graphics for the web, you're a step ahead. If not, you'll appreciate this chapter's pointers on how to convert images for the web, what image formats to use, and how to optimize images for faster download times. The examples in this chapter were created using Adobe Photoshop CS6, but the features I used are nearly identical in both Photoshop CS6 and Photoshop Elements, so you can use the same instructions in either program. (See the sidebar "Comparing Adobe web graphics programs" to find out more about the differences.)

If your images are already in GIF, JPEG, or PNG format and ready for the web, you can jump ahead to the "Inserting Images in Dreamweaver" section, where you find out how to place and align images and use an image as a background. You also discover some of Dreamweaver's built-in image-editing features, which enable you to crop images and even adjust contrast and brightness without ever launching an external image-editing program.

Comparing Adobe web graphics programs

Most professional designers strongly prefer Adobe Photoshop, although I have to say I've been impressed with Photoshop Elements, which is a light version but offers many of the same features for a fraction of the cost. The following is a list of some of the most popular image-editing programs on the market today. All these image programs are available for both Mac and Windows:

✔ **Adobe Photoshop** (www.adobe.com/photoshop): By far the most popular image-editing program on the market, Photoshop is a widely used standard among graphics professionals. With Photoshop, you can create original artwork, edit and enhance photographs, and so much more. Photoshop has a wealth of powerful painting and selection tools, special effects, and filters that enable you to create images far beyond what you can capture on film or create with many other illustration programs.

✔ **Adobe Photoshop Elements** (www.adobe.com/elements): If you don't need all the bells and whistles offered in the full-blown version of Photoshop, Photoshop Elements is a remarkably powerful program — for about a sixth of the price. If you're a professional

designer, you're best served by Photoshop. But if you're a hobbyist or small-business owner and want to create good-looking images without the high cost and learning curve of a professional graphics program, Elements is a great bargain.

✔ **Adobe Fireworks** (www.adobe.com/fireworks): Fireworks was one of the first image-editing programs designed to create and edit web graphics. Created by Macromedia, the program is now part of Adobe Web Suite and is fully integrated with Dreamweaver. Fireworks gives you everything you need to create, edit, and output web graphics, all in one well-designed product. Fireworks lacks many of the advanced image-editing capabilities of Photoshop but shines when creating web graphics and is especially popular among web designers who rave about the capability to create a design in Fireworks that can easily be sliced and converted into a web page in Dreamweaver.

If you have an Internet connection and want to do basic image editing for free, visit www.gimp.org. The site makes it possible to edit and optimize images online without purchasing a software program.

Creating and Optimizing Web Graphics

The most important thing to keep in mind when creating images for the web is that you want to *optimize* your images to make your file sizes as small as possible so that they download as quickly as possible.

How you optimize an image depends on how the image was created and whether you want to save it as a JPEG, PNG, or GIF. You find instructions for optimizing images with Photoshop in the sections that follow, but the bottom line is this: No matter what program, format, or optimization technique you choose, your biggest challenge is finding the best balance between small file size and good image quality. Essentially, the more you optimize, the faster the image will download, but the compression and color reduction techniques used to optimize images can make them look terrible if you go too far.

As a general rule, do any editing, such as adjusting contrast, retouching, or combining images, before you reduce their size or optimize them because you want to work with the highest resolution possible when you're editing. Also, resize an image before you optimize it. You find instructions for resizing an image in the next exercise and instructions for optimizing in the sections that follow.

Resizing graphics and photos

Resizing is important for two reasons: The images must be small enough to be displayed well on a computer monitor, and you want them to download quickly to a user's computer. The smaller the image is, the faster it will download.

Although you can change the display size of an image in a web page by altering the height and width settings in Dreamweaver, you get much better results if you change the dimensions of an image in a program such as Photoshop.

When you alter an image's height and width in the HTML code (by using the height and width settings in Dreamweaver), you simply instruct a web browser to display the image in a different size. Unfortunately, browsers don't do a good job of resizing images because browsers don't change the image itself but just force it to fit in the assigned space when the browser loads the page. If you set the image to display larger than its actual size, the image is likely to look fuzzy or distorted because it doesn't contain enough pixels for all the details to look good in a larger size. If you set the code to display the image smaller than it is, the image is likely to look squished, and you're requiring that your users download an image that's larger than necessary.

Reducing an image's size for use on the web requires two steps. First, you reduce the resolution of an image, which changes the number of pixels in the image. When you're working with images for the web, you want to reduce the resolution to 72 pixels per inch, or ppi. (If you're wondering why 72, see the sidebar that's appropriately named "Should I use 72 ppi or a higher resolution?") Second, you reduce the image's physical size by reducing its dimensions. You want to size your images to fit well in a browser window and to work within the design of your site.

Should I use 72 ppi or a higher resolution?

For years, most web designers have saved images for the web at a resolution of 72 pixels per inch (better known as *ppi*). Most computer monitors displayed no more than 72 ppi, so any resolution higher than that was wasted on the web and you'd be making your visitors download more pixels than they could see.

One of the emerging questions on the web is whether designers should start increasing the resolution of the images we're using to keep pace with the higher resolution offered by the new breed of mobile devices, such Apple's iPhones with ultra-high-density pixel resolution, Retina display laptops, and widescreen monitors.

Of course, other manufacturers followed suit, and we are now seeing that the old 72 ppi standard is quickly becoming outdated. Most modern computer monitors are capable of displaying images at 96 to 100 ppi resolution or higher.

So what should you do? Well, as with everything web-related, there are tradeoffs. More pixels mean better appearance but also an increased image size — and longer page load times. Here are your options:

✔ **Stick with 72 ppi.** *Upside*: It's what most designers still use, and it still looks good in even the latest browsers. You won't have to go back to all your sites and resize and resample your photos. *Downside*: In a few years, your photos and graphics could look grainy and pixelated when compared to higher-resolution sites.

✔ **Make an incremental change to 96 or 100 ppi.** *Upside*: The increased resolution will make your images look better on the more advanced displays, without really hitting your page load times. *Downside*: A few years from now, you may have to go through this process again when even higher resolutions are in vogue.

✔ **Use the @2x tag.** *Upside*: This option enables you to swap a lower resolution image for a higher resolution image using CSS media queries. *Downsides*: Not all devices support this option, so it works only for a limited audience. And Dreamweaver does not support this feature, so you'll have to write the CSS yourself. Here's an example of a background image that use the @2x option:

```
.background-image {
    background: url(../images/cool-
        background.png) repeat;
    background-size: 100px 100px;
}

@media only screen and (-webkit-min-
        device-pixel-ratio: 2) {
    .background-image {
        background: url(../images/
        cool-background@2x.png)
        repeat;
    }
}
```

Follow these steps to lower the resolution and reduce the size of an image in Photoshop. (In Photoshop Elements or Fireworks, you follow a similar process although the specific steps may vary.)

1. **With an image open in Photoshop, choose Image⬩Image Size.**

   The Image Size dialog box opens, as shown in Figure 3-1.

TIP

If you don't want your original image to lose quality (or you just want to play it safe), make a copy of your image and resize the *copy* for your website.

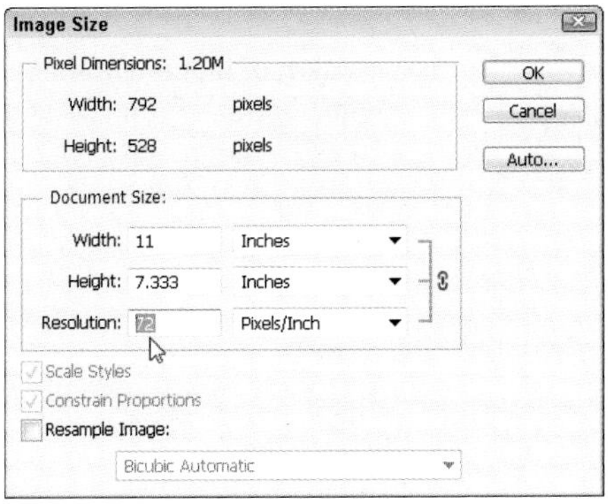

Image Size

Pixel Dimensions: 1.20M

Width: 792 pixels

Height: 528 pixels

OK

Cancel

Auto...

Document Size:

Width: 11 Inches

Height: 7.333 Inches

Resolution: 72 Pixels/Inch

☑ Scale Styles
☑ Constrain Proportions
☐ Resample Image:

Bicubic Automatic

Figure 3-1: Change the image resolution to 72 ppi for a faster download.

2. **To change the resolution of your image, first deselect the Resample Image check box at the bottom of the Image Size dialog box.**

   For best results, you always want the Resample Image check box deselected when you change the resolution.

3. **Click and drag to highlight the number in the Resolution field and replace it by typing the number** 72.

4. **Select the Resample Image check box.**

   With the Resample Image check box deselected, you can't change the Pixel dimensions, so it must be checked when you change the image size.

5. **Enter a height and width for the image in the Height and Width fields.**

   As shown in Figure 3-2, I'm changing the size of this image to 528 pixels high. If the Constrain Proportions check box at the bottom of the dialog box is selected (as it is in this example), any changes you make to the height automatically affect the width (and vice versa) to ensure that the image proportions remain constant. I prefer to work this way, but if you do want to change the image and not maintain the proportions, deselect this box.

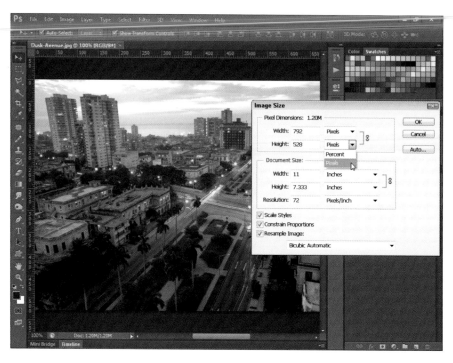

Figure 3-2: Specify a new image size in pixels or as a percentage of the original size.

6. **Click OK to resize the image.**

   If you want to return the image to its previous size, choose Edit⇨Undo Image Size. Beware that when you save the image, the changes become permanent.

Choosing the best image format

One of the most common questions about images for the web concerns when to use GIF or PNG and when to use JPEG. Table 3-1 provides the simple answer.

Table 3-1	Image Formats for the Web
Format	**Best Use**
GIF (`.gif`)	For line art (such as one- or two-color logos), simple drawings, animations, and basically any image that has no gradients or blends. GIF is also the best format when you want to display an image with a transparent background.
Animated GIF (`.gif`)	The simplest way to animate a web page. Animated GIFs work in almost every web browser used on the Internet, even very old browsers. Animated GIFs are a special type of GIF made up of a series of image frames, displayed in succession. These simple animations can include time delays between frames and can loop so that the series of images plays over and over.
PNG (`.png`)	PNG generally produces better-looking images with smaller file sizes than GIF for the same kinds of limited-color images. Really old browsers, such as IE 3, don't support the PNG format, but most web designers today choose the PNG format over GIF because so few people use such old browsers.
JPEG (`.jpg` or `.jpeg`)	JPEG is the best format for colorful, complex images (such as photographs); images containing gradients or color blends; and any other images with millions of colors.

Saving images for the web: The basics

If you're new to saving images for the web, the following basics can help you get the best results from your files, your image-editing program, and ultimately your web pages. You can

- ✔ **Convert an image from any format into the GIF, PNG, or JPEG format.** For example, turn all your TIF, BMP, and PSD image files into a web-friendly file format.

- ✔ **Optimize images that are already in GIF, PNG, or JPEG format.** Even if your files are already in a web-friendly format, following the instructions in this chapter to optimize images with Adobe's Save for Web dialog box further reduces their file sizes for faster download over the Internet.

- ✔ **Use many programs to create web graphics.** However, Photoshop is one of the most popular ones to use. Under the File menu in Photoshop (and Photoshop Elements), you'll find the Save for Web option. (In Photoshop CS5, the option was changed to Save for Web and Devices.) Fireworks provides a similar feature, and although each program's dialog boxes are slightly different, the basic options for compressing and reducing colors (which are covered in this chapter) are the same.

See the upcoming sections "Optimizing JPEG images for the web" and "Optimizing images in GIF and PNG formats" for details about using the Save for Web & Devices feature.

✔ **Make image edits before you optimize.** When you're editing, using the highest quality image possible is always best. Make sure to do all your editing, sharpening, and resizing before you use the Save for Web option. Similarly, if you want to make further changes to an image after you've optimized it, you'll achieve the best results if you go back to a higher resolution version of the image rather than editing the version that's been optimized for the web. (When you use the Save for Web feature, Photoshop creates a new copy of your image and leaves the original unchanged.)

Optimizing JPEG images for the web

The JPEG format is the best choice for optimizing continuous-tone images, such as photographs and images with many colors or gradients. When you optimize a JPEG, you can make the file size smaller by applying compression. The more compression, the smaller the image, but if you compress the image too much, the image can look terrible. The trick is finding the right balance, as you discover in this section.

If you have a digital photograph or another image that you want to prepare for the web, follow these steps to optimize and save it in Photoshop (in Photoshop Elements or Fireworks, the process is similar although the specific steps may vary):

1. **With the image open in Photoshop, choose File➪Save for Web.**

   The Save for Web dialog box appears.

2. **In the top-left corner of the dialog box, choose either the 2-Up or 4-Up tab to display multiple versions of the same image for easy comparison.**

   In the example shown in Figure 3-3, I chose 2-Up, which makes it possible to view the original image on the top and a preview of the same image as it will appear with the specified settings on the bottom. The 4-Up option, as the name implies, displays four different versions for comparison (as shown later in this chapter in Figure 3-4).

Figure 3-3: Use JPEG for photographs and other images with millions of colors.

3. **On the right side of the window, just under Preset, click the small arrow to open the Optimized File Format drop-down list and choose JPEG (this list is open in Figure 3-3).**

4. **Set the compression quality.**

   Use the preset options Low, Medium, High, Very High, or Maximum from the Compression Quality drop-down list. Or use the slider just under the Quality field to make more precise adjustments. (The slider appears when you click the arrow.) Lowering the quality reduces the file size and makes the image download more quickly, but if you lower this number too much, the image will look blurry and blotchy.

   Photoshop uses a compression scale of 0 to 100 for JPEGs in this dialog box, with 0 the lowest possible quality (the highest amount of compression and the smallest file size) and 100 the highest possible quality (the least amount of compression and the biggest file size). Low, Medium, and High represent quality values based on the amount of compression. The more compression applied, the lower the image quality.

5. **Specify other settings as desired (the compression quality and file format are the most important settings).**

6. **Click Save.**

   The Save Optimized As dialog box opens.

7. **Enter a name for the image and save it to the images folder in your website folder.**

   Photoshop saves the optimized image as a copy of the original and leaves the original open in the main Photoshop work area.

Repeat these steps for each image you want to optimize as a JPEG.

At the bottom of the image preview in the Save for Web dialog box, Photoshop includes an estimate of the time required for the image to download at the specified connection speed. In the example shown in Figure 3-3, the estimate is 32 seconds at 56.6 Kbps. As you adjust the compression settings, the size of the image changes and the download estimate will automatically adjust. You can change the connection speed used to make this calculation by clicking the small arrow just to the right of the connection speed and using the drop-down list to select another option, such as 256 Kbps for cable/DSL modem speed. Use this estimate as a guide to help you decide how much you should optimize each image.

Optimizing images in GIF and PNG formats

If you're working with a graphic that can be displayed in 256 colors or less, such as a logo, cartoon character, or drawing, your best bet is to use the PNG format and reduce the total number of colors used in the image as much as possible to reduce the file size. (If you're concerned about visitors using a very, very old web browser, use GIF instead.)

To help make up for the degradation in image quality that can happen when colors are removed, GIF and PNG use a dithering trick. *Dithering* involves alternating pixels in a checkerboard-like pattern to create subtle color variations, even with a limited color palette. The effect can smooth the image's edges and make it appear to have more colors than it actually does.

To convert an image to a GIF or a PNG in Photoshop, follow these steps (in Photoshop Elements or Fireworks, the process is similar although the specific steps may vary):

1. **With the image open in Photoshop, choose File⇨Save for Web.**

   The Save for Web dialog box appears.

2. **In the top-left corner of the dialog box, choose the 2-Up or 4-Up tab to display multiple versions of the same image for easy comparison.**

   In the example shown in Figure 3-4, I chose 4-Up, which makes it possible to view the original image (in the upper-left corner), as well as three different previews of the same image.

3. **Select a preview image to begin changing its settings.**

   Changing the preview images in the 4-Up view enables you to compare the original image with up to three versions using different color, transparency, dither, and other settings, covered in the steps that follow.

4. **On the right side of the dialog box, just under Preset, click the small arrow to open the Optimized File Format drop-down list and choose PNG-8.**

   Although PNG-24 does produce a better quality image, not all web browsers support PNG-24, so PNG-8 is the safer option if you want the image to display consistently for the broadest audience on the web.

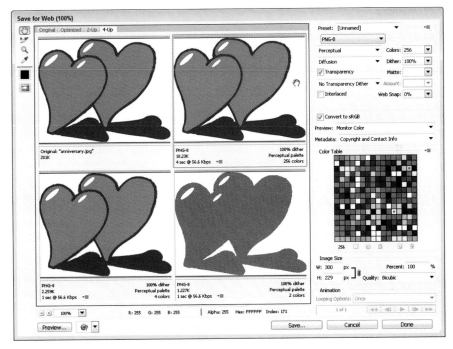

Illustration by Tom McCain

Figure 3-4: GIF and PNG are best for images with limited colors.

5. **In the Colors box, select the number of colors.**

   The fewer colors you use, the smaller the file size and the faster the image will download. But be careful; if you reduce the colors too much (as I have in the bottom-right preview shown in Figure 3-4), you lose details. The ideal number of colors depends on your image; if you go too far, your image will look terrible.

6. **If you want to maintain a transparent area in your image, select the Transparency check box.**

   Any area of the image that was transparent when you created the image in the editor appears transparent in the preview window. If you don't have a transparent area in your image, this setting has no effect.

   Transparency is a good trick for making text or an image appear to float because a transparent background doesn't appear on the web page. You can select transparency as a background option in the New File dialog box when you create a new image in Photoshop or Photoshop Elements.

7. **If you choose Transparency, also specify a Matte color.**

   You want the matte color to match the background of your web page so that the dithering along the transparent edge will blend with the background. If you don't specify a matte color, the transparency is set for a white background, which can cause a halo effect when the image is displayed on a colored background.

8. **Specify other settings as desired.**

   The remainder of the settings in this dialog box can be left at their defaults in Photoshop.

9. **Click Save.**

   The Save Optimized As dialog box opens.

10. **Enter a name for the image and save it into the images folder (or any other folder) in your local site folder.**

Repeat these steps for each image you want to optimize as a GIF or PNG for your site.

Trial and error is a great technique in the Save for Web dialog box. In each of the three preview windows displaying optimized versions of the cool cartoon image in Figure 3-4, I used fewer and fewer colors, which reduced the file size with an increasingly degrading effect.

How small is small enough?

After you know how to optimize GIFs and JPEGs and appreciate the goal of making them as small as possible, you may ask, "How small is small enough?" The answer is mostly subjective, but the following points are good to remember:

- ✔ **The larger your graphics files, the longer people have to wait for them to download.** You may have the most beautiful picture of Mount Fuji on the front page of your website, but if it takes forever to download, most people won't be patient enough to wait to see it.

- ✔ **When you build pages with multiple graphics, consider the cumulative download time of all the graphics on the page.** Even if each individual image is a small file size, the cumulative image size can add up. Unlike most things in life, smaller is definitely better on the web.

- ✔ **Most web pros consider anything from about 75K to 150K a good maximum *cumulative* size for all the elements on a given page.** With the increasing popularity of DSL and cable modems, many websites are starting to become a bit more graphics heavy and go beyond that size limit. However, anything over 150K is pushing the limit, especially if you expect people with dial-up modems (56K and under) or those surfing on mobile phones to stick around long enough to view your pages.

Inserting Images in Dreamweaver

Now for the fun part. Adding an image to your web page may seem almost magical at first because the process is so simple with Dreamweaver. The challenge with web graphics isn't adding them to your pages but creating good-looking images that load quickly in your viewer's browser. You need another program, such as Photoshop, Photoshop Elements, or Fireworks, to create, convert, edit, and optimize images. *Optimizing* images makes file sizes smaller so your images download faster. Dreamweaver provides some basic image-editing tools, but mostly you use Dreamweaver to insert and position images on your page.

Dreamweaver makes placing images on your web pages easy and provides multiple ways to do so:

- ✔ Click the Images icon in the Common Insert panel and then select an image using the Insert Image dialog box.

- ✔ In the Files panel, click and drag an image name onto the page where you want the image to appear.

- ✔ Use the Insert menu, as I explain in the following steps.

If you don't have a web-optimized JPEG, GIF, or PNG image handy, you can download free images that are already optimized by going directly to www. DigitalFamily.com/free. (You find instructions for downloading the free images when you get to this special page on my website.)

To place an image on a web page using the Insert menu, follow these instructions:

1. **Open an existing page or create and save a new page.**

2. **Place your cursor where you want to insert the image on the page.**

   You can insert images into the top left of a new blank file, and you can insert images into <div> tags and elements in a web page, but you can't just place an image in the middle of a page without using additional HTML tags or CSS formatting to position it. See the "Why can't I place images anywhere I want them?" sidebar, later in the chapter, for more on how to position images in a page.

3. **Choose Insert⟹Image⟹Image.**

   The Select Image Source dialog box appears.

4. **Browse to locate the image you want to insert.**

   Depending on your computer system, you can preview images as you insert them in different ways. Here are three common options:

   - **On a PC with Windows XP,** choose Thumbnails from the View menu drop-down list to the right of the Look In field to display thumbnail versions of all the images in any open folder. You can also view a single preview of any selected image in the far right of the dialog box.

   - **On a PC with Windows Vista or Windows 7** (as shown in Figure 3-5), choose one of the icon options (Small Icons, Medium Icons, Large Icons, or Extra Large Icons) from the View menu drop-down list to the right of the Look In field to display thumbnail versions of all the images in any open folder. You can also view a single preview of any selected image to the far right of the dialog box.

   - **On a Mac,** choose the View As Columns option from the top left of the dialog box. You can view a single preview of any selected image in the far right of the dialog box.

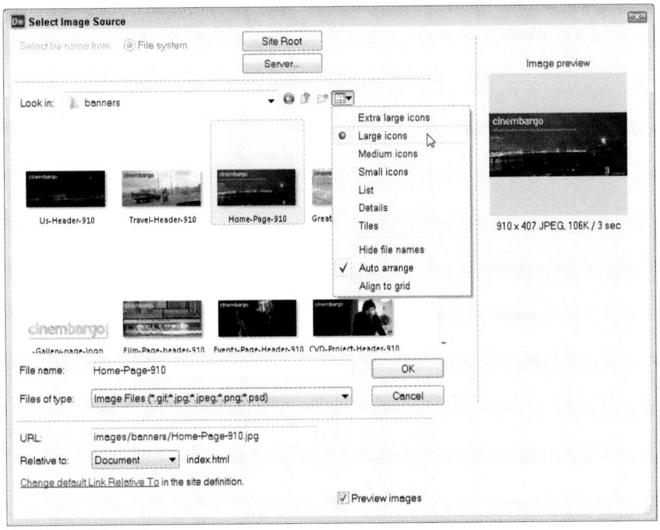

Figure 3-5: Locate and preview images in the Select Image Source dialog box.

Photos by Casey Stoll

5. To insert the image, double-click the image name or click once and then click OK.

If you insert an image into a page and the image isn't saved in your local site folder, Dreamweaver prompts you with a warning dialog box and offers to copy the image into your local site folder. (Find out how to set up a local site folder in the section in Chapter 2 on setting up new or existing sites.) Many designers create a subfolder called *images* inside the local site folder where they store all the images in their site, but you can organize images in multiple subfolders if you prefer.

6. Select the image on your web page to view and edit image properties.

Image options are displayed automatically in the Property inspector at the bottom of the page when an image is selected, as shown in Figure 3-6.

Photo by Casey Stoll

Figure 3-6: The Property inspector provides easy access to common image attributes.

Table 3-2 describes the many image attributes available in the Property inspector when an image is selected. If you don't see all the attributes listed in the table on your screen, double-click the bottom-right corner of the Property inspector to expand it to reveal all the image options shown in Figure 3-6.

Table 3-2	Image Attributes in the Property Inspector	
Abbreviation	**Attribute**	**Function**
Image	N/A	Displays the file size.
ID	Name	Identifies the image uniquely on the page — an important detail if you use behaviors or other scripts that target an image. Can be left blank.
Map	Map Name	Assigns a name to an image map. All image maps require a name.
Hotspot tools	Image Map Coordinates	Creates image map hotspots for links in the shape of a rectangle, an oval, or a polygon.

Abbreviation	Attribute	Function
Src	Source	Automatically sets the source (the filename and path from the current document to the desired image). Required.
Link	Hyperlink	Displays the address or path if the image is used as a link.
Target	Link Target	Controls how a link opens in a web browser. For example, if you want the link to open a new browser window, choose _blank.
Original	N/A	Indentifies the original version of the image, if you're using the Smart Objects features in Photoshop or Firefox. (See your Photoshop or Firefox documentation for more on these features.)
Class	CSS Setting	Enables you to apply any class styles defined in Dreamweaver. To use this option, select any element in the workspace and then select any class style you want to apply in the drop-down list.
Edit	Edit	Launches the image editor associated with Dreamweaver. (You can change these settings in Dreamweaver's Preferences dialog box.)
Edit	Edit Image Settings	Launches the Image Optimization dialog box, where you can make basic edits to an image.
Edit	Update from Original	Ensures that edits are made using the original image. **Note:** This setting works only if you've used an associated Adobe image editor to edit the image before inserting the image on the page.
Icons for	Crop; Resample; Brightness and Contrast; and Sharpen	Make minor alterations to an image in Dreamweaver. **Note:** Any changes made using these options permanently alter the image when the page is saved.
W	Width	Specifies the width of the image based on the actual size of the image dimensions.
H	Height	Specifies the height of the image based on the actual size of the image dimensions.
Alt	Alternate Text	Enables you to add or edit alternate text.

Why can't I place images anywhere I want them?

You can't just place your cursor anywhere on a page and insert an image where you want it. This isn't a limitation of Dreamweaver; the way HTML is displayed on the web restricts how you can place images.

By default, all images, text, and other elements are inserted starting at the top-left corner of the browser window. To create more complex layouts and position images precisely on a page, your best option is to create a layout with CSS (which I cover in Chapters 5-8). You can also use an HTML table to position elements on a web page (which I cover in Chapter 10).

When you insert an image file onto a page, you don't actually add a copy of the image to the page; you create a reference to the image. The underlying code looks much like the code for a link from one page to another. Both image references and links include the name of the file (the page you link to or the image you insert) and the path from the page to that file. Essentially, you're creating an instruction for a web browser to find the image when it displays the page.

To display an image on your web page, you need to upload both the page and the image when you publish your website. If your image files and the pages that refer to those files aren't in the same relative location on your hard drive as they are on your web server, you break the reference to your images, and an ugly Broken Image icon appears on your page. The best way to make sure that your images and files stay where they're supposed to in relation to one another is to let Dreamweaver keep track of them for you. That's why it's so important to complete the site setup process at the beginning of Chapter 2 and to make sure you never move or rename an image, except in the Files panel.

Image Editing in Dreamweaver

Dreamweaver includes basic image-editing features, including the Crop, Resample, Brightness and Contrast, and Sharpen options. You find these tools just below the Class field in the Property inspector, as shown in Figure 3-7. Image-editing features in Dreamweaver enable you to make minor changes to images without opening Fireworks, Photoshop, or any other graphics-editing program.

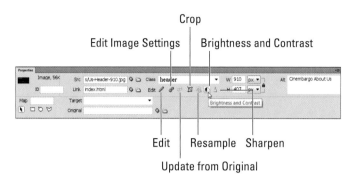

Figure 3-7: Use the image-editing tools to do basic image editing.

Before you get carried away editing your images, remember that Dreamweaver is primarily an application for creating web pages and isn't designed to edit graphics. Although these tools can be useful, they shouldn't take the place of doing serious work on your graphics in a graphics application, such as Fireworks or Photoshop.

When you use Dreamweaver's image-editing tools, beware that you're changing the actual image (not just a copy of it). Make sure you're happy with these changes before you save the page you're working on. You can use the Undo feature in Dreamweaver to revert several steps, but after you save the page, you can't undo changes made to an image with these tools. To protect your original image, save a copy before editing it.

Cropping an image

Essentially, *cropping* an image involves trimming its edges. If you're trying to fit an image into your design and need the image to be just a touch smaller, Dreamweaver's cropping tool can come in handy. To crop a graphic or photo, open the page that contains the image you want to edit, and follow these steps:

1. **Select the image you want to crop by clicking it.**

   The Property inspector changes to display the image's properties.

2. **Click the Crop icon.**

   A dialog box appears, warning you that cropping changes the original image.

   If you're concerned about keeping the entire image available, don't make the change. Instead, make a copy of the image before you crop it.

3. **Click OK in the Dreamweaver dialog box.**

   A solid crop line with selection handles at the sides and corners appears over the image, as shown in Figure 3-8.

4. **Click and drag the selection handles to outline the area of the image you want to keep.**

   Any part of the image outside the crop line (and shaded) is deleted when the crop is completed.

5. **Double-click inside the box or press Enter (Return on a Mac).**

   The image is cropped.

You can undo cropping by choosing Edit⇨Undo Crop. However, after you save the page, changes are applied permanently to the image and can't be undone.

Photo by Casey Stoll

Figure 3-8: Drag the outline edges to define the area to crop.

Adjusting brightness and contrast

Adjusting an image's *brightness* allows you to change the overall amount of light in an image. *Contrast* controls the difference between the light and dark areas of an image.

Using Dreamweaver's editing tools permanently alters the image when the page is saved. If you're concerned, the best thing to do is to make a copy of the image and make your adjustments to the copy.

To adjust brightness and contrast, follow these steps:

1. **In the Document window, select the image you want to alter.**

   The Property inspector shows the image properties.

2. **Click the Brightness and Contrast icon (labeled in Figure 3-7).**

   A dialog box appears, indicating that the changes you make will affect the original file.

3. **Click OK in the Dreamweaver dialog box.**

   The Brightness/Contrast dialog box appears.

4. **Use the sliders to adjust the brightness and contrast settings of the image.**

   Make sure to select the Preview check box if you want to see how the changes affect the image as you move the sliders around.

5. **Click OK.**

   The settings take effect permanently when you save the page.

Sharpening an image

When you apply *sharpening* to an image, you increase the distinction between areas of color. The effect can increase the definition of shapes and lines in an image.

Using Dreamweaver's editing tools permanently alters the image when the page is saved. If you're concerned, the best thing to do is to make a copy of the image and make your adjustments to the copy.

To sharpen an image, follow these steps:

1. **In the Document window, select the image you want to sharpen.**

   The Property inspector shows the image properties.

2. **Click the Sharpen icon (labeled in Figure 3-7).**

   A dialog box appears, warning that your change is made to the original file.

3. **Click OK in the Dreamweaver dialog box.**

   The Sharpen dialog box appears.

4. **Use the slider to adjust the sharpness of the image.**

   Select the Preview check box to see how the changes affect the image as you move the slider.

5. **Click OK.**

   The image is sharpened, and changes to the image become permanent when you save changes to the page.

Opening an image in Photoshop or Fireworks from Dreamweaver

The Property inspector includes an icon that enables you to easily open an image in Photoshop or Fireworks from Dreamweaver. The Edit icon changes to the icon of the program specified in Dreamweaver's preferences. To open an image in your preferred program, simply select the image in Dreamweaver, click the icon in the Property inspector, and watch your image appear as you've commanded.

Adobe has done great work integrating the Photoshop and Fireworks programs into Dreamweaver. When you save changes to the image in Fireworks or Photoshop, they're automatically reflected in the version you've already inserted into a page in Dreamweaver.

To specify the image editor you want to associate with a file type in Dreamweaver's preferences, follow these instructions:

1. **Choose Edit⇨Preferences (Windows) or Dreamweaver⇨Preferences (on a Mac).**

   The Preferences dialog box opens.

2. **On the left, select the File Types/Editors category, as shown in Figure 3-9.**

3. **In the Extensions pane, select an image format.**

   Dreamweaver lists a wide variety of file types here, and you can associate any or all of them with your favorite editors. To associate image editors with these graphic formats, select the GIF, PNG, and JPEG options one at a time and then continue with these steps. In the example shown in Figure 3-9, I've selected the .png format and I'm associating it with Photoshop.

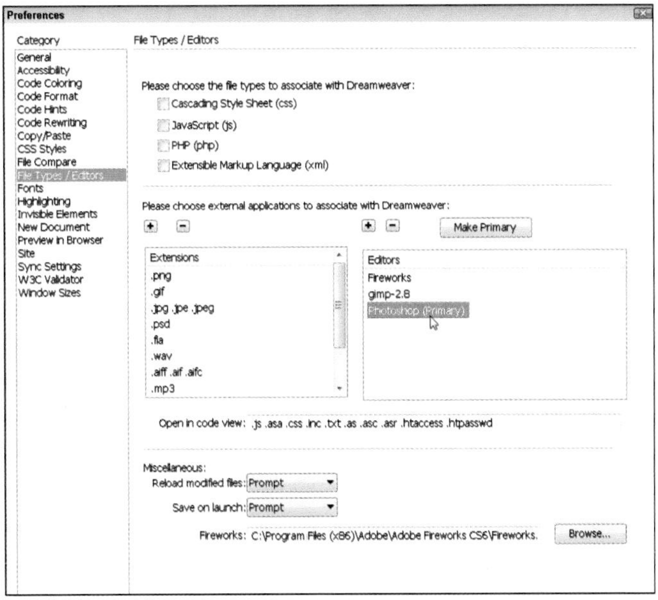

Figure 3-9: Use the preferences settings to associate your favorite image editor.

4. **In the Editors pane, select the editor you want associated with the .png format.**

   In the example shown in Figure 3-9, Photoshop is already included in the list of options, so you can simply click Photoshop to select it. If you want to associate an editor that isn't on this list, click the plus sign (+) just above the Editors pane, browse to find the program on your hard drive, and select it to make it appear on the list.

5. **With the file type and program name selected, click the Make Primary button to associate the editor with the file type.**

   The editor specified as primary is launched automatically when you select an image in Dreamweaver and click the Edit icon in the Property inspector.

6. **Select .jpeg from the Extensions pane and repeat Steps 4 and 5.**

   You can continue with this process for any or all the other formats listed.

   To add additional file formats to Dreamweaver, click the plus sign (+) over the Extensions pane and type the extension, beginning with a dot (.).

Inserting a Background Image

Background images can add depth and richness to a page design. Used cleverly, a background image that downloads quickly and efficiently helps create the illusion that the entire page is one large image. The trick is to use an image with a small file size that creates the impression of a large image. One way this works on the web is to use the default settings for a background image, which cause the image to *tile* (repeat) across and down the page (see Figure 3-10).

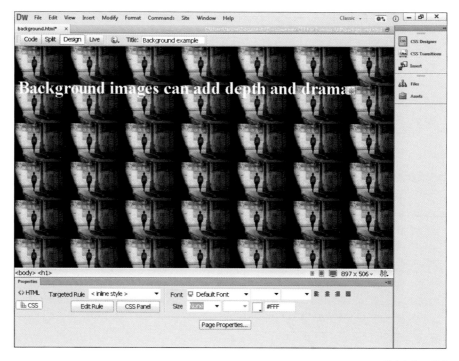

Photo by Casey Stoll

Figure 3-10: You can repeat a background image across and down a page.

Text placed on certain backgrounds (such as the one shown in Figure 3-10) can be difficult to read. Choose your background images carefully and make sure your background and your text have plenty of contrast. Reading on a computer screen is hard enough.

With CSS, you can have far greater control over the display of a background image. When you create a CSS background style, you can insert a background image that doesn't repeat or that repeats only across the Y axis or down the X axis of the page.

To insert a background image in Dreamweaver, choose Modify⇨Page Properties, click the Browse button to the right of the Background Image field (see Figure 3-11), and select the image you want to use as your background. If the image isn't already in your local site folder, Dreamweaver offers to copy it there when you click OK.

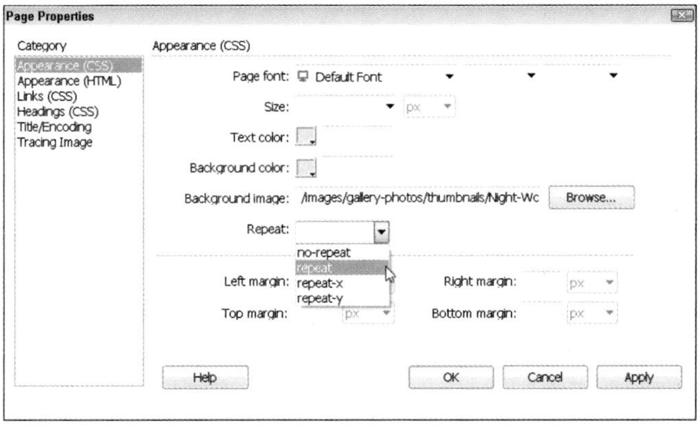

Figure 3-11: Control how a background image is repeated on a page.

When you insert an image using Dreamweaver's Page Properties feature, you can use the Repeat drop-down list to specify how the image repeats on the page, as shown in Figure 3-11. When you specify a repeat option, Dreamweaver automatically creates a style for the page with these background settings. If you use the CSS Definition dialog box to further edit the background options in the body style (covered in Chapter 5), you can also specify where the background image is displayed on a page.

Managing, Testing, and Publishing a Website

*T*he scenario is shocking: You create a page design that looks just perfect in your favorite web browser on your own computer. You publish your site on the Internet and tell all your friends. And the next thing you know, your cousin in Chicago and your friends in Italy are telling you that the site looks terrible, the text is unreadable, and your video files won't play at all.

Don't let this happen to you. Take time to test your work before you publish it to ensure that your site works well in the many different web browsers, operating systems, and monitor sizes that your visitors are likely to use on today's increasingly diverse Internet. Web pages can look very different depending on the browser, especially older versions, and they can fall apart if you design on a giant desktop monitor and then try to use the site on a tiny cell phone screen.

No matter how your pages are viewed, you also want to use Dreamweaver's tools to check that your site code is valid, all the links work, and everything is in tip-top shape. As you work with the files in your site, you may appreciate that Dreamweaver includes tools for managing files and folders so that your links stay current as your site grows. And when you're ready to publish or update your site on the web, Dreamweaver has tools to help you transfer files, too. In this chapter, you discover how to test and publish a website, and you find a few tips I've learned about designing websites that look good to everyone who visits your site.

If you're looking for information about where to host your website, how to choose a web-hosting service, or how to register a domain name, find recommendations and tips for choosing the best services on my site at www.digitalfamily.com/hosting/.

Understanding Why Web Pages Can Look Bad in Some Browsers

A confusing and frustrating aspect of web design is that different browsers and computer systems affect a page's appearance. You can create a page that looks great in Dreamweaver and test it in a browser to confirm that it looks fine only to discover later that the page looks terrible in another web browser or on a different computer system. Web pages can look different from one system to another for many reasons, but the following issues are the most common culprits:

- **Browser differences:** Today, dozens of browsers are in use on the web, not counting the different versions of each browser. For example, at the time of this writing, Internet Explorer (IE) 10 is the newest release from Microsoft, but a significant percentage of web users haven't upgraded yet and are still using IE7 or even earlier versions. (More on browser differences in the next section.)

- **Mobile phones and tablets:** The biggest challenge of today's web is creating websites that look good on tiny mobile phone browsers, as well as giant screens. Just because you can open your website on a smartphone doesn't mean it's usable on the tiny screen. (For more on designing for mobile and other small screen sizes, see Chapter 8.)

- **Unsupported design features:** One of the most exciting improvements in web design in the last several years is the addition of design options such as drop shadows, gradients, transparency, and the capability to use almost any font. You can add these design features to your web pages, even though they won't be visible on older browsers. However, make sure your pages are still *readable*, even if the drop shadows and other features don't work. (See the two upcoming figures for examples of how CSS3 styles aren't displayed in older web browsers.)

✔ **Hardware differences:** Another challenge comes from the differences between Macintosh and Windows computers. For example, most fonts appear smaller on a Macintosh than on a PC. (Times 12 on a PC looks like Times 10 on a Mac, which makes text harder to read and can change the layout of a page.) Image colors and brightness can also vary from one computer to another.

✔ **Individual preferences:** Most web browsers include preference settings that individual users can adjust to suit their needs. For example, someone may increase the text size in his or her browser settings to make text more readable, which may cause the text on your carefully designed pages to wrap and ruin the page design.

✔ **Monitor resolution settings:** In addition, the same web page may look very different on a 21" monitor than it does on a 15" monitor. And even on the same monitor, different resolution settings can alter the way a page looks. On a PC, a common resolution is 1024 x 768; on a Mac, the resolution is generally set much higher, making the design look much smaller, even if the monitor sizes are the same.

As a result of all these differences, the same web page can look very different to the people who visit a website. For example, Figure 4-1 shows a web page displayed in Dreamweaver's Design view with the monitor resolution set to 1024 x 768. The screen is typical for a web page viewed in an old browser on a relatively small, low-resolution monitor.

To get around the limitations of Dreamweaver's Design view, Adobe added the Live view option in Dreamweaver version 5. In version 6, Adobe shortened the name to Live and placed the option to the right of the other view options, Code, Split, and Design. The Live option changes the display engine to the webkit engine, which is used in the Safari and Chrome web browsers. In version 7, Adobe updated the Live view options to provide even better support for CSS3, but Design view still works much like a very old web browser.

For example, Figure 4-2 shows the same page displayed in Figure 4-1 but in the Google Chrome browser on a large monitor set to a higher resolution, 1280 x 800. Note how the Chrome web browser supports my use of an unusual font and the transparent background in the main text box in the middle page. Also note that more of the page is visible on a larger monitor with a higher resolution.

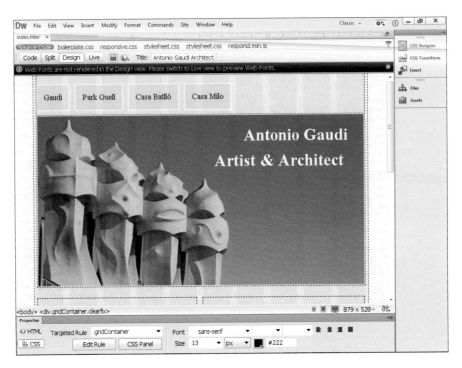

Figure 4-1: A web page in Dreamweaver's Design view with 1024 x 768 resolution.

Figure 4-2: The web page in Figure 4-1 displayed in the Google Chrome browser with the monitor set to 1280 x 800.

This challenging aspect of the web is at the root of many of the limitations and complications of creating good web designs. People who visit your site will use different web browsers and some of them may not be able to see the latest features. Your website will be viewed on very small screens on mobile phones as well as on giant television monitors. With patience, testing, and an understanding of the most problematic tags and styles, you can create great websites that look good to most — if not all — of the people who visit your website.

Understanding browser differences

The many reasons why web pages can look different from one browser to another can be boiled down to the following:

- Over the years, web browsers have evolved to support new web technologies. Thus, many older browsers still in use have trouble displaying some of the latest, most advanced features that you can use on your web pages today, such as rounded corners and drop shadows.

- Compounding this problem, the companies that make web browsers — including Microsoft, Google, and Apple — don't all agree or follow the same rules (although most are getting better at complying with at least most of the standards in their latest browser versions).

- Dozens of browsers are now in use on the web, not counting the different versions of each browser. For example, Google Chrome has become increasingly popular and is one of the best for supporting pages designed to follow modern web design standards. Unfortunately, a significant percentage of Internet users haven't yet changed or upgraded and many people are still using the browser that came with their computer. If that browser is IE6, your pages will face a real challenge because IE6 is notoriously bad at displaying CSS (Cascading Style Sheets) and other modern web features.

Browser limitations and differences are the root of many complications when creating and testing websites. Entire books and websites are dedicated to how best to design for the differences among browsers. I can't possibly cover all the issues or tricks to working around them in this book. However, in this chapter, I do include tips and testing sites to help you ensure that your pages look their best. In addition, throughout this book I try to stick to design strategies and techniques that most browsers in use today support.

The best way to make sure your site looks good to your visitors is to write clean code, test it for errors (using the testing tools included in this chapter), and then preview how the site looks in a variety of web browsers, screen sizes, resolutions, and operating systems. In the following sections, you find instructions for adding browsers to Dreamweaver's preview options and using online services to test in browsers that you don't have on your computer.

Targeting browsers for your design

Some web designers have decided to ignore users with older browsers or to simply include a warning message, such as: "This page looks best in the latest version of Firefox; upgrade now." Other designers carefully test their pages in dozens of browsers to make sure they look good to as many people as possible on the Internet. As you decide how to approach this issue, I suggest taking your audience into account. For example, consider the following scenarios and design accordingly:

- **Your visitors are advanced computer users.** If you run a website for high-end game developers or web geeks and are confident that they update their software regularly, you may not need to concern yourself with older browsers. Similarly, if you're a photographer or designer interested in winning over creative directors, you can probably assume that they have large monitors and fast computers on their desk, but keep in mind they probably also have iPhones and iPads and may be using those to review your work.

- **Your site attracts users from large organizations.** People at large corporations, universities, or other big organizations often are not allowed to update their own software. They're stuck with older browsers until some official decides to update their systems, which can take a notoriously long time. In this scenario, make sure your site is at least readable in older web browsers. That said, if you're designing a site for use by people in only one company or organization, you can often find out exactly what software they are using and design specifically for their systems.

- **Your audience is made up of people with older computers who are unlikely to have upgraded their web browsers.** If you're designing a website for a doctor's office, real estate agency, little league team, or another group likely to attract old and young visitors who may be using older computers at home, you need to design for the broadest possible audience on the Internet. Although web browsers are generally free and relatively easy to install, some people are afraid to download any software over the Internet, and many don't appreciate the benefits of using a newer browser.

The movement toward more standardized web development is growing, but getting your pages to look exactly the same on every computer on the planet is still difficult if not impossible. As a result, most designers strive to create pages that look as good as possible on as many browsers as they consider important, even if the same pages don't look *exactly* the same on all browsers.

Previewing Your Page in a Browser

Although Dreamweaver's Design and Live views display web pages much like old and new web browsers, not all interactive features work in Dreamweaver. To test links, for example, you have to preview your work in a web browser.

You can test your pages using any web browser on your computer, but I recommend that you set up at least two (and preferably, all four) of the latest versions of the most popular browsers: Internet Explorer, Firefox, Chrome, and Safari. (You find instructions for adding browsers to Dreamweaver in the next section.)

The simplest way to preview your work is to save the page you're working on and then click the Preview/Debug in Browser icon (it looks like a small globe), which is located at the top of the workspace, as shown in Figure 4-3. You can also choose File⇨Preview in Browser.

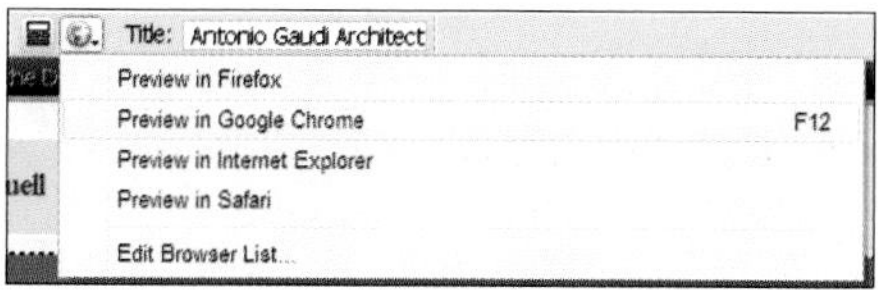

Figure 4-3: The Preview/Debug in Browser icon opens any Dreamweaver page in the selected web browser.

Adding web browsers to the preview feature

To help you test your pages, Dreamweaver makes it possible to add multiple browsers to the preview. The first step is to download and install a variety of browsers on your hard drive (see the sidebar "Downloading new browsers").

After you've installed one or more new browsers on your computer, follow these steps to add them to Dreamweaver's browser preview list:

1. **Choose File⇨Preview in Browser and then choose Edit Browser List from the fly-out menu.**

   The Preferences dialog box opens with the Preview in Browser settings displayed. *Note:* You must have a page open in Dreamweaver for these menu options to be available.

2. **Click the plus sign (+) at the top of the Preferences dialog box.**

   The Add Browser dialog box opens.

3. Enter a name for the browser.

To help make sure you're using the latest browsers, include the version number as well as the name, as I have in Figure 4-4, where I'm adding the latest version of Firefox.

4. Click the Browse button.

The Add Browser dialog box opens.

5. Navigate your hard drive until you find the browser you want to add.

Look for the browser's executable or application file (indicated with an `.exe` extension under Windows and stored in the Applications folder on a Mac). Don't use a shortcut to the actual program file.

You can add a browser to Dreamweaver only if the browser is on your hard drive. (See the nearby sidebar, "Downloading new browsers," for more about finding and downloading new browsers for testing.)

6. Double-click the name of the program file to select it and add the browser to the Application field in the Add Browser dialog box.

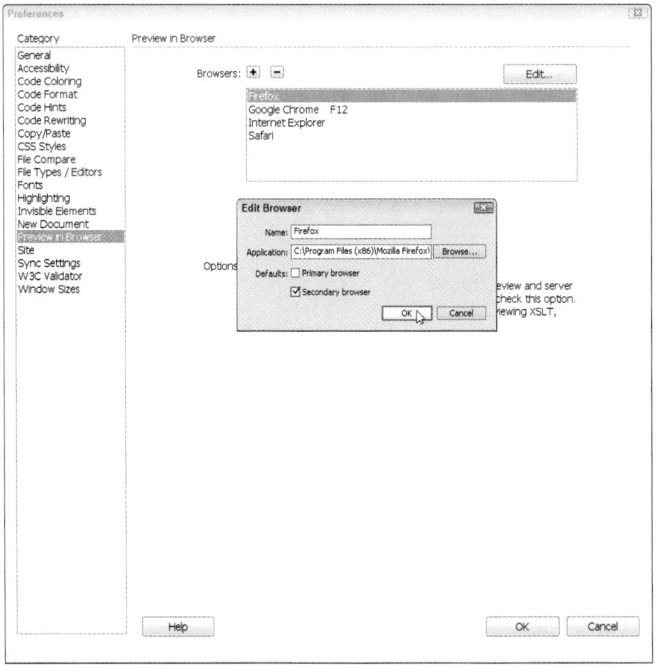

Figure 4-4: Add web browsers to the Preview in Browser list.

Downloading new browsers

So how do you put new browsers on your hard drive so that you can use them to preview your pages? The simplest way is to visit the websites of the companies that create the most popular browsers. You can download the latest version for free from each of these sites, and all four browsers are available for Mac and Windows computers:

✔ Microsoft Internet Explorer: `www.micro soft.com/ie`

✔ Mozilla Firefox: `www.firefox.com`

✔ Apple Safari: `www.apple.com/safari`

✔ Google Chrome: `www.google.com/ chrome`

7. **Click OK to add the browser to the Browsers list in the Preferences dialog box and close the Add Browser dialog box.**

8. **If you want this browser to be the first browser listed in the Browser drop-down list, select the Primary Browser check box. Otherwise, select the Secondary Browser check box.**

   You can also launch the designated primary browser by pressing the F12 key. To launch the secondary browser, press Ctrl+F12 in Windows or ⌘+F12 on a Mac.

9. **Repeat Steps 2–8 to add more browsers to the list.**

10. **After you add all the browsers you want, click OK to close the Preferences dialog box.**

Previewing pages in many web browsers

When you're designing web pages for the broadest audience on the web, it's best to test your site by previewing the pages in a variety of web browsers. The following steps walk you through the process of previewing the same web page in multiple browsers:

1. **Open a web page that you want to preview in Dreamweaver.**

2. **Choose File⇨Preview in Browser, and select a web browser from the list of browser options.**

   You find out how to add more browsers to the Preview in Browser list in the preceding section, "Adding web browsers to the preview feature."

3. **Study and test the page.**

   Carefully test all links, rollovers, and other special effects to make sure that the page appears the way you want it to in this browser.

4. **Close the browser window and return to Dreamweaver to make any necessary changes to the page.**

   Often, you can make the page look better with minor changes, such as swapping the position of an image with a block of text, or adding a paragraph return using a <p> tag after a video.

5. **Preview the same page again in the same browser to make sure the changes you made had the desired effect.**

   Return to Dreamweaver to make further changes as necessary.

6. **Follow Steps 2–5 to preview the same page in another web browser.**

Testing sites with online browser services

Unless you own a dozen computers with different operating systems and a vast collection of web browsers, you can't fully test your website — at least not on your own. Fortunately, a growing number of online services are available to help you preview your pages on many different operating systems and browsers — without your having to manage multiple computers and browsers yourself.

Like many professional web designers, I have three computers on my desk (Macs and Windows), and many different browsers installed on each. I also have an Apple iPad, a Samsung Galaxy tablet, and an iPhone because I like having several options handy to test my pages while I'm developing a design.

After a page design looks good in all the browsers and systems I have on my desk, I upload the site to a server and do a final test in even more browsers using these online services.

Following are some of the best places to test your website online:

- **Browser Sandbox** (spoon.net/browsers/): With Browser Sandbox, you can test a website using any of the eight most popular browsers, but you do have to go through a time-consuming installation process to use them. After you've set up each browser, you can launch it and surf the web as if the browser were installed on your computer. That means you can test interactive features, such as those that require JavaScript, AJAX, forms, and other advanced programming.

- **Cross Browser Testing** (crossbrowsertesting.com): The Cross Browser Testing site takes website testing to another level. Instead of simply providing screenshots of a web page in different browsers, or letting you launch a few browsers in which to test pages, this site lets you take over other computers connected to the Internet so that you can do sophisticated testing of interactive features using a variety of browsers and operating systems. For example, suppose you use a computer that runs Windows 7 and want to see what your site will look like on a Mac. Simply choose to use a computer with the Mac OS and then view your site on that computer in any of a dozen browsers. This high-end service requires that you purchase a monthly subscription but also offers a free 30-day trial period at the time of this writing.

- **Browsershots** (www.browsershots.org): Browsershots is a popular online testing tool. You simply enter a page's URL and choose the options you want to use for testing. Browsershots then tests the page you submitted on each computer system selected with the specified browser and takes a screenshot. Although you can't test interactive features with this service, it's one of the easiest options and provides the largest collection of browsers to choose from. The basic service is free, but testing can take from a few minutes to a few hours. If you don't like waiting, you can upgrade to their priority processing for a fee.

Testing your designs with mobile, tablet, and desktop previews

Dreamweaver CC includes preview features that make it possible to view the same web page in three screen sizes. This capability is useful when you use the latest in CSS options to design HTML pages that use more than one style sheet, each designed for a different screen size.

To switch among the three view sizes, open any page in Dreamweaver, and then click the three small icons at the bottom right of the workspace in turn, as shown in Figure 4-5.

In Chapters 5–8, you find instructions on how to use Dreamweaver's CSS features, including how to use the CSS media query options and the fluid grid layout features to design pages that adapt to different screen sizes. Using media queries is an advanced topic, even for those familiar with the basics of CSS, but if you're interested in designing websites that work on mobile phones, as well as large monitors, it's worth the extra effort to learn how to use these features.

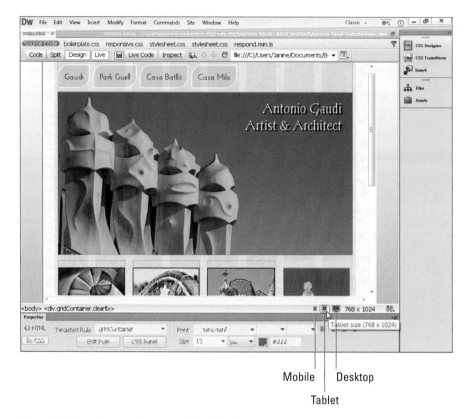

Mobile | Desktop

Tablet

Figure 4-5: A web page as it appears in tablet size.

Figure 4-5 shows a web page when viewed on a tablet-sized screen, and Figure 4-6 shows the same screen on a small mobile device. In Chapter 8, you find instructions for using Dreamweaver's fluid grid layouts to design multiple sets of styles for one page to achieve the kind of variation in page design you see in these two figures.

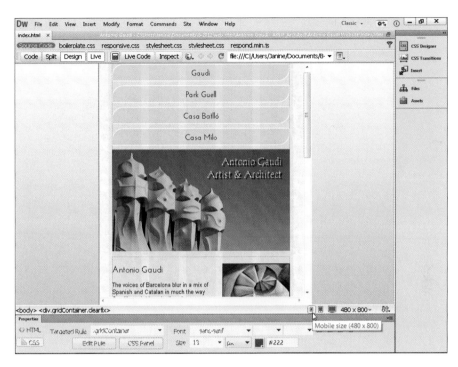

Figure 4-6: A web page as it appears mobile screen size.

Testing Your Work with the Site Reporting Feature

Before you put your site online for the world to see, check your work using the Dreamweaver site reporting feature. You can create a variety of reports to identify problems with external links, redundant and empty tags, untitled documents, and missing alternate text — important errors that are easily missed. Before Dreamweaver added this great feature, finding these kinds of mistakes was a tedious, time-consuming task.

Designing a simple page for mobile devices

You can follow several approaches when designing for different screen sizes. If you have the time, budget, or skills, I recommend that you redesign your site using one of the two most popular approaches to designing for multiple screen sizes: responsive or adaptive, covered in Chapter 8. If you just want to make sure that the most important information on your site is accessible to mobile phone users, I recommend that you create a second very simplified version of your website designed to best serve the limited display options of mobile devices and then link your main website to the alternate mobile design. If you have experience writing server scripts (or can hire someone to do it for you), create an autodetect script that can determine whether visitors to your site are using a mobile device or a computer and then direct them to the best version of your site. (You can learn more about autodetect scripts and mobile web design on my site at `www.DigitalFamily.com/mobile`.)

Consider the following important tips when designing a version of your website for mobile devices:

- The screen size on a mobile device is extremely limited.

- Use a minimum of images because download times are much slower on cell phones.

- Avoid outdated HTML styling and layout options, such as frames and iframes, which may not be displayed at all on mobile devices.

- Adjust your design to require as little scrolling and user movement as possible and make your links big and separated so they can be activated by a fat fingertip. Mobile phone users point not with a mouse but with up and down arrows and at best a touchscreen.

- Always validate your web page code (numerous validation services are available for free online, such as the popular one at `validator.w3.org`). Mobile browsers are even less forgiving than traditional website browsers about errors in your code.

- Avoid using Flash and Flash video because many mobile devices don't support them. Use multimedia sparingly and consider using video-hosting services such as YouTube or Vimeo (covered in Chapter 13). Services such as Vimeo offer sophisticated video servers and optimize video for different devices for you.

To read more about designing for mobile devices, check out my books *iPhone & iPad Web Design For Dummies* and *Mobile Web Design For Dummies* (Wiley).

Follow these steps to produce a site report of your entire website:

1. **In the drop-down list at the top of the Files panel, select the site you want to work on.**

   If you already have the site you want to test open in Dreamweaver, you can skip this step. *Note:* Your site appears in the Files panel list only if you've completed the site setup process covered in Chapter 2.

2. **Make sure any documents you have open in Dreamweaver's workspace are saved by choosing File⇨Save All.**

3. **Choose Site➪Reports.**

   The Reports dialog box appears, as shown in Figure 4-7.

4. **In the Report On drop-down list, choose Entire Current Local Site.**

   I regularly use this option to test an entire site just before publishing it to the web, but you can choose to check only a single page by opening the page in Dreamweaver and then choosing Current Document in the Report On drop-down list. You can also run a report on selected files or on a particular folder. If you choose Selected Files in Site, you must first select the pages you want to check in the Files panel.

5. **In the Select Reports section, click the check boxes to select the reports you want.**

   Table 4-1 describes the kind of report you get with each option. You can select as many reports as you want.

6. **Click the Run button to create the report(s).**

   If you haven't already done so, you may be prompted to save your file, set up your site, or select a folder.

   The Site Results panel appears, displaying a list of problems found on the site. To sort the list by category (filename, line number, or description), click the corresponding column heading.

7. **Double-click any item in the Site Results panel to open the corresponding file in the Document window.**

   The file opens, and the error is highlighted in the workspace.

   You can also right-click (Windows) or Control+click (Mac) any line of the report and choose More Info to find additional details about the specific error or condition.

8. **Use the Property inspector or another Dreamweaver feature to correct the identified problem, and then save the file.**

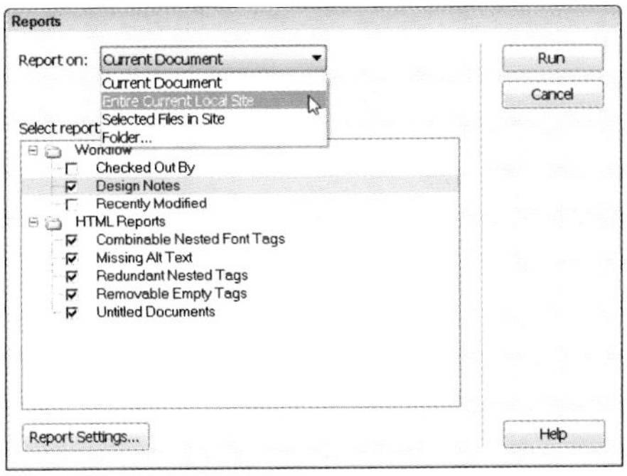

Figure 4-7: Run reports on a single page or the entire site.

Table 4-1	Site Report Options
Report Name	**What It Does**
Checked Out By	Lists files checked out of the site and identifies the person who checked them out. This feature is necessary only if you're working with other web designers on the same site and there's a risk of overwriting each other's work.
Design Notes	Lists Design Notes used in the site.
Recently Modified	Lists files that have been edited within a specified time period. You can set the time period for the report by selecting the Recently Modified check box and then clicking the Report Settings button at the bottom of the dialog box.
Combinable Nested Font Tags	Lists all instances where you can combine nested tags. For example, `<font color="#000000"><font size="2">Great Websites You Should Visit</font></font>` is listed because you can simplify the code by combining the two font tags into `<font color="#000000" size="2">Great Websites You Should Visit</font>`.
Missing Alt Text	Lists all the image tags that do not include Alt text. Alt text is a text description for an image tag included in the HTML code as an alternative if the image is not displayed. Alt text is important to anyone who uses a special browser that reads web pages.
Redundant Nested Tags	Lists all places where you have redundant nested tags. For example, `<h1>Good headlines <h1>are harder to write</h1> than you might think</h1>` is listed because you can simplify the code by removing the second `<h1>` tag to make the code look like this: `<h1>Good headlines are harder to write than you might think</h1>`.
Removable Empty Tags	Lists the empty tags on your site. Empty tags can occur when you delete an image, a text section, or another element without deleting all the tags applied to the element.
Untitled Documents	Lists filenames that don't have a title. The `<title>` tag is easy to forget because it does not appear in the body of the page. Instead, the `<title>` tag specifies the text that appears at the very top of the browser window and the text that appears in the Favorites list when someone bookmarks a page. You can enter a title for any page by entering text in the Title field just above the work area or in the Title field in the Page Properties dialog box.

Finding and Fixing Broken Links

If you're trying to rein in a chaotic website or you just want to check a site for broken links, you'll be pleased to discover Link Checker. You can use this feature to verify the links in a single file or an entire website. Link Checker can also automatically fix all the referring links at once if a link is broken. (You find instructions for creating links in Chapter 2.)

Here's an example of what Link Checker can do. Assume that someone on your team (because you would never do such a thing yourself) changed the name of a file from `new.htm` to `old.htm` without using the Files panel or any of Dreamweaver's automatic link update features. Maybe this person changed the name using another program or simply renamed it in Explorer (Windows) or Finder (Mac) the way you would change the name of most other files on your computer. Changing the filename was easy, but what this person may not have realized is that the links are now broken if he or she didn't change the links to the file when the file was renamed.

If only one page links to the file that your clueless teammate changed, fixing the broken link isn't such a big deal. As long as you remember which file the page links from, you can simply open that page and use the Property inspector to reset the link the same way you created the link in the first place.

But many times, a single page in a website is linked to many other pages. When that's the case, fixing all the link references can be time-consuming and forgetting some is all too easy, which is why Link Checker is so helpful.

Link Checker may not work properly if you're working on a dynamic website that uses a database or a content management system such as WordPress, Joomla!, or Drupal. The Checker works best for sites with static HTML pages and sites created using `.dwt` Dreamweaver templates.

Checking for broken links

To check a site for broken links, follow these steps:

1. **In the drop-down list at the top of the Files panel, select the site you want to work on.**

   If you already have the site open in Dreamweaver, you can skip this step.

   You must have the entire site on your hard drive and you must have completed the site setup process (covered in Chapter 2) for Link Checker to work properly.

2. Choose Site➪Check Links Sitewide.

The Link Checker tab, shown in Figure 4-8, opens in the Results panel at the bottom of the page, just under the Property inspector. The tab displays a list of internal and external links. The tab also lists any pages, images, or other items not linked from any other page and identifies them as unused files. Large unused files, such as images and videos, can waste space on your server, so this list is handy if you want to clean up old files you no longer use on your site.

REMEMBER

Remember, just because you delete a file from your hard drive doesn't mean the file is deleted from the server where you host your website. Make sure you remove files from both the Remote Site window in the Files panel as well as the Local Site panel. (For more on using FTP and synchronization to update or delete files automatically on your server, see the section "Publishing Your Website," later in this chapter.)

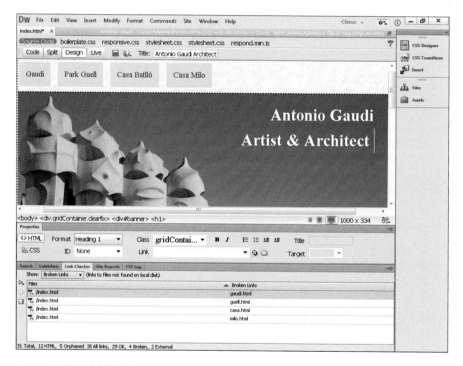

Figure 4-8: The Link Checker report displays broken links, external links, and unused files.

Fixing broken links

Broken links are one of the worst problems you can have on a website. Nothing turns off visitors faster than clicking a link and getting a *File Not Found* error page. After you identify a broken link in a site, fix it as soon as possible. Fortunately, Dreamweaver makes fixing broken links simple by providing quick access to files with broken links and automating the process of fixing multiple links to the same file.

After using the Link Checker tab described in the preceding section to identify broken links, follow these steps to fix them by using the Results panel:

1. **With the Results panel open at the bottom of the page, double-click a filename that Dreamweaver identifies as a broken link.**

   The page and its corresponding Property inspector open. The Results panel remains visible.

2. **Select the broken link or image on the open page.**

   For example, you can fix a broken image by selecting the Broken Image icon on the page and then reinserting the image using the Property inspector to find the correct image file.

3. **In the Property inspector, click the Browse icon (which looks like a folder) to the right of the Link text box.**

   (Instead of using the Browse button to find the correct image, you can type the correct filename and path in the text box.) The Select Image Source dialog box appears.

4. **Select the filename of the correct image and then click OK.**

   The link automatically changes to reflect the new filename and location. If you replace an image, the image file reappears on the page.

   If the link that you correct appears in multiple pages and you fix the link using the broken link's Results panel, Dreamweaver prompts you with a dialog box asking whether you want to fix the remaining broken link references to the file. Click the Yes button to automatically correct all other references. Click the No button to leave the other files unchanged.

Finding files by their addresses

If you're not sure where you saved a file or what you called it, but you can get to it with your browser, you can determine the filename and location by looking at the URL in the browser's address bar. Each folder in a website is included in the address to a page within that folder. Folder names are separated by the forward slash, /, and each filename can be distinguished because it includes an extension. For example, the URL in the browser's address bar of the Speeches page on my site tells me that the file is named `speeches.html`. (See the URL in the top of the figure in this sidebar.)

Similarly, you can identify the name and location of any image you're viewing on a web page. If you're using Google Chrome or Firefox, place your cursor over the image and right-click (Windows) or Control+click (Mac) and then choose Inspect Element. (In Internet Explorer, choose Properties.) The Element Properties dialog box includes the specific URL of the image, which has the name and folder (path). If you're using the Safari browser on a Mac, you won't find this option, but you can Control+click any image and choose Open Image in New Window. Then, in the new window, look in the URL field and you'll find the name and path for the image.

Making Global Changes to Links

If you want to globally change a link to point at a new URL or to some other page on your site, you can use the Change Link Sitewide option to enter the new URL and change every reference automatically. You can use this option to change any kind of link, including mailto, FTP, and script links. For example, if an e-mail address that you use throughout your site changes, you can use this feature to fix it automatically — a real timesaver. You can use this feature also when you want a string of text to link to a different file. For example, you can change every instance of the words *Enter This Month's Contest* to link to /contest/january.htm instead of /contest/december.htm throughout your website.

To change a collection of links with the Change Link Sitewide feature, follow these steps:

1. **Make sure the site you want to work on is displayed in the Files panel.**

   See the preceding exercise for instructions on selecting a site.

2. **Choose Site⇨Change Link Sitewide.**

   The Change Link Sitewide dialog box appears.

3. **Enter the old address and then enter the new address, or click the Browse button to identify files where you want to change the links.**

   You can use this feature to change any link, including e-mail links, links from one page to another within a site, or links to a different website.

4. **Click OK.**

   Dreamweaver updates any documents that include the specified links.

Any changes you make to links using Dreamweaver's automated link features occur only on the local version of your site on your hard drive. Make sure you upload all affected files to your web server to ensure that all changes are included on your published site. To automatically reconcile changes on your local and remote sites, use Dreamweaver's Synchronize Files feature, which I describe later in this chapter.

Managing Files and Folders in Your Site

Dreamweaver includes a variety of tools that help you manage the files, folders, and subfolders within a site without breaking links or image references. You can use the Files panel to rename and rearrange files and folders, as well as create new folders, all with drag-and-drop ease.

You need to complete the simple site setup process for Dreamweaver's Files panel features to work. If you haven't already set up your site, turn to the instructions at the beginning of Chapter 2. (If you're getting tired of my reminding you of this point throughout this book, realize that you'd probably be even more annoyed if you didn't know the site setup process was necessary and couldn't get these features to work.)

Moving and renaming files and folders

To move or rename files and folders in a website, follow these steps:

1. **Open the site you want to work on (if it's not already open in Dreamweaver) by selecting the site name from the drop-down list at the top of the Files panel.**

   When you select a site by clicking the site name, the folders and files in that site appear in the Files panel.

2. **Click the plus sign (Windows) or the small arrow (Mac) to open the local site folder or any subfolder to display the files within the folder.**

   Click the minus sign to close a folder or subfolder.

3. **To *move* a file or folder:**

   a. **In the Files panel, select the file or folder you want to move.**

   b. **Drag the selected file, group of files, or folder onto a folder.**

   Dreamweaver automatically moves the files into the folder and changes all the related links. The Files panel works much like the Explorer window on a PC or Finder on a Mac, except Dreamweaver tracks and fixes links when you move files through the Files panel.

   If you move or rename files or folders in Finder or Explorer instead of in the Files panel, you will break any links set to or from those files and any image references within them.

   When you move a linked file into a new folder in Dreamweaver, the Update Files dialog box appears, listing any linked pages that need to be updated, as shown in Figure 4-9.

   c. **To adjust the links so they don't break, choose Update.**

   If you choose Don't Update, any links to or from that file are left unchanged. Of course, you can always move the file back to its original location to restore the links.

Figure 4-9: You see all files that will be changed during the update process.

4. To *rename* a file or folder:

   a. **In the Files panel, select the file or folder you want to rename.**

   b. **Click twice on any filename or folder name.**

   Much like Finder or Explorer on your computer, you need to click twice with a slight pause between clicks to select the name (instead of double-clicking, which opens the file).

   c. **Choose Update to adjust the links.**

Creating files and creating and deleting folders

In this section, you find out how to create a folder as well as how to delete folders and files:

1. **Open the site you want to work on (if it's not already open in Dreamweaver) by selecting the site name from the drop-down list at the top of the Files panel.**

   When you select a site by clicking the site name, the folders and files in that site appear in the Files panel.

2. **Click the plus sign (Windows) or the small arrow (Mac) to open the local site folder or any subfolder to display the files within the folder.**

   Click the minus sign to close a folder or subfolder.

3. **To *create* a new folder in the Files panel:**

   a. **Right-click (Option-click on a Mac) the main site folder or any subfolder where you want to create a new folder.**

   A list of options appears.

b. **Choose New Folder from the list.**

A new, untitled folder appears inside the folder just selected in the preceding step.

c. **Name the new folder by typing new text to replace the word *Untitled*.**

After you've created a new folder, you can drag files or other folders in the Files panel into the new folder.

4. **To *delete* a folder or file from the Files panel, select the file or folder and then press the Delete or Backspace key.**

This action will permanently delete the folder or file from your hard drive.

Publishing Your Website

If you're looking for the section where you find out how to upload your site (or any or all pages in your site) to your web server, you've found it.

After you create and test your website so that it's ready to publish on the web, you can put Dreamweaver's publishing tools to work. Which features you use depend on the kind of web server you use. If you're using a commercial service provider, you'll most likely need Dreamweaver's FTP features, which I cover in detail in the following section.

Note that you need the following information from your web-hosting service before you can configure Dreamweaver's FTP features. Most service providers send this information in an e-mail message when you first sign up for an account. If you don't have this information, you will need to contact your service provider for it, because it's unique to your account on your web-hosting service. Here's what you need:

✔ The FTP host name.

✔ The path to the web directory (optional but highly recommended), such as `/web/htdocs/jcwarner`.

✔ Your FTP login or user name.

✔ Your FTP password.

⮑ Any special instructions from your server, such as if you need to use passive FTP or any of the other advanced settings covered in Step 11 in the exercise that follows. These settings vary from server to server, so you need to ask your web-hosting service. (If you're having trouble connecting and you're not sure about these options, you can always experiment by selecting and deselecting these options to see whether a setting enables you to connect.)

Setting up Dreamweaver's FTP features

After you gather all your FTP information, you're ready to set up Dreamweaver's FTP publishing features. This process can seem daunting and often takes a few tries to get right, but the good news is that you have to do it only once. (Dreamweaver saves these settings for you so you don't have to set them up every time you want to upload new pages to your site.)

Follow these steps to set up Dreamweaver's FTP features and publish files to a web server:

1. **Choose Site⇨Manage Sites.**

   The Manage Sites dialog box opens.

2. **In the list of defined sites, double-click the name of the site you want to publish.**

   If your site is not listed in this dialog box, you haven't set up your site. Refer to the instructions for site setup in Chapter 2 and then return to complete these steps.

3. **Select Servers from the categories listed in the left panel of the Site Setup dialog box.**

   The server list appears. If you haven't yet set up any web servers in Dreamweaver, this list is blank

4. **Click the small plus sign at the bottom left of the server list area, as shown in Figure 4-10.**

   The Basic category opens in the servers dialog box and FTP is automatically selected. (If you need to use an option other than FTP, see the list explaining all the Dreamweaver options by the Technical Stuff icon at the end of these steps.)

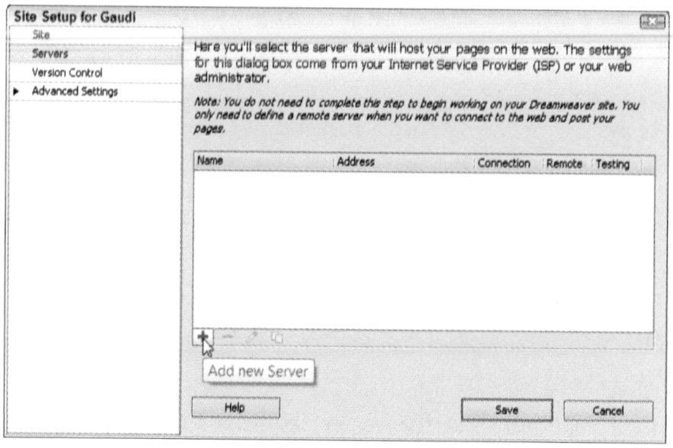

Figure 4-10: Click the small plus sign to open the Basic server configuration dialog box.

5. **Enter a name in the Server Name field.**

   You can name your server anything you like. Choose a name that will enable you to easily choose among the servers you've set up. (If you use only one web server to host your site, the choice doesn't matter as much as it does if you host your site on multiple servers — something generally done only by very large or international sites.)

6. **Enter the FTP address for your web server account.**

   Again this information depends on how your web server is set up, but most use one of the following: `ftp.servername.com`, `ftp.your domainname.com`, or simply `yourdomain.com` without anything at the beginning of the domain.

7. **In the Username and Password fields, type your username (sometimes called a login name) and password.**

   Again, this information is unique to your account on your web server.

8. **Select the Save box to the right of the Password field if you want Dreamweaver to store your access information.**

   This step is handy because you can then automatically connect to the server anytime you want to upload or download pages. However, selecting Save could enable anyone with access to your computer to gain access to your web server.

9. **Click the Test button to make sure you've entered everything correctly.**

   Making a mistake is easy, so the capability to test the connection and make any needed adjustments before you close this dialog box is helpful. If you connect with no problems, you see a message stating that Dreamweaver connected to your web server successfully. (***Note:*** You must save the password to use the test feature, but you can deselect the Save Password box after you test if you prefer not to save the password in the program.)

If you do have trouble connecting to your site, skip ahead to Step 11 for a few advanced options that may help.

10. **In the Root Directory field, type the directory on the remote site in which documents visible to the public are stored (also known as the local site folder).**

    The root directory usually looks something like this: `public_html/` or `www/htdocs/`. Again, how your server directory is set up may vary depending on your service provider.

    If you upload your files to the wrong directory on your server, they won't be visible when you view your site through a browser. The nearby sidebar, "Why can't I see the files on my server?" helps you work around this potentially frustrating problem with tips on identifying where to upload your website after you log into your server and finding the root directory to enter in this field if you can't find it in the information you get from your web-hosting company.

11. **Click the small arrow to the left of More Options, as shown in Figure 4-11.**

    You may not need to change any of these settings, but if you're having trouble connecting to your server, and you're sure you've entered your user name, password, and FTP address correctly, adjusting these settings may enable you to connect.

    I recommend selecting and deselecting each option in this area in turn, and then clicking the Test button after each change, to see if any of these adjustments makes the difference and enables you to connect to your server.

    A little experimentation with settings before waiting on hold with tech support is usually worth the effort. But if you're really having trouble establishing a connection with your server, call or e-mail the tech support staff at your web server. The only people who can help you are those who run your web server, because the settings are specific to your service provider and can vary dramatically from one hosting company to another.

12. **After clicking Test successfully connects to your server, click Save to save your settings.**

Basic	Advanced

Server Name: Gaudi Server

Connect using: FTP

FTP Address: ftp.antoinogaudi.com   Port: 21

Username: anonymous

Password: •••••••• ☑ Save

Test

Root Directory:

Web URL: http://ftp.antoinogaudi.com/

▼ More Options

☑ Use Passive FTP

☐ Use IPV6 Transfer Mode

☐ Use Proxy, as defined in Preferences

☑ Use FTP performance optimization

☐ Use alternative FTP move method

Help	Save	Cancel

Figure 4-11: Enter all the information from your web-hosting company

Dreamweaver saves all your FTP settings (assuming you opted to save the password). After you enter these settings properly and know that the connection works, you never have to enter them again. You can then access your web server from the Files panel in Dreamweaver, as you discover in the exercise that follows.

Dreamweaver provides seven Access options. If you work at a large company or university, you are likely to use one of these options rather than FTP. The options available from the Connect Using drop-down list in the Server Setup dialog box are as follows:

✔ **FTP (File Transfer Protocol):** Select this option to use Dreamweaver's built-in File Transfer Protocol features, which I cover in detail in the following section. You're most likely to need these settings if you're using a commercial web-hosting service.

✔ **SFTP (Secure File Transfer Protocol):** Select this option if your web server requires a more secure connection.

✔ **FTP over SSL/TLS (implicit encryption):** This option provides a more secure FTP connection, but the server can allow the client to work in an unsecure mode.

✔ **FTP over SSL/TLS (explicit encryption):** This option provides a more secure FTP connection and the server drops the connection if it is not deemed secure.

✔ **Local/Network:** Select this option if you're using a web server on a local network, such as your company or university server. For specific settings and requirements, check with your system administrator.

✔ **WebDAV (Web-based Distributed Authoring and Versioning):** Select this option if you're using a server with the WebDAV protocol, such as Microsoft IIS.

✔ **RDS (Rapid Development Services):** Select this option if you're using ColdFusion on a remote server.

Why can't I see my files on the server?

Including the root directory in Dreamweaver's FTP settings is optional, but doing so makes transferring files using Dreamweaver's Upload and Download options easier. Thus, you reduce your chances of uploading your files to the wrong directory on your server, where they won't be visible when you try to view your site through a browser.

To find the root directory and the path to that directory on your server, you may need to log into your web server and do a little experimenting before you can figure out the path to the root directory. To perform these tasks, you need to complete the steps in the "Setting Up Dreamweaver's FTP Features" and "Publishing files to a web server with FTP" sections. Trust me, the effort is worthwhile. Here's why.

When you log into most commercial web servers using the login information they provide you, you access your main folder on their server. This folder often includes several subfolders, such as a folder that stores your e-mail on the server, another folder that stores log reports of traffic to your site, and possibly several others for storing things such as CGI scripts. Among all these subfolders, finding the one in which you

need to upload your pages can be tricky. The subfolder you need is usually named something like `htdocs`, `web`, or `webfiles`. You have to upload your web pages to the right folder so that your website becomes public on the Internet and your pages are visible when you open your domain name in a web browser.

If you're not sure which folder you should use, try uploading just one file to any folder that looks like a good candidate (using the instructions in the "Publishing files to a web server with FTP" section in this chapter). Then visit your domain with a web browser to see if the page is visible. (Each time you upload another page, remember to click the Refresh button in your browser to see any changes.) After you figure out which folder corresponds to your domain name, upload all the rest of your site to that same subfolder, making sure that you mirror the local site folder on your hard drive with the main root folder on your server.

Also note that if you want to use Dreamweaver's synchronization features, also covered in this chapter, you need to include the root directory in the FTP folder.

Publishing files to a web server with FTP

You can upload pages to your server and download pages from your server using the built-in FTP capabilities of Dreamweaver.

To transfer files between your hard drive and a remote server (after you've successfully set up the FTP features covered in the preceding section), follow these steps:

1. **Make sure the site you want to work on is selected in the Files panel.**

2. **In the top left of the Files panel, click the Connect to Remote Server icon (labeled in Figure 4-12).**

   If you're not already connected to the Internet, the Connect to Remote Server icon starts your Internet connection. If you have trouble connecting this way, try establishing your Internet connection as you usually do to check e-mail or surf the web, and then return to Dreamweaver and click the Connect to Remote Server icon after you're connected to the Internet. When your computer is online, Dreamweaver should have no trouble automatically establishing an FTP connection with your host server.

   If you still have trouble establishing a connection to your web server, refer to the preceding section, "Setting up Dreamweaver's FTP features," and make sure that you specified the server information correctly.

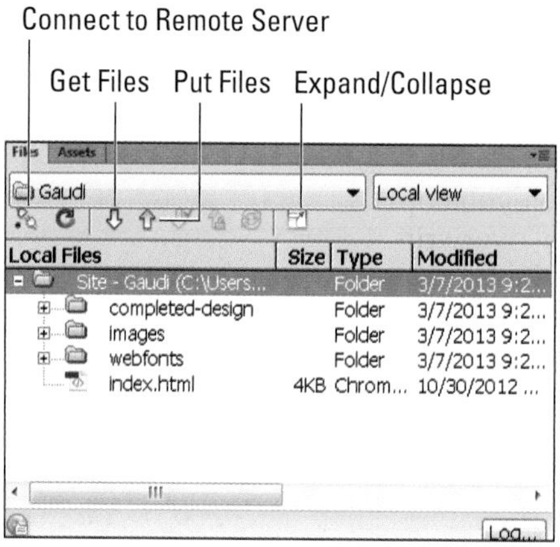

Connect to Remote Server

Get Files   Put Files   Expand/Collapse

Figure 4-12: The row of icons across the top control FTP functions.

3. **After you establish a connection between your computer and your web server, click the Expand/Collapse icon (labeled in Figure 4-12).**

   When you click this icon, Dreamweaver displays both the local folder with your site on your hard drive and the remote folder with the site on your server. I prefer the dual view, because seeing both side-by-side makes moving files from one place to another easier. It also helps me visualize the structure of the site on the server, but it does take up more space on your computer screen.

   You can also view your local site folder by choosing Local View from the drop-down list at the top right (visible in Figure 4-12). Or choose Remote View to see only the files on the server.

4. **To upload a file, select the file from the Local View panel and click the Put Files icon (the up arrow) in the Files panel.**

   The Local View panel displays the files on your hard drive.

   The files are copied automatically from your hard drive to your web server when you transfer them. You can select multiple files or folders to be transferred simultaneously.

   After you upload files to your server, test your work by using a web browser to view them online. Sometimes things that look and work fine on your computer (such as links) won't work on the server.

5. **To download files or folders, select the files or folders from the Remote View panel and click the Get Files icon (the down arrow) in the Files panel.**

   The Remote View panel displays the files on your server.

   The files are copied automatically from your web server to your hard drive when you transfer them.

   Be aware that when you copy files to or from your server, the files you're transferring overwrite the files already at the destination. Dreamweaver notifies you about the overwriting if it notices you're replacing a newer file with an older one, but it can't always correctly assess the proper time differences. Take note of these warnings, but keep in mind that you can get warnings that aren't always accurate when they're based on the age of a file, especially if you use more than one computer to work on your website.

   When the transfer is complete, you can open the files on your hard drive.

6. **To close this dual-panel dialog box and return to Dreamweaver's main workspace, simply click the Expand/Collapse icon again.**

Downloading an existing website

If you want to work on an existing website and you don't already have a copy of it on your computer's hard drive, you can use Dreamweaver to download any or all files in any website (that you have the login information to access). Then you can edit the existing pages, add new pages, or use any of Dreamweaver's other features to check links and manage the site's further development. The first step is to get a copy of the site onto your computer by downloading it from the server.

To download an existing website, follow these steps:

1. **Create a new folder on your computer to store the existing site.**

2. **Use Dreamweaver's site setup features to specify this folder as the local site folder.**

   Follow the instructions at the beginning of Chapter 2 to set up a site, if you're not sure how to do this yet.

3. **Enter the FTP settings in the Basic server dialog box (refer to Figure 4-11).**

   I explain how to do this in the "Setting up Dreamweaver's FTP features" section.

4. **Connect to the remote site by clicking the tiny Connect to Remote Server icon, which looks like the ends of two cables, in the Files panel.**

5. **Click the Get Files icon, which looks like a down arrow, to download the entire site to your local drive.**

Sometimes your web host has files on the remote server that you don't need to download. If you want to download only specific files or folders from the site, select only those files or folders in the Remote Site pane of the Files panel and click the Get Files icon. (See the sidebar "Why can't I see my files on the Server?" to find the folder on your web server that corresponds to the local site folder on your hard drive.) Re-creating the folder structure on your local computer is important because Dreamweaver needs to know the relative location of all the files in your site to set links properly. The safest option is to download the entire site; but if you're working on a large web project, downloading part of the structure will enable you to work on a section of the site without downloading it all.

If you're working on only one page or section of a site, I recommend that you choose to include *dependent files,* meaning any files linked from those pages, as you download them. Choosing this option ensures that the links are set properly when you make changes and that all related files are downloaded to your hard drive.

6. **After you download the site or specific files or folders, you can edit them as you do any other file in Dreamweaver.**

Synchronizing local and remote sites

One of the most valuable features in Dreamweaver's FTP options is the capability to automatically synchronize the files on your hard drive with the files on your server. This cool feature helps you keep track of which pages you've edited and ensures that they've been updated on the server. This capability may not matter much to you the first time you upload your site, or if you have only a few pages in your site. But if you have a large site and make frequent updates, this feature is a wonderful way to make sure you upload all the changes you make to your server. Dreamweaver also confirms which files are updated after you complete the synchronization.

Follow these steps to synchronize your website:

1. **Make sure the site you want to work on is selected and displayed in the Files panel.**

2. **Click the Connect to Remote Server icon (labeled in Figure 4-12), in the top left of the Files panel, to log on to your remote site.**

3. **Click the Expand/Collapse icon (labeled in Figure 4-12) to expand the dialog box and view the remote and local sites simultaneously.**

   The Files panel displays both the remote and local views of the site. (To collapse this dialog box, click the Expand/Collapse icon again.)

4. **Choose Site⇨Synchronize.**

   The Synchronize Files dialog box appears.

5. **In the Synchronize drop-down list, choose whether to synchronize the Entire Site or Selected Files Only.**

6. **In the Direction drop-down list, choose which option you want to use to copy the files:**

   • **Put Newer Files to Remote:** This option copies the most recently modified files from your local site to the remote site. Select the Delete Remote Files Not on Local Drive option *only* if you're sure you want those files removed from your web server.

   • **Get Newer Files from Remote:** This option copies the most recently modified files from your remote site to the local site. If you want to remove those files from your local copy, select the Delete Local Files Not on Remote Server box.

   • **Get and Put Newer Files:** This option updates both the local and remote sites with the most recent versions of all the files.

Be careful of the Delete Remote Files Not on Local Drive feature when using Get or Put. As a general rule, I recommend that you leave this option deselected because you may have folders and files on the server, such as log files, that don't exist on your hard drive, and you don't want to delete them inadvertently.

7. Click the Preview button.

The Site FTP dialog box displays the files that are about to be changed.

Now you have the option to verify the files you want to delete, put, and get. If you don't want Dreamweaver to alter a file, deselect it from the Site FTP dialog box now or forever live with the consequences.

8. Click OK.

All approved changes are automatically made, and Dreamweaver updates the Site FTP dialog box with the status.

9. When the synchronization finishes, you can choose to save or not save the verification information to a local file.

I recommend that you save the verification information because it can be handy if you want to review your changes after synchronization is complete.

Setting cloaking options

The Dreamweaver Cloaking option enables you to exclude folders or files from site-publishing features, meaning they won't be uploaded to the live site when you're synchronizing or uploading a batch of files to the server. If you're wondering why you might want to prevent files from uploading to your web server, consider this: The Cloaking feature is a handy way to prevent large graphics, such as Photoshop files, from being uploaded and taking up room on your server, while still storing your high-resolution graphics in your local site folder so you can easily keep track of them. This capability is useful, for example, if you have a layered `.psd` or `.tiff` file that you want to store near the optimized JPEG versions you use in your site. (You find information about converting images into JPEG and other web-friendly formats in Chapter 3.)

You can use the Cloaking feature to save any type of files in your local site folder, with the assurance that no one can accidentally publish the files with Dreamweaver until you uncloak them and publish them. This feature is best used for large files you don't want on your web server, such as .psd, `.tiff`, `.avi`, and other high-resolution image or video formats.

Using a dedicated FTP program

If you prefer to use a dedicated FTP program instead of Dreamweaver's built-in features, you can download the following FTP programs for the Mac and PC:

✔ FireFTP (`fireftp.mozdev.org/`): This nifty little FTP program is an add-on to Firefox and a great alternative to Dreamweaver's FTP features. Ideal for fixing things when you're on the road and don't have Dreamweaver handy or just want to view the files on your server without using Dreamweaver, this program can be added to any version of Firefox (for free).

✔ Filezilla (`filezilla-project.org`): This popular open source option works on computers running the Windows, Mac, and Linux operating systems.

✔ WS_FTP (`www.ipswitch.com`): A popular FTP program for the PC, WS_FTP is such a sophisticated FTP program that many web designers are willing to pay the cost of this program. A free trial version is also available.

✔ CuteFTP (`www.cuteftp.com`): Another popular Windows FTP program.

✔ Fetch (`www.fetchsoftworks.com`): This FTP program is a popular option for those with a Macintosh computer.

✔ Transmit (`www.panic.com/transmit`): Transmit is another popular FTP program for the Macintosh computer.

Using Design Notes to Keep in Touch

If you sometimes forget the details of your work or neglect to tell your colleagues about updates to pages in your website, the Dreamweaver Design Notes feature may save you some grief. If you're the only person working on a website, you probably don't need the features described in this section because they're intended for use on sites developed by a team of people who need to communicate with each other and make sure they don't overwrite each other's work.

Design Notes are ideal if you want to hide sensitive information from visitors, such as pricing structures or creative strategies, but make that information available to members of your development team. Comments, instructions, and other text saved as a Design Note in Dreamweaver can travel with any HTML file or image, even if the file transfers from one website to another or from Fireworks to Dreamweaver.

Essentially, Design Notes enable you to record information (such as a message to another designer on your team) and associate it with a file or folder.

Design Notes work a lot like the *comment tag* (HTML code that enables you to embed in a page text that won't appear in a browser) but with a bit more privacy. Unlike the comment tag, which is embedded directly in the HTML code of a page (and can be seen if someone views the source code behind a page on the web), Design Notes are never visible to your visitors. The only way for a visitor to view Design Notes is to deliberately type the path to your notes subdirectory and view the notes files directly. You can even explicitly block someone from accessing your files directly, but only if you have administrative access to your server. To be even more secure, you can keep the notes on your hard drive and prevent them from ever being uploaded to your server — though, of course, then your team members won't see your witty remarks.

To access the Design Notes page, choose Design Notes in the Category list in the Site Setup dialog box. The settings on this page enable you to control how Dreamweaver uses Design Notes:

- **Maintain Design Notes:** Select this option to ensure that the Design Note remains attached to the file when you upload, copy, or move it.

- **Enable Upload Design Notes for Sharing:** Choose this option to include Design Notes when you send files to the server by using FTP.

- **Clean Up Design Notes:** Use the Clean Up Design Notes button to delete Design Notes that are not associated with any files in the site.

When you create graphics in Adobe Fireworks, you can save a Design Note for each image file that is also available in Dreamweaver. To use this integrated feature, create a Design Note in Fireworks and associate it with the image. Then when you save the Fireworks image to your local website folder, the Design Note goes with it. When you open the file in Dreamweaver, the Design Note appears when you right-click the image (Control+click on the Mac). This feature is a great way for graphic designers to communicate with other members of the web development team.

Part II

Creating Page Designs with Style

You'll find more tips for writing cleaner, more concise CSS code at http://www.dummies.com/extras/dreamweavercc.

In this part . . .

- Discover the power and advantages of CSS.
- Review all the great CSS features in Dreamweaver.
- Create CSS layouts that work well across the most popular web browsers.
- Add drop shadows, gradients, and other advanced design features.
- Create web pages faster and easier and update multiple pages at once by using Dreamweaver templates.
- Create tables, split and merge cells, and use table attributes.

Introducing Cascading Style Sheets

In This Chapter

▷ Introducing CSS

▷ Comparing internal and external style sheets

▷ Looking at CSS rule options

▷ Working in the CSS Styles panel

▷ Switching between CSS and HTML

▷ Working with style sheets

Want to add a little style to your pages? *Cascading Style Sheets (CSS)* offer the best way to create websites that are accessible, flexible, and designed to work on a wide range of screen sizes and devices. Today, CSS is the clear choice when it comes to formatting web pages.

Unfortunately, most people find working with styles far more complicated and confusing than previous approaches to web design. In my experience, this confusion fades after you learn the basics and start working with styles, but brace yourself as you start into these next few chapters. CSS is confusing to everyone at first. Until you start to understand all the basics, none of it makes much sense.

If you've used a previous version of Dreamweaver, you should note that the CSS features were completely redone in version CC. Many of the dialog boxes that were in previous versions have been removed, and all CSS panels have been revised. The good news is that the new CSS Designer panel is a definite improvement, most notably because all style tools are consolidated into one area of the program, which makes adding and editing styles more efficient. If you've used previous versions of Dreamweaver, however, you may have to unlearn a few habits as you work with the new features. Either way, CSS is a fundamental part of any modern website.

This chapter explains how styles work, the different kinds of styles (and what they're best used for), and how to use the features in Dreamweaver to create and edit styles. In Chapter 6, you apply these basic skills to creating CSS layouts and complete page designs, and in Chapter 7, you discover how to add the latest CSS3 features, including drop shadows and gradients.

Introducing Cascading Style Sheets

The concept of creating styles has been around long before the web. Desktop publishing programs, such as Adobe InDesign, and even word processing programs, such as Microsoft Word, have long used styles to manage the formatting and editing of text on printed pages. In a word processor, you can create and save styles for common features, such as headlines and captions. In print design, styles are great timesavers because they enable you to combine a collection of formatting options, such as Arial, bold, and italic, and then apply all those options at once to any selected text in your document using a single style. In addition, if you change a style, you can apply the change automatically — and everywhere you've used that style in a document.

On the web, you can do all that and more with CSS because you can use style sheets for more than just text formatting. For example, you can use CSS to create styles that align images to the left or right side of a page, add margins and padding space around text and images, and change background and link colors. For all these reasons (and more), CSS is the preferred method of designing web pages among professional web designers.

CSS is a powerful tool because you can use it to make global style changes across an entire website. Suppose, for example, that you create a style for your headlines by redefining the `<h1>` tag to create large, green, bold headlines. Then one fine day, you decide that all your headlines should be purple instead of green. If you aren't using CSS, changing all your headlines could be a huge undertaking — a matter of opening every web page in your site to make changes to the font tags around your headlines. But if you're using CSS in an external style sheet, you can simply change the style that controls the headline in the style sheet and — voilá — your headlines all change from green to purple automatically.

If you ever have to redesign your site (and believe me, every good site goes through periodic redesigns), you can save hours or even days of work if you've created your design with CSS.

Understanding the basics of styles

Many people find CSS confusing at first because it's such a different approach to design than what they may be used to if they've worked in print. Following are four of the more confusing aspects of CSS for beginners:

- **Getting used to thinking about the styles on your site separately from your text, images, and other content:** For example, you can type text right into the design area in Dreamweaver, and you can format that text with HTML tags, such as the heading 1 tag, which adds the <h1> tag to the code next to the text. However, if you want to change the size or color of your text beyond these basic HTML tags, you do that in a separate area of the program (using the CSS panels covered in this chapter) and that style information is not saved anywhere near the text that if formats in the HTML code. In the early days of the web, we used HTML attributes to format text in a page, but the latest versions of Dreamweaver won't even let you use HTML attributes anymore. If you want to change things such as the size or color of text, you have to use CSS.

- **Understanding how you combine CSS and HTML to create web pages:** It's easy to confuse HTML and CSS because they are used so closely together, but they are very different animals and the better you appreciate the difference, the more all of this makes sense. Think of HTML as the building blocks that you use to create the structure of your web page and to put basic space and just a little formatting around your text. For example, when you format a headline with the <h1> tag, it changes to 24 pt and bold because that basic formatting is included in the HTML tag. Similarly, the <div> tag divides elements on a page. However, if you want to change the spacing between the content in <div> tags, or add a border around each box created by a <div> tag, you do that by defining a style and applying it to the <div> tag.

- **Understanding all the different kinds of style selectors you can choose from, such as class, ID, and tag selectors:** No matter how you create your styles, each style definition, or *rule,* contains a selector and a declaration. The *selector* identifies the name and type of style, for example, #container or .caption. (Multiple types of style selectors are available so that you can create different kinds of styles depending on what kind of formatting you want to do with the style.) The *declaration* defines the style and describes its properties, such as bold, blue, or 300 pixels wide. If those terms don't mean much to you yet, don't worry — Dreamweaver's four selector types are described later in the chapter in the "Understanding style selectors" section. And as you discover how styles work, new terms such as *selectors* and *declarations* begin to make a lot more sense.

✔ **Understanding when it's best to create external style sheets, internal style sheets, or inline styles:** *Internal style sheets* are saved in the HTML file where the formatting is applied. *External style sheets* are saved as separate files that can be attached to the pages in your website. External style sheets offer the greatest advantages because they enable you to use the same styles across any or all pages in a website. Sometimes, however, internal style sheets are useful, such as when you want to apply a style to only a single page. The section "Using internal versus external style sheets" explains how best to use the different types of style sheets.

If you're starting to feel baffled already, hang in there. I'm just giving you an overview before I take you farther and farther down the rabbit hole. CSS is a topic that's hard to grasp until you learn a number of basic concepts. Even if you're not quite sure you understand everything I've described, keep reading. As you make your way through the three chapters on CSS, it should all start making more and more sense.

Combining CSS and HTML

Essentially, web pages are created by combing HTML and CSS. You can also add more advanced programming, such as PHP or JavaScript, but the basic structure and formatting of just about every page on the web is created using HTML and CSS. Here's the simplified version of how the two work together:

1. Use HTML to create the structure of a page with tags, such as division (`<div>`), heading (`<h1>`, `<h2>`, and so on), and paragraph (`<p>`).

2. Create styles in CSS that specify the size of these elements, where they appear on a page, and a variety of other formatting options, such as the color, size, and font face.

Similarly, you use HTML to insert images and create links, and then add styles to change formatting options, such as adding more space around your images or removing the underline from your links.

Understanding style selectors

When you create new styles, you first have to choose which selector to use for which job. The selector corresponds to the kind of style you create. Each selector option has its own naming conventions, restrictions, and uses. If you're completely new to working with styles, this may not make much sense yet, but understanding the basics of selectors is a fundamental part of working with styles. I encourage you to read through all these descriptions of selectors so you can appreciate your options before you move on.

Don't feel you have to memorize all this, however. Instead, consider folding down the corner on this page so you can refer to this list of selectors as you create and edit styles later. If you don't have this book handy, you can refer to this page I created as a CSS selector reference on my website: www.digital family.com/tutorials/css-selectors/.

The following sections offer descriptions of each of the four selection types that you can use when you create styles.

Class selectors

The class selector is the most versatile selector option. *Class styles* can format any element (from text to images to multimedia), and you can use them as many times as you like on any page in a website.

Class style names always begin with a period (often called a "dot"). You can create class styles with any name as long as you don't use spaces or special characters. (Hyphens and underscores are okay.) Thus, if you create a style called *caption* for the text that appears under your pictures, it should be written like this with the dot followed by the name:

```
.caption
```

When you create styles with the class selector, you must include a dot at the beginning of the name, but don't include any space between the dot and the style name. In the style sheet, and in Dreamweaver's CSS panels, class style names appear with the dot in front of the name.

However, the dot appears only in your style sheet code. When you *apply* a class style to a <div> tag, or to any other element in a web page, the dot doesn't appear with the name in your HTML code. If you think that's inconsistent, you're not alone, but upon closer inspection of the HTML code, you will notice that all class styles are indicated by the word *class* in HTML code. Thus, if you applied the .caption style to a paragraph tag to format the text under an image, the HTML code would look like this:

```
<p class="caption">Flooding is on the rise, even in places
            that have never flooded before.</p>
```

Class styles must be applied to an element, such as the paragraph tag shown in this example. Class tags can also be used in combination with other styles, making it possible to apply more than one style to an element.

When you create a class style in Dreamweaver, the style is displayed in the CSS Designer panel on the right side of the workspace, as shown in Figure 5-1. You can apply class styles by using the CSS drop-down list in the Property inspector at the bottom of the workspace, also shown in the figure.

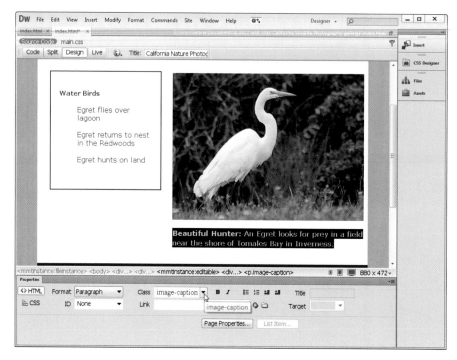

Photo by Janine Warner

Figure 5-1: Styles created with class selectors are available from the CSS drop-down list in the Property inspector.

For more details and step-by-step instructions for creating and applying styles with class selectors, see Chapter 6.

ID selectors

Think of styles created with the *ID selector* as the building blocks of most CSS page layouts. ID styles, unlike other styles, must be unique, so they can be used only once per page. This characteristic makes them well suited to formatting `<div>` tags and other block-level elements that are used to create distinct sections, such the header or footer of a page, which will be used only once. You can create as many ID styles as you want for each page, and you can use them on as many pages as you like, but you can use each one only once on each page.

Being unable to use ID styles more than once per page has some advantages, especially when you are creating complex websites with many compound styles, because this rule can help you avoid style conflicts. But this limitation is also the reason why many designers use the ID selector sparingly, opting instead to create most styles with the class selector, which can be used as many times as you want on any page.

ID styles must begin with a pound, or number, character (#). Similar to class styles, you can name ID styles anything you like as long as you don't use spaces or special characters (again, hyphens and underscores are okay). An ID style used to identify the bottom section of a page could look like this:

```
#footer
```

Similar to class styles, # isn't used in the HTML code. When a style is applied to an element, such as a `<div>` tag, the HTML code looks like this:

```
<div id="footer">Between these tags with the footer ID
        style, you would include any information you want
        at the bottom of the page, such as copyright
        information.</div>
```

Although using ID styles is common practice in many websites, the prede-signed CSS layouts included in Dreamweaver were created by combining a series of `<div>` tags with class styles using names such as `.container`, `.header`, and `.footer` to identify the main sections of the design. In Figure 5-2, you can see how a collection of class, tag, and compound styles are displayed in the CSS Designer panel.

Photos by Janine Warner

Figure 5-2: The CSS Designer panel displays all class, tag, ID, and compound styles available on any open page.

Tag selectors

The tag selector is used to redefine existing HTML tags. Use this option if you want to change the appearance of an existing HTML tag, such as the `<h1>` (heading 1) tag or the `<ul>` (unordered list) tag.

In many cases, redefining existing HTML tags with your desired formatting using CSS has advantages over creating new styles with the class or ID selectors. For example, content formatted with the heading 1 tag is presumed to be the most important text on a page. For that reason, many search engines give priority to text formatted with the `<h1>` tag. Similarly, the hierarchical structure of the `<h1>`–`<h6>` tags helps ensure that, even if visitors to your site change the text size in their web browser, text formatted with the heading 1 tag is still larger relative to text formatted with a heading 2 tag, which is larger than text formatted with the heading 3 tag, and so on.

When you use the tag selector, the style definition is applied automatically to any text or other element that's been formatted with the corresponding tag. Thus, if you've formatted a heading with an `<h1>` tag and then create a new `<h1>` style, the formatting you used to define the style will apply automatically to the heading as soon as the style is created.

As you type the name of any HTML tag in the selector panel in Dreamweaver, a drop-down list appears providing easy access to the HTML tags. This shortcut can save on typing and help ensure that you enter the name correctly. After the tag names appear, simply choose the tag you want to use, as shown in Figure 5-3.

Creating compound styles

The *compound selector* can be used to combine two or more style rules to create a style definition that is displayed only when one style is contained within another. Compound styles are useful, for example, when you want to use the heading 2 tag multiple times to format headlines in different ways on the same web page. For example, you could create one style for headlines that appear in the main story area of a page and another style for headlines that appear in the sidebar on the page but use the heading 2 tag to format both.

Compound styles are created by combining ID, class, or tag styles. Following is an example:

```
.sidebar h2
```

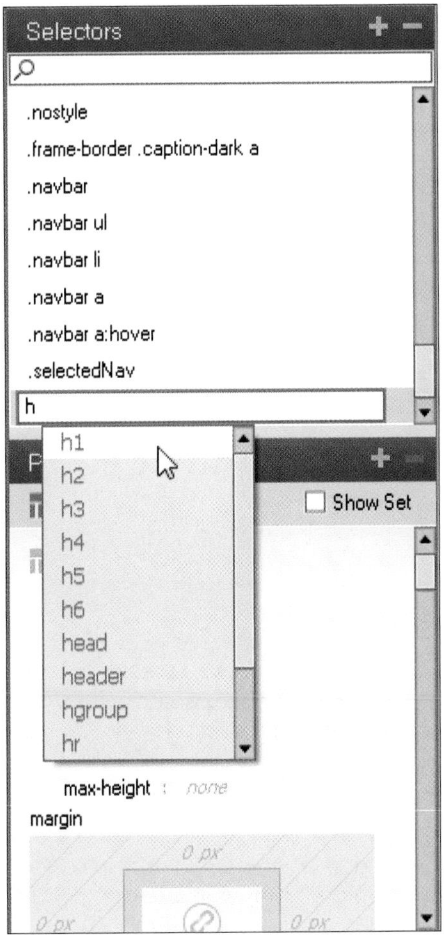

Figure 5-3: Redefine the appearance of any HTML tag by creating a style with a tag selector.

See Figure 5-4 for an example of how the list item tag, the `<li>` tag, appears when it is defined within a class style named `.navbar`. For a compound style, you must

- ✔ Include a space between each name or tag in a compound style
- ✔ Not include the brackets around the tag in a style name

Figure 5-4: Use the compound style selector to combine styles to apply more specific formatting.

In this example, the style definition will apply only to `<li>` tags that appear within another element, such as a `<div>` tag with the `.navbar` class style. Combining styles in this way enables you to use the same HTML tags with different formatting in different parts of the same page. For example, you might define one set of styles for text in an unordered list in your navigation bar, and another set of styles for text in an unordered bulleted list set off in the main text.

If a compound style combines more than one tag, it's written like this:

```
#sidebar h1 a:link
```

Again, you must include a space between each style name or tag. In this example, you see a style that defines the appearance of the active link tag only when the link is located inside an element formatted with the `<h1>` tag that's also inside an element formatted with an ID style named `#sidebar`. A compound style like this enables you to create links in a sidebar headline that look different than links in another part of the sidebar.

Replacing ID and class styles with HTML5 tags

Dreamweaver CC includes two CSS layouts designed with the new HTML5 tags. So many people create class or ID styles with the names *header* and *footer* that the W3C decided to make these and several other new tags standard. Most of the new HTML5 tags are designed, in part, to help make the formatting in web pages more consistent.

After you figure out the differences among these style selector options and when they're best used, you're well on your way to mastering the art of creating and applying styles in Dreamweaver, which is covered in Chapter 6.

Using internal versus external style sheets

In CSS, you have the option of creating internal, external, or inline styles. You can even use a combination of these options, or attach multiple external style sheets to the same web page. Here's an explanation of these options:

- ✔ **Internal styles:** If you create internal styles, the CSS code is stored in the `<head>` area at the top of the HTML page, and you can apply the styles on only that page. If you're just creating a one-page website or styles used on only one page, an internal style sheet is fine, but for most sites, external style sheets offer many advantages.

- ✔ **External styles:** If you save your styles in an external style sheet, they're stored in a separate file with a `.css` extension. You can attach external style sheets to any or all pages in a website in much the same way that you can insert the same image into multiple pages. You can also attach multiple external style sheets to the same page. For example, you can create one style sheet for styles that format text and another for layout styles. You can also create external style sheets for different purposes, such as one for print and one for screen display. For a web designer, external style sheets offer two big advantages: They enable you to create new pages faster and more easily and to update styles across many pages at once.

- ✔ **Inline styles:** Inline styles are created within a document at the place that a style is used and apply only to the element to which they're attached in the document. Inline styles are generally considered the least useful of the three style sheet options because to change the defined style you must change the code that contains the element, which means you lose the benefits of making global updates and creating clean, fast-loading code. For example, creating one style for all your headlines and saving it in an external style sheet is more efficient than applying the style formatting options to each headline separately.

At the top of the CSS Designer panel, shown in Figure 5-5, you find the Sources panel with a drop-down list that makes it easy to specify whether you want to save each new style that you define in an internal or external style sheet. The options are

- **Create a New CSS File:** Launches the Create a New CSS File dialog box, where you can enter a name, specify a few settings, and click OK to both create and attach a new external style sheet.

- **Attach Existing CSS File:** Launches the Create a New CSS File dialog box, making it easy to browse and select any .css file already on your computer's hard drive.

- **Define in Page:** Adds `<style>` tags to the top of the open HTML file, where new styles can be saved in an internal style sheet.

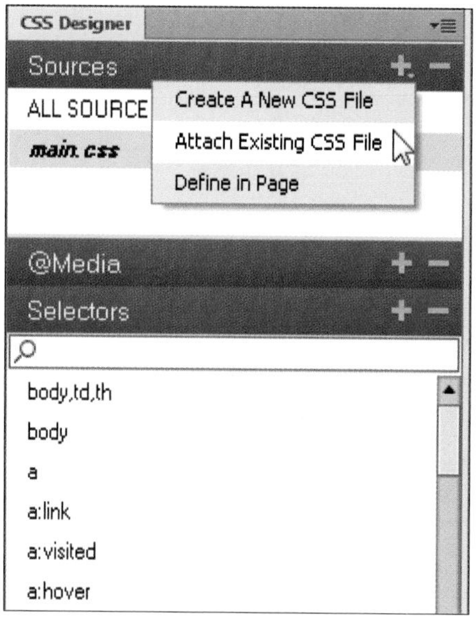

Figure 5-5: When you create new styles you can choose to save them in internal or external style sheets.

 You can attach multiple external style sheets to the same HTML page and you can use internal and external style sheets in the same document. When you create new styles, it's important that you select the name of the style sheet in the Sources panel (refer to Figure 5-5) where you want each new style saved.

If you're creating a style that you're likely to use on more than one page in your site, saving the style to a new or an existing external style sheet is your best choice. If you save a style in an internal style sheet and later want to add it to an external style sheet, you can move the style by dragging the style name in the Selector panel to the name of the style sheet list you want to move it into in the Sources panel.

Looking at the code behind the scenes

Even if you *prefer* not to look at the code behind your web pages, it's helpful to have at least some familiarity with different kinds of tags, CSS, and other code that Dreamweaver creates for you when you design web pages. For example:

```
#container {
  width: 780px;
  margin-right: auto;
  margin-left: auto;
}
.caption {
  font-family:  Verdana, Geneva, sans-serif;
  font-size: .8em;
  font-style: italic;
  font-weight: bold;
}
h1 {
  font-family: Arial, Helvetica, sans-serif;
  font-size: 1.3em;
}
```

These examples show what the CSS code in an internal or external style sheet would look like in Dreamweaver for the following styles:

- ✔ An ID style created with the ID selector, named `#container`, and defined as 780 pixels wide with the left and right margins set to auto (a cool trick for centering a CSS design, covered in Chapter 6).

- ✔ A style created with a class selector, named `.caption`, and defined as Verdana, Geneva, sans-serif, small, italic, and bold.

- ✔ A style created with a tag selector to redefine the HTML tag `<h1>` as follows: Arial, Helvetica, sans-serif, large, and bold. (**Note:** Because the heading tags already include bold formatting, it's not necessary to include bold in the style definition.)

Introducing the CSS Designer Panel

The CSS Designer panel provides a great place to create, attach, view, manage, organize, and edit CSS styles. To open the CSS Designer panel, choose Window⇨CSS Styles. If you've set your layout options to one of the compact layouts or you've diminished the size of the panels in the right side of the workspace, you need to click the small double-arrow at the top of the panel to expand and view the panel.

The CSS Designer panel, a new feature in version CC, combines all Dreamweaver CSS tools in one collection of panels. In Figure 5-6, you see the panels docked on the right side of the page and expanded to take up two columns of space. Like other panels in Dreamweaver, the CSS Designer panel can be adjusted in a number of ways by clicking and dragging the top, bottom, or side of the entire panel set or any of the individual panels, such as the Properties panel, shown in the far right in Figure 5-6.

Figure 5-6: The CSS Designer panel, docked on the right side of the screen in the Designer layout, provides easy access to all CSS features.

Identifying and selecting styles

At the top of the CSS Designer panel, you can view all the style sheets *currently* applied to any open page in Dreamweaver. In Figure 5-6, an internal style sheet (indicated by the `<style>` tag) is selected in the Sources panel. For comparison, refer to Figure 5-5 to see an external style sheet, named main.css, selected in the Sources panel.

When you select a style sheet name in the Sources panel, a list of all style rules defined in that style sheet appears in the Selectors panel, just below the Sources and Media panels.

If you don't see any style rules listed in the Selectors panel, you probably haven't defined any styles in the selected style sheet. Also note that before you can create a style, you must create or attach a style sheet in the Sources panel. You find step-by-step instructions for creating a style sheet as you create styles in Chapter 6.

Reviewing CSS Selector Options

After you determine what selector type is best for your style — and decide whether you want to save it in an external or internal style sheet — you're ready to move on to the CSS rule options and define the color, size, and other formatting options you want to include in your style. You find instructions for creating style rules in Chapter 6. This section continues the overview to help you better understand your choices before you start creating a style.

In previous versions of Dreamweaver, most features that are now included in the CSS Property panel were located in a separate CSS Rule Definition dialog box. Although the new CSS Property panel includes a few new visual tools that can help you better understand how CSS properties work, all these choices can seem a bit daunting at first. As you go through the following sections, keep in mind that my goal is to give you an overview of the options in each category of the CSS Property panel so that you'll have a better understanding as you go through the instructions for using these options in Chapter 6. Again, don't feel that you have to memorize the details of each feature; you can always refer to this section when you're creating styles.

Also remember that you don't *have* to specify any of the settings in this panel. When you leave an option blank, you let the default browser settings (or other styles) already applied to the page take control. For example, if you don't specify a text color when you define a style, any text formatted with the style remains black (the default color in most web browsers) unless another style applied to the text contains formatting instructions for a different color.

In most cases, you select only a few options from one or two categories in the CSS Property panel for each new style you create. I've included the full list here so you can appreciate all your choices.

Not all options in the CSS Property panel are supported by all the web browsers in use today, so the way styles are displayed on a web page can vary depending on the browser. Similarly, some CSS options aren't included in Dreamweaver because they're not commonly supported. The following sections describe the options in each category offered in the CSS Property panel. Remember, if you know how write a CSS rule, you can always edit the CSS code in Dreamweaver's Code view.

The Layout options

At the top of the CSS Designer Properties panel (see Figure 5-7) you find the CSS properties commonly used to create page layouts. You use these options to specify height, width, alignment, positioning, and spacing. As you can read in Chapter 6, these settings are ideal for creating page layouts with class and ID styles to do things such as align images and position `<div>` tags to create multicolumn layouts.

You can use the Layout options in the CSS Property panel to set these values:

- **Width:** Specify a width for any element that can have its dimensions specified, such as a `<div>` tag. Size options are pixel (px), point (pt), pica (pc), percent (%), em, rem, ex, and ch. (See the "Comparing CSS size options" sidebar, later in this chapter, for the basics of sizing with ems, exs, and percentages on the web.)

- **Height:** Specify a height for any element that can have its dimensions specified.

  The Height field is often left empty to enable elements (such as `<div>` tags) to expand to fit their contents.

- **Min and Max Width:** Specify minimum and maximum widths for `<div>` tags and other block elements. These options are useful when you specify the width as a percentage of the browser window. For example, you can set the width of your design to take up 80 percent of the browser window, and then set a Max Width of 1000 px to prevent your layout from getting stretched wider than 1000 pixels, even on a very large monitor.

- **Min and Max Height:** Specify minimum and maximum heights for `<div>` tags and other block elements.

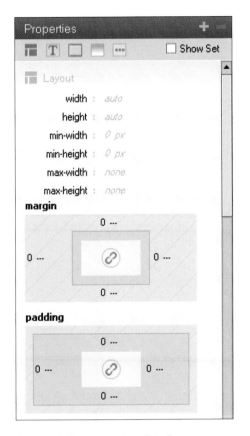

Figure 5-7: The top portion of the Layout options in the CSS Property panel.

✔ **Margin:** Set the amount of space around an element (refer to Figure 5-7). Margins can be used to create space between the edge of an element and other elements on the page, such as between an image and text or between two <div> tags. You can set the margin separately for the top, right, bottom, and left. Padding is measured in pixels, points, inches, centimeters, millimeters, picas, ems, exs, and percentages.

✔ **Padding:** Sets the amount of space within the borders of an element (refer to Figure 5-7). For example, you can use padding to create space between the borders of a <div> tag and its contents. You can set padding separately for the top, right, bottom, and left. Padding is measured in pixels, points, inches, centimeters, millimeters, picas, ems, exs, and percentages.

Setting padding and margin spacing can be tricky. When you add margin and padding to an element, such as an image or <div> tag, you increase the overall size of that element and the amount of space it requires in the layout. For help on setting these options to best fit your designs, see Chapter 6.

✓ **Position:** As shown in Figure 5-8, the Position option, available from the lower part of the Layout section of the Properties panel, alters the way elements are positioned on a page. As you can read in Chapter 6, positioning can dramatically change the way block-level elements (such as table, list, header, paragraph, and <div> tags) appear in a browser.

Positioning is always determined relative to something else, such as another element on the page or the browser window. How you set up positioning depends on where your element is on the page — and on whether the element is inside another element (such as the <h1> tag inside the <div> tag). The Position drop-down menu includes

- **Inherit:** You do not need to specify this default option. Unless another option is selected, each element inherits the positioning of its parent element.

- **Static:** Place the content at its location within the flow of the document. By default, all HTML elements that *can* be positioned are static.

- **Absolute:** Use the top and left coordinates to control the position of an element relative to the upper-left corner of the browser window or the upper-left corner of an element that contains the element. (For example, the positioning of an AP Div contained within another AP Div is based on the position of the first AP Div.)

- **Fixed:** Position an element relative to the top-left corner of the browser. The content of an element using fixed positioning remains constant even if the user scrolls down or across the page.

- **Relative:** Use a position relative to the point where you insert the element into the page or relative to its container.

✓ **Float:** Align elements, such as images and <div> tags, to the left or right of a page or other container causing text or other elements to wrap around it. Click the icons in the Float field, as shown in Figure 5-8, to specify the following four options: Inherit, Right, Left, or None.

✓ **Clear:** Prevent floating content from overlapping an area to the left or right, or to both sides of an element. This option is useful when a floated element, such as a <div> tag used to create a sidebar, overlaps another block-level element, such as a <div> tag used to create the footer of a page.

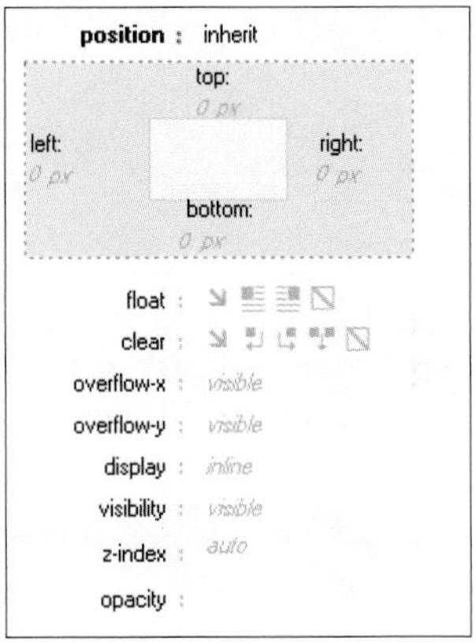

Figure 5-8: The bottom portion of the Layout options in the CSS Property panel.

✔ **Overflow-x and -y:** Tell the browser how to display the contents of an element if the container, such as a `<div>` tag, can't fit the element's entire height or width. Overflow options are

 • **Visible:** Keep content, such as an image or text, visible, even if it expands beyond the defined height or width of a container.

 • **Hidden:** Cut off the content if it exceeds the size of the container. This option doesn't provide scroll bars.

 • **Scroll:** Add scroll bars to the container regardless of whether its content exceeds the element's size.

 • **Auto:** Make scroll bars appear only when the content of a container exceeds its boundaries.

✔ **Display:** Indicate if, or how, to render an element in a browser. For example, you change the positioning of an unordered list from horizontal to vertical by choosing Inline or hide an element, rendering it invisible, by choosing None. You can use the Display option with a scripting language (such as JavaScript) to change the display of elements dynamically. For example, you can cause an element to appear on a page only when a user clicks a button — and then make the element disappear when the button is clicked again.

✔ **Visibility:** Control whether or not the browser displays an element. The Visibility options are

- **Inherit:** The element has the visibility of the element in which it's contained (the default).

- **Visible:** The element is displayed.

- **Hidden:** The element isn't displayed.

- **Collapse:** For use with HTML tables. Collapse can be used to remove a column or row without affecting the rest of the table layout.

An important difference exists between setting the Display to None and setting the Visibility to Hidden. When you set Visibility to Hidden, the element in not displayed on the page but still takes up the same amount of space. In contrast, if you set Display to None, the element is not rendered at all.

✔ **Z-Index:** Control the position of an element on the Z-coordinate, which controls the stacking order of elements in relation to each other. Higher-numbered elements overlap lower-numbered elements. (***Note:*** This setting works only on elements that use absolute or relative positioning settings.)

✔ **Opacity:** Control the opacity level for an element from 0.0 (fully transparent) to 1.0 (fully opaque). For example, if you enter .5 in the opacity field, the opacity of an element will be reduced to 50 percent.

The Text panel

The Text panel features a collection of options that control the display of (you guessed it) the text in your pages. You can access the Text panel options by scrolling down the Property panel until you get below the Layout options, or by clicking the T icon at the top of the panel (see Figure 5-9).

The Text panel includes the following formatting options:

✔ **Color:** Set the text color. You can click the color well and choose a color, use the eyedropper to sample any color on the screen, or enter a hexadecimal color code in the color field. If you enter a hexadecimal color code, include the beginning pound sign (#). For example, you would enter #ffffff for white. You can also abbreviate these codes with shorthand hex notations, such as #fff for white.

✔ **Font-Family:** Define a font family or a series of families. You can add fonts from your local hard drive or from Adobe TypeKit by choosing Manage Fonts in the bottom of the drop-down list and launching the Manage Fonts dialog box, shown in Figure 5-10. (For an explanation of why Dreamweaver includes font collections — and a look at how to create new ones — see the upcoming section, "Why so many fonts?".)

Figure 5-9: The Text panel in the CSS Designer Properties panel.

Figure 5-10: The Manage Fonts dialog box provides access to local fonts and fonts from Adobe TypeKit.

- **Font-Style:** Enter Normal, Italic, or Oblique. However, italic and oblique are rarely different in a web browser, so stick with italic unless you have a specific reason not to.

- **Font-Variant:** Change text to small caps. Test your designs carefully because this attribute is not supported by all browsers.

- **Font-Weight:** Make text appear bold by selecting Bold or Bolder from the drop-down list. You can also enter a number between 100 and 900 to more precisely control how bold the text appears (100 is a light bold, 900 is a dark bold). To remove bold formatting, choose Normal or Lighter.

- **Font-Size:** Define the size of the text. You can choose a specific numeric size or a relative size. Size options are pixel (px), point (pt), pica (pc), percent (%), em, rem, ex, and ch. Pixels, ems, and percentages are the most commonly used options for text sizes. (For more on these options, see the upcoming sidebar, "Comparing CSS size options.")

- **Line-Height:** Specify the height of the line on which the text is placed. (The spacing between lines of text is called *leading*.) Much like text size, you can specify line height in a variety of ways, including pixels, ems, and percentages. It is good practice on the web to add line height because increasing space around your text makes it easier to read on a computer screen. (For more on these options, see the upcoming sidebar, "Comparing CSS size options.")

- **Text-Align:** Left align, right align, center, or justify your text by clicking the corresponding icon (refer to Figure 5-9). The first icon, for Inherit, is the default. For example, you could center the text in the footer of your web page by including Text-Align set to Center in the definition of a style you apply to the `<div>` tag at the bottom of the page. (You find details about styling `<div>` tags to create footers in Chapter 6.)

- **Text-Decoration:** Specify whether text is underlined, overlined (a line appears over the text), displayed with a strikethrough (Line-Through), or displayed with the blink effect (which makes text appear to flash on and off). You can also choose None, which is frequently used to remove the underline from linked text.

Use the decoration options sparingly, if at all. Links are underlined automatically; if you underline text that isn't a link, you risk confusing viewers. Overlined and strikethrough text can be hard to read, so use these options only if they enhance your design. And by all means, resist the blink effect; it's distracting and can make the screen difficult to read.

- **Text-Indent:** Specify the amount that text will be indented from the left side of the page by entering a number in one of the size options, such as pixels, ems, or percentages. (For more on these options, see the upcoming sidebar, "Comparing CSS size options.")

Why so many fonts?

You may have heard that you can now use any font you want on your web pages, thanks to the latest version of Cascading Style Sheets, CSS3. This statement is true (at least for anyone using the latest web browsers) but with some limitations: You must have the legal right to publish the font, and the font must be hosted on a web server. In Chapters 6 and 7, you find detailed instructions for using the @font-face options with the included font collections as well as hosted web services, such as Google Web Fonts.

To help ensure that your text appears as you intend, Dreamweaver includes collections of the most common fonts on Windows and Macintosh computers (popular fonts that your visitors are most likely to have). These fonts are grouped in families, such as

- Gotham, Helvetica Nue, Helvetica, Arial, sans serif
- Cambria, Hoefler Text, Liberation Serif, Times, Times New Roman, Times, and serif

When you apply a collection of fonts, the browser displays the formatted text in the first font available in the list. For example, if you choose the font collection that starts with Gotham and your visitors have Gotham on their hard drives, they see your text in Gotham. If they don't have Gotham, the text is displayed in the next font on the list — in this case, Helvetica Nue. If they don't have that font either, the text is displayed in Helvetica. And if they don't even have Helvetica (which is more common on Macintosh computers), the browser uses Arial (which is common on Windows computers). And finally, if they don't have any of the fonts on the list, the browser looks for any serif font. (*Serif* describes fonts, such as Times, that have those little curly things on the edges of letters; *sans serif* means no curly things, which is what you get with a font such as Arial.)

You can create your own font collections using the Manage Fonts dialog box (refer to Figure 5-10), which is accessible by selecting the Manage Fonts option at the bottom of the Font-Family drop-down list in the Text panel in the CSS Designer panel. This dialog box is covered in more detail in Chapters 6 and 7.

In the early days of the web, the only way to ensure that text appeared in the font you wanted was to create the text as a graphic in a program such as Photoshop or Fireworks, and then insert the graphic with the text into your page. That's still not a bad option for special text, such as logos. For all other text, however, don't save text in an image because graphics take longer to download than text, text saved in a graphic is harder to update later, and search engines can't read the text in an image.

Comparing CSS size options

When you create CSS styles, you can specify sizes for fonts and other elements in so many ways that confusion (and frustration) can set in pretty quickly. When you design web pages, you can choose from many size options, but these are the most popular:

- **Pixels:** Pixels are an easy choice because they offer many designers a familiar size option. In addition, if you specify the text size in pixels, the size won't change (although the display size may change between Mac and Windows computers). Pixels are especially useful when you're working with complex style sheets because you don't have to worry about the cumulative effect of relative sizes, but that's why so many of us are now moving on to rems.

- **Percent-based relative sizes:** Many designers use percentages to make text larger or smaller relative to a base text size. For example, if you define the text in a caption style as 90 percent, it would appear at 90 percent of the size of the rest of the text on the page. You might then make headlines 150 percent and subheads 125 percent. This system is easy to understand but it is no longer the best choice.

- **Em:** For some time, the most popular option among experienced web designers (and anyone who wanted to follow good standards on the web), was the em size. Em is based on the amount of space taken up by the capital letter *M* in the font face specified in a style. Expressing the size of your text using ems may seem complex (especially when you're new to web design), but this option is ideal on the web because the size is adjusted relative to the displayed text size. Ems work much like percentages but they adapt even better to different font face sizes and do a better job of maintaining a good display when users change their font size settings.

- **Ex:** Similar to em, the ex option is based on the size of a lowercase *x* in the specified font face. The em size is generally preferred.

- **Small, medium, and large relative sizes:** Although these relative sizes were popular in the early days of the web, most web designers today prefer to use ems, pixels, or percentages.

The problem with relative sizes, like ems or percentages, is that they are cumulative. If I set the size of all text on the page to 80 percent of the default size, and then I set the size of my captions at 75 percent, the captions will be 75 percent of the 80 percent of the default size, which is a lot smaller than 80 percent of the default size. The same problem exists with ems and exs. If you're creating one simple size, you're fine, but if you're applying multiple styles on a page (as most of us do), the cascading effect of styles causes a problematic cumulative effect.

One of the new options in CSS version 3 is the rem (root em) size option. The key to using rems is to set a base font size. In theory, you can specify any base font size, but in practice, many designers choose 62.5 percent. That seemingly arbitrary size enables you to specify rems in a way that corresponds nicely to pixels. For example, with the base font size set to 62.5 percent, 1.4rem is equivalent to 14 pixels, a popular size for the text used throughout a web page, and 2.4rem is equivalent to 24 pixels.

Here's how these basic styles look when you use rem:

```
html { font-size: 62.5%; }
body { font-size: 1.4rem; }
h1   { font-size: 2.4rem; }
```

Note: Like many of the other new CSS3 features in use on the web, not all web browsers support rems. As of this writing, you can expect good results in most popular browsers, including Safari 5+, Chrome 1+, Firefox 3.6+, and Internet Explorer 9+.

The Text-Shadow section of the Text panel

The Text-Shadow section of the Text panel provides tools for adding text shadows, one of the newest CSS properties included in the CSS3 definition. You find step-by-step instructions for using these options in Chapter 7. The Text-Shadow options are shown in Figure 5-11. The most popular options are the following:

- **H-shadow:** Add a shadow to your text on the horizontal axis. First choose a size option, and then enter a number in the field. For example, enter 2px, to add a horizontal shadow that is 2 pixels wide.

- **V-shadow:** Add a shadow to your text on the vertical axis. First choose a size option, and then enter a number in the field. (See the sidebar "Comparing CSS size options.")

- **Blur:** Control the amount of blur in the shadow. The larger the number, the more the shadow is spread out, or blurred.

- **Color:** Enter a hexadecimal color code to specify the color of the shadow, or use the eyedropper to sample any color on the screen.

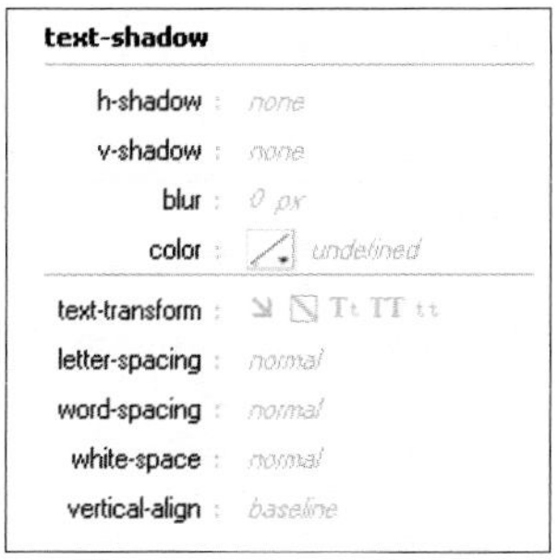

Figure 5-11: The Text-Shadow and other options at the bottom of the Text section in the CSS Designer Properties panel.

The features at the bottom of the Text panel, which are not as common as the other Text panel options, are as follows:

- **Text-Transform:** Change the case of your text. Options are Capitalize (which capitalizes the first letter), Uppercase, and Lowercase. Click the corresponding icon to set this property.

- **Letter-Spacing:** Defines the amount of white space inserted between letters. Size options are pixel (px), point (pt), pica (pc), percent (%), em, rem, ex, and ch. (See the preceding sidebar "Comparing CSS size options.")

✔ **Word-Spacing:** Defines the amount of white space inserted between words. Size options are pixel (px), point (pt), pica (pc), percent (%), em, rem, ex, and ch. (See the preceding sidebar "Comparing CSS size options.")

✔ **White-Space:** Tell the browser how to handle line breaks and spaces in a block of text. Your options are Inherit, Normal, Nowrap, Pre, Pre-line, or Pre-wrap. Nowrap is especially useful because it prevents elements from being separated if they must wrap to fit within a browser window or another container.

✔ **Vertical-Align:** Align inline elements, such as text and images, in relation to the elements that surround them. You can set a numeric value or choose Baseline, Sub, Super, Top, Text-Top, Middle, Bottom, and Text-Bottom.

The Border panel

The Border panel defines the appearance of borders around images, tables, `<div>` tags, and other elements. As shown in Figure 5-12, you can specify border settings on one, two, three, or four sides of an element.

Figure 5-12: The Border section in the CSS Designer Properties panel.

You can use the border settings to create dividing lines between `<div>` tags that create columns or add separating lines above or below elements. The Border panel options are

- **Border-Collapse:** Specify whether table borders are combined into a single border or detached as they appear in standard HTML when you use the `<table>` tag. The choices are Collapse, Separate (the default), and Inherit.

- **Border Spacing:** Set the spacing between borders of adjacent table cells when the Border-Collapse option is set to Separate.

- **Border Color:** Specify the border color for all four sides of an element by entering a hexadecimal color or by clicking the color well and using the color picker.

- **Border Top, Right, Left, and Bottom Color:** Specify different colors for any or all borders of an element.

- **Border Width:** Specify the width, or thickness, of the border. You can choose thin, medium, or thick, or you can specify the size in pixels, ems, or any of the other size options.

- **Border Top, Right, Left, and Bottom Width:** Specify different widths for any or all of the borders of an element.

- **Border Style:** Choose from any of the border style options, including Solid, Dashed, or Double.

- **Border Top, Right, Left, and Bottom Style:** Specify different border styles for any or all borders of an element.

- **Border Radius:** Create rounded corners on your borders. Click to place your cursor in any of the four fields located near the corners of the border preview box and enter a number to specify the amount of the radius. You can choose from any of the CSS size options by using the drop-down list.

The Background panel

Using the Background panel in the CSS Designer panel (see Figure 5-13), you can specify a background color or image for a style — and control how the background is displayed on the page. You can use background style settings for any element of your web page that can display a background — including the `<body>` , `<div>`, heading, and image tags.

Figure 5-13: The Background section in the CSS Designer Properties panel.

For example, you could alter the `<body>` tag to include background settings that apply to the entire page, or you could create a style with the class or ID selector and specify a background that appears only behind an individual `<div>` tag. By including the background in the class or ID style of a `<div>` tag, you can limit the background to appear on-screen only where the `<div>` tag is used. Note that the Background option works with an image only if you first set a margin around the image.

You can choose from these Background options:

- **Background-Color:** Specify the background color of a defined style using one of several methods. You can click the color well and select a pre-defined color or create a custom color. Or use the eyedropper to sample any color on the screen. Finally, you can enter a hexadecimal color code — make sure to include the #, as in #000000 for the color black or #ffffff for the color white. You can also use abbreviated hexadecimal colors, such as #000 or #fff for black and white.

- **Background-Image:** Select an image to serve as the background in your style definition. Enter any URL to an image on your computer or on the Internet, or click the folder icon to browse your hard drive and select an image.

- **Background-Position:** Specify the position of the background image from the left and top of the parent element by entering a number in each field. This option is visible only if you click the small arrow next to the URL field in the Background section to reveal the additional fields that follow.

- **Size:** Select the measurement in pixels, ems, or another option, and then enter the size you want for the background. Leaving the Size field set to auto (the default) displays the image at actual size.

↙ **Background-clip:** Specify whether the background begins the border, the padding, or the content of a box element, such as a `<div>` tag.

↙ **Background-Repeat:** Click the corresponding icon to specify how and whether the background image repeats, or tiles, across and down the page. Background images tile by default, so you must choose an option if you don't want your background to repeat or you want to specify how it repeats. Also note that if the image is larger than the element to which it is applied, only as much of the image as will fit in the display area of the element will be visible. For example, if you use a 600-pixel-wide image as the background of a `<div>` tag that is set to 300 pixels wide, only half the image will be visible. The Repeat options, listed in order of the appearance of their icons, follow:

   • **Inherit:** Unless another option is selected, each element inherits the behavior of its parent element. This default option does not need to be specified.

   • **Repeat:** The background image repeats vertically and horizontally in the background of the element.

   • **Repeat-X:** The background repeats horizontally, but not vertically, in the background of the element.

   • **Repeat-Y:** The background repeats vertically, but not horizontally, in the background of the element.

   • **No-Repeat:** The background is displayed once at the top left of the element.

↙ **Origin:** Specify whether the origin of the background begins at the border, the padding, or the content of a box element, such as a `<div>` tag.

↙ **Attachment:** Determine how the background behaves when the page is scrolled. The options are

   • **Inherit:** Unless another option is selected, each element inherits the behavior of its parent element. This is a default option and does not need to be specified.

   • **Fixed:** The background remains glued to one place in the viewing area and doesn't scroll out of sight, even when the web page is scrolled.

   • **Scroll:** The background scrolls along with the web page.

↙ **Gradient:** Click the color well next to Gradient to open Dreamweaver's new visual gradient selector, shown in Figure 5-14.

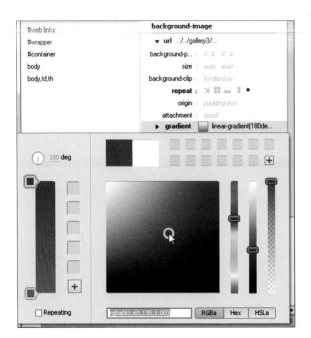

Figure 5-14: The gradient selector opens when you click the color well next to Gradient in the Background panel.

The Box-Shadow panel

The Box-Shadow options (see Figure 5-15) make it possible to add shadows to <div> tags and other box elements. The options are

- **H-shadow:** Add a shadow to your text on the horizontal axis. First choose a size option, and then enter a number in the field. For example, enter 2px to add a horizontal shadow that is 2 pixels wide.

- **V-shadow:** Add a shadow to your text on the vertical axis. First choose a size option, and then enter a number in the field. (See the previous sidebar "Comparing CSS size options.")

- **Blur:** Control the amount of blur in the shadow. The larger the number, the more the shadow is spread out, or blurred.

- **Spread:** Control how far the shadow spreads away from the box element.

- **Color:** Enter a hexadecimal color code to specify the color of the shadow.

- **Type:** Display the shadow in the inset or outset style.

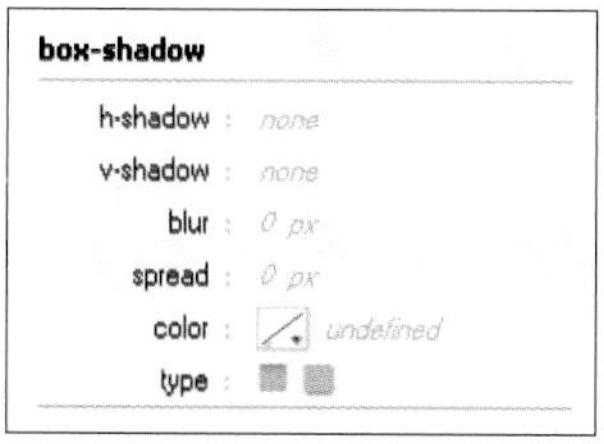

box-shadow

h-shadow :	*none*
v-shadow :	*none*
blur :	*0 px*
spread :	*0 px*
color :	*undefined*
type :	

Figure 5-15: The Box-Shadow section of the CSS Designer Properties panel includes options for adding shadows to box-level elements.

The List panel

The List panel can be used to define the size and type of bullets displayed with list tags. Use the icons at the top of this section to specify whether the bullet should be inside or outside the list. Use the drop-down list next to List-Style-Type to select the style of the bullet. The options are Disc, Circle, Square, Decimal, Lower-Roman, Upper-Roman, Lower-Alpha, Upper-Alpha, or None (see Figure 5-16). Choose None if you want to use the list tag with no bullet, a common option when you're formatting a list of links in a navigation bar (covered in Chapter 6). If you want to use a custom bullet made with your own graphic, choose URL from the drop-down list next the List-Style-Image field and then click the Browse button to select an image.

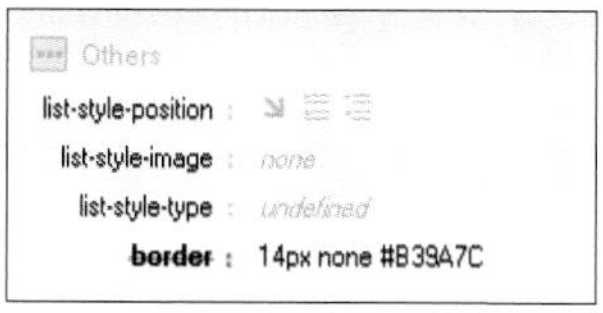

⋯ Others	
list-style-position :	
list-style-image :	*none*
list-style-type :	*undefined*
border :	14px none #B39A7C

Figure 5-16: The List options are at the very bottom of the CSS Designer Properties panel.

The CSS Transitions panel

The CSS Transitions panel, shown in Figure 5-17, provides access to the New Transition dialog box, also shown in Figure 5-17. Use these features to create and manage CSS3 *transitions,* which enable you to add gradually changing interactive effects to elements. For example, you can use a CSS3 transition to slowly change the background color of a `<div>` tag from red to blue.

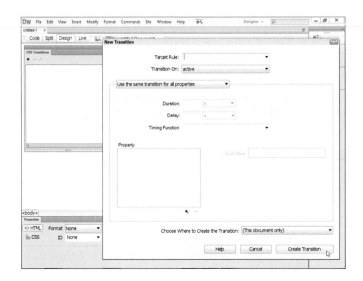

Figure 5-17: Click the plus sign in the top left of the CSS Transitions panel to open the New Transition dialog box, shown on the right.

The CSS Transitions panel is not grouped with the other CSS Designer panels, but you can dock it there after it's opened. To open the CSS Transitions panel, choose Window➪CSS Transitions. To open the New Transition dialog box and create a new transition, click the small plus sign in the top-left corner of the CSS Transitions panel.

The Transition category has the following options:

- **Target Rule:** The CSS style definition, or rule, that contains the properties you want to change with the transition.

- **Transition On:** Choose any option from the drop-down list to specify the action that will trigger the transition. For example, choose Hover if you want the transition to begin when a user rolls a cursor over the element.

- **Property drop-down list:** Specify whether the same transition will apply to all properties defined in the target rule or whether each property will have a different transition.

- **Property:** Specify which CSS property you are targeting with the effect. Click the plus sign (+) to add a property or the minus sign (–) to remove one.

- **End Value:** Enter the final value you want used when the transition is complete.

- **Choose Where to Create the Transition:** Specify whether the transition should be saved in an internal or an external style sheet.

Creating and Editing CSS Styles

In This Chapter

▶ Using class and tag selectors

▶ Creating page layouts with CSS and Div tags

▶ Understanding the box model

▶ Using Dreamweaver's CSS layouts

▶ Creating custom CSS layouts

▶ Styling unordered lists for links

▶ Testing and editing CSS

▶ Comparing margins and padding

▶ Aligning elements

Whether you're new to CSS or you've been struggling (I mean *designing*) with styles for years, Dreamweaver's many CSS features offer welcome assistance. If you've used the CSS tools in previous versions of Dreamweaver, beware that the CSS features were redesigned in version CC. Although the basic rules of CSS remain the same, the way you define style rules in Dreamweaver has changed dramatically.

This chapter walks you through the process of creating and applying styles with the class, tag, and ID selectors using Dreamweaver's new CSS Designer panel. You also find instructions for customizing the CSS layouts included with Dreamweaver. And you discover not only how to create styles for text, but also how to position and align images, text, and other elements on a web page. Finally, you discover how Dreamweaver makes it easy to edit, rename, and even remove styles.

If you're new to CSS or Dreamweaver, I recommend that before you start this chapter you at least skim through Chapter 5, where you find an introduction to CSS and a review of the new CSS Designer panel and how you can use it to create, apply, and edit styles in Dreamweaver.

Brace yourself: You're getting into some of the most complex web design features that Dreamweaver offers, but you're also getting into the core of web design today. If you want to design web pages that can be edited and maintained efficiently, look good in a variety of screen sizes, and meet the latest web standards, CSS is clearly your best option.

Organizing Style Sheets

One of the first decisions to make when you create new styles is whether to save the style information in an internal or an external style sheet. In an *internal style sheet*, the style rule is saved at the top of the same HTML document where you want to apply the style. In an *external style sheet*, new styles are saved in a separate document that can be attached to any or all files in your website.

External style sheets offer the greatest advantages because using one set of styles across many pages is more efficient than creating styles for each page in your site. That said, sometimes internal style sheets are a good choice, such as when you're creating a style that will apply only to elements on one page.

The following sections walk you through the process of creating, attaching, moving, copying, and editing styles in internal or external style sheets. In the first section, you find out how to create internal and external style sheets. The remaining exercises in this chapter work the same way whether you save styles in an internal or an external style sheet. (For more on the differences and relative advantages of internal and external style sheets, see Chapter 5.)

This chapter focuses heavily on the features in the CSS Designer panel, which is new in Dreamweaver CC and replaces nearly all CSS features in previous versions of Dreamweaver. In Chapter 5, you find a detailed review of all sub-panels in the CSS Designer panel. Use that chapter as a reference if you need to check on a specific feature. In this chapter, you find step-by-step exercises designed to show you how the different sections of the CSS Designer panel work together.

If the CSS Designer panel is not already open, you'll need to open it before following along with any of the exercises. To open this feature-rich panel set, choose Window➪CSS Styles.

Creating an internal style sheet

Internal style sheets are saved in the same HTML file where they are applied. Thus, you don't create a file when you create an internal style sheet, as you do when you create an external sheet (covered in the next section). Instead, when you create an internal style sheet, you simply add <style> tags within the <head> tags at the top of the HTML file you have open in Dreamweaver. Then, when you create styles, you save the new style rule definitions within the <style> tags in your file.

Creating a new internal style in Dreamweaver requires just two steps. First click the plus (+) icon in the Sources panel at the top of the CSS Designer panel, shown in Figure 6-1. Then select Define in Page from the drop-down list. You're done. Dreamweaver inserts the <style> tags into the code in your file, and lists the internal style sheet in the Sources panel with the <style> tag, which is also visible in Figure 6-1.

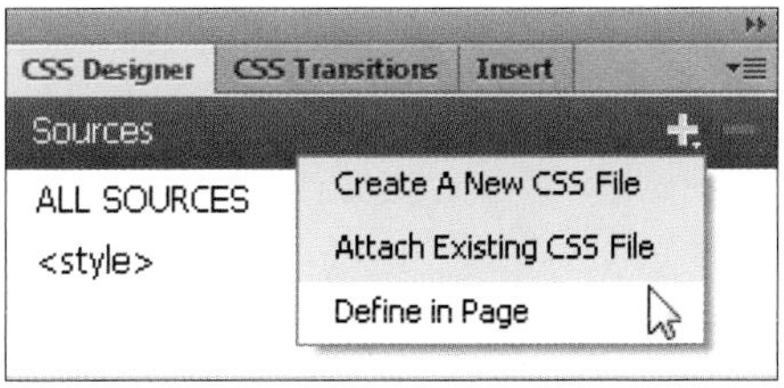

Figure 6-1: Select Define in Page from the CSS Designer Sources panel to create a new internal style sheet.

Creating an external style sheet

At the very top of the CSS Designer panel, you find the Sources panel. This panel displays the name or names of any style sheets available to the open page. This same panel is used to create or link to style sheets as you create or apply styles.

To create an external style sheet, first create and save a new HTML file or open an existing file in Dreamweaver, and then follow these instructions:

1. **Click the plus (+) icon in the Sources panel at the top of the CSS Designer panel, shown in Figure 6-2.**

   A drop-down list opens with three options: Create a New CSS File, Attach Existing CSS File, and Define in Page.

Figure 6-2: You can create a new external style sheet using the Sources panel.

2. **Choose the Create a New CSS File option from the drop-down list.**

   The Create a New CSS File dialog box opens.

3. **Enter a name for your new style sheet file, as shown in Figure 6-3.**

   You can name style sheets anything you like, as long as you don't include spaces or special characters other than the hyphen (-) or underscore (_).

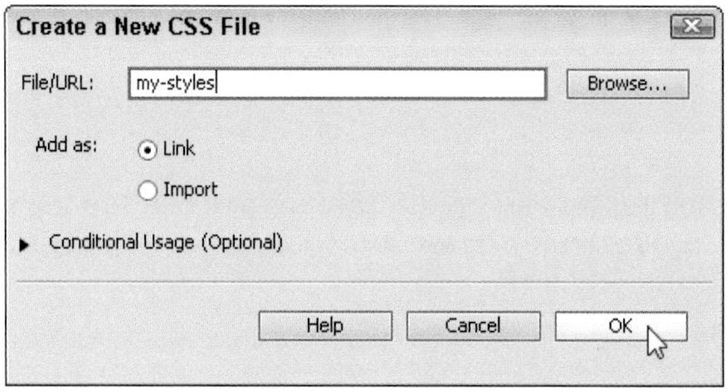

Figure 6-3: Name your new external style sheet in the Create a New CSS File dialog box.

4. **Select the Link option.**

   Link is considered the best practice in most cases and is selected by default in Dreamweaver.

   For the most part, the Import option is used only when would want to apply multiple external style sheets to the page but only want to link to one style sheet. In that case, you could use the Import option to associate multiple style sheets with one.

5. **Click the arrow next to Conditional Usage to view additional settings.**

The Conditional Usage settings are used to set up media queries for style sheets. To learn how, and when, to use media queries, see Chapter 8.

6. **Click OK.**

The style sheet is saved and linked to the HTML page you have open in Dreamweaver. *Note:* If you're working on a new HTML page, make sure that you've saved the page; otherwise, you'll be unable to create and link a new CSS file.

After you create an external style sheet, you can link that same style sheet to as many pages as you like by following the steps in the exercise that immediately follows. You can also add as many style rules as you like to any external style sheet, which is covered in various exercises that follow on creating class, tag, and other types of styles.

Attaching an external style sheet to a page

After you've created an external style sheet, you can attach it to any web page. In the step-by-step instructions that follow, you can use any of the predefined style sheets included in Dreamweaver (as I do in this exercise), or you can use these instructions to attach any style sheet you create using the steps in the previous exercise. Begin by opening the page to which you want to attach the style sheet and then follow these steps:

1. **Click the plus (+) icon in the Sources panel at the top of the CSS Designer panel and choose Attach Existing CSS File from the drop-down list (refer to Figure 6-2).**

The Attach Existing CSS File dialog box opens.

2. **Click the Browse button and locate the CSS file in your local site folder.**

You can also enter a URL if you want to use a remote CSS file located on another website, but it's most common to use a style sheet contained in the website you're working on.

3. **Select the Link or Import option.**

If you're attaching a style sheet to an HTML file, your best choice is almost always to choose Link, which is the default. Choose Import if you want to create one master external style sheet that contains references to other style sheets, an advanced option that enables one style sheet to refer to another.

4. (Optional) Choose options from the Conditional Usage section.

Use the Conditional Usage features to define a media query as you attach your style sheet. Media queries are covered in Chapter 8.

5. Click OK.

The dialog box closes, and Dreamweaver sets the link to the style sheet by adding a line of code to the top of the HTML file. After you link an external style sheet, any applicable styles are automatically applied to the content in the page in Dreamweaver and the selector names of the styles defined in the style sheet become visible in the Selectors panel of the CSS Designer panel set.

You can attach multiple style sheets to the same HTML page, and you can use internal and external style sheets in the same document. For example, you can save your text styles in one style sheet, save your layout styles in another, and then attach both to the same document — which makes all the defined styles available to the page. Similarly, you create different style sheets for different purposes, such as one for printing the file and another for browser display.

Moving and copying styles

After you attach an external style sheet to a document, you can move, copy, and edit styles as follows:

- **Moving styles:** You can move styles from one style sheet to another with click-and-drag ease. First, in the Sources panel, select the name of the style sheet with the styles you want to move. Then, in the Sources panel, drag the name of any style in that style sheet onto the name of the style sheet you want to move it into. In Figure 6-4, I'm moving an h1style from the internal style sheet, identified in the Sources panel with the <style> tag, into an external style sheet named new-styles.css. If you've attached more than one external style sheet to a document, you can also move styles from one external style sheet to another using the same click-and-drag technique.

- **Copying styles:** You can copy styles from one document to another by right-clicking (Control-clicking on a Mac) a style name in the Sources panel and choosing Duplicate. This makes a copy of the style, which you can then edit or move into another style sheet.

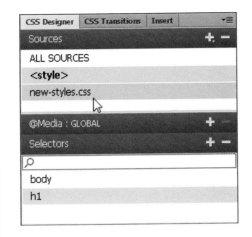

Figure 6-4: Move styles from an internal to an external style sheet.

✏ **Editing styles:** You edit styles in an external style sheet the same way you edit styles in an internal style sheet — by first selecting the name of the style sheet in the Sources panel, then selecting the style name in the Sources panel, and finally editing the style definition in the Properties panel. If you want to edit a CSS file used in a website on a server, you must first download the file to a local hard drive and save it in your site's root folder. (You find detailed instructions for editing CSS files in the next section. You find instructions for uploading and downloading files in Chapter 4.) *Note:* Any changes you make to a style in an external style sheet are applied automatically to all the files to which the external style sheet is attached.

When you edit an HTML page linked to an external style sheet, you must upload both the HTML file and the CSS file to your server before the style changes become visible on your website online. Be sure to save the CSS file when you finish editing it!

Editing styles in code view

Although you don't ever have to look at the code in your CSS files, Dreamweaver does include a great text editor that color-codes CSS selectors and properties to make them easier to read, as you see in this figure.

In Dreamweaver, you can open .css files by double-clicking them or by choosing File⇨Open and then double-clicking the name. The style sheet opens in Code view. When you view an external style sheet using the Code view editor,

you can still use the CSS Designer panel to edit or review the styles in the style sheet — even if the style sheet isn't linked to an HTML page.

If you prefer, you can also edit the code by hand in Code view. The figure shows an example of a style sheet opened in Dreamweaver's Code view. Note that the CSS Designer panel displays all relevant style information and gives you access to the CSS editing tools.

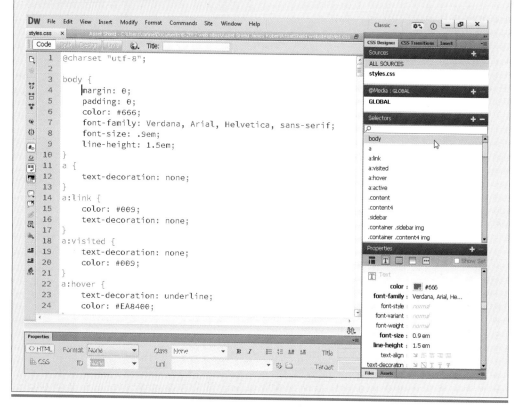

Creating Style Rules

Get ready to create your first styles. Whether you're creating styles using class, tag, or ID selectors, most of the steps are the same.

As you go through the steps to create a style in Dreamweaver, you may be surprised by the number of options in the many panels in the CSS Designer panel group. However, you will use only a few of the available options to create most styles.

You can always refer to Chapter 5 for more detailed descriptions of the different selector types as well as the many options in the Properties panel in the CSS Designer panel, which you can use when you create or edit styles.

Defining styles with the tag selector

You can create completely new styles using the call or ID selectors, but you can also create styles that change the formatting of existing HTML tags. These styles are created using the *tag selector,* which is also known as the *element selector* (because HTML tags are also called HTML elements). When you define a style using the tag selector, you can alter the appearance, position, and other features of any existing HTML tag.

Many HTML tags already include formatting options. For example, the heading tags include formatting to style text using a large bold font. When you create a style with a tag selector, you have to consider the formatting options already associated with that tag. Any options you define will either be added to the existing formatting or override the formatting. For example, in the steps that follow, I create a CSS rule for the <h1> tag, which is displayed using the Times font in most web browsers. In the rule, I change the font by selecting the Gotham font collection included in Dreamweaver. That means Gotham will override Times when the <h1> tag is used in my page. If I want my headlines to be bold, I don't need to include bold in the style definition because bold is in the default style of the <h1> HTML tag. In this case, if I don't want headlines to be bold, I need to add a style rule that removes the bold formatting by setting the Font-Weight to Normal.

You may ask, "Why would I redefine the <h1> tag instead of just creating a new headline style using the class or ID selector?" Although you can define a new class style instead of redefining an HTML tag, sometimes using an existing HTML tag is better. Heading styles are especially important on the web because text formatted in an <h1> tag is well recognized as the most important text on a page. Among other things, text formatted in an <h1> tag may get special consideration from search engines.

When you create a style for an existing HTML tag, you don't need to apply the style itself the way you do with class and ID styles, covered later in this chapter. Wherever you've used the HTML tag, the style definition settings are applied. Thus, in the exercise that follows, as soon as I create a style that redefines the font face, color, and formatting for the <h1> tag, any text that is already formatted with the <h1> tag will automatically change to reflect the new style. Similarly, any time I use the <h1> tag again, it will format the text using the formatting I've defined in the new tag style.

To create a style that redefines an HTML tag (such as the <h1> tag) with the tag selector, first create a file or open an existing one and then follow these steps:

1. **In the Selectors panel of the CSS Designer panel, select the style sheet to which you want to add the new style.**

   If you haven't yet created or attached a style sheet to the page, see the earlier exercises in this chapter for instructions on how to complete this required initial step.

2. **If you want to target the style to a specific media type or screen size, choose or define a media query in the @Media panel.**

   Using media queries with styles is optional. If you do not specify a media query, Dreamweaver will use the Global property and your style will work in all media formats and screen sizes. (You find more on media queries in Chapter 8.)

3. **Click the plus sign (+) in the Selectors panel.**

   A new selector is added to the Selectors panel.

   When you click the plus sign (+) to create a new selector, a few things can happen, depending on what's already on the page open in Dreamweaver. The first time you create a style in a blank web page, Dreamweaver enters body in the Selectors panel, as shown in Figure 6-5. If you're working on a page with text or other content that is formatted with HTML tags or styles, Dreamweaver may add a compound selector based on the elements surrounding whatever you've selected with your cursor. For example, if your curser is resting in a headline formatted with an <h1> tag, and that headline is inside a <div> tag styled with an ID style named #container, Dreamweaver will add a compound selector, like this: #container h1. Remember, you can always change any selector name by double-clicking to select the name in the Selectors panel, and then editing or replacing the name with whatever you want to use for your selector.

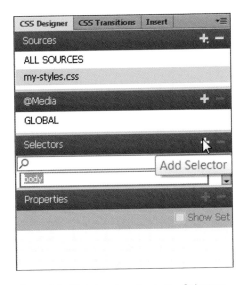

Figure 6-5: Click the plus sign in the Selectors panel to create a new style.

4. **In the Selectors panel, double-click the selector name. Begin to enter the name of the HTML tag, and then select the tag from the drop-down list that appears.**

   You can enter the name of any HTML tag to create a style using the tag selector. As you can see in Figure 6-6, as you type an HTML tag, a drop-down list appears with tags that begin with the same letter you've typed. Selecting the desired tag from the list rather than typing the entire tag name yourself is good practice because you avoid typos.

5. **In the Properties panel, specify the settings you want in your style rule.**

   For this example, I redefined the <h1> tag to use the Gotham font collection, instead of the default browser font, and changed the text color to red. As you see in Figure 6-7, the font and color are immediately applied to the text in the page formatted with the <h1> tag.

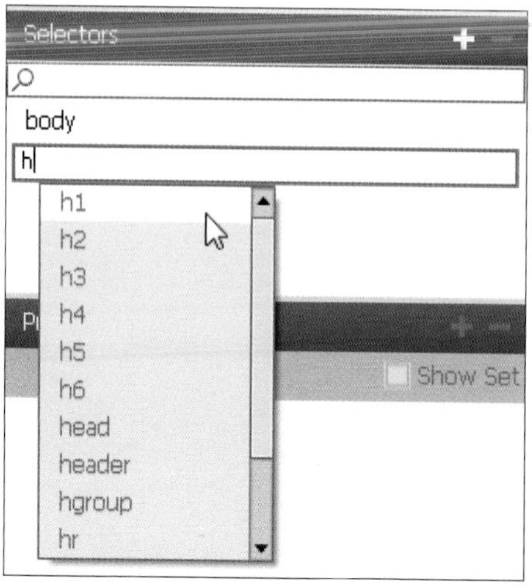

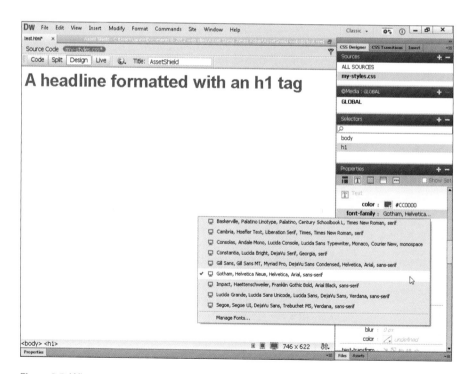

Figure 6-6: Dreamweaver includes code hints for HTML tags.

Figure 6-7: When you create a style using the tag selector, the formatting you define in the style rule is immediately applied to any content formatted with the HTML tag.

If you want to be able to use the same HTML tag with different formatting in different parts of the same page, you can create compound styles, as described in the "Creating compound styles" sidebar. Compound styles are handy, for example, if you want text formatted with the <h2> tag to look different in the main part of your page than it does in a sidebar.

Creating styles with class and ID selectors

Class and ID selectors have many similarities and one key difference. ID styles can only be used once per page but class styles can be used as many times on the same page as you like.

Class and ID styles have the following similarities:

- ✔ You can name styles created with the class and ID selectors anything you like. Seriously, you can name a style Fred if you like, although most of us prefer to use names that have some meaning, such as footer for the name of the style that goes at the foot, or bottom, of the page. You should not include spaces or special characters in style names, although the underscore and hyphen are okay. The use of all lowercase is a common but not required practice.

- ✔ You can apply class and ID styles to any element on a page, but they are most commonly applied to header tags, div tags, unordered list tags, paragraph tags, image tags, and the new HTML5 tags.

- ✔ Using styles created with the class and ID selector is a two-step process. First, you create a new style using the class or ID selector and give it a name; then you apply the style to an element on the page.

In this section, you find step-by-step instructions for creating styles with the class and ID selectors. In the next section, you see how to format text and other elements by applying a style created with the class or ID selector. These same instructions can be used to create and apply any class or ID style in Dreamweaver.

To define a new class or ID style, create and save a new document or open an existing file, and then follow these steps:

1. **If you're defining a new style you want to apply to an existing element, click to place your cursor over the element that you want to format with the new style.**

   Although this step is not required (you can create styles for elements that are not yet on the page), Dreamweaver automatically creates selector names based on the page element that your cursor is currently selecting. In the example shown in this exercise, my cursor is inserted at the beginning of the headline text.

2. **In the Selectors panel of the CSS Designer panel, select the name of style sheet to which you want to add the new style.**

   If you haven't created or attached a style sheet to the page, see the earlier exercises in this chapter for instructions on how to complete this required initial step.

3. **If you want to target the style to a specific media type or screen size, define a media query in the @Media panel.**

   If you don't specify a media query, Dreamweaver will use the Global property and your style will work in all media formats and screen sizes. (You find more on media queries in Chapter 8.)

4. **In the Selectors panel, click the plus sign (+).**

   A new selector is added to the Selectors panel. In Figure 6-8, Dreamweaver has added a compound selector name, which includes all the styles already applied to the headline where my cursor was resting when I started to define the style. (To learn more about using compound styles, see the sidebar, "Creating compound styles," later in this chapter.)

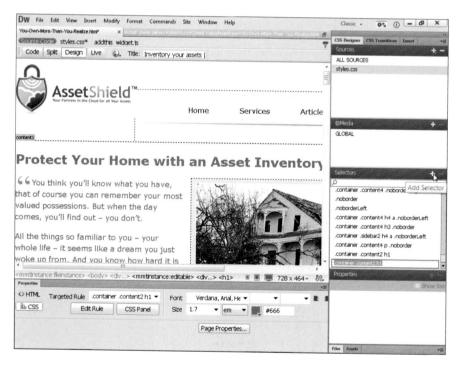

Figure 6-8: Click the plus sign to create your new style.

5. **Double-click the selector name, and edit or replace it with the name you want to use for your style.**

   You can name class and ID styles anything you like, as long as you don't use any spaces or special characters other than the hyphen (-) or underscore (_).

   If you want to create a style using the class selector, you must begin the style name with a dot, or period. If you want to use the ID selector, the style name must begin with a pound sign (#). See Chapter 5 for a detailed explanation of the differences between class and ID styles.

6. **In the Properties panel, specify the settings in your style rule, as shown in Figure 6-9.**

   For this example, I created a style called `.quote-style`. I defined the rule using the following settings in the Text section of the Properties panel:

   - For the **Color** field, I clicked the color well (the square icon) and selected a dark blue color. Sticking to the default color swatches in the color well is the quickest way to choose a color, but you can also create custom colors by clicking the icon that looks like a rainbow-colored globe in the upper-right corner of the color well and selecting a color from the system color picker.

   - In the **Font-Family** field, I chose the Baskerville font collection from Dreamweaver's font list. To format your text with almost any font using the new font embedding options in CSS3, see Chapter 7.

   - In the **Font-Style** drop-down list, I chose Italic as the font style.

   - In the **Font-Size** field, I chose 1.3em for my quote style, which will make the quote text appear just a little larger than the rest of the text on the page. You can specify text sizes in pixels, percentages, ems, and several other measurements. (For an explanation of options, see the section "Understanding CSS size options," in Chapter 5.)

   - In the **Line-Height** field, I chose 1.3em to provide more space between the lines of text, to compensate for the larger size I set in the Font-Size field.

   In this example, I chose to define the style using the class selector (indicated by the period at the beginning of the name) so that I could apply the style to more than one quote on the same HTML page. As you see in the exercise that follows, class and ID selectors are easy to apply to content after you create them because Dreamweaver adds these styles to the Class and ID drop-down lists in the Property inspector, located at the bottom of the workspace.

Figure 6-9: Define style rules using the options in the Properties panel.

Applying class and ID styles

Defining class and ID styles in Dreamweaver is the time-*consuming* part. Applying them after you define them is the time-*saving* part. How you apply a style depends on the kind of style you've created. To apply a class or ID style in Dreamweaver, create a new file or open an existing one and follow these steps:

1. **Click and drag to select the text or other element to which you want to apply a style.**

   In this example, shown in Figure 6-10, I've selected the text to the left of the photograph.

2. In the Property inspector (with the HTML features displayed), select the style from the Class or ID drop-down list.

Note that in the example, I'm selecting a style from the Class drop-down list and Dreamweaver provides a preview of the style by formatting the way the name appears in list based on the style definition. (For example, in Figure 6-10, the `.quote-style` style name is displayed as italic and blue in a large size.) When you choose a style, the selected element (in this case, the text to the left of the image) changes to reflect the application of the style. Figure 6-10 shows the quote style created in the preceding section applied to the text.

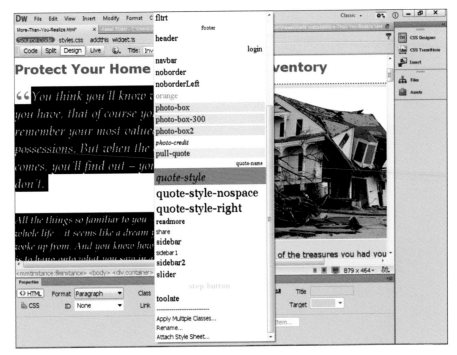

Photo by istockphoto.com

Figure 6-10: To apply a class style, select an element in the main workspace, and then choose the style from the Class list.

Resetting HTML elements with CSS

Because not all browsers interpret HTML and CSS in the same way, many web designers begin designing pages by creating styles that remove any border, padding, or margins included in an HTML tag by defining a style that sets those values to 0 (as you see in the following example).

Resetting common HTML tags to remove any padding or margins means that all your tags start with the same blank slate. In this way, you help ensure that any styles you create will be displayed more consistently across different web browsers.

In the CSS layouts included in Dreamweaver, you find styles that reset common tags, including the heading and list tags. In this example, I've set the border, padding, and margins to 0 to ensure a more consistent display across different web browsers:

```
h1, h2, h3, h4, h5, h6, p, ul, ol, li, {
border:0; margin:0; padding:0;
```

Creating Layouts with CSS and Div Tags

The key to understanding how CSS works in a page layout is to think in terms of designing with a series of infinitely adjustable containers, or *boxes*. Indeed, this approach to web design is commonly called the *box model*.

Think of the box model this way: First you use HTML tags, such as the <div> (division) tag or <p> (paragraph) tag, to create boxes around each section of your content. Then you use CSS to style each box, using CSS rules to control the position, width, and alignment of each box by specifying such settings as Width, Margin, Padding, Float, and Border. The combined effect is one beautiful page, created by combining CSS styles with HTML tags.

Although you can use any HTML tag as part of your page layout, the <div> tag is used most often to create the boxes for main sections of a page, such as the banner area, commonly used at the top of a page, the main content area, the sidebars, and the footer. Think of <div> tags as generic containers designed to contain text, images, or other content. Essentially, <div> tags create divisions on the page, separating one section of content from another. Unlike other HTML tags, <div> has no inherent formatting features. Unless CSS is applied to a <div> tag, it's invisible on a page when viewed in most web browsers; yet the tag has a powerful purpose because you can easily format with CSS any content surrounded by opening and closing <div> tags.

Splitting the view

If you're creating a series of `<div>` tags to position content on a web page, you may find it easier to keep track of the `<div>` tags if you use Dreamweaver's Split view, as shown in the figure. Split view enables you to see Code view and Design view simultaneously. To split the workspace area, choose View⇨Code and Design or click the Split button, located just under the Insert panel at the top of the workspace.

If you select an image, text, or another element on a page in Design view, it's highlighted

automatically in Code view — a great feature that makes it easier to find your place in the code when you're trying to troubleshoot what's happening behind the scenes. I like to use Split view to keep an eye on the code as I create page designs — especially when I'm inserting `<div>` tags. When you're using only Design view, keeping track of how `<div>` tags are arranged and nested can be hard.

Adobe uses the box model to create all the CSS layouts included in Dreamweaver. In these layouts, each <div> tag on the page has a corresponding style. As a result, to change the size or positioning of the header, footer, or any of the other main areas of the page separated by <div> tags, you need to edit the corresponding style. You find detailed instructions for how to identify and edit these styles in the sections that follow.

Using Dreamweaver's CSS Layouts

Dreamweaver includes two CSS layouts designed with HTML5 tags that you can customize to create a seemingly infinite variety of page designs. These layouts give you a head start when you create a new page, and they're designed to work well in a variety of web browsers, so they can help you avoid common problems caused by the different ways web browsers display HTML5 and CSS. For all these reasons, I recommend starting your design work in Dreamweaver with a CSS layout chosen in the New Document window, especially if you want to use HTML5.

One of the challenges with CSS is that it continues to change and design features are introduced with each new version. Unfortunately, browser support — which can make the difference between a beautiful web page and a jumbled, unreadable design — hasn't always kept up, and the companies that make browsers haven't always agreed on how to display CSS. (You find more about browser differences and testing in Chapter 4.)

To help you get around the problems caused by browser differences, Adobe dedicated the equivalent of decades of time (at least in Internet years) to designing CSS layouts with HTML5 that display well in many different web browsers, even older versions of browsers.

Before you rush off to check out these cool CSS layouts in Dreamweaver, let me warn you: They're not much to look at when you first open them. They're intentionally designed with the most basic of formatting options and a dull green color scheme — but fortunately color styles are some of the easiest styles to alter in CSS.

No matter what your experience level, the following sections are designed to help you appreciate how Dreamweaver's CSS layouts work and to help you create your own page designs by customizing the layouts step by step. You find out how to change the width of columns, the formatting styles for text, and the alignment of any element on the page in one of Dreamweaver's layouts. If you're new to CSS, altering one of these layouts may seem confusing at first; trust me, altering an existing layout is much easier than creating a design from scratch.

Creating a new page with a CSS layout

To create a new page using one of Dreamweaver's CSS layouts, follow these instructions:

1. **Choose File⇨New.**

   The New Document dialog box appears.

2. **Choose Blank Page from the left column and HTML from the Page Type column in the middle.**

   Alternatively, you can choose an option in the bottom part of the Page Type section that corresponds to the programming language used on your site, such as ASP.NET, PHP, or ColdFusion, and then progress to Step 3. (If you're not familiar with these programming options, stick with HTML.)

3. **In the Layout section, select either CSS layout.**

   For this example, I chose 2 Column Fixed, Right Sidebar, Header and Footer. In Figure 6-11, note that when you select a CSS layout, a preview of the layout is displayed at the top right of the dialog box.

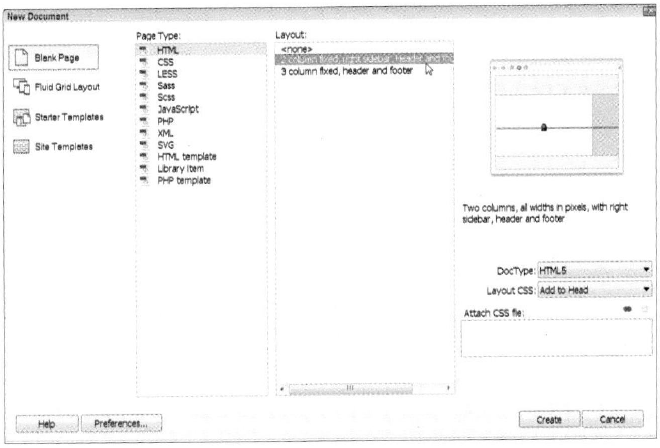

Figure 6-11: When you select the name of a CSS layout, a preview appears in the top-right corner.

4. **From the Layout CSS drop-down list, choose the type of style sheet you want to create as you design the page:**

 * **Add to Head** creates an internal style sheet and includes all the styles for the layout in the header area of the new document.

 * **Create New File** creates a new external style sheet with all the page styles as you create the new document with the design.

 * **Link to Existing File** adds the style sheet information for the new document to an existing external style sheet.

 Note: You can always change how the style sheet is set up later by moving styles from an internal style sheet to an external one or from one external style sheet to another. (You can find instructions for creating external style sheets and moving styles at the end of Chapter 5.)

5. **Click Create.**

 The new page is created and opened in the main workspace.

6. **Choose File⇨Save to save the page and styles.**

 If you saved the styles in an external style sheet, a second box prompts you to save the style sheet separately. If the styles are contained in an internal style sheet, they're saved automatically when you save the page.

 Save all the pages of a website, including external styles sheets, in your local site folder. (For more about defining a website and specifying a local site folder in Dreamweaver, see Chapter 2.)

Editing the styles in a CSS layout

After you create a new page with a CSS layout, you have a seemingly infinite number of options for editing it, but first you have to determine which styles in the style sheet correspond to the elements you want to edit.

The steps in the following sections explain how to edit the overall design of a page created with a Dreamweaver CSS layout. I've broken the process into several step lists to help you follow along more easily. *Note:* The steps assume you're proceeding through the sections in order.

As you can probably imagine, you can edit the styles in a CSS layout in many ways to create your own designs, but the process I explain in the following sections should serve you well as you get started with any of these layouts.

After you adjust the existing styles to get the basic page design the way you want it, you can create as many additional styles as you desire.

Checking out the available styles and making basic edits

You can use these same basic instructions with any CSS layout included in Dreamweaver. To edit styles in a CSS layout, follow these steps:

1. **Open a page file that's based in a Dreamweaver CSS layout, and choose Window⇨CSS Styles (or click the CSS Designer tab to expand the panel).**

   The CSS Designer panel opens or expands.

2. **Click to select the name of the style sheet in the Sources panel at the top of CSS Designer.**

   All the styles associated with the new page are listed in the Selectors panel, as shown in Figure 6-12.

   To change any element in the design of this page, you edit the corresponding style.

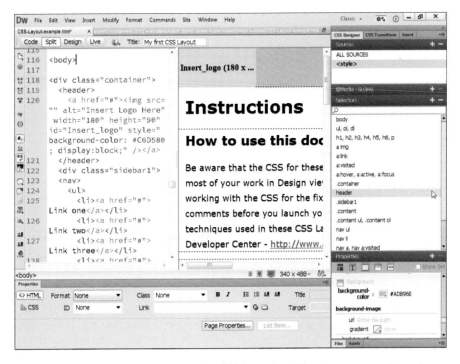

Figure 6-12: Alter the formatting options in a CSS layout by editing the corresponding style definition in the CSS Designer panel.

3. **Select the name of any style listed in the CSS Designer Selectors panel.**

   The corresponding CSS rules defined for the style are displayed in the Properties panel, at the bottom of the CSS Designer panel (refer to Figure 6-12). Clicking through the list of styles and reviewing their corresponding rules is a good way to get a quick overview of the design and to see where the various page-formatting options are stored.

The HTML5 `header`, `.nav`, and `footer` tags control the main sections of the page. For example, the `header` style, which is shown in Figure 6-12, includes a rule that makes the background color green. Thus, to change the color of the header area at the top of the page, you change the background color setting in the `header` rule. (You find detailed instructions for editing the `header` and other main styles in this CSS layout in the "Customizing content areas" section, later in this chapter.)

Editing page-wide settings

To edit page-wide settings — such as the background color of the page or the main font face, size, and color of the text used throughout the page — follow these steps:

1. **In the CSS Designer Selectors panel, select the style named body.**

   The properties defined in the selected style rule are displayed in the Properties panel, as shown in Figure 6-13.

2. **Click the T icon at the top of the Properties panel, and change or add your desired font and other text settings.**

   You can change the font face, size, style, and weight. To change the space between lines of text, change the line height.

3. **Scroll down to the Background area of the Properties panel and use the color well in the Background-Color field to specify a color for the entire background of the page.**

   Alternatively, you can enter any hexadecimal color code in the Background-Color field or use the eyedropper to sample any color on the screen. To add a background image, click in the URL field in the Background section and then click the Browse button that appears and select the image that you want to serve as the background. Use the Background-Repeat icons to specify how the background image should repeat (if at all) on the page.

4. **Make any other changes or additions to the style rule.**

Changes to style rules in the Properties panel are automatically saved and applied to content formatted with the rule.

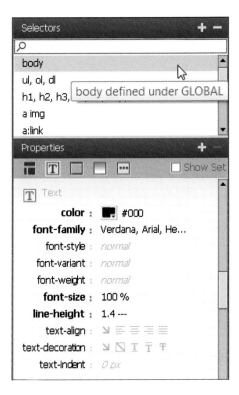

Figure 6-13: Define page-wide settings in the style for the <body> tag.

Creating compound styles

Compound styles make it possible to create more specific styles. Of the many uses for compound styles, one of my favorites is the capability to create tag styles that appear differently in different parts of the same page.

When you redefine a tag (as with the unordered list and link tags), the new style applies to all uses of that tag within a page, unless you define the tag as a compound style by including the name of its container in the style name.

For example, in the "Creating a Navigation Bar from an Unordered List of Links" section, instead of creating a new tag style with just the name of the <ul> tag, I created a compound style called #navbar ul to redefine the <ul> tag *only* when it's contained within a <div> tag with an ID of navbar.

When you create compound styles like this, make sure you separate each style name by a single space. In this example, I also created styles for the <li> and <link> tags in the same way, creating styles with the names #navbar a:link, #navbar a:hover, and #navbar ul li. You can create compound styles with multiple tags and style names to create more specific CSS rules.

Customizing content areas

To change the width or other settings of the main content areas, which control the overall size of the page and the header, footer, and sidebar, follow these steps:

1. **To change the width of the entire main design area:**

   a. **Click the `.container` style in the Selectors panel of the CSS Designer panel.**

   The properties of the `.container` style rule are displayed in the Properties panel, where you can also edit the style.

   b. **Change the size in the Width field or type a new number for your desired page width.**

   The width of the page design is automatically changed based on the size you entered. When you alter the width of the `.container` style, as I did here, you change the width of the entire design because all the `<div>` tags and other elements are contained in the `<div>` formatted with the `.container` style — and they're all set to expand to fill the `.container` `<div>`. (For more on the best width for a web page, see the sidebar "How wide should I make my web page's design?")

2. **To alter the size of the content area of the page, select the style named `.content` and specify the size and other options you desire in the Properties panel.**

   If you change the width of the content area in a layout that includes a sidebar, you must change the width of the sidebar as well. For example, in the layout used in this exercise, the content section is 780 pixels wide and the sidebar is 180 pixels wide, and they fit perfectly in the 960-pixel-wide container. Thus, if you increase the width of the content style by 30 pixels, you'll need to decrease the width of the sidebar by 30 pixels so that the total remains 960 pixels.

3. **To change the background color of any style on the page, click the name of the corresponding style and change the settings in the Background section of the Properties panel.**

   For example, in the CSS layouts in Dreamweaver, the sidebar is defined in a style named `.sidebar1`. Thus, to change the background color, I clicked `.sidebar1` in the Selectors panel, selected the Background category in the Properties panel, and then clicked the color well (as shown in Figure 6-14) and selected the color I wanted. Similarly, to change the background color of the header, select the style named header in the Selectors panel and use the color well in the Properties panel.

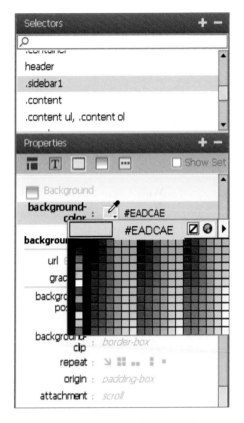

Figure 6-14: Change the background color in the Properties panel.

4. **To add an image to the header:**

    a. **Select the placeholder image labeled Insert Logo and press the Delete or Backspace key.**

    b. **Choose Insert ⇨Image⇨Image and select an image using the Select Image Source dialog box.**

5. **Replace text and insert images in the sidebar and main content areas.**

    You can add or replace text and insert images in any page created from a CSS layout, just as you would in any other web page.

6. **Choose File⇨Save All to save the page and styles.**

You can combine CSS layouts with Dreamweaver's template features to create a *template* — a page design you can use to create additional pages without repeating all the steps to customize the styles for each page. (As you discover in Chapter 9, Dreamweaver's template features offer many advantages when you're designing a site with more than a few pages; for example, you can make changes that affect many pages at once.)

Here's a related tip: If you intend to use the design as a template, make sure you save your styles in an external style sheet so you can edit the style rules outside the template. (Find instructions for creating external style sheets and for moving internal styles into an external style sheet in Chapter 5.)

Creating a Navigation Bar from an Unordered List of Links

Here's a great CSS trick for turning a bulleted list (or unordered list) into a navigation bar with a simple rollover effect. Using a bulleted list for navigation bars is a well-accepted convention for websites that meet current accessibility standards. A bulleted list is a logical choice for navigation elements; even if the style rules are removed, the links still stand out from the rest of the elements on the page and are clearly grouped together in a list.

In Figure 6-15, for example, you see how the links, which are contained in an unordered list, appear without styles applied to them. In Figure 6-16, those same links are still contained in the unordered list, but the application of the styles changes their appearance dramatically.

To see how any web page looks without its styles applied when using the Firefox web browser, as shown in Figures 6-15, choose View➪Page Style➪No Style.

Thanks to CSS, you can gain the benefits of styling a list of links with the unordered list tag and still format your links with any style you choose. For the same reason, most designers use the heading tags to format headlines and then create styles to change the way they appear. Formatting a list of links with the unordered list tag adds meaning to the code, but you don't have to keep those boring bullets, and you can align your links horizontally or vertically. CSS applied to text also enables you to create a rollover effect because you can change the style of the different link states, as you see in the following exercise.

You can use the following steps to add a list of links to any CSS layout included in Dreamweaver, as well as to any custom CSS layout you create yourself.

Photos by istockphoto.com

Figure 6-15: The same web page shown in Figure 6-16 with the No Style option selected in the Firefox browser.

Photos by istockphoto.com

Figure 6-16: The same page shown in Figure 6-15 but with styles applied.

To create a navigation bar using CSS to redefine the unordered list and link tags, follow these steps:

1. **Click to place your cursor where you want to create your navigation bar in the page.**

When you're creating a list of links to serve as your navigation bar, it's good practice to position those links at the top or side of the page, where visitors to your site can find them easily.

2. **Enter the text you want to serve as the links, separating each by pressing the Return or Enter key to create a paragraph return.**

To format the links as an unordered list, separate each line of text that you want to link with a <p> tag.

You can type any text you want, but the general recommendation is to keep the main navigation links in your site very short. For example, use a single word when possible (such as *Home*) instead of something longer (such as *The front page of the site*).

3. **Create links by selecting each piece of text in turn, clicking the Hyperlink icon in the Common Insert panel, and then selecting the page you want to link to or entering a URL.**

Essentially, you set these links as you would set any other links in your site. (You find detailed instructions for creating a variety of different types of links, including links to other websites and e-mail links, in Chapter 2.)

4. **Drag to select the entire set of links, and then click the Unordered List icon in the Property inspector, as shown in Figure 6-17.**

A bullet point appears at the beginning of each link. If any link isn't set off with a separate bullet, click to delete the space between it and the link before it, and then press Return or Enter to separate the links with a paragraph return (which will be automatically converted into a bullet in the unordered list).

5. **To add a <div> tag around a list of links (or any other content that is already on a page), select the content and then click the Div icon in the Common Insert panel.**

The Insert Div dialog box opens.

Adding a <div> tag around the unordered list of links is helpful if you want to add formatting, such as the background color that fills the entire navigation row in this example.

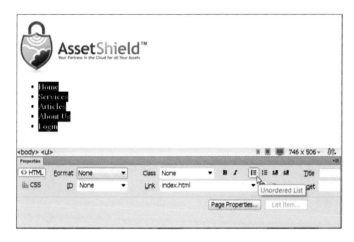

Figure 6-17: Formatting a collection of links as an unordered list.

6. **Choose Wrap Around Selection from the Insert drop-down list, as shown in Figure 6-18.**

   For more precise control over where you add a new `<div>` tag, you can choose options from the Insert drop-down list at the top of the Insert Div dialog box. Choosing the Wrap Around Selection option, for example, adds open and close `<div>` tags to the code before and after the selected content, in this case, the bulleted list of links.

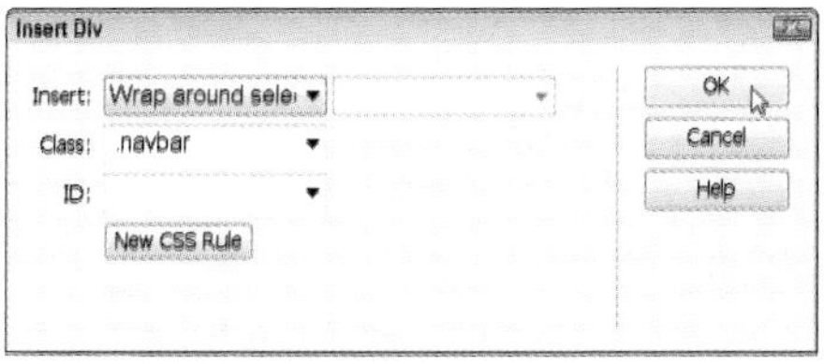

Figure 6-18: Adding a <div> tag around content to create a class style.

7. **Enter a name in the Class field or the ID field.**

   A `<div>` tag with the class or ID name you entered is added automatically to the page surrounding the list of links.

   In this example, I chose to create a class style with the name `.navbar` (as shown in Figure 6-18).

You can create a class or ID style to format the `<div>` tag that surrounds your list of links. If you plan to have only one navigation bar on the page, an ID style is a fine option. If you plan to repeat the navigation bar in more than one place (as I did in this example by adding a navigation bar to the top and bottom of each page), create a class style so you can use it twice on the same page. (For more about the differences between class and ID styles, see Chapter 5.)

8. **At the bottom of the Insert Div dialog box, click the New CSS Rule button.**

   The new CSS rule name is added to the list of style names in the CSS Designer Selectors panel.

9. **In the Properties panel, specify your desired settings for color, background, size, margins, and padding.**

   The style formatting is automatically applied to the content of the `<div>` tag because you applied the style as you created it in Steps 5–7.

10. **To create a compound style that will format the unordered list only when it is used in the navigation bar, create a compound style that includes the class name `.navbar`:**

    a. **Place your cursor anywhere in the bulleted list.**

    b. **Click the plus sign (+) at the top of the Selectors panel.**

    c. **In the Selector Name field, make sure that Dreamweaver automatically entered .navbar ul as the name of a new style in the Selectors panel.**

       If the name of the new style is not .navbar ul, double-click to select the name and change it to .navbar ul. (For an explanation of how compound styles like this work, see the sidebar "Creating compound styles.")

    d. **In the Properties panel, set the margins and padding to** 0.

11. **Create a compound style to redefine the list item tags:**

    a. **Place your cursor anywhere in the bulleted list.**

    b. **Click the plus sign at the top of the Selectors panel.**

    c. **In the Selector Name field, make sure that Dreamweaver automatically entered .navbar ul li as the name of a new style in the Selectors panel.**

       If the name of the new style is not .navbar ul li, double-click to select the name and change it to .navbar ul li.

d. In the Properties panel, set the Display to Inline.

This step changes the style of the `<li>` tag and the list of text changes from vertical to horizontal.

e. Change the List Style Type to None to remove the bullet.

f. Set the left and right margins to 20 pixels.

This step separates the list items from one another in the horizontal list. You can change the setting to create the amount of space between links that best fits your design.

12. Create a style to redefine the link tag:

a. Click to place your cursor within a link in the navbar.

b. Click the plus sign at the top of the Selectors panel.

Dreamweaver automatically enters a compound style name: .navbar ul li a:link

c. If you want to change the style name, double-click the name in the Selectors panel and enter the name you want to use.

You can make compound styles as specific as you choose. For example, the style `.navbar a:link` will change the appearance of any links in the `.navbar` `<div>`. However, if you create the style `.navbar ul li a:link`, that style will apply only to links that appear in the `.navbar` `<div>` and inside the unordered list tags. Because these are the only links I use in the `.navbar` `<div>`, I don't need to be so specific; both styles will work the same in this example.

d. In the Text section of the Properties panel, set Text-Decoration to None.

This step removes the underline from linked text.

e. Still in the Text section, choose a color from the color well to specify the color of links when they're loaded on a page.

Make sure to select a color that provides good contrast with the background color of the page so that the links are easy to read.

13. Create a new style to redefine the hover-link tag so that the link color will change when a user rolls a cursor over the link:

a. Click the plus sign at the top of the Selectors panel.

b. In the Selector Name field, enter .navbar a:hover.

Again, I could create a more specific compound link by entering .navbar ul li a:hover, but it's not necessary here.

Comparing block and inline elements

As a general rule, HTML tags can be divided into block elements and inline elements. *Block elements,* such as the `<div>` tag, interrupt the flow of the page, creating a box or block around which other page elements align. In HTML, block elements include the paragraph (`<p>`) tag, which creates a line break before and after it's used and doesn't allow anything to appear alongside it. Heading tags, such as `<h1>`, `<h2>`, and `<h3>`, and list tags, such as `<ul>` and `<ol>`, are also block elements.

In contrast, *inline elements* follow the flow with text. For example, the `<strong>` and `<em>` tags, which apply bold and italics, respectively, are inline elements. You can place these elements one after another, and a new line break doesn't appear between each element. They simply flow with the text. For that reason, the `<span>` tag, which is an inline element, is a good choice for applying styles that you want to affect a small amount of text within a block, such as when you want to add a little color to text contained within `<p>` tags. Dreamweaver often adds `<span>` tags when you apply a class style to text in the middle of a paragraph.

   c. **In the Text section of the Properties panel, set Text-Decoration to None.**

   This step removes the underline from linked text. If you prefer to have the underline appear when a user rolls a cursor over a link, select Underline.

   d. **Still in the Text section, choose a color from the color well to specify the link's color when users roll their cursor over the link.**

   The more dramatic the color difference between the `a:link` and `a:hover` colors, the more dramatic the rollover effect.

14. **Create a new style to redefine the visited link tag so the link color changes after a user clicks a link:**

   a. **Click the plus sign at the top of the Selectors panel.**

   b. **In the Selector Name field, enter .navbar a:visited.**

   c. **In the Text section of the Properties panel, set Text-Decoration to None.**

   d. **Still in the Text section, choose a color from the color well to specify the link's color after it's been visited.**

   If you want the color to remain the same, set the `a:visited` link to the same color as the `a:link`.

15. **Click the Live button at the top of the workspace or click the Preview button to view the page in a browser to see the effect of the link styles, as shown in Figure 6-19.**

Figure 6-19: Click the Live button to preview the hover color in link styles.

Comparing Margins and Padding in CSS

When creating or editing CSS styles, new web designers are often confused by how and when to use margins and padding. Both settings add space between elements — for example, a margin between text and an image or a little padding between the border of a `<div>` tag and its contents. Here's how margins and padding work:

- **Padding** adds space inside an element. Think of padding as a way to add a cushion around the inside of a box so your content doesn't bump into the sides of your box.

- **Margins** add space outside an element. Think of margins as a way to add space between boxes, on the sides of images, or around any other element on a page, so things don't bump into each other.

Figure 6-20 shows a `<div>` tag with a corresponding ID style that creates the thin black border around the `<div>` tag and defines it as follows:

500 pixels wide

25 pixels of padding inside the `<div>` tag border

50 pixels of margin spacing outside the `<div>` tag border

2-pixel border around the entire `<div>` tag

How wide should I make my web page's design?

For nearly a decade now, most web designers have been setting the width of their web pages to 960 or 960 pixels wide. That size is based on the most common screen resolution on most computer desks. If you want your web pages to look good on computers with monitors set to 1024 by 768, design your pages to take up 960 to 980 pixels and you leave enough room for the borders of a web browser. This size also displays well on iPads and many other tablets. However, if you want your pages to look as good on tiny smartphone screens as they do on large monitors, consider creating multiple style sheets and designing your pages to work at more than just one fixed width. In Chapter 8, you find out how to create responsive web designs that work on small and large screens.

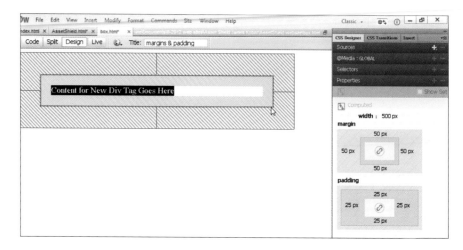

Figure 6-20: Padding is added to the inside of an element and margins are added to the outside; both add to the width needed for an element on a page.

Here's the confusing part:

- **Padding adds to the specified width.** If you specify a width for a `<div>` tag (or any other box element) — as I have in Figure 6-20 — the padding increases the total width. In my example, the `<div>` tag will fill 550 pixels of space on the page: 500 pixels for the width plus 25 pixels on each side of padding.

- **Margins add to the total space taken up by an element in a page.** The margins of the `<div>` tag style are set to 50 pixels, so the `<div>` tag is positioned 50 pixels from the top and left of the page and no other element will appear on-screen closer than 50 pixels on the right or at the bottom. Adding margin space prevents elements from bumping up against each other, but you need to remember, that the `<div>` tag will then effectively take up all that space on the page — the combined width, plus padding, plus margins.

- **Borders add to the specified element width.** The ID style for the `<div>` tag also includes border settings, which cause the dark border to surround the `<div>` tag. In this example, I created 1 2-pixel border, which adds 4 pixels to the width. If you choose the thick border setting, it adds 4 pixels to each side of the `<div>` tag (8 pixels total).

Thus the <div> tag fills a total space on the page of 654 pixels:

500 pixel width

50 pixels total of padding (25 pixels on each side)

4 pixels of border

100 pixels total of margin (50 pixels on each side)

Aligning and Centering Elements in CSS

In addition to formatting text, you can use CSS to align elements and position them in relation to one another on a page. In this section, you find out how to use floats to align images and other elements, how to use margin settings to center an element, such as a <div> tag on a page, and how to use the text alignment option to center text or other elements contained in a <div> tag.

Centering a page layout with CSS margins

Many web page designs are centered on the page so they seem to float between the sides of the browser window no matter how wide or narrow the window becomes. This helps create the illusion that the design fills the page, even if the browser window is much wider than the page design.

Most web page designs created with CSS achieve this effect by creating one <div> tag that surrounds all the page content and then applying a style to that <div> tag that includes a style rule that centers that <div> tag. As you discover in the following step-by-step instructions, creating a style to center a <div> tag is not as obvious as you might imagine but is easy to implement after you understand the technique.

Common practice is to use an ID style for the <div> tag that centers your design, and to name it #wrapper or #container. However, you can achieve the same effect with class styles named .container or .wrapper. I like to name the style I use for this purpose #container because the style *contains* all the other tags and content on the page.

If your page isn't already set up with a <div> tag around all your content, here's a tip for adding one. First click and drag to select all text, images, and other content on the page. Then choose Insert➪Layout Objects➪Div Tag. In the Insert Div Tag dialog box, make sure the Wrap around Selection option is selected from the Insert drop-down list. Leave the rest of the fields blank and click OK to add a <div> tag around all the contents of your page, and you're ready for the steps that follow.

When margins collapse

A little-understood rule of HTML called Margin Collapse is not specific to CSS but does affect how margins in CSS are displayed in a web browser. Margin Collapse causes top and bottom margins between elements to overlap. The goal of Margin Collapse is to keep elements that appear one above the other, such as paragraphs created with `<p>` tags, from displaying with twice as much space as you'd want between them.

Not doubling the margins is useful with the paragraph tag, but it can cause confusing problems when you set margin space above and below adjacent elements, such as `<div>` tags, and the total margin space doesn't add up the way you'd expect. For example, suppose that you have two `<div>` tags, one above the other, and have set the bottom margin of the top `<div>` to 10 pixels and the top margin of the `<div>` below it to 20 pixels. You'd expect those pixels to combine to create 30 pixels of space between the two `<div>` tags (because you'd get 30 pixels of space if those same margins were set on the left and right and the `<div>` tags were side-by-side). However, with `<div>` tags stacked on top of each other, the Margin Collapse rule causes the margins to overlap, resulting in a space that is equal to the larger of the two margins. In this case, the 10-pixel and 20-pixel margins combine to take up 20 pixels of space between the `<div>` tags, not the 30 pixels of space you might expect, because 20 pixels is the largest of the two margins.

The exception to the Margin Collapse rule? (Of course, there's an exception to this rule.) If you add a border or padding in addition to margins between `<div>` tags, the Margin Collapse rule is ignored and the margin space will be the total of the two margins, plus the padding or border size. In that case, the total space created by the margins will add up just like you might expect.

To center an entire page design, make sure that a `<div>` tag surrounds all of the contents of the page, and follow these steps:

1. **Click the plus sign in the CSS Designer Selectors panel.**

   Depending on what is on the page, a new style name or a blank field where you can enter a style name is added to the Selectors panel.

2. **Double-click to select the name that Dreamweaver added to the panel and change it to the name you want for your new style, or click to select the blank field and enter a name.**

   If no name is added, enter the name you desire in the empty field. You can name the style anything you like, but make sure to enter a period before the name if you create a class style, or a # sign for an ID style.

3. **In the Properties panel, specify the width, margins, and any other formatting settings you want to define.**

   As shown in Figure 6-21, I set the width for the container <div> tag to 980 pixels. Here's the trick to centering a <div> tag like this: Set the left and right margins to Auto. That way, a browser automatically adds an equal amount of margin space to each side of the <div> tag, effectively centering it on the page.

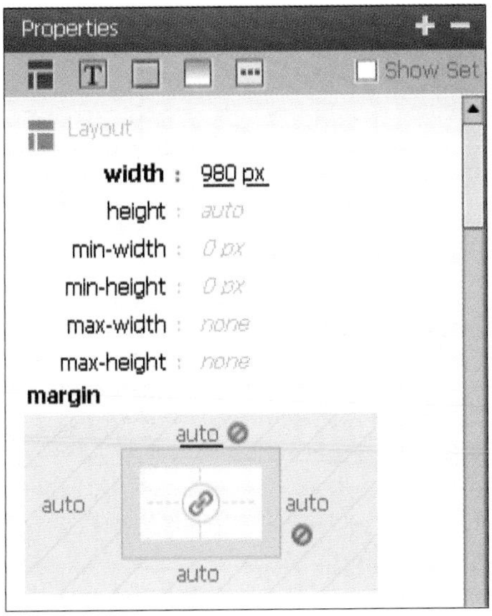

Figure 6-21: To center a <div> tag, set the left and right margins to Auto.

4. **Select the ID that surrounds all the content on the page.**

   To make sure you've selected the right <div> tag, click to place your cursor anywhere in the main part of the page, and then click the <div> tag listed to the farthest left in the Quick Tag Selector at the bottom of the workspace.

5. **With the <div> tag selected, select the name of the style you created from the ID drop-down list in the Property inspector.**

   The style rules you defined when you created the style are automatically applied to the <div> tag. In this example, the result is that the size of the <div> tag is changed to 980 pixels wide and the <div> tag and all its contents are centered on the page.

Not all features work when Dreamweaver is set to Live view. Although Live view (activated by the Live button at the top of the workspace) is a great way to preview how your page designs will look in most modern web browsers, the use of the Live view feature makes many of Dreamweaver's editing tools unusable. If, for example, the Property inspector appears dimmed when you want to use it, make sure that the Live button is deselected.

Aligning the contents of an element

If you want to align the contents of an element, for example, centering text within a `<div>` tag, you can use the text align option. This technique is also useful for aligning a horizontal list of navigation links to the right side of a page. A common approach to using this option is to create an ID or a class style that you will apply to an entire `<div>` tag and include the text alignment option as part of the style rule.

Aligning elements with floats

Designers often align an image, a `<div>` tag, or another element to the left or right of a web page and then wrap any text or other content around that element. In Figure 6-22, I've used a style to align the image to the right of the column so that the text wraps next to it on the left. In the steps that follow, you find out how to create styles like this one.

CSS offers many advantages when it comes to aligning elements like this, but the way you set up these styles is not as obvious as you might expect at first because you use the float option.

After you understand that you can float elements, such as images, to the left or right side of a page, it's pretty easy to create styles that accomplish this goal. In this exercise, you learn to create two styles that are ideal for aligning images to the left and right of a page, complete with a little margin just where you need it.

In all my sites, I create two styles like this, one to align images and other elements to the left, and another to align to the right. It is good practice to define these two alignment styles using the class selector and to save them in an external style sheet so that they can be used multiple times in any or all pages in your site. *Note:* The CSS layouts included in Dreamweaver CC already have float styles that you can use to align elements to the right and left. These class styles are named `.fltlft` (for, you guessed it, float left) and `.fltrt` (for float right).

Image from istockphoto.com

Figure 6-22: When you align an image to the left or right using floats, adjacent text wraps around the image.

To create two class styles that you can use to align images and other elements to the left and right of a page, follow these steps:

1. **Click the plus sign in the CSS Designer Selectors panel.**

   Depending on what is on the page, a new style name or a blank field where you can enter a style name is added to the Selectors panel.

2. **Double-click to select the name that Dreamweaver added to the panel and change it to the name you want for your new style, or click to select the blank field and enter a name.**

   If no name is added, enter the name you desire in the empty field. You can name the style anything you like, but make sure to enter a period before the name if you create a class style or a # sign for an ID style.

3. **Double-click the new name and edit it as desired.**

   Although you can name these styles whatever you prefer, alignment styles are commonly named with the abbreviated fltrt and fltlft, which stand for float right and float left respectively.

For example, if you create a style to align elements to the left, you would name it `.fltlft`.

4. **In the Properties panel, click the icon that sets Float to Left, as shown in Figure 6-23.**

Figure 6-23: To define alignment in a style rule, select the Float Left or Float Right icon.

5. **Use the Margin settings in the Properties panel to create a margin around the floated element.**

   It's good practice to add margin space to the opposite side from the float setting. For example, if you're creating a style to float an image to the left, add 5 or 10 pixels of space to the Right margin field. Then, when you use the style to align an image to the left side of the page, a margin will also be created between the image and any text or other element that wraps next to the image.

6. **Select the image or other element you want to align in the page.**

7. **Select the name of the style you created from the Class drop-down in the Property inspector.**

   The style rules you defined when you created the style are automatically applied. If you had selected an image in a page of text, the image would move to the left side of the page and the text would wrap around it with a margin between the image and text.

8. **Repeat Steps 1–7, once with the float set to Right and 5 to 10 pixels of margin space in the Left margin field in the Box category, and again with the Float set to Left and 5 to 10 pixels of margin space in the Right margin field in the Box category.**

Editing, Renaming, and Removing Styles

After you create and apply a few styles, you're likely to want to go back and edit some of them. Fortunately, Dreamweaver makes it easy to rename, edit, and even remove styles, as you learn in the sections that follow.

Editing a style

You can change the attributes of any style after you create it by editing its style definition. This is where some of the biggest advantages of Cascading Style Sheets come into play. You can make global changes to a page (or even to an entire website) by changing a style; when you edit the style, the changes are applied automatically to every element that uses the style.

One of the reasons why external style sheets are so valuable is that you can create styles that are used on any *or* all pages in a site. Beware, however, that this capability can also lead to problems. If you decide to edit a style when you use it on a new page, don't forget that you'll be changing the formatting everywhere else you've already used that style.

You can create new styles by duplicating an existing style, giving it a new name, and then altering the style definitions. This time-saving trick is useful when you want to create a new style that's similar to an existing one.

To edit any existing style (whether it was created using the class, tag, or ID selector), follow these steps:

1. **Open the CSS Designer panel by choosing Window➪CSS Styles.**

2. **In the CSS Designer Selectors panel, select the name of an existing style.**

   The style rules are displayed in the Properties panel.

   If you want to edit a style that has already been used to format text, images, or other content in the page open in Dreamweaver, select the content. The name of the style applied to that content will be displayed in the Selectors panel, making it easy to find and edit.

3. **Edit the settings for the style to your liking.**

- **If you edit a style in the CSS Rule Definition dialog box,** changes are applied automatically when you click the Apply button or when you click OK.

- **If you edit a style definition in the Properties panel,** the changes are applied automatically as soon as you press the Return or Enter key or click outside the formatting field in the panel.

Renaming existing styles

You can rename a style in the CSS Designer Selectors panel by double-clicking to select the name and then typing a new name.

If you change a name in the Selectors panel, you must also change the name in the corresponding page code, or reapply the style using the Property inspector — which can get complicated if you've used the style in many places.

For example, let's say you create a class style and name it #footer. You then apply the style to the <div> tag that surrounds the content at the bottom of your web page using the Property inspector (as I did in the first exercises in this chapter). Then suppose you decide to change the name of the style to #copyright because you want to add another <div> that you'll use as the footer later. Changing the name from #footer to #copyright in the CSS Designer Selectors panel is easy enough, but then you have to make sure to update every place you've used that style in your site — either by reapplying the style using the Property inspector or by changing the name in the code wherever the style has been applied.

If you want to change the name of a class style, Dreamweaver includes a feature that updates the corresponding code automatically, but only for class styles and only if you change the name using the right-click (or Control-click) option described in the instructions that follow. If you change the name of an ID style, you must reset the style using the Property inspector, or change the corresponding references in the code manually using Code view or the Quick Tag Editor.

Removing or changing a style

If you want to remove or change a style applied to any text, image, or other element on your page, here are two options:

✔ Select the text, image, or other element. Then open the Class or ID drop-down lists in the Property inspector and choose None from the top of the list of styles.

✏ Select the element, and then right-click (Control-click on a Mac) the tag that the style is applied to in the tag selector at the very bottom of the workspace (just above the Properties inspector), as shown in Figure 6-24. When you right-click the name of a tag in the tag selector, a list opens with many options; choose the corresponding option for the selected style. In the example shown in Figure 6-24, I selected the <p> tag that surrounds the first paragraph and chose the Set Class option to open a list of all class styles in the site. To change or remove a style this way, simply select the style you want and it will replace any style that has already been applied.

For a list of more advanced CSS training resources online and offline, visit www.DigitalFamily.com/css and look for the article titled "Where to learn more advanced CSS techniques."

Image from istockphoto.com

Figure 6-24: Right-click the element name in the tag selector to change or remove any style or HTML tag.

Designing with CSS3

In This Chapter

▶ Comparing browser support for CSS3

▶ Adding text and drop shadows

▶ Making rounded corners

▶ Using almost any font you want

W hen most designers learn about the new features in CSS3, including drop shadows, gradients, and vastly improved font support, their reaction is: "It's about time!" These long-awaited design improvements provide a compelling reason to graduate to using CSS3 right away, even though older web browsers won't display all of these fancy new features. The good news is that if a browser doesn't support a new CSS rule, such as rounded corners, it simply ignores the style information. Visitors with older browsers may see square corners on the borders of your <div> tags instead of rounded ones, or common fonts such as Times or Arial in place of the more obscure fonts you may prefer to use in your page designs.

I recommend you start using CSS3 style rules even if some of your visitors can't see them because CSS3 is clearly the wave of the future. As people update their web browsers and new computers replace old ones, CSS3 will become increasingly well supported. So why wait? Your most savvy visitors will appreciate the design enhancements and faster download time today, and everyone else will come around before too long.

That said, you may not want to add every new CSS3 feature to your pages right away (some are better supported than others, even in the latest browsers). In this chapter, I introduce the most popular CSS3 features, including adding drop shadows to text and images, creating rounded corners on <div> tags, and using almost any font you want.

Comparing Browser Support for CSS3

To help you appreciate how a page designed with CSS3 looks in different web browsers, I used the latest version of Google Chrome to preview the page shown in Figure 7-1 and then used Design view in Dreamweaver to preview the same page in Figure 7-2. Note that Figure 7-1 shows a custom font, drop shadows, and rounded corners created using new properties available in CSS3 — Google Chrome is well known for its excellent support of CSS3. In contrast, Figure 7-2 shows how the page looks in an older web browser that does not support CSS3 rules, such as Internet Explorer version 6.0. Many web designers agree that it's okay to create web pages that don't look the same in all browsers, as long as the text is still readable by all your visitors.

Photo by Charlie Simpson

Figure 7-1: Google Chrome displays all CSS3 features used in this design.

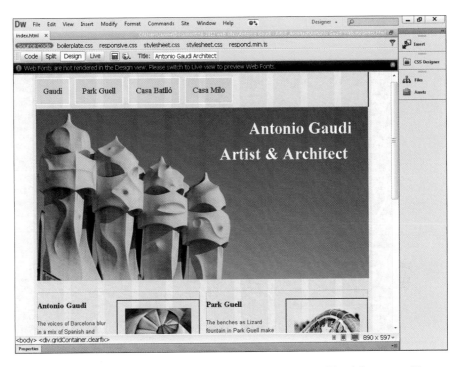

Figure 7-2: Design view in Dreamweaver displays the page like an old web browser, without the custom fonts, drop shadows, and other CSS3 features.

To get a better idea of how your pages will look in Dreamweaver, click the Live view icon at the top of the workspace. When you display a page using the Live view option, Dreamweaver works much like the Google Chrome and Apple Safari web browsers.

In Chapters 5 and 6, I cover the basics of CSS. If you're new to working with style sheets, I recommend that you start with the basics in those chapters before moving on to the more advanced CSS3 features covered in this chapter. In Chapter 4, you find more tips and resources for testing your web pages in different web browsers.

TECHNICAL STUFF

Why so many ways to write CSS3 code?

The World Wide Web Consortium (W3C) is continually working on CSS and HTML standards. Because approval of new tags and rules can take years, many browser companies start implementing new features before they are officially approved. When they use a specification that isn't fully approved, browser companies add a special prefix to the new rules to distinguish them from other code that has been approved. As a result, you sometimes need to include different versions of the same style rules in your code if you want your styles to work in all the most popular web browsers.

For example, the following code creates a rounded corner using CSS3. The three lines of code do the same thing — they set the radius to 10 pixels. The first line is written for Safari, the second for Firefox, and the third follows the currently proposed W3C specification, which

is already supported by a growing number of browsers. (Note that in CSS, comments are surrounded by /* */ in the code and the text in the comments is not required.)

```
-webkit-border-radius: 10px; /* Safari 3
        and 4 */
-moz-border-radius: 10px; /* Firefox 1+ */
border-radius: 10px; /* Internet Explorer
        9, Safari 5, Chrome */
```

Some designers shy away from using code until it's approved, preferring to wait until the standards are official because the specifications might change. However, CSS degrades gracefully in browsers (a fancy way of saying that if the browser doesn't support a new CSS rule, it's ignored), and CSS3 offers so many exciting new features and so few negative side effects — if you design your pages carefully — that many of us agree there is no reason to hold back.

Adding drop and text shadows

You can enhance your designs and give your pages greater depth by adding drop shadows to images, `<div>` tags, and other elements. Adding text shadows makes your words easier to read, especially if your design has a complex background or the foreground and background colors lack contrast, as shown in Figure 7-3.

Dreamweaver CC provides better support and integration of CSS3 drop shadows and text shadows from the new CSS Designer panel, covered in this section.

You can create class or ID styles with text shadows, and you can add text shadows to existing HTML elements by defining a tag style, such as the heading 1 style I used in Figure 7-3. The CSS3 code that creates that text shadow is

```
h1 {text-shadow: 2px 2px 2px #000;}
```

Gaudi

Park Guell

Casa Batlló

Casa Milo

Antonio Gaudi
Artist & Architect

Photo by iStockphoto.com

Figure 7-3: Text shadows make text more readable, especially when the text overlaps a background image.

The numbers in the code specify that the text shadow should extend 2 pixels to the right and 2 pixels below the text with a 2-pixel blur. In addition, the shadow is created with the color black, specified by the abbreviated hexadecimal color code #000.

When creating rules for text shadows you can specify up to four values:

- ✔ horizontal and vertical: The first two number values are required and specify the horizontal and vertical offsets — the distance the drop shadow extends below the text (vertical) and to the right of the text (horizontal).

- ✔ blur radius: The third value specifies the amount of blur in the shadow. If you don't include blur radius, the default is 0, which makes the shadow appear as a solid color.

- ✔ color: The fourth value specifies the color of the shadow and can be defined using a hexadecimal color code or an RGBa color code.

Choosing an RGBa color for the Color option gives you greater control over the shadow's appearance because you can add transparency.

You can add a text shadow using the Properties panel at the bottom of the CSS Designer panel, as shown in Figure 7-4. To do so, follow these steps:

1. **Scroll down to the Text-Shadow section of the CSS Designer Properties panel.**

2. **Enter the size of the shadow you want to display using the H-shadow (horizontal) and V-shadow (vertical) fields.**

3. **Add the amount of blur you want for your text shadow by entering a size in the Blur field.**

4. **Click the color well and select the color your want to use in the text shadow.**

Figure 7-4: You can add drop shadows to images, <div> tags, and other elements using CSS3.

Adding drop shadows to images and divs

In addition to text shadows, CSS3 gives you the power to add shadows to images, boxes created using `<div>` tags, and other elements. In Figure 7-5, for example, I'm using the CSS Designer panel to define a rule that adds a drop shadow to all images on this page.

Figure 7-5: Add drop shadows to images, <div> tags, and more by adding a box-shadow rule.

Style rules that are part of the CSS3 definition, such as drop shadows, are visible in Dreamweaver only when you select the Live view option. In Figure 7-5, the cursor is over the Live button, changing the display area from regular Design view to Live view so that the drop shadows are visible.

The following style adds a drop shadow to all images on a page:

```
img {box-shadow: 3px 3px 3px 3px #000;}
```

Much like the text shadow covered in the preceding section, the first two values specify how much the shadow extends on the x- and y-axis. The third value describes the amount of blur. The `box-shadow` rule includes a fourth setting that specifies the spread radius of the shadow. At the end of the list, the hexadecimal color code defines the color of the shadow.

Again, much like the `text-shadow` rule, you can use the Properties panel in the CSS Designer panel to define a `box-shadow` rule. Scroll down to the box-shadow section, and then fill in each of the definition options shown in Figure 7-5.

By default, drop shadows using the `box-shadow` rule in CSS3 appear to the right and below any element to which they are applied. However, you can specify that the shadow be inset instead of outset by clicking the corresponding icon at the bottom of the box shadow settings, shown in Figure 7-5.

Softening Edges with Rounded Corners

Another popular CSS3 rule, `border-radius`, enables you to add rounded corners to the borders of `<div>` tags and other box elements. Using CSS3, you can specify how much corners are rounded, and you can apply the style to any or all corners of an element.

In Figure 7-6, you see a `<div>` tag with a border and a colored background, as well as the `border-radius` style rule applied to the top-left and bottom-right corners.

You can use the new rem measurement to design rounded corners that scale with the size of the text. The rem measurement is a popular choice among designers who value creating pages that look good on small and large screens and for designs that adapt gracefully when a visitor to a site chooses to increase the text size to make a page more readable. For more on the rem and other sizes in CSS, see Chapter 5.

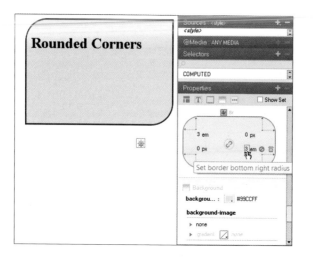

Figure 7-6: The radius of the rounded corner.

Enhancing Your Site with Custom Fonts

The few fonts that come installed on most Windows and Mac computers are woefully inadequate. Serious designers spend hours searching for just the right font to convey the feeling they want to elicit in a design, which is why so many of us are excited that CSS3 offers a better solution.

The @font-face option, new in CSS3, enables you to link to any font available from a web server. Add a little drop shadow and other styling elements with CSS3, and you can create fantastic font effects without resorting to the old workaround: using images with styled text created in Photoshop. The @font-face rule offers many advantages because using text instead of images on your pages means they load faster and are easier to update.

Using text with the @font-face rule instead of text in an image offers many advantages, including the following:

- Text loads more quickly than images.
- Text formatted with HTML and CSS is easier to update than text in an image.
- Including keywords in text on a page instead of hiding them in images can improve your search engine rank.

> ✔ Using text in place of images makes your web pages more accessible to anyone with a disability who uses a screen reader or other special browser.
>
> ✔ Text is selectable and resizable.

How does the @font-face rule work?

Using the `@font-face` rule requires just two steps. First, you use the `@font-face` rule to link to a font hosted on a web server. Then, you use that font in the `font-family` property in your CSS rule. And finally, you use that rule to format some or all of the text in your web page.

Armed with those basic instructions, it's tempting to assume that you can just upload any font on your hard drive to your web server and link to it with the `@font-face` rule. Unfortunately, like so many things on the web, hosting and using fonts in web pages are more complicated than they should be. For example, even if you have the rights to host a font on your server, you may not have all the variations of that font needed to display the letters properly on Mac and Windows computers or to work in all web browsers.

The solution? Most of us use a font service, such as the following:

> ✔ **Font Squirrel** (`www.fontsquirrel.com`)**:** Font Squirrel features a collection of free fonts in font kits. You have to download the kits and then upload and host them on your own server, but the price is right — free. Font Squirrel also provides a font generator that you can use to create the four font types you need to support the most popular web browsers. This service is useful if you have the rights to a font and want to host it yourself.
>
> ✔ **Google Web Fonts** (`www.google.com/webfonts`)**:** The easiest site to use (as you see in the step-by-step instructions that follow), Google Web Fonts offers a limited collection of fonts but you can use all their fonts for free.
>
> ✔ **Typekit** (`www.typekit.com`)**:** Adobe Typekit offers a wide range of high-quality fonts and is the clear choice of many professional designers. You can try this service for free, but if you get much traffic, want to use all their fonts, or want to use fonts on more than one website, you'll have to pay a monthly subscription fee.

These popular services take different approaches to making fonts available to web designers. Font Squirrel lets you download fonts that you can then upload to your own web server. (They manage the rights and font options for you.) Google Web Fonts makes it easy to link to fonts hosted on their server. Typekit follows a more complicated approach to protect the copyright of font holders.

Much of the confusion among web designers about using the `@font-face` rule stems from the fact that the most popular font services take such different approaches to managing and using web fonts.

No matter which service you use, the basic concept is the same, but as you go through the exercise that follows, keep in mind that how you use a web font depends on the service that hosts the font.

Using custom fonts from the Google Web Fonts site

Follow these steps to add any of the fonts from the Google Web Fonts site to your pages:

1. **Open a web browser and visit** `www.google.com/webfonts`.

2. **Search through the fonts available on the site by selecting the type and style of font you're looking for, as shown in Figure 7-7.**

   To narrow your search, use Filters (in the left column). You can change the text that is displayed in each font by editing the Preview Text field at the top of the screen.

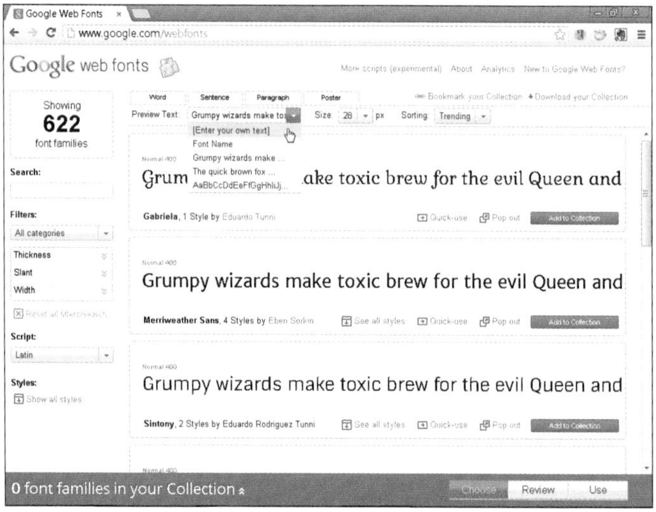

Figure 7-7: Search the Google Web Fonts collection of free fonts for your web pages.

3. **Find a font you like, and then click the blue Add to Collection button in the bottom-right, just below each font name.**

4. **Click the check boxes next to each of the font styles that you want to use on your web page.**

   Most fonts in the Google Font Directory have only one style. Although you may be tempted to choose all styles, it's best to select only the ones you'll use. As Google warns, the more font styles you choose, the longer it will take to download your web page.

5. **Scroll down the page and select the Latin option (for English).**

   If you need the additional characters for another language, select the Latin Extended option instead.

6. **Scroll further down the page to the blue box with three tabs; click the first tab to link the font to your website.**

   Google provides three options: Standard, @import, and JavaScript, as shown in Figure 7-8. You find detailed descriptions of all three on the Google site.

Figure 7-8: Copy a snippet of code from the Google Web Fonts site to link to each font.

7. Copy the link from the Standard tab field on Google just as you would copy any other text or code from a web page.

8. **In Dreamweaver, paste the link into the head area of your web page between the open** `<head>` **and close** `</head>` **tags.**

9. **Return to the Google Web Fonts site and at the bottom of the page, copy the name of the font family.**

   You can find the name of the font family in the Integrate the Fonts into Your CSS area.

   In your style definition, you must include the name of the font exactly as Google writes it. I find that copy-and-paste is the best way to make sure the font name matches.

10. **In Dreamweaver, paste the name of the font family into the CSS rule where you want to use the font.**

11. **Apply the rule to text in your web page.**

   If you use the font in a Tag selector style, such as the `<h1>` tag, when you apply the tag to text, the font will be automatically applied as part of the rule. If you use the font in a class or ID style, the style must then be applied to a tag that surrounds the text, such as a `<p>` tag or a `<div>` tag. You discover more about class, ID, and tag styles in Chapter 5.

12. **Publish the page to a web server and then preview the page in a web browser to see the font.**

   Note that when you use Google Web Fonts you may not see the font displayed in Dreamweaver, even if you use the Live view option. To ensure that the font works on your page, you may need to transfer the page to a web server using FTP and preview the page after it's published online. You find out more about using Dreamweaver's FTP features in Chapter 4.

Creating Responsive Designs with Fluid Grid Layouts

. . . .

In This Chapter

▷ Future-proofing your site with responsive design

▷ Comparing responsive and adaptive sites

▷ Using Dreamweaver's fluid grid layouts

▷ Targeting style sheets with media queries

. . . .

*T*he biggest challenge of web design today is that your pages are as likely to be projected on a giant computer monitor as on a tiny cell phone screen. As a result, creating websites that look good to all visitors is more complex — and more important — than ever.

When people first started using mobile phones to connect to websites, many of us created special versions of our sites specifically optimized to work only on small mobile devices. Today, some sites still use this approach, creating one simple mobile site that works in parallel to the main website, but two other approaches to designing for small and large screens are available — adaptive and responsive design.

Adaptive design was developed to meet the diverse needs of a growing number of cell phones with different capabilities and screen sizes. *Adaptive design* requires that you create many different versions of each web page, use complicated programming to detect each device that visits the site, and deliver a version of each page optimized for the specific size and features of that cell phone visitor. Adaptive design is complicated, expensive, and generally used only by large, well-financed websites.

Fortunately, a new, simpler approach called responsive design is quickly gaining popularity. With *responsive design,* you create one web page and then use multiple sets of CSS rules to change the format and layout based on the size of the browser window.

Following are two big advantages to responsive design over adaptive design:

- **Responsive designs are based on screen size, not device capabilities.** Adaptive design requires that you maintain a complex database of the mobile devices in use on the web, including the screen size and capabilities. Such databases are expensive to create or purchase, and they must be updated every time a new phone or device comes on the market. Responsive designs are adjusted based on the size of a browser window, so it doesn't matter what type of mobile device your visitor users.

- **Adaptive design requires complex programming on the server.** An adaptive website requires complex programming — and advanced programming skills — to assemble a web page to match the size and capabilities of each device. Responsive design is accomplished with HTML and CSS, and all adjustments to the page design are done in the web browser, so there is no need for complex programming on the server.

Understanding Responsive Web Design

The best way to understand how responsive design works is to visit a website designed with this approach, such as the Antonio Gaudi site shown in Figure 8-2, which is available on my website at `www.digitalfamily.com/g`. With the Gaudi website open on your computer, drag the right edge of the browser window from right to left, slowly making the browser window smaller, and you'll see how the page design changes automatically as the browser window becomes smaller.

Responsive designs are created by combining one well-crafted HTML page with multiple sets of CSS styles, and then using media queries to target each set of styles. *Media queries* are CSS rules that inform a web browser about which set of styles should be applied to the page when the browser window is within a specified size. Essentially, media queries cause the styles applied to a page to change based on the width of the browser window.

When you create responsive designs using the fluid grid layout features covered in this chapter, Dreamweaver generates three sets of styles and corresponding media queries:

✔ **Mobile layout:** Targets CSS rules that apply when the browser window is 480 pixels and below.

✔ **Tablet layout:** Targets CSS rules that apply when the browser window is 481 to 768 pixels. This layout inherits all styles from the mobile layout and adds styles that apply to the page only when the browser window is in the tablet size range.

✔ **Desktop layout:** Targets CSS rules that apply when the browser window is 769 to 1232 pixels. This layout inherits all styles from the mobile and tablet layouts and adds styles that apply to the page only when the browser window is in the desktop size range.

As you design your fluid grid layouts, remember that you are not creating three completely different web pages. Instead, you're creating one HTML file that can respond and adjust to fit each of the target screen sizes defined in the media queries. That means you need to position all `<div>` tags and other elements in your HTML document in a way that they can be reduced, enlarged, and rearranged to work in all three of the layouts you create. As a result, one of the biggest complexities as you develop responsive designs is coming up with a basic page structure that lends itself to working on all three screen sizes.

In the step-by-step exercises that follow, you create your own fluid grid layout and design three sets of styles. Before you do, however, look at the design in Figures 8-1 and 8-2. In Figure 8-1, you see how the same boxes, created using the same `<div>` tags or HTML5 elements, are rearranged to create the three layouts shown in Figure 8-2.

As you study these designs, consider that only one HTML page is used to create all three page layouts and that this design follows common best practices:

✔ **The mobile version:** The smallest version is designed as a single-column layout, with each box stacked one on top of the other.

✔ **The tablet version:** The midsized version is designed with narrow columns arranged side by side.

✔ **The desktop version:** The largest version is designed with wide columns, and the images within those columns are aligned so that the text wraps around each image.

Creating responsive designs requires some planning, and often some trial and error. However, your reward will be that you create an efficient web design, meaning you have only one page of content you need to update, yet that one page looks good on virtually every device anyone may use to visit your website.

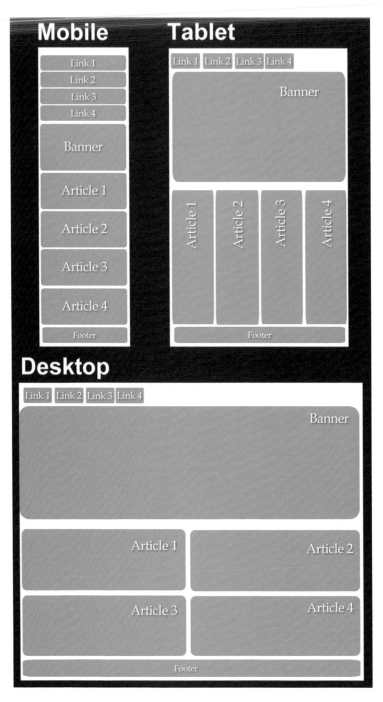

Figure 8-1: Responsive design makes it possible to turn one HTML document into three layouts.

Figure 8-2: This design was created from the HTML layout featured in Figure 8-1.

Creating mobile websites versus native apps

Many designers are confused by the difference between a mobile website and an application and why you should create one or the other. Here's a quick look at the differences.

Native apps are programs that you download from the iTunes or Android app stores. Native apps are programs designed to work on specific mobile devices, such as iPhones, iPads, and any of the many tablets and phones that use Android, Windows Mobile, or other mobile operating systems.

Mobile websites, in contrast, are similar to other websites in that you view them in a web browser while you're connected to the Internet. What makes a mobile website different than other websites is that it is carefully designed to look good, and be easily usable, on small mobile screens.

In general, creating a native app is far more expensive than creating a mobile website for several reasons, most notably that you have to create different versions of each native app — one for iPhones, another for iPads, another for devices that use Android software, another for Windows Mobile, yet another Blackberry devices, and so on.

In contrast, if you design the mobile version of your website using the responsive design strategy covered in this chapter, you create just one version of each page, and then design it to work on all mobile devices, no matter what operating software they use.

So why does anyone create a native app instead of a responsive website? Apps enable you to create more complex programs and they are the best option when you're creating a highly interactive game, such as Angry Birds. But many developers are realizing that apps have been overhyped by Apple's "there's an app for that" advertising campaign. A growing number of companies that designed native apps for the mobile audience are now shifting their focus and creating mobile websites instead.

I recommend that you create a native app only if you have a compelling reason, such as the creation of a video game. For everyone else, your goal should be to make sure your website works well on small and large screens, and that is best done today by taking the responsive approach to creating websites, covered in this chapter.

Although you can create many kinds of designs, using different combinations of columns, the basic structure of any responsive site follows this example: The `<div>` tags and other elements have to be positioned on the page in such a way that you can use only CSS to rearrange them to be displayed well at each size (for mobile phones, tablets, and desktops).

Designing Pages with Fluid Grid Layouts

Recognizing the growing popularity of responsive web design, Adobe added a new feature set to Dreamweaver CS6, and improved it in version CC. The fluid grid layout features, which are available from the File menu and the New

Document window, make it easier to create multiple page layouts simultaneously by automatically generating three sets of CSS styles and their corresponding media queries when you create a new web page.

Creating a new fluid grid layout

Before you dive into creating a design as complicated as the one shown in Figures 8-1 and 8-2, consider trying a simpler design such as the one featured in this series of tutorials. These tutorials are designed to be followed one after another. Combined, they complete the process of designing one fluid grid layout. I've broken the steps down into sections to make it easier for you to understand how the files in each of these layouts work together.

Start by creating a simple, one-column fluid grid layout, following these instructions.

1. **Choose File⇨New.**

   The New Document window opens. ***Note:*** Make sure you have completed the site setup process covered in Chapter 2 before you start working on a new fluid grid layout.

2. **From the left side of the screen, select Fluid Grid Layout.**

   The New Document window options change to the fluid grid options shown in Figure 8-3.

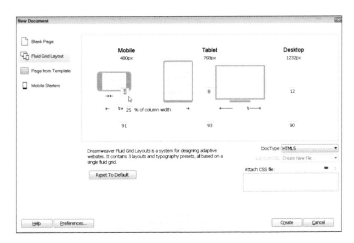

Figure 8-3: The fluid grid layout options as they appear in the New Document window.

3. **Specify the number of columns you want in each of the three layouts.**

   To add or remove columns, select the text field over each column in turn and enter the number of columns you want. In Figure 8-3, I've selected the text field for the mobile layout, which is set to 4 columns by default.

4. **Specify the percentage of the browser window you want each layout to cover.**

   Select the text field below each layout in turn and enter a number representing the percentage of space you want the layout to cover when the design is viewed in a browser window. For example, by default the desktop layout is set to take up 90 percent of the available space, but you could change it to 95 percent to give yourself a little more design space and reduce the margin space on each side of the layout.

5. **Change the percent of column width to alter the amount of margin space between each column.**

   By default, Dreamweaver sets each margin to take up 25 percent of the available space.

6. **Use the drop-down list to specify a doctype.**

   By default, fluid grid layouts are created using the HTML5 doctype. Unless you need to change the doctype to be more compatible with other formatting used in your website, HMTL5 is the recommended option for responsive web designs.

7. **Click Create.**

   The Save As dialog opens ready to save a CSS file.

8. **Enter a name for your CSS file and click Save.**

   A new HTML file opens in the Dreamweaver workspace, but is not yet saved. The CSS file you named is saved and its name becomes visible in the Files panel.

   Note: Unlike the process of creating other types of pages in Dreamweaver, the CSS file is saved first and the HTML file is saved in a later step.

9. **Choose File⇨Save**

   The Save As dialog box opens.

10. **Enter a name for your HTML file, and click OK.**

    The Save As dialog box closes and a notice appears in Dreamweaver informing you that your fluid grid layout requires two additional files: boilerplate.css and respond.min.js.

11. **Click OK to copy the boilerplate.css and respond.min.js files to your site folder.**

    All three files are added to the Files panel and you return to your newly named HTML file open in the Dreamweaver workspace, as shown in Figure 8-4.

12. **Give the page a title by entering text in the Title field at the top of the workspace.**

And that completes the process of creating a new set of files for your fluid grid layout. Continue through the rest of the exercises in this chapter to add content and format your designs.

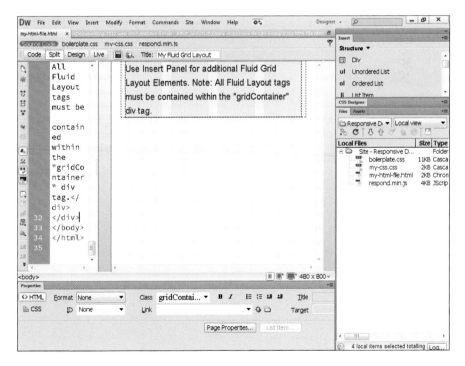

Figure 8-4: When you create and save a new fluid grid layout, four files are saved and added to the Files panel.

Adding fluid elements to a layout

After you create a fluid grid layout, the next step is to add <div> tags or other elements to make up the sections of the design. You have two options when you design pages in Dreamweaver CC: use <div> tags or use HTML5 tags. Both work similarly in these fluid layouts, but using HTML5 tags, such as the <header> and <footer> tags, has some advantage, because the tags add additional meaning and structure to your web page.

To add <div> tags, HTML5 tags, and other elements to a fluid grid layout, follow these instructions:

1. **Choose Insert⇨Structure⇨Navigation.**

   Alternatively, you can click Navigation in the Structure Insert panel.

2. **Select the Insert as Fluid Element check box in the Insert dialog box, as shown in Figure 8-5.**

   When you use the fluid grid layout features, you must select this option when you add tags.

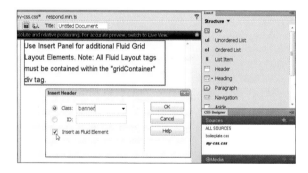

Figure 8-5: You must select the Insert as Fluid Element check box when you insert tags in a fluid grid layout.

3. **In the Insert dialog box, select whether you want to use the class or ID selector to create a new style for the tag you're inserting and then enter a name for the new style.**

Even when you insert HTML5 tags, you must create a corresponding class or ID style that can be used to format the element in all three layouts.

Class style names must begin with a dot (.) and ID style names must begin with the pound sign (#).

4. **Click OK.**

   The tag is added to the layout, forming a new box in the layout, and the corresponding style name is added three times to the CSS layout.

5. **Select the initial `<div>` tag that was included in the layout and then click the small trash can icon that appears at the bottom right of the `<div>` tag to delete it.**

   Although you can keep the initial `<div>` tag included in fluid grid layouts, or you can rename the style applied to it, I find it simplest to just delete it and add my own elements and styles.

6. **Choose Insert⇨Structure⇨Article.**

   The Insert Article dialog box opens (similar to the Insert Header dialog box; refer to Figure 8-5).

7. **Select the Insert as Fluid Element check box in the Insert dialog box.**

8. **In the Insert dialog box, select whether you want to use the class or ID selector to create a new style for the tag you are inserting and enter a name for the new style.**

9. **Click OK.**

   The tag is added to the layout, forming a new box in the layout, and the corresponding style name is added three times to the CSS layout.

10. **Add as many elements as you want for your layout by repeating Steps 6–9.**

    I added five HTML5 elements to my fluid grid layout by clicking their corresponding icons in the Structure Insert panel: one navigation, one header, two articles, and one footer, as shown in Figure 8-6.

    Note that in the code, as shown in Figure 8-6, Dreamweaver adds the prefix *fluid-* to the name of each style you create for your fluid grid layouts.

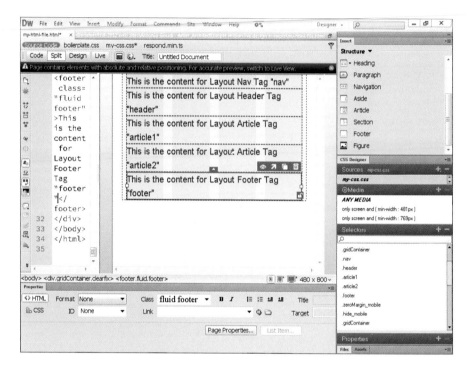

Figure 8-6: A series of HTML5 tags has been inserted into the page to make up the basic structure of a fluid grid layout.

Positioning elements to create three layouts in one fluid grid

What makes fluid grid layouts so powerful is that you can change the position and size of elements so that they are arranged differently for each of the three layouts, creating designs that are optimized for mobile, tablet, and desktop screens. To change an element's width or position, you use Dreamweaver's visual tools.

Editing the mobile layout

Dreamweaver sets up the styles in such a way that they cascade through each of the three layouts. That means you should get the mobile design the way you want it first. Then move on to the tablet layout and change only the elements that you want to appear differently on the tablet. Finally, view the page as it will appear on a desktop computer and, again, change only the elements that you want to be displayed differently in the largest version.

To edit the mobile layout, follow these instructions.

1. **Select the Mobile Size option at the bottom of the workspace, as shown in Figure 8-7.**

   The workspace area changes to display the page in the mobile preview, formatted with the corresponding set of styles.

   Note: The three small icons at the bottom right of the workspace provide access to the mobile, tablet, and desktop previews. When you switch from one to the other, you change not only the size of the display area but also the corresponding set of styles applied to your page.

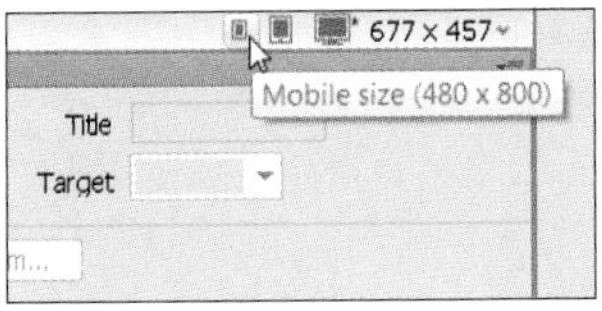

Figure 8-7: These three small icons provide access to the Mobile, Tablet, and Desktop View options.

2. **Add text and images to the elements in your fluid grid layout just as you would add content to any other page in Dreamweaver.**

   You can copy and paste text as well as apply HTML tags and CSS formatting following the instructions in the earlier chapters of this book.

3. **Select an element in the design area.**

   The corresponding CSS style is displayed in the Selectors panel, where you can edit it. In this example, I selected the header.

4. **Create, edit, and apply styles to text and images as you would in any other page design in Dreamweaver.**

   I specified a height for the header and added a background image, as shown in Figure 8-8.

   After you have finished working on the mobile design, move on to the next lesson to edit the tablet design. Note that you can always come back and edit the mobile design further by clicking the Mobile icon at the bottom right of the Document window.

   Styles that you want to apply to all three layouts should be created when the mobile layout is selected because these styles will apply to all three designs unless overridden by another style created in the tablet or desktop layouts.

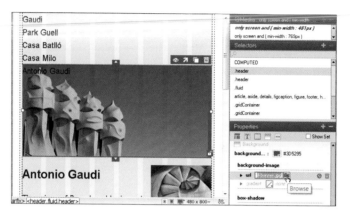

Figure 8-8: Fluid grid layouts work best when you design the mobile version first.

Editing the tablet layout

After you get the mobile layout the way you want it, move on to the tablet size layout and edit the styles that apply to that layout.

To edit the tablet layout, follow these instructions.

1. **Select the Tablet Size option, at the bottom right of the workspace.**

   The workspace area changes to display the page in the tablet preview, formatted with the corresponding set of styles.

2. **Select an element that you want to change into a column and use the handles on the right side to drag the column to the desired width.**

   Dreamweaver provides a collection of visual editing tools that make it easier to adjust the size and positioning of fluid grid elements, such as the column I'm creating in Figure 8-9.

   If you drag the handle of any fluid grid element from left to right, you add margin space that forces the element to stay to the right of the layout. If you drag a handle from right to left, you resize the element, as I'm doing in Figure 8-9.

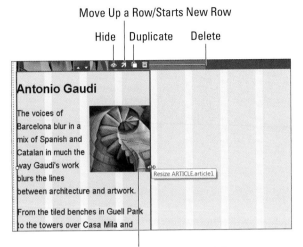

Figure 8-9: Drag the handles on any fluid grid element to resize it.

3. **Select a resized element that you want to reposition, and then click the Move Up a Row arrow (labeled in Figure 8-9).**

The element moves up and aligns itself next to the element above it, as you see in Figure 8-10. In this example, I created two columns by first reducing the width of each element by half (using the drag features covered in Step 2), and then using the Move Up a Row arrow on the second element to bring it up to the right of the first element.

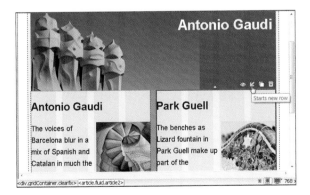

Figure 8-10: Use the Move Up a Row/Starts New Row arrows to create multiple column designs.

4. **To move an element down, click the Starts New Row arrow (labeled in Figure 8-9).**

   In Figure 8-10 my cursor is hovering over the Starts New Row arrow, which would reverse the action I took in Step 3.

   Note: Click each of the four icons labeled in Figure 8-9 to hide an element, move it up or down, duplicate or delete it.

When you use the visual tools covered in Steps 2–4 to resize and reposition elements, Dreamweaver adds corresponding style definitions to the CSS, but only for the set of styles that affect the Tablet design. As you see in the desktop exercise that follows, the columns that I created for the tablet layout will not affect the desktop layout.

Editing the desktop layout

After you get the mobile and tablet layouts the way you want them, move on to the desktop size layout and edit the styles that apply to the largest of the three layouts.

To edit the desktop layout, follow these instructions.

1. **Select the Desktop Size option at the bottom right of the workspace.**

   The workspace area changes to display the page in the desktop preview, formatted with the corresponding set of styles.

2. **Select a Swap arrow in the middle of any two elements to switch the positions of the two elements.**

   In Figure 8-11, the Article1 and Article2 elements can be swapped by simply clicking the Swap arrow between them.

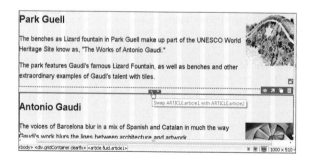

Figure 8-11: Click the Swap arrow between elements to switch them.

3. **Format the text, images, and other elements as desired for the desktop design.**

   All other visual formatting options covered in the preceding exercise, in which you created a tablet layout, are available. For example, you can drag the handle from right to left to resize an element in the desktop layout, just as you did in the tablet layout.

4. **Choose File⇨Save All to save all the files in the fluid grid layout.**

   When you're editing a fluid grid layout, you're making changes to the HTML file as well as to an external style sheet. Using the Save All option ensures that you have saved all the necessary files before you preview them or publish your site to a web server.

Switching among layouts to continue editing

It's good practice to design fluid grid layouts in the order of the three preceding exercises: first the mobile version, then the tablet version, and finally the desktop version. You can, however, switch among these three layouts as you refine your designs.

Keep in mind the following few general rules and best practices:

- ✔ Fluid grid layouts are created using media queries. Those media queries act as dividers between each of the sets of styles that format the mobile, tablet, and desktop layouts.

- ✔ If you study the corresponding styles that format these fluid grid layouts, you will find three sets of styles, each using the same names. Thus, when you edit styles, you need to take care that you're editing the styles that correspond to the layout you want to work on: Select the corresponding element in the workspace with the targeted layout displayed.

- ✔ If you view the corresponding styles that are automatically created in code view, you will see that widths and other sizes are specified to the fourth decimal point, for example, width: 48.2758%. Resist the urge to round off these numbers. If you change these numbers in code view, Dreamweaver will no longer automatically adjust them for you. These sizes are set as percentages so that the layout will adjust fluidly.

- ✔ When you create styles that you want to apply to all three layouts, first select Any Media from the @Media panel in the CSS Designer panel, as shown in Figure 8-12.

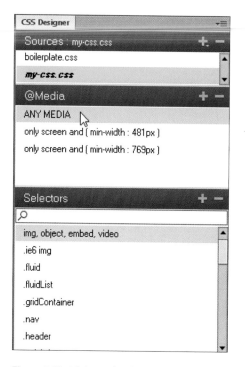

Figure 8-12: All the styles that correspond to these fluid grid layouts are available from the CSS Designer panel.

Creating Custom Media Queries

When you create pages using fluid grid layout features, Dreamweaver automatically creates the corresponding media queries for you, but you can create your own custom media queries and use them to target your own CSS rules.

Many large, complicated websites, such as the Boston Globe, use six or more media queries to target different screen sizes. Visit www.BostonGlobe.com on your computer and then drag the edge of the browser window from right to left, slowly making the browser window smaller, and you'll see how the media queries are triggered and six different sets of styles are applied to the page causing it to change as the browser window gets smaller or larger.

Media queries have been in use on the web for more than a decade for other uses, such as creating an alternative page design optimized for printing. A media query is made up of a media type, such as screen or print (the two most common), and an optional expression that checks for particular features, such as the height or width. The most commonly used media types are

- all: Suitable for all devices
- print: Designed for print preview and for display when a page is printed
- screen: For content displayed on any screen

The handheld media type is almost never used anymore and was best used only for cell phones and other devices with small screens, limited bandwidth, and monochrome displays that support only bitmapped graphics. iOS devices and most smartphones are categorized as screen media types.

Applying styles to your page designs

You can apply style sheets as external files by linking them or importing them, or you can include them as internal styles in the head region of your page's HTML code. You can even target devices using inline styles — a handy option if you want to apply a specific rule only to certain devices.

You can use a combination of these options, and you can import, or link, multiple external style sheets to the same web page. After you've defined the media type with the media features you want to target, you specify how the styles should be applied to the page.

Using media queries in external style sheets

You can use media queries with external style sheets in two ways. The first option is to link to one external style sheet with multiple sets of styles separated by media queries. That's how Dreamweaver links the styles when you create a fluid grid layout.

The second option is to link two or more separate external style sheets to each HTML page and include the media queries in each style sheet. Either way, the code for the CSS and HTML are saved in separate files, and the <link> tag connects them.

Whether you save all media queries and related styles in one file or in separate CSS files, you can link additional style sheets to any HTML page as well. For example, you can include a separate set of styles in a separate style sheet that is designed to format the page when it is sent to a printer.

Creating media queries in Dreamweaver

You can create as many media queries as you like in Dreamweaver and you can include them in one CSS file or many. To create a new media query in Dreamweaver, follow these steps:

1. **Open the CSS Designer panel by choosing Window⬧CSS Styles.**

2. **Select an existing style sheet in the Sources panel, or create a new one by clicking the plus sign (+) in the Sources panel, as shown in Figure 8-13.**

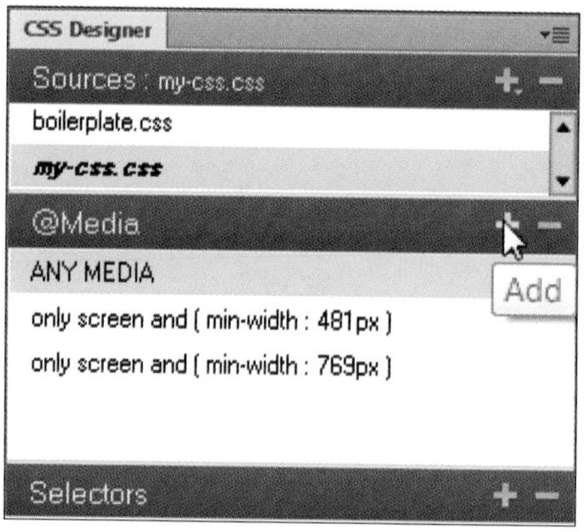

Figure 8-13: Click + in the @media panel to add a new media query.

3. **Click the plus sign (+) in the @Media panel in the CSS Designer panel.**

   The Define Media Queries dialog box opens.

4. **Select Media from the first drop-down list and Screen from the second drop-down list (refer to Figure 8-14).**

5. **Move your cursor to the right of each the drop-down lists to make the plus sign appear, and then click the plus sign to add a new field.**

   A new field appears in the Media Queries dialog box so that you can specify the orientation. This field is optional but is commonly used if you want to create different designs for landscape and portrait views on a tablet or a smartphone. If you don't want to create additional layouts based on orientation, you can remove this field by clicking the minus sign (–), as shown in Figure 8-14.

Note: The plus and minus signs become visible only when you roll your cursor over the right side of the dialog box.

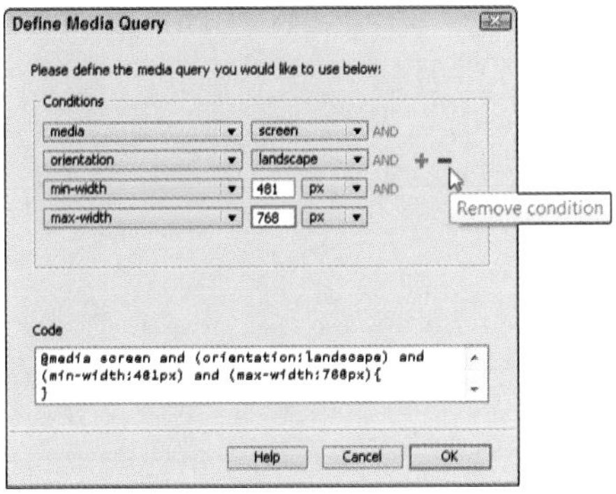

Figure 8-14: Specify the type, size, and other properties of each media query.

6. **Move your cursor to the right of the drop-down lists, click the plus sign a second time to add a field, and enter a minimum width condition.**

   The Min-Width field appears in the Media Queries dialog box so that you can specify the minimum width you want to use to target the query. The minimum width is important because the media query targets the styles based on the minimum to maximum width range you specify, covered in the next step.

7. **Move your cursor to the right of the drop-down lists, click the plus sign a third time to add a field, and enter the maximum width condition.**

   The Max-Width field appears in the dialog box so that you can specify the maximum width you want to use to target the query.

8. **Click OK.**

   The Media Queries dialog box closes and the media query is generated and added to the style sheet you selected in the Sources panel in the CSS Designer panel.

9. **To add additional media queries to any selected style sheet, repeat Steps 3–8. To add media queries to a different style sheet, repeat Steps 2–8.**

Although you can save media queries in as many different styles sheets as you want, saving them all in one external style sheet is more efficient because each style sheet must be downloaded from the server separately, requiring more bandwidth. Downloading one long style sheet with multiple media queries is a little more efficient than downloading multiple style sheets — and when you're delivering content to mobile devices, which often have more limited bandwidth than desktop devices, you want to use as little bandwidth as possible.

9

Saving Time with Templates and More

In This Chapter

▶ Creating pages quickly with a template

▶ Using templates to change to multiple pages automatically

▶ Using the library for frequently used elements

▶ Designing a web page with the Tracing Image feature

Strive for consistency in all your designs — except when you're trying to be unpredictable. A little surprise here and there can keep your website lively. But most websites work best and are easiest to navigate when they follow a consistent design theme. Case in point: Most readers take for granted that books don't change their designs from page to page and that newspapers don't change headline fonts and logos every day.

Publishers of books and newspapers are consistent not because these print publications are old fashioned but to make it easier for readers to find what they're looking for and to help the publications feel familiar. That doesn't mean you should limit modern web design to what's possible in print, but it does mean that we can all learn a thing or two from hundreds of years of print design. Using the same fonts, styles, and colors across a website creates the feeling that all the pages belong together and gives readers the sense that they are in a familiar place, an important quality for the web.

AssetShield™
Your Fortress in the Cloud for all Your Assets

Home

ntent1

Headline

❝ Quote. ❞
- quote name

Ad

Quote. ❞
- quote name

❞
- quote name

Dreamweaver offers several features to help you develop and maintain a consistent look and feel across your site. In this chapter, you discover three of my favorite Dreamweaver features: templates, library items, and the Tracing Image feature.

Both the templates and library items help you work more efficiently and make changes to sections of a site faster and easier. These features work well with CSS, and as you discover in this chapter, you can work even more efficiently by combining CSS with templates and library items.

Tracing images, covered at the end of the chapter, are handy design tools that you can insert into the background of a page to guide your design work. Tracing images aren't visible when the page is viewed in a web browser, but they are useful if you like to create your designs in a program such as Fireworks or Photoshop before you build your web pages in Dreamweaver.

Templating Your Pages

You can choose from many kinds of templates to create websites; and you can find many places on the web where you can buy templates or even download them for free. At its simplest, a *template* is a ready-made page design, usually created in a way that makes it easy to add your own text and images and to create pages based on the template. Some templates are easily customizable so that you can change design elements, such as colors, images, or fonts; others are harder to edit or change.

Not all templates are created equal. Keep in mind that you need the right program for each kind of template. For example, templates designed for a program such as WordPress or Flash won't work in Dreamweaver. (See Chapter 1 for more about the different kinds of templates you can use in all sorts of different websites.)

In this chapter, I focus on Dreamweaver's `.dwt` templates, which you can use to create pages quickly as well as to make global changes across all the pages created from a template.

Dreamweaver templates are best used in the following scenarios:

> ⮡ **Templates are definitely the way to go when you're creating a number of pages that share the same characteristics, such as the same background color, navigation links, or logo.** I recommend that you use a template anytime you create a site with more than a few pages. For example, you might create a template that includes your logo, a row of

links at the top and bottom of each page, and styles for the site's main text colors and fonts, such as the template shown in Figure 9-1.

After you create a template with all these features, you can use it as the basis for all the other pages in your site, such as the page shown in Figure 9-2. This approach enables you to quickly and easily create a series of pages that share the same navigation, logo, and so on. Best of all, if you ever decide to change one of these elements, such as your logo, you can change it once in the template and automatically update all the pages created from the template in your site.

✔ **If you want to use different design elements in different sections, you can create more than one template for a site.** For example, if you're creating a website for a bed-and-breakfast inn, you might create one template for all the pages where you want to show off the rooms in the inn and another for a collection of pages that feature great places to hike in the area.

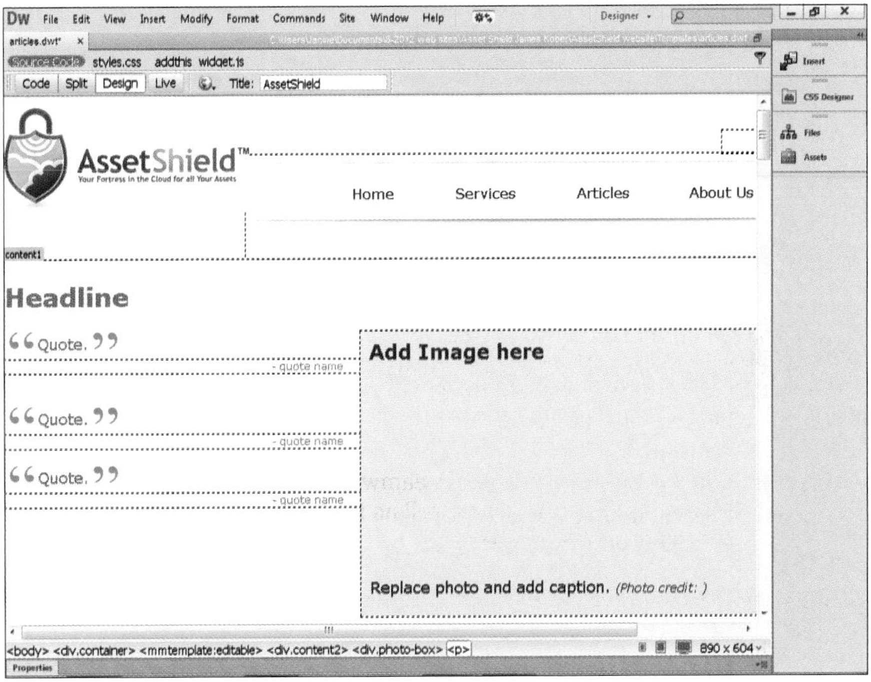

Figure 9-1: Create a simple template page such as this one, and then use it to create similar pages.

Figure 9-2: Consistent elements, such as the logo and navigation links, remain the same while the main area of the page can vary dramatically.

When creating multiple templates for a website, you may want to use a *nested* template, a template whose design and editable regions are based on another template. For example, you can create a main template for elements that appear on every page across an entire site, such as navigation bar. Then add to the main template several secondary nested templates that have design variations for each section of a site.

✔ **Templates are valuable when you're working with a team of people with varying skill levels.** Say you're building a site for a pet store and want to let the employees update their own pet stories without messing up the page design. The fact that templates have locked regions can protect the most important elements of a page, making it easy for sales staff to add new information without accidentally breaking navigation elements or other consistent features. You can also design templates that work with Adobe Contribute, a much simpler and less expensive program, to make it easier for people who are not web designers to update a website. (See the nearby sidebar, "Easily update Dreamweaver sites with Adobe Contribute.")

Easily update Dreamweaver sites with Adobe Contribute

Adobe Contribute was created so that people who don't know much about web design can easily *contribute* to a website. Contribute works well not as a standalone program but as a kind of assistant to Dreamweaver, or better said, as the ideal tool for an assistant, such as your client's assistant who may need to update the website after it's built in Dreamweaver. Adobe has carefully integrated a number of features in Contribute that can be set up in Dreamweaver to make that collaboration work smoothly.

For example, using Dreamweaver's .dwt template features, you can designate areas of each page that can be edited by users of Contribute.

You can also lock sections of a page so that they can't be edited in Contribute, which is a great way to protect elements you don't want changed, such as logos and navigation links, while making it easy for contributors to edit text and images in designated areas.

If you're working with other developers of a site who use Contribute, make sure you select the Enable Contribute Compatibility check box in the Contribute category of the Site Setup dialog box, covered in Chapter 4. To learn more about Adobe Contribute, visit www.adobe.com/products/contribute.html.

The most powerful aspect of Dreamweaver's template feature is the capability to make global changes to every page created from a template. Even if you're working alone on a site, this aspect of templates can save hours (or even days) of time as the site grows and changes over time.

Creating Templates

Creating a template is as easy as creating any other file in Dreamweaver. You can create an HTML Template page much as you would any other page by using the New Document dialog box. You can also turn any existing page into a template by choosing File⇨Save As and saving the file as a template in the Templates folder.

Dreamweaver templates are distinguished by the extension .dwt (Dreamweaver Web Template), and by their location in the directory structure. Dreamweaver template files must be stored in a special folder named Templates (with a capital *T*) at the root level of the site.

When you create a template for the first time in a website, Dreamweaver automatically creates a Templates folder in your local site folder and stores all your .dwt template files in this folder. Templates must be kept in this common Templates folder and the folder must be kept at the top level or root level of your website (meaning you can't move the Templates folder into another folder) for the automated features in Dreamweaver to work properly.

If you haven't gone through the setup process to define your local site folder yet, see Chapter 2 and complete those setup steps first. Dreamweaver's template features work only after you've completed the site setup process.

Creating editable and uneditable regions

Perhaps the most difficult concept to grasp when it comes to templates is how editable and uneditable regions work and why they're important. I provide the short answer here, and get into the details later in this chapter.

When you create a template design, every aspect of the design is locked (uneditable) until you designate some part of the page as an *editable region* — an area of the template page that can be changed in any page created from the template.

Many people are confused at first by the idea that they would want to make any part of a page uneditable, but this concept is key to how templates work. Before you begin creating pages, you need to understand that when you create new pages from a template, only the areas you've designated as editable regions can be altered. The uneditable regions stay the same on every page, making it possible later to change the protected sections of those pages all at once.

For example, suppose you create a design for an online magazine with the logo and navigation bar at the top of the page and room for each article in the middle. You leave the section at the top uneditable because you want it to remain the same on every page. Then you create a design area in the middle of the page where a story and photo can be added to each page created from the template, and you designate that area as an editable region. Then when you create new pages from the template, you can replace the photo and story on each page because they're in editable regions, but you can't change the logo, navigation links, or copyright because they're in uneditable regions.

Now imagine that you've used this template to create dozens, or even thousands, of pages, each with a different story and photo in the editable region but with the same logo and navigation in the uneditable top region. Then one day your editor decides to change the company logo and add a new link. Thanks to that uneditable region in your template, this change is no problem. You simply open the original template file and edit the logo and add the link to that one template page. Then, when you save the template, Dreamweaver offers to update every page created from the template. You save a ton of time because you don't have to replace the logo and link on each page separately — although I leave it to you whether you tell your editor how easy and fast the process was.

Why the head section is editable by default

In a new template, all elements are locked by default except for the document head section, which is indicated by the `<head>`, `</head>` tags at the very top of any HTML page. Keep in mind the head section of any page is not visible in Dreamweaver's Design view or in the main area of a web browser. Within the `<head>` tags you find things like `<title>` tags, `<meta>` tags, style definitions, and scripts.

When you create a new template, Dreamweaver creates two editable regions in the head area of the page. The first editable region is around the `<title>` tags and enables you to change the title in each page created from a template. (Using a different title customized to the content of each page is a good practice.) The second editable region is in the head section of the page for any scripts, links to CSS files, or other elements that must be added to the top of the HTML file. For example, when you use behaviors on a page (covered in Chapter 11), Dreamweaver inserts code in the page where you apply the behavior, but it also adds a script to the head section of the page to make the behaviors work. Similarly, if you add multimedia files, such as Flash or Flash video, to a page, Dreamweaver adds special code to the head section to make the multimedia files play properly. For all these reasons, editable regions are automatically added to the head area when you create a template or save a page as a template.

In previous versions of Dreamweaver, if you created a template from an existing HTML page using the File⇨Save As feature to save the file as a `.dwt` template file, editable regions were not added to the head section automatically. If you're working with a template created in a previous version of Dreamweaver, you may run into this problem and find that you are unable to edit the title of any page created from the template or add features that use JavaScript or other elements that must be saved in the top of the file. To solve this problem, you can re-create the template from a new file in Dreamweaver CC or manually add the template code to the head region of the existing template file by copying it from the head region of any new template you create. If you choose the latter method, be sure to copy the code exactly.

You could make the same kinds of global changes to any element that you keep in an uneditable region of your template. The key is to find the right balance between designing a page you can edit for your daily work on the site and locking the areas of the page that you are the most likely to want to change later.

To help you fully appreciate how editable and noneditable regions differ, keep in mind that if you make changes to the editable region in the template, those changes aren't applied to any page created from the template. This point is important because you wouldn't want to make a global change that overwrites all the individual stories and photos you've inserted into each page in your magazine, for example.

To summarize: Locked (uneditable) areas of a template can be changed only in the template itself, and those changes can be applied automatically to all the pages created from that template. Editable areas of a template can be changed in any page created from the template, but those areas can't be updated automatically by changing the template.

If you're still a little confused after all this theory, don't worry; you see all this in action in the sections that follow.

Creating a new Dreamweaver template

You create a new template in Dreamweaver by using the same New Document dialog box that you use to create any other type of page. To create a Dreamweaver template, follow these steps:

1. **Choose File⇨New.**

   The New Document dialog box opens.

2. **In the list on the left, click the Blank Page option, as shown in Figure 9-3.**

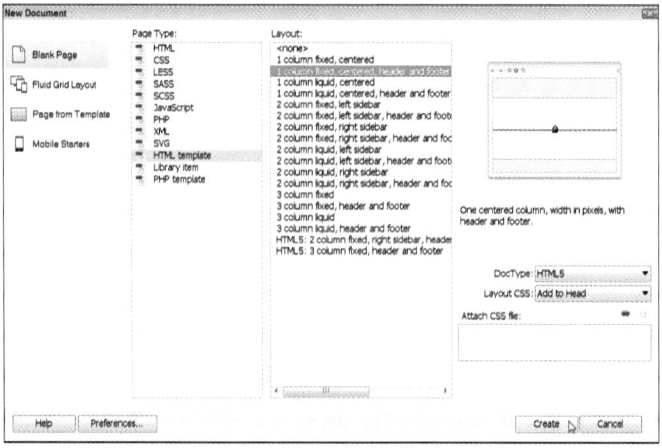

Figure 9-3: Use the New Document dialog box to create new HTML templates.

3. **In the Page Type list, choose HTML Template.**

4. **In the Layout area, choose <none> to create a blank page or select a predesigned CSS layout.**

Dreamweaver's many CSS layout options, covered in Chapter 6, provide a great head start to creating a new page design. In this example, I selected a CSS layout called "1 column, fixed, centered, header and footer," as the basis for my new template design.

5. **Click the Create button.**

A new blank template is created and opens in the main work area, and the New Document dialog box closes.

6. **Choose File⇨Save.**

You get a warning (if you haven't disabled it), stating that the template doesn't have any editable regions and asking whether you really want to save it. Click OK to close the warning dialog box and continue. Dreamweaver gives you this warning because a template with no editable regions isn't useful. You find instructions for creating editable regions in Step 9.

7. **Click OK to save the page as is for now.**

The Save as Template window appears with the Templates folder open. If you don't already have a folder named Templates in your local site folder, Dreamweaver will create one for you when you create and save your first template.

To work properly, Dreamweaver templates must be saved in a folder named Templates (with a capital *T*) in your local site folder, which is visible in the Files panel. If you change the folder name or move the Templates folder into a subfolder, your templates will no longer work properly.

8. **Create a design for the page by adding images, text, and other elements as you would in any other Dreamweaver file.**

You find instructions for adding all these features to your pages throughout this book. Again, remember that you create a page design in a template just like you would in any other web page. Whether you include images and text that will be replaced in pages created from the template or just create the skeleton of a page is up to you.

9. **To create an editable region:**

   a. **Select any image, text block, or content area.**

   Often the best option is to select an entire area of a page so that everything in that section becomes editable. If you've designed your pages with <div> tags and CSS, as covered in Chapter 6, a good option is to select the <div> tag for an entire section, such as the <div> tag styled with the mainContent class style that I've selected in this example.

A handy way to select a section surrounded by a `<div>` tag is to place your cursor anywhere in that area of the page, and then use the tag selector at the bottom of the workspace to select the `<div>` tag.

b. **Choose Insert➪Template➪Editable Region (as shown in Figure 9-4).**

The New Editable Region dialog box opens.

c. **Give the new editable region a name.**

I recommend something that identifies the type of content, such as *headline* or *main-content.* The region you define as editable becomes an area that can be changed in any page created from the template. You can have multiple editable regions in one template. Each editable region must have a different name; names can't use spaces or special characters, but underscores and hyphens are okay.

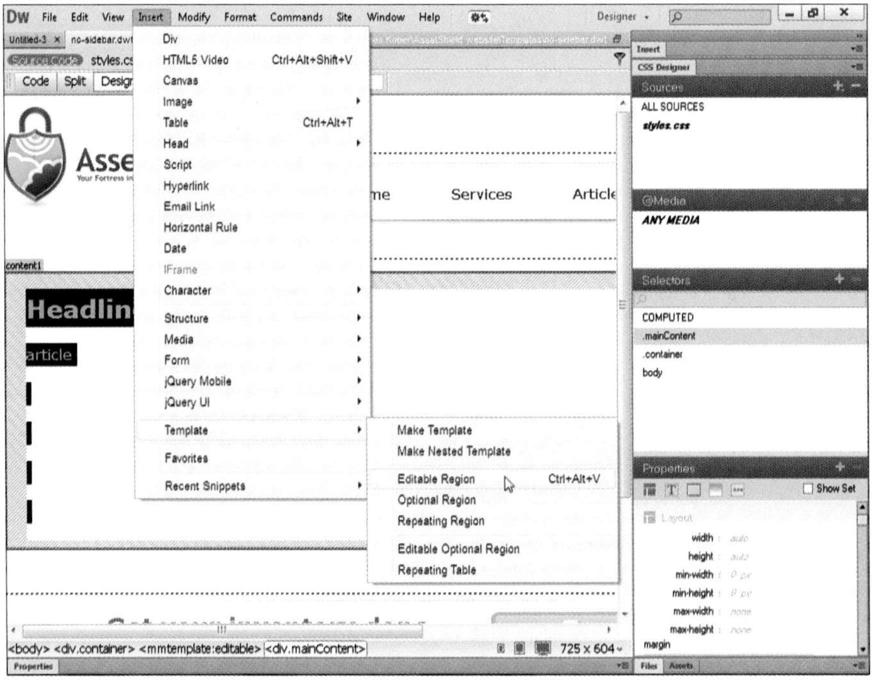

Figure 9-4: Make a selected element an editable region by using the Insert menu.

d. Click OK.

An aqua blue box (with an aqua blue tab at the top left of the box) surrounds the editable region (refer to Figure 9-1). The name you entered into the New Editable Region dialog box appears on the tab.

10. **When you finish designing the page and add all the editable regions you want, choose File⇨Save to save your template.**

When you save a new template page or you save an existing page as a template, Dreamweaver automatically adds the .dwt extension and saves the file into the Templates folder.

If you save a template before you specify any editable regions, Dreamweaver gives you a warning because templates aren't useful without editable regions. You don't have to create editable regions before you save a template, but you can't make any changes in any pages created from a template until you create one or more editable regions. You can always go back and add editable regions later. Saving your work before you create editable regions is generally good practice.

Adobe added a new Templates Insert panel in Dreamweaver CC. You can use this new panel instead of the menu items when working with templates. The features work the same: Just click the corresponding icon in the Templates Insert panel, such as the Editable Region icon shown in Figure 9-5.

Figure 9-5: You can create an editable region also by clicking the icon in the Templates Insert panel.

Saving any page as a template

Sometimes you get partway through designing a page before you realize that you'll probably want more pages that are similar. If you turn the page into a template, you can create the rest of the pages a lot more efficiently. Similarly, you may want to turn a page that someone else designed into a template that you can use throughout your website. No matter the page's origin, creating a template from an existing page is almost as easy as creating a template from scratch.

To save a page as a template, follow these steps:

1. **Open the page that you want to turn into a template.**

   Choose File➪Open and browse to find your file. Or open the site in the Files panel and double-click the file to open it.

2. **Choose File➪Save as Template.**

   The Save dialog box appears.

3. **In the Site drop-down list, choose a site.**

   The menu lists all the sites you've set up in Dreamweaver. By default, the site you've set up and opened in the Files panel is selected when the dialog box opens. If you're working on a new site or haven't yet set up your site, flip to Chapter 2 for information on the site setup process.

   You can use the Save as Template option to save a page as a template into any defined site, which makes it possible to save a page that you design for one site as a template in another site.

4. **In the Save As text box, type a name for the template.**

   You don't have to add a description. However, if you're working on a big site with many templates, descriptions can help you keep track of which templates go with which sections of your site.

5. **Click the Save button.**

   If you haven't disabled the warning (stating that the template doesn't have any editable regions and asking whether you really want to save it), click Yes to continue.

   Note that the file now has the .dwt extension, indicating that it's a template.

6. **Click OK in the Dreamweaver dialog box that appears to update links in the template.**

   Because your original file probably wasn't saved in the Templates folder, any links to other pages or images must be updated when the file is saved. After you click OK, Dreamweaver corrects any links in the file as it saves the file in the Templates folder.

7. **Make any changes that you want, and then choose File⇨Save.**

   You edit a template just as you edit any other page in Dreamweaver.

8. **To create an editable region:**

   a. **Select any content area, image, or text.**

   b. **Choose Insert⇨Template⇨Editable Region (refer to Figure 9-4).**

      The New Editable Region dialog box opens.

   c. **Give the new region a name.**

      You can name the region anything you like — just don't use spaces or punctuation. The region you define as editable becomes an area that can be changed in any page created from the template. You can create multiple editable regions in any template.

   d. **Click OK.**

      The editable region is enclosed in a highlighted area with a tab at the top left, identified by the name you gave the region.

9. **When you finish designing the page, choose File⇨Save to save your completed template.**

Making attributes editable

In addition to making any element in a page editable, you can also make the attributes of any element editable. This step is necessary only if you want to make an attribute editable when the tag itself is not editable (for example, when you want the ability to change the background image of a `<div>` tag but not the `<div>` tag itself).

Editable attributes are especially handy when you want to identify the open page of a site by changing the color of the link to that page. For example, suppose that all your links are blue in the navigation bar, but you want each page link to change to the color red when that page is open. By making only the color attribute of the link editable, you can change the blue color of, say, the About Us link to red when a visitor is on the corresponding About Us page.

To create editable attributes in a template, follow these steps:

1. **In any Dreamweaver template, select an item to which you want to give an editable attribute.**

   In the example shown in Figure 9-6, I selected the navigation link About Us and am in the process of making one of the its attributes editable.

   To make sure you've selected a link and not just the text, click anywhere in the linked text and then use the Tag Selector at the bottom of the workspace to select the `<a>` tag.

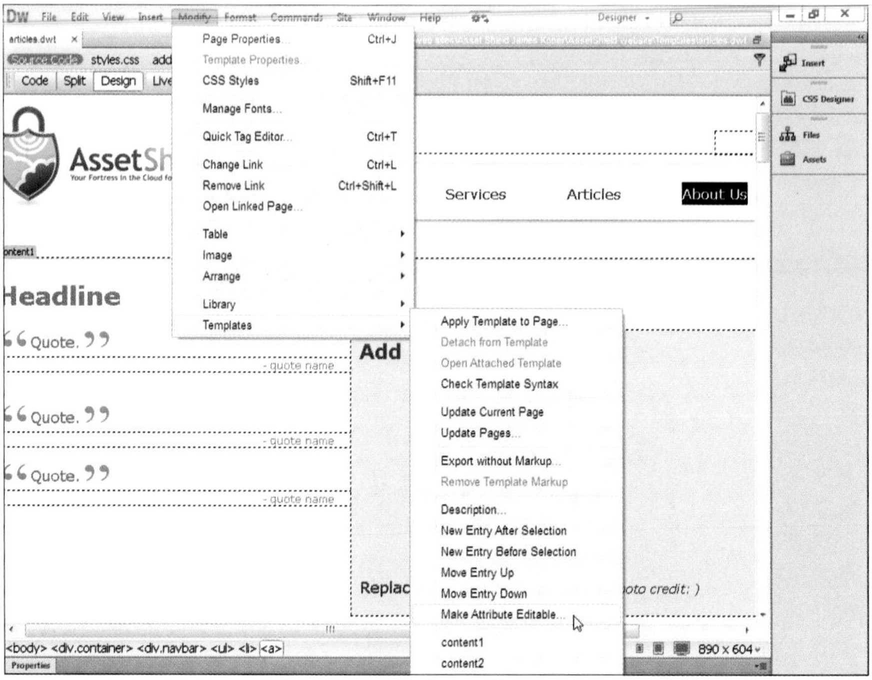

Figure 9-6: Select any link, image, or other tag and use the Modify menu to make the attributes of that tag editable.

2. **Choose Modify⇨Templates⇨Make Attribute Editable.**

   The Editable Tag Attributes dialog box appears, as shown in Figure 9-7.

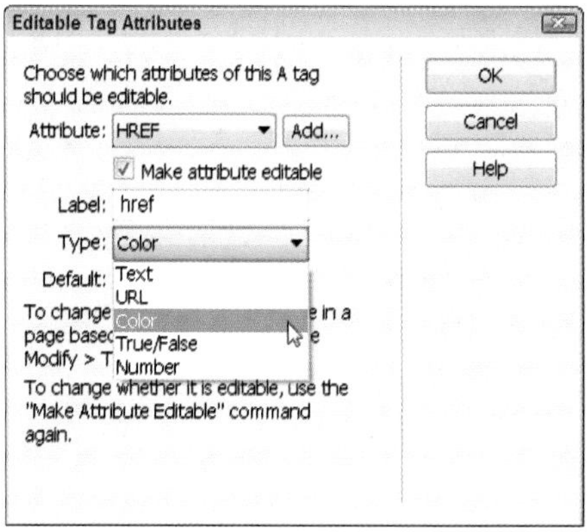

Figure 9-7: Identify which attributes you want to make editable.

3. **From the Attribute drop-down list, choose the attribute you want to make editable.**

   The attribute options vary depending on whether you select an image, a link, text, or another element on the page.

   In this example, I selected the HREF attribute to be able to change the color of the link, as shown in Figure 9-7. The link tag is one of the most confusing HTML tags because it's known as the anchor tag and displayed as just an `<a>` in the Tag Selector. However, the full tag is `<a href>`, and in the Editable Tag Attributes dialog box, it's identified as HREF.

   If the attribute you want isn't listed, click the Add button and then enter the name of the attribute.

4. **Select the Make Attribute Editable check box.**

   The options for that attribute become active in the bottom of the dialog box.

5. **In the Type drop-down list, select an attribute type.**

   As shown in Figure 9-7, the link tag has several attributes. I selected Color in this example.

6. **Click OK to make the attribute editable and close the dialog box.**

To change an editable attribute in a page created from a template, follow these steps:

1. **Create a new page from the template, or open any page that was created with the template.**

   For details on creating a page from the template, see the next section.

2. **Choose Modify⇨Template Properties.**

   The Template Properties dialog box opens, listing any editable attributes.

3. **Select the attribute you want to edit to see your options in the bottom of the dialog box.**

   To change the color of the link, which I set up as an editable attribute in the preceding steps, I selected href to display the template properties. I then clicked the color swatch in the bottom left of the Template Properties dialog box and selected a color.

4. **Click OK to close the dialog box and save the setting.**

   The new setting is applied when the dialog box closes. In this example, the color of the About Us link changed to the new color after the dialog box closed.

Creating a Page from a Template

After you create a template, it's time to put it to use. You can use one template to create all the pages in your website or create different templates for different sections. For example, in the site featured in this chapter — at www. assetshield.com — I created two templates, one for the main pages and another for the article pages, which include a sidebar that provides links to all articles. Whether you create one template or a collection of templates for your site, creating a page from a template is similar to creating any other page in Dreamweaver.

To use a template to create a page, follow these steps:

1. **Choose File⇨New.**

   The New Document window opens.

2. **In the list on the left, click the Page from Template option, as shown in Figure 9-8.**

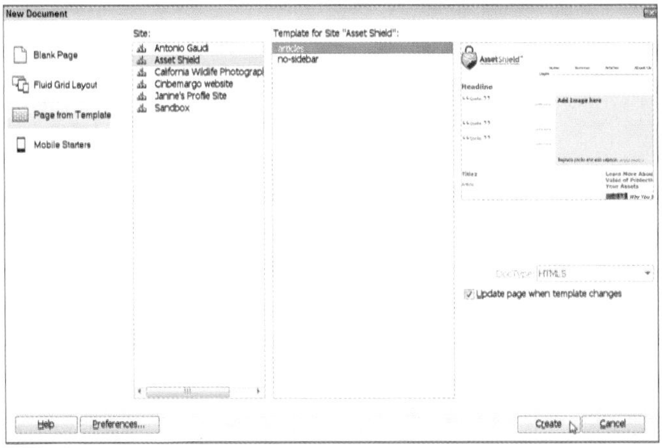

Figure 9-8: Use the New Document dialog box to review and select any template saved in any defined website.

3. **In the Site list, choose the name of the site that contains a template you want to use.**

   The templates in the selected site appear in the Template for Site section just to the right of the Site list in the New Document window (refer to Figure 9-8).

4. **In the Template for Site list, select the template you want to use.**

Note that when you click the name of a template, a preview of the selected template appears on the far right of the New Document window. In the example shown in Figure 9-8, I selected the articles page template.

5. **Click the Create button.**

   A new page is created from the template and appears in the main work area.

6. **Edit any region of the page that's editable with Dreamweaver's regular editing features and save the file as you would save any other HTML page.**

When you create new pages from a template, you can change only the editable regions in each file created from the template. When you edit a template, only the regions that aren't defined as editable can be used to make global changes to all the pages created from the template. In the template shown in this example, only the main content area of the design can be edited in the page created from the template. The banner area at the top, the navigation on the left, and the footer with the copyright and address at the bottom are all locked regions that can be edited only in the template itself.

Making Global Changes with Templates

The great advantage of templates is that you can automatically apply changes to all the pages created with a template by altering the original template. For example, in the AssetShield website featured in this chapter, the navigation links are saved in an uneditable region of each template. Thus, if we decide to add a new section to the site later, we can automate the process by making the change in the template. Add the new navigation link to the row of links at the top of the template, and Dreamweaver can add the new link to all the pages in the site created from that template automatically.

To edit and update all pages in a site that were created from a template, follow these steps:

1. **Open the template file.**

   Note that template files are distinguishable by the `.dwt` extension and are saved in the Templates folder.

If you're not sure which template was used to create a page, check its name in the top-right corner of the page. If you don't see the template name, choose View➪Visual Aids➪Invisible Elements to turn on the feature that displays the template name. Alternatively, you can open a template from any page created from a template by following the steps in the next section.

2. **Use Dreamweaver's editing features to make any changes you want to the template.**

   Remember that only changes to uneditable regions are updated automatically. In this example, the logo and navigation elements are locked regions and can be edited to make global changes. Thus, if I add a new link to the row of links at the top of the page, it will be added to all the pages created from the template.

3. **Choose File⇨Save.**

   The Update Template Files dialog box appears, as shown in Figure 9-9, listing all the pages created from the template.

4. **Click the Update button to modify all pages listed in the Update Template Files dialog box.**

   (Click the Don't Update button to leave these pages unchanged.) If you click Update, Dreamweaver automatically changes all the pages listed in the Update Template Files dialog box to reflect any changes made to uneditable regions of the template.

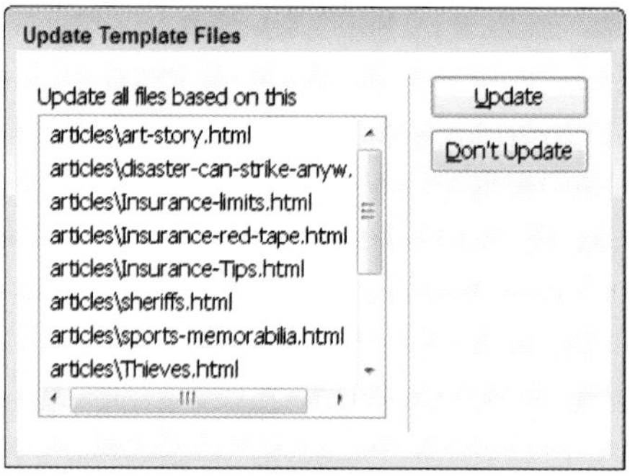

Figure 9-9: You can update all files created from a template automatically.

Opening a template from any page created from a template

If you're not sure which template was used to create a page, you can open the template while you have the page open, make changes to the template, and update all the pages created with it by following these steps:

1. **Open a document that uses the template that you want to change.**

2. **Choose Modify⇨Templates⇨Open Attached Template, as shown in Figure 9-10.**

   The template opens.

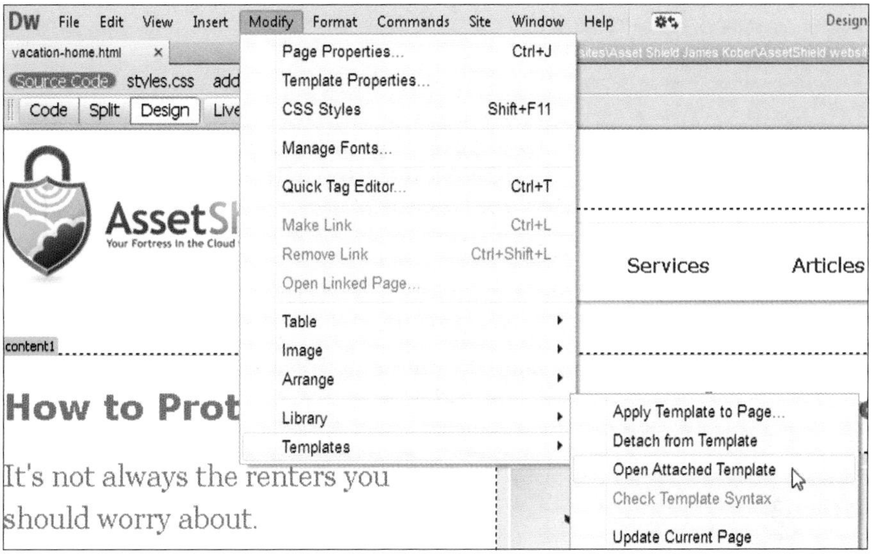

| Dw | File | Edit | View | Insert | Modify | Format | Commands | Site | Window | Help | ⚙⚓ | | Design |

Page Properties...   Ctrl+J

Template Properties...

CSS Styles   Shift+F11

Manage Fonts...

Quick Tag Editor...   Ctrl+T

Make Link   Ctrl+L

Remove Link   Ctrl+Shift+L

Open Linked Page...

Table ▶

Image ▶

Arrange ▶

Library ▶

Templates ▶   Apply Template to Page...

Detach from Template

Open Attached Template

Check Template Syntax

Update Current Page

Services   Articles

content1

How to Prot

It's not always the renters you

should worry about.

Figure 9-10: Open an attached template from within any page created from a template.

3. **Use Dreamweaver's regular editing functions to modify the template as you would edit any page or template.**

4. **Choose File⇨Save.**

 If you've altered the template, the Update Template Files dialog box appears (refer to Figure 9-9).

5. **Click the Update button to modify all the pages listed in the Update Template Files dialog box.**

 (Click the Don't Update button to leave these pages unchanged.) If you choose Update, Dreamweaver automatically changes all the pages listed in the Update Template Files dialog box.

If you edit a template and have an open page that was created from that template, the changes are automatically applied to the open page but you need to save the page before closing it to save the changes.

You can also apply changes to all the pages created from a template by using the Update Pages option. To do so, open the template, and then make and save your changes without applying those changes to pages created with the template. Anytime later, choose Modify⇨Templates⇨Update Pages to apply the update.

Reusing Elements with the Library Feature

The library feature is handy when you have a single element you want to reuse on many pages, such as a copyright statement you want to appear at the bottom of every page across a site with multiple templates.

A *library item* is a snippet of code that can contain almost anything, including images, videos, text, and links. However, you can't use features created with Dreamweaver's Behaviors or Spry menu, which use JavaScript.

After you save a section of code in the library, you can insert it into any page with drag-and-drop ease. If you ever need to change a library item (by adding or changing a link, for example), simply edit the stored library item, and Dreamweaver automatically updates the contents of the library item on any or all pages where it appears throughout the site.

Like Dreamweaver templates, library items are a great way to store frequently used items and make global changes to those items if you need to update them in the future. You have more flexibility with library items than templates because they're elements you can place anywhere on any page, even multiple times. However, Libraries aren't shared among sites the way templates are, and you can't save an entire page layout as a library item.

Another limitation is that library items can't contain their own style sheets because the code for styles can appear only as part of the head area of an HTML file, and library items are just snippets of code, not complete HTML pages, like templates. You can attach an external style sheet to a library item to see how the styles affect the display of the library item, but the same styles must be available on each page where the library item is used for the styles to be applied. (For more on style sheets, see Chapters 5–7.)

Creating and Using Library Items

The following sections show you the steps for creating a library item, adding one to a page, and editing and updating a library item across multiple pages. For these steps to work properly, you must do them in order. Before creating or using library items, you must first set up the site and open it in the Files panel. (See Chapter 2 for instructions on setting up a site in Dreamweaver.)

Creating a library item within an existing page works well because you can see how the item looks before you add it to the library. You can edit an item after it's in the library, but it may not look just as it will on a web page. For example, library items don't include <body> tags when they're saved in the library, so link colors are displayed as default blue when viewed in the library, even if the link colors have been changed to, say, purple in the <body> tag of the page.

Creating a library item

To create a library item that you can use on multiple pages on your site, follow these steps:

1. **Open any existing file that has images, text, or other elements on the page that you want to save as a library item.**

2. **From this page, select an element or collection of elements that you want to save as a library item, such as the copyright information that appears at the bottom of the page.**

3. **Choose Modify⇨Library⇨Add Object to Library.**

   The Library Assets panel opens and displays any existing library items. Your new library item appears as *Untitled.*

4. **Select Untitled and replace it by typing a new name as you would name any file in Explorer on a PC or the Finder on a Mac.**

   When you create a library item, Dreamweaver automatically saves it to the library. Naming library items makes them easier to identify when you want to use them. You can then easily apply library items to any new or existing page in your site by following the steps in the next section.

Adding a library item to a page

You can easily add elements from the library to your pages by simply dragging them from the Assets panel to the page. When you add a library item to a page, the content is inserted into the document and a connection is established between the content on the page and the item in the library. This connection is important because it enables you to edit the library item later and apply the changes to all pages where the item appears, but it also means that you can't edit the item on the page where it's inserted. You must edit library items from within the library, as you see shortly.

To add a library item to a page, follow these steps:

1. **Create a new document in Dreamweaver or open any existing file.**

2. **From the Files panel, click the Assets tab, and then click the Library icon.**

   The library opens in the Assets panel (see Figure 9-11).

Figure 9-11: The Assets panel provides access to the library items list.

3. **Drag an item from the library to the Document window.**

   Alternatively, you can select an item in the library and click the Insert button. The item automatically appears on the page. After you insert a library item on a page, you can use any of Dreamweaver's formatting features to position it on the page.

Highlighting library items

Library items are highlighted to distinguish them from other elements on a page. In the Preferences dialog box, you can customize the highlight color for library items as well as show or hide the highlight color. To change or hide library highlighting, follow these steps:

1. **Choose Edit⇨Preferences (Windows) or Dreamweaver⇨Preferences (Mac).**

   The Preferences dialog box appears.

2. **In the Category section on the left, select Highlighting.**

3. **Click the color box to select a color for library items and then select the Show box to display the library highlight color on your pages.**

   Leave the box blank if you don't want to display the highlight color.

4. **Click OK to close the Preferences dialog box.**

Making global changes with library items

The Dreamweaver library feature saves time because you can make changes to library items and automatically apply those changes to any or all pages where the library item appears. To edit a library item, follow these steps:

1. **From the Files panel, click the Assets tab and then click the Library icon.**

   The library opens in the Assets panel (refer to Figure 9-11).

2. **Double-click any item listed in the library to open the item.**

   Dreamweaver opens a new window where you can edit the library item.

   Because the library item is just a snippet of code, it won't have a `<body>` tag in which to specify background, link, or text colors. Don't worry about this: The library item acquires the right settings from the tags on the page where you insert it.

3. **Change the library item as you would edit any element in Dreamweaver.**

   For example, you can change a link, edit the wording of text, change the font or size, and even add images, text, and other elements.

4. **Choose File➪Save to save changes to the original item.**

   The Update Library Items dialog box opens, displaying a list of all the pages where the library item appears.

5. **To apply the changes you made to the library item on all listed pages, click the Update button.**

   If you don't want to apply the changes to all the pages where the library item appears, click the Don't Update button.

   If you clicked the Update button, the Update Pages dialog box appears and shows the progress of the updating. You can stop the update from this dialog box, if necessary.

If you want to create a new library item based on an existing one without altering the original, follow Steps 1–3, and in place of Step 4, choose File➪Save As and give the item a new name.

Editing one instance of a library item

If you want to alter a library item on a specific page or on a few pages, you can override the automated library feature by detaching it, or breaking the link between the original item in the library and the item inserted into the page.

After you break a connection, you can no longer update that page's library item automatically.

To detach an instance of a library item so that it can be edited independently, follow these steps:

1. **Open any file that contains a library item and select the library item.**

    The Property inspector displays the library item options, as shown in Figure 9-12.

2. **Click the Detach from Original button.**

    A warning message appears, letting you know that if you proceed with detaching the library item from the original, you can no longer update this occurrence of it when the original is edited.

3. **Click OK to detach the library item.**

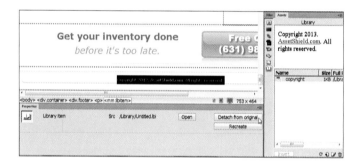

Figure 9-12: You can detach a library item in the Property inspector.

Using a Tracing Image to Guide Your Design Work

The Tracing Image feature is especially popular among designers. The concept, which dates back to the earliest days of design, enables you to use graphics as guides for your page designs, much as you might copy a cartoon through thin transparent paper.

The Tracing Image feature is ideal for people who like to first create a design in a program, such as Photoshop or Fireworks, and then model their web page after it. By using the Tracing Image feature, you can insert any web-ready image into the background of any Dreamweaver page. Then you can position <div> tags or insert tables or other elements on top of the tracing image, making it easier to re-create your design in Dreamweaver. You can use JPG, GIF, or PNG images as tracing images and you can create them in any graphics application that supports these formats.

Although the tracing image appears in the background of a page, it doesn't take the place of a background image and won't appear in a browser.

To add a tracing image to your page, follow these steps:

1. **Create a new page or open an existing page in Dreamweaver.**

2. **Choose View⇨Tracing Image⇨Load.**

   The Select Image Source dialog box opens.

3. **Select the image you want to serve as your tracing image and click OK.**

   The Page Properties dialog box opens with the Tracing Image category selected, as shown in Figure 9-13.

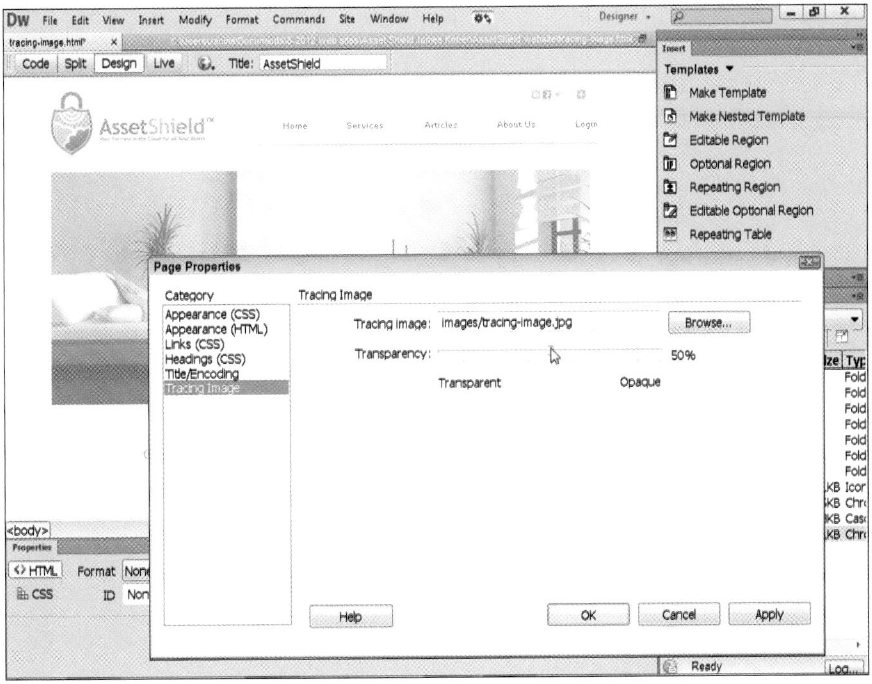

Photo by istockphoto.com

Figure 9-13: The Page Properties dialog box lets you set the options for a tracing image, which you can use as a guide when designing your page.

4. **Click the Browse button to locate the image you want to use as a tracing image.**

   The Select Image Source dialog box appears.

5. **Click the image you want to trace from, and then click Apply to preview how the image looks behind the page.**

6. **Set the opacity for the tracing image with the Transparency slider.**

   Lowering the transparency level causes the tracing image to appear faded, which makes distinguishing between the tracing image and content on the page easy. You can set the transparency level to suit your preferences, but somewhere around 50 percent works well with most images.

7. **Click OK.**

   The tracing image appears in the Document window, and the dialog box closes.

You have a few other options with the Tracing Image feature. Choose View➪Tracing Image to reveal the following options:

- **Show:** Hides the tracing image if you want to check your work without the image but don't want to remove it.

- **Align with Selection:** Enables you to automatically line up the tracing image with a selected element on a page.

- **Adjust Position:** Enables you to use the arrow keys or enter X, Y coordinates to control the position of the tracing image behind the page.

- **Reset Position:** Resets the tracing image to 0, 0 on the X, Y coordinates.

- **Load:** Enables you to add or replace a tracing image.

After you have the tracing image in place, you can use it as a guide while you design your page. Because the tracing image is behind the page, it won't interfere with your design work, and you can add any elements over the tracing image that you could add to any other web page. Use the tracing image as a reference as you insert and position <div> tags, images, and other elements.

10

Coming to the HTML Table

In This Chapter

▷ Introducing HTML tables

▷ Creating tables in Dreamweaver CC

▷ Sorting table data

▷ Nesting tables

*H*TML Tables offer an ideal formatting option when you need to format tabular data, such as the contents of an Excel spreadsheet or any other data that is best displayed in consistent columns and rows.

In the early days of the web, tables were used to create page designs, but that method is no longer recommended with the advent of CSS. (See the sidebar, "Why tables were used for creating page layouts," later in this chapter.) Even though tables are no longer *recommended* for creating page layouts, you may find this chapter helpful if you're working on a site that was designed the old-fashioned way.

In this chapter, you discover how to create and edit tables in Dreamweaver in the few cases where tables are still the best solution — when you need to format or sort tabular data in columns and rows.

Understanding HTML Tables

Tables are made up of three basic elements: rows, columns, and cells. If you've ever worked with a spreadsheet program, you're probably familiar with tables. Working with tabular data in HTML tables is similar to working with a spreadsheet: In most cases, you'll want to create a row of headings along the left side or top of a table and then create columns and rows that can be populated with text, images, and other data, as shown in Figure 10-1.

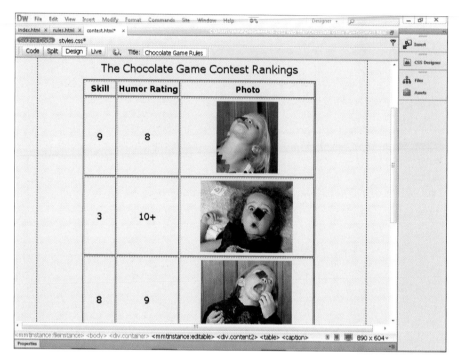

Photos by Janine Warner

Figure 10-1: Dreamweaver makes it easy to create and edit HTML tables, which are ideal for formatting tabular data.

The code behind an HTML table is a complex series of `<tr>`, `<th>`, and `<td>` tags that indicate table rows, table header, and table data cells, respectively. Figuring out how to type those tags so that they create a series of little boxes on a web page was never an intuitive process. If you wanted to merge or split cells to create rows or columns with varying numbers of cells, you faced a truly complex challenge.

Thanks to the cybergurus at Adobe, Dreamweaver makes this process much easier. With Dreamweaver, you can

✔ Create tables and modify both the appearance and the structure of a table by simply clicking and dragging its edges.

✔ Insert any type of content into a cell, such as images, text, and multimedia files — even nested tables.

✔ Add or remove columns and rows in a table using the Table option in the Modify menu.

✔ Use the Property inspector to merge and split cells, add color to the background or borders, and change the vertical and horizontal alignment of elements within a cell.

Why tables were used for creating page layouts

In the early days of web design, HTML tables offered one of the only options for creating complex page layouts. By splitting and merging table cells and using them as containers for text and images, web developers could create intricate page designs despite the limits of HTML.

Using tables to create designs was far from ideal, and most of us found this solution frustrating. But because tables were all we had, we had to be clever, and we often resorted to imperfect tricks, such as

✔ Using a clear GIF to control spacing

✔ Using carefully designed background images to add graphic elements and the illusion of layers to specific parts of a page.

✔ Inserting tables within tables to create ever more elaborate designs.

If you implemented all these tricks, you could use tables to position text, images, and other elements, anywhere you wanted on a page (well, almost anywhere). For example, you could use a table to align two columns of text side by side and then merge the cells at the top to create a wider space for a headline across the

top to create a two-column layout like you might see in a newspaper or magazine. Because you could make the borders of a table invisible, you could use tables to create page designs without the table itself being visible on the page. Back in the day, we were all rather proud of ourselves for figuring out these clever workarounds.

Today CSS has completely changed the way designers create web pages, and tables are no longer the recommended solution for creating page layouts, except when you need to format tabular data, such as a list of numbers you would display in columns and rows in a spreadsheet or data exported from a database.

Today, most professional designers use CSS to create overall page designs because pages designed with CSS download faster, are easier to update, and are more flexible and accessible than tables ever were. Chapters 5 and 6 are dedicated to showing you how to design web pages with CSS; Chapter 7 introduces you to the latest developments in web design with CSS3, which provides design options we only dreamed of back in the days when we created page layouts with tables.

Creating Tables in Dreamweaver

You can insert a table by clicking the Table icon in the Layout Insert panel or by using the Insert menu, as shown in the step-by step instructions that follow. Don't worry about perfecting the settings; you change all of these options later (with the exception of the accessibility settings, which can be edited only in Code view after you've created a table). The sections that follow explain how to further edit and refine the appearance of a table after you've created it.

To create a table in Dreamweaver:

1. **Choose Insert↷Table, or click the Table icon in the Common or Layout Insert panel.**

   The Table dialog box appears, as shown in Figure 10-2.

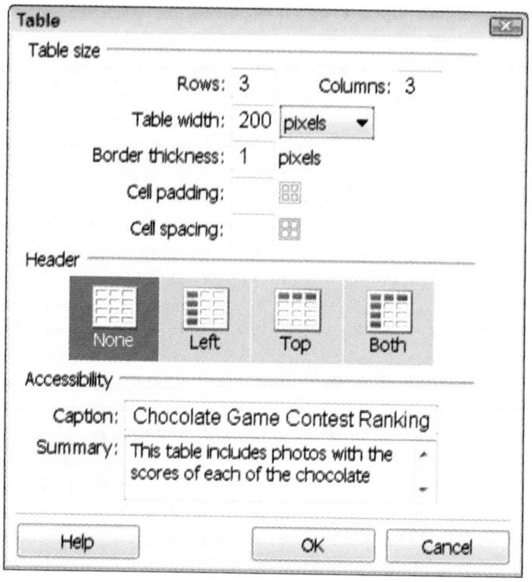

Figure 10-2: Use the Table dialog box to specify table settings.

2. **In the Rows and Columns fields, specify the number of rows and columns, respectively, you want in your table.**

3. **In the Table Width field, enter the width of the table and then select Percent or Pixels from the drop-down list.**

   If you choose Pixels, the table will be created in a fixed size. If you choose Percent, the table will expand or contract in size based on the size of the browser window. For example, if you create a table and set the size to 80 percent, the table will fill 80 percent of the browser window space.

4. **In the Border Thickness field, specify the thickness of the border of your table in pixels.**

   You can enter a 0 in this field to create a table with no visible border.

5. **In the Cell Padding and Cell Spacing fields, enter the number of pixels of cell padding and cell spacing, respectively, for your table.**

The padding and spacing fields can be left blank to create a table with no extra padding or spacing. Alternatively, you can create a CSS style that specifies spacing.

6. **Choose a Header option by clicking the icon that represents the header position you want in your table.**

   In Figure 10-2, I selected the Top option under Header to create a row of Header cells across the top of my table.

7. **(Optional) In the Accessibility fields, add a caption and a summary.**

   These fields provide extra information that can be useful to the hearing impaired and other people who are surfing the web using screen readers or other web browsers that read web pages aloud. You find more information about accessibility issues in the section, "Making tables more accessible," later in this chapter.

8. **Click OK.**

   The table is added to the page in Dreamweaver and the Table dialog box closes.

9. **To add text to a table, click to place your cursor in any table cell and then type the data you want in that cell. Repeat for each cell.**

   Alternatively, you can use Edit⇨Paste Special to insert columnar data from another program, such as Excel.

10. **To insert an image into a cell, click to place your cursor in any table cell and then choose Insert⇨Image⇨Image. Repeat for each cell.**

    Alternatively, you can use Image icon in the Common Insert panel.

11. **Apply formatting options, such as bold or italic, to selected cells and their contents by choosing the option from the Property inspector.**

    The "Specifying cell options," "Aligning table content in columns and rows," and "Merging and splitting table cells" sections, which follow, explain the basics of table formatting.

You can edit all table options, except the Accessibility options, in the Property inspector after you create a table. When you select a table or cell by clicking it in Dreamweaver's workspace, the attributes appear in the Property inspector at the bottom of the work area. Click the border of any table to select the entire table, and the Property inspector displays the table options, as shown in Figure 10-3. To view all options, click the expander arrow in the lower-right corner of the Property inspector. (All these options are described in the next section.)

The Chocolate Game Contest Ranking

```
<body> <table>                                              908 x 506
Properties
     Table          Rows 3    W 500   pixels      CellPad          Align Default         Class None
                    Cols 3                         CellSpace        Border 1
```

Photo by Janine Warner

Figure 10-3: The Property inspector displays table properties when a table is selected.

Sometimes selecting the entire table and not just an individual cell is tricky. If you're having trouble selecting the table, simply place your cursor anywhere in the table and choose Modify⇨Table⇨Select Table.

Changing your table's appearance

When you select a table in Dreamweaver, the Property inspector gives you access to the following options for customizing your table's appearance:

- **Table:** Provides a text area where you can enter a name for a table. This name, or ID, is useful for targeting the table in scripts.

- **Rows:** Displays the number of rows in the table. You can alter the size of the table by changing the number. Be careful, though: If you enter a number that is smaller than the number of rows in your table, Dreamweaver deletes the bottom rows — contents and all.

- **Cols:** Displays the number of columns in the table. You can alter the size of the table by changing the number. Again, if you enter a number less than the number of columns in your table, Dreamweaver deletes the columns on the right side of the table — contents and all.

- **W (width):** Displays the width of the table. You can alter the width by changing the number. You can specify the width as a percentage or a value in pixels. Values expressed as a percentage increase or decrease the table's size relative to the size of the user's browser window or any enclosing container, such as another table or a `<div>` tag.

Table dimensions expressed as a percentage enable you to create a table that changes in size when the browser window is resized. For example, if you want a table to always take up 75 percent of the browser window, no matter how big the user's monitor or display area, set the size as a percentage. If you want a table to always be the same size regardless of the browser window size, choose pixels rather than percentages for your table width.

If a table is inserted in another container, such as a `<div>` tag or a table with a fixed width, the table is sized based not on the browser window but on the container.

Note: Beginning in Dreamweaver CS4, you no longer find an H (height) field. As a best practice, most designers don't specify table height because the table's contents may change from one visitor to another. For example, the font size of text depends on a user's system and settings.

✔ **CellPad:** Specifies the space between the contents of a cell and its border.

✔ **CellSpace:** Specifies the space between table cells.

✔ **Align:** Controls the alignment of the table on the web page. The options are Default, Left, Center, and Right. As a general rule, the Default setting aligns the table from the left side of the browser window or other container.

✔ **Border:** Controls the size of the border around the table. The larger the number, the thicker the border. If you want the border to be invisible, set it to 0.

✔ **Class:** Provides easy access to style sheet options. (See Chapters 5–7 for more on CSS.)

✔ **Clear and Convert:** The icons in the lower-left area of the Property inspector (click the expander arrow in the lower-right corner to view them) provide these formatting options:

• **Clear Row Heights** and **Clear Column Widths** enable you to remove all height and width values at one time.

• **Convert Table Widths to Pixels** and **Convert Table Widths to Percent** enable you to automatically change Width settings from percentages to pixels. Pixels specify a fixed width; a percent setting means the browser automatically adjusts the specified percentage of the browser display area.

You can also apply formatting options and change the attributes of any element — such as text, an image, or a multimedia file — within a table cell. To do so, select the element and then use the options in the CSS or HTML Property inspector to make your desired changes, just as you would if the element weren't in a table cell. See "Specifying cell options," later in this section, for more details.

Making tables more accessible

A few simple behind-the-scenes elements can make your tables more accessible to people who are blind or have limited sight and view web pages with screen readers. *Screen readers* are special browsers that read the contents of a web page aloud.

One important element is the table header (<th>) tag for table headings. The <th> tag adds bold formatting and centering to content, and identifies the content as the header of the row or column.

For example, suppose you have a table like the one in the Chocolate Game Rules website, which includes a list of contestants and their game scores (refer to Figures 10-1). Identifying text in the top row with the table header tag tells the screen reader to repeat the heading before each column name and number. Thus, instead of just reading a long list of names and numbers, the screen reader will identify each cell by the name of the header as it reads through the contents.

You don't have to make all your table headings bold and centered just because you use the table header tag. Like any other HTML tag, you can alter the formatting of the <th> tag by creating a tag style (as I explain in Chapter 5).

Dreamweaver also includes Accessibility options at the bottom of the Table dialog box when you first insert a new table (refer to Figure 10-2). Here's what those options do:

- ✔ **Caption:** If you enter a table caption, it's displayed within the table. You can specify where the caption appears with the Align Caption option.

- ✔ **Summary:** The Table Summary doesn't appear in a web browser but prompts a screen reader to describe the table for visitors who can't see the contents of the table. This gives your visitors overall context before they hear the entire table read out loud.

If you don't include these Accessibility settings as you insert your table, you can't go back to a dialog box with these options in Dreamweaver to insert them later. To add a label and summary to a table after you insert it into a page in Dreamweaver, you have to re-create the table or add the code manually in Code view.

Make sure the table fits the contents

Be aware that table cells automatically adjust to accommodate whatever you insert into them. For example, if you create a cell that's 100 pixels wide and then insert a 300-pixel-wide image, the table cell expands to fit the image. This behavior can cause problems if the overall size of the table isn't set wide enough to accommodate all the objects within the table cells. When you build your tables, be aware of the size of the images and multimedia files you're inserting into cells or you may end up with a mess on your hands.

For example, if you set a table to a total width of 400 pixels and then insert 600 pixels worth of images, the table is forced to adjust in a way that contradicts the settings. Some content may get cut off or expand beyond the desired width of the page layout. Worse yet, the table may not appear the same in all browsers because different browsers try to accommodate these errors in different ways, which can lead to unpredictable results.

Specifying cell options

In addition to changing overall table settings, you can specify options for individual cells in a table. When you select a cell, which you can do by clicking to place the cursor anywhere inside the cell area, the Property inspector changes to display the individual properties for that cell (see Figure 10-4), such as the formatting and alignment of the contents of a particular cell.

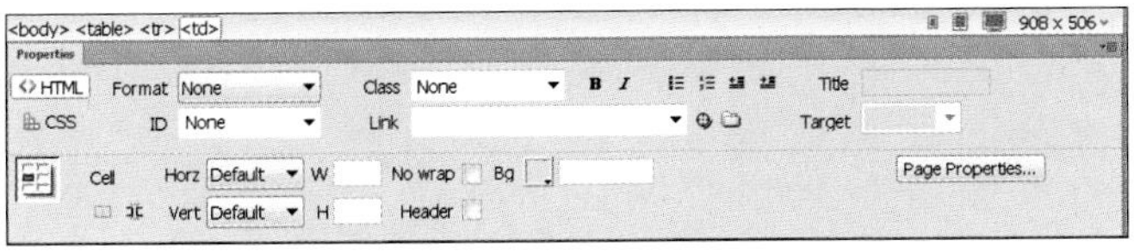

Figure 10-4: The Property inspector (in CSS mode) displays cell properties when <td> or <th> tags are selected.

Beginning in Dreamweaver CS4, the Property inspector features both HTML and CSS settings. CSS settings are generally preferred and work the same for the contents of a table cell as they do for content anywhere else on a web page. (See Chapters 5–7 for more on using CSS.)

You can also change multiple cells at the same time. For example, suppose that you want to format some (but not all) cells in your table with a certain background color and style of text. You can apply the same properties to multiple cells by selecting more than one cell at a time before choosing the settings in the Property inspector. Any properties you change in the Property inspector apply to all selected cells. Here are tips for selecting cells:

- **To select adjacent cells,** press the Shift key while clicking to select cells.

- **To select multiple cells that aren't adjacent,** press the Ctrl key (the ⌘ key on the Mac) and click each cell you want to select.

- **If you're having trouble selecting an individual cell because it contains an image,** click the image and then use the ← or → key on your keyboard to move the cursor and deselect the image, which activates the Property inspector and displays the options for that cell.

When one or more adjacent cells are selected, the top half of the Property inspector controls the formatting of text and URLs in the table cells. The lower half of the Property inspector provides the table cell attribute options (refer to Figure 10-4), as follows:

- **Merge Selected Cells Using Spans icon:** Merges two or more cells. To merge cells, you must first select two or more cells by clicking and dragging or by pressing the Shift or Ctrl key while selecting multiple cells.

- **Split Cell into Rows or Columns icon:** Splits one cell into two. When you select this option, a dialog box lets you specify whether you want to split the row (split the cell horizontally) or the column (split the cell vertically). You can then specify the number of columns or rows, which controls how many times the cell divides. Note that you can apply the Split Cell option to only one cell at a time.

  See the "Merging and splitting table cells" section, later in this chapter, for more details about working with these options.

- **Horz** and **Vert:** Controls the horizontal alignment or vertical alignment, respectively, of the cell contents. See the next section, "Aligning table content in columns and rows," for tips on working with the Horz and Vert alignment options.

- **W and H:** Controls the cell's width or height, respectively.

- **No Wrap:** Prevents word wrapping in the cell. The cell widens to accommodate all text while you type or paste it into a cell. (Normally, the excess text just moves down to the next line and increases the height of the cell.)

✔ **Header:** Formats a cell's contents by using a header tag, which displays the text in bold and centered by default in most web browsers.

✔ **Bg (color):** Click in the color well to select a background color from the color palette or enter a hexadecimal color code in the text field. If you use the color palette, the hexadecimal code is entered automatically in the Bg color field. Make sure you include the # sign if you add your own hexadecimal color or the color will not display properly in many browsers.

Although the alignment, color, and formatting options in the Property inspector are handy, using CSS is the preferred option. You learn more about working with CSS and creating styles to alter the appearance of HTML tags, such as the table tags, in Chapters 5–7.

Aligning table content in columns and rows

Clean alignment of elements in columns and rows makes your table neat and easy to read. Achieving that look can be tricky, however, because you don't have as much control in HTML as you have in a program such as Excel, where you can align numbers to the decimal point, for example. In an HTML table, you can align the content of columns to the left, right, or center. The following steps explain the basics of aligning rows and columns in your table (and you find tips for solving common alignment problems, too):

1. **Select the column or row for which you want to change the alignment.**

   Place the cursor in the first cell in the column or row you want to align; then, click and drag to highlight all the columns or rows that you want to change.

2. **Choose an alignment option from the Horz (horizontal) or Vert (vertical) drop-down lists in the Property inspector, as shown in Figure 10-5.**

   The content of the cell adjusts to match the selected alignment option.

   Alternatively, you can access many formatting options, including alignment options, by selecting a table and then right-clicking (Windows) or Control-clicking (Mac).

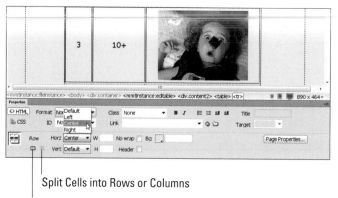

Split Cells into Rows or Columns

Merge Selected Cells

Figure 10-5: You can specify the horizontal and vertical alignment of cell contents using the Property inspector.

If you follow the preceding steps but table contents still aren't aligning, try the following tips:

- **If you use the same number of digits after the decimal point in all your numbers, you can get them to line up in a column.** For example, if one price is $12.99 and another is $14, express the latter as $14.00; then, when you right align, the numbers line up properly. (If your columns still aren't lining up the way you want them to, consider using a monospace font, such as Courier, which lines up better.)

- **If you're having trouble aligning the contents of adjacent cells, set the vertical alignment to Top.** A common frustration when you're building tables is that you have two or more rows side by side with text in one and images in the other, and you want the top of the image and the top of the text to line up. Often they don't line up because they're different lengths, and the table is trying to adjust the contents to best use the space within their respective cells. The solution is simple: Select all the cells you want to align, and in the Property inspector, change the vertical alignment to Top. Seemingly like magic, all the content jumps to the top of the cells and lines up perfectly. This is such a common problem that I routinely set the vertical alignment of table cells to Top.

- **Make sure you use the same formatting, paragraph, and break tags if you want the contents of adjacent cells to line up.** Another situation in which the contents of adjacent cells don't line up properly occurs when you include paragraph tags around the text or an image in one cell but not in another. Use Split view (by clicking on the Split button at the top of the workspace) and make sure that the code in both cells matches. If you have <p> tags around the contents in one cell and not in another, make sure to include them in the second cell or remove them from the first so that both cells match.

Merging and splitting table cells

Sometimes, the easiest way to modify the number of cells in a table is to *merge* cells (combine two or more cells into one) or *split* cells (split one cell into two or more rows or columns). With this technique, you can vary the space in table sections and customize table structures. For example, you may want a long cell space across the top of your table for a banner and then multiple cells below it so that you can control the spacing between columns of text or images. The following two sets of steps show you how to merge and split cells in a table.

To merge cells in an existing table, follow these steps:

1. **Highlight two or more adjacent cells by clicking and dragging the mouse from the first cell to the last.**

   You can merge only cells that are adjacent to one another.

2. **Click the Merge Selected Cells Using Spans icon, in the lower-left region of the Property inspector (labeled in Figure 10-5), to merge the selected cells into a single cell.**

   The cells are merged into a single cell by using the colspan or rowspan attributes. These HTML attributes make a single cell merge with adjacent cells by spanning extra rows or columns in the table.

To split a cell, create a new table or open a page with an existing table and follow these steps:

1. **Click to place the cursor inside any cell you want to split.**

2. **Click the Split Cell into Rows or Columns icon, in the lower-left region of the Property inspector (labeled in Figure 10-5).**

   The Split Cell dialog box appears.

3. **Select Rows or Columns in the dialog box, depending on how you want to divide the cell.**

   You can split a cell into any number of new rows or columns.

4. **Type the number of rows or columns you want to create.**

   The selected cell is split into the number of rows or columns you entered.

Sorting Table Data

When you're working with lots of columnar data, you want to be able to sort that data just as you do in a spreadsheet program, such as Excel. In Dreamweaver, you can sort data even after you format it in HTML but you don't have as many options as you do in Excel. For example, you can sort an entire table based on a specified row, but you can't sort different rows individually.

To use the Sort Table Data feature, create a new, blank HTML page, add a table with several rows and columns, and add some content. (I explain how in the preceding section.) You may also open an existing page with a table of columnar data. Then, follow these steps:

1. **Select the table you want to sort.**

   To select a table for sorting, simply place the cursor in any cell of the table you want to sort.

2. **Choose Commands⇨Sort Table.**

   The Sort Table dialog box appears, as shown in Figure 10-6.

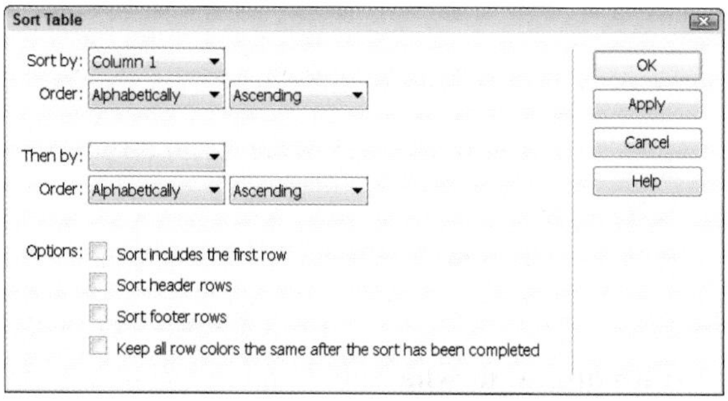

Figure 10-6: You can sort cell contents alphabetically or numerically, even after they're formatted in HTML.

3. **Specify which column you want to sort by and then choose Alphabetically or Numerically and then Ascending or Descending.**

   You can set up one or two sorts to happen simultaneously and opt whether to include the first row and whether to keep the `<tr>` (table row) attributes with a sorted row by selecting Keep All Row Colors the Same.

4. **Click OK.**

   The selected cells are sorted, just as they are in a program such as Excel. (Pretty cool, huh?)

Nesting Tables within Tables

Placing tables within tables, or *nested tables,* can help you create extremely complex designs. For example, with a table that contains scores of all the baseball games in a season, you could add a smaller table inside one cell to include detailed stats of an exceptional game. You create nested tables by inserting a table within a cell of another table.

The best web designs communicate the information to your audience in the most elegant and understandable way and are easy to download. To make sure that your designs don't get too messy, remember these guidelines:

- ✔ A table within a table within a table is nested three levels deep. Anything more than that gets hairy.

- ✔ Pages that use nested tables take longer to download because browsers have to interpret each table individually before rendering the page. For some designs, the slightly longer download time is worth it, but in most cases, you're better off adding or merging cells in one table, as I explain in the section "Merging and splitting table cells," earlier in this chapter. One situation that makes a nested table worth the added download time is when you want to place a table of financial or other data in the midst of a complex page design.

To place a table inside another table, follow these steps:

1. **Click to place the cursor where you want to create the first table.**

2. **Choose Insert⇨Table.**

   The Insert Table dialog box appears.

3. **Type the number of columns and rows you need for your design.**

4. **Set the Width option to whatever is appropriate for your design and then click OK.**

   The table is sized automatically to the width you set.

5. **Type the information that you want in the table cells.**

6. **Click to place the cursor in the cell in which you want to place the second table.**

7. **Repeat Steps 2–5.**

   The new table appears inside the cell of the first table.

Part III
Making Your Site Cool with Advanced Features

Find tips for managing the images, videos, and other multimedia in your web pages at http://www.dummies.com/extras/dreamweavercc.

In this part . . .

- Add dynamic, interactive features to your web pages with Dreamweaver's behaviors.

- Create advanced features for your site, such as drop-down menus and collapsible panels.

- Add multimedia files, such as sound, video, and Flash animations, to your web pages.

- Discover the Dreamweaver tools for creating radio buttons, check boxes, and submit buttons for interactive forms for your website.

Adding Interactivity with Behaviors

In This Chapter

▸ Adding behaviors to your web page

▸ Creating image rollovers

▸ Using the Swap Image behavior

▸ Launching a new browser window

▸ Editing your behaviors

▸ Enhancing Dreamweaver with extensions

*W*ant to add cool effects such as rollovers and pop-up windows? Dreamweaver's behaviors make it easy to create these kinds of interactive features without having to learn the JavaScript scripting language.

Behaviors are ready-to-use scripts that you can customize to create a variety of interactive features. You can apply behaviors to almost any element on an HTML page and even to the entire page itself. For example, you can use the Swap Image behavior to create an interactive slide show within a page, or you can apply the Open Browser Window behavior to open a new browser window when you want to reveal more information or display a larger version of an image.

In this chapter, I introduce you to the Behaviors panel and show you how to use some of Dreamweaver's most popular options. Dreamweaver CC includes 16 options in the Behaviors panel (along with some new CSS3 effects, such as Puff or Pulsate), and you can download and install many more. For instructions on installation, see the "Installing New Extensions for Behaviors" section, at the end of this chapter.

Brushing Up on Behavior Basics

When you start working with behaviors in Dreamweaver, you can get up and running more easily if you begin with this basic introduction to how behaviors work and the terminology they use. When you set up a behavior, you can choose from a number of *triggers,* or *events,* such as `OnMouseOver` or `OnClick` (the two most popular options). Consider this slightly corny example: If you tickle someone and make the person laugh, you used an event to trigger an action. Dreamweaver would call the tickling the *event* and the laughter the *action.* The combination is a Dreamweaver *behavior.*

You may already be familiar with the *rollover* behavior, which causes one image to be replaced with another when someone rolls the cursor over an image. In a rollover, putting your mouse cursor over an image is the *event.* The *action* is the switching of the original image for the second image. In Figure 11-1, you see the effect of a rollover as the main image in the page is changed to another image. Dreamweaver's Swap Image behavior makes it easy to create a gallery of images, like the series of galleries I created in the Cinembargo website shown in the figure.

Rollovers are commonly used when you want to show off two or more images on a web page. You can create a simple rollover effect that uses two images, or you can create more complex designs when you use the Swap Image behavior to cause any or all the images on a page to change. As you discover in the exercises that follow, the most important factor is to make sure the images that you swap are exactly the same size.

The rollover behavior used to be a popular way to create rollover effects on links, but a better option has emerged. As you discover in Chapter 6, you can create links with rollover effects using CSS, which is more search engine friendly, easier to update, and more accessible to people who use screen readers.

Artwork by istockphoto.com

Figure 11-1: When a cursor rolls over the images at the bottom on this page, the Swap Image behavior causes the larger image to change.

Creating a Simple Rollover Image

Rollover images, as the name implies, are designed to react when someone rolls a cursor over an image. The effect can be as dramatic as a picture of a dog being replaced by a picture of a lion, or as subtle as the color of a word changing as one image replaces another. Rollovers are such a popular feature that Dreamweaver includes a special dialog box just for rollovers: the Insert Rollover Image dialog box.

You can create more complex rollover image effects with the Swap Image option from the Behaviors panel, covered in the section that follows. The Swap Image option enables you to change multiple images at the same time.

To create a simple rollover effect with two images using Dreamweaver's Insert Image Rollover dialog box, follow these steps:

1. **Place your cursor on the page where you want the rollover to appear.**

   Rollover effects require at least two images: one for the initial state and one for the rollover state. You can use two different images or two similar ones, but both should have the same dimensions. Otherwise, you see strange scaling effects because both images must be displayed in exactly the same space on the page.

2. **Choose Insert⇨Image⇨Rollover Image.**

   Alternatively, you can use the drop-down list available from the Images icon in the Common Insert panel and select Rollover Image.

   The Insert Rollover Image dialog box appears, as shown in Figure 11-2.

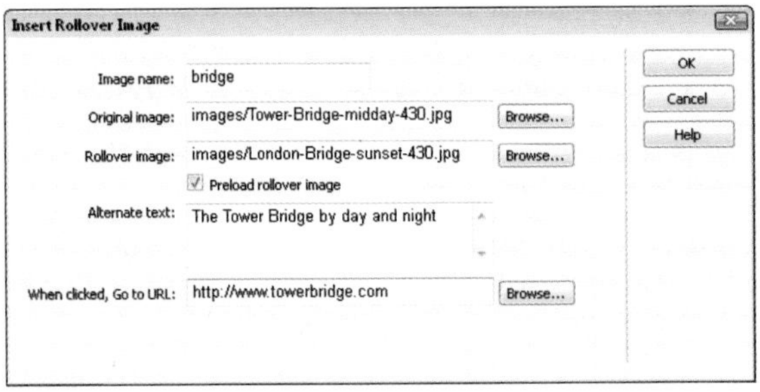

Figure 11-2: Select the original and the rollover images.

3. **In the Image Name box, name your image.**

Before you can apply a behavior to an element, such as an image, the element must have a name so that the behavior script can reference it. You can name elements anything you like as long as you don't use spaces or special characters.

4. **In the Original Image box, specify the first image you want visible. Use the Browse button to locate and select the image.**

If the images aren't already in your local site folder, Dreamweaver copies them into your site when you create the rollover. (If you haven't already set up your site in Dreamweaver, see Chapter 2 for more on this important preliminary step.)

5. **In the Rollover Image box, enter the image you want to become visible when a visitor moves the cursor over the first image.**

Again, you can use the Browse button to locate and select the image.

6. **Select the Preload Rollover Image check box to load all rollover images into the browser's cache when the page first loads.**

If you don't choose to do this step, your visitors may experience a delay because the second image won't be downloaded until a cursor is rolled over the original image.

7. **In the Alternate Text field, enter a description of the images.**

Alternate text is optional but recommended because the use of keywords can enhance search engine optimization. Similarly, Alternate text is a key part of web accessibility because this text is read aloud by special browsers called screen readers, which are used by people who are blind and others with limited sight or mobility. Alternate text is displayed only in the browser if the images are not visible.

8. **In the When Clicked, Go to URL box, enter any web address or browse to locate another page in your site to which you want to link.**

If you don't specify a URL, Dreamweaver automatically inserts the # sign as a placeholder in the code.

The # sign is a common technique for creating links that don't link anywhere. Because rollover images that don't link to another page have many great uses, this technique is useful. Just remember that if you do want your rollover to link, you need to replace the # sign with a link to another page. See Chapter 2 for details about setting links.

9. **Click OK.**

   The images are set up automatically as a rollover.

10. **To see the rollover in action, save the file and then click the globe icon at the top of the workspace to preview your page in a web browser.**

You can see how your rollover works in Dreamweaver's Design view or by using the Live view option. When you click the Live button at the top left of the workspace, you essentially turn Dreamweaver into a web browser that displays pages much like the Chrome browser I used for the screenshots shown in Figure 11-3.

When you're previewing a page on your computer that includes a rollover image (or any other feature that requires JavaScript or special programming), some web browsers, including Internet Explorer, will display a warning stating that you must allow ActiveX controls to view the page. This is a security warning that appears only when the page is opened on the same computer where the page is saved. If you publish the page to a web server and then view it over an Internet connection, you and your site visitors will not see this error.

Peeking at JavaScript code

JavaScript is the code behind Dreamweaver behaviors. Writing JavaScript is more complex than writing HTML code, but not as difficult as writing in a programming language, such as C# or Java. (No, Java and JavaScript aren't the same.) Dreamweaver takes most of the challenge out of JavaScript by giving you a graphic interface that doesn't require you to write the complicated code yourself. When you use behaviors, Dreamweaver automatically writes the code for you behind the scenes.

To fully appreciate what Dreamweaver can do for you, you may want to switch to Code view after setting up a behavior, and then click the JavaScript file in the files list at the top of the workspace. You'll see the complex code required when you use JavaScript. If you don't like what you see, don't worry: Go back to Design view and you can continue to let Dreamweaver take care of the code for you. (I just want you to see how lucky you are that Dreamweaver includes these features.)

Artwork by istockphoto.com

Figure 11-3: In a simple rollover, rolling your cursor over an image, such as the one shown on the top, reveals a second image, shown on the bottom.

Adding Behaviors to a Web Page

Dreamweaver offers a number of behaviors you can choose from, including the Swap Image behavior and the Open Browser Window behavior, which are covered in detail in the next two sections. The process of adding other behaviors is similar to process for these two, but each behavior has its quirks. The tips and tricks you find here can help you get started with behaviors, find the location of most behavior features, and match behaviors with triggers using the Behaviors panel.

You can download many more behaviors from the Adobe Exchange website. You find instructions in the "Installing New Extensions for Behaviors" section, at the end of this chapter.

Creating swaps with multiple images

Before you start creating a more complex page design with Dreamweaver's Swap Image behavior, look at a finished page. In that way, you can see the result before you get into the details. In Figure 11-4, note the collection of thumbnail images on the bottom of the page and a larger version of one of those images in the main area of the page.

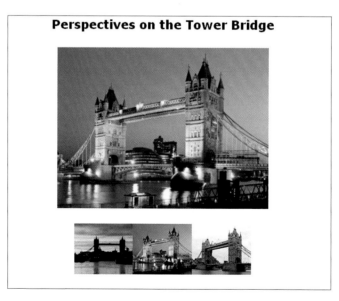

Artwork by istockphoto.com

Figure 11-4: The Swap Image behavior is a great option for creating interactive image galleries.

In Figure 11-5, when I roll my cursor over a different thumbnail image on the bottom, the larger image displayed above it changes to correspond to that thumbnail. With the Swap Image behavior, you can replace any or all images on a page.

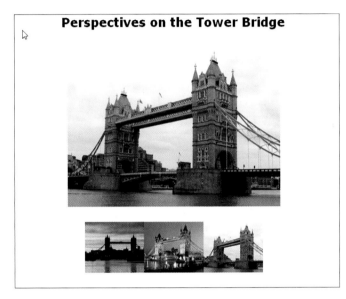

Perspectives on the Tower Bridge

Artwork by istockphoto.com

Figure 11-5: When you preview a behavior in a browser, you can see the effect of the Swap Image behavior when the cursor is rolled over an image.

When you use the Swap Image behavior, it's important to make all images that you will swap the same size (height and width). If the images are not the same size, all images except the first one will be stretched or compressed to fit the space taken up by the first image inserted into the page.

If you're using the Swap Image behavior with a series of images that are not all the same height and width, you have a few of options:

- Crop the larger ones so that all images are the same size.
- Make horizontal and vertical images take up the same space in your design by combining two vertical images for every horizontal one. Simply create a file in a program such as Photoshop, insert two vertical images into the same file side by side, and then size that image so that the file is the same size as one horizontal image.

✓ Create one image file the size of your largest image, set the background to a neutral color, such as black or white, and then insert all other images onto the background so that you can save them all with the same file size.

Follow these steps to use the Swap Image behavior:

1. **Create a page design with all the images you want displayed initially.**

   Each of the three photos in the page design for the Tower Bridge in London has two copies: one thumbnail and one larger version. When the page first loads in a web browser, all three thumbnail images are positioned on the bottom of the page, with the first of the corresponding larger versions displayed in the main area just above the thumbnails.

   You can use the Swap Image behavior to change images on any web page no matter how the layout is created. In the design featured in this section, I used CSS to create a layout with separate `<div>` tags for the row of thumbnails on the bottom and another `<div>` tag for the bigger image above the thumbnails. These divs are positioned with CSS. (Find instructions for creating CSS layouts in Chapter 6.)

2. **Name your images in the Property inspector, as shown in Figure 11-6.**

   To target your images with JavaScript, which is how behaviors work, first give each image a unique ID. The image ID isn't the same as the image filename or the text `<alt>` tag, although you can use the same or similar names. In this example, I gave each thumbnail image an ID that matched the text on the small image, to make indentifying the thumbnails easy. Image IDs should not have spaces or any special characters.

   Although you can use any name you want for image IDs (as long as you don't include spaces or special characters), I like to name the main image something simple and distinctive, such as `targetImage` or `mainImage`, as shown in Figure 11-6, to make it easier to keep track of which image I'm replacing each time.

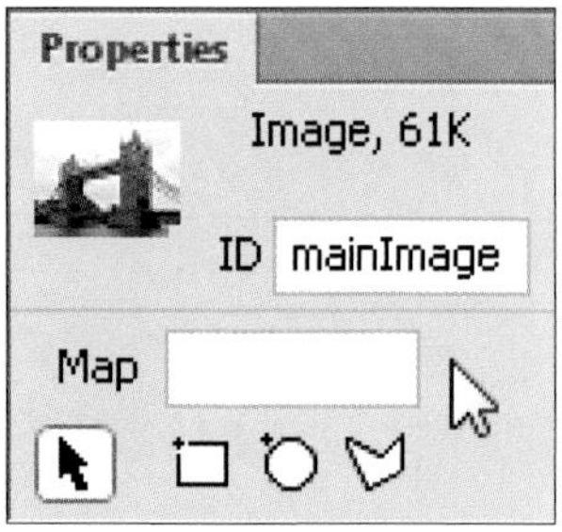

Figure 11-6: In the top left of the Property inspector, enter an ID for each image.

3. **Choose Window⇨Behaviors.**

   The Behaviors panel opens. You can drag the Behaviors panel elsewhere on the page, and you can expand it by dragging its bottom or side. You may also want to close any other open panels to make more room by clicking the dark gray bar at the top of any panel.

4. **Select an image.**

   First select the image in the page that will serve as the trigger for the action. In this example, I'm using the thumbnail images as triggers, so I select them one at a time. I started with the Tower Bridge at sunset thumbnail, but because it triggers the image that appears when the page is first displayed, I'm going to use the second one as the example here. You repeat this same process for each thumbnail. In the example shown in Figures 11-7, I've selected the second thumbnail image, with the ID dusk.

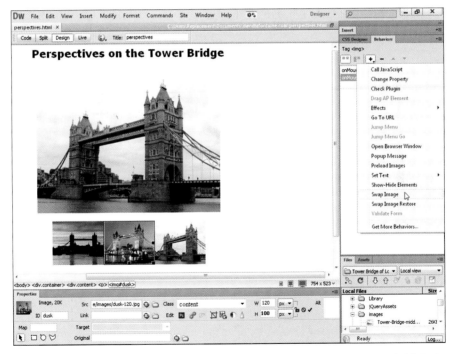

Artwork by istockphoto.com and David LaFontaine

Figure 11-7: With a thumbnail image selected, click + to open the drop-down list in the Behaviors panel, and then select Swap Image.

5. **Choose the Swap Image behavior.**

   With the trigger image selected in the workspace, I click the plus sign in the Behaviors panel to open the drop-down list of actions, and choose the action I want to apply. I chose Swap Image, which opens the Swap Image dialog box.

6. **Specify the images to swap in the Swap Image dialog box.**

   a. **In the Images list, select the ID for the image that will be** *replaced.*

      In Figure 11-8, I'm replacing the main image, which I've given the ID `"mainImage"`. (The main image is identified with an asterisk, *, because the image was inserted into the page.) The process is the same when you have more than two images.

   b. **Click the Browse button to select the image that replaces the main image.**

      I selected the `Tower-Bridge-dusk-430.jpg` image, which I carefully named to correspond to the matching thumbnail, which has the `dusk` ID. Now when a user rolls a cursor over the `dusk` thumbnail image, the big photo of the Tower Bridge at sunset will be replaced with the big photo of the Tower Bridge at dusk.

      Note: If the image is not already saved in the local site folder, Dreamweaver will offer to copy it there for you.

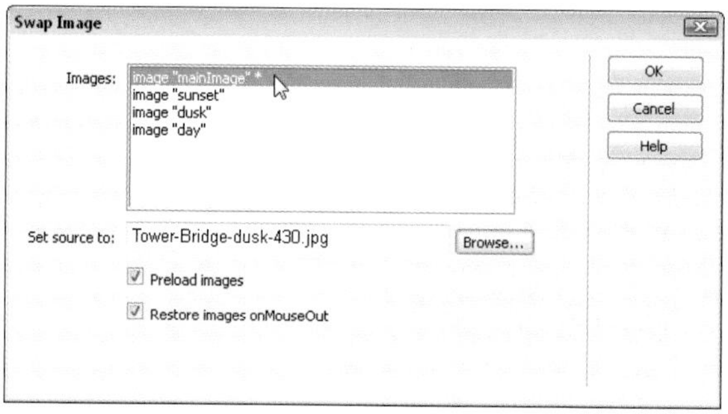

Figure 11-8: Select the ID of the image that you want to replace before using the Browse button to select the image you want to swap in.

7. **At the bottom of the Swap Image dialog box, select the Preload Images option to instruct the browser to load all images into the cache when the page is loaded.**

   If you don't select this option, a delay may occur when the image swap is used.

8. **If you want, deselect the Restore Images OnMouseOut option.**

   The Restore Images OnMouseOut option means that when an event is completed (such as when the mouse is moved off the triggering thumbnail), the original image is replaced. By default, Dreamweaver preselects this option for the Swap Image behavior. You may want to deselect this option if you find that replacing the original image each time you roll the cursor over another thumbnail is distracting.

9. **After you specify all the settings for the behavior, click OK.**

   The new behavior appears in the Behaviors panel.

10. **Specify an event for the behavior.**

    After the action is applied, you can go back and specify which event will trigger the action (as shown in Figure 11-9). By default, Dreamweaver applies the OnMouseOver event when you use the Swap Image action, but you can change that event to any available one, such as OnClick, which requires that the user click the image to trigger the Swap Image action. In this example, I left the event set to OnMouseOver.

Show All Events

Figure 11-9: When you set up a behavior, you can specify any available action to trigger an event.

The list of behaviors and events varies depending on the element selected and the applied behavior. For more information about events and what each one accomplishes, see the "Choosing an event for a behavior" sidebar, elsewhere in this chapter.

You can display or hide events by clicking the Show All Events icon in the top left of the Behaviors panel. Note that if you're using Windows, you also see a collection of events that begin with an `<a>` and are for elements that are linked.

11. **Apply additional behaviors.**

    To apply the Swap Image behavior to other images on a page, repeat Steps 5–10, clicking to select the image you want to serve as a trigger and then specifying the corresponding image that should be swapped. In this example, I selected each thumbnail in turn and set up a Swap Image behavior that replaced `mainImage` with the corresponding larger version of the photo in the thumbnail.

12. **Test your work in a browser.**

    You can't see the effects of behaviors like this one until you click the Live view button at the top left of the workspace in Dreamweaver or preview your page in a web browser, such as Firefox or Internet Explorer.

Choosing an event for a behavior

Events, in interactive webspeak, are things a user does to trigger a behavior or an action in a web page. Clicking an image is an event, as is loading a page into a browser or pressing a key on the keyboard. Different browser versions support different events (the more recent the browser, the more events available). Some events are available only for certain kinds of objects or behaviors. If an event can't be used with a selected element or behavior, it appears dimmed. This list describes the most common events:

✔ onBlur: Triggered when the specified element stops being the focus of user interaction. For example, when a user clicks outside a text field after clicking in the text field, the browser generates an onBlur event for the text field. onBlur is the opposite of onFocus.

✔ onClick: Triggered when the user clicks an element, such as a link, a button, or an image.

✔ onDblClick: Triggered when the user double-clicks the specified element.

✔ onError: Triggered when a browser error occurs while a page or an image is loading. This event can be caused, for example, when an image or a URL can't be found on the server.

✔ onFocus: Triggered when the specified element becomes the focus of user interaction. For example, clicking in or tabbing to a text field of a form generates an onFocus event.

✔ onKeyDown: Triggered as soon as the user presses any key on the keyboard. (The user doesn't have to release the key for this event to be generated.)

✔ `onKeyPress`: Triggered when the user presses and releases any key on the keyboard. This event is like a combination of the `onKeyDown` and `onKeyUp` events.

✔ `onKeyUp`: Triggered when the user releases a key on the keyboard after pressing it.

✔ `onLoad`: Triggered when an image or the entire page finishes loading.

✔ `onMouseDown`: Triggered when the user presses the mouse button. (The user doesn't have to release the mouse button to generate this event.)

✔ `onMouseMove`: Triggered when the user moves the mouse while pointing to the specified element and the pointer doesn't move away from the element (that is, the pointer stays within its boundaries).

✔ `onMouseOut`: Triggered when the pointer moves off the specified element (usually a link).

✔ `onMouseOver`: Triggered when the mouse pointer moves over the specified element. Opposite of `onMouseOut`.

✔ `onMouseUp`: Triggered when a mouse button that's been pressed is released.

Using the Open Browser Window behavior

You can use behaviors in Dreamweaver to create many interactive features, such as opening a new browser window when someone clicks an image or a text link. As you can see in Figure 11-10, opening a new window is a great way to make supplemental information available without losing the original page a visitor was viewing. The Open Browser Window behavior enables you to specify the size of the new window and to display it over the existing window.

To add the Open Browser Window behavior to a selected image or text on a page, follow these steps:

1. **Create the page that will open in the new browser window.**

   For the Tower Bridge site, I created a new HTML page for the Additional History page, and inserted the text and images that correspond to that section. The main image on the Tower Bridge at Sunset page serves as the trigger. The goal is that when a user clicks the trigger image, a smaller browser window will open to reveal the content for that section.

   When you name files that will be used in behaviors, such as a page that will open when the Open Browser Window behavior is used, avoid using slashes anywhere in a filename or numbers at the beginning of a filename (you can use numbers anywhere else in the name). It's also best to avoid hyphens and underscores.

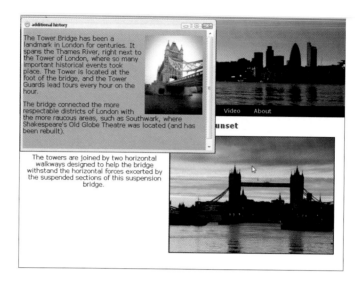

Artwork by istockphoto.com

Figure 11-10: Clicking the image on this page opens a new browser window with a corresponding page that provides additional information.

2. **Select the image, text, or another element you want to serve as the trigger for the action.**

   You can select any image, text, or other element on a page and apply a behavior to it the same way.

3. **Choose Window⇨Behaviors to open the Behaviors panel.**

4. **Click the plus sign (+) and choose the behavior you want from the drop-down list.**

   In this example, I selected the Open Browser Window behavior, as shown in Figure 11-11.

   If a behavior appears dimmed, it can't be associated with the selected element. For example, the Swap Image behavior can be applied only to an image, so it appears dimmed if you've selected text or another element.

5. **In the Open Browser Window dialog box, as shown in Figure 11-12, specify the settings.**

   You can set a number of options that control how the new browser window appears:

   • **Use the Browse button to the right of the URL to Display box to select the page you want to open in the new browser window.** (You can also enter a URL in this box to open a page in another website.)

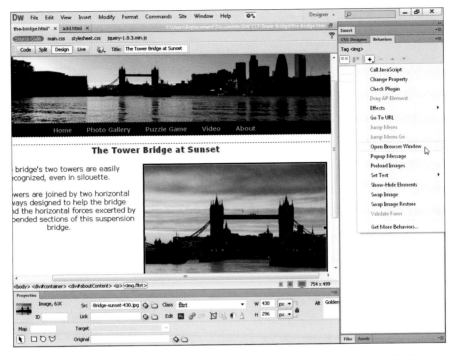

Artwork by istockphoto.com, David LaFontaine

Figure 11-11: Select the image or text link to serve as the trigger, click + in the Behaviors panel, and choose the desired behavior.

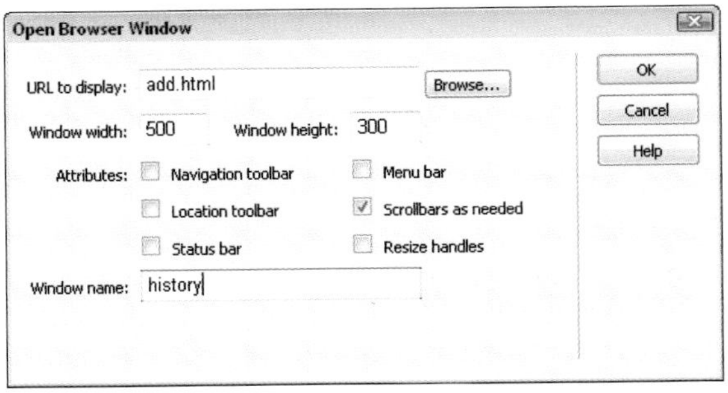

Figure 11-12: Specify settings for the display of the window.

- **Set the window width and height to specify the exact pixel size of the new browser window that will open.** In this example, we set the width so that the archival photo of the Tower Bridge fits nicely next to the text.

- **Select the options Navigation Toolbar, Location Toolbar, Status Bar, Menu Bar, Scrollbars as Needed, or Resize Handles if you want the new browser window to include any of these features.** I selected Scrollbars as Needed in case my visitor's browser window is smaller than the size I specified for the text and photo package, but I left all the others deselected because I want a clean, simple browser window without any menus or other features.

- **Name the new window, an important step if you want to target that same window to load other pages into it.**

6. **After you specify all the settings for the behavior, click OK.**

   The new behavior appears in the Behaviors panel.

7. **To change the event that triggers your behavior, select the current event from the left side of the Behaviors panel and then choose the event you want to replace it with from the drop-down list.**

   You can select any available event to serve as the trigger for the behavior. However, not all events are available for all behaviors. For more information about events and what each one accomplishes, see the "Choosing an event for a behavior" sidebar, elsewhere in this chapter.

8. **To test the action, save the file and then choose File⇨Preview in Browser.**

   Click the image to test whether a new browser window opens.

Attaching Multiple Behaviors

You can attach multiple behaviors to the same element on a page (as long as they don't conflict, of course). For example, you can attach one action that's triggered when users click an image and another when they move their cursors over the image. You can also trigger the same action by using multiple events. For example, you can open the same page in a new browser window when a user triggers any number of events.

To attach additional behaviors to an element, click the plus sign in the Behaviors panel and select another option from the drop-down list. Repeat this process as many times as you want.

Editing a Behavior

You can always go back and edit a behavior after you create it. You can choose a different event to trigger the behavior, choose a different action, or remove behaviors. You can also change behavior options after a behavior is applied.

To edit a behavior, follow these steps:

1. **Select an object with a behavior attached.**

2. **Choose Window⟳Behaviors to open the Behaviors panel.**

   A list of all behaviors associated with the selected element appears. Here are some options you can choose in the Behaviors panel:

   - **Change a triggering event.** Choose a different event by clicking the specified event in the Behaviors panel and then selecting another option from the drop-down list that appears.

   - **Remove a behavior.** Click the action name in the Behaviors panel to select it and then click the minus sign at the top of the panel. The behavior disappears.

   - **Change parameters for an action.** Double-click the gear icon next to the action name and change the parameters in the dialog box that opens.

   - **Change the order of actions when multiple actions are set.** Select an action name and then click the up arrow icon to Move Event Value Up or the down arrow icon to Move Event Value Down in the list of actions.

Installing New Extensions for Behaviors

Even with all the cool features in Dreamweaver, a day will almost certainly come when you'll want to do things that Dreamweaver can't do with the features that shipped with the program. Fortunately, the programmers who created Dreamweaver made it possible for other programmers to add features with Extension Manager. The result? You can add new functionality by adding extensions from a variety of third-party sources.

You can find extensions that do everything from adding highly customizable drop-down and fly-out menus to full-featured shopping cart systems. Keep in mind, however, that not all extensions are well supported and few come with good instructions. They're not all free, either. Some cost hundreds of dollars, but most are in the $20–$50 range. When you visit the Dreamweaver Exchange site, you'll find reviews and rankings to help you sort through the best options.

In the following steps, I explain how you find, download, and install a free Dreamweaver extension. Although how extensions work after they're installed can differ dramatically, the basic process of adding them to Dreamweaver is nearly the same.

1. **Visit the Dreamweaver Exchange site.**

   Do one of the following to get to the Dreamweaver Exchange site:

   - Choose Get More Behaviors from the bottom of the Add Behavior drop-down list in the Behaviors panel.

   - Visit www.adobe.com/exchange and follow the link to the Dreamweaver section.

   - Click the link in the bottom right of the Dreamweaver Welcome screen.

   Note: If you launch Dreamweaver and find a link to download an update for Dreamweaver instead of the link to the Exchange site, by all means download and install the update first. After you're finished, the update link is replaced by the link to the Exchange site.

2. **Sort through the many available extensions.**

   You'll find a wide range of extensions on the Dreamweaver Exchange site. You can search through extensions by category, keyword, and ranking options. Many extensions featured on the Exchange site include links to their creators' sites, where you'll often find even more extensions.

3. **Select an extension and review its features.**

   When you click a link to an extension on the Exchange site, you'll find more information about the extension, including system requirements and the version of Dreamweaver for which the extension was designed. In general, you can use extensions designed for earlier versions of Dreamweaver in more recent versions. Be aware, however, that extensions designed for later versions of Dreamweaver usually won't work in earlier versions of the program, and some extensions will work only on the Windows platform.

   Before you leave the extension's page, I highly recommend that you take the time to read the special instructions in the middle of the page. Some extensions include important instructions, such as where you find the new feature in the Dreamweaver interface after it's installed and warnings that some functions of an extension will work only when previewed on a live web server (this is true for the random image extension, for example).

4. **To download an extension, click the Download button (for free extensions) or the Buy button next to the extension name and save the extension to your hard drive.**

   Depending on how the extension is hosted on the exchange, you may be redirected to another page where you have to click Download again to download the extension.

5. **Choose Help⇨Manage Extensions to open the installation dialog box.**

   Most extensions require that you close Dreamweaver before installation, and most install with the click of a button. Dreamweaver's Extension Manager launches automatically to install most extensions.

6. **In the Extension Manager dialog box, choose File⇨Install Extension and then browse your drive to select the extension file you downloaded.**

   After the installation is complete, Dreamweaver displays instructions for using the extension. These instructions are usually the same as the ones included in the middle of the page on the Exchange site.

   Pay special attention to the part of the instructions that tells you where you'll find your newly installed extensions. Extensions may be added to menus, dialog boxes, and other parts of Dreamweaver depending on their functionality and how the programmer set them up. Finding them can be hard if you don't know where to look.

7. **Launch Dreamweaver and find the new menu option, button, or other interface feature that controls your new extension.**

   In many cases, all you have to do is open an existing page or create a new page in Dreamweaver and then open the newly added dialog box or select the new option from a menu.

Adobe is constantly updating the Exchange site, which is available by clicking the Dreamweaver link at www.adobe.com/exchange. Visit it regularly to find new extensions you can download and install to enhance Dreamweaver's feature set.

12

Using jQuery UI and Mobile Widgets

In This Chapter

▶ Designing collapsible panels

▶ Creating tabbed panels

▶ Using jQuery mobile widgets

*I*n addition to using HTML and CSS, many web designers use JavaScript to add interactive features, such as collapsible panels and other interactive features that can be opened and closed without reloading a web page. jQuery is also popular for creating interactive features in mobile web designs.

To make it easier to provide these complex and popular features, Dreamweaver includes a collection of widgets in the jQuery UI Insert panel that you can use on web pages, and a second collection in the jQuery Mobile Insert panel that is optimized for mobile designs. In this chapter, you find instructions for using these widgets to create collapsible panels with tabs, as well as instructions for using mobile jQuery features — even if you don't know how to write JavaScript.

Making Magic with jQuery

JavaScript has become an increasingly important part of the web, and the jQuery framework is one of the more popular JavaScript frameworks because it enables you to create highly interactive web page features that load quickly. jQuery also enables designers to open and close panels and extend drop-down menus without reloading the page.

To save you from having to write the code for these kinds of features, Dreamweaver includes two collections of jQuery widgets that instantly add things such as collapsible panels to your pages as well as editing tools for customizing these features without knowing JavaScript. To view the list of jQuery UI widgets available in Dreamweaver, open the jQuery UI Insert panel by choosing jQuery UI from the Insert panel drop-down menu shown in Figure 12-1. To view the jQuery Mobile widgets, choose jQuery Mobile from the Insert panel list.

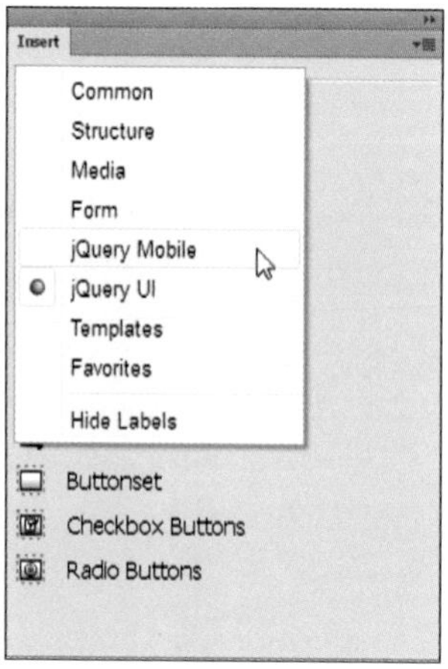

Figure 12-1: The jQuery UI and jQuery Mobile Insert panels provide quick access to many jQuery options.

Creating Collapsible Panels

The jQuery UI accordion widget makes it easy to add collapsible panels that site visitors can open and close without refreshing the web page. This jQuery feature enables you to make better use of the space on a page by displaying more information in less space in a browser window.

In Figure 12-2, you can see how I used the accordion collapsible panels to contain the name, photo, and habitat preferences of each songbird in this nature website. The result is that you can easily see the names of all the birds on one page. To view the description of any bird, a user need only click the tab at the top of the panel (where the bird's name appears), and the panel opens instantly.

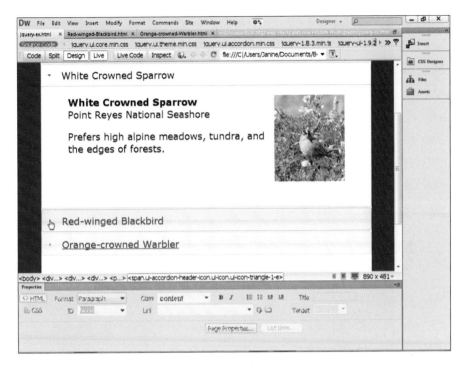

Figure 12-2: The jQuery accordion widget adds a series of collapsible panels to a web page.

In Figure 12-3, the photo and description for the orange-crowned warbler is open while the others on the page are closed. The beauty of jQuery is that the page doesn't have to be reloaded for the panels to open or close. Click once on a tab and a panel opens instantly. Click another tab, and that panel opens as the previously opened panel closes. Collapsible panels can be used to display text and images as well as multimedia files such as audio, video, and Flash files.

To view an accordion panel (or many other advanced features in Dreamweaver) as it will appear in a web browser, you need to click the Live view button at the top left of the Dreamweaver workspace.

After you create a set of accordion panels with the jQuery UI menu in Dreamweaver, you can change a number of panel settings by using the Property inspector, as shown in the instructions that follow.

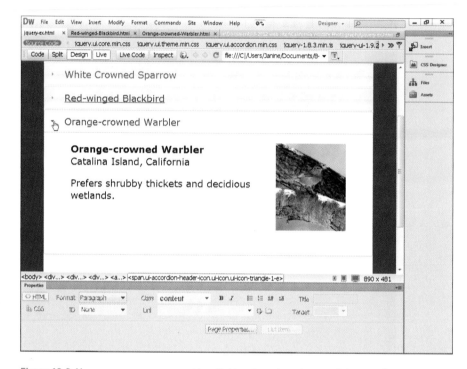

Figure 12-3: Users can open any panel by clicking the tab at the top of the panel.

Follow these steps to create an accordion panel set:

1. **Place your cursor on a page where you want the accordion panels to appear.**

2. **Choose Insert⇨jQuery UI⇨Accordion, or click the Accordion item in the jQuery UI Insert panel.**

   A jQuery UI collapsible accordion panel group with three panels appears in the page, as shown in Figure 12-4.

3. **Select the word *Section* at the top of each panel, and replace it with the text you want to appear in the panel's Tab area.**

   By default, the text in the Tab area is plain text, but you can change that by altering the corresponding CSS rule or formatting the text using HTML tags, such as the heading tags.

4. **Select the word *Content* in the main area of the each panel, and enter any text or images you want to display.**

Figure 12-4: When you create an accordion panel set, three panels are automatically included.

You can paste text into a panel just as you'd paste text anywhere else on the page. Similarly, you insert images into panels just as you would anywhere else on a page: Place your cursor in the panel, choose Insert⊏⊃Image⊏⊃Image, and select the GIF, JPEG, or PNG file you want to display. You can also select a Photoshop file if you want to use Dreamweaver to optimize your images. (See Chapter 3 if you need help preparing or converting images into these formats.)

When you paste text into a panel, choose Edit⊏⊃Paste Special to choose the amount of formatting you want to preserve in the text you paste in Dreamweaver. Limiting the amount of formatting preserved can cut down on potential style conflicts.

5. **To change the panel settings, click the blue jQuery Accordion tab at the top of the panels in the design area.**

When you click the blue tab, the panel settings appear in the Property inspector, as shown in Figure 12-5. (Correctly clicking the blue tab can be tricky, so make sure you click the blue area.) Click anywhere else on the page, and the inspector returns to its default settings.

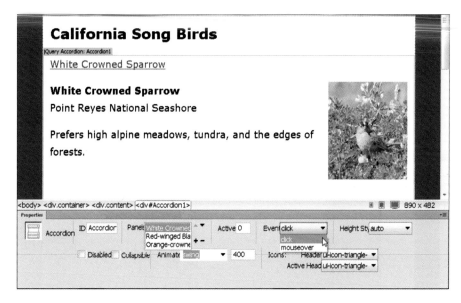

Figure 12-5: Edit the accordion options in the Property inspector.

6. **Add or remove panels using the Panels field in the Property inspector.**

   To add a panel, click the plus sign (+) to the right of the Panels field. To remove a panel from an accordion set, first select the panel name in the Panels drop-down list in the Property inspector and then click the minus sign (–).

   You can add another panel by clicking the plus sign again.

7. **Change how panels are opened by using the Event drop-down menu.**

   The Event settings control whether the panels open when a user clicks on a panel tab (Click) or rolls a cursor over the panel tab (Mouseover).

8. **Set other panel options, as desired.**

   The accordion options in the Property inspector are optional, and include the capability to disable any or all panels (Disable) and animate the way panels open and close (Animate drop-down list).

9. **Choose File⇨Save to save the page; when the Copy Dependent Files dialog box appears, click OK to generate all the related files.**

   For the Spry features to work, you must upload these files to your web server when you upload the web page.

10. **To change the appearance of the panel, such as the font face or text color, edit the corresponding CSS rule.**

    Note: You can't edit the corresponding styles for an accordion panel until the page has been saved and Dreamweaver has generated the corresponding CSS and JavaScript files. For more about how to edit CSS rules in Dreamweaver, see Chapters 5–7.

11. **To see how the panels will appear in a web browser, click the globe icon at the top of the workspace and select the browser you want to use to preview the page.**

When you're using your computer to preview a page that has an interactive feature (such as an accordion panel) requiring JavaScript or another programming, some web browsers, including Internet Explorer, will display a warning stating that you must allow ActiveX controls to view the page. This is a security warning that appears only when the page is opened on the same computer where the page is saved. If you publish the page to a web server and then view it over an Internet connection, this error will not appear for you or your site visitors.

Creating Tabbed Panels

The jQuery UI Tab option makes it easy to add a series of panels that display or hide content corresponding to a series of tabs, as shown in Figure 12-6. Similar to the collapsible panels, this jQuery UI feature lets you display more information in less space within a browser window.

Figure 12-6: Tabbed panels enable you to change the content displayed on a web page when a visitor clicks a tab.

Similar to the accordion panels, tabbed panels can be used to display text, images, and multimedia.

When you create tabbed panels with the jQuery UI widget in Dreamweaver, you can specify the order of the tabs, effectively controlling what content appears when the page is first loaded.

Follow these steps to create a tabbed panel group:

1. **Place your cursor on a page where you want the tabbed panel to appear.**

2. **Choose Insert⇔jQuery UI⇔Tabs, or click the Tabs item in the jQuery UI Insert panel.**

   A tabbed panel is inserted into the page and the corresponding CSS files appear in the CSS Designer Source panel, as shown in Figure 12-7.

3. **In the main workspace, select the *Tab1, Tab2,* and *Tab 3* text in turn, and then replace each tab heading with the text you want to appear in the panel's tab area.**

   You can edit the contents of the tabs only in the workspace, not in the Property inspector. By default, the text in the Tab area is bold and black, but you can change that formatting by altering the corresponding CSS rule.

4. **To adjust the size of each tab, select the tab and then use the Height and Width settings in the Property inspector.**

   With an individual tab selected, the Property inspector displays the settings for that tab specifically. In Figure 12-8, I've changed the width of the tab from 100 pixels to 200 pixels to make room for the longer name, *Hummingbird.*

Figure 12-7: The jQuery UI Tabs widget adds a tabbed panel group to a web page.

Figure 12-8: You may need to change the width of each tab to better fit the text.

5. **To add content, select the word *Content* in the main area of any selected tab panel and then enter text, images, or multimedia.**

   You can copy text into a panel by pasting it just as you'd paste text anywhere else on the page. Similarly, insert images into panels just as you would anywhere else on a page: Choose Insert➪Image➪Image and then select the GIF, JPEG, or PNG file you want to display. You can also add multimedia, such as Flash video files, or Photoshop files if you want to use Dreamweaver to optimize your images. (Find instructions for adding multimedia to web pages in Chapter 13.)

6. **To change the appearance of a tab or a panel, such as the font face or color, edit the corresponding CSS rule.**

   For example, to edit the text color or font in the tabs, select the box around the tab and the `box around` style is automatically selected in the CSS Designer Selector panel. You find detailed instructions for creating and editing styles in Chapters 5–7.

7. **To edit the number or order of tabbed panels, click the blue jQuery Tabs tab at the top of the panel set in the design area.**

   When you click the blue tab, the panel settings appear in the Property inspector (refer to Figure 12-9). Click outside the blue boxed area, and the Property inspector returns to its default settings.

8. **To add tabs, click the plus sign (+) icon in the Property inspector.**

   New tabs appear in the workspace.

9. **To change the order of tabs, select the tab name in the Property inspector and then use the arrows in the Panels field to move the panel.**

Figure 12-9: Click the blue tab at the top of the panel group to reveal panel settings in the Property inspector.

Panel names move up and down the menu as the order is changed. Panels and their corresponding tabs appear in the web page in the order in which they appear in the Property inspector.

10. **Select the panel in the Panels drop-down list that you want to display when the page is loaded into a web browser.**

    The drop-down list corresponds to the names you give each tab in the workspace.

11. **Choose File⇨Save to save the page; when the Copy Dependent Files dialog box appears, click OK to automatically generate all the related files.**

    For the jQuery UI features to work, you must upload these files to your web server when you upload the web page.

12. **Click the globe icon at the top of the workspace and select a browser to preview your work in a browser.**

    Depending on your web browser, you may have to allow ActiveX controls to preview the page on your computer.

Using jQuery Mobile Widgets

The Insert menu also includes a collection of jQuery mobile widgets you can use to create form elements and other features commonly used in mobile web apps. For example, you can use the jQuery mobile widget to add mobile-friendly form elements, such as text areas and check boxes.

Before you can use any of the jQuery mobile widgets, you must first define a jQuery Mobile page by choosing Page, the item in the list of jQuery mobile widgets shown in Figure 12-10.

To use the jQuery mobile widgets, follow these steps:

1. **Create a web page in Dreamweaver.**

   You find instructions for the many ways to create web pages in Dreamweaver in Chapter 2.

2. **Click to place your cursor in the top-left of the new page, and then choose Page in the jQuery Mobile Insert panel (refer to Figure 12-10).**

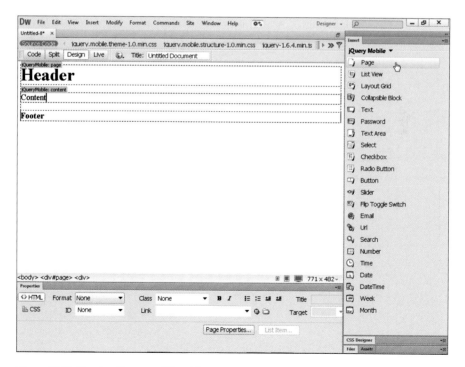

Figure 12-10: Use the jQuery mobile widgets to create mobile web pages and simple web applications.

The jQuery Mobile files dialog box opens.

3. **Change the default settings in the jQuery Mobile files dialog box (or leave them set to the defaults), and click OK.**

   The Page dialog box opens.

4. **Enter a name in the ID field, and select or deselect the check boxes next to Header and Footer based on whether you want header and footer sections in your mobile page.**

5. **Replace the *Header, Content,* and *Footer* text with the text, images, and other elements you want in your mobile page.**

   You can add text and insert images and other elements into a jQuery mobile page just as you would any other page in Dreamweaver.

   The text should be short and the images should be small for displaying on small mobile screens.

6. **Click the Mobile Size icon in the bottom-right of the workspace to view the page in a smaller window, as shown in Figure 12-11.**

   The Mobile Size option enables you to view the page in a manner similar to how it will appear on a small mobile device.

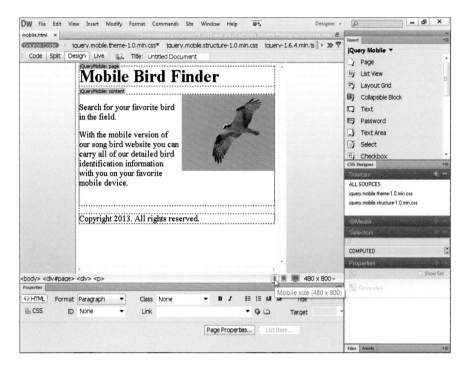

Figure 12-11: Use the Mobile View option to display your mobile page in a smaller size in Dreamweaver's workspace.

7. **Add other jQuery Mobile options as desired.**

   The rest of the jQuery Mobile options in the Mobile jQuery Insert panel are optional. Use them to add additional features to your mobile page, including form elements such as password fields, radio buttons, and text areas.

8. **Choose File⇨Save to save the page; when the Copy Dependent Files dialog box appears, click OK to generate all the related files.**

   For the jQuery Mobile features to work, you must upload these files to your web server when you upload the web page.

9. **To preview your work in a browser, click the globe icon at the top of the workspace and select a browser.**

To test a mobile website or web app on a mobile device, publish the page and all related files to a web server, and then view the page in a web browser on an iPhone, an Android device, a Blackberry, or another mobile device.

Showing Off with Multimedia

In This Chapter

▶ Understanding multimedia

▶ Hosting videos using an online service

▶ Hosting audio files with SoundCloud

▶ Working with Adobe Flash

▶ Working with Adobe Edge Animate

▶ Comparing audio and video formats

▶ Adding audio and video files to web pages

Multimedia, especially video and complex animations, were the exception on the web — and for good reasons. Producing decent video was expensive, video was difficult to edit and upload, and most users connected by dial-up phone lines, which made downloading and watching video a slow and laborious process. But recent years have seen a revolution as all these bottlenecks have been resolved, one by one. Video cameras have become cheaper (or integrated into our smartphones), editing programs have become more powerful yet easier to use, and the majority of users now connect at broadband speeds that formerly were available only to scientists at nuclear-research labs.

As a result, the growth of video being created and watched online has been massive. Even formal corporate sites now routinely offer videos explaining who they are and why their products are so great. As users have come to expect multimedia on the sites that they visit, designers must become more adept at navigating the dizzying variety of file formats, image resolutions, and delivery quirks.

One of the biggest challenges for Dreamweaver has been how to handle the rapid changes in audio, video, and animation. Dreamweaver CC integrates some of the new tools in Adobe Creative Cloud to ensure that the multimedia that you embed in your pages can be enjoyed by the widest possible audience.

Dreamweaver CC also includes some exciting new tools to help designers deal with the problems and uncertainties inherent in dealing with the still-evolving HTML5 video standard.

Not all websites warrant multimedia; if your goal is to provide information in the fastest way possible to the broadest audience, text is still generally the best option. If you want to provide a richer experience for your users, to *show* rather than just *tell,* or to entertain as well as inform, adding audio, video, and animation can help you share more information more vividly and even make you look more professional. For example, a video demonstrating how to do the foxtrot is far more useful to a user than any number of paragraphs of explanation, even if they're accompanied by a black-and-white diagram of footprints and arrows like the ones students of the Arthur Murray dance studio puzzled over.

The most complicated aspect of multimedia on the web is choosing the best format for your audience, which is why you'll find a primer on audio and video formats in this chapter. You can't create or edit multimedia files in Dreamweaver. (You'll need a specialized video, audio, or animation program for that.) But after your files are ready, Dreamweaver makes adding them to your web pages relatively easy.

As you discover in this chapter, inserting video, audio, Flash, or HTML5 animation files is similar to adding image files to web pages, but with many more options, such as settings that control whether a video starts automatically or only when the user clicks the play button.

Many people surf the web in their offices, in libraries, and in other locations where unexpected sound can be jarring, disruptive, or worse. Always give people a warning before you play video or audio and always give users a way to turn off audio quickly when necessary.

In this chapter, you also find instructions for using third-party services, such as YouTube or Vimeo, to host videos. With this approach, you upload your video to YouTube, Vimeo, or another service and then use Dreamweaver to add a snippet of code into your site so that the video plays on your page (even though the video is hosted elsewhere). An advantage of this approach is that YouTube and other video sites are better at delivering video on the web than most of the commercial web servers that you're likely to use to host your site.

Understanding Multimedia Players

When you add sound, video, or any other kind of multimedia to a website, your visitors may need a special player (sometimes with an associated plug-in) to play or view your files.

Players are small programs that work alone or with a web browser to add support for functions, such as playing sound, video, and animation files. Some of the best-known multimedia players are Flash Player, Windows Media Player, and Apple QuickTime.

The challenge is that not everyone on the web uses the same player, and viewers must have the correct player to view your multimedia files. As a result, you need one or more strategies to help visitors play your multimedia easily, such as the following:

- Many web developers offer audio and video in two or three formats so users can choose the one that best fits the players they already have.

- Some developers also include the same multimedia files in different file sizes so that visitors with slower connection speeds don't have to wait as long. Optimizing multimedia for the web works much as it does with images: The smaller the file size, the lower the quality but the faster the file downloads.

- Many web developers also include information about how visitors can download and install the best player if they need it to view the files.

You can use Dreamweaver to insert or link to any type of multimedia file, but only you can choose the format that's best for your audience. Although dozens of plug-ins are available for web pages, the most common plug-ins on the web today are Flash, Windows Media, and QuickTime.

In general, I recommend that you avoid the more obscure players unless you're offering specialized content that users have a good reason to download, such as a three-dimensional game that requires a special program to run.

Using YouTube, Vimeo, and Other Online Services to Host Videos

One of the most complex and confusing aspects of the general migration by website owners and designers to using the HTML5 standard is the integration of video on web pages. Millions of words have been written about the corporate wars being waged in courtrooms over patents, licensing fees, and technical specifications for the various "flavors" of HTML5 video.

For this reason, we suggest that designers who are just beginning to integrate multimedia into their creations simplify by using one of the popular video-hosting sites, such as YouTube or Vimeo. These hosting services handle the storage, bandwidth, compression, formatting, and delivery of video assets to your users. All you have to do is upload your video files and then include special code from that site in the HTML code of your web pages. The video plays within your pages, even though it's not hosted on your web server.

If you're designing a site that includes video that is confidential, sensitive, or used to meet business objectives (such as sell products or embed advertising messages), you will probably be best served by using a content delivery network (CDN). Services such as BrightCove, Akamai, and Amazon Web Services not only handle bandwidth and delivery but also offer the option of transcoding (video geekspeak for reformatting video) your video clips to the correct format so that they play seamlessly on a desktop computer, a tablet, and a smartphone.

YouTube is a great option if you want your video to reach the widest audience for free, but you give up some of your rights to your video in exchange for having it hosted on the site. Similarly, when you add a video to your site from YouTube, you're stuck with the YouTube player, which includes the YouTube logo, as well as ads that might be shown on top of, or next to, your video. Make sure to read through the terms and conditions on any video site you use so that you fully understand the rights that you may be giving away and how the site may use your video in the future.

Vimeo has won the loyalty of increasing numbers of video professionals because it offers a reasonably priced professional level of service that makes it easier to control the rights to your own videos and offers the option of adding videos to your pages without the Vimeo logo or links to other videos on the site.

Today YouTube and Vimeo seem to offer the best options for most small- to medium-sized websites, but competitors are emerging. The services that these video companies offer keep changing, so you may want to research the best services for your needs before you decide where to host your videos.

The advantages of hosting video on a site such as YouTube or Vimeo include the following:

- ✔ **Better video compression:** Both YouTube and Vimeo optimize your video when you upload it to their servers, and they often to a better job than you could yourself.

- ✔ **Delivery of the right version to each visitor:** YouTube detects the connection speed and device of your visitors and delivers video accordingly. If you visit YouTube with an iPhone, you see the video in MP4 format. View the same video with a computer, and you see the Flash version. Similarly, if you have a fast 3G connection, you see a higher-resolution version. View the video with a slower connection, and you see a lower-quality version that loads faster.

✔ **Bandwidth cost management:** These services can help you save money. If your videos become popular and you host your own video, you may exceed the bandwidth limits of your web host and incur additional fees. Because video uses more bandwidth than other types of content, over-ages can get costly. Hosting your video on YouTube or Vimeo means you'll never be surprised by extra bandwidth fees for video.

Hosting video on YouTube or Vimeo is easy. Here's how it works:

1. **Create an account on the site by filling out a form (or log on to your account if you already have one).**

   If you want to use the professional-level services on Vimeo, you also must pay a fee.

2. **Upload your files to the site through your web browser.**

   In this process, the video is uploaded and encoded, which can take a few minutes depending on the site and how busy it is.

3. **Follow the site's instructions for copying the code needed to embed your video on your website.**

   For example, in YouTube, click the Embed button, which displays a dialog box so that you can control how the video is displayed to your users, as shown in Figure 13-1.

Figure 13-1: Use the Video Size menu to choose a display size for your video.

4. **Open your web page in Dreamweaver. In the HTML code on your page, click where you want the video to appear, and then paste the code snippet.**

TIP

Use Dreamweaver's Split view to make it easy to find the right place to paste the code, and make sure you paste the code into Dreamweaver in Code view, not Design view.

Using SoundCloud to Host Audio Files

Finding a free place on the Internet to host your audio files has been much more difficult than hosting video files. This seems illogical, because video files are so much larger than audio files and thus more difficult to store, retrieve, and deliver, but the problem has been that music pirates have used audio-hosting sites to illegally distribute copyrighted content.

Luckily, the web startup SoundCloud has figured out a way to defeat (or at least slow down) the pirates, allowing site owners and podcasters a free and easy way to share their creations. The site includes neat tools that allow your friends or contacts to comment on specific portions of your audio file that they like and to easily share their opinions with others. You can upload, embed, and promote your audio files through Facebook, Twitter, Tumblr, and Google+. (For more tips on promoting your videos and your website, see Chapter 15.)

To sign up for a free SoundCloud account, follow these steps:

1. **Open a browser and navigate to** `http://soundcloud.com`.

   The SoundCloud home page opens as shown in Figure 13-2.

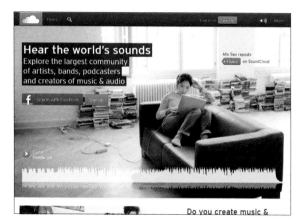

Figure 13-2: A large, thriving community of musicians, podcasters, and audio artists sharing their creations on SoundCloud.

2. **Click the Sign Up button.**

   A window opens, allowing you to sign in using your Facebook Profile ID or your e-mail address. If you've already signed up for an account, choose the Log In tab at the top of the Sign Up dialog box and sign in.

3. **Follow the site's instructions for uploading your audio file.**

   SoundCloud allows you to choose the genre for your audio file (such as a podcast interview or a work-in-progress guitar solo) and type tags so other people can discover your audio file as well.

4. **After your file has been uploaded, you can choose to publicize it and share it with friends by posting the file's SoundCloud link on Facebook, Tumblr, Twitter, or Google+.**

Using Adobe Flash

Adobe Flash has long been a favorite among web designers, but it has lost its dominance of the market, because Flash files don't work on Apple's popular iPhone, iPad, and iPod touch devices. That said, Flash is still well supported by desktop computers connected to the web (more than 90 percent of Internet users already have the Flash plug-in) and is still popular with professional video producers (such as the major TV networks or movie studios) because of its tools to prevent piracy, track what users do with the video, and monetize via advertising.

Because Flash is not supported by Apple's devices, designers have turned to HTML5, CSS3, and JavaScript. You can find out more about using the new CSS3 features in Chapter 7. Writing JavaScript is beyond the scope of this book, but Dreamweaver's behaviors, covered in Chapter 11, provide a great alternative and make it easier to create interactive design elements, such as slide shows and drop-down menus, without using Flash.

Dreamweaver supports both of the popular Flash file types:

- ✔ **Flash files:** (extension `.swf`) The most versatile Flash format is the SWF file (pronounced "swiff"). Often referred to simply as a *Flash file,* this format is sometimes called a Flash movie, even when it doesn't include video. Flash files with a `.swf` extension can include illustrations, photos, animation sequences, and video. In Dreamweaver, choose Insert➪Media➪Flash SWF for this format. You find detailed instructions for working with this type of Flash file in the following section.

- ✔ **Flash video:** (extension `.flv`) As the name implies, Flash video is a video format, although it can also be used for audio files. To convert video into the Flash video format, you need the Adobe Media Encoder. In Dreamweaver, use the Insert➪Media➪Flash Video option for this format. You find detailed instructions for working with `.flv` Flash files in the "Adding Flash audio and video files" section later in this chapter.

Flash files (with the `.swf` extension) are so flexible and so fast on the Internet in part because Flash uses vector graphics instead of bitmaps. Therefore, the graphics in Flash are based on mathematical descriptions *(vectors)* instead of pixels *(bitmaps),* and those vector equations take up far less space than bitmapped images. Vector graphics can also be scaled up or down in size without affecting the image quality or the size of the downloaded file. This capability to scale makes Flash ideally suited for the many different monitor sizes that web viewers use. You can even project Flash graphics on a wall or movie screen without losing quality, although any photographs or video files integrated into a Flash file may lose quality or look distorted at higher or lower resolutions.

To create a Flash file, you need Adobe Flash or a similar program that supports the Flash format. Because Flash is an open standard, you can create Flash files with a variety of programs, including Adobe Illustrator, which has an Export to SWF option.

Flash is great overall, but be aware of these important drawbacks:

✔ Flash is not supported by most mobile web browsers, including the iPhone or iPad. As a result, if you try to view a site created with Flash on some mobile devices, you see only a blank screen. To get around this problem, more and more web designers are creating a second version of their Flash sites designed for mobile phones and linking it to their main site. These second sites are often simplified versions of the main site, optimized with the information most likely to be useful to mobile users.

✔ If you need printouts for some reason, Flash may not print as well as you would hope.

✔ Flash may cause accessibility problems. Screen readers and other specialized viewers can't read the text in a Flash file any better than they can read text in an image file. To make Flash files more accessible, include detailed alternative text.

✔ Flash sites are generally more complicated to edit or update than sites created using HTML and CSS.

✔ Search engines may not read text in Flash files, which can hurt your page ranking in search results (although including alternative text can help with this limitation and Google is improving its capability to index Flash pages).

✔ Sites created entirely in Flash are harder to link to, especially if you want to link to a particular page within a site and not just to the front page of the site. Similarly, it's harder (or impossible) to bookmark specific pages within a site designed with Flash.

Inserting Flash SWF files

Flash files, often called Flash *movies,* use the `.swf` extension and can include animations, graphics, photos, and even video. Thanks to Dreamweaver, these files are relatively easy to insert into a web page. In this section, I assume you have a completed Flash file (an animation or other Flash movie), and you want to add it to your web page.

You insert a Flash file much as you insert an image file. But because a Flash file can do so much more than a still image, you have a variety of settings and options for controlling how your Flash file plays.

Before you start, make sure to save the Flash file you want to insert in the main folder for your website (that is, the local site folder you set up, as I explain in Chapter 2). I recommend creating a multimedia subfolder in your main website folder for audio and other multimedia files, just as most designers create an image folder for image files.

To add a Flash file to a website, open an existing page or create a new document and save the file. Then follow these steps:

1. **Click where you want the Flash file to appear on your web page.**

2. **If the Insert panel is not already open, choose Window⇨Insert. Then use the drop-down list to select the Media panel, as shown in Figure 13-3.**

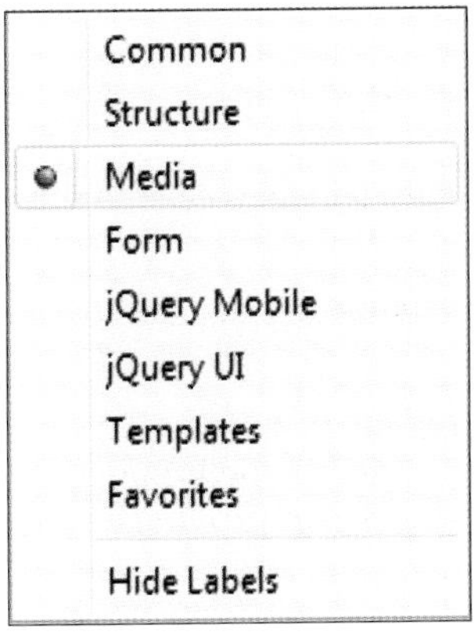

Common
Structure
● Media
Form
jQuery Mobile
jQuery UI
Templates
Favorites
Hide Labels

Figure 13-3: To insert a Flash file, open the Media panel.

3. **From the Media drop-down list in the Media Insert panel, shown in Figure 13-4, choose the Flash SWF option.**

   You can also choose Insert⏷Media⏷Flash SWF. The Select SWF dialog box appears.

Insert	
Media ▼	
🔲	Edge Animate Composition
🔲	HTML5 Video
🔊	HTML5 Audio
🔲	Flash SWF
🔲	Flash Video
🔌	Plugin

   Figure 13-4: You can use Dreamweaver to insert Flash animation files and Flash video files.

4. **Browse to locate the Flash file that you want to insert in your page, select the file, and click OK.**

   The Object Tag Accessibility Attributes dialog box opens.

5. **In the Object Tag Accessibility Attributes dialog box, enter a title that describes the Flash file and click OK.**

   The dialog box closes, and the Flash file is inserted into your document.

You can also specify an access key and tab index in the Object Tag Accessibility Attributes dialog box. These optional settings make it easier for visitors with disabilities to navigate your website with special browsers. You can learn more about designing accessible websites at www.w3.org/WAI/intro/accessibility.php.

When you first insert a Flash file, Dreamweaver displays it as a gray box on your web page. To display the Flash file as it will appear in a web browser when viewed with the Flash player, click anywhere in the gray box to select the Flash file and then click the Play button in the Property inspector. (*Note: The Play and Stop buttons are available only under Windows.*) If you have the Flash player installed on your computer, the Flash file will play when you preview the page in a browser. You can also choose Live view to see how Flash will play, although more complex Flash movies may cause this function to stop, skip, or otherwise misbehave.

Setting Flash properties

Like most HTML tags, the tags that link Flash and other multimedia files to web pages have *attributes* (also called properties) that define how a file is displayed within a browser, controlling such actions as whether an animation plays automatically when a page is loaded or only when a visitor clicks a link. Dreamweaver automatically sets some of these options, such as the height and width of the Flash file, but you may want to specify others.

To display Flash attributes in the Property inspector, as shown in Figure 13-5, select the gray box that represents a Flash file after it's inserted into a web page.

Figure 13-5: Select any Flash file to view or change its settings in the Property inspector.

If you don't see all the options in the Property inspector, click the expander arrow in the lower-right corner to display the more advanced options. If you still don't see all the options, you may be dealing with a `.flv` file, not a `.swf` file.

The following describes the Flash options included in the Property inspector:

- ✔ **ID field:** Use the text field in the upper-left corner of the Property inspector, just to the right of the Flash icon, to assign a name to the file. (In Figure 13-5, we named the Flash file GiantPen.) You can enter any name; just don't use spaces or special characters other than the hyphen or underscore. The name is important if you want to refer to the file in JavaScript or other programming, but you can leave this field blank if you're not using a script with your Flash file.

- ✔ **W (width):** Use this option to specify the width of the file. The file is measured in pixels.

- ✔ **H (height):** Use this option to specify the height of the file. The file is measured in pixels.

- ✔ **Reset Size icon:** (This small icon, which looks like a circle with an arrow in it, is visible only if you've changed the size of a Flash file.) You can change the display size of a Flash file by clicking and dragging one of its corners or by entering a number in the height or width fields. When the size of a Flash file has been altered, a small, circular icon appears just to the right of the height and width fields. Clicking this circular icon reverts the Flash file to its original size. You can resize Flash files, unlike images, video, and many other file types, without affecting image quality because they're vector-based. To keep the file proportionate, hold down the Shift key while you drag to resize the file.

- **File:** Dreamweaver automatically fills in this field when you insert a Flash file with the filename and path. You risk breaking the link to your Flash file if you alter this field.

- **Src:** Use this option to enter the name of the Flash file and the path to its location, including any folders or subdirectories.

- **Bg:** Click the color swatch to change the background color that appears behind the Flash file, or enter a pound sign (#) followed by a hexadecimal color code.

- **Edit:** Click this button to open a Flash source file with the Adobe Flash program, where you can edit the file. Note that you can edit only the Flash source file. After saving the Flash file for web use with the `.swf` extension, return to the original Flash file to edit it again.

- **Class:** Use this drop-down list to apply any class styles defined for the document.

- **Loop:** Selecting this check box causes the Flash file to repeat, or *loop*. If you don't select this box, the Flash movie stops after it reaches the last frame.

- **Autoplay:** Selecting this check box causes the Flash movie to play as soon as it is downloaded to the viewer's computer. If you don't select this box, whatever option you've set in the Flash file itself (such as `onMouseOver` or `onMouseDown`) is required to start the movie.

- **V Space (vertical space):** If you want blank space above or below the file, enter the number of pixels.

- **H Space (horizontal space):** If you want blank space on either side of the file, enter the number of pixels.

- **Quality:** This option enables you to prioritize the anti-aliasing options of your images versus the speed of playback. *Anti-aliasing,* which makes your files appear smoother, can slow down the rendering of each frame because the computer must first smooth the edges. The Quality parameter enables you to regulate how much the process is slowed by letting you set priorities based on the importance of appearance versus playback speed. You can choose from these Quality options:

  - **Low:** Anti-aliasing is never used. Playback speed has priority over appearance.

- **High:** Anti-aliasing is always used. Appearance has priority over playback speed.

- **Auto High:** With this option, playback is set to begin with anti-aliasing turned on. However, if the frame rate supported by the user's computer drops too low, anti-aliasing automatically turns off to improve playback speed. This option emphasizes playback speed and appearance equally at first but sacrifices appearance for the sake of playback speed, if necessary.

- **Auto Low:** Playback begins with anti-aliasing turned off. If the Flash player detects that the processor can handle anti-aliasing, it is turned on. Use this option to emphasize speed at first but improve appearance whenever possible.

✔ **Scale:** Specify this option only if you change the file's original height and width settings. The Scale parameter enables you to define how the Flash movie appears within those settings. The following options in the Scale drop-down list enable you to set preferences for how a scaled Flash movie appears in the window:

- **Default (show all):** The entire movie appears in the specified area. The width and height proportions of the original movie are maintained and no distortion occurs, but borders may appear on two sides of the movie to fill the space.

- **No Border:** This option enables you to scale a Flash movie to fill a specified area. No borders appear and the original aspect ratio is maintained, but some cropping may occur.

- **Exact Fit:** The Flash movie appears in the specified width and height. However, the original aspect ratio may not be maintained, so the movie may look squished.

✔ **Align:** This option controls the alignment of the file on the page. This setting works the same for plug-in files as for images.

✔ **Wmode:** Choose the Window option to display the Flash file in a rectangular window on a web page. Choose Opaque to hide everything behind a Flash file when you move or resize it using JavaScript. Choose Transparent to show the background of the HTML page through any transparent portions of the Flash file.

✔ **Play button:** Click the green Play button to play a Flash file in Dreamweaver. Note that when the Play button is activated, the button changes to Stop. *Note:* The Play button is available only under Windows.

✔ **Parameters:** This button provides access to a dialog box where you can enter parameters specific to your Flash files.

Using scripts to make Flash function better

When you insert Flash or other multimedia files with Dreamweaver, the program creates a collection of JavaScript files that help the Flash file play properly.

The files are named according to the format `swfobject_modified.js` and are stored in a Scripts folder, which Dreamweaver automatically creates in your local site folder. The first time Dreamweaver creates this file, a dialog box alerts you that you need to upload the script for your multimedia file to work properly. Make sure you include this script when you publish your site on your web server.

If you don't include the script, your multimedia file may not play properly, or your visitors may be required to click the green Play button twice before the file begins to play. (Remember, the Play and Stop buttons are available only under Windows.)

 With each new version of Dreamweaver, Adobe has changed the scripts included with Flash and other multimedia files. If you're editing a site that was created with an earlier version of Dreamweaver, update these scripts by deleting and then reinserting the multimedia file to generate new scripts. Then, make sure you upload the page with the Flash or other multimedia file, as well as the Scripts folder.

Working with Adobe Edge Animate Files

Ever since Apple's wildly popular iPhone and iPad famously refused to support Flash, Adobe has been working on providing alternatives to video producers, animators, and web designers. Edge Animate is a software program that allows designers who are familiar with the Flash interface to create animations and then export them as bundled `.oam` files that are easy to insert into your web pages, using the new Dreamweaver CC functions.

The `.oam` files contain the images and the JavaScript, HTML5, and CSS code that Dreamweaver uses to display the animation in your web page. To add the `.oam` files to a page in Dreamweaver, use the following steps:

1. **Click where you want the Edge Animate file to appear on your web page.**

2. **If the Insert panel is not already open, choose Window⇨Insert. Then use the drop-down list to select the Media panel (refer to Figure 13-3).**

3. **In the Media drop-down list, choose the Edge Animate Composition option.**

   You can also choose Insert⇨Media⇨Edge Animate Composition, or press Ctrl+Alt+Shift+E. The Select Edge Animate Package dialog box appears.

4. **Browse to locate the Edge Animate package file that you want to insert in your page, select the file, and click OK.**

5. **If you have accessibility options turned on, you're prompted to add alternative text to describe the Edge Animate file. Enter a description of the file and click OK.**

   The dialog box closes, and the Edge Animate file is inserted into your document. Dreamweaver also copies the requisite jQuery, CSS, HTML, and image files to the root folder of your site, as shown in Figure 13-6.

6. **Click the Live view button at the top of the workspace to view the inserted animation, as shown in Figure 13-7.**

   (Unlike Flash, there is no button to play the animation to see if it works.) Note the extensive list of files listed next to the Source Code button above the page design. If you want to see the example HTML5 animation in action, go to www.davidlafontaine.com/case-studies.

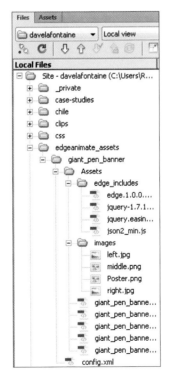

Figure 13-6: The necessary files are copied into a subdirectory in your site root folder.

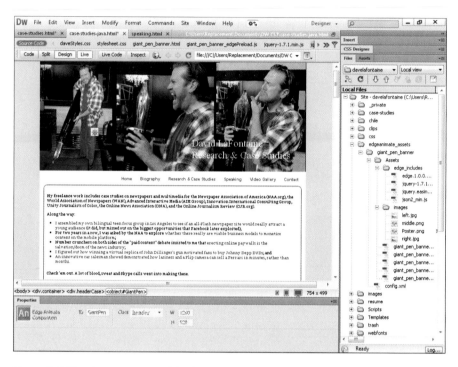

Figure 13-7: The three segments of the banner zoom across the page, and then the text bounces down from above.

Finding Flash resources online

One of the best places to read more about creating Flash files is on the Internet, where a wide range of websites offers everything from predesigned Flash files you can easily customize to great ideas for getting the most from this award-winning technology. You may find these websites useful if you want to find out more about Flash:

✔ www.adobe.com: At the Adobe site, you'll find loads of tips and tricks for creating and using Flash files (as well as many inspiring examples of Flash in action).

✔ www.swishzone.com: If you're looking for an alternative to Adobe Flash, Swish

from Swishzone.com is a great little program that's more reasonably priced.

✔ www.flashkit.com: You'll find a wide range of resources for Flash developers at the Flash Kit site.

✔ www.gotoandlearn.com: Go to gotoAndLearn when you want free Flash tutorials as well as videos about developing Flash animations and working with ActionScript, the programming language used in Flash.

Dreamweaver includes just a few options in the Property inspector to modify Edge animations on your web pages. You can assign a class style to the Edge Animate file, but we recommend that you not adjust the height or width of the animation with the dialog boxes in the Property inspector, unless you are expert at manually editing the CSS, jQuery, and HTML files.

Working with Video and Audio on the Web

As bandwidth has grown on the web, the use of video files has grown more dramatically than almost any other multimedia file type. From YouTube to small personal websites, millions of video files are added to the web every day. However, conflicting video formats that are fighting to be the standard under HTML5 are making life more difficult for web designers. Some browsers support the increasingly common MP4 video format, while others are choosing to support formats such as Ogg Theora or WebM, which are free and open-source alternatives.

For those who use a more traditional video format, such as Windows Media Video or Apple QuickTime, see the instructions for adding files in those formats in the section, "Inserting audio and video files," later in this chapter. You can specify video and audio settings, such as Autoplay, by changing setting parameters, an option that is a little more complicated if you use any format other than Flash video. You find instructions for managing these settings in Dreamweaver in the "Setting options for audio and video files," later in this chapter.

The first challenge to working with multimedia is choosing the right format and optimizing your video so it downloads quickly and still looks good. Unfortunately, no single video format works perfectly for everyone on the web, but most new computers come with preinstalled video and audio players that play the most common file formats. If you use a Windows computer, you probably have Windows Media Player. If you use a Mac, you have QuickTime. Both video players can handle multiple video formats, so anyone with a relatively new computer can likely view video in common formats.

Comparing popular video formats

You can convert video from one file format to another relatively easily with most video-editing programs. You can open a video in AVI (Audio Video Interleave) format in a program, such as Adobe Premier Elements (a good video editor for beginners), and then choose File⇨Export to convert it to any of a dozen formatting and compression options. For example, you could convert an AVI file to the .mp4 format with the compression setting for a smartphone or into the QuickTime format with the compression setting for a cable modem.

Streaming media plays faster

To *stream* multimedia means to play a file while it's downloading from the server. This trick is valuable on the web because video and audio files can take a long time to download. Here's how streaming works. When you click a link to a video file, your computer begins to download it from the server. If the video is hosted on a web server that supports streaming, the video or audio file begins to play as soon as enough of the file downloads successfully to ensure an uninterrupted experience.

If you don't use streaming, the entire file may have to download before the media can play. Although the download time for streaming or nonstreaming files may be the same, streaming can greatly reduce the time your visitors wait before they can start viewing a video online. Because web servers that stream video are very expensive, Flash offers an option called *Progressive Download*. This option offers many of the same advantages of streaming because a video embedded with the Progressive setting will start playing before the entire file is downloaded. However, the option has some limitations. For example, you can't fast forward or back up as well with a video that is downloading using Progressive settings as you can with a video hosted on a web server that supports streaming.

Editing video can get complicated, and optimizing video for the best quality with the fastest download time is both an art and a science, but the most basic process of converting a video file isn't difficult after you understand the conversion options.

Table 13-1 provides a brief description of the most common digital video formats, their file extensions, and a web address where you can find out more about each option.

Table 13-1		Common Digital Video Formats		
Format	*File Extension*	*Website*	*Description*	*Browser Support*
Flash video	.flv	www.adobe.com	You can create Flash videos with Adobe Flash. Because the Flash player is almost ubiquitous on the web, many developers still consider Flash a viable option.	Through browser plug-in. Nearly universal support through 95 percent market penetration on desktops. On mobile platforms, however, Flash is famously not supported.

Format	File Exten-sion	Website	Description	Browser Support
WebM	`.webm`	`www.webm project. org`	WebM is an open-source video format championed by Google. Although WebM is still somewhat rare, many designers are starting to take it seriously due to the increasing popularity of Android mobile devices.	Chrome, Firefox 4 and later, Internet Explorer 9 (although this requires separate installations), Opera 10 or later, and Safari 3.1 or later.
Ogg Theora	`.ogv`, `.ogg`	`http:// xiph.org`	Ogg Theora is another open-source video format, this one championed by Wikipedia, for use in delivering its video content. Also favored by the Firefox development team.	Firefox 3.5 and later, Chrome 3 and later, Opera 10. Not supported by Internet Explorer or Safari.
MP4	`.mp4`	No official site for this technology	Part of MPEG-4, the MP4 format can be used for audio or video. This format is becoming increasingly popular, partly because most mobile phones, including the iPhone, support it, making it a good alternative to `.flv`.	Chrome 3.0 or later, Internet Explorer and Safari (all versions). Not supported by Firefox or Opera.

(continued)

Table 13-1 *(continued)*

Format	File Extension	Website	Description	Browser Support
Windows Media Video	.wmv	www.micro soft.com/ windows/ windows media	Defined by Microsoft and popular on the PC, the Windows Media Video format supports streaming and plays with Windows Media Player as well as many other popular players.	Nearly universal support. Safari or browsers on a Mac may need a plug-in.
QuickTime	.qt, .mov	www.quick time.com	The QuickTime player is built into the Macintosh operating system and is used by most Mac programs that include video or animation.	Nearly universal support. Older versions of Windows may experience pixelated playback and heavy artifacting.
AVI	.avi	No one site about AVI exists, but you can find information if you search for *AVI* at www. microsoft. com.	Created by Microsoft, AVI (Audio Video Interleave) is an uncompressed video format that is fine if you're viewing video on a CD or on your hard drive, where the file doesn't have to download. For Internet use, however, AVI tends to result in unwieldy file sizes.	Not supported on the Mac platform. Specialized plug-in required.

Format	File Exten-sion	Website	Description	Browser Support
			If your files are in AVI, convert them to one of the other formats before adding them to your website. Otherwise, you force your visitors to download unnecessarily large video files.	

Comparing popular audio formats

Audio works much like video on the web. You can link to a sound file or embed the file into your page; either way, your visitors need to have the right player to listen to the file. You find instructions for adding both audio and video files to your pages in the following section, "Adding Audio and Video Files to Web Pages."

Table 13-2 provides a brief description of the most common digital audio formats, their file extensions, and a web address where you can find out more about each option.

Table 13-2		Common Digital Audio Formats	
Format	**File Exten-sion**	**Website**	**Description**
MP4	`.mp4`	No official site for this technology	Part of MPEG-4, the MP4 format can be used for audio or video. This format is becoming increasingly popular, partly because most mobile phones, including the iPhone, support it, making it a good alternative to `.flv`.

(continued)

Table 13-2 (continued)

Format	File Extension	Website	Description
MP3	.mp3	No official site for this technology	One of the most successful audio compression formats, MP3 supports streaming audio. Most music you can download from the Internet is in MP3 format, and it's clearly the first choice of many web developers. Most popular multimedia players on the web can play MP3 files.
Ogg Vorbis	.ogg	http://xiph.org	Ogg Vorbis is an open-source alternative to MP3 that was created when developers feared that exorbitant licensing fees were about to be imposed. It remains something of a rarity on the web, although it is commonly used in video games and on Wikipedia. It is supported by all the major web browsers, although Apple's iPhone and iPad need special applications to play Ogg Vorbis files.
Windows Audio	.wma	www.microsoft.com/windows/windowsmedia	Microsoft's Windows Audio format supports streaming and can be played with Windows Media Player as well as many other popular players. It also offers digital rights management functionality.
WAV	.wav	No official website exists for WAV files, but you can find some documentation at www.microsoft.com if you search for WAV.	The WAV file format is popular in digital media because it offers the highest sound quality possible. Audio files in this format are often too big for use on the web, averaging 12MB for a minute of audio. (In comparison, an MP3 file that is five times longer can be less than one-third the size.) Although WAV files are commonly used on the Internet because of their nearly universal compatibility, I recommend that you convert WAV files (especially for long audio clips) to one of the other audio formats.

Adding Audio and Video Files to Web Pages

Like other multimedia files, you can link to an audio or a video file or you can insert multimedia files into a page. Linking to a multimedia file is as easy as linking to any other file, as you see in the instructions that follow. Inserting an audio or a video file is a little more complicated, but it lets a visitor play the file without leaving the web page. Inserting audio and video files is covered in this section. If you're using Flash video or audio, see the "Adding Flash audio and video files" section, later in this chapter.

Linking to audio and video files

To use Dreamweaver to link to a video or an audio file, follow these steps:

1. **Select the text, image, or other element you want to use to create a link.**

   If you're linking to a video file, a good trick is to take a single still image from the video and insert that into your web page. Then create a link from that image to the video file.

2. **Choose Insert⇨Hyperlink or click the Hyperlink icon in the Common Insert panel.**

   The Hyperlink dialog box opens, as shown in Figure 13-8.

   Alternatively, you can click the Browse icon just to the right of the Link field in the Property inspector. (The Browse icon looks like a small file folder.)

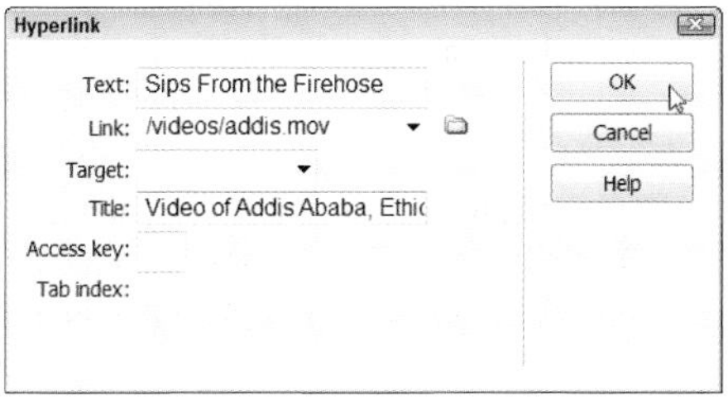

   ![Hyperlink dialog box showing fields: Text: Sips From the Firehose, Link: /videos/addis.mov, Target:, Title: Video of Addis Ababa, Ethic, Access key:, Tab index: with buttons OK, Cancel, Help]

   Figure 13-8: Link to an audio or a video file just as you'd create a link to another web page.

3. **In the Text field, enter the text you want to serve as a link.**

   If you selected a section of text on the page before opening the Hyperlink dialog box, that text automatically appears in the Text field.

4. **In the Link field, enter the URL where the audio or video file is located.**

   Alternatively, click the Browse icon (the file folder icon) to the right of the Link field and browse your hard drive to find the video or audio file you want to link to.

   As with any other file you link to, make sure you've saved your audio or video files into your local site folder (which I explain how to set up in Chapter 2).

   Note that you can link to an audio or a video file on another website, but you need to have the exact URL of the file's location.

5. **(Optional) Use the Target field in the Hyperlink dialog box to define where your linked page opens.**

   To open the linked page in a new browser window or in a new tab within a browser, choose the _blank option. The New option is not recommended because it is not standard. Choose _self to open the linked page in the same window (the default). Choose _top to force the page to open in a fresh browser window, even if the page is displayed in a frame. The _parent option is almost never used anymore, but if your page is in a frameset, you can select this option to open the linked page a level above the current page in the frame structure.

6. **(Optional) Fill in the title, access key, and tab index.**

   The Title, Access Key, and Tab Index fields in the Hyperlink dialog box are optional. These settings make it easier for visitors with disabilities to navigate your website with special browsers. You can learn more about website accessibility at `www.w3.org/WAI/intro/accessibility.php`.

7. **When you have finished specifying settings, click OK and then choose File ⇨Save to save the page.**

   The dialog box closes, and the link is created automatically.

8. **Click the Preview (globe) icon (at the top of the work area) to open the page in a browser, where you can test the link to your multimedia file.**

   Dreamweaver launches your specified web browser and displays the page. If you have the necessary player, the file downloads, your player launches, and your file automatically plays.

Many people like to have multimedia files, such as video, pop up in a new browser window. To do this, create an HTML file and embed your multimedia file in it. Then use the Open Browser Window behavior in Dreamweaver to create a pop-up window that displays your multimedia page. For more on how to work with Dreamweaver behaviors, see Chapter 11.

You can link to video files instead of embedding them (just as you would link to any file), but the advantage of embedding your audio or video file directly into the page is that the file will play in your web page instead of opening in a separate window or player.

Inserting audio and video files

Although you can use Dreamweaver to insert video files directly into a web page, our best advice is to use one of the video-hosting services, such as YouTube or Vimeo (covered earlier in this chapter). Dreamweaver's media features support all the audio and video files in Tables 13-1 and 13-2.

When you select Media from the Insert menu, you find multiple video and audio options. The Flash video format is covered in detail later in this chapter. If you want to insert video files that are in one of the older and more proprietary formats, such as Windows Media Video (.wmv) or QuickTime (.mov), you choose the Plugin option from the Media drop-down list in the Insert menu.

If you want to use the latest video formats using the HTML5 video tag, you can insert video in the MP4, WebM, or Ogg Theora formats (included in Table 13-1), by following these steps:

1. **Click where you want the file to appear on your web page.**

2. **Choose Insert⇨Media⇨HTML5 Video (see Figure 13-9).**

   You can also click the drop-down list in the Insert panel, choose Media, and then select HTML 5 Video. A small gray box containing a film icon appears in your design.

3. **Click the small gray box containing a film icon.**

   The Video properties are displayed in the Property Inspector at the bottom of the screen.

4. **In the Source field in the Property inspector, enter the URL to your video file or select the Browse icon and then select a video file on your hard drive.**

   After you selected the file, the path and filename appear in the Source window, as shown in Figure 13-10.

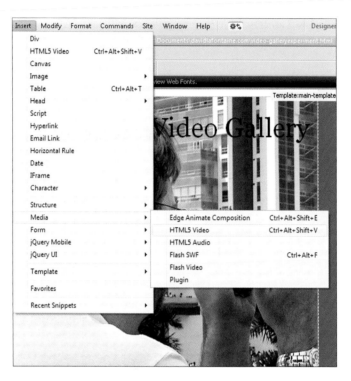

Figure 13-9: Choose from a variety of multimedia file formats.

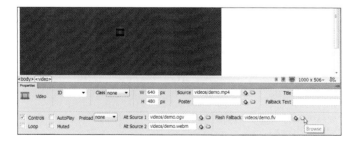

Figure 13-10: When you use the HTML5 option, you can embed videos in multiple formats using the Property inspector.

5. **(Optional) Use the Alt Source 1 and Alt Source 2 fields to enter the URL or browse and select video in additional formats.**

One of the complexities of using the HTML5 video tag is that you can use it with three video formats: mp4, Ogg Theora, and WebM. If you want your video to play in all popular web browsers, you need to include the video in all three formats. In Figure 13-10, you see that all three source fields are filled in with videos in each of these formats. Additionally, you can include a Flash video for older web browsers in the Flash Fallback field.

If you think it's crazy to have to embed four different video files in four different formats, you're not alone. This complexity is due to the lack of agreement among browser companies about what format is best for video.

TIP

Another advantage of using Vimeo or YouTube, to host your videos is that you can upload a video in just one format, and YouTube and Vimeo convert it and deliver it in all these formats automatically.

6. **Enter the height and width in the H and W fields, respectively, of the Property inspector.**

When you add audio or video, Dreamweaver doesn't automatically determine the height and width of the file, so you need to add the dimensions in the Property inspector after you insert the file. You find a description of these and other options in the next sections, "Setting options for audio and video files."

7. **Save the page and click the Preview (globe) icon (at the top of the work area) to open the page in a browser, to ensure compatibility.**

As noted in Tables 13-1 and 13-2, not all video formats will play in all browsers. Test your video to make sure that it plays at least in the browser that you're targeting as your primary destination. If you've set the file to Autoplay, your file plays automatically when the page loads into the browser. Otherwise, your browser inserts a simple controller so that you can start, pause, fast-forward, and rewind the video. To change video and audio settings that aren't included in the Property inspector, such as Autoplay, see the next section.

Setting options for audio and video files

When you select an inserted multimedia file, such as a sound or a video file, the Property inspector displays the options for the file (refer to Figure 13-10). The height and width are the most important settings. Unlike image files or Flash files, Dreamweaver can't automatically detect the height and width of other audio or video formats, so it's important to set these options in the Property inspector. To determine the height and width of a video file, you may need to open the file in a video-editing program.

The following describes the multimedia options available from the Property inspector:

- ✔ **ID field:** Use the text field in the upper-left corner of the Property inspector, just to the right of the plug-in icon, if you want to assign a name to the file. If you leave this field blank, Dreamweaver doesn't enter a name automatically unless you are using a file in a Flash format. The name is important only if you want to refer to the file in JavaScript.

- ✔ **Class:** Use the Class drop-down list to apply styles defined using the class selector.

- ✔ **W (width) and H (height):** Specify the measurement of the file in pixels. If you make the video much bigger than its actual size or fail to maintain its proportions, the video may be distorted or lack quality.

- ✔ **Source:** This option specifies the name and path to the file. You can type a filename or click the Browse icon (which looks like a small folder) to browse for the file. This field is filled in automatically when you embed the file.

- ✔ **Poster:** Specify an image to fill the space where your video will play so that your users have something to look at while the video loads.

- ✔ **Title:** Specify an identifying name for your video.

- ✔ **Fallback Text:** Display a short phrase to users who have incompatible browsers, such as "This video requires you to use the Firefox browser."

- ✔ **Controls:** Hide or display the video or audio controls for a file.

- ✔ **Loop:** Control whether a video file or an audio file loops, or continues to play over and over.

- ✔ **AutoPlay:** Play the file as soon as the page loads. We don't recommend this setting because many people browse the web from their office or other quiet location and resent being blasted with music when a page loads.

- ✔ **Muted:** Controls whether a video file or an audio file is muted at the beginning of playback.

- ✔ **Preload:** Use the drop-down list to choose the information that appears on the screen while your HTML5 multimedia file is loading. The None option leaves the space blank, Auto displays a percentage loaded indicator, and Metadata displays the file size, format, and other information relevant to your file.

- ✔ **Alt Source 1:** If you have an alternative version of your video (such as in WebM or MP4), choose it by following the process you used for the Source setting.

  ✔ **Alt Source 2:** If you have a third version of your video, choose it by following the process you used for the Source setting.

  ✔ **Flash Fallback:** If all else fails, choose the `.flv` file on your computer to
  serve as the ultimate backup to the HTML5 video files.

Be careful about combining these options. For example, if you turn off
AutoPlay and Controls, your visitor can never play your file. By default, the
controls are visible unless you deselect the box next to the Controls parameter. Similarly, if you turn off Controls and set your file to Mute, your users
can never hear what the audio track is playing.

Adding Flash audio and video files

Flash video has long been the video format of choice because so many
people have Flash Player and it is such a small and easy download for those
who don't have it. Adobe owns both Flash and Dreamweaver, so you find
much better support for Flash files in Dreamweaver.

The Insert FLV dialog box makes it easy to set parameters for Flash.
Dreamweaver can even automatically detect the size of Flash video files. You
can also use Flash to create and insert audio files, displaying only the player
(called a *skin* in Flash).

Follow these steps to insert a Flash video file into a web page:

  1. **Click where you want the file to appear on your web page.**

  2. **Choose Insert⇨Media⇨Flash Video.**

     (Alternatively, you can choose Flash Video from the list in the
     Media Insert panel.) The Insert FLV dialog box appears, as shown
     in Figure 13-11.

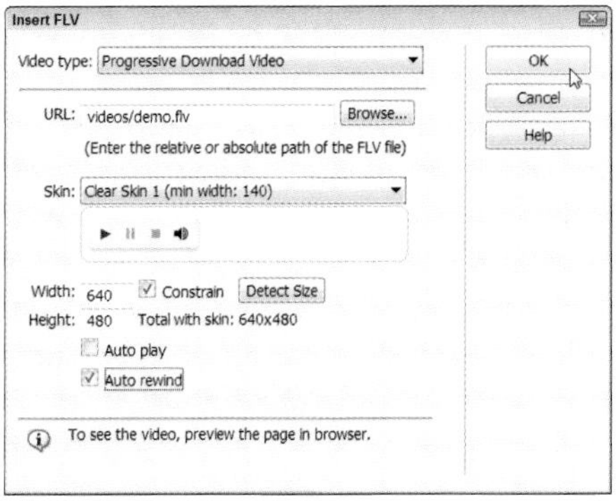

Figure 13-11: Specify how a Flash video will be
displayed in a web page.

3. **At the top of the dialog box, specify Streaming Video or Progressive Download Video.**

   You must have special server software to handle streaming video. Check with your Internet hosting service or system administrator to find out whether your web server supports streaming Flash files. If not, choose Progressive Download Video, which offers some of the advantages of streaming and works on any web server. For more on this topic, read the sidebar "Streaming media plays faster," earlier in this chapter.

4. **Click the Browse button to the right of the URL field and browse to find the Flash FLV file you want to add to the page. Select the file and click OK.**

   Dreamweaver automatically adds the filename and path to your Flash file in the URL field.

5. **Choose a skin from the Skin drop-down list.**

   Dreamweaver calls the play and audio controls for a Flash file a *skin*. As you can see in Figure 13-11, a preview of the selected skin appears in the dialog box so you can better decide which one is best for your Flash file and your design. You can also create custom skins in Adobe Flash.

6. **Click the Detect Size button to insert the height and width of the inserted Flash file (if Dreamweaver hasn't already done so).**

7. **If you want the Flash video to play as soon as the page is loaded, select the Auto Play check box.**

8. **If you want the video to rewind after play is complete, select the Auto Rewind check box.**

9. **Click OK to insert the Flash file and close the dialog box.**

   The Flash file appears on the page, represented by a gray box that's the height and width of the file.

When you insert a Flash video file and include a skin for the player, Dreamweaver creates a Flash file for the player with the .swf extension and saves the file in your local site folder. This Flash file contains the player controls and *must* be uploaded to your website when you publish the page with the Flash file for the player controls to work.

You can change the skin by clicking to select the inserted Flash file and using the Skin drop-down list in the Property inspector to select another option, as shown in Figure 13-12. Each time you choose a skin, Dreamweaver creates a new .swf file. You can delete any skins that aren't being used.

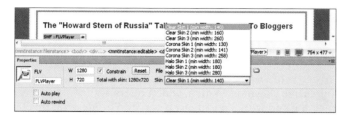

Figure 13-12: Use the Property inspector to alter the settings for a Flash video.

If you want to find out about other Flash options, visit `www.adobe.com` and search for *Flash Object and Embed tag attributes.* Or go directly to `http://kb2.adobe.com/cps/127/tn_12701.html`.

If you want a more customized player than the one available in Dreamweaver (for example, if you want to allow your users to click to see the video full-screen) and don't want to build one in Flash, check out the variety of players in Adobe's online Dreamweaver Exchange marketplace, at `http://www.adobe.com/cfusion/exchange/index.cfm?event=productHome&exc=3`.

Part IV
The Part of Tens

Enjoy an additional *Dreamweaver CC For Dummies* Part of Tens chapter on timesaving web design tips at http://www.dummies.com/extras/dreamweavercc.

In this part . . .

- ✔ Check out a collection of websites that can help you with some of the things you won't find in Dreamweaver, such as domain registration.

- ✔ Add detailed traffic tracking and e-commerce features to your website.

- ✔ Design and manage e-mail newsletters and other bulk e-mail messages.

- ✔ Discover ten ways to promote your website and attract the audience that your site deserves by using social media sites and search engine optimization (SEO).

Ten Resources You May Need

In This Chapter

▷ Finding domain registration services

▷ Adding a favicon image to the address bar

▷ Creating interactive forms

▷ Selling stuff on the web

▷ Sharing what's on your screen

▷ Keeping track of visitors to your traffic

▷ Using a heat map to see how visitors use your site

▷ Surveying your site visitors

▷ Following web standards with the W3C

▷ Adding new features to Dreamweaver with extensions

A lthough Dreamweaver is a wonderful tool for creating websites, it can't do everything you need to put a site online. For example, you can't register a domain name using Dreamweaver and you can't create a *favicon,* a special kind of tiny icon image that appears at the top of a web browser, usually in the address bar or the corresponding tab.

I added this chapter to offer you a handy list of online resources that can help you finish your site when you need to go beyond the features in Dreamweaver.

Registering a Domain Name

The address for your website is its *domain name*. The domain name is what visitors need to know to find your website. For example, you can visit my Digital Family website at www.DigitalFamily.com.

Even before you start building your website, I recommend that you register your own domain name. The process is simple, painless, and costs less than $10 per year at most registrars, but it can take from a few hours to a few days for the domain registration process to be completed.

You can register any domain name that hasn't already been taken by someone else. Just visit any domain registrar, such as www.godaddy.com or www.1and1.com, and enter the domain name you want in the search field on the main page of the registrar's site. If the name you want is no longer available, most registration services will give you a list of recommended alternatives.

Most domain registration services also provide web-hosting services, but you don't have to host your site at the same place where you register the name. You can set up a web server anywhere you want and then use the domain management settings at your domain registration service to point your name to the server where your website is hosted.

After you buy that killer new domain name that will undoubtedly lead to a life of fame and fortune and a ten-figure exit strategy, you'll probably be bombarded with offers to buy all the variants of your website's name. Before you go splurging on the .tv, .org, .net, and .biz versions of your site, you should know that most people still default to the good old .com when looking for a site with a catchy name.

When you enter a domain name into a web browser, everything before the extension (the .com, .net, or .org part) can be written in uppercase or lowercase, and it will work just fine. However, if you want to go to a specific page within a website, such as www.digitalfamily.com/store, the text that comes after the extension is often case sensitive. Because the part before the .com doesn't matter, I find it easier to recognize domain names when they're written with capital letters. So, for example, I use *www.DigitalFamily.com* on my business cards instead of *www.digitalfamily.com*.

Dressing Up the Address Bar with a Favicon

Have you ever wondered how to add a *favicon* — a custom graphic that appears in the address bar at the top of browsers such as Internet Explorer or Firefox — to your site? Google adds a capital *G*, Adobe adds its logo, I use a small piece of my logo for the favicon on my DigitalFamily website (shown in Figure 14-1). You can add an image, too. But first you have to get the image in the right format.

Figure 14-1: Distinguish your site by adding a favicon.

You can use a number of online services to create favicons. A popular service is available at `www.Favicon.com`. To use the service, open the main page of the `Favicon.com` site in a web browser and upload a graphic. It will be automatically converted into a favicon with the `.ico` extension for free. Then you simply download the new image to your hard drive, and then upload it to the root level (the main site folder) of your website (that is, the one that corresponds to your local site folder). The next time you view your page in a browser, the image appears automatically in the address bar.

Add Forms with Online Services

Forms follow function, to paraphrase the old saying. On the web, many of the most advanced and interactive features you can add to a web page require *forms* — structures for collecting, from site visitors, information that can then be used in a variety of ways. Forms are commonly used to create guest books, contact forms, search engine entry fields, order forms, chat rooms, and discussion areas.

Dreamweaver makes it relatively easy to create form elements, such as check boxes, radio buttons, and drop-down lists, but if you want your form to actually *do* something, you have to pair it with a program on your web server.

One of the most confusing aspects of working with forms is that they don't do much until you connect them to a script (essentially a program that executes a limited set of commands). These programs, or scripts, enable form processing.

For example, when you fill in a contact form on most web pages, a script collects the information you entered and either saves it to a database or sends it to a specified address by e-mail. Similarly, if you enter text in a search field and press Search, the text you enter gets processed by a program that conducts the search and delivers a page with the results. The more complicated the form and the processing required, the more complicated the programming.

You can create your own forms in HTML, write your own scripts, and even download form scripts from the web, but unless you're an experienced programmer or a system administrator, you're likely to have a hard time making your own forms work on your website. How you install a script on your server depends on how your server is set up and often requires special access and experience configuring programs on a web server — topics that are way beyond the scope of this book.

Today, unless you are working on a large site or need a highly customized form, your best option is to use an online service. Here are two of the most popular ways to set up forms on a website (without needing programming skills):

- ✔ Email Me Form at `www.emailmeform.com/`
- ✔ Adobe Acrobat Forms Central at `www.acrobat.com/FormsCentral`

When you use either of these online services, you use a script that is hosted on their web server and linked to the form that you to add to your website. Not having to host a script on your own server removes most of the headaches when it comes to creating a wide variety of forms.

To use these services, set up an account, choose the type of form you want to create, and then copy and paste a little code into the HTML of your blog or your website. It's that simple.

Selling Stuff on the Web

You can sell things online in many ways. As a general rule, I recommend that you start simple and add more complex and expensive options after you know that you'll make money with your site.

At the simple end of the spectrum, you can add a purchase button or a simple e-commerce shopping cart with the services offered at www.PayPal.com and checkout.google.com. These services require no upfront costs and are as easy as copying and pasting to use, but they are suited only for relatively small shopping carts. For a slightly more advanced, Dreamweaver-compatible solution, consider www.cartweaver.com.

If you're selling hundreds of products, you'll want to move up the scale in complexity and price and choose a service such as www.bigcommerce.com or www.shopify.com. At the high end of the shopping service, you could create a site as complex as Amazon.com with the tools offered at www.Magento.com.

Sharing Your Computer Screen Remotely

Often when you're designing a website, you'll want to show your site to someone (a client, a friend) before you publish it on the public web. That's where remote screen sharing can come in handy.

With a growing list of online collaboration tools, you can show what you're doing on your computer to anyone who has access to the Internet. At the high-end of the spectrum, Adobe Connect, at www.adobe.com/adobeconnect, provides a collaborative sharing environment with chat features and the capability to moderate questions, making it ideal for large presentations and online classes and webinars.

If you just want to share your screen with one other person, my favorite tool is Skype. I've long loved Skype for its capability to make phone calls over the Internet for little or no cost, but the latest version includes a Share My Screen option that is free and super easy to use. Both computers must have the Skype software and accounts on Skype (download the program and set up your account for free at www.skype.com). After you've logged in and initiated a call between your two computers, click the Sharing icon (just to the right of the Video icon) and choose Share My Screen from the pop-up window.

Another useful sharing service can be found at https://join.me, a quick and easy-to-use service that works on Mac and Windows computers, as well as many mobile devices.

Keeping Track of Traffic

Most web-hosting services provide basic log reports and traffic information, but if you want more detailed reports about how people are finding your website and what they're doing after they arrive, consider using a service such as Google Analytics (www.google.com/analytics), StatCounter.com (www.statcounter.com), or WebSTAT.com (www.webstat.com).

To use any of these services, set up an account and copy a bit of code from the site to your web pages. (The procedure is a simple copy and paste that you can do in Code view in Dreamweaver.) Google Analytics, StatCounter, and other services then use that bit of code to track your traffic.

Visit any of the services, such as Google Analytics (the most popular of these tools), for a demo and a sample report that illustrates the kind of information you can collect, including what search terms someone used to find your site through a search engine. Studying how people use your website is one of the best ways to determine how to improve your site's content and design.

For instructions on how to copy and paste code from a site such as Google Analytics into the pages of your site in Dreamweaver, read the tutorial on Google Analytics on my website at www.DigitalFamily.com/dreamweaver.

Taking Your Site's Temperature with a Heat Map

Adding a heat map to your website is a great way to discover what people find most interesting on each page of your site. Analytics, covered in the preceding section, measure overall traffic patterns on the different pages of your site; a heat map shows you the popularity of the different elements on each page of your website.

When you add a heat map to your site, you get a visual snapshot showing "hot areas" — the links, text, images, and other elements on a page that attract the most attention from your visitors. To learn more about how heat maps work, visit www.clickdensity.com or www.crazyegg.com, shown in Figure 14-2.

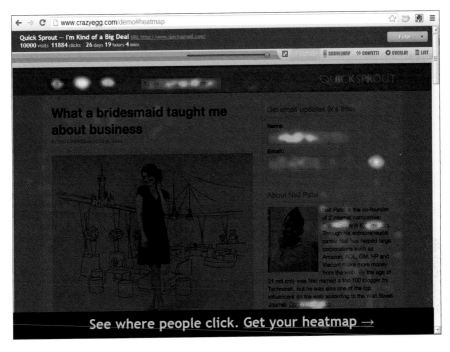

Figure 14-2: Heat maps show you where visitors go on your pages.

Surveying Your Visitors

Want to know what your visitors really think? Ask them. You can create a free online survey at www.SurveyMonkey.com and link to it from your website. With SurveyMonkey, you create the survey using a web browser. The site then automatically tallies the results and presents them in a series of reports and pie charts. The survey results are a great way to impress your board of directors at the next annual meeting.

Prefer to create an interactive quiz that you can embed directly into the pages of your site? Visit www.quizrevolution.com, where you can design quizzes with a service that automatically scores each quiz taker and includes the option to add bonus instructions or tips.

Keeping Up with Web Standards at W3.org

If you want to keep up with the latest developments in web design and make sure you're following standards, you'll find no better place than www. W3.org, the official website of the organization that sets web standards. This nonprofit site provides loads of information, including the full specification for HTML and CSS.

In Chapter 4, you find instructions for testing your web pages with Dreamweaver's validation tools. For more advanced testing, or for testing sites you've already published to the web, the W3C offers online testing tools. You can use these sites to test your web pages for compliance with W3C standards by entering a page's URL in the CSS validator at http://jigsaw. w3.org/css-validator/ or the MarkUp validator at http://validator .w3.org/.

Extending Dreamweaver at Adobe.com

Visit the Dreamweaver Exchange Site at www.adobeexchange.com/ to find a vast collection of extensions you can use to add behaviors and other features to Dreamweaver. To install them, use Extension Manager, which I cover in Chapter 11.

While you're at the site, check out the growing collection of Adobe tutorials, updates, and resources at www.adobe.com/devnet/dreamweaver. Among the resources, check out the new CSS section, where you'll find the latest in CSS tips, tricks, and workarounds.

Ten Ways to Promote Your Site

In This Chapter

▷ Optimizing your site for search engines

▷ Paying for keywords on search engines

▷ Building contacts on social networking sites

▷ Ranking on social bookmarking sites

▷ Adding social media share buttons to your site

▷ Attracting return visitors with regular updates

▷ Getting mentioned in traditional media

▷ Spreading the word with viral marketing

▷ Blogging

▷ Finding useful ideas on other websites

*W*hat if you build a website and nobody comes? Unfortunately, that problem is all too common, which is why I've chosen to end this book by pointing you to a few places where you can promote your website. Driving large amounts of traffic to the pages of a site often requires an investment of time, a compelling product or message, money, a viral hit, or dumb luck. Improve your odds and save your budget with this chapter's tips, which are designed to help you attract the right visitors to your website.

Scoring High in Search Engines

Search engine optimization, or *SEO,* has evolved from an esoteric dark art to the hottest buzzword on the web. Basically, SEO is a process designed to help you attract more attention from search engines such as Google, Bing, and Yahoo! The goal is to get your site higher on the search results page than your competitors.

Why all this search engine secrecy?

Because much money can be made when your site appears at the top of search results lists, web marketers spend countless hours testing how search engines work to come up with their best guesses about the criteria that search engines are using and how best to move their sites up the list. The people who run sites such as Google and Bing, however, want to deliver the best results when someone conducts a search — not just a list of the sites that reflect the ability of smart web marketers to figure out how to trick their way into the top position. The result is a cat-and-mouse game, with search engines changing the rules to thwart the most calculated efforts of specialists in SEO, and people who specialize in SEO charging big bucks to figure out the secret formula that can put you on top of the search results.

Scoring high in web searches is complicated because millions of sites vie for the top spots and search engines use complex formulas to determine which website should match any given keyword search. Search engines also guard their formulas for prioritizing websites and search ranking more carefully than Coca-Cola guards its recipe. And if all that secrecy doesn't make search engine optimization complicated enough, most search engines change their formulas regularly. (*How* regularly is also secret, although major updates and changes are often publicly announced.)

Building a website today without considering SEO is like opening a store in a dark alley with no advertising. Letting people know that your site exists is vital. A good way to start is to create a Google Webmaster Tools account at www.google.com/webmasters/.

A detailed explanation of SEO and how best to optimize your pages is beyond the scope of this book, but I've added a section on my website with a collection of the most important tips and instructions for making sure your website is optimized for search engines. Visit www.digitalfamily.com/tutorials/seo-and-dreamweaver/.

Buying Traffic (Yes, You Really Can!)

In addition to the natural results that search engines deliver when someone does a keyword search, buying keywords on search engines helps to ensure that your site is listed when someone searches for words that are relevant to your site, although the process is far more complex than most people realize. Search engine ads generally appear at the top and right side of most search result pages.

Not all keywords sell for the same price. Using a complex bidding process, most search engines charge significantly more for the most popular keywords. Adding to the complexity, the results of those keywords for your site can vary dramatically based on a dizzying array of factors. For example, the expensive keyword *Hawaii* may bring the most amount of traffic to your site, but the lower-priced keyword phrase *best Hawaiian luau* may result in more reservations to your hotel. Because it's possible to measure not only the traffic from a keyword search but also the actions of the person who clicks that keyword, you can calculate and compare the effectiveness of nearly every aspect of search engine advertising.

Again, this process can be highly complex. Just consider the following:

✔ **The real art of developing a list of keywords for search engine advertising requires more than just brainstorming a few words related to your business.** The best SEO companies come up with hundreds or thousands of keywords and phrases and then track the results to find the best return on each dollar spent for the keywords (for example, how many paying customers arrive via each keyword or phrase and how much they buy). Thus, running a campaign with 10,000 words might not cost much more than running a campaign with 100 words and might prove much more effective over time.

✔ **The most sophisticated ad campaigns involve creating special web pages to go with each keyword ad.** For example, you can create a special page (often called a *landing page*) on your Hawaiian hotel site for people who click the search term *scuba diving* that is different from the page for those who click the search term *luau.*

You can learn more about how to make the most of your keyword ads by carefully reading the instructions and tips on any site where you plan to advertise.

Google AdSense offers the largest online advertising program for keywords. Just visit www.google.com/adsense to find detailed instructions and a number of tips and tools to help you develop the best campaign and measure the results.

In addition to buying ads on Google, you can include Google Ads on your own website to earn advertising income. This program is called Google AdWords, and you can learn more about it at adwords.google.com. Google often gives away $100 coupons in AdWords to web developers who use their Webmaster Tools (including Google Analytics). Signing up for a Google Webmaster Tools account at www.google.com/webmasters/ is also a valuable way to build traffic to your website.

Using Social Networking Sites for Promotion

Social networking, the art of meeting and building contacts through social media websites, has become the most popular activity on the Internet. As we live more of our lives online, social networks have become a powerful way to build connections, attract new clients, find discounts, or get a new job. On the most popular social media sites, you can create personal profiles as well as professional pages, which are an increasingly important way to drive traffic to your website and promote your business, brand, or organization.

Here's what you can expect to find among the most popular social networking sites:

- **Facebook** (www.facebook.com): Facebook wins top place as the largest social networking site on the web, and its broad appeal makes it an excellent place to promote your website. Facebook was originally considered a vanity site and a place for college students, but its professional power is growing with its ever-expanding audience. With more than 1 billion members, Facebook is by far the most important, and most active, of the social media sites to date.

- **LinkedIn** (www.linkedin.com): LinkedIn is the site for *professional* connections and online business networking. If you're online to develop business contacts with other professionals, especially if you're job hunting or trying to attract new business clients, LinkedIn is a powerful place to promote yourself and your website. Unlike Facebook and Myspace, LinkedIn is all business.

- **Twitter** (www.twitter.com): Once derided as an insipid waste of time, where people fired off short messages about trivial details of life, Twitter has evolved into an international force to be reckoned with. Best described as microblogging, Twitter makes it easy to connect with people online and share brief bursts of information, called *Tweets.* Twitter limits you to no more than 140 characters per post, but that brevity seems to be the secret to Twitter's success. Athletes, celebrities, politicians, and all types of so-called experts use Twitter to connect directly with their audiences, one brief message at a time. It takes a while to get the hang of the terse, abbreviation-heavy Tweetspeak language, which includes the use of special characters, such as the hash tag (#) to indicate a topic (such as *#Dreamweaver* in posts about the software) or the at sign (@) in posts about a person. (As in, follow me @janinewarner.)

  Because you can post to Twitter from a computer, a cell phone, or any other Internet-enabled device, and because the posts are so brief, people tend to update Twitter more frequently than other services, making it a great place to follow trends, news events, and other information in real time. Like all social networks, Twitter is constantly evolving, so it's a good idea to read other people's posts for a while to get the hang of it before you start to participate. Follow a few friends or experts to see how they use the service.

- **Google**+ (www.plus.google.com): The newest entry in the social media scene is Google's competitor to Facebook, known as Google+. Launched in the summer of 2011, Google+ quickly turned into a must-have for every self-respecting web geek because membership was initially limited only to people who managed to finagle an invitation. The principal difference between Google+ and other social networking sites (such as Facebook) is that Google+ starts out by encouraging you to put your friends into circles. Google circles provide a way to organize the people you know into categories, allowing you to choose what information and updates you share with each group.

- **Pinterest** (www.pinterest.com): This highly visual site exploded on the social media scene and became the fastest growing site in 2012. Especially popular among designers, artists, fashionistas, and other creative people, Pinterest makes it easy to "pin" and share images in collections called *boards,* as shown in Figure 15-1.

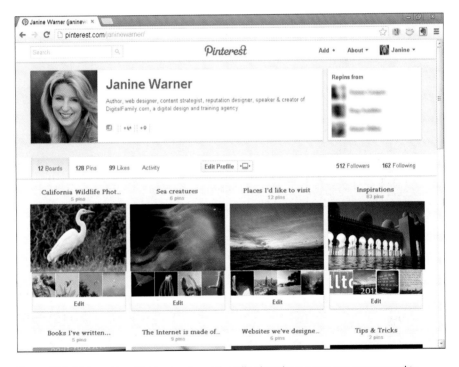

Figure 15-1: Pinterest is a highly visual social media site where users are encouraged to share images.

  ✔ **Myspace** (www.myspace.com): Once the most popular social networking site, Myspace now exists mostly to help musicians promote new songs and for movie studios to release movie trailers. Myspace's redesign attracted some new attention to this site, but it's still not clear if the site has much to offer to anyone who is not promoting music or videos.

Increasing Your Ranking on Social Bookmarking Sites

Social bookmarking sites rank the popularity of web pages by the number of votes they get. As a result, these sites are excellent resources for people who want to keep up with what's popular online. Most enable anyone to vote on a site.

Getting your site listed on social bookmarking sites is a highly effective way to increase traffic. Dozens of these sites and services exist (with more sure to come), and they feature catchy and unusual names, such as Delicious (delicious.com), StumbleUpon (www.stumbleupon.com), and reddit (www.reddit.com).

Although you can submit your own pages on any of these sites, that practice is generally frowned upon and you can be banned if you do it too frequently. Besides, your one little vote won't make much difference. A better method is to add a button to your site from each of these services so that visitors can easily vote for you. If you're a blogger, you can add a button each time you post. You can get the buttons (called *chiclets*) for free and add them to your pages by simply inserting a little code you generate on the social networking site.

Spreading the Love with Social Media Share Buttons

Want to know about one of the best ways to attract new visitors to your website? Make sure that current visitors can easily tell a friend about your site by enabling them to share your site's content on Facebook, Twitter, and other social media sites. Simply add social media share buttons to your pages. You'll find many services designed to help facilitate the connection between your site and social media sites, but www.addthis.com (see Figure 15-2) and share.lockerz.com are among my favorites. Simply sign up for a free account and then copy and paste a little code to your web page. Your visitors can then click an icon on your page to add a post about your site to their pages on social media sites.

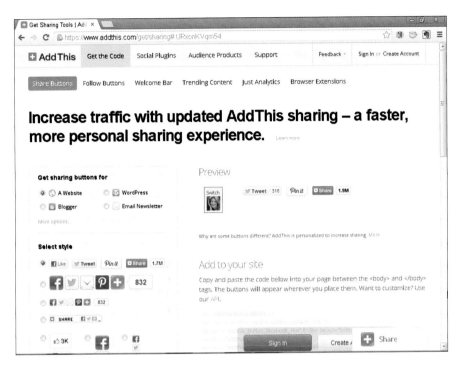

Figure 15-2: Include social media share buttons so your site visitors can tell their friends about you.

Enticing Visitors to Return for Updates

One of the best ways to improve traffic to your site is through repeat visitors, and regular updates to your site can make all the difference. If you want your visitors to know when to look for updates, consider making regular changes to your website. Add a post to your blog every Thursday morning, for example, or post your newest photos to your site every Saturday. Regular updates help get people in the habit of visiting your site.

Regularly updating your site can also help improve your ranking on Google, which seems to favor sites that have fresh content. Adding new posts, articles, and images can help attract more people to your site — as well as keep them coming back.

Marketing a Website to the Media

Attracting traditional media attention to your website is like attracting it to any other business. The trick is to tell a good story and get the attention of someone who can write about it in a publication that your target audience reads. If you're looking for press coverage, make sure to include a Press section on your website with contact information, story ideas, and any other press coverage you've received.

Don't wait for journalists to come to you! You should never pester a reporter with a barrage of e-mails, press releases, or phone calls, but a well-timed or well-pitched message can get the attention of a reporter *and* the desired result — your web address in the press. One good way to find journalists who might be interested in your site is to visit related sites and study their Press sections to find out who has been writing about the site. Note not only the publication but also the writer. Then send a note directly to that person with a message that starts like this:

> Dear *fabulous technology journalist* <insert *that person's name,* of course, such as Dear David Pogue>:

> I enjoyed reading the article you wrote on the XYZ company and thought that you might be interested in what we're doing.

Keep your message brief, and try to include a news hook and a story idea that go beyond just promoting your business. For example, rather than tell a reporter that you have the best B&B site in northern California, pitch a story about the best hikes in the area. With any luck, the article on great hikes will include a quote from you and a mention of your B&B's website (especially if the reporter can send readers to your online list of hiking tips).

Unleashing the Power of Viral Marketing

Viral marketing is another marketing industry buzzword for the digital age. The idea is that a message (a video, an article, or a photo, for example) is so exciting, fun, and compelling that people share it by passing it on to their friends, who then pass it on to their friends, until the message spreads like a virus. Such messages are often sent by e-mail, blogs, or chat, which can make the ever-expanding effect happen at an almost instantaneous pace.

Tap in to the power of viral marketing, and you can become an overnight sensation. Humor seems to be the most effective strategy. Among the mainstays of the viral phenomena are those silly photos of cats with clever sayings. Known as the LOL cats, these photos have spawned several websites, such as `www.icanhascheezburger.com`. Funny video clips — the kind you would expect to see featured on a show such as *America's Funniest Home Videos* — are also highly viral because they're shared around the web.

To use viral marketing to attract traffic to your website, include a section with funny photos, industry jokes, or a top-ten list, and you might just get visitors to tell their friends about your site.

Blogging, Blogging, Blogging

Blogs are designed for frequent updates, so creating a blog for your website makes it easy to add fresh content. If you become a blogger, you'll also join the ranks of a prolific group of writers who regularly refer their readers to each other's website.

Don't launch a blog without considering the commitment it requires. For your blog to attract traffic and serve as an effective marketing tool, you must

- Feature interesting, relevant information for your audience.
- Update the blog regularly.
- Take the time to participate in other blogs. Adding relevant tips and thoughtful comments to other people's blogs is an excellent way to get their visitors to come to your website.

Check out *Blogging For Dummies,* 4th Edition, by Susannah Gardner and Shane Birley, if you're interested in exploring blogging.

Gathering Ideas from Other Websites

One of the best ways to create good habits in web design is to visit the websites of others and study what works and what doesn't on their pages. In particular:

- Pay special attention to the title of the page, descriptive text, and keywords used throughout the site.
- Ask yourself what you like about the site and why you like it.
- Determine whether you can easily find the information you're most interested in and how easily you can navigate around the site.

Sometimes the best way to discover the problems in your own website is to look for problems on someone else's site and then return to yours with a fresh perspective. The Internet changes every day. Keeping an eye on what other sites are doing is a great way to stay informed about new technologies, new social media sites, and other ways of promoting your site.

Index

• *M* •

Macs
  installing required software for
    templates, 14
  local site folder, 38
  previewing images, 76
  Windows hardware versus, 91
Magento, 359
main pages, 56
MAMP.com, 14
Manage Fonts dialog box, 146–147
Manage Sites dialog box, 39–41
Map (Map Name) attribute, Property
    Inspector, 78
Margin Collapse rule, HTML, 198
Margin option, CSS Property panel, 143
margins
  centering page layouts with CSS, 197–200
  changing with Page Properties dialog box,
    48–49
  in CSS styles, 195–197
markup, HTML, 17
MarkUp validator, W3.org, 362
matte colors, in images, 74
Max Height option, CSS Property panel, 142
Max Width option, CSS Property panel, 142
Max-Width field, Media Queries
    dialog box, 239
media, marketing websites to, 370
Media Insert panel, 32, 329–330
@media panel, 238
media queries, CSS, 220–221, 236–240
menu bar, 29
Merge Selected Cells Using Spans icon,
    Property inspector, 276, 279
meta tags, 61–62
Microsoft Internet Explorer, 97
Microsoft Windows
  Apple Mac hardware versus, 91
  installing required software for
    templates, 14
  local site folder, 38
  previewing images, 76
  viewing file extensions, 45

Microsoft Windows 7, 76
Microsoft Windows Vista, 76
Microsoft Windows XP, 76
Microsoft Word, 52
Min Height option, CSS Property panel, 142
Min Width option, CSS Property panel, 142
minus sign (–)
  Manage Sites dialog box, 40
  removing accordion panel, 312
  removing orientation field from Media
    Queries dialog box, 238–239
Min-Width field, Media Queries
    dialog box, 239
Missing Alt Text option, Site Reporting
    feature, 104
Mobile button, status bar, 34
mobile devices
  adaptive versus responsive design, 219–220
  Adobe Flash, 328
  designing simple pages for, 102
  testing sites for, 99–101
mobile layout styles, 220–224, 230–232
Mobile Size icon, Page dialog box, 317
Mobile Starters option, New Document
    window, 43
mobile websites, 224
monitors
  adaptive versus responsive design, 219–220
  custom media queries, CSS, 236
  differences in web page appearance
    depending on resolution, 91–92
  fluid grid layouts, 220–224
  recommended page width, 195
  remote screen sharing, 359
  screen readers, 274
  testing sites for different sizes, 99–101
.mov (QuickTime) format, 340
Move Up a Row arrow, workspace, 232–233
Mozilla Firefox, 97
MP3 format, 342
MP4 format, 339, 341, 345–347
multimedia
  adding audio and video files to web
    pages, 343–351
  Adobe Edge Animate files, 334–337

ple & Mac

ad For Dummies,
h Edition
8-1-118-49823-1

hone 5 For Dummies,
h Edition
8-1-118-35201-4

acBook For Dummies,
h Edition
8-1-118-20920-2

X Mountain Lion
r Dummies
8-1-118-39418-2

ogging & Social Media

cebook For Dummies,
h Edition
8-1-118-09562-1

om Blogging
r Dummies
8-1-118-03843-7

nterest For Dummies
8-1-118-32800-2

ordPress For Dummies,
h Edition
8-1-118-38318-6

usiness

ommodities For Dummies,
d Edition
8-1-118-01687-9

vesting For Dummies,
h Edition
8-0-470-90545-6

Personal Finance
For Dummies,
7th Edition
978-1-118-11785-9

QuickBooks 2013
For Dummies
978-1-118-35641-8

Small Business Marketing Kit
For Dummies,
3rd Edition
978-1-118-31183-7

Careers

Job Interviews
For Dummies,
4th Edition
978-1-118-11290-8

Job Searching with
Social Media
For Dummies
978-0-470-93072-4

Personal Branding
For Dummies
978-1-118-11792-7

Resumes For Dummies,
6th Edition
978-0-470-87361-8

Success as a Mediator
For Dummies
978-1-118-07862-4

Diet & Nutrition

Belly Fat Diet For Dummies
978-1-118-34585-6

Eating Clean For Dummies
978-1-118-00013-7

Nutrition For Dummies,
5th Edition
978-0-470-93231-5

Digital Photography

Digital Photography
For Dummies,
7th Edition
978-1-118-09203-3

Digital SLR Cameras &
Photography For Dummies,
4th Edition
978-1-118-14489-3

Photoshop Elements 11
For Dummies
978-1-118-40821-6

Gardening

Herb Gardening
For Dummies,
2nd Edition
978-0-470-61778-6

Vegetable Gardening
For Dummies,
2nd Edition
978-0-470-49870-5

Health

Anti-Inflammation Diet
For Dummies
978-1-118-02381-5

Diabetes For Dummies,
3rd Edition
978-0-470-27086-8

Living Paleo For Dummies
978-1-118-29405-5

Hobbies

Beekeeping
For Dummies
978-0-470-43065-1

eBay For Dummies,
7th Edition
978-1-118-09806-6

Raising Chickens
For Dummies
978-0-470-46544-8

Wine For Dummies,
5th Edition
978-1-118-28872-6

Writing Young Adult Fiction
For Dummies
978-0-470-94954-2

Language &
Foreign Language

500 Spanish Verbs
For Dummies
978-1-118-02382-2

English Grammar
For Dummies,
2nd Edition
978-0-470-54664-2

French All-in One
For Dummies
978-1-118-22815-9

German Essentials
For Dummies
978-1-118-18422-6

Italian For Dummies,
2nd Edition
978-1-118-00465-4

e **Available in print and e-book formats.**

ailable wherever books are sold. For more information or to order direct: U.S. customers visit www.Dummies.com or call 1-877-762-2974.
U.K. customers visit www.Wileyeurope.com or call (0) 1243 843291. Canadian customers visit www.Wiley.ca or call 1-800-567-4797.
Connect with us online at www.facebook.com/fordummies or @fordummies

Math & Science

Algebra I For Dummies,
2nd Edition
978-0-470-55964-2

Anatomy and Physiology
For Dummies,
2nd Edition
978-0-470-92326-9

Astronomy For Dummies,
3rd Edition
978-1-118-37697-3

Biology For Dummies,
2nd Edition
978-0-470-59875-7

Chemistry For Dummies,
2nd Edition
978-1-1180-0730-3

Pre-Algebra Essentials
For Dummies
978-0-470-61838-7

Microsoft Office

Excel 2013 For Dummies
978-1-118-51012-4

Office 2013 All-in-One
For Dummies
978-1-118-51636-2

PowerPoint 2013
For Dummies
978-1-118-50253-2

Word 2013 For Dummies
978-1-118-49123-2

Music

Blues Harmonica
For Dummies
978-1-118-25269-7

Guitar For Dummies,
3rd Edition
978-1-118-11554-1

iPod & iTunes
For Dummies,
10th Edition
978-1-118-50864-0

Programming

Android Application
Development For
Dummies, 2nd Edition
978-1-118-38710-8

iOS 6 Application
Development For Dummies
978-1-118-50880-0

Java For Dummies,
5th Edition
978-0-470-37173-2

Religion & Inspiration

The Bible For Dummies
978-0-7645-5296-0

Buddhism For Dummies,
2nd Edition
978-1-118-02379-2

Catholicism For Dummies,
2nd Edition
978-1-118-07778-8

Self-Help & Relationships

Bipolar Disorder
For Dummies,
2nd Edition
978-1-118-33882-7

Meditation For Dummies,
3rd Edition
978-1-118-29144-3

Seniors

Computers For Seniors
For Dummies,
3rd Edition
978-1-118-11553-4

iPad For Seniors
For Dummies,
5th Edition
978-1-118-49708-1

Social Security
For Dummies
978-1-118-20573-0

Smartphones & Tablets

Android Phones
For Dummies
978-1-118-16952-0

Kindle Fire HD
For Dummies
978-1-118-42223-6

NOOK HD For Dummies,
Portable Edition
978-1-118-39498-4

Surface For Dummies
978-1-118-49634-3

Test Prep

ACT For Dummies,
5th Edition
978-1-118-01259-8

ASVAB For Dummies,
3rd Edition
978-0-470-63760-9

GRE For Dummies,
7th Edition
978-0-470-88921-3

Officer Candidate Tests,
For Dummies
978-0-470-59876-4

Physician's Assistant Exam
For Dummies
978-1-118-11556-5

Series 7 Exam
For Dummies
978-0-470-09932-2

Windows 8

Windows 8 For Dummies
978-1-118-13461-0

Windows 8 For Dummies,
Book + DVD Bundle
978-1-118-27167-4

Windows 8 All-in-One
For Dummies
978-1-118-11920-4

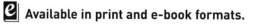 **Available in print and e-book formats.**

Take Dummies with you everywhere you go!

Whether you're excited about e-books, want more from the web, must have your mobile apps, or swept up in social media, Dummies makes everything easier .

Visit Us

Like Us

Follow Us

Watch Us

Join Us

Pin Us

Circle Us

Shop Us

Dummies products make life easier

- DIY
- Consumer Electronics
- Crafts
- Software
- Cookware
- Hobbies
- Videos
- Music
- Games
- and More!

For more information, go to **Dummies.com**® and search the store by category.

Born in Scotland, Andrew worked as a research scientist for almost a decade, on projects including DNA synthesis, forensics, and drug development. His short fiction has featured in several anthologies published by Fox Spirit books and his fantasy novel serial on Wattpad amassed nearly 175,000 reads.

The Hunter is his debut novel.

Praise for *The Hunter*:

'Reid's debut hits like a spin-kick. *The Hunter* is razor-sharp action from start to finish.'
James Swallow, bestselling author of *Nomad*

'Non-stop action all the way, packed with graphic violence and mayhem, hi-tech chicanery and suavely dangerous villains bent on taking over the world.'
Irish Independent

'This is top drawer stuff, and should give Lee Child and Simon Kernick a few sleepless nights.'
James Oswald, bestselling author of the Inspector McLean series

'*The Hunter* is an exhilarating, action-packed, gripping tale. Andrew Reid has written a real page turner that thrills and entertains from start to finish.'
Adam Hamdy, author of the Pendulum series

THE
HUNTER
ANDREW REID

HEADLINE

First published in 2018 by
HEADLINE PUBLISHING GROUP

First published in paperback in 2018 by
HEADLINE PUBLISHING GROUP

3

Cataloguing in Publication Data is available from the British Library

ISBN 978 1 4722 5635 5

Typeset in Adobe Garamond by Avon DataSet Ltd,
Bidford-on-Avon, Warwickshire

Printed and bound in Great Britain by CPI Group (UK) Ltd,
Croydon, CR0 4YY

HEADLINE PUBLISHING GROUP
An Hachette UK Company
Carmelite House
50 Victoria Embankment
London EC4Y 0DZ

www.headline.co.uk
www.hachette.co.uk

For Lisa

. . . there is an area of town for degenerates and an area of town for the working class. There is nothing positive gained from having them so close to us. It's a burden and a liability having them so close to us. Believe me, if they added the smallest iota of value I'd consider thinking different . . .

Silicon Valley CEO, 2013

Chapter 1

On the highway, the snow is already thick enough that Cameron can't make out the center line. There are tracks where other cars have been – trucks, maybe, from the width of them – but they're fading fast into the static fuzz of the blizzard. About a mile back, they'd passed two cars pulled over, the syncopated orange blink of their hazard lights soaked up by the falling snow. The barrier is still there, the white-crested strip of silver just visible on the right-hand side of the car, and Cameron can't help but think about what happens when a car hits it. They're built to break, to take an impact, bolts popping free and a few hundred feet of steel bending like a weighted rope as it soaks up the force needed to decelerate two tons and change without killing everyone inside. Even in the best-case scenario, if you had no choice but to hit it, you want to hit it as slow as you can. Right now, the speedometer reads eighty-two miles per hour.

The whole car lurches forward as Nate puts his foot down, and for a dizzy instant the back of the car feels as though it is sliding free of the road. According to the radio, the worst of the weather was supposed to be hitting over to the east. Either the forecast was lying or everyone due east is digging in right now to welcome in the end times. Cameron's gut goes cold, and she glances across at her brother. Not for the first time tonight, she wonders what the hell his problem is. There's no emergency that she knows of. Just some business opportunity he pitched her a couple of days ago that turned into a dinner meeting. He's always had a good head for that kind of thing. He left a high-paying position with a multinational biotech firm to join her team, taking the computer systems he'd built to track epidemics and using them to predict how brands go viral instead. Ever since, he's been a key player in landing some of her best endorsement deals – but it's late in the year to be thinking about signing something new. She only agreed to go with him because she trusted his instincts. Now, though, she's starting to wonder if there's something else going on.

'You sure you should be going this fast?' she asks.

Nate doesn't answer. He's got a hard-jawed look that doesn't suit his face, and he glances up at the mirror quickly before hunching back over the wheel. He's gripping it in both hands, like a learner driver, his chin thrust forward. He's wearing a big jacket that hides his skinny frame, and even though the aircon in the car is blasting them with heat, he's got a scarf jammed up tight around his neck like any second now he expects to be out in the cold. Cameron clears her throat.

'Nate. Slow the car down. Now.' She can hear her mom in her voice. Something about it always goes south when she tries to sound like a hard-ass. Normally she hates the sound of it, but then maybe it's the kind of push that Nate needs right now.

He swallows hard before he answers. Nervous. Guilty. 'You ever get into trouble, Cam?' He doesn't look at her.

2

Oh Nate, she thinks, *what have you got into?*

'Enough.' Fighters get into nothing but trouble. Even with a good manager, a really good lawyer, and as clean a promoter as she could find, there had still been a few close moments that she'd rather not have to remember. One time she'd got back from a weigh-in to find a picture tucked inside her kit bag, next to her wraps. It was a picture of her parents' home: cheap paper, a little blurred from the printer, but unmistakable for what it was. There had been a phone number on the back. Cameron had been so angry that she had sidestepped everyone – her lawyer, her manager, even Nate – to get it dealt with quickly. That decision had been a whole other kind of trouble, and it had taught her one thing. 'Enough to know you can't outrun it,' she says.

Nate nods, swallows again. Worries at his lip like he's trying to work something out. Cameron has seen that look before. More brains than sense, their dad always said, but then Nate overthinking every damn detail has saved her career more than once. Clauses in contracts that her manager had missed; a guy in the crowd he'd seen in another fighter's entourage weeks before, waiting to spray oil of wintergreen in her face during the walk-in. His face is blue in the light from the low-beams reflected back through the windshield by the falling snow. 'I'm not trying to outrun it, Cam.'

'Trying to get us killed?' She tries to say it lightly, make it a joke, but it catches in her throat and comes out high and scared.

When he answers, his voice is far away. Like he's forgotten that they're pushing ninety along a skating rink disguised as a highway. 'You ever wonder if it's possible to just . . . disappear?'

3

Don't let him do this. Cameron checks that her seat belt is fastened. She's already running through the options, her brain switching on to automatic. Can't pull the handbrake. Can't fight over the wheel. Both of those would crash the car. She could hit him, catch the angle of his jaw with just the right amount of force to cold-cock him, and get a hold of the wheel. The only thing that stays her hand is that it's Nate. Geeky, dumb, dependable, big brother Nate. In her whole life, he has never once let her down. Not one time.

'Whatever's happening, Nate, you can talk to me.'

Nate turns and looks at her, the long angles of his face softening. It's not fondness. It's like he's relieved. 'You know, I really can't.'

The way he looks at her snaps something inside of Cameron. It's like the last time he'll see her. *Do something.* She reaches down past the handbrake and pops his seat belt, the buckle whipping across his chest and catching under his left armpit. There's a sour twist of triumph, an echo of the feeling she gets when she outmaneuvers someone on the mat. He has to slow down now. The crash would kill him.

Nate nods at her like they've just shook hands on a deal, like this was what he was waiting for, then wrenches the wheel two-handed, a quick swing to the right that takes them on to the verge and then back again, hard over to the left.

The Lexus fishtails in answer, and as their forward momentum suddenly becomes sideways the car flips, driver-side wheels peeling reluctantly off the tarmac then springing skywards as it turns up and over.

It's like a hip throw. Cameron feels the jolt, the sudden violent motion, and in its wake the drawn-out moment of

4

almost weightlessness as the whole car goes over.

Time goes slower when you're upside down. Cameron sees the snow spiraling through the windshield, like it's the whole world turning and not her, and she has more than enough time to recognize that queasy lurch of shock, the dawning awareness that you're no longer in control of the fight. That what comes next is a world of hurt, and there isn't a damn thing you can do about it.

When the car lands on its roof, it's like being hit with a sledgehammer. Cameron sees nothing but sparks, like purple snow swirling across her vision; feels nothing but the impact, a bone-deep jolt that shakes every single joint in her body loose. She's never been hit so hard in her life and then she's weightless again as the car bounces and makes another three-sixty turn about its long axis.

They tumble twice more, or fifty times – she can't keep track of how many it really is – and at the last something in the roof gives way with a shriek and some fucker chooses that exact moment to kick her in the head.

Cameron is eight years old again, and she's just lost her first fight. In fairness, nobody ever wins when they fight gravity. She lay for a long time on the asphalt not daring to move, because moving made her leg hurt more than anything had ever hurt before.

It was Nate who came looking for her, eleven years old and not quite strong enough to carry Cameron's weight but he did it anyway, hauling her crying on to his back and walking her home, step by heavy step. Cameron's crying from the pain and doesn't hear him wheezing, struggling for every breath, doesn't realize

5

what's happened until they get home and the ambulance comes and it's not for her.

She asks her mom why he did it, lying in bed with her bandaged ankle like a hot coal at the end of her leg. She asks why he carried her all that way when he knew it was hurting him.

'Because he's your brother,' she says, almost scolding her, as though she's shocked it needs to be said at all.

Cameron wakes up to blinking lights, red and blue flicker; the crunch of boots on fresh snow; the buzz of radio static and the ticks and creaks of metal under stress. There's a hiss of hydraulic pressure, loud enough to startle her fully awake, and she realizes that she's upside down in the wreckage, halfway out of her seat belt, pinned in place between the buckled seat back and what's left of the glove compartment. She's not sure if there's no pain at all, or just too much of it to process.

'Nate?'

It comes out as a whisper. She tries to take a deeper breath, but there's not enough room for her chest to expand. A couple more inches and she wouldn't be breathing at all. She'll take the whisper.

'Nate?'

There's a wedge of fresh air down by her right arm, cubes of safety glass crusted round the edge of what once was a window like salt round the rim of a cocktail glass. A pair of boots appear, turn into gloved hands as whoever's out there gets down on their knees, and finally a face. Cameron can't make out much of his face – he's nothing more than a pink blur right now – but she knows it's not Nate.

'Ho-ho-holy shit,' he says, and Cameron tries not to panic, tries to keep her shit together enough that she doesn't hyperventilate. Control your breathing when you're in a tight spot: that's what she knows, what she clings to. Make the best of the air you've got. He's looking away now, fumbling for something, and Cameron thinks of the hydraulic hiss she heard. The jaws of life. They're going to cut her out of the car. She's going to live.

The man grunts, sliding down on to his side so he can get an arm inside the car. His forearm presses up against Cameron's, and the contact sends pain coursing through her. Every last scrap of self-control she had is taken from her by it, and she twitches and shrieks in her panic as his arm moves further into the car. He's holding something up by her face, and Cameron turns towards it. Whatever it is – water, painkillers, a bandage to stem some bleeding she hasn't noticed – it has to be important enough that he'd ram his arm into a car wreck to get it to her.

The flash goes off right in her face, and the reflex jerk of her body sends a fresh wave of pain through her. His arm snakes back out of the wreck and Cameron is dimly aware of the sound of him checking the photo and laughing to himself.

'Can't believe he did it,' he says. He's got a deep voice. Not local. 'He actually fucking did it.'

More footsteps, and a conversation that Cameron is just too angry to follow. She breathes slow through her nose, brings it all back under control. She's going to live. She's going to live, even if it's only just long enough to take that phone and feed it to its owner.

Time passes, and another face appears at the broken window. She didn't hear them coming, and she can't be sure she was conscious the whole time.

'Miss? Can you hear me?'

Cameron takes as deep a breath as her situation will allow. 'Yeah.'

'Great. That's great.' He sounds like a trainer complimenting her on a good combination. 'My name's Mike. Can you tell me yours?'

'Cameron.'

'Cameron. Okay. This is going to sound real funny, but don't try to move. We're going to get you out of there.'

'What about my brother?'

'Your brother?'

'My brother.' The confusion in his voice throws her. 'The – the driver. Is he alive?'

There's a long pause before he answers.

'Miss, you're the only person in the car.'

Cameron has questions – was he thrown clear? Have they started a search? – but something tightens in her chest and all she can do is gasp, her hands scrabbling against plastic and metal as though to somehow make up for the fact she can't breathe by grabbing hold of the air. She hears Mike swearing, and a flurry of movement, and with one final thought – *I'm tapping, you bastard, I'm tapping* – she sinks into darkness.

Chapter 2

There's nothing lost that can't be found again. Nothing ever disappears entirely. Money, assets, people: they all leave traces of their existence, scraps that – if you look at them all from the right angle, piece them together the right way – tell you how they passed out of view, and where they went. Like a puzzle. You work at it hard enough and clever enough, then the thing you're looking for will pop up as though you've called it.

That's been the truth of Cameron's world in the eighteen months since the crash. The eighteen months since her brother drove their car off the road and almost killed her. The eighteen months since she woke up and Nate was gone, vanished into a blizzard.

There's nothing lost that can't be found again. Not even Nate.

The light on Cameron's phone is blinking. She can see it in the corner of her eye, because she's been watching for it all along. Waiting for it has been a distraction, which goes a long way to solving the mystery of how she ended up caught in a headlock, side on, with only the frame of her arms to keep it from closing on her. She wants to tap out, to check out that blinking light, but there's such a thing as pride. She tightens her grip on the frame, left wrist in right hand, feeling the tension and the opposition of weight against her forearm. She focuses on it, all her attention now bent on this one, simple motion. Somewhere behind her over her left shoulder, a voice reminds her to breathe, to take her time. That this is easy, that to overthink it is to kill it. Listening to it makes her falter.

Her forearm trembles under the strain, and for a moment all she can think of is the fracture lines that thread the length of her radius, the pins they put in there to hold the puzzle-piece shards of bone in place while her body tried to fuse it all back together again. About what will happen to all those pins when her arm gives way.

Fuck it.

She can feel her jaw twitch, the unconscious acknowledgement that this is a bad idea, as she leans her weight into her right shoulder, swings her hips away and pushes up with her arm. They can put the pins back later if they need to. Her opponent is two hundred and fifty pounds and change, and as she pushes the bony blade of her forearm up into his neck all that weight stops working for him and starts working against him. He grunts, tries to force the headlock closed with strength alone, but physics is on her side. The biomechanical connection between arm, shoulder, and neck means that the more he pulls, the further his windpipe turns towards her arm. As he recoils from the sensation of being choked, he falls back and her legs scissor about his neck so that Cameron can reintroduce him to the same feeling from a brand-new angle. She counts to three in her head before he taps her on the leg and she lets go.

'Good.' The same soft voice that was telling her to breathe, now louder. Ludo, who runs the gym. 'Good escape.'

Cameron sits up, takes a kneeling position across from her training partner. He's an older guy, heavyset but not out of shape. He's flushed from all the grappling, but his breathing is steady. Ludo brought him along for the session and Cameron has already forgotten his name. She bows, lower than she needs to, and he bobs awkwardly in return. 'Thank you,' she says. 'Sorry to drag you out so far.'

'No, no. It's no problem.' He gets to his feet with surprising speed for a big man. Standing at six-two, he has a clear six inches on Cameron and still manages to look bashful. 'It's an honor to train with you.'

'Anytime, big guy.' She gives him *the smile*, the crooked half-cocked grin that she started off wearing as a shield whenever a camera was pointed at her, which ended up becoming her trademark look. Of all the things she lost, of all the things that have been taken from her, that smile is the one thing she would have missed the least. Figures.

There's a beat as his eyes flick up and look past her shoulder, and she can almost see Ludo nod his permission, before he swallows hard and braces himself. 'Can I have your autograph?'

'Yeah.' Cameron nods, relieved. The last guy Ludo brought had asked her out. 'Yeah, absolutely. You got something I can sign?'

'I-I'll go get it.' He hustles off to the men's room like there's a special offer on. Cameron watches him go, conscious of Ludo watching her.

'It wasn't a good escape,' she says. It wasn't. She can see the phone blinking at her, the urgent flicker of the green light, but she makes herself stay on the mat. Respect is the first thing you learn there. 'It didn't flow. I let doubt creep in. I left a gap.'

'It was a good escape.' Ludo paces round the edge of the mat and into her peripheral vision. He moves like a lion tamer pacing the circus ring, always measuring the distance. He doesn't quite meet her eyes, and she feels something tense up inside of her at that careful avoidance. The feeling that if he looked straight at her, he would see the truth; that he would see every one of her fears. 'You're careful of loading your injured arm. That you finished the escape is good.'

'It was sloppy.' Cameron shakes off the encouragement with a gesture towards the men's room. 'If he'd done the same, you would have chewed him out for it.'

'I would have.' Ludo nods. 'I would. Do you know why I asked him to come train with you?'

'He weighs a shit ton and he's a big enough fan that he'd take a two-hour drive before sun-up to get here?'

Ludo considers it for a moment. 'Well, yes and . . . yes. I chose him because he understands what we're doing here. He gets it.' His eyes lift to meet Cameron's, and she realizes that she was wrong before to think he'd see too far into her. Instead, she can see too far into him. 'That on the mat you're only ever fighting one person. Yourself.'

'Thanks, Yoda.'

He looks away again. 'I was wondering what had happened to the old Cam.'

'She got crushed by a car.'

Ludo's jaw tightens, and though neither of them moves Cameron can feel him pull away. He's not the only one who measures out distances. He lifts his chin. 'You should answer your phone. You've been staring at it since you came in here.'

'Thanks, Ludo.' Cameron bows, quick and formal, before stepping off the mat.

She unlocks her phone and checks the message: it's an automated notification from her computer at home. Cameron might need to sleep or train, but her computer is always working. That was one of the first things she learned after the crash. Sitting in a hospital bed trying to search for any news of Nate online, feeling the pain building as she tried to hold off pushing the button that would flood her system with morphine and send her crashing back into insensibility. The nurse on her ward brought up a guy from IT to show her how to automate it, and Cameron had never looked back. Community college had a bunch of coding classes that ran in the evenings, and the tutors had relished the opportunity to teach someone with Cameron's single-mindedness. Now, she's always connected. Always on.

Always searching.

The message is just an image, a little distorted on the small screen, but even so she can feel the thrill of victory as she recognizes the man pictured. It's a high angle, but his widow's peak and round face are unmistakable. *I've got you*, she thinks.

'Now there's a look I haven't seen in a long time,' Ludo says. Cameron starts, and looks up to find that Ludo has followed her off the mat. He's still keeping his distance, careful to stand so he's not able to see the screen on her phone. Even off the mat, he respects her boundaries.

'What look?'

'You used to get that look in the ring. Like you were about to pounce whether the ref called go or not. Tunnel vision.'

'Something like that.' She holds the phone up so he can see for a second. 'See this guy? He's wanted for a series of high-value frauds across ten states. Anyone that finds him is in for one hell of a payday.'

Ludo frowns. 'Bounty hunting.'

'It's called skip tracing.' Cameron shakes the phone, frustrated by the look he gives her. 'Ludo, this guy's a ghost. Most people when they skip town make maybe one or two new identities. He has hundreds. Similar names, similar social security numbers, all of them spread across the US. Almost all of them have assets. Some of them have jobs. Some even have death certificates. All of them are dead ends. Nobody has been able to pin him down in a year.'

'Until now.'

'Until now,' Cameron says. She looks down at the phone and swipes past the picture to the location details. West coast, of course, because God forbid her travel costs ever be anything less than the lion's share of her expenses. Another thing that's changed. All her sponsors had moved on after the crash ended her fight career, and while they'd been gracious enough to let her down easy by covering most of her hospital bill, Cameron had been forced to severely adjust her 'let someone else deal with it' approach to finances. It had been a crash course, but it had helped her in the end. She'd caught herself on the horns of a whole bunch of dead-end skips early on, and the experience had given her a good eye for spotting bad leads. In this business, *stay hungry* wasn't just some motto to wear on your workout top.

Everyone expected her to get over it, to move on. Everyone else did. Kids, weddings, divorces, the next fight. All Cameron had was the hunt.

The picture has come in from San Francisco, which makes a twisted kind of sense. If you're good with computers and want to get lost, head for a tech hub. Half the skips she's found to date have been guys that made the wrong call and tried to hole up in some tiny Midwestern hamlet with populations that barely scrape out of triple digits. One of them even made the local newspaper's 'Getting to Know Our Neighbor' section. He'd been gone two days before Cameron showed up on his doorstep, the local sheriff in tow.

'. . . find him?'

Cameron snaps out of her reverie and looks up at Ludo. 'Sorry?'

Ludo smirks. 'Tunnel vision. How did you find him?'

'Facial recognition. Got a program hooked up to webcam feeds from all over the US: parks, zoos, city squares.' She doesn't tell him she set it up to hunt for Nate. She doesn't need to. He knows why she retrained, burning through eighty- to a hundred-hour weeks building the rest of the skills she needed. *You're only ever fighting one person.* Cameron has only ever been hunting one, too. The other skips are just practice. It feels like Ludo can see right through her, and she covers by over-talking. 'Lot of local government overspent on kit to keep their budgets from getting cut, so there are plenty of twenty-four-hour high-definition feeds running, and all of them are completely open.'

Ludo's smirk fades as she talks, and before Cameron can say any more he's already shaking his head to stop her.

'I have no idea what you just said, but my son would probably love it.'

'Every family has a black sheep,' Cameron says. Ethan is fourteen and a handy resource. Cameron doesn't want to tell Ludo that his son was the one who hooked her up with the facial recognition software.

He spreads his hands. 'They love what they love.'

'Nate would like him.'

'He loves his computers.' Ludo doesn't specify who he's talking about. A lot of people make a point of using the past tense around her, but Ludo knows it pushes her buttons. He already has his escape lined up. 'You can't force it,' he says. 'Besides, Cleo's got enough fight in her for both of them. She told me she wants to grow up to be you.'

Cameron laughs. Ludo's daughter is five, and wears a permanent scowl like it's her armor against the world. 'With you training her? She's aiming too low.'

'So, you found him. What now?'

'Now I need to go print out a list of all the local aliases that could be him, and check them out.'

'You got a computer program for that, too?'

'I've got feet. Guys like this, you get one chance to catch them.' Cameron checks her watch. Eight a.m. Maybe enough time to build a list and winnow it down to the most likely candidates. 'I can be on a red-eye tonight.'

Ludo frowns. 'Take care of yourself. You need help, you let me know.'

Anyone else, Cameron would blow off. For Ludo, she takes it with a nod. Ask anyone in the Boston martial arts scene to name a trainer, *the* trainer, nine times out of ten Ludo's name would be the first out of their mouths. It had taken Cameron a long time to understand why that was. He didn't have any winners coming out of his club or any titles to speak of. Before the crash, his was the only club that ever turned her down for sessions. Afterwards, Ludo was the first and only one to ask if she'd like to train again. He'd come down to the hospital himself while she was still trying to get used to walking. After that, Cameron got it.

You're only ever fighting one person.

'Think fast, Cam.'

Cameron looks up to see her sparring partner returning, pen and pristine flier in hand. She recognizes it immediately: a promotional handbill from the last bout she fought, a month before the crash: Cameron in the foreground, fists raised; her opponent in miniature over her left shoulder, arms crossed. She can see the watermark, a matte crosshair against the glossy black background, and for a brief moment considers how much it must have cost to print them up like that just to match her brand. If her manager had had his way, they'd have had her in an orange vest and her opponent sporting a pair of antlers.

The big guy has come prepared: he's got a silver marker that will show up nicely against the black. She cracks *the smile* and too late realizes she can't remember his name. *Think fast.* Ludo knows it too, and he's grinning like the devil.

'Hey,' the guy says. 'Sorry I took so long. Didn't want to sweat all over it.'

'No problem.' Cameron takes the flier and the pen. 'You want this made out to you?'

'Please.'

'Just don't let me see this on the Internet going for a hundred bucks.' She shakes the pen to get the ink flowing while he makes vague sounds of protest at both the accusation and the value. Bending down to write, she pauses. 'You know, I've never been the best speller. Could you just spell your name for me real quick?'

There would be a beat of silence if Ludo wasn't coughing into it.

'Well, first there's an A, then there's an L.'

Cameron signs it quickly. 'I'm really sorry, Al.'

Al shakes his head as she hands the flier back to him, both of them taking care not to smudge the still-wet ink. 'No worries,' he says. 'It happens to me a lot.'

Cameron laughs, more genuine this time. 'You ever want to partner up again, let Ludo know. You're always welcome.'

'Really?' His face lights up like it's Christmas, and Cameron almost remembers what it was like to have fans. Back in the day, Al wouldn't have had two seconds of her time.

'Really.' She glances up at the clock again, and feels the weight of all those aliases pressing down on her. It's going to be tight. 'But right now, I've gotta run.' She grabs her bag and offers him a fist bump as she passes. 'See you, Ludo.'

Ludo gives her a lazy salute in answer, and she's out the door.

Chapter 3

The plane's wheels hit tarmac at six forty-two a.m., and by seven fifteen Cameron is on her second coffee of the day. Every part of her body hurts, every fiber of her being crying out for some good, healing sleep. For the moment, it'll have to make do with too-hot liquid caffeine spiked with so much sugar it makes her gums ache to drink it. She managed two hours of shut-eye on the flight: trapped in the zig-zag fold of an economy-class seat, semi-lucid dreaming the tilt of a horizon through half-shut lids, a pulsing, flickering orange glow that followed the curve of the Earth, her dread of it growing strong enough to make her spasm awake before the flight was half-gone. Her neighbor had no such problem. Sagged so deep in his seat it was hard to tell if he was wearing his rumpled beige suit or if it had been laid over him, his breath whistling raggedly through his nose, he was dead to the world. Cameron had shut her eyes and tried her best to get somewhere in the vicinity of sleep, but once her brain acknowledged that it could hear that whistling, it was all she could think about. She'd waved down a cup of water from a harassed-looking flight attendant, beat her neck pillow into something approximating an actual shape, and tried to block it out by focusing on the task at hand.

When Nate vanished, the first thing Cameron had found out about skip tracing was that it was an easy job to get started in. Anyone with a little seed money could sign up to the kind of services that trace cellphones and bank transactions, or websites that scrape all the metadata that people sign away every time they skip the Terms of Service and click *Accept*. It was easy to get started as a skip tracer, but hard to get good at it. Most low-level skip jobs were chasing down years-old debts that had been passed from one collection agency to the next. They usually ended with someone's grandma waking up one morning to a stern letter, or two guys on a doorstep with a van looking to take away a flatscreen television in lieu of what they were owed. Most skip tracing was easy work, the sort of pattern recognition you could do from your armchair, and none of it was any use for finding Nate. He went from living a completely ordinary life to a ghost: no bank activity, no phone calls in his name, no social media, no loyalty cards. Off the grid.

Training herself to find him had meant going after the hardest skips, the sort of people you didn't find while sitting in your armchair. You had to get out in the world. You had to hunt. And even if it meant spending money you didn't have on a last-minute flight across the country, you had to be willing to take a risk.

In the morning press of people taking the BART train into the city, Cameron could almost bring herself to feel good about it. Of the thirty or so aliases that her target had scattered about the Bay area, only one of them struck her as being real. Almost all of them had digital trails – social security, travel cards, phone bills, lists of associates, previous addresses – and once she started looking through them side-by-side, the more obvious it became that what she was looking at wasn't so much evidence of a person as the appearance of a person. Only one of them was different.

Half-complete, lacking a phone or social security, it wasn't even close to a new identity. It was the sort of thing that flagged on her radar as an obvious fake, a rushed job left hanging when fleeing the law was more important than making sure you had submitted all the forms you needed. She'd seen more than enough of them in the past eighteen months: some from the skips she'd taken on, most from the ever-growing list of aliases that Nate might have taken, every Nate, Nathan, Nolan, Noah that had popped into existence since the crash.

Samuel Gorton. Not enough information under the name to pin him down, but it had been a start. Cameron had raced the clock counting down to her flight, printing off a map and sticking pins in it wherever she found an alias that could easily pass as both. As *Gorton*, he had no fixed address, but there was a *Gordon* listed as residing in an apartment near the financial district. *Samuel* had no employment records, but *Samantha* was in high demand as a freelance accountant, finding tax loopholes for the kinds of people who were willing to drop a significant annual stipend on someone who could clear even bigger debts off of their ledgers: more than enough to cover the rent for an apartment in a tall shiny building in the heart of the city.

So, a patchwork person. *E Pluribus Unum*. Hunting down Sam wasn't about finding the needle in a haystack: it was

21

about taking a step back and seeing that he *is* the haystack. Hidden behind a cluster of names, all of them incomplete, he was free to seed a more complete identity in any part of the country and send every skip tracer and bounty hunter off on a wild goose chase. Everyone, that is, but Cameron.

Because she's seen it before.

Six months ago, hunting across the South for a guy with a stolen check printer and enough aliases that he'd turn a corner and already be somebody else. The only reason Cameron found him was because she'd got lucky, had been in the same town the day he lifted a case of ink and paper from the local bank's supplies. Until then, he'd been nothing more than a rumor, a shell game of false identities constantly shuffled and discarded when you weren't paying attention. While the police were arresting him, she cloned his phone and copied everything she could off of his laptop, studied it for weeks until she knew how he had done it. Because if he could hide like that, so could someone like Sam Gorton. Or even Nate.

Cameron waits almost two hours before heading to the address to find Gorton. Timing isn't just about being early. When you've only got one shot to take, you pick your moment and make it when it suits you best. Instead of heading straight there, she occupied a stool in a busy coffee shop, nursing her third tall cup of the day while trying to figure out if the barista who kept staring recognized her or was just giving her the stink eye for not drinking up and leaving. Hard to tell with the beard, and the distracting sight of his lean, muscular arms going through the motions of making coffee with aggressive efficiency. He had good arms. Cameron sighed – *another time, another life* – and went through the notes on her phone one more time. She stayed off the Internet, had turned it off before take-off. You never knew what kind of flags you could trip looking somebody up. She'd met a guy who'd stayed hidden on the grid for almost a decade because he'd rebuilt the front end of a tracing website – a big one – and had the presence of mind to build in a warning system should he ever need it. Could have made a fortune brokering that information to other fugitives, selling it on, but he'd had a weird sense of justice about it. Not everyone deserved a warning.

The morning rush doesn't peter out. It builds, and Cameron starts to pick up a lot of talk about a protest that is due in the afternoon. A protest means crowds, and a lot of chances for someone to vanish. *Better beat the rush*. Cameron buys a pastry to go – half apology for hogging the stool, half recognition that coffee alone is not going to be enough to get her through the day – and makes her way down the street to the address she has matched to Sam Gorton.

The apartment building has a keypad entry, but a van is double-parked in front of the lobby entrance and the door is jammed open, a strip of metal bent double and stuck beneath it. No desk or super in sight, and there are enough scratches and scrapes to suggest it's a common enough event and everyone has given up caring.

Cameron takes her time, makes her way round the back of the building and into the narrow strip of alley that edges past the ramp to an underground parking lot. Unlike the pristine face of the building, the alley side is a cement grey box filled high with shadows. City maintenance obviously comes around semi-regularly because it's not banked shoulder-high in accumulated crap, but from the crunch of old glass and the reek Cameron can tell that they do the very least their job demands. She can't blame them. There's a lot of city to clean. A pile of cardboard boxes in one corner catches her eye, an old comforter thrown over the top in a shape that looks oddly human from the right angle, and Cameron stands silent, waiting to see if the owner is still in residence, or if the hunched-over suggestion of a shape is just her wanting to see it. There's no sound, no movement, no huff of breath. Cameron relaxes. A green reflective plate above the door tells her that this alley is a fire exit. She makes a mental note: there are no ladders, no outside balconies. A runner will have to choose between here and the front door.

Sam Gorton won't be a runner. He doesn't look or act the part. Runners are all young, nervy types, the ones who skip on an uncle's credit card and go to bed every night feeling the heat prickling warm on the back of their neck. Nobody goes to the lengths that this guy has to live their life out of a bag already packed. He lives comfortable. He sleeps well. He won't be a runner.

Cameron doesn't do another circuit of the building. The important part of casing a place is not overdoing it. You can walk the block all day, but when it comes down to it there isn't much of your plan that can change. Knock on their door, confirm their identity, and call law enforcement to follow up with the arrest. Easier to arrange for a deputy to be on-site or nearby, but Cameron prefers to handle the first part herself. When she first started the job, she'd been stiffed on the credit for a collar by a sheriff looking to bolster his department's records in the run-up to re-election. Lesson learned, she doesn't bother calling ahead unless the skip looks like trouble.

Finance nerds don't pack heat. All Cameron has to do is dress smart, look serious, talk a tough game. He might try and buy her off, talk his way out of it, but he isn't likely to have a holdout stashed somewhere close to hand.

Cameron makes her way back round to the front of the building and goes inside. On her way in, she kicks the metal strip out from under the door, picks it up and pockets it while the door swings closed behind her. Straight past the elevator there's a door to the staircase. Through it, she starts down the half-flight and the tight turn that leads to the fire-exit doors at the back of the building. The door opens out on a press-to-open bar. Cameron unbends the metal strip into a right angle and jams it behind the bar. Before it will open, someone is going to have to find the strip and jerk it loose. Twenty seconds of work, which is more than enough to eat up any lead a runner might get on the staircase. He won't be a runner, but Cameron has a row of pins in her arm as a reminder about the value of her expectations. It feels like a shitty thing to do, but then half of the active tracers she knows would have just put a padlock on it and bet on the building never catching fire. She can clear it later once the skip is in custody. *No harm, no foul.*

Cameron goes back to the elevator and hits the button for the ninth floor, then all of the buttons for everything above it. It's a cramped little box for the size of the apartment building it's meant to service, mirrored walls to give the illusion of space, and Cameron wonders if there's a freight elevator somewhere for people to move furniture with, and if she should have cased that, too. *He won't be a runner*, she tells herself.

25

The corridor on nine is clean and quiet, and built to last: the paint on the walls is the kind of industrial taupe that you could scrub with a brush dipped in bleach if you needed to; the carpet is dark brown and cut-pile, laid wall-to-wall. All of the lighting is recessed, flush with the walls. Aside from the brass door numbers and peepholes, everything about the place is put together with an eye for function over style. *Well, nobody pays more for a fancy corridor.* Cameron can barely hear her own footsteps on the carpet, and she suspects a layer of rubber has been laid underneath. *Not getting woken up at three a.m. by asshole neighbors, now that's a selling point.* No nightingale floor for Sam Gorton. It should be a comfort, but the silence is unsettling. No conversations, no clatter or argument, no sound of kids. No cooking smells. She can feel the hair rising on the back of her neck. It feels like the peepholes are cameras, watching her pass. It's like the tunnel before the fight: there's a feeling of dislocation when you walk down it, of unreality. Like when the lift doors opened, she left the real world behind.

Sam Gorton's apartment is halfway down the hall on the left. Cameron takes a moment to take a deep breath and collect herself – *the place is too new to be haunted, get a grip* – before knocking.

No answer. Cameron knocks again, three smart raps with the middle knuckle, not too impatient, polite and crisp. *I know you're there.* That's the kind of knock it is. *And I hate to insist, but get your ass up and open the door.*

Between knocks, Cameron listens. She can hear something from inside, the low mechanical hum of air conditioning, but no movement, no thud of footsteps. No rush to answer or escape. She knocks again.

Cameron can't say what it is that makes her reach for the door handle – instinct, habit, the urge to rattle it and dispel the tension that's still pressing at the edge of her senses – but when she does it turns in her hand and the door swings open. The apartment is light inside, tall windows letting in the warm morning light.

'Sam Gorton?' Cameron calls from the hallway. The hum of fans is louder – too loud for air conditioning, and she can hear the tick and whir of a computer working – but there's nothing past that. She edges forward and puts her head round the door.

Sam Gorton is not going to be a runner. He's seated at a desk at the far end of the room, a bullet hole in his forehead. A black monolith of computer equipment is set up behind him, still running, completely oblivious to the dead man, and the dried blood spattered across his face.

Cameron pulls her head back out into the corridor. 'Shit.' A skip is simple. You find the thing that's missing – person, object, money – you get paid. A dead body is complex. There will be a police statement, forensics, red tape.

There's no one else here. All she would have to do is wipe her prints off the door and she could walk away. *And leave a paper trail that sees you taking a day trip cross-country, and a barista as witness that you were in the vicinity, dumbass.* 'Fuck.'

There is, at least, the skip. All she needs is a photograph, time stamped, to show that she found him first. That's it. Get a photo, call the cops, let them tidy up the mess while you get your payday. Taking the first step is the hard part. Cameron rolls her shoulders, bows her head, closes her eyes. Like in the locker room before they come in to check her gloves, when it's

27

just her and the glare of white tiles. Like in the cage, with a couple of thousand voices screaming, chanting, trying to rattle her, trying to psych her out. There's only silence here, and it's deafening.

You can do this. Cam bunches her hands into fists, feels the scar that runs the length of her left arm go tight in answer. 'You can do this.' She opens her eyes, and makes her way into the flat.

Chapter 4

Cameron doesn't need to check Sam Gorton's pulse. With half the back of his head missing and most of his brain on the floor behind him, he's either dead or planning a run for Congress. The bullet hole is low on his forehead, and the impact has smashed the bridge of his nose and the orbit of his right eye: both are tilted in towards it, like they're sinking. She can still tell that it's him, just, and she holds her breath while taking a handful of pictures on her phone. She needs a wallet, really, some form of ID to tie him to his aliases, but the police can handle that. She's not touching him. Even with the desk between her and the body, it's still freaking her out.

He's tremendously pale, all the blood that isn't on the floor sunk down inside him without a heartbeat to move it, and the fish-belly whiteness of him puts Cameron in mind of a waxwork. There's very little smell – a touch of something sour in the air, but not enough to catch in the back of her nose and mouth, nothing that would turn her stomach, and Cameron suspects that might be because of the bank of computer equipment that's still running at his back. There are three

29

stacks, each one with at least ten boxes stacked in them, fans running full-tilt as they work. It's noticeably colder at the desk. They've kept the corpse cool, preserved it in a cocoon of HEPA-filtered air, as though performing some kind of final service for their operator.

Cameron isn't a coroner, but she can tell that he wasn't killed recently. He's not dripping, at least. She's not sure how long blood takes to congeal but she's had enough cuts to know that it takes its sweet time clotting. And he hasn't been here a while, either. She has video footage of him at a zoo that's less than two days old, so taking off a couple of hours' travel time to get back to his apartment, sit down, get shot . . . he died sometime in the last twelve to thirty-six hours.

That's enough. Cameron can leave the rest to the cops. She walks in a slow circle, debating whether to call her lawyer first, or 911. She considers checking for another number, one that will get her to the desk sergeant of the nearest precinct, something to start the ball rolling on them seeing her as a professional having a shitty day rather than the closest available suspect. But it means she's going to be sitting on hold waiting for that one line to free up, standing in a room with a dead body trying not to sit on or lean or touch anything, and the low, industrial hum of the fans slowly building in her ears until she freaks out. They're already chewing at her nerves and it hasn't been five minutes. As she makes her mind up in favour of 911, something catches her eye.

There's a gun on the floor.

It's not quite hidden by the corner of the sofa that sits hard against one wall, below the windows on the long side of the room. Just the back side of the grip is showing, the rounded-

30

off corners of the magazine butt. It's like whoever shot Sam Gorton – and they would have been standing not far from where Cameron is standing now – tossed it casually to one side when the job was done, not caring where it landed. Cameron might not have noticed it was there at all, her eyes might have passed over the abstraction of its shape caught in the shadows and just not registered what it was, but for the jolt of recognition that brings the full focus of her attention to bear. The gun is hers.

It's a 9mm Beretta Cougar. There's a piece of grip tape – more than one, a double thickness layer – laid across the top of the backstrap, right where the gun sits snug against the base of the thumb. Cameron knows this because she put it there when she'd first got it and found that apart from being fit for purpose in every other way, it didn't sit right in her hand while shooting.

'Oh shit.'

She goes over, crouches down by the sofa to get a better look. Not touching anything. Conscious that her feet are leaving prints right now, that she's left prints and traces of herself on the door, the lift, the lobby. *Christ, you even blocked an exit.*

It's definitely her gun. The one that right now should be sitting in a locked box in her apartment, on a shelf in her closet next to a holster that she's never once felt the need to put on except to check for the fit. *Get a gun. Get certified.* That was the one thing everyone in the business seemed to agree on, repeated to one another like it was Gospel. Said it so often that Cameron had started to believe it herself. Even if you never need to draw it, it's better that the knowledge is there.

She should have known better. The fighter in her should have known better. You don't work combinations to leave them unused. You don't learn holds without thinking about the counters. You build a bag of tools with the intention of using them, of keeping them ready at all times, because the thing that you do half-assed is one day going to come back and bite you.

Get a gun. Get certified. Get set up.

Cameron picks up the gun, thumbs the safety on. It feels heavy in her hand and she pops the magazine to check. It's loaded. She works the slide and catches the bullet that falls out. Nine-millimeter soft point. They'd been on the shelf marked *Home Defense*, the cheapest ones in the store: hence she'd gravitated towards them. There's a nub of grey at the tip, softer metal designed to bloom on impact, transferring all its kinetic energy to the first person it hits. Minimum chance of it going through them and into someone else, maximum chance of stopping them with the first shot. No wonder Sam Gorton was missing the back of his head. Whoever had done this had been thorough, had put a lot of effort into getting hold of her gun, her bullets. Putting Sam Gorton in front of a camera knowing she would be the one to see it. *Who the hell did you piss off this badly, Cam?*

She thumbs the bullet back into the magazine, slides it into the grip, pushes it home with a click. She checks the safety again before opening her briefcase and putting it inside. Risky to carry without a permit, but there's no way she's leaving it here. There's a whole bay of water out there that will solve this part of the problem for her, at the very least. If she's being set up, there are three things that need to happen for it to stick:

means, motive, and opportunity. She can get rid of the first at her earliest opportunity.

Out in the corridor, the elevator bell sounds.

Cameron's gut twists as she revises the count upwards. Four things need to happen for it to stick: she needs to be caught. There's a crackle of police-band chatter, muted by the walls, and the soft tread of feet approaching. *Do something.* Her whole body feels like it has frozen up. It's that helpless feeling, the one where you realize that you've been outmaneuvered, and the worst part of it is not seeing it until it's way too late. Like the flick of a steering wheel, hard over to one side, and then back the other way. The memory is a cold shot of adrenaline straight into the base of her brain. *Get. The Fuck. Up.* Her hands close the briefcase on automatic, flick the combination to something other than 'spring open the instant you touch the hasps', and she stands, phone in one hand, briefcase heavy in the other. Thumbs the screen. Nine. One. One. Green for go. It rings twice as the footsteps slow in the corridor and Cameron thinks she can hear the pop of a hasp on a holster. Shit. Shit. Shit.

'Nine-one-one, what is your emergency?'

Get a grip, Cam. It takes her a beat, long enough for the operator to start repeating herself.

'Nine-one-one, can I help—'

'Sorry. I've just found a dead body. He's been shot.'

'Where are you calling from?'

'I'm in an apartment building, it's on—'

'Ma'am, I need you to turn around and show me your hands.' The cop's voice comes from the doorway. He says it a little too fast and Cameron's mouth goes dry, like she just bit down on a cotton pad. She can almost feel the gun pointed at the back of her head.

'Is there someone else there?' Cameron hits the speaker button as she turns with her phone hand held up and out, screen turned towards the cop to show him what it is, or – more specifically – what it isn't. The cop is standing square inside the door, gun held in both hands, the muzzle pointed down at the floor. His finger is outside the trigger guard. He's about five-ten, Latino, broad-shouldered in his uniform, and from the way his jaw is working it's almost as if she has a gun drawn on him. He looks terrified, but at least he's not terrified and aiming down his sights at her.

'There's an officer in the doorway.' Cameron says it loud enough that the operator can hear her. 'He has asked me to turn and show him my hands.'

'Can you put him on the phone?'

'I've put the call on speaker.'

The gun barrel goes down a little further and the officer visibly relaxes. 'You're calling nine-one-one?'

'I came up here to find the door open and this guy dead. What else was I going to do?'

He nods, a curt acknowledgement, and holsters his weapon before holding his other hand out for the phone. Cameron can see his gun hand doesn't stray too far from his hip, so she keeps her distance as she hands it over. Every nerve she has is singing, the fight-or-flight response desperate to be set loose, but he's de-escalating and Cameron wants more than anything to keep it that way.

He switches off the speakerphone and exchanges a quick call-and-response verification with the operator before identifying himself as Ray Perada. Cameron makes a mental note of the name.

'There's an apparently deceased male, gunshot wound to the head. One female witness present. Yes. Yeah, he's dead. Back of his head's gone.' He stops and looks Cameron up and down, then sniffs the air and screws up his face. 'Doesn't seem recent. If you can pass it on to the coroner's office, I'll start with the witness. Yeah. Yeah. Thanks, dispatch, will do.' He presses a button to hang up the phone, and gives Cameron an apologetic smile that, for a brief moment, gives her hope. 'So,' he says, 'can you tell me what's going on here?'

'Your guess is as good as mine, officer. I came here to verify an ID for a contract—'

'You're a notary?'

'No, the contract was for a skip trace.'

'Okay.' He nods again, this time with the disapproval that all cops have for part-timers and private contractors. She can almost feel the disdain thickening in the air between them. 'You're a bounty hunter. What'd this guy skip out on?'

'Multiple frauds, with a total in excess of five million dollars.'

'And you get how much for finding him?'

'Flat fee plus a percentage of losses recouped.'

'Hell of a payday for you, then.'

'Recouped, Officer Perada.'

'Which means what, exactly?' She can tell he's just rattling her cage, blowing off the head of steam he'd built up coming through the door.

'I'll cover the specifics when you take a proper statement, officer, but to put it bluntly: he's no good to me dead.' It's clear from the sour look on Perada's face that he doesn't approve. He glances over at the body as she says it, and Cameron silently curses herself for not adopting an old-school respect for the dead man. All cops are Catholic, whether they start out that way or not. All that time spent thinking about other people's guilt puts their minds on to a parallel course. By that measure, speaking ill of the dead was probably about as bad a choice as telling him about the gun in her bag. 'Sorry.'

'It's okay, Miss . . .'

'King.' She doesn't offer her first name. 'Do you know how long we'll have to stay here?'

Perada shakes his head. 'Coroner's office will update us on a—'

Cameron's phone rings in his hand. He starts, like he's forgotten it was there, and looks down at the screen by reflex. 'Nate,' he says, before remembering himself and holding it out for her to take.

Nate.

The shift in her gut – shock, fear – is so sudden she can't hide it. Something in her face or the way she stands tips Perada off that there's something wrong, and it spooks him. He stands a fraction taller, and the motion pulls the phone out of Cameron's reach.

'Officer Perada,' Cameron says, picking her way around the words like she's stepping through a minefield. 'I need to answer that call.'

'Ma'am, the only thing you need to do is stay right where you are.' His free hand is back down close to his hip now, the phone held out like he can ward her off with it. It's still ringing.

Nate. It's been almost two years. No word or trace of him, and suddenly he's calling her. The break on this case, the body, the gun, this call – she doesn't know how, but they feel connected. There has to be a connection.

'Ma'am.' Perada has his hand on his gun now. He looks more nervous than when he came in. Cameron tries to think how long her phone has been ringing. *How long before it rings out? How long before I lose him again?*

Cameron makes her choice. Perada sees it in her face, and pulls his gun.

Kicks used to be Cameron's weak point. It took a couple of losses for her to decide to put that right. She'd worked at them constantly ever since, until her high kick became something she was known for. Drop a hand out of guard, take a step the wrong way, and she would pull the trigger. Someone once filmed it with a high-speed camera, and they ended up checking their kit three times to make sure it wasn't broken. The instant her foot was off the ground, the rest of the kick looked like it was travelling at normal speed.

When her foot hits Perada, his gun isn't even clear of his holster. The shock of impact gives him a slack-jawed look as he goes sideways, and he hits the floor with a boneless thump. Cameron catches the phone mid-air as it falls from his hand and hits green as fast as her thumb can find it.

'Nate?'

There's a pause before he answers, his breath loud on the line. 'Cam. Where are you?'

Cameron can hear the growing thunder of her heartbeat as she processes the question, the long-brewed anger roiling up inside of her. 'Where am I? Where the fuck are you? What the hell is going on, Nate?'

'Cam, this is important. Where are you?'

'Important? No shit it's important. I just cold-cocked a cop to take this call.'

'Shit, Cam.' Another pause. He goes off the line a second, comes back sounding distracted. There's street noise in the background: cars, pedestrian chatter. *He's here in the city.* She doesn't know how she knows it, save for a feeling in her gut. 'Are you sure it's a cop?'

'Uniform and badge says yes.' She looks down at Perada, at the standard issue belt and gear. If he's not a cop, he's gone to a great deal of expense to look the part. A cheap suit and a badge would have been enough to play detective. 'And he identified himself to nine-one-one. Where have you been, Nate?'

'Cam, I left to protect you. I wouldn't call you if it wasn't important.'

'Protect me? You nearly killed me.'

'You're in danger, Cam.' He takes a long, shaky breath. A car horn blares somewhere, and Cameron's head comes up as she hears a faint echo of the noise from outside. *He's close.* 'Cameron, listen to me. Listen carefully. You have to get out of there. Just go. Do you understand?'

'Who did this, Nate?'

'Cam, I'm sorry this is happening.'

'Nate—'

'Don't try to find me. Listen. You have to get out of there. Just go.'

Cameron bristles at the interruption. He won't even let her speak. 'When I find you, Nate, I'm going to—'

'They're coming, Cam. Get out.' The line goes dead.

38

'Mother*fucker*.' Cameron throws her phone at the floor and tries not to stamp on it. Nate's alive. He's alive, and Cameron is angrier than she can ever remember being in her entire life. A dead body, a cop laid out, and all he has to say is *get out*? Cameron yells, a loud, primal roar, her blood fizzing, and she kicks the wall hard enough that it puts a boot-sized hole in the drywall. She pulls her foot free and stands with her eyes closed, thinking. *Processing*. Getting a handle.

Faintly, Cameron can hear sirens. She knows that they're coming for her.

Get out. She takes a deep breath. Of the building, maybe. Of reach of the police department, certainly. But as for the rest of it, she's going nowhere. Nate is alive – in this city – and Cameron is going to find him.

Chapter 5

Coming to isn't the worst part of Ray Perada's morning. Getting kicked in the head wasn't exactly high on his bucket list of things to do before hitting forty, either, but none of it matches up to the shit-eating grin the desk sergeant has on his face when Perada goes to sign in.

'Heard you had a rough day.' Bulwell is a department legend, and not in the good way. Somewhere in his early fifties he just stopped caring, and now he's spinning out the last few years between him and the two beers per guest tab that will pass for a retirement party sitting at the front desk making sure everyone knows exactly how little he cares.

'Depends on your definition of a rough day.' Ray uses his own pen when he puts his name in the daybook. Everything gets logged on the computer, but the department is still holding on to paper copies. Two years previously some punk kid with a computer got his nose put out of joint over a misdemeanor possessions charge. He hacked in and froze the system for a month, flushed everything from the day of his arrest. Most cops would've found it funny, but in the process he zeroed the overtime of everyone who'd worked a shift that month. Serial killers got less manpower assigned to them.

While Ray is signing, Bulwell's smile drops off of his face like hot bird shit down a windshield. Normally Ray would've ignored whatever crack Bulwell had lined up for him – something about wetbacks, usually – but the ache in his jaw has lit a fire in him today.

'How'd you figure?' Bulwell is staring down from on high with a face like a thunderstorm. He can't work out what it is, can't leave it either. Perada meets it with a shrug.

'I dunno, Sarge. Most of the guys here, if they got assaulted by a perp they'd call it an occupational hazard. Guys like you fill out an insurance form every time you have to walk more than ten feet.'

'Least I didn't get my ass kicked.'

'Are you kidding? Anyone trying to kick your ass would lose their foot in it up to the ankle.'

Ray can almost hear the cogs turning in Bulwell's head as he thinks it through. 'Yeah, you're real clever, Perada.' A smile like a grease stain lights up his face. 'Clever guy like you around, I'd better watch my back.'

It feels like an itch scratching at the nape of Ray's neck, the thought of all the talk that has gone on behind his back since the shooting board ruled in his favor. You don't need to be paranoid to think like that. Cops talk, and if you're not hearing it then it's definitely about you. Bulwell can see how much it rattles Ray and nods, satisfied. 'Captain wants to see you,' he says. 'Got some brass in there with him, waiting. See how clever you are once they're done with you.'

Ray sucks in a taut breath and walks off, stiff with embarrassment and rage. They used to play up the brotherhood thing at the academy, that the badge was a promise shared by all that wear it. They failed to mention that the slightest tarnish was enough to see that promise broken. Bulwell's laughter follows Ray all the way into the station house, and not a soul lifts their gaze to acknowledge him.

True to the man's word, Captain Adams is not alone in her office. She answers Ray's knock with a brusqueness and volume that suggests she's not happy with having had to wait for him, and he hustles in as quick as his sore jaw will let him. She's sitting at her desk looking more like a judge than a captain, whip-thin and straight-backed, not an ounce of softness in her. *Yeah*, Ray thinks. *She's mad as hell.*

'Officer Perada,' she says. 'Have a seat.'

'Yes, ma'am.' There's one pulled out ready for him. He sits down, and waits in silence. Adams doesn't acknowledge or introduce either of the people that are in the room with her. One of them is the deputy chief of police: Ray recognizes him, and his heart sinks. The last time he saw the deputy chief, it was at a hearing that had ended up costing him six months of appointments with the department shrink and buried all hope of seeing a promotion. *Just when you think things can't get any worse.* The other is a civilian. Gingham shirt, brown jacket, jeans, enough hair product in play to support a small salon, cleaning his thick-framed glasses to avoid eye contact: everything about him screams Silicon Valley wunderkind, the kind that puts in a complaint whenever the bus drivers strike or they see a homeless person rooting through a dumpster. He gives Adams a look. 'Is this a disciplinary meeting, ma'am?'

'Not as such, Perada.' She looks uncomfortable, but doesn't elaborate. 'I understand you took a hell of a knock this morning. Have you seen a doctor?'

'Yes, ma'am. The EMT wanted to have me admitted for X-rays, but I wanted to file my report as soon as possible.'

'Department policy mandates a full check-up after a head injury. You feel dizzy, you vomit, you let someone know, you understand?'

'Yes, ma'am.'

Adams shifts in her seat, like she's got something jammed under her, and it dawns on Ray that she might be angry, but it isn't with him. She slides a piece of paper across the desk. 'Six weeks. Full pay, any and all healthcare costs covered. Effective immediately.' She says it fast and terse, like she's ripping off a plaster. 'We've cleared it with your union official as acceptable terms.' He looks at the paper. It's exactly as she describes: six weeks of 'administrative leave', full pay, full health cover, no strings. She's signed it, the deputy chief has signed it, his union rep has signed it. There's no space for his signature; giving him eyes on the hard copy is just a formality.

'I don't understand.'

'How are you sleeping, Ray?' The deputy chief has a deep voice. He's a big man, as big as Bulwell at the front desk, but all of his weight is hard-packed, the suet-soaked muscle of a bare-knuckle fighter. The question might have sounded avuncular, even concerned, if Ray's hackles hadn't already been rising.

'I sleep fine, sir,' Ray says. 'My last psych evaluation cleared me for service.'

'I understand it might be difficult for you to accept this,' the deputy chief says, as though Ray hasn't said a word, 'but having an officer involved in another incident so soon after returning to active duty could raise some questions about whether or not we rushed things.'

'Nothing was rushed, sir. I'm absolutely fine.' It feels like the truth right up until he says it. Some things you never recover from. They are fixed points: immutable, unfading. But you say the words anyway.

'I understand that. Captain Adams agrees with you. But we have to consider things from the point of view of the department. We have to maintain . . .' He screws up his face, searching for the word, 'public trust.'

'So you're benching me.'

The deputy chief bristles at that. 'Now look—'

'It could have gone worse for you.' The Silicon Valley wonk talks over him, and while the deputy chief turns the color of a fire truck, he doesn't protest. 'The woman who assaulted you could've taken your gun. She could have decided that leaving you alive was a liability. She has already killed one person that we know of.'

Sitting on the desk is the cop's equivalent of Wonka's Golden Ticket, six weeks of all-expenses paid time for Ray to sit on his ass and not give a shit. It feels like a slap in the face, and while he can't take it out on his captain or the deputy chief, a civilian will do just fine.

'Who the hell are you?' Ray asks.

'I'm a consultant working with the—'

'Start with your name, then we can work to whatever asshole title you've got.' Ray shakes his head. 'How do you know she's a killer? Forensics won't even have finished taking photos yet.'

'It's fairly obvious that she went there to kill—'

44

'The dead guy in the chair? You been out there to see him? That body was a day old. Dry blood, very little in the way of smell. Perp was in a beige pant suit and didn't have a drop of blood on her. And I still want your name.'

'Perada, stand down.' Captain Adams interrupts, close to shouting in the cramped office. 'He's a representative from Carrington Medical. He needs to be here, and if you've got a problem with that you can take it up with the mayor.'

Carrington. With departmental funding being slashed left and right, having a private medical firm offer to pick up the tab for health coverage was a boon to the force and a PR coup for them. Ray had made good use of it, and had never once given a thought to what strings might be attached. It goes a long way to explaining why the deputy chief and the captain are kissing his ass instead of handing him it.

Silicon Valley gives Ray a smug look. If Adams isn't going to back him up, there's no point in fighting it. 'Understood, ma'am.' Ray stands, and takes the paper from the table. 'I'll get my statement filed before the end of this shift.'

Adams closes her eyes, gives the tiniest shake of her head, like she herself can't believe what she's doing. 'Effective immediately, Officer Perada. Get changed, get those X-rays taken, and go home. Get some rest.'

Ray looks from her, to the deputy chief, to Silicon Valley. Both of his superiors avoid his gaze. Silicon Valley looks straight through him. *No statement.* A dead body, a manhunt for the only potential witness: the whole station should be buzzing with it. Instead, the mayor's office is involved, nobody's saying a word, and he's got six weeks to forget all about it. It stinks, and Adams knows it. 'Yes, ma'am.'

He has no intention of forgetting about it. Benched, disgraced, dismissed. None of that matters. Inside, he's still a cop. Ray double-times it to the locker room to get out of his uniform.

He beats Silicon Valley out to the street by ten minutes. Enough time to buy a hotdog from the stand that does swift business twenty feet from the entrance to the station, and to work through his doubts about what he's about to get himself into. He's heard of guys working off the books plenty of times, but none of the stories ever turn out well. Even firing off a couple of snaps of a cheating husband is suspension material if you get caught doing it. Time was he would have shared the same dim opinion that all cops have for moonlighting, but this is different. A man is dead, and with the only possible witness in the wind someone's got both the interest and the pull to make it all go away. And as much as he suspects he's going to regret it, Ray is going to find out.

Any reservations he has evaporate when Silicon Valley trips down the steps and jumps into a taxi. It's been waiting for him, it seems: he doesn't flag it down, the light is off, and there's no apparent conversation. As soon as he hits the sidewalk, it pulls up curb-side. The instant the door is closed, it peels away. Ray makes a note of the number to check later, but suspects that it will bounce back as legit. He crumples the greasy paper up into a ball and holds up a hand to flag down a taxi of his own.

Chapter 6

Cameron checks the nameplate twice before she rings the doorbell. With the nickname 'Pickaxe', she expected Antonelli to live in a cramped room above a crumbling boxing gym, some brick-and-whitewash relic of the seventies waiting for the inexorable rumble of bulldozers. Instead it's a pretty little box of a place, like a full-size doll's house with a flight of steps leading up off the pavement to a cherry-wood door polished to the color of ox blood. A pair of big potted plants flank the door, and Cameron can't quite bring herself to believe that Antonelli has the patience to look after them. The shortest fighter in the division's history, Sophia Antonelli built her entire career off the back of her singular ring persona. Once she stepped through the ropes (and later, into the cage) she switched on a laser-focus anger that made every other fighter look casual by comparison. She got her nickname early when what would have been an axe kick for someone taller turned into an uppercut as her rising heel caught a charging opponent under the chin and put them down six seconds into their first round. Her promoter spent a year trying to push the Italian angle before he conceded that the name just wasn't going away.

Aside from the location, something else catches Cameron's eye: below *Antonelli*, there's another name. *Jones*.

They kept that quiet, she thinks, and hits the button a second time.

Ophelia Jones comes to the door in sweatpants and a 49ers shirt that hangs loose about her shoulders. She's almost a head taller than Cameron, and she stands with the easy confidence of someone whose arms are long enough to connect a punch without ever letting you get close. She's a fighter, too. No nickname – hard to brand initials with a loaded history – and no trademark style. Just a lot of experience and hard work which might not bring in the endorsement dollars but count for as much, if not more, in Cameron's book.

'Hey, Ophelia.' Cameron tries to smile like she hasn't just fled the scene of a crime. 'Is . . . is Sophia in?'

'Who wants to know?' It's a flat, hostile, *get the fuck off my doorstep* question. Aside from their relationship, there's one important fact about Sophia Antonelli and Ophelia Jones that Cameron has been trying not to think too much about: both of them have lost fights against her. And when the crash put an end to Cameron's career, they were forever denied the chance of a rematch. Ophelia grins, the hostility evaporating. 'I'm just fucking with you, Cam, of course she is. Come here.' Cameron sags in relief into Ophelia's long-armed embrace. The experience is like being crushed in a really happy vice, and Cam grunts out a laugh as Ophelia lifts her off of her feet and carries her inside.

'Hey, Pickaxe!' Ophelia yells, back-heeling the door shut behind her. 'Guess what we just got delivered!'

'Pickaxe?' Sophia yells from somewhere at the far end of the hall, probably the kitchen from the clatter of pans that follows. She storms into the hall with the same quick, short steps that make her so hard to gauge in the ring. 'When was the last time you— holy shit, is that Cameron King?'

'Hey, Sophia.' She almost coughs Sophia's name as Ophelia puts her down and her breath drops back into her in a rush. Sophia is on her before she has a chance to really recover, and all Cameron can do is laugh and weakly pat her old rival's back as her ribs creak under the strain of a second hug.

'What are you doing here? Finally realized there's a whole other coast, decided to come pay us a visit? How are you?'

For a brief, precious moment, their warmth feels right, like she has escaped from the nightmare of her own life. That this is sanctuary, and that if she wanted to she could stay forever. Cameron savors it for the three heartbeats it takes for her to remember that it's the opposite. This isn't sanctuary. It's their home, and by going to them, she puts their jobs – their livelihood – in danger.

'Sophia, I'm really sorry to do this, but I'm in trouble.'

Antonelli's smile falters a little, but she recovers quickly. Cameron catches the look that passes between her and Ophelia, the unspoken communication between them. 'What kind of trouble? You need money?'

It's not an unreasonable question. Once you stop fighting, the money dries up fast. Management and tax make purses a lot thinner than advertised, and the fast cycle of events means that endorsement deals have a lot of exit points baked into their contracts. When she'd been fighting, Cameron had tried her best to pass on as much work – coaching, punditry, teaching – to ex-fighters that were feeling the bite. 'It's not money. It's . . . work. I was meant to be out of here on a flight tonight so I didn't book a hotel. I just need to charge up my phone and laptop and make a few calls.'

Ophelia claps her on the shoulder as she sails past. She has an arm of solid oak; Cameron can recall the time in the ring when she'd tried to break it. 'Shit, Cam. Is that all? I'll even throw in a pot of coffee. Gluten-free madeleines, too.'

Sophia waits until she hears Ophelia in the kitchen. Even then she steps closer and lowers her voice. 'What's really going on, Cam?'

'It's Nate.' Saying it out loud makes it feel like madness, like the whole thing is a bad dream she's waiting to wake up from.

Sophia's eyes widen. 'He's alive? You found him?'

'He's alive, but he found me. Called me. Sophia . . .' She can barely find the breath to say it. 'A man is dead. Nate's involved somehow. And someone is trying to set me up.'

'Set you up? How?'

'The dead guy. He stole money from a bunch of banks, all corporate fraud stuff. I was looking for him. When I tracked him down, he'd been shot and my gun was on the floor.'

'Your gun.' It comes out flat, full of doubt.

'I know how it sounds, Sophia. Someone took it from my house. I didn't even know it was gone.'

'What did you do?' She barely waits for Cameron to answer. 'You called nine-one-one and reported the body, right?'

'I—'

'Cam?'

'It's complicated, okay? I called nine-one-one but a cop showed up while I was on the call.'

Sophia doesn't say a word. She knows there's more, and she can wait it out. *Patience*. That was what had changed

50

since they fought. Sophia of old would have charged in, demanding the rest; now she's waiting, calculating. *Working out if she's going to have to ask you to leave before madeleines and coffee.*

'Everything was going fine,' Cameron says. 'The cop talked to nine-one-one, called in people to take care of the body, holstered his sidearm. Then Nate called my phone. He's here in the city, Sophia. I'm sure of it. If I can just run a check to find the phone he rang from—'

'What about the cop?' Sophia asks.

Cameron swallows. 'He wouldn't give me the phone back. When I saw it was Nate, I panicked.'

Sophia puts her face in her palms, draws them down her face with a weary sigh. 'Don't say it, Cam.'

'He drew his gun, so I kicked him.'

'Oh no, Cam. No.' Sophia's eyes go wide. 'There must be an APB or something out on you now.'

'I don't know.' Cameron shakes her head. 'Look, I know this is bad and if you want me to I will leave right now. I just hoped I could charge up my phone and—'

'How did he take it?'

Cameron stops. 'Nate?'

'Not Nate, the cop. How did he take the kick? You can't just say you kicked a guy and leave it at that.'

'He went down like he'd been darted. Didn't see it coming, might not even know what hit him.'

Sophia grins, her face lighting up as she punches Cameron on the shoulder. 'Still got it, Cam. Arm full of pins, and you've still got it. You should get back in the ring. We could call you the Bionic Woman. How about Cyborg?'

'We could call you Car Crash,' Ophelia calls from the end of the hall. 'From the sound of things, it suits you. Coffee's ready.'

'You heard all that?'

'I heard it.'

Cameron looks at the door as Ophelia vanishes back into the kitchen. 'How could she hear all that?'

Sophia shrugs. 'Beats me. I could live to a hundred, and that woman will still surprise me.'

Their kitchen has the minimalist look of a professional chef's dream workplace. Most of the surfaces are clear space in stainless steel, and everything that isn't stored away is neatly racked along one wall. A coffee machine sits incongruously on the island in the middle of the room, dredged up from the back of whatever cupboard it had been hiding in to serve their guest. The madeleines are on a plate next to it, and Ophelia is wasting no time in waiting: she has a mug already brimming and a madeleine half-eaten in her other hand.

'Cheat day?' Cameron asks.

Ophelia nods, swallows. 'Now you're here, it is.'

'Glad I could help.' She looks around, taking it all in. Both women look really fit. Their industrial kitchen helps explain it. 'This is amazing. You guys got really serious.'

'Yeah.' Sophia looks away, almost embarrassed. 'Cam, when your sponsorship fell through, our managers just . . . you know. It's a business. You've got to take every opportunity you can.'

'Don't worry about it.' Cameron waves the apology away. It's not that it didn't hurt. There's just nothing she can do about it. 'Take every cent you can get. You never know . . .'

'. . . when you're going to get hurt,' Ophelia finishes for her. 'We had a talk after you . . . after the crash. About what we would do if one of us got hurt. We decided to put a few things in place: savings, investments, and this place. Full nutrition planning. Personal physio.' She looks up, gestures at the ceiling. 'Our own gym.'

Cameron won't pretend she hasn't been following their fights. Both women have been winning, and winning with ease. They've taken their training up a notch, and it has shown in their records. The way their careers are going, there's only one conclusion. 'So. What happens when you end up on a card against each other?'

Sophia grins. 'Fight of the decade. We'll keep dodging until the purse is too big to ignore.'

'Do your managers know about . . .'

'Yeah, yeah. Both teams do. Closely guarded secret. Non-disclosure contracts, the works.'

'Still, aren't you worried about it coming out?'

'Nope.' Ophelia's grin is wide enough to match Sophia's now. 'One guy even wrote a blog about what amazing "friends" we had become and how we are role models for good sports-manship. I swear I could kiss her in the street and people would say it was CPR or something.'

'Amazing.' Cameron takes a long drink of her coffee, the two women watching her closely. 'What?' she asks, eventually.

'Aren't you going to flip out or something?' Sophia asks.

'It's just . . . you're the first fighter that we've really told,' Ophelia finishes for her.

'I just kicked a cop in the head and fled a crime scene. I'm not sure I'm in a position to judge anyone.' Cameron shrugs.

'But even if I was, it doesn't change a thing. I'm happy for you guys. And I'm looking forward to seeing that fight.'

'Would be better if you were still around,' Sophia says.

'I'm still around.' Cameron drains her mug, and takes the offered refill. 'Just cheering you guys on.'

'You're still a fighter, Cam. Even if you don't believe it.' For a moment, it's as though Ophelia is facing her in the ring. Her focus is so complete. 'And while it goes against every instinct you have, you need to let go of this idea that you're going to find Nate. He almost got you killed once, and now this? Walk away, Cam.'

Cameron grips her mug in her hands so hard that she thinks it might shatter. Walk away. It is as easy, and as hard, as that. 'I know, Ophelia.' Her voice comes out small. 'I should.' She feels like anything but a fighter as she says it. 'But he's my brother. I can't just walk away from this.'

Ophelia nods, not agreeing but understanding. It takes a moment for Sophia to break the silence that settles over them.

'So.' She puts her mug down. 'Phone and laptop. I'll put them on to charge. Maybe you should give your lawyer a quick call while you're waiting?'

It's good advice. Cameron feels a pang of guilt for putting this on them. 'You sure you don't want me to go? This probably counts as aiding and abetting.'

Sophia shakes her head. '*De nada*. Besides, we've got good lawyers. All this goes south, we'll say you threatened to kick the crap out of us.'

54

Chapter 7

It took more money than Ray was truly comfortable parting with to keep the taxi driver on Silicon Valley's tail. He flashed the badge, which had the opposite effect intended: 'this ain't the movies' turned into 'now I *know* you shouldn't be doing this.' He'd fully expected to get turned out on to the sidewalk, for the cabbie to blurt his number into the radio and see his administrative leave bumped up to a full suspension, but his luck – or the mercenary nature of cabbies – held true. All Ray had to do was let slip his suspicions about the cab Silicon Valley had taken not being legit, and his driver came on-side, even offering some opinions on what he was going to do to an off-the-books driver when they caught him. Still took the time to lighten Ray's wallet, though.

Silicon Valley gets dropped off a block into the Mission district and starts down the road on foot. Ray's driver pulls up at the sidewalk and drops him off before peeling away so fast that Ray loses a chunk of coat to the door slamming shut on it. Ray stumbles, straightening fast at the thought of losing his mark, then spots him crossing the street further up. Another man – taller, bigger, with a shaved head – steps down from the curb to meet him, offering a handshake and a deferential nod to what is probably a question. He's wearing black shirt, pants, and boots: military fatigues that make him stand out like a bruise. The combination of his outfit and the fact that he walks into the street completely oblivious to hazards set Ray's nerves to singing. *Walking like he owns the place.* He's seen it before. Whenever brass enter a perimeter they like to pace it out, mark it as their territory. If they could piss on all the lampposts, they would. The block might not know it yet, but they are on lockdown.

As he walks, Ray cases it out. Silicon Valley and his pal in the Action Man fatigues vanish into an unmarked van on one side of the street. It has some patched bodywork, but the wheels are in good condition. Surveillance vehicle. No holes or windows in the side, so whatever they are watching is up ahead. When Ray passes, he is careful not to look back, taking his phone out as he walks with the goal of looking too busy to be a threat whilst making a quick call to a buddy in the department car pool. When it connects, his ear is filled with the comforting sound of the shit music that the mechanics blast twenty-four seven.

'Yo Perada. What you want this time?'

'Vin. We got a banged-up van on the books rigged for surveillance? Plate starting five, victor, foxtrot, papa.'

'Hold on. Homeland just got authorization to park what looks like a whole fleet of unmarked vehicles with us. You should see these things, Ray. If federal overfunding is the disease, these bad boys are the symptom. Tinted windows, heated seats, enough kit stowed in the back the rear suspension will be shot in six months. Your tax dollars at work, man.'

'Doesn't sound like my guys. They've got a beat-up Ford, looks ready for scrap.'

'Old school.' He can almost hear Vin nodding in approval down the line. 'Nope, Fed cars are all here, nothing else is out on loan.'

'Thanks, Vin. I owe you.'

'Always, buddy.'

As he makes it to the end of the block, Ray thinks it through. Surveillance sitting down the street looking forwards means that they are probably looking across at his side. None of the houses on the van's side of the street look vacant, so there's probably no one in any of the buildings. No clean view into windows, so they're casing an entrance. The neighborhood is upscale enough that the van might be the only surveillance they have. Anywhere more rundown, they would have put people on the head and tail of the street pretending to be joggers or some shit; here, it was a risk, because strangers standing idly at the end of the block would spook the residents. Black fatigues. Like SWAT. The rest of the team would be at the back of the building, or sitting in vans one block over ready to move.

Ray turns left at the end of the block and dials the precinct again, a different extension.

'Hey, Perada.' A woman's voice, Ray's name almost a sigh of exasperation.

'Kaz! How'd you know it was me?'

'Vin called me. Said you were looking for a favor and I should probably brace myself.'

'The man knows. Look, have we got anything big going down today?'

'Aside from the giant protest that's going through half the city? The one with the mayor and a couple of counter-protests to juggle?'

'Aside from that.'

'Good day to get a paid holiday, that's all I'm sayin'.'

'Hey, I don't like it any more than you.'

'Yeah, you sound real choked up. And no, we've got nothing happening.'

'No busts or agency stuff? No out-of-towners breathing down your neck?'

'None that I know of.' She isn't holding back. The last time the FBI had come in asking for cooperation, they'd stomped around the precinct making sure everyone knew how in charge they were. By the end of it, Karen in dispatch had been ready to commit treason on the next suit-and-tie-wearing asshole she saw. That she wasn't audibly grinding her teeth down the line was a good sign.

'You're one of the good ones, Kaz.'

'Don't I know it. What else do you want?'

Ray grinned. 'How'd you know.'

'You always say thanks when you're done. At least that's what I heard.'

'Uh, yeah.' In the background, Ray can hear someone spitting out their coffee. He sighs and looks at his shoes, feeling the heat climb in his cheeks. He'd dated one of the girls in dispatch for a couple of weeks, back before the fallout from the shooting inquiry had marked Ray as *Do Not Touch*. It never went anywhere, but apparently her supervisor had bullied some details out of her. 'So if you've got a black and white handy, could you get them to just check out a block for me? See if they can find an excuse to take a closer look at a van, make sure there's nothing going down.'

'Okay, Ray. Give me the details. But you owe me.'

'Do you take doughnuts?'

'Yeah, if they're bottle-shaped and filled with bourbon.'

The line goes dead and Ray drops Kaz the details as a text. He's almost to the end of the block and when he walks round it he starts back down the next street, parallel to the one he came from. There are no pedestrians, no cars that seem out of place. A little traffic goes by, but no one seems to be circling. For a moment, it feels like paranoia. His therapist said there might be moments of hyper-awareness, moments where his body would suddenly expect danger, and to try and give that feeling context; mundane events might take on a significance that they did not deserve. It feels like vertigo: that dizziness, that vulnerability; the realization that all of it might just be in his head. *And half the station will know it, when that black and white turns up nothing.* Ray feels like throwing up, and he stops to bend forward, hands on thighs, not knowing if it's to steady himself or just to make sure it will clear his shoes. *Breathe.* He counts backwards from ten. At seven, a faint buzz of static interrupts the count and grounds Ray's nerves, all of the doubt flooding out through the soles of his feet and leaving him listening intently for the source of the sound.

His phone vibrates in his hand. He answers the call, keeping his voice low. There's an alley a little way down that echoes with the sound of a man's voice, and Ray doesn't want him to know he's coming.

'Hello?'

'Ray, whatever the fuck you're doing, get out of there.'

'Kaz?'

'Your black and white isn't coming, Ray. I just got my ass chewed out for trying to send one your way, and the captain is on her way down to find out who asked for it.'

Ray's heart starts pounding when she mentions the captain. 'Shit, Kaz, sorry I got you into this.'

'Don't apologize,' she says. 'Whatever it is you're into, we're not allowed to touch it. If you don't get the fuck out, you're on your own.'

Ray tries to thank her, to apologize again, but she has already hung up. *You're on your own.* Whatever it is Silicon Valley is doing, it has its hooks buried deep into the department, and suddenly Ray understands the reason for his Golden Ticket. They've all read his psych. eval., his resolution to be not just a better cop, but the best cop. *You got that time off because they can't be sure you'll look the other way.*

He could turn around right now and walk away. Whatever this is, there's a world of trouble waiting for him on the far side of it. All he has to do is turn on his heel, and it will pass him by. But being a cop doesn't stop when the uniform comes off, and it sure as shit doesn't stop when other cops start looking the other way. Ray never went looking for redemption, but he knows what the right thing to do is.

When he clears the entrance of the alley, he freezes and backs up out of sight. Halfway down it, there's a guy dressed in black fatigues, kit bag at his feet, radio held up to one ear, and a submachine gun slung on a shoulder strap hanging at his right elbow. Ray can't identify the weapon. From the glance he got, it's a cut-down, space-age piece of kit, but it's unmistakably built like a submachine gun: short barrel, stock, big mag, suppressor. Ray's service weapon is locked up at the precinct, but – against his therapist's advice – he's still carrying. He pulls the snub-nosed revolver from the waistband holster at the small of his back and checks the weapon. It's almost childishly small in Ray's hands, but it's a design that's seen few alterations since the fifties and needed none of them. In an alleyway at short range, all the tech in the world isn't going to change the fact that Ray has his gun ready and the other guy is scratching his ass. He gets his badge out, clips it on to his jacket pocket before taking a quick, deep breath and starting round the corner.

There's no fear in him. There should be. His guts should be doing somersaults, but instead all he feels is anger. His jawline still aches from the kick that perp had hit him with this morning, her foot coming up out of nowhere, and the pain of it focuses all his concentration down to a single thought: this is a second chance. Radio Guy is still focused on the alley, the back of the buildings ahead. Ray closes, finger off of the trigger, gun angled down. No need to escalate. Ray's footsteps echo off the brickwork, and Radio Guy's head comes up in answer.

'Sir.' Polite, but firm. Ray puts his gut into it. *Cop voice.* 'I'm going to ask you to keep your hands in plain sight, and turn around slowly.'

Radio Guy startles a little, hands twitching down, but he's not a dummy. They go out to the sides, palms open, fingers spread, and he turns slowly. He's square-jawed, blond and thinning, and wears a neat mustache above a shit-eating grin that borders on insolent. 'Shouldn't you be in uniform, officer?'

'It's at the dry cleaners. You mind explaining what all this hardware is for?'

'You're interrupting an active op, officer. Walk away now and I might think more kindly when I mention this to your captain.'

'Nice try, smartass. I called dispatch. No active ops cleared with them. You're working off the books, you and your buddies in the van that's the other side of the block.' Radio Guy's eyes widen. 'Yeah, I made them, too. Probably got another van circling a couple of blocks away, five or six guys loaded for rapid response?' Radio Guy says nothing, but the grin evaporating off his face gives it away. 'Yeah. So maybe you cut the shit and tell me what you're doing here.'

Radio Guy relaxes a little, steps forward. 'Look, officer, I can expl—'

He lunges for Ray's gun, taking a long step forward and snapping his hand out snake-quick to knock the pistol's barrel to the side. Ray has been waiting for it, could see it coming the instant Radio Guy grinned at him. A step back is all it takes, and the grasping hand whips the air six inches short of its target. In answer, Ray brings the gun up into line, his finger on the trigger, the sights lined up on the bridge of Radio Guy's nose. Rear sight, front sight, target. A couple of ounces of pressure is all it will take to turn the other man's day to shit and he knows it. His face is milk-white. 'Put your hands behind your head.' Compliance is instantaneous. 'On your knees.'

Ray strips the SMG from the man's side, popping the shoulder strap one-handed. The gun is very light, all plastic and air. Half the weight of it must be just the bullets. 'What the hell is this?' Radio Guy doesn't answer. On his belt he has a handful of plastic cable ties, and a folded square of black cloth that Ray takes a moment to place. It's a black bag, ready to be flicked open and thrown over someone's head. They're not here on a surveillance job. They're here for a rendition. *And that's a two-man job.*

Ray snatches up the SMG and runs, just as the air where he had been standing fills with bullets. There's very little noise – the suppressed gunfire sounds like someone riffling the edge of a deck of cards – but from the crack of impact chewing up the cement and the yelp of warning from Radio Guy, Ray can tell it was close. He hits the enclosure at the end of the alley and dives sideways, getting out of their line of sight. There are some trash cans and a few pieces of old furniture here, but nothing big enough to use as cover. There are a few windows where the houses back on to the courtyard, but all of them are too small and too high to reach. Nobody wants a clear view of their trash cans. The handful of service doors stand resolutely shut. *Trapped.*

A mocking burst of gunfire bounces off the wall facing the alley mouth. Ray puts the SMG down, gets his phone out. There's no bars of signal, but he tries calling it anyway. He should have signal, but there's nothing. *They knew you were coming*, he thinks. *They radioed ahead. Baited you in.* Cut lines of communication, encircle, neutralize. Rendition tactics.

He picks up the SMG, pops the clip, checks it. Loaded. Twenty rounds, give or take. He puts it back, works the bolt, checks for a selector switch. There's a space between panic and madness, an unreal spread of seconds that feels like it goes on forever. Ray has been here before. He puts the SMG down, barrel pointing towards the alley mouth – *front towards enemy*, he thinks – and lifts his back-up.

Five bullets. They might have cut off his phone, but he can still send a message. Ray aims up at the windows, angling his shots high. It's irresponsible, stupid, and dangerous, but he's out of options. There's little hope of back-up, but he'll take an open door if he can get it. He prays that the shots don't hit anyone.

Five shots. One by one, he works his way across the lowest row of windows, a bullet for each. Without a suppressor, even his small gun makes an almighty crack in the enclosed space behind the buildings. The handclaps of a giant, controlled and evenly spaced with the rhythm of long practice.

From the alley, silence. Not even footsteps. Ray figures they have taken cover, made themselves ready for a surprise. *Whatever wins you time.*

The SMG is in his hands now, lighter than a gun has any right to be. He isn't ready. Nobody ever is. He looks up at the broken windows, the last shards of falling glass like an impossible summer snowfall. 'Come on,' he says, to no one but himself.

Chapter 8

Cameron didn't call her lawyer right away. The first number she dialed, her fingers punching it in on autopilot so it was ringing before she had even realized who she was calling, was her mom's.

For a couple of heartbeats Cameron tries to tell herself she doesn't even know why she did it. They declared their son dead when the first searches turned up no sign of him, buried an empty casket when the snow thawed. But she knows why. A year and a half of arguments, of them begging her to just stop looking, to accept that he was most likely killed. She couldn't bring herself to tell them that he did it, that he drove them both out into the blizzard knowing that he was going to crash the car. They don't know that she found out that the scarf that he was wearing was actually an airbag collar, designed to be better than a crash helmet. That chasing its purchase and import details down hadn't found Nate, but had given Cameron the conviction that she hadn't hallucinated the whole thing. That knowledge hadn't helped her in arguing with them. If anything, it had made things worse. Ever since, there had been a wall of silence between Cameron and her parents, all three of them too proud, too hurt to back down.

Nate's alive, was what she wanted to say. And *I'm sorry*.

'Hello?' Her mom's voice down the line, quiet from the four and a half thousand miles of distance. 'Hello?'

Cameron hangs up, then lifts the receiver to dial her lawyer instead. She can't bring herself to drag her parents into it. Not until she knows what Nate is into. Not until she has him there to explain himself.

A few minutes later, Cameron regrets not staying on the line with her mom. Dale Cross is pushing sixty, and with no kids he has a lot of spare energy to spend on lecturing his clients instead. All she can do is nod and throw in the odd verbal acknowledgement to let him know that she is still on the line, experiencing every second of the slow-motion explosion as his disbelief blossoms into straight-up anger. *Tell me everything*, he'd said. *Don't leave anything out*. So she did. *Almost*. She can't tell him about the gun. After she mentions that she's dragged two of her old rivals into it, she doesn't get the chance.

'They don't have privilege, Cam. The first touch of this on them, their counsel will advise them to flip on you so fast it will make your head spin.'

'I—'

'I would give you the same advice, if you were in their position.' He sighs down the line, a long, withering exhalation. 'Jesus, Cam. You couldn't have done something simpler, like running a gym? Or a bar?'

'You know why.'

A long pause. He knows why. He's schooled himself not to say Nate's name, as if by not saying it she will somehow decide to move on. 'Cam. He doesn't want to be found.'

'I don't care what he wants.'

'He almost killed you.'

'Nate called me when I went to the apartment.'

There's a long silence on the other end of the line. Cameron realizes how insane it sounds, all her desperate searching, her obsession, and then it's Nate that calls her. When Dale finally speaks, his reasonable tone is gone. His voice is hard, taut with resolve. 'Cam. I am telling you right now, get your ass down to a police station. Turn yourself in. Call me from there and I will be on a flight this afternoon.'

There is a noise from the back of the house: a crack, the sharp sound of glass breaking, then four more cracks, louder than the first. *Gunfire.* Cameron sits up tall, neck craned as if she can somehow spot danger through a wall, and takes the phone away from her ear. Her lawyer has heard it, too.

'Cam, what was that noi—'

'Dale, thanks for the advice. I'll . . . I'll call you back.'

'Cam, don't—'

She hangs up the phone and it rings in her hand. She hits green and lifts it back to her ear. 'Dale, I'm sorry, I—'

'Cam?' Her mother's voice down the line. Cameron's throat tightens, and it takes her a second to answer. She can still feel the gunfire echoing in her ears. *You don't have time for this*, she thinks.

'Hi, Mom.' It comes out weak, like her mom has just caught her with one hand in the cookie jar.

'Are you out of state? I didn't recognize the number—'

'Mom, I dialed the wrong number. I'm really sorry but I've got to go.'

'Not even two minutes to talk to me? It's been weeks, Cam.'

Cameron bristles at the question and bites down on the instinct to counterpunch, argue back. 'Mom, I promise I will call you when I can.'

A pause. Quiet on the end of the phone. Cameron knows she's made a mistake not rising to the bait. You spar with someone long enough, they know your patterns. 'Cameron, are you in trouble?'

I found a dead body. I kicked a cop in the head. Someone just fired a gun. Just one would be more trouble than Cameron has ever seen in her life, but all three of them are tied to the one thing she can't say: *Nate's alive, and he called me.*

'I love you, Mom,' she says, and hangs up.

Cameron heads for the kitchen, and the back of the house. Antonelli and Jones meet her on the way: Ophelia looks shocked; Sophia looks outraged.

'Do you have a back window?'

'Not anymore, from the sounds of it,' Sophia says. 'It's back here.'

'What's happening?' Ophelia asks.

'It sounded like a gunshot.' Cameron tosses the phone to her as she passes and Sophia falls in behind her. 'Call nine-one-one.'

'Where are you going?'

'To take a look.'

There's a utility room at the back of the house that has very recently lost a window. Glass crunches under Cameron's feet the instant she is through the door – shards cast a surprising distance – and she edges past the worst of it to reach the broken pane.

'Where does this look out?'

'Courtyard at the back. Where we put out the trash.'

Standing next to the window, Cameron leans over and peeks out past the frame and the last, clinging remnants of broken glass. A bitter taste catches in the back of her throat at what she sees. In the yard below, a man is crouched by the corner leading on to the alleyway with a gun in his hands. As she sees him, he levels the gun around the corner and fires blind, three shots that – thanks to the squat cylinder on the end of the barrel – make almost no noise at all. He whips the gun back as more shots sound in reply, chips of brickwork spinning loose from the corner as he flinches aside. Cameron catches a proper glimpse of his face, sees the bruise along his jawline. It's the cop from the flat. *Perada*. More shots catch the brickwork, and as they do Cameron sees movement in the alley. Someone moving up, under cover of fire. *He's in trouble.*

'Is there a door down to there?'

'There is, but—'

Cameron barges past Sophia, and all her friend can do is point down a short flight of stairs that lead to the back of the house. As Cameron rattles down the steps she's already working through the questions in her head, the most important ones rising to the top, the words already forming on her lips. *How did you find me?*

She hits the bottom of the steps and works the lock, pushing the door open a hand's width, keeping her body angled out of sight behind the wood. There's a good chance a bullet would go straight through it, but she'll be damned if she's going to offer anyone a target.

'Hey, asshole!' Cameron yells. 'Get in here.' She gives the door a kick and runs back up the stairs, out of the line of fire. Behind her, the door bangs off the wall outside and is answered by running footsteps and a burst of automatic fire. The cop swings through the door, pulling it shut behind him. Cameron watches as he works the lock, ducking on instinct as a handful of shots slap against the door. None of them make it through, which surprises her. He leans his forehead against the wall for a moment, eyes closed, and takes a deep breath. Cameron doesn't interrupt him. There's value in that space, that rest, even if it's just a second's worth. Sometimes it's all you need to get centered. He straightens, collecting himself, and looks straight up at her.

'You.' There isn't a hint of surprise in his voice. 'That figures.'

Cameron feels momentarily embarrassed, then anger at the embarrassment. 'How the fuck did you find me? Who are those guys?'

Perada climbs the stairs, fiddling with the gun in his hands. It looks too small, like a toy gun, but Cameron has no doubt that it's the real thing.

'I didn't find you,' he says. 'But they did. I've been following them. There's two out back and a van out front. They're kitted up to kidnap someone.'

Ophelia's voice rings out. 'Cam! I couldn't get hold of nine-one-one. Something's wrong with the phone.'

Perada is already nodding before Cameron can reply. 'They've cut the line. Mobile, too. They'll wait for their team to get here, then they're coming in.'

Cameron's throat feels dry. *Kidnap*. She guesses this is some kind of back-up plan, seeing as she managed to avoid arrest. The thought comes again: *who the hell did you piss off?* 'Cavalry's coming, though, right?' He just looks at her, and Cameron knows it isn't. 'Shit. How long have I got?'

He tips his head, holds the gun ready across his chest, barrel down, trigger finger flat along the top of the trigger guard. *Letting the training take over.* 'One minute. Maybe two.'

Cameron nods. Cut off, front and back. Nowhere to go. She turns back into the house. 'Come with me.'

Sophia and Ophelia are waiting for her back in the hall. Neither of them startles at the sight of Perada, gun in hand. Sophia looks him up and down once, and from her expression finds him sorely wanting. 'Is this the guy that shot out our windows?'

'Yeah.' Cameron's gut feels tight. 'He's the cop I told you about. Look, I'm sorry about this, but you know how I said I was in trouble?' They nod. 'I've brought it with me.'

'What kind of trouble?'

Cameron looks at Perada, who fills them in. 'Private military. They've come for her.' He points at Cameron. 'They're armed and apparently willing to use lethal force.'

Sophia lets out a low whistle. 'Right now?'

Cameron nods. 'Right now.'

'Cool.' It's not the response Cameron is expecting. She looks at Ophelia, who shrugs in answer, as if to say, *you know how she is.*

Footsteps hammer up the steps out front. A heartbeat, and the concussive thud of a ram hard against the woodwork, a blow that shakes the door on its hinges. Ophelia's face goes flat with rage. 'Do they know how much that door cost?'

71

'Is there another way out of here?' Cameron asks.

Sophia just laughs at her. She's already on her way to the front door, Ophelia falling in behind her, fists tight at her sides. Perada watches them go with a look of pure confusion, clinging to his gun like it's the only sane thing left in the world. 'What are they doing?'

Cameron knows the look she saw on Sophia's face. Pure, undiluted rage. 'I think they've gone to welcome their guests.'

Sophia flicks the latch open just as the ram hits again, and the door springs open faster than any of the men on the other side can react. Ophelia grabs the ram as it hits the top end of its swing and hauls their point man inside. Sophia slams the door shut behind him and locks it.

What follows is an education in how to beat a man senseless. There's not enough space in the hall for a clean swing, so the two women pound him with elbows and knees, the blows passing him back and forth between them like the world's fastest tennis rally. He tries to get his arms up, but gets tangled up in the bulk of his tactical vest and the sling that his weapon hangs from. He's wearing body armor and a helmet, but Sophia's hits are rising at just the right angle to capitalize on the two-inch gap where his neck is exposed. His attempts to cover up are over in the first three hits: another three and he's a ragdoll sliding boneless to the floor.

'Motherfucker!' Ophelia yells, all calm gone in a flash, standing over him looking for all the world like she's going to finish the job. 'You know how much that door cost?' He groans, and she kicks him, hard. 'Hand planed, you son of a bitch!'

'Get down!' Perada yells. Whether it's instinct or a cue that Cameron missed, they hit the floor as the men outside open fire, the muffled sound of automatic weapons and the snare-drum beat of bullets hammering into the door. Very little of it gets through the dense wood, but Cameron still feels the whip of air as a bullet passes overhead.

She can't breathe. There are more outside the door. There are more out back. She wants there to be a way out, some secret route, but there won't be. She can feel it coming: the helplessness, the inevitability, the fear of the pain to follow; two-fifty and change is leaning on her arm, and every single pin is going to come loose.

'Fuck it.' It comes out hard and low. 'You said a van, right?'

Perada is prone, his plastic science-fiction gun held out in front of him, aimed at the door, waiting for something to happen. He's on the defensive, and Cameron knows it is a mistake. The thin blue line, outflanked and outnumbered. 'What?'

'They've got a van, out front. The boss will be in it, right?'

He gets this look on his face, like he's remembering something. 'Yeah, that prick is in there.'

Prick? It's a question to save for later. Cameron gets up into a crouch. 'Come on.'

'Where are we going?'

'Up.' She waves her hand at Ophelia and Sophia, both still prone. 'Grab his radio.'

Sophia hauls the radio off the man's belt, stripping a microphone along with it and Ray takes his gun. Ophelia helps her to her feet, and ducks again to reach for the fallen man. 'He's got grenades,' she says, looking up at Cameron in shock. 'What kind of asshole brings—'

73

There's a crack from the front room, the sound of broken glass and the thud of something bouncing off the hardwood floor. Ophelia's eyes widen in realization as Sophia – quicker on the uptake – barges into her, pushing her towards the staircase. Perada hauls on Cameron's arm and she turns reluctantly, too focused on seeing her friends safe. *You did this*, she thinks. *You brought this down on them.*

'Move!' Perada tries to yell at her, but the sound of it is lost as the grenade detonates, the door to the front room bowing on its hinges and springing free, setting loose a blast of burning hot air that hits them like a fist. A muffled blanket of silence wraps itself round Cameron's head and the sensation fills her with panic. She casts about trying to get her bearings, but she feels unsteady on her feet, seasick, the stairs suddenly treacherous beneath her feet. She has to close her eyes and hold them shut to keep from falling, and the sensation of a hand grabbing her forearm startles her.

'You okay?' Cameron opens her eyes and finds Perada's face, close to hers. A high-pitched ringing fills her ears, her whole body is shaking, she feels anything but okay. 'We need to move,' he says.

Cameron nods. 'Up.' She looks back to see Ophelia holding Sophia upright, her partner's arm held across her shoulders. Blood is streaming from Sophia's ear, and the sight of it brings the world back into focus. 'Come on.'

Chapter 9

Ray hits the first-floor landing with lead in his feet. It's a feeling he knows, one that he's been trained to recognize. That first flush of adrenaline, the fight or flight response – that heart-pounding, ultra-aware state, the hormonal equivalent of a shot of nitrous straight into the intake manifold – is only good for a few minutes before it leaves you high and dry. Every single fiber of your body is going absolutely flat out to keep your ass alive, and there's a cost to that effort. You can't suppress it and you sure as hell can't stop it. All you can do is ride it out, knowing in advance that it's not going to last. They tried it with the army, putting boys into combat on a stomach full of pills that hopped their whole bodies up close to the limit and kept them there, combat-ready, storing up the crash to hit them days later. Years later. Rumor was they'd stocked up in the PD after 9/11, back when the departments had been flush with funding and access to everything the army had, all in the name of safety. Caches of pills in every precinct, enough that if the day came they needed all hands on a quadruple shift, everyone would be too busy grinning to call a union rep. Ray could do with a couple right about now.

Cameron King looks like she's already had her dose for the day. The other two women, the ones who just kicked the ever-loving shit out of a dude whose tactical armor did nothing to protect him, stumble up the stairs in a daze, their eyes on nothing, feet moving on automatic. King pushes past Ray with her head up, eyes bright and alert, like a concussive blast is her equivalent of three shots of espresso. She drags him in her wake through to the front room, where tall windows hang draped with white net curtains, spilling light across an unmade king-size bed. The air in the room is fresh, a sharp contrast to the smoke and panic of the hall and stairs, and Ray goes dizzy with the sensation of having woken from a nightmare.

King snaps him out of it with a tug on his elbow. There isn't much to her, but she's got a grip like a vice. She pulls him towards the middle window. 'Is that the van?'

The van that Silicon Valley asshole got into is still there. There's no driver visible in the front seat, but Ray can just make out something that could be a shoulder, an arm, visible on the far side of it. Someone standing on the sidewalk, watching the street. 'That's the van,' he says.

'Think you can hit it from here?'

Ray starts. 'You want me to shoot into the street?'

'No, I want you to shoot that fucking van, before we get an assault team up our ass.'

He hefts the submachine gun. It's light enough that it feels like it should kick to vertical off a single shot, but having fired it he knows there's virtually no upwards movement on recoil. It's precision engineering, the sort of thing that costs more than his monthly paycheck – *probably why you've never seen it before* – and he is certain it can make the shot. Whether he can make it, though, is a different question entirely. Firing blind down that alley was different. They made the choice for him. Ray swallows hard, feels King's gaze hard on him, and wonders what would happen if he gave her the gun. She looks as though she'd spray the street opposite with automatic fire if she thought it would help. 'I can make the shot,' he says.

Ray moves one window over to angle his shot along the length of the truck. King wants to shift them on to the back foot, make them back off. It's the right call. If Silicon Valley is still in there, the last thing he expects is to be used for target practice. All Ray has to do is scare them. *Shoot into the engine block, the seats. No through-and-through. No casualties.* The stock comes up snug against his shoulder and he aims down the sight at the broad target of the windshield. No need to take off the suppressor. They'll know where the fire is coming from. All he has to do is spook them with the first shot, then rattle the cage until they bug out.

He pulls the trigger. The window in front of him shatters, and across the street the windshield of the van spiderwebs in answer. Ray leans back from the falling glass and aims again, flicking the selector switch to three-round bursts. He puts the first one low into the radiator, then another through the windshield, and another into the engine.

Yells from below – not inside, but below – and the window-sill bursts into a shower of stone chips and dust as answering fire comes upwards. Ray shuffles back from it, taken aback. It's full automatic spray, uncontrolled and sudden. All those bullets that didn't find the masonry are going to come back down in about half a minute's time, and the thought feels unreal, hypothetical, like a question chalked up on the board at the end of a training session. *You put a hundred rounds into the air on a windy day in a built-up area: what are the chances you've just killed someone?*

King steps past him and tosses something underhand out of the window. He sees the lever fly just as he realizes what it is: one of the grenades they peeled off of the point man downstairs. 'What the fuck are you—'

His question goes unfinished as the grenade goes off with a flat *crump*, the sound muted by the open space it tries to fill. There are cries from below – panic, pain – and a shot whips past Ray's head to bury itself in the wall behind him. He ducks, and more shots fly through where he'd been standing a moment before. The big bald guy down by the van has opened up, trying to give his team some cover to retreat.

Ray moves one window right in a low crouch, out of the line of fire, and without needing to be asked pops up over the sill to fire down at the van again. *You're in the fight now, and there's only one way to end it.* There's someone in the driver's seat now, hunched over trying to start it, so he aims low, hitting the front tire and the engine block. One of the shots ricochets off something hard inside the van and shatters the driver-side window, and Ray sees the driver bailing into the back. Steam rises from the hood, and Ray shifts his sights towards the back of the van, the doors still resolutely shut.

King pulls at his arm again. 'They're leaving,' she says, and he glances back at her to see that she's jammed the radio earpiece into her ear and is listening to the frantic radio chatter, wide-eyed and grinning like the devil himself. Ray hears the screech of tires peeled raw on asphalt, and she nods to acknowledge it. 'That's their back-up coming to pull them out.'

Downstairs, a door bangs open and Ray turns, bringing the gun round, but stops short of moving towards the door. He can hear the too-loud voices calling out instructions, gruff and clipped, the sound of defeat and confusion. Three of them are yelling at each other, over each other, as they pull out their fallen man.

A second vehicle brakes hard out on the street, doors slam open, and the ceiling above Ray's head begins to fall around his ears as the assault team cover their retreat with automatic fire. King gets to the door before him, and Ray bundles through after her, half-expecting to feel a ricochet hit him in the back.

Out on the landing, the two women are sitting on the floor, backs to the wall, their eyes closed. The shorter of the two has her head on the other's shoulder, her skin is gray with plaster dust, the blood from her ear set bright against it.

King listens to the radio for a moment, then nods to herself, peeling out the earpiece. 'It's done,' she says. 'They're gone.'

The taller woman opens her eyes. 'Cam. What the hell have you got yourself into?'

'I don't know.' King looks around, lost. *There's the drop*. Ray can see the fight going out of her, her shoulders falling under the sudden weight of fatigue. 'I didn't think—'

The woman laughs, a short, harsh sound. 'They'd send a SWAT team? Seems like they don't know you like I do, Cam. If they did, they'd have sent an attack chopper.'

The gun hangs in Ray's hands like a dead weight. The police will be on their way now, for sure. It doesn't matter how high up Silicon Valley's hold on the department is. Chaos like this can't be ignored. Half the street will be calling 911 and the other half will be live-streaming the aftermath of those grenades on their phones.

He can already guess at what will happen, though. If he sticks around to give his version of events, it won't make it off of the captain's desk. Silicon Valley will slide right out of the picture. Ray doesn't have a single witness to back up his testimony. A couple of rich-ass pro fighters and a murder suspect, the same one he just managed to let escape that morning, and not a single one of the gunmen to prove who attacked them. He can already imagine what the excuses will be: betting rings, gang violence, an Internal Affairs investigation gone sour. He'll spend the next six months suspended while they go over every line of his psych evaluations looking for something to screw him with. Even if they don't find something, he'll still be let go. *It's in everyone's best interests.* He can hear them saying it. *Department morale would suffer. Let's not drag this out.* The only way he's going to get to the truth and have any chance of proving it is if he can find out what they want with Cameron King. And that means leaving before the cavalry arrives. 'We have to go.' The words are out before he realizes that he's even going to say them. 'The police will be here soon.'

'I thought you were the police.' King is wary. He doesn't blame her.

'I am.' He grips the gun, suddenly more sure of himself than he has been in a long time. 'But whoever comes might not be. I was ordered to forget about a dead man this morning, on the orders of someone who ended up here looking for you. Until I find out who he is, who he's compromised, I can't go back.'

'You sound like you're scared.'

You would too if you thought you'd been set up. 'You don't sound scared enough.'

In the distance, the shrill wail of sirens, the insistent brass of a fire engine's horn as it shoulders its way past parade-day traffic. King looks at him for a long moment, sizing him up, waiting for his composure to break. For the first time in a long while, Ray holds firm.

'Okay,' she says. 'Let's go.'

Chapter 10

They walk north towards the sirens, against all sense, but there's a reason for it. They're coming south and west from the Folsom Street station. That isn't far from Market Street, where the protest will be marching soon, and Cameron wants to be there when it happens.

The assault team made their move because they were on a quiet street, away from possible interference. It only took one cop turning up, off duty and in civilian clothes, to disrupt them. The more people she can surround herself with, the less likely they are to try again.

There was something in that that felt off to Cameron. She doesn't have any experience of SWAT tactics, but she knows what a lack of discipline looks like. When Ophelia and Sophia had hauled the guy with the ram inside to beat him unconscious, the look on the faces of his back-up had been one of pure surprise. That they'd immediately followed one of their own with direct fire and a grenade spoke volumes about how little he'd been worth to them. Coming back for him felt less like not leaving a man behind and more like they'd been ordered to remove the evidence.

They'd set her up at the scene of a murder. When she'd gone to ground, tried to find a way out, they had come for her again. Twice she'd tried to escape, and twice she'd handed them the initiative. Cameron could feel her back teeth grind as that thought circled round again. She wasn't going to give them a third opportunity.

The cop Perada – Ray – leads the way. Cameron had been tempted to ditch him, leave him to look after Sophia and Ophelia, but he seems really keen to avoid waiting for other cops, and a little local knowledge made navigating the streets a lot easier. She'd heard of people that could memorize a street map, which was straight-up magic as far as she was concerned. She knows vaguely which side of the city the bay is, which side is the ocean, and after that it has all been guesswork. She'd run her phone's battery almost to zero just trying to find Sophia's house. If they'd been tracking her cell, she'd made damn sure they knew where to find her.

Ray stops, and turns to look back along the street they've come down. A pitiful, stooping figure is heading their way, pushing a cart full of cardboard. They passed him before, on their way here, and Cameron could tell then from how thin he was, from the heavy curve of his spine, that he is no threat. Across the street there's an ATM, and Ray tilts his head towards it. 'You sure we should be doing this?'

'We don't have much of a choice.'

They ditched most of their stuff on the way. When you learn all about how to track people down, you spend a lot of time learning about how not to be tracked. The machine gun and grenades had been wiped clean and left on the doorstep to explain the automatic fire that had shredded Sophia and

Ophelia's home. Getting rid of it had almost been a relief to Ray, but he straight-up refused to ditch his back-up gun. It could be traced to him, for a start. Her pistol had been disassembled and dumped in pieces down a sewer grate. Cameron had pulled the batteries and SIM cards from their phones, smashed the phones, and scattered the pieces. She'd pulled the lining out of her briefcase, found the deadstick that was hidden there, and with a heavy heart plugged it into her laptop. It was an oversized USB stick, custom made to render a laptop useless the moment you insert it. There was a good ten seconds during which she thought it would do nothing at all, before it fired a jolt of current through the circuitry and – with a crisp, fizzing sound and the smell of burnt plastic – bricked it. Now, she made an inventory of everything they had left between them. Clothes, shoes, wallets, keys, cards. Still too many things they could be tracked with.

'This is it,' she said. 'The last step. Whoever was following me before is still tracking me. More likely both of us. They'll follow the trail of broken bits and pieces here, and even if they don't, when we use that ATM it's going to be like I set off a flare.'

Ray frowns. 'Has anyone ever told you that paranoia isn't a healthy mindset?'

'Nobody that didn't want to get knocked out again.'

He goes to the crossing and looks both ways. *Regular boy scout.* 'Ray. I'm saying that you can get off here. You don't need to come with me.'

It crosses his face. She can see it, the same relief that came when he pulled the action of the machine gun to pieces passing across his face before being replaced by something else,

84

something she can't read. 'No,' he says. 'Thanks for the offer, but I'm coming with you.'

'Some of the things I'm going to do aren't strictly legal.'

He does a good job of not looking disgusted. 'I can handle that.'

As he says it, Cameron starts over the crosswalk before the signal. Ray makes a noise of protest, and she turns, walking backwards the rest of the way. 'I'm not saying you can't, Ray, but you're going to need to convince yourself first.'

The lights change, and Ray hurries after her.

Cameron gets to the ATM, puts in her card, hopes that they haven't done anything to her account. If her card is frozen, at the very least it will tell her something about how much reach they have, how much power they can bring to bear in their pursuit. She's been running it over and over in her head, and it feels like everything they've done so far has been about position. You want to dominate someone, you need to control their movement. The body and the set-up sent her towards her friends, the nearest source of help; the assault team putting a grenade through the front window stripped that help away from her. They were herding her, pushing her into the corner. She knows what happens to fighters who let themselves get cornered.

She withdraws a thousand dollars, the largest sum the ATM will give her. It spits out the notes in a thick bundle, and she pockets them before pulling her card and bending it in half. She does the same with her business account, not enough in it after flights to make anything like the full withdrawal, but it's better than nothing at all. She waves Ray forward to do the same as she works both cards back and forth until the plastic turns white and she can start tearing them in half.

'Uh.' Ray's voice interrupts her work.

'What?'

'How much should I—'

'All that you can. We're going to need it.'

There's a pause, then the hesitant beep of keys being pressed. Cameron has her cards quartered now, the chip embedded in the card well and truly beyond repair, and she slings the pieces into the trash can nearby. She hears the whir of the ATM counting out cash, and turns back to find Ray checking the bills, lips moving as he counts under his breath. It doesn't take long.

'Seventy dollars?'

He looks up, embarrassed and defiant in equal measure. 'Give me a break, it's the end of the month.'

'I thought cops were supposed to be careful.'

'And I signed up thinking we got paid more.' He folds the cash and sticks it in his trouser pocket. 'You think I'm not careful? You should see my rent agreement.'

'They bleeding you dry?'

'Hey, don't joke about it. One of the guys in janitorial had a problem making rent three months back, ended up giving blood to make up the shortfall.'

'He told you that?'

'He fainted on a shift. Pretty much begged us not to take him to the ER.'

Cameron still has the smaller fold of bills in her hand, and she holds it out to him. 'Here. Hold on to this. Just in case we get split up and you need it.'

He hesitates on the edge of protest, but takes it. 'So what now?'

'New clothes.'

He shakes his head. 'To go with the tinfoil hats?'

She stares straight at him. 'Wouldn't be more obvious than your cop haircut.'

'I don't have a—'

'Ray, you might as well be wearing your badge on your forehead.' Cameron holds up a hand. 'May I?'

'I don't—'

She reaches out and messes his hair up, her fingers curling in on themselves as she draws her hand back, confirming the unpleasant feel of whatever cheap-ass styling wax sits in a jumbo tub on his bathroom shelf. It looks a little better, but even with his hair a mess he still radiates a cop vibe. 'There.'

Ray does not look impressed. 'So . . . we're going shopping?'

In the distance, Cameron can hear the sound of the protest warming up, overlapping voices rising and falling like the sound of waves. She can imagine the crowds, and all the opportunities they'll offer to slip a tail. It's almost the exact situation she would least like to have to find someone in. Get out of the corner. Take the initiative. Turn the fight around. If she plays it right, she might even get to see who's hunting her. She can feel the smile creeping on to her face just thinking about it. 'Not exactly. Come on.'

Ray freezes with his pants round his ankles. For a moment he forgets the reason he's here, the memory of eight grams of lead fizzing past his face, the involuntary twitch that followed uselessly – like he could dodge bullets – and all he can think of is the embarrassment of exposure. California penal code 314: even though it would only be a misdemeanor charge, it could see his name permanently attached to the sex offenders' register. The thought makes him feel sick, instantly, physically sick, and he squats, reaching for his belt.

'What's the hold-up, Ray?' Cameron is halfway through swapping clothes with a girl called Harmony, who is looking at her new ensemble with an expression that suggests the hundred dollars she's getting for the deal is not nearly enough.

'You're sure we need to do this?'

'I'm sure. Now take your damn pants off.'

Ray grimaces and drops his pants again, steps out of them.

'Your boxers, too.' Even the guy Ray is swapping with, a RayBan-wearing tanning booth advert called Chris, starts at that.

'Guys, if you think two men getting naked in an alley is the wildest thing that's ever happened on the west coast, you've got it way wrong.'

Harmony snorts in disgust. 'Not with this many cops out. Loads of private security too. All the big companies want to protect their assets from people waving cardboard signs.'

Cameron's stomach tenses a little. 'Are they televising all this?'

Harmony shrugs, non-committal. 'There's plenty of news crews out there. Lots of sponsors with banners up so they get airtime.' She says the last like it leaves a bad taste in her mouth, then nods at her friend. 'He got interviewed.'

Chris grins. 'I did! I should call my mom and tell her to look out for it.'

'He's a magnet for TV crews,' Harmony says. 'Straight, white, great teeth. Might as well have had him march by himself.'

'How do I look?' Cameron interrupts before the face of corporate America gets his feelings hurt and decides he wants his 501s back. Harmony's battered sneakers are a tight fit, but her white T-shirt, rainbow flag motif printed as a whole can of paint in mid-flight across the front, feels like it sits perfectly across her chest and shoulders. Harmony's jeans are ripped to shit, and the only solace Cameron has in wearing them is that she didn't go the whole way and make them into a pair of hi-cut shorts.

'Woah.' Chris is the first one to say anything. 'What happened to your arm?'

There isn't enough jewelry or make-up in the world to cover it, so aside from wearing long sleeves, Cameron has never tried to hide it. She still forgets the reaction people have to her scar, though. A finger-thick welt of too-pink tissue, it runs from her elbow to her wrist, criss-crossed and punctured by the tracks of all the pins and drains that it took to put her arm back together again.

'Cat got me.' Cameron doesn't even glance down at it anymore, make apologies for its existence. It's part of her. 'Took her to the vet, scratched the hell out of me.'

'Hey, no offence, but that is one motherfu—'

'Chris.' Harmony's voice is soft as she puts her hand on his arm. 'Put your shirt on.'

'Sorry.'

Cameron waves it away, and catches Harmony's eye before the girl looks down and away. There's something about survivors, something you recognize in one another. Not shared, but acknowledged.

'How about me?' Ray asks, and Cameron winces at how fake the question is. He's not dumb enough to have missed anything, and the conflict resolution hammered into him at the academy is kicking in. It's a safe bet he always plays good cop. Forced cheer, self-effacing. The sort of guy who buys donuts for everyone on the last Friday of every month.

'You look like an off-duty cop,' Harmony says. Ray's face drops.

'A more fashionable one,' Cameron offers, to take the sting out of it.

Chris claps Ray firmly on the shoulder. 'You look good, man. Roll up those jeans and you're set.' Cameron tries her best to keep the grin off her face as Ray stoops to do it and Chris winks at Harmony.

Chapter 11

Cameron ducks out of the alleyway and out into the press of people that line the street. She can feel the lenses already, the cameras turning this way and that, background shots for live reporters, directors scanning for interesting faces. She can imagine what facial recognition can do with those kinds of images. Her own set-up had been crude, a facsimile of a much broader kind of surveillance, a precision tool built to find people. If they can see her, they can find her. She moves light and quick on her feet, weaving through the press of people, making contact briefly if at all, bobbing her head this way and that to minimize the time she spends with her face still and exposed.

And realizes that she's only making it worse.

This isn't a chase. No one is hot on her heels. It's a pursuit, and that kind of hunting is as old as humankind. We don't run after prey, or spring out at it, we have no claws to speak of, and our senses are blunt and crude compared to other predators. All we have is a tendency towards stubbornness, and excellent pattern recognition. It's why everyone sees the cop in Ray, no matter how hard he tries to hide it. Right now,

Cameron doesn't fit, and it wouldn't take a supercomputer to pick her out. Her movements – erratic, quick, evasive – would draw the eye of any decent spotter.

She slows down, smiles, joins in with a group of people whooping and clapping at a witty placard that's attracting a lot of camera flashes and feels the shift in the crowd around her. Nobody does a double-take, their brains flagging up the movement of an outsider and demanding they take a second look. She fits.

Cameron looks back to see Ray already comfortable with the crowd, posing for a photo with a woman dressed as the Statue of Liberty. They talk between clicks of the shutter, and she laughs as he offers her a very serious handshake, which she accepts before demanding he give her a high five. Someone takes a picture of them doing it and it sets the hair on the back of Cameron's neck to prickling. She turns in a slow circle, looking for anyone filtering their way. Anyone that stands out. When she looks back, Lady Liberty is looking straight at her. She gives Ray a friendly pat on the chest before letting him go.

'Old friend?' Cameron asks.

'New one.' Ray shows her a card, handed to him by the woman. 'She was asking if you were okay, and if you were, you should give her a call.'

Cameron blinks for a moment, the thought that there still exists a world where people aren't shooting at her a revelation, and takes the card. 'Thanks.'

'Don't mention it.' Ray is smiling blandly, looking up and out over the crowd at the parade going past. He circles her waist with one arm and steers her forward to stand next to a dour-faced man holding a prophetic Bible verse on it. He's incongruous enough against the crowd that people passing see him and not Cameron. 'Our friends from earlier are here. Up ahead,' he says. They haven't seen us.'

Cameron grinds a string of curses between her back teeth. 'You sure it's them?'

'You'll see,' Ray says. He smirks to himself. 'They don't exactly fit in.'

They move past the cover the would-be prophet offers and Cameron picks them up quickly. The big guy with the bald head who'd been by the van is now standing completely still in a sea of people, scanning the crowd for any sight of them. His face and posture radiate rage and disgust, and there's a pool of space growing around him as people actively move out of his way. It wouldn't be a problem knowing where he is, save for the fact that they're stuck on the same side of the street and the natural movement of the crowd will eventually pull them on to him.

'Come on.' Cameron heads for the edge of the sidewalk, where a uniformed cop is nodding along to a beat that no one else is hearing, thumbs hooked into his belt, his gaze distant, apparently not too worried about the tide of liberal elitism that's slowly working its way along the street. She pushes Ray towards him, as they might as well make his aura of cop work for them for a change.

'Hey, buddy,' Ray says. The cop startles, but relaxes when he turns. They give each other *the nod*, that shared moment of recognition that everyone does when they see one of their own.

'Hey.' The cop screws up his face, looks out over the crowd. 'Good day to be off duty.'

Ray scowls. 'Mandatory. Had an op last month, can't go back 'til the stitches heal. No overtime. Medical bills are screwing me.'

Instant sympathy. 'Tell your union rep. They got a deal going with . . .' He snaps his fingers. 'Carrington Medical. Them and the city.'

'Thanks!' Ray indicates the Bullet-Headed Hate Machine with a tip of his head. 'What's the deal with Elite Force Delta? Shouldn't he be off hitting a tire with a hammer or something?'

The cop glances warily at Cameron, lowers his voice as he leans in. 'There's been an attack.'

'At the protest?'

'No, but not too far. They think the protest march was the target, and something went south before they could get here. No fatalities, but shots fired, at least one explosion. Everyone's been ordered to sit on it to keep a lid on any panic, but the city have rolled out some extra manpower.'

'He ain't PD.'

The cop shakes his head. 'Don't ever get sick again, bud. These guys are private military: Trident or Axion or whatever they're called now. Mayor thinks we need the back-up. "In case of an escalation," they say.'

'Shit,' Ray says. 'Can't afford hazard pay, but they'll pay to put mercs on the street? Thanks for the good news, man.'

'For the price of a coffee, I'll throw in this week's horoscope.'

'Stay safe, brother.'

'You too.' They shake hands and the cop turns back to the parade. Ray's face screws up tight as he looks down past where Bullet Head is standing. He lets out a low whistle. 'Private military,' he says, and glances at Cameron. 'How did they find us?'

'They haven't. Not yet. They're fishing. You ever see a guy go into a river to shake off tracker dogs?'

'Sure. On TV.'

'Doesn't work. Guy in the water travels pretty slow. Slow enough that they can put men and dogs the length of the river, walk back and forward until they catch the scent again.'

'The parade is the river.'

'Really big crowd to get lost in.' Cameron tries to put confidence that she isn't feeling into her voice. 'They would have had to come, even just to rule it out.'

'So how do we get past them?'

Cameron gestures towards the parade as it passes. Harmony wasn't joking about the corporate touch. Everything fronting on to the street that can support a banner has sprouted one, all sporting big company names: Warton Technical, Carrington Medical, Syntech. A Coca Cola stand is up and running, handing out free bottles of water and bananas in branded bags. 'How would you get across that street?'

'Without them making me? Sneak across behind a cop car or one of the ambulances.'

'Lot of open space between the curb and the back end of the vehicle,' Cameron says. Pattern recognition again. Even if the cops stationed on the sidewalk let them past without issue, all they have to do is step into the open and they're breaking the pattern, creating an anomaly to catch Bullet Head's gaze.

Ray shrugs. 'We wait for a crossing, then. They do let people cross.'

'Not often enough.' Cameron slips a handful of bills from the wedge in her pocket. She can tell it's a lot more than she would like to be getting rid of from the thickness of the wad, but she needs to be sure it'll have the intended effect. Distractions don't work if you need more than one try to get it right. 'Free money!'

She yells it at the top of her voice and pitches the wad of cash up and out, high enough that it separates in the breeze overhead. Between the placards and the waving, uplifted arms, it seems like there are a lot more bills falling than there really are, and the protest falls apart as a large section of it surges towards the money with a roar of approval. Cameron dodges a few outstretched arms, already grabbing eagerly at the air, and pushes Ray back away from the street.

The reaction from their hunters is instantaneous. Bullet Head's hand goes to the side of his head, relaying orders, while a handful of men swarm past him to make a beeline for the disruption. On the far side, a second team breaks cover and rushes in to cut off any chance of escape. Even Bullet Head forgets to hang back, and his tunnel vision as he charges into the crowd is so bad that Cameron and Ray pass through his peripheral vision unnoticed.

Another block down, the police manning the sidewalk take advantage of the stopped parade to let people cross from one side to the other. Cameron and Ray cross, and head off at right angles to the flow of the parade, making their way back north and towards the financial district.

Chapter 12

Ray doesn't need to ask Cameron where she's headed. They're going back to the crime scene where he first ran into her. She's taking a roundabout route, but he can still tell where they're going because it's one of the first rules of investigation. You get stuck, hit a roadblock, come up dry on ideas, you go right back to the very beginning and go over everything again. And again, until you find out what you missed the first ten times you looked at it. There's always something. Another angle, another clue. It's why cold cases get solved decades after the crime has happened: because someone took the time to go back to the start of the investigation and looked at it with a fresh perspective.

He also knows that it's a dumb idea. It's as obvious as daylight, and if the guys that are after her were to make a list of places they might pick up her trail again, that crime scene is top of the list. At the very least, she seems conscious of that fact, as he can see her getting jumpier with every step they take.

'Hey.' He touches her elbow as he says it, and the speed with which she turns tells him he came close to losing the hand. 'What's the plan, Cam?'

'Don't call me that.'

Ray bristles at the correction. 'Look. We shouldn't be here. You know that. So spare me the etiquette lesson and tell me what we're doing going back to look at the dark spot on a carpet where a dead guy was.'

'It's not what you think.'

'I'm telling you, getting stuck in another building is not on my to-do list.'

'It was a set-up, Ray. There's nothing that can help us. The dead guy, the computers, the gun—'

'We didn't find a gun.'

He can tell she took it from the look on her face. Her jaw works for a moment. 'If it's any comfort, I didn't kill him.' She says it very carefully.

Ray can feel the jump in his chest, that kick of discovery when two statements don't quite line up, or you look at the crime scene photos *just so* and what was once a random scrape reveals itself to be at just the right height to have been caused by the bumper of a car. She tampered with the crime scene. Cameron is standing as far away from him now as she was in the apartment, waiting to see what he's going to do with the information. If he tries to take her down now, it will likely be the last he sees of her. He knows how fast she can kick, and how hard.

'What's your play, Cameron?' It comes out flat. *Give me something. Tell me why I should be backing you up and not calling this in the first chance I get?*

She sighs. 'I need to find a payphone.'

'We've passed a few already.'

'A specific payphone. One close to where Sam Gorton was killed.'

'That's his name?'

'One of them. He was wanted for fraud, but had so many fake identities it made him really hard to . . .' She trails off, frowning. She thinks for a moment, then looks up at Ray. 'Really hard to find,' she finishes.

'What is it?'

'Nothing.' She shakes her head. 'When I . . . answered my phone, I heard something on the line. A car horn. I could hear it in the apartment, too. He was close.'

When you kicked me in the head. Ray bites down on it, finds a name instead. Remembers seeing it flash up on the screen as the phone buzzed in his hand. 'Who's Nate?'

'He's my brother,' Cameron says. 'He disappeared two years ago.'

Ray feels like he is standing on the edge of an open pit, and every question he asks is just falling away into darkness. He can't tell if she's lying, or mad, or both. 'Let me get this straight: you come out here looking for this Gorton guy. How much did he take you for, anyway?'

'He didn't take me for anything. I'm a skip tracer, remember?'

'So you were playing detective. Fine.' Ray can't keep the scorn out of his voice. 'But when you got here, Gorton has a bullet hole in his forehead, there's a gun on the floor – which you decide to get rid of – and then your missing brother calls you on a payphone that somehow manages to show up with his name?'

Cameron's jaw tightens. 'I have a hunch. He's involved with this somehow, enough that he couldn't approach me directly. He called . . . he told me to run, to get away, but he knew that I wouldn't. He's left me something. He wants me to find it.'

'How do you know that?'

'Because I've spent every day since he vanished looking for him.' It comes out quick, like she's ashamed to say it. 'He knew I wouldn't be able to walk away.'

That Ray can believe. He knows what it's like to keep your phone on, to never put it on silent, because you still believe there's a chance that you'll get the call, hear that voice come on to the line to tell you that it's okay, that they're not really gone. That you're not to blame. He takes a long, shuddering breath. He knows that feeling well enough to stick with her. Maybe helping someone else find that kind of peace is just as good as getting it for yourself.

'Can you trust him?' Ray asks.

'What?'

'Your brother. Can you trust him?'

Cameron goes silent and stares at the ground, cradling her left elbow in her right arm as though it's injured. 'Nate always looked after me. Even when I didn't want him to. Even when I didn't realize he was doing it. He has always had my back.' She looks up at Ray, meets his eyes. 'I trust him. I don't know what he's doing, but I trust him.'

Ray sighs. 'Okay. You're not looking for a payphone.'

Cameron's eyes narrow. 'What am I missing?'

'You're not from here. I know what you're thinking. Any other city in the world, he'd call you from somewhere nearby, let you find the phone he called from, leave a message taped under it. Here, nobody ever passes up an opportunity to do things the hard and convoluted way. You ever hear of a dead drop?'

'Sure. It's a spy thing, a way of handing over a message without ever meeting.'

100

'Not just a spy thing. Tech geeks love them. Think they're cool.' Ray nods to himself. 'Your brother was a geek, right?'

'That's one way to put it, yeah.'

'Then get your money ready. We're going to need a new computer.' He catches himself savoring Cameron's puzzled look. 'Or maybe just a chisel.'

They pick up a mobile phone and an adapter cable from a store they find nearby. The guy behind the counter is chatty, asks them if they've heard about the explosion and crashes any chance they have of answering by continuing with his theory that the government are behind it. Spraying chemicals into the air isn't working like they'd hoped, so now they're drumming up fear and panic with false flag attacks. He's too busy telling them about his online discussion group – *The Cause*, said so deliberately that they can't miss the capital letters – to let Cameron know if the phone is charged, so she opens it right there in the shop to discover that it is. Dropping a sixty-dollar chunk of her remaining funds on an off-brand touchscreen phone is a painful hit, and having to charge it up to full would have been the finishing touch to the icing on a shit-frosted cake. She has forward momentum, a lead spooled out ahead of Bullet Head and his friends, and she doesn't want to lose any of it. She drums her fingers on the counter as Ray talks the guy into looking something up online for him and printing him off a copy, the sheet of paper changing hands with a couple more bills on the way. The store is so dark that walking out of it is like walking out of a cave, and Cameron shields her eyes as she recoils from the glare of the sunlight. Cars and people are rolling by as though it's a completely ordinary day, like she hasn't fled two crime scenes since breakfast. Like there isn't a squad of heavily armed mercenaries out there tightening the net.

'So what is that?' Even as Cameron asks the question, she can see the gray blocks criss-crossed by white lines, a map of the Bay area south of the Golden Gate Bridge. A handful of black blobs are scattered across it. 'Map to the stars?'

Ray grunts. 'Yeah, right. Like anyone famous lives here.' He holds the map out so she can see it better. 'Landmines, from the last time the Packers were here.'

'The Packers?'

'You don't mess with Wisconsin.' Ray gets a pen from one pocket and draws a cross on the map. The crime scene. 'Okay. Your brother calls you here. You say you heard something down the phone that made you think he was close by?'

'Yeah. A car horn.'

'Right.' Ray folds the paper, dropping the area down to a quarter page. 'So he can't be far away. You don't hear a car horn ten blocks away, not during the day. Here.' He unfolds the paper again, checks the scale with his thumb, then leans against the wall to draw a quick circle on the map. 'Ten blocks is about a klick. Put that as our radius around the crime scene, and we have got . . .'

Cameron looks at the area he's marked. 'Three sites.'

Ray nods. 'Rincon Park is a stretch, but it's on the way.'

'We should try the one closer to Sam Gorton's apartment.' A car revs its engine nearby, and Cameron feels the hair on the back of her neck rising. She recognizes that it's the fear that's making her jump ahead, and fights it down. If they stay calm, and work quickly, they can do this. 'But you're right. We should try them all.'

When she sees the first dead drop, she understands why Ray wanted a chisel. It's a USB stick, half sunk into the tree, fixed in place with grainy resin that's been mixed to look like a lump of granite.

'If I can pull the USB key out of the stone, do I get to be CEO of a software empire?' Cameron asks.

'I hear that's how Zuckerberg got started.'

Cameron turns on the phone and unwinds the cable they bought.

'Better start praying this isn't just a bunch of malware and porn,' she says.

'Are you kidding? The porn is the best part.'

'Come for the espionage, stay for the dick pics?'

'Something like that.'

She plugs the drive in the wall into the cable attached to her phone. Nothing happens at first, and the drop in her gut manages to pack a day's work of defeat into a half-second beat before the phone screen lights up and indicates that it has found a new drive. Cameron feels a fleeting moment of triumph before she scrolls through the drive's contents. Pictures, mostly, a bunch of archived files that she wouldn't open even on this burner phone, and a mess of old text files dating back five years or more.

'Well?' Ray asks.

'We should have asked him to print off where the pay-phones are,' Cameron says, unplugging the phone with a jerk of the cable.

The second dead drop is closer to the crime scene, and Ray can feel how jumpy Cameron is getting with every minute that passes. He can't blame her. He's feeling it himself with the extra police presence on the streets, and every time they pass another patrol car he braces himself for the shout of recognition, for someone to come chasing after him.

They get to the drop and he knows even before Cameron plugs it in that it's going to be a bust. It's a half-assed job, a USB stick glued into a groove that's been gouged out of a wooden facing on the side of a building. A tight-faced woman gives them a dirty look through the glass, and Ray puts his hand out to stop Cameron from even trying to connect.

'This isn't it,' he says. A thought occurs to him, one that he's not a big fan of. It isn't going to be the third one, either. If Cameron's brother is a hard-core geek, it isn't going to be one of the drops you can find online. They're going to have to go and see a specialist.

'Are you sure?'

'You think Mary Poppins here will tell us she's seen anyone using this in the last day or so?' Ray gestures at the window, and the woman inside gives him the finger in answer. Cameron's face falls.

'You're right,' she says. 'He wouldn't risk it. Where's number three?'

'It's not going to be the third one either,' Ray says.

'So we're right back where we started.' Cameron looks ready to drop-kick the mobile phone. 'That's great, Ray. Just great.'

'I know where we have to go,' he says.

'You said that before, remember?'

'Yeah, but this time I don't want to go there.' He takes a deep breath. *Volk. The Ghost.* 'How much money have you got left?'

Cameron's mouth twists. 'Five, six hundred.'

'It's going to cost us more than that,' Ray says.

Chapter 13

Cameron follows Ray down a flight of metal steps that end when they butt up against an eight-foot slab of brushed steel that looks more like the business end of a bank vault than a door. There's a hatch at eye height, and even though there's no obvious camera watching them approach, it snaps open as Ray hits the bottom step. With it open, Cameron can just make out the sound of music from inside, the sort of high-BPM Eurotrash techno they'd blast out pre-fight to fill the arena with noise. It was a great trick for the announcers: too loud to even yell a conversation over, so when they cut it for the main event the crowd would already be silent.

'What is this, Ray, a speakeasy?'

'He wishes.'

'What's the password?' The voice at the door isn't the deep, heavy voice of a bouncer. He doesn't sound American, but that's as far as Cameron can place it off a single question.

'City Health Inspector.'

'You change departments, Officer Perada?'

'They keep asking,' Ray says. 'Are you going to let us in?'

'That depends on what you— hey!' There's a thud as

someone else pushes up against the inside of the door, another pair of eyes appearing at the hatch. Cameron hears swearing, her name mentioned and a brief, enthusiastic argument which sounds like German. The only word she recognizes is *Jägerin*, but that's enough. There's a click and several grating thuds as the bolts in the door retract, and it swings open so fast that Ray has to jump to keep it from hitting him. In the doorway are two very tall young men, both dark-haired, one sporting a neat goatee. Both of them are grinning from ear to ear.

'Officer Perada,' the clean-shaven one says, holding his hand out. 'What a pleasure to see you again.'

'Mister Volk.'

'Please, call me Ghost.'

'Ghost?' Cameron asks. Aside from being pale, he doesn't look very ghostly. He has the sort of build that suggests he either lifts weights or has spent a few years carrying a growing calf on his shoulders three hours a day.

'It's from a computer game,' his friend says. 'He loves computer games.' He thrusts out his hand. 'My name is Pedro. It's an honor to meet you, Cameron King. I'm a huge fan.'

'Oh, cool.' The ground feels a little steadier under Cameron's feet. A fan. She can handle fans. She shakes his hand and tries her best to put *the smile* on her face. 'Nice to meet you, Pedro.'

'If it's not too much trouble, could I ask you to punch me?'

Ray starts next to her, but Cameron doesn't flinch. One of *those* fans. 'If you've got a couple of grand and an insurance waiver, sure.'

Pedro gives her an awkward two-handed wave by way of apology for asking, and Ghost rolls his eyes. 'Well, now that he's got that out of his system, can I invite you both in? I don't like being outside on such an unusually busy day.' He steps back, and when Cameron looks to Ray the cop just shrugs and gestures her forward.

Inside the basement, the techno is a lot louder than Cameron expected. Ghost sees her frowning and gives Pedro a look: he strides off past a stack of computer cases, and a few seconds later the music drops fractionally in volume.

Ghost's basement is big. The door opens on to a mezzanine deck that loops round the upper floor of the room, and it overlooks a space that Cameron could only describe as what happens when someone starts building an office and halfway through decides what they really wanted was an arcade instead.

'Do you know where you are, Cameron King?' Ghost asks, his voice just shy of a yell.

'Neon lights, techno music, and a bunch of pinball machines,' Cameron says. 'All you need is a skate ramp and we'd be in 1995.'

'I like it! 1995!' Ghost laughs, spreads his hands. 'This is my humble home, the center of my empire.'

Cameron notices the way he's standing, square on to them, hands spread like a barrier. Whatever his empire consists of, he's not letting them get any closer to it. 'How do you know this guy, Ray?'

'Ghost is a security consultant. IT and communications specialist. He finds holes in systems that companies don't know they have, and fixes them.'

'For a price,' Ghost adds.

'For a price,' Ray nods. 'He helped the department out a few years ago, found a flaw that gave full access to our computer system. We would have been completely exposed if it got out.'

Something changes in Ghost's face as Ray describes it. His expression hardens, and she knows instantly where the story is going. 'You arrested him for finding it, didn't you?'

Ray sighs. 'Yeah. Not my call, but a warrant was put out for his arrest.'

'And with that arrest on his record, his consultancy work goes down the toilet.' Cameron slow claps it out. 'Well done. I hope whoever thought that was a great idea got a commendation.'

'Actually it got the captain a dressing-down from the DA,' Ray says. 'Turned out Ghost has a lot more pull than she thought.'

Ghost coughs, interrupting. 'Since then, I've tried to avoid the attention of the police. I certainly didn't expect my arresting officer to show his face.'

'We need your help, Ghost,' Ray says. 'This is off the books.'

'That would explain your outfit.'

'I'm serious. I'm in some deep shit here and I'm trying to dig my way out of it. Now, Cameron thinks that someone might have left some information for her on a dead drop. We've tried the public ones, but this is a whole different ball game we're playing.' Ray holds out the map, the circle he marked on it face-up. 'I need to know if there's a drop we don't know about within five to ten blocks of this location.'

Ghost doesn't take the map, but bends forward slightly to peer down his nose at it. 'That cross,' he says. 'Does that mean something?'

'No,' Ray says.

He's testing you, Cameron thinks. *Seeing what you'll hold back, what you'll give up.* 'I found a body there. Shot dead.'

A flicker of a smile at the corners of the German's mouth. 'Lying will get you nothing, Officer Perada. Not when you're out of uniform.'

'I also kicked him in the head,' Cameron says.

Ghost laughs, sudden and loud over the music, and nods. 'I know,' he says. 'I know you did, because Pedro and I have been listening to the police band all morning.'

Cameron can see Ray bristling, his embarrassment turning to anger, and can tell he's on the verge of walking out. She steps in front of him, forcing Ghost's eyes on to her.

'You work in IT, right?' Cameron asks. 'Communications?'

'In a broad sense.'

'You ever hear of my brother? Nate King?'

Ghost's smile vanishes, gone in an instant. When he answers, his face is a mask. 'I knew Nate King.'

'You know what happened to him?'

'A car crash. It ended your career, and killed him.'

'It didn't kill him, Ghost. He disappeared. Until today.'

'You saw him?'

'He called me.' Cameron pulls the map from Ray's hand and points at the crime scene. 'He wasn't far from here when he called. I'm sure of it. He's left something for me, and I need to know what it is.'

Ghost reaches out and takes the map from her. 'Do you

110

have a pen?' Cameron passes the pen to him and he marks the map, writing something down beside the mark. 'You'll find it in a parking garage, just a block over. First floor up, at the far end. Near the stairs. It's easy to miss, so be sure to look closely.' He folds the paper once and hands it back to Cameron. 'But I can give you some advice, if you will have it.'

'What is it?'

'Forget your brother,' Ghost says. 'And whatever he left behind for you.'

'What's that supposed to mean?' Ray asks, as Cameron weighs the piece of paper in her hands. It feels heavier than when she last held it.

'I mean this: if Nate King had been the one who found your department's back door, then your captain would not have got off so lightly.' Ghost waits until Cameron looks back up at him, and holds her eye. 'Everything he ever did, was to serve his own purpose.'

'Thank you,' Cameron says. She knew Nate wasn't big on making friends, but Ghost's cold regard is something else entirely. 'But he's my brother.'

'I understand,' Ghost says. 'It is always different with family.' He looks past her at Ray, and his face brightens. 'But we are forgetting something. The matter of my payment.'

'Don't look at me, Ghost, she has the money.'

'Oh no, Officer Perada, I didn't expect you to pay me,' Ghost says. 'I was just enjoying the sight of that bruise one last time.'

'I've got five hundred dollars,' Cameron offers.

'Miss King, I wouldn't get out of bed for five hundred dollars.' Ghost smiles as he says it, and tilts his head in the direction Pedro went when they came in, and Cameron gets it.

'Five hundred dollars, and I punch your friend so hard he sees stars,' Cameron says.

Ghost grins as widely as Cameron has ever seen a man grin. 'Done!' he cries. 'Just wait here and I'll get him.'

Chapter 14

It's on the first floor of a parking garage, just like Ghost promised, at the far end from the ramp, embedded in a crack in the wall six feet up. A USB stick, just like the others, set dead center in the filler used to repair the crack, with only the plug left sticking out. Unlike the others, someone has gone to some trouble to hide this drop. They've sanded the metal of the plug with fine-grained sandpaper, and it blends almost perfectly against the grey wall it is sticking out of. If she hadn't known to look for something out of the ordinary, Cameron might never have seen it at all.

The garage is unmanned, almost completely automatic. Sensors above each parking bay show red or green to show which spaces are taken, and there are cameras mounted in the corners overhead, squat little boxes tucked safe behind protective mesh. As far as she can see, the dead drop is sitting in a blind spot between the two nearest cameras. Hidden from view.

'Got it.' Moments after Cameron plugs in, she knows she has the right drop. She taps through the dialogue boxes on the screen, holds down on a folder marked *CAM*. Another dialogue box appears, covering up the folder icon.

Password:

'You're shitting me.'

'What is it?' Ray asks.

'He put a password on it.'

'So? Just grab the files, we can unlock them later.'

'I need to put in a password before I can move the files.'

Ray makes a strangled noise. 'Fucking nerds. Don't suppose he clued you in on what it was?'

Cameron doesn't reply, already running through the options: old memories of Nate, things he would have thought were important, things that he knows she will remember. *Carrying her home on his back. The ambulance outside waiting to take him away. The day he left for college. The night he crashed the car.* The memories settle cold in her gut, and she can feel her concentration falter. 'I don't know what it is,' she says, her lips pressed tight around the words. Scratching the surface of those memories is like prying open a wound. *He never let me down until that night.* 'Give me a minute.'

Everything he ever did, was to serve his own purpose. That was what Ghost had said. Cameron puts a hand to the wall to catch herself, her legs weak. *He crashed the car on purpose. He left you.*

'Cameron?'

'I said give me a minute.' Ray's concern brings Cameron back to herself, to the problem at hand. *This is the way you find him. This is how you get answers.* The password won't be short. Nate had strong feelings about short passwords. He was always keen on telling people about them, his great conversation-killer. Two beers into any event, he'd be there holding forth on how quickly you could brute-force a six-digit password.

That the more characters you added to the string, the harder it got to crack. He was very fond of the word *exponential*.

His second-favorite two-beer rant was on the vast number of people who still default to the word *password* when it came to securing their private information. Cameron chews on that thought. Nate was always a fan of the ironic. There was a time she would have typed in *password* without a second thought and laughed as it opened. It's exactly the kind of joke he would have played on her, but that was before the crash. Cameron doesn't know what's happened to him or where he's been, but the Nate of now isn't playing around. There's no room for jokes in him. It will be a long password, and she'll get one shot at answering it.

Cameron, listen to me. Listen carefully.

He told her. Of course he had. Make it something innocuous, a simple string that you could pass on without anyone ever guessing what it was. *You have to get out of there.* No contraction. He'd done it deliberately. She closes her eyes, tries to hear the sound of his voice down the line again. The pit of her stomach lurches as she reaches for it.

'Cameron,' Ray says.

'Quiet. I have to think.'

'Think fast,' he says. 'We've got company.' She cracks an eyelid, sees Ray leaning over the half-wall that overhangs the entrance ramp, hears the thunk of the barrier lifting. 'BMW. Looks like two guys.' Tires squeal as they turn on the painted surface beyond the barrier and the engine roar echoes up through the levels of the garage.

'How did they find us?' Even as she says it, Cameron knows it doesn't matter how. They're coming.

Her pulse quickens. It's not a natural acceleration, but a clenched-fist gear shift, the gas pedal pressed straight to the floor. What did he say to her? What was it? She tries to picture his face, picture him saying the words, but all she can think of is him nodding at her, the snow through the driver-side window white streaks on black, and the cold-water sensation as he jerks the wheel and the traction goes from under her. All she can think of are the questions she wants to ask him. *Why did you do it? What did you see coming that I didn't?*

'Cameron.' Ray leans hard on her name. 'We've got to go.' There's a stairwell ten steps away. She knows they could make it if they go now. They could give up, and disappear, and that would be it.

Why did you do it?

Cameron has no intention of giving up.

'Ten seconds,' she says.

'We don't have ten seconds.'

Her hands are shaking. She grips the phone hard to keep her fingers steady. They're coming. She can't keep her mind on the task. All she can think about is the car. *They'll want to pull up close*, she thinks. *They don't know we aren't armed. They'll use the car to give themselves cover, use the size and speed to intimidate. They'll stay in the car as long as they can.*

'We have to get out of here,' Ray says.

The words stick, like she's heard them before. She can hear Nate saying them. 'That's it,' she says. She starts typing.

Youhavetogetoutoftherejustgo

She types it in as one long string. *Do you understand?* That was what he had said.

The car engine revs, deep and muscular. Close. It's on the ramp to their level now. Cameron hits the accept button as the tires squeal, spinning as they fight for a grip on the concrete.

The file transfers.

She looks up to see the BMW speeding along the garage towards them. Collision course. An intimidation play. They'll stay in the car as long as they can. She's already running as she pulls the phone free from the dead drop. Not sideways, away from the threat, but straight at them. When they rush you, you rush them right back. *Break their rhythm. Take back the initiative.* The hood of the car looks like it's an acre across. There's no room to dodge it. If it doesn't stop, she'll have to try and jump high enough that it doesn't break both her legs.

The guy behind the wheel panics. No time to confer, no time to decide. Only room for reaction. His eyes go wide and white and he stamps on the brakes. The nose of the car dips sharply as it shrieks to a stop.

The passenger-side door is already opening before the car is stopped and Cameron takes the jump anyway, a tiny shift in direction all she needs to launch herself over the bonnet and catch the door two-footed, all of her weight behind the kick. One foot connects with a gun hand, and the guy holding it pulls the trigger in reflex. The crack of the gunshot is loud in the enclosed space, a bark of noise that rings in Cameron's ears and makes her skin prickle with fear and anger. She doesn't feel the jolt and scrape of landing, all of her attention focused on the gun hand. He's pulling it back inside the car and she aims a kick at it, right leg cocked up towards it and hammered out with vicious quickness. The door frame catches him square across the back of the hand and he drops the gun. Cameron scrambles after it, throwing herself forward on forearms that feel like they're on fire and lunging to catch the gun before it can skitter away behind the rear wheels. She gets it, letting her momentum carry her forward and over, rolling on to her back and bringing the gun up two-handed as the driver rounds the front of the car.

He isn't well trained, and that's what saves her. Her gun isn't centered on him when she brings her arms up in front of her. Her aim is about twenty degrees out of line when he clears the bonnet. But then neither is his. Instead of coming round the corner with his gun already aimed down the length of car, he arrives facing the way he's moving, arms long and rigid like he's at the shooting range. He starts the long right-angle turn to bring his gun to bear, and Cameron has already got him clean in her sights, arms braced against the angle of her knee. He sees it, knows that she cannot miss him at this range, and makes the wrong choice. He pulls the trigger, too early to ever have a chance of hitting her, blind panic making him desperate, and Cameron fires in answer.

The shot kicks high and right of center mass, catching him a hand's breadth below his left collarbone. The shot goes straight through him, the bullet barely slowed by layers of skin, muscle and lung. Cameron sees the bloom behind him, the spray of blood that mists the air in the bullet's wake as it exits, and the stunned look on his face as the first wave of realization hits him. He goes slack-jawed at the jolt, and Cameron can almost see the wheels turning in his head.

All he has to do is fall. Let gravity and fate's good graces take over. His friend in the car can help him, hold the wound closed while waiting for help to arrive. Emergency services will be on high alert, so it won't be long. All he has to do is let go, and fall. For the second time in as many seconds, he makes the wrong choice. His hands tighten on his gun and he lifts it back into line, seeking vengeance.

Cameron's second and third shots are not off-center. The second bullet flies past the top of his gun and hits him dead in the center of his chest, shattering the sternum and collapsing the ribs inwards, burying itself in the meat of his heart. It does not come out of his back. Her third bullet goes higher, her aim kicking upwards with the recoil of the gun. It hits him under the chin, the entry hole a dark spot of color, and travels up and through his head, tumbling as it hits the bone at the base of his brain. The spray that fills the air behind him is pink-red, blood and brain matter, his medulla oblongata reduced to liquid by the passing bullet, the shards of bone that spin in its wake. It's the part of the brain responsible for the reflexes. Responsible for breathing. If putting a bullet in his heart wasn't enough to stop him, then this makes it a certainty.

His body falls, the slack weight of his arms pulling him forwards, crumpling at knees and waist and neck. His face sags, already empty of life. It's not like seeing someone fold up after a knockout, or feeling them slip away in a submission hold. There's no return from this.

Cameron struggles to her feet, tries not to see the look of open-mouthed shock on Ray's face as she catches sight of him standing off to the side, caught halfway to the stairwell because he was already running the second she pulled the connection. She turns on the balls of her feet, the gun heavy in her hands, and levels it at the passenger window of the BMW. She doesn't need to aim at this distance, but she does it anyway, her eyes focused on the front sight, the tiny stub of metal pin-sharp in her vision.

'Get your hands up and get the fuck out of the car!' She bellows it at the window, her voice raw, cracking on the swear word. The guy in the passenger seat is an out-of-focus blur, his hands two pale patches either side of his face. His voice is high, muffled by the car door.

'Don't shoot. Please. I'm coming out. Don't shoot.'

Cameron pops the door handle, hauls it open. Swung fully out, the bulk of the door means that she doesn't have to look at the dead man, the blood pooling around him. She can smell it, the air thick with a coppery tang that lies like a blanket under the acrid taste of gun smoke that swirls blue-grey in the draft of the door opening.

'Get the fuck out!' Cameron yells it in his face. He's wearing a tactical vest, black webbing, radio kit, pouches bulked out across the front of it. Black shirt underneath. She grabs him by the vest and hauls him out of his seat, one foot braced against the side of the car. He sprawls on the garage floor face-down, and Cameron aims down at him, the gun pointing directly at the back of his head.

'Cameron.' Ray's voice breaks her aim. 'Put the gun down.' She looks up and he's standing right next to the dead man, a gun in his hands, angled downwards. Not aiming straight at her, but held in such a way that he could be, very quickly. 'Put it down, Cameron. Now.'

Chapter 15

Ray knows that he should arrest her. He should take her back to the precinct, process her, and let the system do what it was built to do. Find the truth. That's what he believes in. *Believed in*. Ray can feel the gun twist in his hand, the grip slick with sweat. Cameron doesn't move an inch, her own gun still aiming downwards, only her gaze lifting in response to his challenge. Her gaze is like a rock. No twitching, no nervous sideways flick. She looks straight at him, and Ray can read nothing in her eyes. No remorse. No rage. In the space of three breaths, she is completely in control of herself. He has the drop on her. She knows it. She also knows he's not going to shoot her. That he can't. Because his faith – his faith in the system he swore to uphold – has been shaken.

Ray feels a tremor building in his left thigh, his nerves and his body betraying him, giving way under the pressure. He knows for certain now: he was never ready to come back to active duty. They rushed him back. His mouth feels like it has been pasted shut, and he has to work to regain his voice.

'I know what it's like,' he says.

'Know what?'

'What it's like to kill someone.' He lowers the gun a few inches, edges forward. 'This is the first time, right?'

Cameron blinks, a rapid flutter of eyelids. 'What?'

She's not processing. Confusion is a common symptom. The first crack in your armor. Everything moves so fast, it's hard to catch up.

'This is the first time you've killed someone.' He thinks about stepping closer, and decides against it. He remembers how fast her kick was. Out of reach is a good distance. 'Cameron, I need you to take your finger off the trigger. Keep it on him, by all means. Keep him covered. But I need you to take your finger off the trigger.'

Her head jerks almost involuntarily and she grins, a terrifying flash of even, white teeth. 'You afraid I'm going to shoot him?'

'I'm afraid that these are exactly the type of assholes who'd modify guns to fire on a hair trigger, and that if you don't, so much as a cough is going to kill him.'

Cameron nods and eases her finger out of the trigger guard, laying it flat along the line of the gun. The movement pulls the gun to one side, and she's no longer aiming directly at the man's head.

'Thank you.' Ray flicks the safety on his own gun, and lowers it completely. A show of trust. A de-escalation. He feels the stickiness of the blood pool reaching his sneakers, steps away a shade too slowly to avoid getting it on them. A de-escalation. Try telling that to the dead guy, see what he thinks.

'You said you know what it's like.'

'I do.'

'So tell me what it's like.'

Ray takes a deep, shuddering breath. 'You try and justify it. You never stop trying to justify it. "It was them or me", or "It was just bad luck."' He pauses, finds the words ready to be spoken without even trying to recall them. '"The panel concludes that in the time between the officer's reaction, the pull of the trigger, and the bullet's impact, the suspect was able to turn sufficiently that the fatal wound was sustained to the rear portion of their right lumbar region. The panel concludes, therefore, that this was a clean shoot."' He's shaking by the time he's done saying it.

'Doesn't sound like you agree,' Cameron says. The guy lying on the ground at her feet moves his arm, a slow but very deliberate attempt to get his hand closer to his side. Before Ray can call it, Cameron moves her foot and steps on his hand. 'Don't think I've forgotten you,' she says. The noise he makes when she rocks forward and puts her weight into it – a scream through gritted teeth – makes Ray go cold.

Ray takes a deep breath. 'I don't.' It's the first time he's ever said it out loud. When they investigate a shooting, they make you go over it again and again. They reconstruct the scene, using computers and math and angles to build back from a body, a brass casing and a handful of bullet fragments to model an event that stands free of any witness interference. They show you it, show it to your lawyers, your co-workers, and they say to you, *walk us through it, one more time*. The scene they built absolved him in the eyes of the law. And by the time they were finished running him through it, he could almost accept that was how it had gone down. Enough that he breezed through the mandatory therapy sessions, enough that he was given a clean bill of health and put back to work. 'It wasn't a clean shoot,' he says.

He would have missed the reaction if he hadn't been looking straight at her. Something in Cameron's face gives, and he sees that swell of pity pass across her face before she smothers it down, her brow creasing with the effort.

'Why are you telling me this?'

'Because I didn't want to see you kill a man in cold blood,' Ray says.

'I wasn't going to shoot him,' she says. 'Not without a good reason.'

'You were close,' Ray says. 'I could see it.'

Cameron shakes her head, but Ray knows what he saw. Her blood was up. He knows what that does to a person when they've got a gun in their hand.

'That's not why you told me,' Cameron says. 'You knew he was safe. What else is going on, Ray?'

Ray can't find an answer. When he caught the smell of gunpowder, saw the blood pooling, it took him back to something he thought he had managed to put behind him. He'd realized that he wasn't ready. Cleared in the eyes of all the experts, the tribunals, the counsellors, his colleagues, but he still wasn't ready. They should have seen it.

Maybe they did see it, and they sent you back out anyway.

He pulls that thought tight to his chest, like he's gone all in on aces and eights, and there's only the river to come. A dead man's hand. They put him back on duty when they knew he wasn't ready for it, and every cop in the precinct knew it: the captain, Bulwell, even Kaz. Ray takes a deep breath, holds on to it. *You knew they were covering something up*, he thinks. *Maybe it wasn't duty they thought you couldn't handle.*

The feeling is like discovering a tick burrowed in tight under your skin: that there's something rotten in the department, and everyone knows it but you. Dispatch had tried to wave him off responding to the call-out to the apartment, but he'd been on the end of the block when it came through. Silicon Valley had been keen to fit Cameron King up for a murder with a broken timeline. Was someone else meant to find Sam Gorton's body first? After he died, did they wait for her to show up before calling it in? Even if it means turning a blind eye here, he's going to find out who the hell is pulling the department's strings. Until he can, the precinct is burned. A no-go area.

Ray gestures to the man stuck under Cameron's heel. 'We should see what he has to say. If they know we're here, they won't be the only ones sent after us. We need to get moving.'

Cameron looks down at the man on the ground, then up at the car. 'Hey.' She addresses it to the captive. 'You come kitted out for a kidnap?'

He stays silent until she leans on his hand again. 'Yes! Yes! Christ!'

'Back seat? Trunk?'

'Back seat. Look, jus—' He loses his voice. Ray hears something pop: maybe a knuckle, maybe the scaphoid bone. Six months to heal, if he's lucky.

'Shut up,' Cameron says. 'Ray, check what they've got in the back seat.'

'We're taking the car?'

'We're taking the car.'

'You want me to drive?'

She gives him an unreadable look. 'I'll drive,' she says.

125

Chapter 16

Cameron drives the BMW out of the garage and on to an empty street. The car judders as she peels out, lurching hard enough that the rear end scrapes on the ramp upwards. She bites down on a curse, the sort of thing she would have yelled in private, a curse aimed at all things four-wheeled and dumb as shit. It's a stick shift, and while she knows how to drive one in theory, it's been a long time since she had to do it in practice. Ray is sitting in the back of the car, and Cameron is amazed at how loud someone can be when saying nothing. Their would-be kidnapper, now prisoner, makes the sort of noise that suggests he was the one that signed off on the rental. He's in the passenger seat, zip-tied at ankle and wrist, held in place with loops of duct tape. Most of it is across his chest, holding him tight to his seat; the tape around his knees has another length passed down between his legs, securing it to the lever underneath. A final piece is round his neck, loose enough that he can breathe but little more than that. With the back of his head pinned to the headrest, he has to look down his own nose to see ahead. It gives him the air of a man who regrets ever getting on the rollercoaster but can't get off, and Cameron thinks that it suits him, given the circumstances.

For the sake of good road safety, they put his seat belt on for him.

'You okay there?' He doesn't answer. She fumbles the first couple of gear changes, but it's slowly coming back. The light ahead changes to red, and she sighs at having to put her foot back on the clutch. 'How do people cope with this shit?'

'I did offer,' Ray says.

'You did.'

When he told her to put down the gun, she'd expected a stand-off. Instead, she'd looked up into the eyes of someone on the verge of a breakdown. He'd remembered his training, kept control of his voice and his posture, and yet he'd been shaking. His voice had cracked, and when he told her why, she had understood. When she shot the driver, she'd sent Ray back to the moment he shot a man. Three bullets, two casualties. He'd tried to make it sound like he was trying to help her, but he was talking himself down more than her. There was something else. Some question he kept to himself, odd pauses as he worried at it in the privacy of his own thoughts. Cameron hopes that he'll solve it in his own time. The first shots have been fired, and this is far from over. She wants to be sure that if it comes down to it, he won't freeze up.

She turns the corner on to a wider road, signposted towards the outer city limits. She's picking the route by feel, mostly. The car has a satnav, but she's disabled it. Too easy to hijack, to track from a distance, or spoof new directions to it and force them into a trap. Once they realize their team hasn't picked her up, they'll send back-up. When they find the body, they'll go straight for the car. As long as they are in it, she has to assume that they're on borrowed time. No dead ends, no stops, no doubling back. A wide loop that swings out and round, and they can ditch it somewhere and double-time it on foot to a BART link to vanish back into the heart of the city. Leave their passenger somewhere where he'll be found. Eventually.

'How did you find me?'

'What?'

'Sorry, weren't you paying attention?' Cameron jerks the wheel, making the car swerve suddenly. She glances across at her would-be kidnapper, sees that he has gone grey in the face. She knows how terrifying it is to be helpless. 'Maybe you should be. How did you find me?'

'I didn't.' It comes out in a rush. He's breathing hard and tight with panic, and it makes him speak in staccato fragments. 'I didn't find you. We were given— we were given a location. Told to pick you up. They said,' he shakes his head, as much as the tape will allow, 'they said it'd be an easy job. Said you were running scared.'

'How'd they contact you?'

'R-radio.' He drops his chin towards his chest, to where the earpiece is hanging by its cord. She took it off of him just in case he found a way to broadcast an alarm. Some models could be programmed to do it with a channel switch, or the press of a button.

'Channel?' She gives the wheel a nudge as she asks it, to put him off thinking too long on the answer.

'Seven! Jesus fuck!' His eyes are close to popping clean out of his head. 'Seven.'

Cameron checks the radio. It's still set to channel seven. She didn't hear any mayday being sent, but then she'd been half-deaf from the gun going off. 'Who are you working for?'

'I'm with Axion. Axion.'

'Axion?' Ray speaks from the back seat. 'The security company? I thought they worked bank contracts, all that armored van stuff?'

'No, they do lots of stuff. Transplant runs. Personal security.'

'And kidnapping, apparently,' Ray adds.

'Dude, I swear, I didn't think it'd be like this.'

'What's your background?' Ray asks. 'Army? Marine corps? You look young for an ex-cop.' Cameron takes the opportunity to check the road signs ahead, thinks about getting off the 101. They're making good time heading south, but the car will be easy to spot.

Especially if they're airborne.

'I answered an ad. They said there'd be training on the—'

He yells as Cameron turns hard, hauling the car across two lanes to get to an exit. She puts her foot down as they hit the ramp.

'Cameron, what the fuck?'

'They wanted us to take the car,' she says.

'They what?'

'Look out the window, see if there's anything over us.'

'Over us? Like a chopper?'

'Chopper, drone, whatever. Something that can fly and keep pace.'

'Cameron, I—'

'Just look, Ray.' She turns off the ramp and starts off down a road that lies at roughly ninety degrees to the path they were on. She flicks the trip meter to zero. A couple of miles should keep them off the same roads they drove out on. In the back, the electric window whirs as Ray lowers it, and the car's cabin fills with noise and wind. The meter ticks over to one mile before Ray brings his head back inside and closes the window. It's like putting on ear defenders: once closed, the car is silent save for the low rumble of the engine. 'Well?'

'There's something up there,' he says. 'It's not a chopper.'

Cameron shakes her head. 'Drone. I fucking knew it.'

'Like a Predator drone?' Ray sounds doubtful. 'It looks pretty small.'

'It doesn't need to be big,' Cameron says. 'Not if you're tracking someone. You put a mark on the roof of their car, follow the car from the air.'

'Like numbers on police units.'

'Right. Nobody ever thinks to look up to see if they're being followed.'

'There was no mark on the roof of the car.'

'It doesn't have to be visible. You could use ultraviolet or infra-red active paint. Looks like a clear coat to the naked eye, lights up like Christmas to the right kind of camera.' Cameron looks across at her passenger, who is trying to lean as far away from her as his bonds will allow. 'What about your partner? Did he answer an ad, too?'

'I never met him before today. I got a message saying I'd be picked up, he was waiting downstairs. He seemed pretty tough. Said we were on a mission.'

'Who's your manager? You must know someone.'

130

'I got sent down to Bakersfield on a training course. Full board and pay, maybe fifty other guys on the same deal. I got back two weeks ago. They gave me my kit bag, told me to keep it ready, they'd be in touch.' He bites down on a sob. 'This was my first . . . God. It wasn't meant to be like this. I thought I'd be—'

'You thought you'd be four nights a week on your ass guarding some gate, yeah. Whatever. Let me guess, they told you there'd be simulations, exercises. High-pressure situations that would test how well you'd done at training.'

'They said we'd be assessed—'

Cameron turns back towards the city, leaning back in her seat to address Ray. 'They must have sent out a bunch of cars to different locations. Dead drops, known associates, anywhere they thought we might go. Send out a bunch of rookies, guys who barely know what end of the gun goes bang, hand us a free ride. Put a ring of spotters round the city, see which car breaks from the pattern. Tells them where we are and where we've been.'

'I guess they want to find your brother too,' Ray says.

Cameron nods. 'And what he's told me. This is their plan B. They weren't trying to catch me this time. They're fishing.' She clicks her tongue, frustrated. If they can get under cover quickly, they might be lucky and be able to slip the drone. Throwing a net around the city takes a lot of organization. If they're spread thin enough, she and Ray might be able to ditch the car and walk away.

'At least your brother used a password,' Ray says. Cameron curses. She had forgotten about the USB key. By taking the car, they'd given away the location, and probably what it contained.

'Shit. We need to go back and destroy it.'

'Do we?'

'If they listened in on Nate's phone call, then they could guess—'

Cameron is interrupted by a shadow sliding into her peripheral vision. Her first instinct is to dodge, and she hits the brakes hard. The car that had been coasting in her blind spot lunges past the driver-side door, swerving hard as its driver tries to respond. Cameron keeps her head up, seat belt smarting across her chest as it holds her against the deceleration and watches the other car go past their front bumper and over to the passenger side. She drops into second and jams her foot on the accelerator. The car revs hard, and she is pressed into her seat as it lurches forward. As they come up alongside the other car, she can see the rear windows lowering.

'Ray?'

'I see it.' He doesn't bother with the window. She hears the snick of the safety going off and the rear door opens. 'Brake when I shoot!' She glances back to see him head down, holding the door right-handed, the gun pointed down and back under his right elbow. In the other car the driver is waving at them to pull over, the barrel of a pump-action shotgun visible on the far side of him. The instant they pull level with the other car, Ray fires three times. The rear tire of the other car bursts with a bang as loud as the gunfire, and Cameron hits the brakes a second time.

The other car fishtails, almost recovers, then spins out, doing a one-eighty as it curves back across the front of the BMW. Cameron can see the driver struggling to regain control, his passenger fighting to retrieve a gun that has leapt out of his hands like a live fish. She punches the accelerator again as they clear the driver-side bumper.

'Brass!' Ray yells, and Cameron flinches away as he starts firing through the rear window, arms straight, the spent casings ejected into the front of the car past Cameron's right ear. The window behind her shatters, and in her mirror she catches a glimpse of steam rising from the other car. It struggles to move forward, a groggy final effort to try and beat the ten-count, and falls away, unable to give chase. The car is quieter than she expects with the window gone, and she realizes that the sound of gunfire behind her head has left her half-deaf.

'Motherfucker.' Cameron can barely believe what she sees in the street ahead. Bullet Head is standing in the middle of her lane, not two hundred yards away. He doesn't have a gun: he's just standing there with his arms loose at his sides, shoulders hunched forward, daring her to hit him. He's standing like he has faith in human nature, that she will brake or swerve to avoid hitting him. Maybe he thinks it's instinct, or that she has somehow forgotten how clearly the stakes have been laid out. Cameron keeps the car in a low gear and puts her foot on the gas. Next to her, their duct-taped prisoner starts yelling, an incomprehensible rush of words.

Ray grabs the back of her seat, by her shoulder. 'Cameron, you're not going to—'

'If he doesn't move, it's his own fault.'

She braces herself for the impact, back glued to her seat, arms braced against the steering wheel, elbows and knees bent. They're almost on Bullet Head, and he hasn't moved. This isn't the same as the garage. There's no gun, no threat. Just a man in the street, waiting for her to mow him down.

Chapter 17

Cameron has her arms tight across her chest and her feet free of the pedals when the grenade goes off underneath them. Between the skid and the explosion, it's like a giant hand comes up under the right-hand side of the car and flips it, sending them tumbling. They go up and over, and Cameron holds tight against the weightless feeling that comes with it. She knows what's coming.

The car lands three-quarters of the way through the flip, the corner of the roof catching the first impact. The airbag goes off in Cameron's face and her window implodes at the same time. As they go over on to the roof, the frame on her side buckles awkwardly. Everything in the car's frame is built to take a head-on collision, to crumple and fold neatly about the driver without flinging the engine into their lap or putting the steering column through their chest like a lance. All that weight on the roof, on the columns that are meant to stay rigid around the driver, is too much for it to take. The force goes into the door, which folds like paper and pops clean open.

As the car slides the last few feet, the scream of metal on tarmac so loud that she can feel it trying to turn her bones to powder, Cameron is already scrabbling to find the release on her safety belt. Upside down, she's half hanging out of it, pinned in place by the two lengths of strap that are bunched together across her waist. She can see Bullet Head's feet and legs, the angle of her head making it look like he's standing balanced on a sheer cliff. She doesn't know what's happened to Ray or their prisoner, doesn't dare look away from the waiting figure outside the car. She can't hear anything but the pings and creaks of settling damage, the metal ticking like footsteps on a hard wooden floor. The car reeks like a mechanic's workshop, of oil and grease, and over it all is the distinctive cut of gasoline. Cameron finds the release, braces with her bad arm and her knee under the steering column, and presses it.

It isn't until she gets right side up that the dizziness hits her. She turns round to get out of the car, and the pavement keeps on turning under her hands, far enough round that she has to brace herself against the car to keep from falling sideways – or down, she can't quite tell – into the steering wheel.

Cameron almost loses her footing as she climbs out of the car, her feet sliding on the broken glass. She catches herself on the buckled remains of the door and is struck by how heavy her arm feels, how hard it is to close her hand on the metal. She can't decide if it's the shock of the crash or the fatigue piling up that's most responsible, but she knows that she doesn't have much left in the tank. Bullet Head is just standing there, waiting for her. It's only a matter of time before he gets bored and stops gloating – any sensible thug would've kicked her in the face before she could climb out of the car – but she'll take all the rest that she can get.

'You look like shit,' he says, and something in his voice brings Cameron's head up fast, twin spikes of pain shooting up the length of her neck as the muscles there spasm, still stiff from the crash impact. She ignores them. She's heard his voice before.

'What did you just say to me?'

'I said you look like shit, Cameron King.'

'You motherfucker.' She knows exactly who he is. *Ho-ho-holy shit.* An arm pushing past her, the flash of a photo being taken. When she woke up in the hospital, her lawyer was the first person she'd called. He'd sat on every news outlet and photo agency for a full day afterwards waiting to find out who had taken that picture of her. It never showed, and she'd assumed that either no one was willing to touch it, or he'd not got a shot worth selling. 'It was you that took that photo.'

He snorts in disbelief. 'You remember that?'

'Hard to fucking forget.' If she had felt drained when she climbed out of the car, she didn't feel it now. The anger is burning through layers of fatigue like a blowtorch on full blast, fueled by the immediate need to tear this guy's boiled-egg head off his steroid-swollen neck and take a steaming shit down the neck hole.

He searches for something clever to say. She can see the change in his expression as he thinks it up, like watching a light go on in the echoing void where his brain should be. 'You know,' he says, 'we should really stop meeting like this.' He gestures at the car, like he's not sure she'll get it.

'Yeah?' Cameron pushes herself up off the door and stands tall. Her hands lift into a guard on instinct. 'I got an idea of how I can make that happen.'

'Oh?' He feigns surprise, but his stance changes. He starts rolling his shoulders, loosening them up for the fight. *Boxer?* Cameron can't help but think it. 'You want a fight now?'

'There's not going to be a fight, dickhead.' Cameron watches him limber up, watches as he punches the air in front of his chest. Short, choppy arm movements, each one coupled with a quick turn at the waist. She knew a boxer who did the same thing. In front of a heavy bag, at the start of fights: always the same kind of movement. But this guy's feet are all wrong. He's standing flat-footed, feet almost a yard apart. Like he couldn't care less about moving them. *Not a boxer. Arrogant, in good shape, swings like a boxer: he's probably military. Don't need to be able to throw a punch well if you're pulling a trigger.* She takes a careful step forward, away from the glass, towards him. He doesn't adjust. Doesn't seem to care how far away she is. Cameron speaks low, keeps the anger tight and focused. 'I'm going to kick your balls straight into your brain pan, and then I'm gonna have a sandwich.'

'Is that right?' He keeps punching at the air, less a warm-up and more an intimidation tactic. He's got long, muscular arms, and each swing is like a challenge, a reminder. If he gets a clean hit on her, if he gets a good grip; either way, she's fucked. Cameron doesn't recall the arm that pushed past her being like a tree trunk, but then she'd had other things on her mind at the time. 'Come on, then.'

Cameron takes another step forward.

Time and distance are everything in a fight. It's why his stance, his apparent unwillingness to move even an inch, is strange. He's a big guy with a long step and a longer arm. He could be on her in two steps if he wanted to. He's got one hell of a reach, and Cameron is right on the edge of it.

She wants him to move. Wants him to take the bait and launch a big, fight-ending right so that she can slip it and kick his knee clean out of joint. He isn't taking the bait, though. He just waits, and he looks as though he's happy to keep waiting. Cameron doesn't like it much, but she's going to have to go to him.

She gets up on to the balls of her feet, her calves protesting every bounce, and starts moving round him. The way he's standing is an invitation to kick him square in the crotch, but a shot in the balls isn't going to stop him straight off. Big guys don't fold up that easily. It takes them a long time to realize what's happened. All it will do is set him up to grab or punch, and piss him off into the bargain. So she goes round him instead, and though she has further to go, the stupid way he's standing makes him slower on the turn.

The instant the weight shifts on his feet, Cameron changes direction and skips in, kicking hard, her foot swinging round at ankle height to scythe one of his legs out from under him. Break his base, put him off-balance. *Wipe that grin off his face.*

Her kick misses. Quick as a snake, he lifts his foot just far enough that the kick goes under it. He sets his foot back down and keeps on turning to face her. He's fast. He's really fucking fast and when he sees Cameron's surprise it makes him grin even more. *Maybe you're just slow.* Cameron crushes that thought the instant it appears. Doubt will end the fight for her if she lets it.

She speeds up, keeps going round him, watching the shuffle of his feet as he follows. He's lighter on his feet than she thought, and that makes her cagey. Still, he doesn't chase her, doesn't capitalize on the opening she gave him, and even if it's a choice born of mocking confidence, it's still a mistake. He might be fast, but that cockiness makes him a rookie.

She feints with the low kick again, turns her hip and lifts it into a high kick at the last moment. There's not a great deal of power in it, it's not hard to block, but it's something fighters can walk straight into if they're not watching for it. The sort of thing you throw at a promising beginner, or a sparring partner who thinks they've seen everything you've got.

It doesn't land. He almost catches it full in the face, his feet planted square on to her, but at the last second he jerks his head and neck back. He's shit-quick, but the movement is awkward as hell and even though the blow doesn't land it still rattles him. His smile vanishes and his whole face flushes red. She can see a vein in his forehead bulge, pressing hard against the skin. He lifts his fists, holding them up six inches from his own face. If he wasn't so quick, she'd kick his forearm or elbow and he'd punch himself and break his own nose.

'Come on, then.' She taunts him as she moves, circling round behind him. 'Move your fucking feet, you pussy.'

She only dodges the punch because she knows it is coming, sees the decision being made long before he starts to move. It's a straight right, something she should be able to get past and build on, but his arm is like a steel girder, fist thrust forward with so much momentum that it's all she can do to get clear of it by ducking on the blind side of his arm. She senses the follow-up coming more than sees it, and dives forward as he stiffens his punching arm and swings it like a log through the air where she was standing a moment before. She bangs her forearm hard on the road when she lands, but she rolls through it and is back up and facing him again.

He charges at her, launching forward in a lumbering run that she answers with a kick, a big step in and a kick at chest height, the full force of her weight behind it. Anyone else running on to it would have caught her foot in their sternum. He shifts as it comes in, feet sliding as he turns around the kick, catching hold of her leg in both hands. He pulls, and Cameron's head snaps back as he uses his grip to throw her past him. It's pure rage – if he had kept his cool the fight would have been over the instant he got a hold of her leg – and while she lands badly, it isn't the end of the world. When she gets her feet under her, one of her ankles is so painful to stand on that she sees stars bursting in her vision.

Cameron knows that she's going to lose the fight. It's a hard truth to take but it's better to accept it. Nobody ever got out of a chokehold by denying that it was happening. It's not that he's big. She's trained with big guys before. Beaten them, on occasion. It's not that he's better than her, either. From what she's seen of him so far, she's surprised he can make a fist. It's their difference in speed that's going to win it for him. He's fresh, and she's not. To beat him, she needs an opening to bridge the gap between them. Each time she's tried to close it, she's moved so slowly his reactions have been able to save him. He's too fast and Cameron is too tired, and in recognizing it she accepts that there's no way she can win this. And if she knows she can't win the fight, there's not much point in prolonging it.

She closes with him again, hands up in a guard, and feints another kick at him. He doesn't flinch for it, or when she

141

switches her stance and feints off the other foot. He doesn't even blink, and Cameron realizes that he's trusting his reflexes entirely, only moving when a blow gets close enough to hit him. *This is it.* She comes in a third time and throws a high kick with her left foot that whiffs short of target, the motion turning her so far that she ends up facing the opposite way. As soon as she loses sight of him, she pulls the same foot in and kicks back and up towards head height. It almost hits Bullet Head in the face: coming forward after the first kick he walks straight on to the second, and he leans so far back to avoid it that he stumbles away from her.

Cameron takes the opportunity to sprint for the car. There's a gun in there, and if she can get to it then his speed won't matter. Fast as he is, he's not going to dodge a lump of copper-wrapped lead travelling at nine hundred feet per second.

She ducks as she reaches the car, catches the upturned frame with one hand and turns on her back as she slides in the driver-side door. The inside of the car is hot and close, and the smell of petrol is very strong. She looks at Ray in the back seat – he's still upside down in his seat belt, knees trapped by the seat back in front of him, his head pushed over to one side hard against the roof. There's no blood, and no gun in sight. Cameron paws round the roof, feeling for it. No luck. *No fucking luck.* She tries to work herself forward on her elbows to check the roof behind Ray's head, but a hand closes around her ankle and pulls hard. She cries out, gets both arms round the driver's seat, kicks at the hand that's pulling at her. He's going to drag her out of the car, and there's nothing she can do about it. Cameron fumbles for the phone in her pocket, tosses it into the back next to Ray. All she needs to do is make sure he doesn't come looking for it. Bullet Head's fist interrupts her train of thought by coming down like a hammer on her injured ankle. White specks burst in her vision as her grip fails, and the pain is so intense it feels as though everything below her knee has been flash-frozen. Bullet Head hauls her out of the car, and the bump of her head against the door frame jolts Cameron back to her senses. She pushes off the ground with her hands, not caring what the glass does to them, and climbs the arm that's holding on to her, hauling herself up on two fistfuls of shirt. He tries to peel her off, his other hand coming across her back and grabbing the crappy-quality shirt she's wearing: it gives way before she does, tearing at the shoulder as Cameron gets her hands to his face.

She forgets about the pain in her ankle, the glass cuts in her hands, the bruising echo of falling that lies like a mantle across her shoulders. Her whole world, her universe, shrinks down to her two hands, and his head. She gets her right arm round his head, her elbow locking right where the back of the skull meets his neck, and grabs hold of her left hand before sinking her left thumb into his eye and pressing as hard as she can.

Her thumb goes in a long way. She feels something give way, a hot rush of fluid, and crooks her thumb to try and lock it hard against the inside of his skull. Bullet Head is screaming now, shrieking in horror and pain, and the hold on her ankle gives way as he lets go to thrash at her with his hands. Every time he pulls at her, it jerks her thumb and he shrieks even louder.

Cameron's hand slips a little, her grip loosening. He's thrashing around too hard for her to do anything now but hold on until she can't any more. She knows she's going to lose. At the very least, he'll have paid dearly for it. Her hands slip more, the pressure coming off of Bullet Head's eye socket, and he reaches up with both hands and peels her free, lifting her over his head with a roar of pure animal rage.

Cameron knows what's coming. In spite of herself, she laughs.

'I got you, you bas—'

He throws her, one step and a heave, and she folds into a V-shape as she flies clean over the crashed car and bounces off the tarmac on the far side. She's still conscious when she lands, but the world is fuzzy, out of focus. She tries to say something, to prove to herself that she's still there, but the words won't form in her mouth. She can hear a car coming, rolling up to a stop, and for a moment she feels something that's uncannily like hope. *Here comes the cavalry.*

A pair of shoes appear in her vision, someone standing over her.

'Miss King.' It's not a comforting tone, but Cameron can't bring herself to feel much about it either way. She feels numb. 'You've given us quite a chase.'

'What should we do, sir?' Another voice, off to her left.

'Get her in the van. Prep her.'

A pause. 'And the rest, sir?'

The first speaker sighs. 'Get Samson up and get someone to look at that eye. Torch the rest.'

Cameron blinks, and she comes to, flat on her back on a gurney. She can't lift her head. Someone leans over her and a needle pierces her arm. 'This'll help you rest,' they say. They're not kidding. When she closes her eyes, she sinks into total darkness.

Chapter 18

Ray doesn't come to slowly. He jerks awake like he's just been shocked, flailing his arms up and trying to push away the roof where it is pressed against his neck and cheek. It takes him a second to realize he's upside down, pinned by his own weight, his inner ear and brain compensating to try and make sense of an inverted world.

He's still in the car.

He remembers the crash. The drawn-out feeling of it lifting underneath him, a rollercoaster gut-drop as it turned over and then the hammer of his cranium pounding hard on the anvil of the roof. Unconsciousness was like blinking. He's tensed up like the car is going to turn again, his whole body tricked into waiting for an impact that has come and gone while he was out. Ray doesn't know how long it has been, but the smell and the hot, close feel of the car tell him that it's been long enough.

He does a quick inventory of limbs. Both arms, still with hands; legs cramped tight against the back of the seat in front, but otherwise whole. There's a sharp pain along the outer curve of his right elbow, an old strain pulled fresh, but it's

145

almost a comfort to know that's the least of it. Ray puts one arm up over his head, forearm braced against his weight, and feels for the seat belt release with the other. It doesn't budge. He thinks it might be his weight on it and jumps, legs pushing hard against the seat back, but it does nothing except dislodge the gun that was caught behind his knee and send it rattling past his face, making him flinch.

'Did you hear that?'

Ray hadn't made sense of what he could see through the windows, but as soon as he hears the voice, the two gray pillars on the other side of the car resolve themselves into legs, calves turned away from the car.

'Hear what?' Another voice, behind him. He can't turn enough to see where exactly they are standing, but he can tell that it's close.

'I'll take that as a no. You think there's enough fuel to burn all this?'

Ray hangs frozen in place, waiting for the other to answer.

'Nope. Tank must've been pretty empty. Most of it ran down the chassis, dripped off the front. I'll grab a can and we can splash it up inside the cab, toss in a road flare. Do it once, do it right.'

'Cool.'

The guy behind him walks away, and Ray reaches to get a hold of the gun. The scrape as he lifts it feels loud enough to echo inside the car. He watches the other man's legs, the impatient twitch in one of them as he waits for his buddy to get back with the petrol. They probably checked him already, crouched down and told themselves he was out or dead, and not likely to wake up soon. Ray eases the slide back on the

146

pistol just enough to see the gleam of brass from the chambered round, and lets it slip forward before taking aim at the weight-bearing leg. One shot. He knows he kept count when he fired at the other car, but the numbers escape him. He knows he went down to single figures, but the crash has taken the exact number from him. Even if he could pop the clip in silence, he can almost hear the thump of a trunk closing, the other guy coming back to throw gasoline in through the broken windows. Ray mouths a prayer to Saint Jude, his father's favorite, a prayer for lost causes and the fate of all gamblers, and thumbs the hammer back to cock the gun.

'What the fu—'

The shot takes Grey Pants high in the meat of his calf and he drops with a yell, not enough weight on his other leg to keep him standing. He grabs the popped driver's seat door and catches himself, his back blocking out all but a wedge of light. Ray aims past the driver's headrest – *at least Cameron got out* – and shoots center of mass. Spine, heart, lungs; whatever it hits, the guy's grip on the door slips free and he goes down on his face and doesn't move.

A shot hits the door behind him, a hailstone smack against the metal as it ricochets off at a shallow angle. Rather than struggle to turn, Ray hooks his feet under the seat in front and heaves, pulling himself up with his legs and pushing with his left arm until he's sitting upside down in his seat. He arches his back as far as he can, head tilted right over, trying to catch the other guy coming through what he can see of the cut-off, crumpled wedge of glass that was the rear windshield. His gun hand is shaking as he tries to get it over to aim, and he almost drops it when his hold slips, smashing his face hard against the car roof. Another pair of shots smack the door, and a third takes out the window. Something jolts hard against Ray's calf, and it feels like someone has drawn a line on his leg with a hot coal. He yells out loud, a quick, panicked bark, and puts the barrel of the gun over his right shoulder to fire off three shots blind, as fast as he can fire them.

His gambler's luck holds, the shots rewarded with a yelp – not pain but shock – and he takes the opportunity the other man's distraction gives to hammer the seat belt release with the butt of the pistol, roaring as he lays into it.

The belt comes free and whips across his chest, setting him free to fall down and sideways just as two more bullets bite into the seat back where his legs were a moment before. Ray turns and pushes himself backwards on his elbows, away from the window, aims the gun towards the back of the car. There's a shape that could be a man, crouched, and Ray puts his sights on it, not willing to wait for a muzzle flash and a bullet in his face to confirm it. The front sight comes into sharp focus, centered on the bulk of the shape, a clear shot. He pulls the trigger.

Nothing happens. The gun is empty. Normally the slide would have stayed back, but when he hit the seat belt release it had sprung forward again, and he had missed it.

'Shit.' He pops the clip, finds it as empty as it seems. 'Shit.'

The rear windshield shatters, and Ray throws himself sideways as though he can somehow dodge the gunfire, burrowing tight against the driver-side door, trying to present as small a target as he can. 'Jesus Christ.' More shots, and he puts his head down. *This is how you die, shot and incinerated in a crashed car.* The thought has him hyperventilating, his skin too tight and too hot. He thrashes his free hand around, looking for something – anything – to hold on to.

He finds the phone, the one Cameron had in her pocket, and his panic doubles at the realization that she's gone, and he doesn't know where. As he pushes it away, his hand bumps into a clip, still heavy with bullets.

Everything he has focuses down on this one thing. He sucks in a shuddering, swift breath, holds it tight. The clip comes up as the gun turns to meet it; it slides into place with the oily resistance of metal parts machined to a close tolerance, accelerating home as their precise, matching nature irons out the fractional misalignments that human hands cannot avoid. He jerks the slide back to chamber the first round, feels the whole gun kick in his hand as it returns, signaling its readiness as weapon and savior. He turns the gun and takes aim, only to realize that the kneeling human shape he could just make out is now prone, and there is no more gunfire.

'Officer . . . Perada?' A new voice, male. Higher than the other two, and hesitant, as though unsure of the name.

Ray keeps his gun trained on the figure. 'That's right.' He shouts it, and is surprised to hear how raw it sounds. His jaw won't keep still, not without him clenching it, and he feels suddenly very cold.

'The man who was firing at you has been neutralized. I, uh . . . I mean you no harm.'

'Right.' Ray can't keep the skepticism from his voice.

'What I mean is, I would like to help you. And I really don't want to get shot.'

'How do you plan on helping me?'

'Well, I would say I can get you out of the car—'

'I got that covered. What else?'

'I have some medical supplies. Sounds like you're hurt.'

'You just happened to have those.' The sights of the gun blur a little, then jump with the effort of bringing them back into focus.

'I do. And I have a good reason for it.'

Ray sniffs, wipes at his face and realizes that he is weeping. He rubs the heel of his hand over his eyes and takes a deep breath. 'Okay,' he says. 'Okay.'

'I'm going to come over to you,' the voice says. 'Like I said, I don't want to get shot.'

'Hold up.' Ray thumbs the magazine eject, catching the magazine as it falls free of the pistol. Racks the slide back all the way, and as the bullet clatters off to the side, locks it in place. Last of all, he flips the gun over and sticks his little finger into the chamber, making sure it is clear. 'There,' he calls. 'Safe as I can make it.'

'Thank you, Officer Perada.' Ray starts as the man speaks just next to him, and he realizes that he walked over while Ray was dealing with the pistol. Either he is very quick and quiet, or it took Ray a long time. He makes a fist of his trembling hand and suspects it to be the latter.

The door opens with some effort from the man pulling on it, a screech of metal before it springs open and he staggers back to avoid being hit by it. Ray looks up to see a tall, skinny figure with long, sun-blond hair and a familiar-looking face. He's wearing a light grey suit, powder-blue shirt, and no tie, and looks like he has just strolled out of a meeting populated entirely by people who make million-dollar cell-phone apps. In one hand he's carrying a black duffel bag.

The man offers him his hand. 'I'm Nate, Cameron's brother.' Ray clasps it, and finds himself holding a hand that feels fragile, like it could shatter under his grip. Cameron's brother might look like her, but that's where the resemblance ends. Something shifts down by Ray's waist, and he puts his free hand on the door frame, stopping Nate from pulling him out.

'What's wrong?' Nate asks.

'These medical supplies you mentioned,' Ray says, 'they come with a pair of pants?'

Nate frowns, confused. 'I don't . . . no, they don't.'

'Can you pull a pair off the other guy for me?' Ray tips his head in the direction Nate came from. 'Because I'm pretty sure I just pissed myself.'

Chapter 19

Nate King makes Ray walk a forced march for two whole blocks before letting him change his jeans. Ray can hear the sirens and knows that he should be happy that they're not currently being arrested and that none of his peers are going to see him like this, but he can't shake the indignity of waddling in the other man's wake or the feeling that having to endure it is somehow Nate's fault. His wet jeans cooled fast, faster than he'd thought they would, and the fabric clings to every inch of skin it touches, pulling at it as it dries, and by the time they stop Ray feels as though he will never be able to get clean again. He's got them halfway off when Nate starts talking. He's wheezing from the walk but he pushes the words out anyway, impatient to question Ray.

'Have you been to the hospital recently?'

'What?' Ray doesn't look up at him. As the jeans crumple round his ankles, drops of cold piss bead on the inside seam and Ray almost falls over trying to keep it from touching his leg.

'A hospital.' Nate shifts his feet, impatient. He coughs once, a convulsive, wet sound that makes Ray feel like backing away from him. 'Or a doctor's appointment. Or the dentist. Any medical appointments in the last twelve months, you need to let me know about it.'

Ray had needed a full work-up before going back to active duty, but between the piss and Nate's tone, he doesn't feel like sharing. 'Fuck you, man, you want to check my credit score too?'

'That's not a denial, so I'll take it as a yes,' Nate says. 'You get a shot any time you were in?'

'You want to know if I got a shot?'

'Did they give you a vitamin shot, an anesthetic, something like that? Any injection at all.' Ray thinks about it, and while he's thinking Nate puts the bag he's holding down and steps closer. 'Ray. This is important.'

Ray worries the corner of his mouth. They did give him a shot, not that he thought anything of it at the time. 'Flu shot. Said it was city-funded, part of a new initiative to help lower the amount of hours lost to sick leave.'

'When they waived the insurance, they made you sign for it.'

It's not a question. 'Yeah.' He frowns. 'Standard procedure, they told me. Part of the insurance fee waiver.'

'Did you read the fine print?'

He hadn't even thought about it. They'd held the clipboard out with a fluorescent orange sticker on the page to show him where to sign. 'Does anyone? Hospital charges twenty bucks for the shot, eighty for the needle and another hundred for the nurse to stick it in your arm.'

'Yeah, that's how they get you.' Nate squats down and opens the bag that's in front of him. 'Which arm was it?' Ray points to his left arm, just below the shoulder. 'Thanks. Can you hold it out for me?'

Ray holds his arm out, and Nate pulls a handful of circuitry and wiring from the bag, resting it on top as he lays it out and checks it over. Ray isn't an expert on these things, and the sight of a circuit board connected by colored wires to a hand-sized rectangle wrapped in black tape makes his stomach go cold.

'Is that a—'

'A bomb?' Nate laughs, and picks up the black brick in one hand. 'Battery pack. Need to keep the power supply separate as it can interfere with the signal.' He puts it down and with two fingers follows the line of the cable up to the circuit board. 'This is basically a small computer. Cost you twenty bucks, you could watch movies on it if you set it up right. And on the other side' – he flips it over to reveal an eight-by-eight grid of off-white squares – 'we have a very basic display.' There is another cable snaking away from the board, slender and red-coated, and at the end of it is a flattened black egg of plastic. Nate picks it up. 'And this is where the magic happens. You ever build a crystal radio when you were little, Ray?'

'I used to beat up kids who did,' Ray offers.

'Right. You got one of those cards where you can pay for your coffee just by holding it near the magic money box?'

'You went a bit too far the other way on the example, but yeah, I do.'

'Right. It uses a thing called RFID.'

'Like FasTrak.'

'Just like that. The chip passes within range of a reader, it can read it.'

'You're saying there's a chip in my arm?'

Nate pauses, tilts his head in a way that suggests he wants to fire up a set of slides and give a twenty-minute primer on the topic. 'I suspect there is, yes. Arm up, please.'

Ray's arm had dropped while they were talking. He held it up and out, and pointed right where the injection had gone in. 'That's where she got me. If they put a chip in, I'd be able to feel it, right?'

'Not this type of chip. The case has a biocompatible mixture of organic and inorganic compounds which when combined with a living substrate . . .' Nate's head twitches again, like dumbing the answer down pains him. 'It's built to feel like living tissue. It beds in after you inject it. And it doesn't necessarily stay at the injection site.' He presses a button on the circuit board and the LED grid floods green.

'Green is good, right?'

'Green is good.' Nate waves the plastic egg in Ray's direction, and the outer ring of LEDs shift to a bright pink color.

Ray sniffs. 'And I'm guessing Unicorn Shit Pink is bad.'

'Magenta. And you're two for two.' Nate doesn't look up from the screen. He pulls his hand away until the board is full green again, and edges it towards Ray until the color appears again. 'Would you like to go for Double Jeopardy where the scores can really change?'

Ray stiffens. 'Range is about four feet. Which means unless they've laid down a carpet of readers this chip they put in me is pretty fucking useless.'

Nate tips his head. 'Not useless. They did a trial in Europe a couple of years back, a tech company fitted all their staff

155

with them. Wave your hand at a locked door, the door opens. No need for ID cards. These ones are the next generation. Try making a fist for me.' Ray closes his hand into a fist. Nothing happens. 'Now flex your elbow?' As he does, the whole board turns pink for a moment, then falls back, ring by ring, to the resting state.

'What the shit? Did I do that?'

'Yes, but not voluntarily. The chip in your arm piggybacks off of muscle motion. It goes from being passive – pretty fucking useless, as you put it, except that's not remotely the truth – to being active. The more you move, the bigger the signal.'

'So what's the active range?'

'Ten feet? Twenty? Maybe more. We could measure it but it'd be a waste of time.'

Twenty feet. A thrill of panic makes Ray shake himself uneasily, and he jumps outright when the reader flushes pink in response. 'This is some fucking bullshit, man. You're saying they low-jacked me? Like I'm on fucking house arrest?'

Nate stands still, coughs into his fist as he waits for Ray to calm down. It isn't easy, but Ray takes some deep breaths, puts on his best parade face.

'Twenty feet,' Ray says. His chest feels tight as he says it, but he keeps it together. 'So they have, like, chip readers installed in all the buildings? How'd they sell that?'

'They don't just install them in buildings,' Nate says. He pauses, and takes a deep breath. 'Do you know how many homeless people there are in the city, Officer Perada?'

Ray shrugs. There's an official figure but the numbers slid right past him at the last department presentation. 'Four thousand,' he says.

'Closer to seven thousand, officially,' Nate says. 'The real number is higher. And while many people see them as a problem in the city, Carrington came to see them as an asset.'

'They've been putting this shit in all the homeless people, too?'

'Actually, a great deal more than just a simple chip.' Nate waves his homebrew electronic, and the LEDs flicker in response. 'Imagine this reader, but about the size of two half-dollars stacked. Small enough you could install it in a person. Cut a little notch in their abdomen, slide it in with the subcutaneous fat, they might even forget it was there.'

'You're shitting me.'

'Readers installed in thousands of people,' Nate says. 'A flexible, mobile and virtually undetectable network, relaying information from all across the city back to us.'

Ray feels sick at the thought. 'What'd you hand out to get them to sign up for that?'

'Whatever they wanted,' Nate says. 'Nobody asked for anything substantial. It's amazing what people will sell their souls for.'

Ray simmers at how casually Nate talks about it. Like seven thousand people on the streets were an untapped asset. The flesh of his arm itches, like the memory of a mosquito bite. He draws in a long, tight breath through his nose. 'Switch that off and get this thing out of me.'

'I told you, it's biocompatible. It's made to—'

'They made it hard to find. I get it, Nate. I do. Now get it the fuck out of me.'

Nate makes no move to switch off the machine. 'It's not as simple as that.'

'What, you need to dig it out or something?' Ray is breathing hard now, chest forward, his whole body in full fight response and nothing in him trying to hold it back. He can feel the scale of the betrayal like a chasm opening up at his feet, his anger the last thin bridge keeping him from falling head first into it. 'You got a knife? Find wherever the signal is strongest. We can do it right here.'

'It's specifically designed to avoid detection and removal.' Nate sweeps the detector the length of Ray's arm demonstratively. There's an even signal. 'Once it's injected, it stops being an implant and starts being . . . you.'

Ray looks down the length of his left arm and finds that he can't feel it, can't move it. It hangs there like a prosthesis, an immobile and completely alien lump of flesh. The feeling passes after a moment – he flexes his fingers and feels the alternating tension of tendons in motion, the skin of his fingertips against the ball of his thumb. He tries not to look at the readout on the LED screen, and realizes that Nate is talking to him.

'—take the idea of mimicking biological systems to the next step and just bootstrap off the cells that are there already. So over the course of a few weeks your body absorbed the casing and built a new one itself.' Nate coughs into his hand. 'Yourself, I should say.'

'That is some fucked-up space-age bullshit,' Ray says.

'It's the truth,' Nate says. He crouches again to put the detector away in the bag at his feet. 'Carrington are on the bleeding edge with this stuff. All of their embedded tracking technology? It's the tip of the iceberg.'

'How do you know all this?'

'I was wondering when you'd ask.' Nate grins, a quick, nervous flash of even, model-white teeth. Seeing them makes Ray really aware of how unwell Nate looks. They're the healthiest thing about him. He's gaunt, and even with the fake tan his color is off, like he's been ill a long time. 'There's no easy way to say this. I helped develop the technology.'

Ray points to his arm. 'You did this?'

That earns a scoff. 'No, not by myself. In fact the tracker itself was almost finished when I was recruited. I was hired because I was good with programming distributed systems . . .' Nate trails off and tilts his head to one side, hands still hidden in the bag at his feet. 'Look, do you want the chip disabled or not? We don't have a great deal of time before they realize you're not dead or in police custody and start looking for you.'

'Of course I want it ou—' Ray's voice fails him when he sees what Nate is pulling from the bag. It's a portable defibrillator, one of the automatic ones that gets packed into high-end first aid kits to justify the price point. It's a bright orange plastic box with a built-in handle, and two buttons on the front. One is green, circular, and is marked with the universal power symbol. The other is a red triangle with a lightning bolt. As if the meaning is somehow unclear, it also has *SHOCK* written on it in bold letters. Ray works his mouth for a moment, finding it suddenly dry. 'What are you gonna do with that?'

'One pad on your shoulder,' Nate says. 'The other on your hand. The electricity will route to the shortest path, which will be the biotracker.'

'Hold up. Can't those things kill you?'

'Absolutely. We're lucky it wasn't injected into your side or chest, or else surgery would be the only option.'

'Woah, okay,' Ray holds his hands out to ward Nate off. 'So you're saying surgery is an option?'

Nate shrugs. 'It is, but I don't have the equipment or the expertise for it. I mean, I could saw your arm off if you want.' He is opening the defibrillator as he talks, and Ray can make out the cartoon diagrams on the back of each pad – red under the left armpit, yellow high on the right side of the chest. 'This is the best and quickest way, Ray. Believe me. It's going to hurt a lot, and you're probably going to struggle with that arm for a while, but if we don't do it? I walk away. I can't let them find me. You'll have to take your chances with them, and Cameron . . .'

'What about her?'

'I was hoping you could help me get her back,' Nate says.

'You know where she is?'

'I know where they've taken her.'

That swings it. Ray swallows hard, holds his hand out for the pads. 'I'll do it,' he says. Nate passes them over, and Ray is surprised by how flimsy they feel, how thin the cables are. In his mind they should be substantial, as though the weight of them slamming into someone's chest after the yell of 'Clear!' is an essential part of the procedure. 'One on my hand, one on the shoulder?'

'That's right.'

The pads have an adhesive layer on them, and Ray peels off the cover before sticking one to the back of his hand. It feels tight on the skin, tighter when he pulls his arm across his body to stick the other pad high on his left shoulder.

'You think this will leave a scar?'

Nate gives him a blank look. 'I'll be amazed if it doesn't.' He passes over the defibrillator. 'Green for power, red for go. I've set it to full power, so it might take a second to hit full charge.'

Ray feels the weight of the case in his hands. It's a lot heavier than he expected. 'How much power is full power?'

'It's best not to think about it.'

Ray presses the green button. The power light jumps on, startling him, and there's a faint flashgun whine from somewhere in the middle of the casing. The note rises out of hearing, and a second green light flickers on next to the word *READY*. He looks up at Nate. 'You might want to back off for this.'

Nate nods, but doesn't move.

Ray takes a deep breath, closes his eyes, and jabs the red button. Nothing happens. He opens his eyes again and frowns down at the green *READY* light. 'I think it's bro—'

Ray's entire left side goes rigid, and the jolt that follows is like being drop-kicked. There's a surge of pain unlike anything he's ever felt, and his mouth fills with a strong metallic taste. The paralysis drops as fast as it came on, and Ray's legs fold underneath him. He lands on his right side, muscle spasms making him jerk like a landed fish. His field of vision feels narrow, and he can just make out Nate coming over, holding something near his arm.

'Looks like we got part of it,' Nate says. Ray tries to speak, but the best he can manage is halfway between a grunt and a moan. 'But not all.' Nate fishes the defibrillator box out from under Ray's right side, and Ray's world tightens down to the

161

sound of it charging. 'We'd better hit it again to make sure. Are you ready?'

Ray can't find voice enough to protest, or even swear at him. The ready light comes on, and Nate hits the button.

Chapter 20

Cameron and Nate are sitting on a porch watching the sun setting over water, passing a beer back and forth between them. They stole it from right under Pop's nose, Nate distracting him with a question about electronics while Cameron eased the fridge open to keep the bottles from clinking. He'll be mad as hell when he finds out about it, but right now they have a beer, the porch, and what feels like the whole world spread out in front of them.

She's sixteen. Nate is back for the summer, his first college year under his belt. Neither of them know it, but this is the last summer they'll spend together as a family. Nate got placed in a summer program: advanced coding, or some other nerd bullshit. Industry money putting the best and brightest on the fast track to grad school. If Cameron had sensed it, even a little, she would have said something to him.

They drink in the grinning, companionable silence of a brother and sister until Nate has a coughing fit. Chronic organ dysfunction, the doctor called it. Mom says it's like he's got a cold that never goes away, but Cameron knows it's worse than that. He's stick thin, like he struggles to put on weight. She's seen what he coughs up from time to time. Nate sticks his hand out and she passes him the bottle: he makes a face as he takes a long pull from it, like the beer has gone sour. He throws the bottle, beer and all, into the lake and Cameron watches it vanish with a sound like a trout snapping a fly off the surface.

There's a jug on the table next to the bed they've put Cameron on. It's full of water cold enough that the plastic has beads of condensation gathering on it, and yet Cameron can't help but feel it's only been put there as decoration. With the restraints pinning her arms to the bed rails and the broad strap across her chest holding her down, there's little chance of her ever reaching it to pour herself a drink.

It looks like a private room in a hospital: peach-colored paint on the walls, fluorescent lighting, the hum of an industrial ventilation system circulating dust- and allergen-free air around the room, but really she could be anywhere. She missed the journey, the indignities of being put in a gown, bandaged up, and strapped in. There's no clock, no natural light, no indication of time passing other than her own growing discomfort. Sometime after she noticed the jug of water she stopped being directly angry at her situation and more concerned about how thirsty she was, how dry her lips and mouth were because of the air conditioning. She'd have yelled in protest, but for the mile-wide stubborn streak that she's clinging on to. Cameron has deep reserves inside of her dedicated wholly to digging her heels in. Instead of yelling, or whimpering, or wasting energy trying to reach that water, she tries to take stock of her situation.

There's an intravenous line running into her right arm. The plastic tubing runs up to a bag hanging from a metal stand, already empty. Whatever was in it has run completely into her: she can see blood backfilling into the plastic tubing, her body pushing back against the weight of fluid. She hopes it was just saline that was in the bag.

On her left, near where an intravenous line would go, is a small, circular patch of flesh-colored Band-Aid. If she turns her arm in the restraint, she can see another applied to the outside of her arm. There's one on the back of her hand, just visible. They stitch a line down her arm, following the lightning-strike path of her surgical scars. Just seeing them focused around her wound makes the skin on either side of it itch.

Cameron kicks off the covers to see her legs. The crash and the fight have not been kind to her, and both shins are covered from knee to ankle with purple-black bruises. She tests the flexion in her knees, and turns her ankles from side to side, testing the range of motion and feeling the tension of a strain in both of them. Nothing broken, though. *Small graces*. She frowns, and feels the tension of a bandage tight around her brow. The touch of it on her face – near her eyes – is disturbingly personal, and it feels like more of an insult than all the rest.

'Hey!' she yells, and her voice comes out clear and loud. 'What the fuck are you doing to me?'

There is a click, and the soft buzz of a loudspeaker on the wall up and to the left of where she is lying. Cameron doesn't doubt that there's a camera next to it. 'Please remain calm,' the voice says. It is a woman's voice, and the toneless, practiced neutrality of it only serves to make Cameron even more angry.

'Bitch, you unstrap my hands I'll show you how fucking calm I am.'

The voice continues, undeterred. 'You have sustained multiple severe injuries and have been restrained to keep you from any risk of making them worse. If you cannot control yourself, you will be sedated.'

That gives Cameron pause. Whatever is happening to her, she doesn't want to sleep through any more of it. Information is key. The more she can get, the better her chances are of getting out of this. Even bruised to shit, Cameron's certain she can give whoever has to come in to sedate her their worst day at work, ever, but as tempting as that is it would be a hollow victory. Better to keep a clear head, so that when she comes back to burn all this down she doesn't leave a single thing standing above ground level. 'Who are you?'

'We are here to help you,' the voice says. 'We are here to help everyone.'

The loudspeaker clicks off, leaving Cameron with the air conditioning and the odd stress on that last word. *Everyone.* The only people who say they can help everyone are zealots and used car salesmen. If this is leading up to her being offered a dented Pinto on layaway, Cameron is impressed. Kidnapping and private medical facilities are a real step up from filming an ad on the lot and running it hourly on the local cable channels.

She lies still, thinking it over. The dead guy in the flat, the cop, the assault team, the chase, the fight. All to get a hold of her. Could have sent a private jet and a check if they wanted an after-dinner speaker, but instead . . . they'd played this *game* with her. They'd known where she was every step of the way. It was the only way they could have gotten ahead of her like that, kept the pressure on her. She hadn't slipped them

166

at the parade; they had let her go. Waited until they were in a quieter spot, away from the crowds. Like a cat batting a three-quarters dead mouse into one final dash for freedom, the chase had meant more to them than the capture, and that meant that they hadn't really wanted to catch her at all.

They wanted Nate.

It was why they'd brought her here to do it. Because they knew Nate was here in San Francisco, so close that they could almost touch him, and the threat against her might be the tipping point they needed to draw him out of hiding. And yet he hadn't taken the bait. The call, the dead drop: he had something on them, whoever they were, and he had tried to pass it on to her. Some kind of leverage that would hold them at bay. And Cameron knew then why he'd crashed the car with her in it, why he'd disappeared that night. Why she'd recognized Bullet Head's voice when he spoke. Nate had been working for them. And now he'd gone and pulled another disappearing trick, and they were casting about for anything they could use to get him back.

The door, on Cameron's left as she lies in the bed, opens and a man walks in. He is dressed in a tan blazer and gray tie over a white, high-collared shirt, and navy pants. He's very tan, with thick-rimmed glasses, and his brown hair is long and slicked back from his forehead. *Silicon Valley.* Maybe this is the same guy Ray mentioned before, the one who'd been in the van outside Sophia and Ophelia's house. He's put a great deal of effort into his look, and Cameron wonders if his personal shopper knows that he doesn't quite have the build to carry it off. He's handsome enough, but he has a very thin neck that the stark wedge of collar does nothing but accentuate.

Whatever position he holds, no one has had the stones to tell him that it looks as though a strong wind would decapitate him, and it's a hint of weakness that makes Cameron feel a little less scared of him.

'Miss King.' He gestures towards the jug by her bed. 'Would you care for a drink of water?'

'Not right now.'

'My name is Miller. I won't insult you by saying these are pleasant circumstances, but I have to say I'm very pleased to meet you.'

'Pleased enough to take these restraints off?'

'Eventually, yes.' He tilts his head like a bird watching for worms in the long grass after rain. 'Although I would like to talk to you a little first.'

'About Nate?'

He doesn't even blink. 'About what we do here.'

'Which is where, exactly?'

'This is a hospital.' He shrugs. 'Not general population, but a hospital nonetheless. Mostly research and drug testing, but they do have facilities for some private patients.'

Cameron leans her head back, looks up at the ceiling. 'Carrington Medical,' she says.

'You've heard the name.'

'The name was on one of the banners at the protest.'

'We at Carrington are pleased to support both the city and the values of its residents. We even have a float for Pride, when it comes round.'

'Hiding in plain sight.'

She hears him laugh at that, a dry, brief noise. 'I think they prefer to call it "Public Relations".'

Cameron lifts her head again. 'You're not from public relations, though.'

'No.' He shakes his head. 'I'm not. But their involvement is important. They do excellent work in letting the public get used to our research in the fields of rapid wound recovery and muscle repair. We've had so many wounded soldiers thank us for our efforts.'

Cameron waves her left arm as much as the restraints will allow. 'Is that what all these Band-Aids are for? Wound recovery?'

'Band-Aids.' He gives her a tight, humorless smile. 'Actually, each one of them is a microneedle applicator, a polylactic acid polymer that delivers—'

'Hey!' Cameron barks the interruption at him. 'I don't give a fuck what they are, I want them off me.'

He clasps his hands together and gives her that sharp, white-lipped smile again. Whoever Miller is, he doesn't like being interrupted. 'Very well. Do you have any idea why you are here?'

'I'm here because my brother either double-crossed, stole from you, or straight-up quit, and you baited me down here to try and find him.'

Miller's smile warms up a little. 'You're almost right,' he says. 'Except we didn't set you up.'

'You're saying Nate did?'

'We're almost certain that is the case.'

Cameron shakes her head. 'He called me. He tried to warn me.'

'Exactly. He called you, and in doing so triggered our surveillance of you.' Miller's hands tighten momentarily into fists, as though the memory annoys him. 'We had been keeping tabs on you ever since he went rogue, in case he tried to contact you.'

'You're saying he knew that this would happen?'

'As I've said, it's our best approximation. It is the first time he's surfaced since he vanished three months ago. From what we know of him, it would be foolhardy to think it was anything other than intentional.'

'And so you sent your goons after me.'

Miller nods. 'We created a high-pressure scenario with the intention of drawing your brother out of hiding. We hoped he would attempt to rescue you.'

'Motherfucker, I don't know if you're up on your recent history but my brother once crashed a car with me in it on purpose.'

'Yes, we know all about that,' Miller says. 'We asked him to do it.'

'You did what?'

'We headhunted your brother to work for us on a very special project,' Miller says. He gestures a lot, like he's giving a TED talk. 'One that requires absolute internal secrecy. When we spoke to him, we found that he talked about you a great deal. Enough that even though he was enthusiastic about coming on board, we proposed a test. Something to clear away the doubts we had regarding his loyalty.'

'You told him to crash the car.'

'We told him to kill you.'

Cameron feels fear settle like a blanket thrown over her. Miller says it like he's recalling his coffee order from this morning. All of a sudden Nate's strange behavior that night makes sense. The way he'd looked at her when she popped his seat belt. *Fair's fair*. She works her dry lips, trying to find something to say.

'But he didn't kill me.'

'No, he didn't,' Miller says. 'In fairness, the crash left him a little too disoriented to check for himself. In any case, the attempt itself was proof enough for me. When he walked away and left you, I was convinced.'

There's more to come. Cameron can tell from the way he's standing, waiting for her to prompt him onwards. 'But you were wrong.'

'I was wrong,' Miller says, nodding in agreement. 'Not only has he betrayed us, but the first sign of him resurfacing has been to contact you. And so, here we are.'

Cameron shrugs. 'Where the fuck are we?'

'I'm going to be straight with you, Miss King. We wanted your brother, but instead we got you. You may not agree with us, but we feel that it's actually turned out to be a positive outcome.'

'You're damn right I don't.'

'Your brother was – is – a very talented man,' Miller says. 'He helped this company make great forward progress, and we expected a great deal more from him. Until three months ago, when he left our employment.'

'He quit?'

'He disappeared, Miss King. No phone calls, no ATM withdrawals, no bus tickets, no security camera footage, not even from the lobby of his building. It was like he simply ceased to exist. We even entertained the possibility that he might have been killed, until he called you.'

171

'Who would want to kill him?' Miller rubs his hands together and looks away, and Cameron bristles at his reticence. 'Hey. You said you were going to be straight with me.'

Miller nods. 'I did, yes.' He looks past her and takes a long breath, like a pitcher on the mound waiting for the catcher's call. 'We do a lot of sensitive work here at Carrington,' he says. 'Sensitive enough that it has gained the attention of several government agencies. Foreign and domestic. They are all very keen to retain exclusive rights to it.'

'You think he's gone over to one of them.'

Miller tips his head again, like he's about to guess her weight or her star sign. She knew a fight manager just like him, the kind of guy who could tell you to the nearest thousand dollars how much a fighter's career was worth. Cameron wouldn't have trusted him as far as she could throw his deadbeat ass, and so far Miller has shown he deserves less than half that. 'Do you know who the dead man was?' he asks.

'He was a finance geek. Wanted for fraud. The bounty on him was worth half a million.'

'Ah yes, the bounty. Would it interest you to know that it was faked?'

'Faked?' Cameron doesn't trust Miller an inch and yet she knows that right now he's telling the truth. He wouldn't be enjoying himself so much otherwise.

'Faked. By the US government. He wasn't wanted for fraud, I can tell you that for certain. There was a kill order on his head. He was an arms dealer operating within the US military supply chain. Weapons being marked in their crates as damaged goods and instead of being destroyed, sold on to foreign powers.'

'How do you know that?'

'Because the military came to Carrington first.'

'They came to a medical company?'

'I think you understand already that we're more than a medical company.'

'So why didn't you find him?'

'They wanted us to do it for free. As a "show of good faith".' Miller shakes his head. 'Absolutely no understanding of modern business.'

'So why farm it out as a fake bounty?' Cameron shakes her head. 'All it would have taken was for one person to slip up and it would have been a huge scandal.'

'They weren't looking for Gorton anymore,' Miller says. 'Or, perhaps I should say, they found him and then they used him as bait. For whatever reason, Miss King, what they really wanted, was you.'

Cameron remembers catching sight of her gun on the floor in the apartment. The strap across her chest flexes, following the motion. 'I was never going to get paid, was I?'

'I doubt it,' Miller says. 'But there is a way to salvage this.'

Cameron sighs. 'Man, I've had the shit kicked out of me, I'm tied to a fucking table and now you're telling me I'm never getting paid. If you've got a way to salvage this, I'm all ears.'

Miller grins at that. 'We want to hire you to track down your brother.'

Chapter 21

It's a close-run thing, but Cameron is certain this is the strangest way she's ever been offered a job. Maybe the second. There was that one time a TV producer thought that getting his dick out halfway through a meeting was a good move. It wasn't a good move. Cameron looks from one arm to the other, making a show of it as she turns her wrist against each of the restraints. She looks up at Miller. 'If you want to talk business,' she says, 'then take these off.'

Miller rolls his shoulders, bobs his head about as though thinking about it. 'And you promise to behave?'

Cameron has zero intention of behaving. Even with a grab bag of injuries courtesy of Bullet Head, she's fairly certain she still has the strength to tie a knot in Miller's pencil neck. 'Call it an act of faith.'

He offers the same thin, humorless smile as before and reaches for a buzzer set in the wall by the door. It occurs to Cameron that Miller isn't comfortable unless he gets the last word in, and that smug-ass smile is the only thing he has to cover the fact he can't think of anything smart to say.

A nurse comes in, and Cameron recognizes her for the real

deal. Petite, with swimmer's shoulders, she looks as though she's turned enough patients to last her two lifetimes. For a moment Cameron wonders if she's going to be bad cop to Miller's hands-off and smug cop, but it's unfounded. She's polite and businesslike, and has the restraints off in short order. She reaches to support Cameron's neck as she sits up, and Cameron waves her off. 'Thanks. I'm okay.'

Sitting up, Cameron feels a million miles short of okay. Without the bed to hold the lion's share of her weight, it feels like her ribcage is going to peel free of her spine and drop clean out of her ass. There's a lot of tension on her right-hand side when she breathes, and her hand goes to it automatically.

'Be careful,' the nurse says. 'You bruised a couple of ribs.'

Cameron nods, holds her breath as she walks the very tips of her fingers along the bandages she can feel under the gown, feels the shift as they find the injury, a sensation of ultra-awareness that makes her eyesight go pin-sharp. 'Not broken?'

'I can show you the X-rays, if you like. You were lucky.'

'Yeah, I'm real lucky.' Cameron laughs, and it really fucking hurts to laugh. 'You want to go half and half with me on the Powerball?'

The nurse suppresses a smile, and Miller coughs, keen to be the center of attention again. 'So, you have your act of faith,' he says. 'Shall we talk business?'

Cameron takes as deep a breath as her ribs will allow, and reaches for the water by the bed. She doesn't make it. She winces when her arm is halfway extended, and by the time that passes the nurse is already putting the plastic cup, three-quarters full, in her hand. 'Thanks again.' Cameron tilts her head to check the nurse's name, but she has no visible ID. 'You, uh, don't have a name tag.'

'Terri.'

'Thanks, Terri.'

'No problem.'

Cameron takes a long drink of water. It's cold enough to make her teeth ache, and the only thing more pleasant is enjoying the sight of Miller simmering as she makes him wait. She holds on to the empty cup. 'I have a question,' she says.

'Go on.'

'What do you need me for? You tracked my ass down like it was child's play.'

'We had something of an advantage,' Miller says. 'The project your brother was working on for us? Subdermal tracking chips.'

Cameron looks at the Band-Aids that are running down the length of her left arm. Subdermal. Under the skin. 'You fucking piece of—'

She is off the bed so quickly that her feet go from under her and she almost falls on her ass. She catches hold of the railing on the bed and the pain that jumps from her right hip up to her shoulder is so sharp that she yells out, the sound raw with anger. Terri moves to help her up and earns a snarl for her efforts.

'You put a fucking chip in my arm?'

'Actually, we put several chips in your arm.' Miller clasps his hands together. 'The pins they used to hold your bones together gave us a unique frame to work with. A test bed for our new prototypes.'

176

Cameron steadies herself on the side of the bed. As her weight shifts, she can feel stitches pull on her side. *Surgical stitches.* 'What have you done to me?'

'Faith only goes so far, Miss King.' Miller dips into his pocket with one hand and comes back with a thin, black rod, like a TV remote. A tiny red light shows on one side of it. 'I have no doubt you'd have tried to attack me, if you could stand.'

'I would kick your ass into orbit if I could.'

'Which is why we put this in, too.' Miller presses a button on the remote, and all the muscles down Cameron's left side go rigid. Her mouth floods with a metallic taste, and all she can think of as she falls is the time that Nate dared her to touch her tongue to a nine-volt battery and how the flavor of it had lingered for hours. She can't lift her hands to catch herself, and the fall ends with her smacking face-first into the floor. It's not the first time she's had her nose broken, and the fire of it – a sphere of pain in the center of her face – is at least something familiar to cling to. *You're still you. No matter what they do to you.* She tastes blood, and – even as she realizes how pointless a worry it is – hopes that her teeth are all right.

Miller tuts aloud. 'Sorry. I thought the bed would . . . Terri, would you, please?'

Terri turns her over with the brisk efficiency of someone who's done it a lot, and she has, at least, the decency to look embarrassed while she does it. Miller is grinning, his mouth a wide slash of unnatural brightness, veneers so bright they look luminous in his face. He waves the remote at her.

'We developed a new kind of pacemaker several years ago,' he says. 'Much smaller than a standard one, programmable via wireless connection. You'll find it halfway down your left side. It's not subtle, I'll admit, but it gets the job done.' Miller waves the control at her, making sure he has Cameron's full attention. 'Let me lay it out for you. Your brother has some plan, some scheme that somehow involves you. You can either choose to help us track him down using the resources we will provide, or we can dump you back in the city as bait. You try to run, go to the police or the press, then I will tape this button down and you will get to discover how much fun permanent nerve damage is.'

Cameron wants to tell him to go fuck himself, but her jaw aches and her teeth feel like they've been glued together. She makes do with hissing at him, the sound coming out as a bubbling whistle through her inflamed sinuses. He tuts again, unimpressed. 'Fix that for me, would you?'

Terri's forearm blocks the view of his face as she grabs Cameron's nose and re-aligns it with a single, crisp motion. The crunch of shifting cartilage is loud in the room, the sound of fresh snow trod underfoot, and the pain sends a thrill of sensation through Cameron's whole body, a flashgun blast of feeling that silhouettes the numbness that still fills her left arm. She lifts her head and looks at Terri. She doesn't seem the evil corporation type, and yet here she is.

'How'd they get their hooks in you?' Cameron asks.

Terri meets the accusation in her gaze with a flat look. 'Hey, my rent went up four times in two years,' she says. 'And there aren't any apartments going on the moral high ground.'

Cameron shakes her head as Terri helps her back on to the bed. She doesn't have the strength to do anything else. It's the hardest thing to give in, but sometimes you have to tap out.

You take that loss, and come back when you're stronger. 'You should get out of here,' she says. She doesn't care that Miller hears. 'Before it gets bloody.'

'Bit late for that,' Terri says.

Miller taps the railing at the bottom of the bed with the remote control, and it sends a note ringing through Cameron's whole body. She feels like throwing up, and would if she had the strength to do it.

'Get some rest,' Miller says. 'You look like you need it. We'll get started in the morning.'

Cameron seethes, the anger boiling up from deep inside of her, filling her with a sudden burst of energy. Ludo would be disappointed – you don't fight sad, you don't fight scared, and you never fight angry – but Ludo isn't here. 'Hey Miller,' she says.

'Yes, Miss King?'

Cameron knows that it's a mistake, but she doesn't care. 'Someday I'm going to take that little box off you, and I'm going to make you swallow it.'

'Hm.' It's not an unhappy noise. Miller sounds like a mechanic, all patience and abstraction, watching as the flaw in a running engine reveals itself. Like he doesn't mind the work it will take to fix, because half the battle is knowing that it's there. He brandishes the remote, and Cameron braces herself as a light on the side of it flickers back into life. 'Let's try that again, shall we?'

Chapter 22

It's hard to see, but if Ray turns his arm at just the right angle the scar is visible again. He should feel good that it's so hard to see, but instead it unnerves him. Knowing that it's there, even if no one can see it – especially if no one can see it – makes his skin itch so bad that he wants to claw it out.

Ferning. That's what it's called, or the closest thing to it. When lightning strikes you, the electrical discharge works its way down your body seeking out the path of least resistance, burning as it goes. The scar it leaves behind looks like a fern growing under your skin. Ray's scar has the same characteristics but looks like anything but a fern. The faint lines that hang subdermal and indelible are more like the lines on a circuit board, tight grids of right-angles and the long, straight roads that chain them together. The scarring runs along the outside edge of his bicep, snakes round behind his arm above the elbow and reappears on the inside of his forearm, fading as it heads down towards his wrist. Nate has told him it's a good sign that it didn't get as far as his hand and that Ray shouldn't expect any loss of sensation, but it's zero comfort. The marks are alien, obscene in their electronic likeness, and the revulsion he feels borders on mania. There's a distant voice screaming in the back of his head that the current from the defibrillator didn't get it all, that something is left, that it's growing back. *Cut it off. You won't be rid of it otherwise.* He knows where to get a knife. Alcohol, dressings, drugs for the pain. *It'll come back if you don't.* Ray takes a sharp breath, surprised that he's even thinking of something like that, and feels a spike of pain high in his chest. *Maybe even that wouldn't be enough.*

Congratulations. That's what Nate had said when he came to. *You're off the grid.* It was a half-truth, if even that. He'd explained how there were systems in place to support the implant program, systems like cell phone tracking that would eventually be superseded but for the moment were maintained to catch and monitor failures and build a list of unregistered assets. Ray catches himself on that one. People. Not assets. There was something in the way Nate had talked about it that marked him as one of the same breed as Silicon Valley. The kind of asshole who saw people as units instead of humans, a morass of data and variables to be corralled and categorized.

Still, Ray couldn't deny the sense that gave shape to the other man's cold disregard for mankind. *Off the grid* was something that took real effort. Traffic cameras. Phone networks. Automated turnstiles on public transport. ATMs. Anything that could be used to pick you out of a crowd and log your location was a potential threat. That other people simply couldn't bring themselves to accept that these things even counted as a threat, that they handed over everything about themselves so freely, put them below Nate's contempt. Ray took the point even as he felt the weight of his own ignorance settling on him like guilt: people were becoming

'Only on the bad days,' Nate explains, hooking the pipe over his ears and fitting it to his nose. There's a short hiss of gas and Ray sees Nate's posture ease as he breathes in.

'You get bad days often?'

'More than I'd like.'

'There a cure for what you've got?'

Nate looks straight at him. 'Yes,' he says.

'So what are you taking for it?'

'I'm not.'

'Expensive?' Ray asks.

'Hard to get a hold of.'

Ray finally takes the hint and backs off. Nate goes back to flicking through a stack of handwritten notes, ciphered text from what Ray can see of it, and occasionally glancing at an impossibly new-looking laptop by his side. The computer is connected to a router directly, the wireless aerial removed completely, and the router itself is plugged into a long piece of telephone wire that snakes off across the plastic and up the near wall to disappear through a hole. The hole looks recent to Ray's eye, a comet's tail of white dust still fresh on the wall beneath it, and he wonders when Nate found time to drill it, and why the security guard has never heard or spotted it. All that cement dust in the air wouldn't have helped Nate's cough much. Someone is backing Nate King, and it sets alarm bells ringing in Ray's head that he hasn't said anything about it.

Ray clears his throat. 'So this is what off the grid looks like.'

Nate bangs his hand flat on the pile of notes and looks up at Ray sharply. He smothers the look quickly and follows the line of Ray's gaze to the hole in the wall, the wire vanishing through it. 'Internet access and air conditioning,' he says. 'That has to be worth two stars at least.'

It's a weak deflection, and Ray isn't going to let him have it. 'You've been set up here for a while?'

Nate shakes his head. 'I have a bunch of places set up around the city. Some are more permanent, others' – he gestures around them – 'are little more than an access point. No more than two trips before I change. No more than thirty-six hours in one place. Never use them in the same sequence. And I always check before approaching. If anything seems off – anything at all – I consider it burnt.'

'Well, that doesn't seem paranoid in the slightest.'

'You've experienced their attention, so you have an inkling of what they're capable of. What you call paranoia, I call caution.' Nate puts the paper he's holding down and rolls up his right sleeve. His arm is thin and so white his veins show through the skin. There's a blue tint to the base of Nate's fingernails that makes Ray feel uneasy, and he tries to focus on what Nate is showing him. As Nate turns his wrist in the light, Ray sees the same criss-cross scarring that marks his own arm. 'If anything, staying here is reckless. But I have to see this finished.'

Something in the declaration rings false to Ray's ears. It's a gut feeling, the sense you get when you go to canvass the neighbors and one of them answers every question a little too readily. Like he's practiced for this moment. *Pour a little cold water on his moment. See how he takes it.* 'And this is how you're going to finish it? Running jackrabbit from cover to cover, hoping the hawks don't notice you?'

Nate doesn't even flinch.

'If that's what I need to do, then yes. Hit and run. Survive to keep fighting. Guerilla tactics are the only course when you're an army of one.'

'Two, now,' Ray says. Nate gives him a tight, non-committal smile. Ray can feel his hackles rising, even as he recognizes the manipulation. *He's waiting for something.* An act of faith, something given freely. Instead, Ray pushes him again. 'It would have been three, if they hadn't taken Cameron.'

'I couldn't have stopped them.'

'You could have tried,' Ray says. 'You know why they want her?'

'I know why they want her.'

'They're trying to get to you.'

He looks away. 'Yes.'

'And you know what they'll do to her.'

'Hold her. Wait for me to make contact.'

'Bullshit they will.' Ray leans closer. 'They're not going to wait. They'll torture her, and they'll make sure you know about it. Audio, video, whatever. They'll record it and put it up online somewhere you're sure to look. They won't strike up a rapport, get her talking with a beer and a pack of cigarettes. I've met their new hires. All that kind of guy knows is how to follow an order and which end of a knife to use on someone.'

Nate's eyes dart to the laptop and back, his mouth set in a tight line, lips white. 'That is a possible outcome,' he says. The prospect of Cameron being tortured seems to have troubled him more than anything else so far.

'So what the fuck are you going to do about it?' Ray asks. 'Keep moving every six hours in the hope that if we run in circles fast enough they'll get dizzy trying to follow us? Keep picking cowardice and calling it caution?'

Nate doesn't look at him. 'I'm doing what I can,' he says, quietly. 'It doesn't look like it, but I have . . . something.'

Ray digs in his pocket for the mobile phone Cameron left in the car. 'We've got this,' he says. 'Whatever it is.'

Nate sits up straight, staring a hole in the phone Ray is holding. 'What is that?'

'The dead drop,' Ray says. 'Cameron knew she wasn't getting away. She didn't want them to find out what you had.'

Nate slaps the laptop shut and swears, then bangs his fist on the closed lid of the machine. 'You didn't think to tell me you've had that all this time?'

Ray waits, trying to weigh up the situation. Whatever Nate had left for Cameron, it wasn't dirt on Carrington Medical. He hadn't seemed too upset that she'd been taken, and everything since then has lacked urgency. Until now.

Ray takes a quick stock of their surroundings. No gun in reach of Nate's hands, and although Ray is sitting awkwardly, he's damn sure he can be faster than an invalid if he needs to be. 'What's on this phone, Nate?'

He can see Nate visibly trying to calm himself, to regain control. He's not flushed, but given the guy looks like a waxwork Ray can tell that he's still panicking. 'It's a back-up plan. Something I left for Cameron, in case the worst happened.'

'I asked what's on the phone, man,' Ray says. 'Don't make me ask again.'

'It's a virus. One that, if it gets plugged into a computer on Carrington's network, will shut down their security systems.'

Ray is gripping the phone so tight he feels like it might crack in his grip. 'You knew they were going to take her?'

'I made sure that if they did, she would have a way out,' Nate hisses, pointing at the phone. 'But she doesn't have it now, does she?' He looks around, like he's lost something, opens the laptop and taps at the keys. 'I've wasted all this time waiting for it to activate and you've had it in your fucking pocket this whole time.'

'You've been waiting.' Ray looks around. 'That's what we've been doing? You think Cameron was just going to walk out by herself?'

Nate shakes his head, agitated, ignoring the question. He gets up on to his hands and knees and reaches for the phone handset connected to the router. It's an all-weather handset built for construction use, the hard plastic angles and oversized rubber keypad refugees from somewhere in the mid-eighties. He's breathing hard, a wheeze catching at the back of his throat, but he forces the words out. 'We're going to have to move. I need to call in a favor, but first you need to call your family.'

'My family?'

'Your parents, your ex-wife, any kids you have.'

'Where'd you get the idea I have an ex-wife?'

Nate nods towards Ray's hand. 'No ring. Cops either stay married forever or collect messy divorces like baseball cards.'

Ray snorts dismissively, but Nate waits him out. Eventually he cracks and reaches for the handset. 'Never got as far as the wedding ceremony,' he says. 'I think she'll be just fine on her own.'

'I'm sorry. Phone your parents.'

Ray's hand stops short of grasping the telephone. 'And tell them what?'

Nate sits back. His expression doesn't change, but Ray can feel the shift in the air between them, the sudden tension that tightens across the gap.

'It's very important,' Nate says, 'that we don't waste time playing games with one another. I know where my sister is being held. I need your help in getting her back. I can't do that if your family could be used as leverage. You already know what you're going to tell them.'

Ray knows. He's known ever since he saw his mother getting spat on in the line for groceries, his father punched and told to go back where he came from. His whole family has known there might come a day when the whole world would go mad, and they would have to vanish before someone else turned up with a black van to make sure they vanished for good. He nods and looks down at his palms. Smooth. No calluses. Nothing like his father's. 'You know, I saw a program once about all these doomsday preppers, all these rich white boys getting tooled up so that when the world ends they're ready for it.' He turns his hands over and closes them into fists for a moment, imagining a black bag going over his father's head. His mother's. 'They never stopped to think that maybe rich white boys *were* the apocalypse.' Ray takes the handset.

He knows what surveillance means. An automated system, the successor to PRISM or whatever else the NSA was low-jacking the whole country with, lines of code running phone calls, texts and emails past a line of trigger words that flag individually for more direct action. He can't shake the image of an insertion team sitting in a cramped van across the street from his parents' place, itching to breach.

He's been on one of those teams himself. You gear up in a hurry and get briefed on the way. If you're lucky, you get to glance at a floorplan. It's a box full of sweat and nervous fear, because when you breach there could be anything waiting for you on the far side. Some deaf old grandma with her TV too loud and thirty cats in lieu of friends, or an LMG bolted to the floor and loaded with armor-piercing rounds. It's a pressure cooker, and there isn't a cop or operator alive that doesn't feel it crawl under their skin and make them want to shoot first. Ray swallows hard, and starts dialing.

'How long have I got?'

Nate shrugs. 'Twenty seconds, maybe thirty.'

'That's a lot of leeway.'

'Depends on what you say. Even the best software can't be everywhere at once. The more you give yourself away, the more it will shift resources towards pinning you down.'

'Right.'

The phone rings once and Ray's father answers it. He must have been sitting right next to the landline. Ray can see him in his mind's eye, snatching the phone up so that he can get the conversation over with. He can hear the sports channel in the background.

'Yeah.' For the longest time he thought his dad couldn't speak English. Turned out he just didn't like talking much.

'Hey.' Ray reflects his curtness back at him. 'Got a bad line here. How about you?'

His father doesn't answer. Ray hears the TV noise cut out as the old man switches it off. They'd talked once, before Ray left for the police academy, about what they would say if the time came. What had been a faint, awkward memory was now a thunderhead darkening the horizon.

'Clear as day here. What you selling today?'

'A better America. You know, like it used to be.'

'Yeah, when's that happening? Tomorrow?'

'Today.' Another silence. Nate holds up a warning, finger to wrist, and Ray nods at him. 'You understand what I'm selling.'

'Yeah. I hear you.' His father's voice sounds strange, like it's the first time Ray has ever heard it. It's because he sounds scared. 'How long for delivery?'

How long until the all-clear, is what he's asking. Ray's mouth feels like it's gone bone dry. The way things are going, he could be dead tomorrow.

'Call it a week,' Ray says. 'We'll let you know if it's longer. You take care of yourself.'

'You too.'

His father hangs up the phone. Ray stares down at the handset as though he's holding a detonator. His father. His mother. His sisters. Their kids. For as long as this lasts, they'll be running. The shock of it almost sees him dial the number again, to take it back, but instead he thinks of the scarring on his arm, about the thing they put in there. That grew inside of him. The world is ending, or at the very least changing beyond his ability to recognize it. At least his family has had some warning of it.

'Is it done?' Nate asks.

Ray nods. 'They're in the wind.' He stands and stretches, brings his arm up and massages the residual pain of the electric shock out of his bicep with his thumb. 'Now if I heard you right, you said you know where Cameron is?'

Nate has already gathered up his papers. 'I know where they're keeping her.'

'Great.' All of a sudden, things feel simpler. For many reasons, he really, really wants to find that Silicon Valley asshole and punch him so hard that the next time he takes a shit it'll have teeth in it. And Nate knows where to find him. 'So what are we waiting for?'

Chapter 23

They don't restrain her anymore. It's not a show of respect.
With the bullshit taser they've buried in her side, they don't
need to. From the moment Cameron wakes up, coming out
of a dreamless dark into pin-sharp, panicked clarity, she is
keenly aware of the stitches in her side, and the tingling
sensation that swept from her wrist up to her shoulder a split
second before the paralysis hit. She can feel the implant in
there, an alien presence that in her lowest moments makes
self-mutilation seem like something she'd sign up for.

She moves carefully through the facility, between the
rooms they've assigned her, wary of the nurses and handlers
who move freely in and out of the space, taking measurements,
making notes, always watching her. They're not interested in
breaking her. They seem perfectly happy to accept her anger,
as long as it doesn't turn into action against them. Terri tried
to get on her good side by pointedly taking the batteries out
of the remote Miller had left with her, but Cameron chalks
that up as another trick and ignores her.

A meal comes, one of the eight that appear in every twenty-
four hours. There are no clocks and no natural light, but

Cameron has an instinctive feel for the time passing which is reinforced by the staff rotation. They aren't disciplined about covering their watches and phone screens, for one thing, and the night shift is perceptibly lighter and less responsive than the daytime workers. All of them complain about the air conditioning, the constant running of the fans like a ferryboat hum, making everything vibrate softly and drawing a chill into the air. Two days have passed, and she's already tuned into their rhythms.

Cameron drew up the diet plan herself. It's halfway between a fighter's diet and a bodybuilder's. There's a lot of protein in it. A lot of fish. Apparently someone in the building feels bad about cooking meals with an offensive level of blandness and has included a slice of lemon, which she dutifully eats with the same mechanical action as the rest of it. Every meal comes with a pint flask of cold protein-rich slurry that she chokes down in a single effort. It is chalky to an extreme, and drinking it leaves her mouth feeling as though it's been lined with aluminum foil for hours afterwards. It is without a doubt the single most disgusting thing Cameron has ever drunk, beaten only by the faint memory of finding an ancient bottle of cream liqueur as a teenager and, in spite of the fact it had split into two layers, declaring it *still good*.

She eats it – all of it – because it's one thing she can control. *They asked him to kill you, and he tried*. Nate has pissed away every good memory she had of him, every good moment they shared. Carrington have taken everything else. All Cameron has left is this one sliver of opportunity: that they are keen for her to recover. She runs through her physiotherapy exercises to warm herself up, and pushes on into a basic workout. She knows it won't keep her mind from racing, won't dull the pain of betrayal or hold back the rage she can feel fizzing up inside of her, but it does give her focus. An opportunity will present itself, given time. All she has to do is be ready for it.

Cameron is in the ad-hoc gym they've provided when she realizes that Miller is on his way. It's like instinct: the subconscious register of a footfall outside, or the first faint smell of coffee and tobacco and body wash combined in such a way that the hairs on the back of her neck stand up. She looks up to the door in expectation of his arrival, and for a moment she considers the possibility of putting the barbell she's holding clean through his head before he can drop her. She wouldn't even have to run over there. She could throw it like a spear, and hope her sore ribs don't put off her aim. Cameron can feel a tension gathering at the top of her spine – the adrenaline building, ready to flood through her – as she weighs up her chances. They aren't good. *Not yet.* She lets the bar drop back on to the rack, and steps clear of it as Miller enters the gym. *Don't give him anything to work with. No sign of weakness.*

Miller comes in smiling, the air of a professional PR bullshit artist about him. 'Cameron. How are we this morning?'

Cameron wipes her face with a towel, using it as cover, time to master her expression. 'Is it morning still?'

'You can't tell?' There's a sour edge to it, and when he looks aside Cameron struggles not to smirk. He's a constant source of questions, a walking progress survey, and it annoys him when every answer she gives is vague enough that he can't be certain she's lying.

'You're the ones with battleship grey walls and no clocks,'

Cameron says. 'Did you run a casino in a previous life? Because I judge these things by the same signs that everyone else does: sun rising, birds tweeting, presence of coffee. Oh yeah, and not being held prisoner. That's a big one.'

Miller gestures at the weight bench. 'You seem to be adjusting well.'

Cameron sniffs. 'The sword is the soul.'

'What?'

'Body and mind,' Cameron says. 'They're all linked.' *Christ, this is the sort of shit Ludo spouts.* If it means getting back to being fit enough to make a run for it, Cameron is happy to go full hippy. 'You want me sharp, this is how I get sharp.'

'Hm.' Miller sounds doubtful, but doesn't argue. Instead he hefts a laptop bag, holds it out to her. 'I would have thought this would be of more use to you,' he says.

Cameron takes it, and finds her laptop inside. It is suspiciously clean, like someone has taken a pack of wet wipes to the casing. 'I bricked this,' she says.

'Actually, you bricked some of it,' Miller says. 'You burned out the USB port and a significant chunk of the motherboard, but the hard drive survived. We got one of our tech guys to fix it. He says it took five hours, which probably means it took two and the rest he spent staring at a vending machine trying to decide which snack to get.'

Cameron opens the laptop, powering it on, and lets out a low whistle when it takes ten seconds to boot up instead of ten minutes. 'Tell him thanks for the upgrade.'

Miller frowns. 'He did say something about it being an insult to his sensibilities.'

'So what's the WiFi password?'

'Your computer will connect to the internal system, but for security reasons we keep our building's server physically separate from the outside world. Whatever information you need you can request, and we'll upload it as necessary.'

'Your building's server isn't connected to the Internet?'

'Correct.'

'So . . . you have someone who actually lifts the memory from one computer and plugs it into the server when you need it transferred?' Cameron mimes the action, stunned by the madness of it.

'We have a robot.'

'That's handy,' she says. 'Keeps it from telling you how dumb that is all day.'

'Miss King, when I said that more than one government agency is interested in our work, I was not boasting. You'd be surprised how much more effective a computer system can be when it is not constantly fighting off attempts to hack into it.'

Cameron waves away the explanation, and looks at the handful of tools she has sitting on her desktop. Links to financial tracking services; real-time transaction monitoring; a search engine that runs down aliases and returns a value for how complete they are: all of them are useless without the Internet. Facial recognition, though, will run just fine on archived footage. *And what about unsecured camera access?* Cameron smothers the smirk that comes on the tail of that thought and tries to look businesslike. 'Fine, whatever. Get me everything you collected from back when my brother "vanished".'

'You think we missed something?'

'I know you missed something,' she says. 'People don't just disappear. They leave a trail.'

'I don't see how going back that far helps you find him.'

Cameron sighs. 'You want me to find Nate?'

'Yes. But—'

'Then take your twenty questions, and push them all the way up your ass,' she says. 'If he found a way to get off your grid that works, then it stands to reason he's still using the same method. So when I get out of here and start looking for him, I'm not just looking at random.'

Miller nods. 'You're right. I'm sorry.'

'You're sorry? Take this fucking implant out of my side, I'll show you sorry.'

'No,' he says, and Cameron stops fiddling with the laptop to pay attention to the tone of his voice. 'I am sorry, but you won't be leaving here to hunt your brother.'

The anger in Cameron's gut flares up, but she keeps a lid on it. It's exactly the kind of bullshit she expects from Miller. 'You don't want to risk him getting his hands on me.'

'His actions suggest you have value to him, and as such that makes you an asset,' Miller says. 'Once you've completed your preliminary report on how your brother got away, you'll be advising Samson in the field.'

'Samson?'

'Our prodigal son. You came close to blinding him.'

Bullet Head. 'Hell of a name to give to a bald guy.'

Miller shrugs it off. 'We can't be blamed for the choices our parents make,' he says. 'But he has made a very quick recovery. He won't recover the eye you took, but he'll be back on his feet in a few days.' The offhand way Miller talks makes it sound like they're discussing a lab rat. Samson could be his first or his last name; it doesn't matter to Miller. All he's lacking is a clipboard and a pen to take down notes. 'What did you think of him?'

'You want me to give you feedback on the guy who tried to beat me to death?'

Miller waves the question away. 'Just your general impression of him.'

'Was he meant to be your headliner?' Cameron laughs. 'What was he, army?'

'Special Forces, originally,' Miller says. 'He left under some unfortunate circumstances and we picked him up not long after. I take it you weren't impressed.'

'No, no, I was impressed. Your boy was faster than shit through a tin horn, but he wasted every opportunity to end the fight for the sake of showing off.'

'You felt he was overconfident.'

'Overconfident? Look, whatever shithole barracks you found him in, you should send him back. Whatever you're paying him, it's not worth it.' Cameron clicks her teeth. 'As soon as he lost his temper, he stopped being an asset and became a liability. If I hadn't got a hold of his head, he probably would have killed me.'

Miller coughs and looks away, shooting his cuffs as though his shirt isn't sitting right inside his suit jacket. Cameron sees it, and pounces.

'You can't send him back, can you?' Miller doesn't answer, but a muscle in his jaw twitches, betraying him. 'What was it? Dishonorable discharge? Drugs? Did he kill someone?'

'Your assessment is very close to the truth,' Miller says. 'He has some issues with holding back.'

'Your asset couldn't control himself.' Cameron shakes her head. 'You're a business guy, right? Don't you spend millions on risk analysis?' Miller shrugs. 'Didn't you stop and think that maybe putting an arrogant man-baby on point was a bad idea? All I had to do was embarrass him and he lost his shit.'

'He almost killed you.'

'Yeah. Your first-in-class prize specimen almost took out someone half his weight and a foot shorter than him after she crawled out of a car wreck.' Cameron slow claps it out, and Miller's expression is like sour milk.

'If you'd been fully fit,' he asks, 'would you have beaten him?'

'Fully fit?' Something flares inside Cameron at that. An old pride, something that she had almost forgotten. 'If I was still fighting?'

'Yes.'

Cameron wants to shake her head and say no. He had been damn fast. Even at her best, she wouldn't have wanted to fight him. Fighting outside your weight class was dumb enough without picking a heavyweight as your opponent.

'I would have destroyed him,' she says.

Miller falls silent, runs his thumb along the line of his jaw, then looks up at her. It's as though her answer confirmed something, answered a question that he had held back from asking. 'Excellent,' he says. 'Perfect, in fact.' He rubs his hands together and they make a dry, papery sound, like he's spent too much of his life in air-conditioned rooms. 'We had conceived of your pursuit as a milk run for Samson. A simple exercise to demonstrate his field-readiness. And yet it proved to be the exact opposite. You are correct about his limitations, and our part in creating them.'

'What are you selling, Miller?'

He spreads his hands wide, palms open, the picture of innocence. 'I was hoping you might agree to replace him.'

'You were hoping?' Cameron holds up her left arm. 'Spare me the soft sell. Try some honesty for once. Take your boy's place or you'll zap me so hard I'll spend the rest of my days eating through a tube, right?'

'The implant in your side is for your own safety.' Miller says it with complete conviction, the kind of sales-floor firmness that comes from long practice. Cameron can sense the edge to it, the admonishing, predatory tilt in his expression that makes her keenly aware of what a single press of a button can do to her, and that Miller could, if he wanted to, press it on a whim. 'When our business with your brother is concluded, when we find out what he wants with you, then there'll be no need for it to remain active.'

Cameron bites down on an insult and stays quiet. He can have his power trip. Miller doesn't realize it, but he's given her a spark of hope in the shape of her laptop. If he's too busy talking shit to notice, then all the better.

'If we were to go out and recruit someone, we would be looking for a candidate just like you,' Miller says. 'Martial arts training from childhood. A successful fighting career. And after it a second career that – while less profitable – has broadened your range of skills. Skip tracing, surveillance and pursuit, subterfuge . . . not to mention your obvious knack for improvisation.'

'I'm not interested,' Cameron says.

'We're changing the world, here, Miss King,' Miller says. 'Once we roll out our program nationwide, we will be in a unique position. Everyone who accepts Carrington as their care provider will be willingly opting to become a living part of the largest monitoring and surveillance network ever built. The losses we make on their insurance will be insignificant in comparison to the value of the information it generates.'

'What are you going to do, lease it out to the NSA or something?'

Miller grunts in disgust. 'The government is a shambles. All of them scrambling to try and climb a little higher than the person next to them. They don't protect the people. Not like we would. Once it goes national – once it goes global – Carrington will be able to completely and genuinely ensure the safety of every man, woman and child in the United States.'

The scale of it is beyond what Cameron expected. He sounds insane. 'All safe under your watchful eye. So what do you need me for?'

'A ground team. To protect our assets and, where necessary, identify and neutralize any attempts to bypass or imitate our system.'

'You want me to crush any resistance.'

'Right now, you're part of the flock,' Miller says, sidestepping the lethal implication. 'How would you like to be one of the shepherds?'

'I'm not interested.' Part of her wants to show willing, string him along, but her instincts tell her he would sense the feint. *Keep him at arm's length*, she thinks. *Make him reach for it, until he thinks the tiniest amount of give is a breakthrough.*

'You don't want to think about it?'

'Look, Miller, you can either stay and give me the hard sell, or I can get to work.' Cameron gestures at the laptop screen. 'Do you want me to find Nate, or not?'

Miller nods, his mouth a tight little line, like she's hurt his feelings. Cameron doesn't buy it for a second. 'I'll leave you to it.'

Cameron ignores him until he goes. When he's out of the room, she finds the program she's been waiting to activate since the laptop booted up. *Access Unsecured Cameras.*

eight six two. She chants them silently in her head, committing them to memory. The less she writes down, the less she records, the less likely it is anyone will see what she's doing.

She can't really hide the fact she's accessing cameras via their internal network, but she can keep everyone who could be watching her too busy to dig in and check. Nate is the key to that. Treating the job of tracking Nate down like any other skip would be too simple – you set a bunch of searches running and sift through the hits you get looking for leads – so it's up to her to get creative.

She opens the internal email they've added to her laptop and puts in a long request about the data from Nate's disappearance. She asks for everything they can put their hands on from six weeks prior to that date, including internal surveillance and traffic cameras from the city. *He didn't just vanish at the drop of a hat*, she writes. *There would have been changes, and a signal to start him off*. She puts in a demand for a floor plan like it's an afterthought, piled in amongst a barrage of questions about Nate's routines, where he worked, where he had access to and how much time he spent off-site. Elevator Nine Eight Six One/Two is a good start, but it won't be of any use to her until she can work out where it is. She signs off with a reminder to send her some headphones, and access to the police band. If nobody in the building is covering their camera up, they sure as shit aren't muting their mics, either.

For the first time, Cameron feels like she's pulling ahead of Miller. The nutrition plan and the workouts were just the foundation, something to keep her anchored. Now, though, she has purpose. Direction. Something to work towards. You don't win a fight by being the strongest or the quickest. People think you train hard, you hit the heavy bag a whole bunch of times, skip rope, maybe spar some and that makes you ready. It doesn't make you ready. All it does is make you fit. What they don't see is the prep work. The research, the frame-by-frame breakdown of their fights and your own, the creation of a strategy that you carry into the ring. You don't win fights with your fists. You win them with your head. By knowing more than your opponent. Cameron knows what Miller is missing. She knows why Nate pulled her into this, what he wanted her for.

He wanted her in here with Miller.

That was what his song and dance routine with the password and the dead drop was all about. He knew she was looking for him, had been looking for him ever since the crash, and he played her with it. By baiting her with just enough information to put her on his scent, he had tricked her into downloading the data off of a USB stick without thinking twice about what it was and why he had left it for her to find.

In the heat of the moment, she had thought it was some great secret waiting to be spilled, the truth of where he had been all these years, something so hot that he could not possibly deliver it in person. The whole thing is like a bitter taste at the back of her throat, that she had been holding so tight to the hope of seeing him again, she'd walked right into it. It only struck her when Miller boasted to her that their servers were completely cut off from the outside world, rendering them immune to cyber-attack.

Nate had known that calling her would set Carrington on her heels. Since she was the one he was meant to kill, the one he'd left alive, it would be impossible for them not to come after her. The data on the USB stick – the data she had downloaded – was meant to be in her possession when they caught her.

It's a virus.

Nate isn't working for a foreign power. Cameron can picture what it is like: a virus like a warhead, a sleek mass of code designed to inject itself into the Carrington system and start shutting down vital components without damaging the bulk of the system's code. A smart-target missile that takes down the security systems, but leaves the rest of the server complete. Vulnerable, ready to be salvaged.

Cameron has heard of that kind of virus before. Stuxnet was a cyber-weapon created by the US government to derail the Iranian nuclear program. Nate is working for a US agency. Whatever Carrington did to piss them off, it must have been really bad. Instead of dishing out a fat government contract, they've flipped Nate and given him the means to hobble his former master. He was never trying to help Cameron. He needed to inject the virus into Carrington's system, and Cameron was his route to making that happen.

Except he hadn't counted on Ray helping her, and that she would leave the data with him.

A chill floods her gut thinking about that. If Ray is alive, then he's in danger. And Cameron has no way of warning him.

Someone clears their throat to get Cameron's attention. She looks up a shade too quickly, closing the laptop on reflex, and curses herself for being so obvious. Thankfully, it isn't Miller. It's Terri, and she is standing in the doorway with a blood-pressure cuff in one hand and a metal tray in the other. Blood tests.

'Is this a bad time?' she asks.

Cameron stares at her. 'You want to take a wild guess at the answer to that?'

Terri takes that without blinking and walks over to where Cameron is sitting. She puts the tray down, pulls up a chair, and sits. Cameron holds out her left arm, and Terri inspects it briefly before slipping the cuff on.

'How does it feel?' she asks. 'Any numbness? Tremors?'

Cameron takes a deep breath in and lets it whistle out through her nose. The swelling from the break has reduced, but isn't completely gone yet. 'If I say yes, does that mean I get all the shit you've put in me pulled out?'

Terri takes her blood pressure in silence, and Cameron wonders why she doesn't do it on the right arm as well. If she was worried about circulation in the limb, it would be one way to check it.

The blood test comes next, and Terri turns the crook of Cameron's arm upwards and slips a tiny needle into a vein with quick, professional ease.

'Ten out of ten,' Cameron murmurs.

'Sorry?'

Cameron shakes her head. 'Old habit. You wouldn't believe how many times someone has missed that vein,' she says. 'I used to give a score out of ten.'

Terri nods, understanding. 'Not everyone has the knack. They've got these new needles that are meant to make it easier.'

Cameron looks at the needle in her arm. 'It doesn't look special.'

'I don't use them,' Terri says. 'It feels like cheating. Like if I used them, I'd forget how to do it properly.'

Cameron watches the vial filling with her blood and feels an odd kind of pride in that sentiment. It sounds a lot like something Ludo would say. *Stick to the fundamentals. You can't build anything if your base is weak.*

'What is it?' Terri asks.

Cameron realizes she is smiling, and smothers it. 'Nothing. Something an old friend told me.'

Terri pauses, on the verge of saying something, then busies herself drawing out the needle and putting a folded wad of dressing in its place. She holds the dressing in position with her thumb, pressing hard into Cameron's flesh.

'You know I saw you fight once.' Terri speaks in a low voice, not looking at Cameron. 'At the Oracle, five years ago. Got my brother some great seats for his birthday.'

Cameron knows which fight she is talking about. She'd been talked into filling a card against Susan Monroe after her opponent pulled out with a training injury. With a weight deficit of almost ten pounds and two inches of reach on her, Monroe had not anticipated a tough time. An excellent grappler, she came close to pulling a submission out of Cameron in both the first and second rounds. In the first round the bell had saved Cameron; in the second, Cameron had held the fraction of an angle against a hold that should have put her out of the fight. Instead, she had held it, getting angrier and angrier at herself for being so dumb as to wind up in the same situation twice in ten minutes. Three seconds into the third round Monroe had rushed her, greedy for the win, and Cameron kicked her in the head so hard that the whiplash tore a muscle in Monroe's neck. She went down and didn't get up until the medics lifted her on to a gurney.

'Must have been a hell of a show.'

Terri grins, but doesn't look up. 'He still talks about it. Says it was the best fight he's ever seen.' Cameron almost says something sarcastic, but bites down on it. This has the air of a confession, and she can sense Terri is building up to something.

Terri reaches for some tape to hold the gauze in place, and Cameron sees her slip something else off of the tray, palming it into her gloved hand. 'Never been a big fan of fights, but I did take one thing home from that night,' she says. As she fixes the gauze in place, she takes whatever it is she's holding and presses it hard against Cameron's skin, just below the edge of the tape. 'You never gave up.' It's barely a whisper. She sits back, pulls Cameron's right hand over to cover her own, and speaks in a normal voice again. 'Keep pressure on that until you get sick of holding it.'

Cameron presses down on the gauze and the packet beside it, the desire to peek making it feel hot against her fingertips. 'Is that a real length of time?'

'Proven science,' Terri says. She gathers her stuff and gets up, ready to leave.

'Hey, Terri?'

'Yeah?'

'You sound rough.' It startles her, and Cameron makes a point of holding her gaze, of not looking down at her arm. 'If you've got a cold coming on I don't want you coughing your germs at me. Take a day off or something.'

Terri's eyes widen, but she recovers quickly. 'I'm fine,' she says, waving it off as she walks to the door. 'It's just a sore throat.'

'I'm serious,' Cameron says, her voice rising as Terri leaves. 'You make me sick I'm gonna sue.'

When she's certain that Terri has gone, Cameron takes her hand off the gauze and tape, and transfers the package to the keyboard of her laptop. It's a square of film, no more than an inch across, and trapped inside it is a spiral of wire with a tiny metal dot at its center. It's an RFID chip. There's a sticker on the other side, and Cameron turns it over to find written in tiny, cramped capital letters: *CHIP CLONE: T. JOHNSON* and below it, in another hand: *9861*.

Nine Eight Six One. *Jackpot.* It didn't occur to Cameron that doors might need a chip as well as a keycode to open them, but if they put a chip in her it makes sense that they're doing it to everyone else on staff. Cameron wants to run after the nurse and hug her. It doesn't fix the problem of the taser buried in her side, but it's a start. On the laptop screen, the active cameras are arranged in a grid, waiting to be picked.

It's a start, but it's not enough. You win fights with your head. By knowing more than your opponent. Cameron clicks on the first camera, and gets to work.

Chapter 25

Ray wasn't sure what he expected. A glistening skyscraper, maybe. A polished crystal shard driven like a spike into the ground, indomitable in its glass-clad armor, deflecting everything, even light. Or a military-style compound complete with high razor-wire fences and a watchtower, jeeps endlessly patrolling, weaving and circling their way through the pattern of telephone poles set in the ground to keep helicopters from landing.

The home of Carrington Medical, Axion, or whoever their enemy is, looks like neither of the scenarios he imagined. What it looks like is a cluster of cement blocks that were dropped in the middle of a scrub patch of abandoned industrial real estate, and have slowly clumped together to keep themselves warm through the night. It looks like the kind of place your uncle would drive an hour out of town to so that he could load up on discount house paint, and not even offer to buy you a soda from the dust-clogged vending machine by way of an apology.

There's a cursory attempt at a fence, loose squares of galvanized mesh hanging limp from battered-looking metal posts that sit too awkwardly to have been set in concrete. It's the sort of thing that keeps most of the big animals out of the trash cans at night, and little else.

All told, it looks like the least secure location in the world, and Ray feels like an idiot for having bought into Nate King's insistence on a cautious approach. They're sitting far enough out that they need binoculars to really add some detail to how unimpressive it all is, and Nate is still twitching like a cat at the sound of distant cars passing.

'Are you sure this is the place?' Ray asks. 'It doesn't look like much of anything.' Nate says nothing, so Ray starts to get up, making to stretch out some of the road-tired feeling that has crept into his lower back. Nate catches hold of his side and drags him back down to ground level.

'This is the place,' he hisses. 'Keep your head and your voice down.'

'What, you worried the two-man team of rent-a-cops they hire to look after the place is going to come point a flashlight at us?'

'You don't see it?'

Ray sighs. 'What I see is a waste of my fucking time.'

'And you call yourself a cop? Look at it. Look how inconspicuous it is. You think that's an accident? It doesn't just blend in. It's genuinely, completely uninteresting. Your gaze slides off it looking for something better to see.'

'I noticed that.'

'Yeah, well that should start your alarm bells ringing. You ever see a place that shabby that didn't have some story hanging off of it? Someone's bankruptcy, some local family feud, the whole business written off. Here? Nothing. The whole thing is just camouflage.' Nate pauses, waiting for a reaction, but Ray gives him nothing. It's all conjecture. Maybe somebody local could point to the place and tell you the story; it's far enough off the beaten path that it's more likely than not people just forgot about it. Nate presses on. 'Look again. You see any birds down there?'

Ray pauses, lifts his binoculars, and looks again. It's not something he ever gives much thought to, but there are always birds. Little ones, dipping low to the ground, chasing down insects or interesting scraps. Big ones, attracted to anything above a storey in height, craning their necks as they search for anything they can grab hold of. Raptors, riding the thermals upwards, hanging casual in the air as they wait out their prey. Here at Carrington there's no sign of any of them, no signs of life at all. It is as still and as silent as the grave.

Ray takes another long look at the site. He's still not convinced. It's just another shit-smear industrial lot rotting at the edge of the city. Not even the birds give a fuck about it. 'Nate, this is a waste of time. The biggest secret they've got down there is a filing cabinet full of sales receipts from 1972.'

'I thought you'd say that.' Nate turns, looking down the length of the access road, the long dusty strip of nothing that leads down from a freeway turn-off. A battered car has turned on to it and is making its way towards the site. 'Here he comes now.'

'Who the hell is that?' Ray asks.

'Pizza delivery.'

Ray looks down at the car in disbelief for a moment before checking through the binoculars. On the sky-blue panel door

213

a faded pizza store decal is just visible. 'You ordered a pizza. Unbelievable.'

'You need to see this,' Nate says. 'You need to see what we're up against.'

Ray's fingers brush the spot where faint scars mark the ghost of his implant. 'I know what we're up against,' he says. 'I just don't think this is—'

'Look.' Nate is pointing, and as Ray follows the line of his finger he sees a black minivan, windows tinted, accelerating down the site road towards the car. Ray didn't catch which building it came from, and it's almost as though it just sprung up out of the earth.

'Who is that? The fucking A-Team?'

'Site security,' Nate says. 'Watch.'

The black van brakes in a cloud of dust, swerving to block the road, and men with assault rifles pile out of the side door, leveling them at the beat-up car. The pizza guy slams on the brakes and stops about a hundred feet short of the van.

'This shit can't be happening,' Ray says. There's enough firepower down there to kit out a SEAL team. 'I'm going to call it in.'

'Call what in?' Nate asks. 'Even if your colleagues would listen to you, it's private property. As far as the law is concerned he's trespassing.'

It's the first time Ray has thought of it as that. *The facility.* There's a palpable air of danger to its blandness now, an edge he hadn't felt before. The pizza delivery guy, now out of the car and waving his arms in surrender, could disappear into those cement blocks and no one would ever think twice about checking for him. The thought lies heavy and cold in Ray's gut. Nate might well have condemned an innocent man just to make a point.

'What will they do with him?'

'Standard procedure with strays is to stick them in a dark room and threaten the shit out of them. They'll turn his life inside out just to make sure he isn't anyone important, and when they confirm the only danger he presents is being too high to beat the thirty-minute promise they'll make him sign a non-disclosure the length of his arm and take him home.'

'They going to chip him, too?'

'If he wasn't already, he'll walk out of there with a chip in his arm or thigh. They'll make it seem like they're doing him a favor.' Nate nods towards the wreck of his car. 'Maybe even offer to get that fixed up if he takes something more substantial. They fit homeless guys with signal repeaters in exchange for food, shelter, healthcare. Whatever they need.'

Ray bristles, his voice rising. 'You let an innocent man get Gitmo'd just so I'd believe you?' Nate doesn't react to it. Ray stares at him for a long time, and Nate sits there watching the black bag go over the pizza kid's head, the restraints go on, and the van door closing with the same cold expression. 'You know, I'm starting to wonder why the fuck your sister would ever want to find you.'

That gets a reaction. Nate turns to look straight at Ray, his expression tight with anger. He coughs in spite of himself, fighting to try and keep it down. 'You don't know a thing about me, Ray Perada.'

'Yeah?' Ray says. 'I know a piece of shit when it stinks up the place.'

215

'You think I threw that guy to the wolves?' Nate asks. 'Wake up. People have been getting chipped in this city for months, willingly. You think this is a problem? This is a dry run for what they plan on doing. Imagine this: a nationwide rollout of Carrington Medical's new medical aid program. Agree to have a chip installed, and they will beat down any insurance roadblock that stands in your way. Agree to the advanced chip – the one that collects and passes on signals – and you don't worry about insurance again. How many people are going to say no to that?'

Ray shakes his head. 'That won't happen. People will see through it.'

'They won't. They haven't. Ring up every family that's had a cancer death in the past five years and promise them free screening for life if they use our new easy-testing subdermal implant. They'll queue round the block.'

Ray knows the kind of person he's reminded of when Nate speaks. There are guys on the narcotics task force like him. All veterans of the much vaunted and ultimately futile war on drugs, burned out and cynical, their morality worn thin by decades of exposure to the very worst of human nature. The sort of cop who thinks the ends justify the means.

Ray swallows hard. Nate is playing him. *Right now, you're the pizza guy.* He wants Cameron, but it sure as shit isn't to help shut down his old boss's surveillance network. There's something else, and for all his prodding Ray can't get it out of him. *If you don't do it, he'll send someone else.* 'I understand.'

Something down on the access road catches Ray's attention and he lifts his binoculars to see it. The rendition-in-progress has halted momentarily as one of the crew has gone back to the ruined delivery car to fetch the pizza. They're taking it with them.

'What did you order?'

'Double pineapple, arugula, anchovies,' Nate says. 'No cheese.'

Ray lets out a low whistle. 'Shit. You sure they're not going to kill him after he turns up with the pizza?'

'Not unless they make him eat the pizza.' Nate shuffles back down the rise, putting himself out of line of sight of the access road and the buildings. 'Come on. We've seen enough, and there's a lot still to do before tomorrow.'

Chapter 26

Ray adjusts the bag in his lap, shifts in his seat, and looks out of the window. Nobody on the bus is talking. They were expressly told not to. A pinch-faced bus guard, skin so tight over the bones of his face it made him look like he was wearing a mask, had laid it out for them. He'd opened with an appetizer of human resource welcome-speak, *we know it's a great opportunity, we know you're all excited*, and followed with the meat-and-potatoes main course: *in the interest of security you are not allowed to speak in transit*. Between the threat and the group of lantern-jawed men watching them board, it felt more like a prison detail than a new-hire induction day. Ray always wondered what it would be like to be on the receiving end of that treatment, and now he knows: it turns people into livestock, and the short ride out to the Carrington Medical buildings is made long by the attention of the guards. Each boring moment stretches out with the threat of dismissal, and as they turn away from the bustle of the highway and down on to the access road an unpleasant sensation rises in the back of Ray's throat. Do cows know when they're being taken to slaughter?

He plays along with the others, acts curious about the landscape. He can see an abandoned shack, whitewash peeling, and another in the distance. They look identical, and when he looks across the aisle he can see others dotted about the landscape. Camouflage, or something like it. This is the most uninteresting place in the world, and Ray finds his focus drifting.

Cameron. Ray can remember waking in the car now, a gap in his memory filling with a hazy recollection of half-grasped moments of awareness. He remembers seeing her crawl from the car, getting up and standing on legs that looked ready to collapse out from under her to fight Bullet Head. Big bastard. There's a gap in what he recalls of the fight, but he knows he saw her land, ragdoll-limp, at the very end of it. He thought she was dead. With all the shit she's brought down on him since they met, Ray could be – should be – anywhere else. But she got out of the car, and she didn't run, even though she could – should – have. She fought, and Ray owes her for that.

Don't get caught. Don't get shot. Don't get lost. Ray takes a deep breath and smothers the sigh that threatens to follow it. *Simple enough.* Find Cameron and work out who her brother is working for, and what they want with her. *Less straightforward.* Oh yeah, and escape.

He can feel the sweat making his shirt stick to him already.

They pass the point where the pizza guy got stopped, and Ray tries not to look too much like a man about to vomit. Up by the driver, a panel lights up green and the guard next to him visibly relaxes, clipboard lowering from where he was clutching it like a shield. He gets to his feet and clears his throat, as though he doesn't already have everyone's full attention, and offers the seated rows the most insincere smile Ray has seen short of the SFPD public relations department.

'Thank you, everyone, for your patience. We apologize for the strict security protocols. We've had some information about our products and services slip out through leaks, so an ability to be tight-lipped is a quality we cherish in all our staff.' He looks at the driver again, who nods in confirmation. 'You may now talk amongst yourselves, if you wish.'

There's a long silence as the bus absorbs the sudden freedom before a soft murmur of introductions begins. The guy sitting next to Ray is wearing a suit that probably cost the same as Ray's rent and is groomed in that exact, polished way that suggests he either has a team of stylists to hand or got up at four a.m. to get started on it. When he turns to Ray he extends one tanned hand, turned slightly to show off the Ivy League ring he's wearing.

'David Farrow, Strategies. I used to be in Assets, but I divested.' He smiles, his straight, even teeth so white they almost glow. Ray tries to suppress the cop instinct – *what is this guy hiding?* – and puts on a grateful-for-the attention face.

'I'm George. Perez.' Ray says it like he's apologizing. 'My name is George Perez.'

'What do you do, George?' It's both question and threat, the old high school leveler carried up to the corporate world. *Which group do you belong to?* and *Am I ruining my reputation by talking to you?*

'I work in data entry and compliance.'

It's not bad work, according to Nate. Spend your days looking at code, spreadsheets, making sure everything is complete, hunting down discrepancies. It's well-paid and rewards a certain level of concentration and analytical thought. In a crowd where everyone wants to be a world-changing innovator you might as well say you catch other people's shits for a living. Farrow's smile doesn't drop, but he does withdraw his hand with haste and turn away to find someone worthier of his time.

By the time they get through the chain-link fence, draw to a stop and line up to get off the bus, word has spread of Ray's status at the bottom of the programmer food chain. He stays in his seat as David slips out ahead of him into the aisle, and then waits quietly for everyone to filter past. They close ranks to make sure he ends up at the back. Nobody asks his name. They barely even look at him. Ray is musing on the idea of a computer tech as the ultimate undercover role until one of the others mutters 'George' to himself, shaking his head as he passes. *Oh yeah, there is that.* Every other person on the bus is white, and his low-level job isn't the only prejudice here. *We'll see how fucking clever you are when I come back and arrest every one of your asses*, he thinks.

Inside, the building is massively more hi-tech than the exterior implies. The lobby they walk through is a kaleidoscope room of granite and steel, dominated by security screening apparatus. There's a metal detector and a body scan to go through, and more than one person has their bag confiscated. Ray's lunch bag and thermos, the latter three-quarters full of a clear beef soup from a pop-up place on the way to the bus, are given a quick once over and handed back without incident. Ray is almost suspicious until he glances back and catches sight of the monitors: there's security camera footage of him from this morning, the girl behind the counter caught freeze-

221

frame pouring soup straight into the thermos for him. On the screen next to it, there's a string of ID photos: Ray's, the girl's, the guy behind him in the queue, the woman leaving with her dog tucked under one arm. Everyone that is in the shot is listed on the second screen, and all of them have a green border. *Safe*. One of the staff catches Ray looking and he moves on quickly.

More surprising than the fact they have access to all this information is that George Perez gets a green flag. Nate King couldn't have known they would meet, and whoever is bankrolling him must have either built a new identity from the ground up in days, or found funds enough to buy one off the shelf. They must have some serious pull to make that happen, and not for the first time Ray wonders who Nate King is working for. They want this incursion to happen, and Ray knows he's being thrown into a meat grinder as part of some grand plan they have, but he owes Cameron too much to walk away.

They filter out of the lobby and are escorted by a team of six handlers along a battleship grey corridor to a warehouse space, an open floor with a high ceiling bounded by wide doorways, built to allow heavy plant to move in and out. Ray is struck by the livestock comparison again. Like the first cows to arrive at market, all the new hires huddle together in a tight group, not quite in the middle of the space. The floor is clean enough that whenever someone moves their shoes squeak. Overhead, six massive vents are pulling air fast enough that the whole room seems to tremble with their thrumming.

Ray raises his hand. One of the handlers lifts his chin in acknowledgement, but otherwise does not move.

'Hey, you know where the toilets are?'

That gets the handler moving. He walks the space between the door they came in and the group with a deliberate slowness, not obviously armed but making a big show of how badly his suit jacket fits him, how awkward it is for him to move his left arm while walking. *Maybe you can wait to go to the toilet*, is the message. Ray can feel the rest of the new hires silently urging him to drop it.

'What?' The handler stands too close, deliberately. Ray can tell that he's a smoker from his breath.

'The toilets,' Ray says. 'That morning coffee really loosened things up, you know what I'm saying?'

The handler's eyes go distant as an instruction is relayed to him through his earpiece. He nods once, to himself, a firm, militaristic jerk of the head as though his unit has been ordered to move out. Ray guesses that he spends a lot of time imagining what it would be like to shoot someone. 'Fine. Does anyone else need to use the head?'

'I could use a break,' Farrow pipes up, and Ray curses inwardly as he steps forward.

'No one else?' The handler makes a challenge of it and everyone else catches on. It's just Ray and David. The handler jerks his head at them. 'This way,' he says, walking them off to one side of the warehouse and out into another anonymous corridor.

Ray walks straight past the bathroom, as it resembles every other door that they pass on the way: a plain panel of wood painted the same color as the walls and fitted with an electronic keypad instead of a lock. The handler calls him back and punches in a four-digit code that opens the door to a small, sparse and very, very clean bathroom. There is a single stall, and two urinals. Ray steps across the threshold as though stepping on to the surface of the moon: it's the first men's room he's ever seen that doesn't smell of week-old piss. Either their cleaning staff is round the clock on call, or he's about to christen the porcelain with its first ever use.

'Be quick,' the handler says.

'Don't burst a valve.' David grins companionably at the man and is met with a stone-faced response. Ray is already heading for one of the urinals. He'd planned on getting rid of the handler, but the Strategies hire tagging along makes things a great deal more complicated.

Come on, Ray. Think.

He gets to the urinal and hears a burst of static from the doorway, someone talking so loud down the radio channel that the handler's earpiece is audible to both him and David. The handler mutters something into a mic sewn into his cuff and almost leaves before realizing that Ray and David are still at the urinals, both of them half-turned to see what the fuss is.

He scowls. 'Finish up, both of you. You need to go back.'

Ray doesn't even start, let alone finish. David, as he pisses, leans over to whisper conspiratorially, 'Are you the plant?'

Ray's jaw locks tight for a moment, every muscle in his body keying up for fight or flight. 'What?'

'The Carrington plant.'

Ray realizes why the Strategies hire followed him. It's an old urban legend that sometimes filters down to rookie cops: that the brass put a mole in with interviewees and new hires to see which of them really has the right stuff. An idea occurs to him.

'Good job, Farrow.' Ray uses his most serious, most official voice, and David beams at the validation. 'Now phase two begins. Are you ready?'

David nods at him like a puppy, and Ray shoves him, hard. He bangs off the modesty panel that borders the urinal, and the push is enough to spoil his aim and make him piss on the floor between them.

'Hey!' Ray yells, his voice rising. He switches tone again, going for the most aggressive gangbanger accent he can muster. 'The fuck you think you're doing?'

The handler is at his shoulder in an instant, but the spilled piss does its job. He ignores Ray and stares down at the floor, his face twisted in disgust.

'What the fuck is this?'

David, too shocked to do anything other than stand there with his pecker hanging out, holds his palms up in the universal symbol for innocence. 'Look, I can explain—'

Ray interrupts by punching the handler in the gut. It's not a department-sanctioned control maneuver, the sort of thing they teach in the academy as an eight-week course before giving you a semiautomatic handgun to use instead. It's quick and nasty, the kind of punch you learn from long experience of punching people and being punched in turn. It's a tight, fast hook, elbow out, turning through the hips and coming up on to the balls of the feet to really drive the blow deep into the soft mass of the man's midriff. All of the air goes out of him in a great huff of breath, his eyes popping as though they're about to jump straight out of his head, and Ray capitalizes on that moment of surprise. He steps in, grabs the handler by his jacket front and with a grunt of effort that rings off the walls

225

throws him up and over his hip, the kind of clumsy-ass throw that's only useful if the other person is too willing or too winded to stop you doing it. There's no space for him to land neatly, so instead the handler smacks face first into the urinal, bounces off of the wall and Ray gets the hell out of the way as gravity takes him all the way down to the floor.

'Fuck!' Ray can't tell if David says it, or if he says it himself.

Ray hauls the unconscious handler away from the broken urinal and into the middle of the room before turning him over and checking his pulse. He's still breathing, and after a moment Ray finds his heartbeat. His face is a mess, but Ray tries not to think too closely on it. *You were always going to get your hands dirty doing this*, he thinks. It was never going to be bloodless. There comes a time when you get so far, turning back would be just as bloody. Ray shakes his head as he opens the handler's jacket and starts an inventory of his stuff. Baton. Taser. Gun. Radio. Mobile phone. Zip ties, bundled in a loop on the side of his belt. For a guy working internal security, he's tooled up for some serious work.

A glance up at David tells Ray he's not coping too well. He's managed to zip himself up, but is backed up into the corner and looks set to bolt.

'Hey, Strategies? Farrow!' Ray snaps his fingers and the other man jumps. 'You still with me?'

'Y-yeah.'

'I really am a plant,' Ray says. 'Genuinely. Good spot. But here's the thing. I'm not a plant for Carrington. I'm a cop.' For a moment Ray thinks David really is going to run, so he stays very still and lays it out for him. 'You've fallen in with some bad people.' Ray gestures at the gear, all laid out on the floor. 'Look at all this crap. You think he was carrying all this around because he likes the look? These guys are fucking crazy.'

'I don't think . . . I didn't . . .' For a guy that claims he specializes in strategy, David is taking a long time to process it. Time that Ray doesn't have.

'Into the stall, David.'

That puts some life into him. 'No way. If you're a cop, you have to—'

'I don't have to do a damn thing other than offer you one of two options. Sit quietly in that stall with a zip tie round your wrist and what's left of my soup until someone comes to find you, or I Taser your ass and leave you spooning with Chuckles McSquarejaw here.'

David thinks about it. The safe territory of a multiple-choice quiz seems to ground him. 'What kind of soup is it?'

Chapter 27

Cameron can feel trouble coming as though it is rising up through the Earth's crust, a seismic tilt of tectonic plates that begins low in her hips and rises up through her spine, her center of gravity shifting to cope with the new normal. With that sensation is the dread that everyone who's ever been on the West Coast feels when the earth starts to move under them. It's not a fight-or-flight fear, not an instinct. It's the cost of self-awareness: that some dangers are unknowable, and just too large to fight against. It's knowing that everything is about to go to shit, and that there's not a great deal you can do about it.

Ever since Carrington picked her up, Cameron has been well acquainted with that sensation.

She's sitting cross-legged on her bed with the laptop balanced on one knee, much as she has been for the past twelve hours, flicking between the data they've gathered on Nate and the internal cameras that she has been able to connect to, her fingers running on automatic as she switches between the two, eyes taking it all in, waiting for aberrations to leap out at her. Meditating is not the word for what she's doing. *Simmering* would be closer to it.

There's nothing on the Nate side of things. No change in his routine, no sudden shifts in behavior. He was chipped, just like the rest of them, and yet even with all that extra data available, Cameron can't figure out how he escaped. Whatever game he was playing, it was well hidden. He must have been so careful, the whole thing orchestrated in the tiny gaps where his signal stuttered or jumped. She'd queried that, and there were dead spots in their coverage, kinks still in the process of being ironed out. Nate had known all about where they were, and how to exploit them. He was always the smartass, full of schemes to get them both into and out of trouble. Knowing that he'd turned that talent against her sits sour in her belly.

The internal cameras at Carrington are what get Cameron's attention. She can tell from the expressions on people's faces alone that something is happening, and that it isn't good news. People talk out of frame, check their phones and are frustrated by what they find. In the background of one, what looks like a security detail comes into shot, moving with purpose. Cameron catches sight of a few employees putting their things together, and then shutting down their computers. Getting ready to leave, or maybe to evacuate. Something big is going down, big enough that it has filtered down to the rank and file. There will be a lot of confusion right now. A lot of chances to slip away.

The chip in her side – the leash they have her on – is a problem that still needs dealing with, but she's not going to solve it sitting on her ass. Out in the world there are doctors, vets, surgical tools, X-rays. Hell, a roll of Reynolds Wrap and a cell phone signal jammer might do the trick. It's probably how Nate managed to drop off their system until he could get his own dealt with permanently.

She flicks from camera to camera, trying to follow the security team that she saw. Three men, in full tactical gear, with automatic weapons. She catches them once or twice as she works her way through, then loses them completely. Cameron can see the security cameras, but she can't move them. She can't pause or wind back the footage. In her head she's been building a picture of the building's layout, trying to link together camera ID numbers with the floors she sees the same people on. The team are moving on the ground floor, or maybe the first. It's hard to tell.

A flicker of movement on the grid of active cameras catches her eye, and the picture goes dead, a flash of white and then static. *Weird.* She scrolls down the list of cameras and finds a couple more are already dead. They're all ground floor, from what she remembers seeing on them. She scrolls up just in time to see a figure taking aim at another one, and before she can click on the picture it dies, too.

Cameron's pulse picks up. Someone is inside Carrington, and they are taking out cameras as they go. She closes the dead camera feed and tries to find the next one in line, taking a guess at which direction they're headed in.

She guesses right. Just as they appear in frame to take aim, she automatically hits the button to take a screenshot.

'Holy shit,' Cameron says to herself. She only saw his face for a fraction of a second, and has to go back and look at the picture she took before she can convince herself she actually saw his face.

Ray Perada.

He's sporting a weak mustache and a haircut that suggests the barber was blind or in a hurry, but it's definitely Perada. Cameron finds that she is grinning at how impossibly good it feels to know that he's alive, and that he's here for her. That he found her, that he got in at all . . . It means that he's not alone, and there's only one person she can think of that would help him.

Nate has sent him in. He must have tracked him down after Carrington took her, found out that the data had stayed behind. And now Ray is his back-up plan, another pawn pushed across the board to set off whatever he wants the virus to do. Ray probably thinks that he's here to get Cameron out. Cameron knows that he's been set up to fail.

She is off the bed and into a pair of sneakers before she even knows it. She pauses a second, instinctively looking for her wallet, keys, phone, but none of those exist here. Sweatpants, vest, shoes. That's all she's got.

She goes back to the laptop, and back to the grid of cameras, looking for the security team. If she could work out where Ray is from that, then security can too. In her head, Cameron tries to plot the course Ray is following, using the cameras he's taken out as reference points. Without a map of the building it's guesswork, but it's all she has. *Where's he going?* He's coming for her, so she guesses down into the basement levels is his rough destination. The lifts are coded, so he'll be heading for any stairwell he can find that will take him down to where she is being held captive. She wonders if Nate knew where they'd hold her, or if Ray shook it out of someone.

There's just one problem with the stairwell: the three-man security team is headed that way as well. Even if Cameron could reach them, they can just zap her with the pacemaker before she can do anything to back Ray up. Still, he's going to be three on one if she doesn't do anything about it.

Nine Eight Six One. Terri's cloned ID chip. Ray has to go past a lift to get to the stairwell. If Cameron can be quick enough, she just might make it.

She picks up the laptop, tucking it under her arm before she opens the door, and sets off at a sprint. No one has been sent to check on her yet, but she can't stay put and hope he'll be okay. The chip in her arm is still tracking her and the pacemaker they've put in her side can still be used to disable her, but only when someone pushes the button to make that happen. All she has to do is avoid running into anyone sporting a Carrington ID and she'll stay in the game. And she has to stay in the game. Because if Ray came here to rescue her, Cameron is going to have to rescue him first.

Chapter 28

The handclap displacement of a bullet passing through the air inches from Ray's head is an uncomfortably familiar feeling. For a half-second he's back in the alleyway, listening to the calm discussion of two men who are making their businesslike way along it to kill him dead, before he shakes off the feeling and presses himself back into the broad doorway he's using as cover.

Things are a little different this time. Firstly, there aren't two of them. There are three, if the number of voices he counted was correct. Secondly, there are no exits. Every door he has tried has been locked, and he can't risk stepping out into the corridor to kick one in. If he moves too far out of cover, he'll instantly make a target of himself. Thirdly, he isn't nearly as scared as he was before. He feels numb to it, like the factors weighed against his survival are just a calculation, a sum that he has to find a solution to. *Maybe this is what happens when you know you're going to die. Maybe you just forget to be scared.*

A foot squeaks on the corridor floor. Ray takes the Taser he's carrying and pokes it out past the edge of the door frame.

The point man will be in the middle of the corridor, aiming down sight, waiting for any movement. He angles the Taser slightly, a blind guess, and pulls the trigger.

The Taser launches its probes with a sound like someone popping a bubble of chewing gum. The wires spool out and the grip lights up, crackling in Ray's hand as it starts to discharge through the target. A direct hit. The point man opens up, an involuntary squeeze of the trigger on his automatic weapon as bullets fly down the corridor before stitching a line along the ceiling as he falls. There are shouts from his back-up, keen to offer supporting fire but unable to shoot past for fear of hitting him. There's a solid thump as he lands and a grunt as his friends pull him back down on to the stairs. One of them is panicking, and Ray grins as he puts his arm round the door to throw the Taser grip towards them.

'Fire in the hole!' He yells it just as the grip clatters off of the floor and there is a flurry of sudden movement as the men try to get away from what they think is a grenade. Ray is about to duck and run when more fire opens up from the stairwell, a man's voice yelling in defiance over the report of his weapon. *Trust my luck to find the one gung-ho asshole who won't put his head down*, Ray thinks.

This is the only way down. Ray pulls the pistol he took from the handler and checks that the safety is off. It's a compact Ruger LC9, a slim piece chosen to fit under a suit jacket. Ray's not a fan, but he'll do what he can with it. Lethal force is a big step, but he can't avoid taking it. He only knows one route down to Cameron, and that's the stairs. He only has Nate's word on it, but considering how everything seems to revolve around getting to her, it's one word he can trust. Ray closes his eyes and tries to think, to find anything that he can use to get out of this. *At least they don't have grenades of their own.*

There's a crisp ripping noise, like someone peeling off a length of Velcro, before something small is slid along the length of the corridor floor towards where Ray is hiding.

They have grenades of their own.

Ray has no answer to this realization other than to stand frozen in place as he waits for the flash and the blast to hit him. He can't even find his voice to swear one last time.

And then he's falling, stumbling sideways as the wall slides away, turning as something takes hold of his shirt and hauls him backwards so suddenly that the heels of his shoes scream as they are pulled along the floor.

Ray hits the back wall of an elevator just as the flashbang goes off, the ice-white flare of burning magnesium silhouetting a figure against the open door for a moment before his body reacts to shield his eyes from damage. Painted in purple and blue across the back of his eyelids like an inkblot test, the figure is unmistakable.

'Cameron?'

'Shh.' He hears the doors sliding shut. Then, closer, a whisper. 'We're waiting them out,' she says. 'Don't make a sound.'

What Ray thinks is blindness is simply darkness: there are no lights in the elevator. He blinks away the last of the after-images to discover only black, although after a short time his eyes adjust and he can make out the faint impression of light from the corridor creeping in under the door. After a minute of waiting, shadows move along the bottom of the elevator door, stop in front of it. *They're outside*. Ray tenses, sits up with his gun in line, arms braced against his knees, ready to open fire. The instant the door opens, they're going to walk into a full clip.

Cameron's hand settles on his shoulder, urging him to wait. On the other side, he can just make out the sounds of a muffled conversation.

. . . think he has the code for this?

. . . doesn't have a chip. Must've run for it—

A fist bangs against the elevator door, making Ray jump, but the footsteps move on. Cameron's hand stays on his shoulder for a full count of ten before relaxing.

'They're gone,' she says in a normal voice.

'How do you know that?'

'All the elevators are coded,' she says. 'If they weren't, they'd be opening the doors with a crowbar to see if you were in here.' An oblong slice of blue-white light illuminates the elevator as she opens up a laptop. It lights up her face from below as she works on it, as though she's about to tell a scary story. Instead, she nods to herself. 'Looks like they're moving on.'

'If the whole floor is locked down how do we—'

Cameron holds something up to the elevator panel and the lights in the elevator go on. Ray doesn't cover his eyes fast enough, and the after-effects of the flashbang make the experience painful to the point that he feels close to vomiting.

'Sorry,' Cameron says. 'I should have told you I was putting the lights on.' As she pulls him to his feet, he can't suppress a burp of gas, the sour acid stench of it rising in his throat. Cameron steps neatly to the side, supporting him with one hand holding the back of his shirt. Ray shakes his head.

'Some rescue mission this turned out to be,' he says.

Cameron gives him a smile and a thumbs up. 'Better than none.' She lets him go and turns to punch in a code on the elevator keypad. After a brief pause, the elevator starts to descend. After all the evasion he's put up with from Nate, seeing her punch in that code like she's been here forever makes his hackles rise.

'They give you a key to the front door, too?'

Cameron has the good grace to look uncomfortable. 'Not exactly,' she says. 'I got some help with the elevators.'

'Wait, there's people on our side in here?'

'Not really,' Cameron says. 'She's a fan.'

'Well, whatever you got, I hope it's enough to get us past these guards,' Ray says. 'Your brother said light security, not three-man roving teams with automatic weapons and flashbangs.'

Cameron doesn't look at him. 'I hope so, too.'

Chapter 29

Cameron is wary of Ray on the way down to the basement. It's not the gun he's holding. It's the way he's watching her. Like a lion tamer edging round the bars of a cage, trying to get to the door. She can feel his suspicion like a wall between them. When she first saw his face pop up on the laptop, she had wanted to hug him. The urge to do it had withered the moment she punched that code in and saw his expression shift. He thinks that she's betraying him, that he's being toyed with. She knows that feeling all too well: to come so far, only to find the person you were looking for is long gone.

Ray looks away. 'So I guess your brother fucked us both over.'

The relief feels like a wave cresting. 'Yeah. When did he find you?'

'He pulled me from the car wreck,' Ray says. 'After you were gone.'

'I thought they killed you.' Cameron doesn't apologize. She hadn't expected to live, either, once that fight was done.

Ray swallows, his throat working as though he's choking down the worst-tasting mouthful of his life. 'I saw you fall,' he says. 'I was certain . . . I knew for sure you were dead. I knew it. And then your brother told me that you were alive, and that he had a way to reach you . . .'

'It smelled like bullshit.'

He nods. 'Reeked of it. But I had to come. I saw you fall.' He doesn't need to say what that looked like. Cameron can see it in his face. 'I thought maybe if I found you . . .' He trails off, embarrassed.

Coming in after her was the wrong call. He knows it, probably suspected it from the get-go, but he'd still gone ahead and made it. That was worth a lot to Cameron. 'Thank you, Ray. It's good to see a friend again.'

Ray holds his hands out as though trying to grab hold of something, trying to find its shape. The truth, perhaps. Or, from his perspective, a betrayal. 'You know, I thought when I found you – if I found you, you'd be . . .'

'Starved? Tortured?'

'In a body cast, at least.' Ray gestures towards her. 'You look like you've stepped off the cover of a workout plan for people who hate carbs.'

'They didn't torture me,' Cameron says. It feels like she's pulling the words up out of a well, they take such a long time coming. 'They . . . put a chip in my arm. Told me they wanted me to find Nate for them.'

The elevator arriving is a relief, the jolt of tension in the cable offsetting the silence that follows. As the doors slide open, Ray unbuttons one shirt cuff and pulls up his sleeve. High on his arm, running from the elbow up along his bicep, is a burn pattern that looks like someone once pressed a red-hot circuit board to his arm. The shape of it, the thin spiral of an aerial running down towards a thicker central core, looks familiar to Cameron's eye.

'You had a chip in you?'

'A tracer,' Ray says. 'They scammed me into it through my medical insurance. Didn't know about it until your brother told me. Probably how they tracked us.' He doesn't apologize, either. They're beyond that now. 'But I burned it out. We can burn it out of you, too.'

The scarring is an electrical burn. Nate must have hooked him up to a defibrillator or something and burned the tracer out of him. At the very worst, he's lost a little sensation in his hand, maybe even some fine motor control. A small price to pay for freedom. Cameron suspects that in her case it's impossible. Even if they could find enough power to burn all the chips they've implanted, she has pins and screws embedded in the bones the entire length of her bad arm. Put enough current through it and she might lose the whole limb.

'I don't think that will work for me,' she says. She starts out of the lift and into the corridor beyond. Down in the lowest basement level, the neutral lighting and blank walls have given way to painted mesh and open pipework. There's no aircon down here, and there are patches of damp where water has pooled on the bare cement. 'What's your plan to get out of here?'

Ray starts. 'Oh,' he says, patting at his pockets as though searching for his keys. Whatever he's looking for, he finds it in his left pants pocket. 'Here.' He offers her a lump of plastic and metal, something that was once part of a thermos flask lid. In the center of it, there's a tiny memory card. She knows immediately it must be the one from her phone. The last time

Cameron saw her phone, she was throwing it at Ray's head in the hope that he would be able to do something with it. She is shaking as she takes it out and holds it carefully between forefinger and thumb, wary of breaking it with the pressure of her grip. 'It's not information. It's a—'

'A virus,' Cameron says. 'Military-grade software designed to target Carrington's server. They keep it offline, disconnected from the Internet. That's why Nate set me up in the first place. He wanted Carrington to find it on me.'

'Nate came up with a plan,' Ray says. 'Something about a diversion to keep security occupied, and that he would pick us up as soon as we cleared the building.'

'Motherfucker!' Cameron almost throws the memory card, but instead turns and kicks out at the wall, her heel catching a section of pipework hard enough that the welded joint holding it in place breaks and the whole thing springs loose from its bindings with a squeal of metal on metal.

Ray is looking at the pipe with a look of horror. 'What the hell, Cameron?'

She can't think of anything she can say that will put him at ease. All she has is the truth. 'My brother betrayed me,' she says. 'He betrayed us.'

That seems to bring him back to himself. 'Yeah. I can believe that,' he says. 'Your brother was very keen to keep me in the dark about who he's working for and why he needs you. The only thing I learned for certain is that you are really, really important to him.'

Cameron nods slowly, taking that in. He'd crashed the car to please Carrington, and now he was playing games to please someone else. *Why are you dragging me into this, Nate?* Had he always just hated her, or something? She tries to speak, but her throat feels suddenly tight and she has to cough to find her voice. 'When he realized I'd left it with you,' she says. 'He didn't plan to send you as a back-up. This isn't a rescue. He's thrown you to the lions, too.'

'Wolves.'

Cameron comes to a dead stop. 'You want me to kick you again, Ray?'

'No, ma'am.'

'He wanted this virus planted,' Cameron says. 'And that's all. You and I were never meant to walk out of here.'

She starts walking again. After ten more paces, Ray plucks up the courage to speak. 'Where are we going?'

'Regrouping,' Cameron says. 'There should be a place for us . . .' She turns a corner and sees a shabby-looking door in one wall breaking the flow of pipework. 'Right there.'

'What is it?' Ray follows her towards the door. 'Looks like storage space.'

'Kind of.' Cameron tries the door. It's locked, but it also trembles in its frame when she rattles the handle. Deep in the heart of their own building, why pay money for a secure door? 'Back it up a sec.' She lifts her right foot and kicks the door once, smartly, just below the handle. Something metal pings off into the room and the door pops open.

Inside, the room is bigger than Cameron expected. The majority of the wall space is taken up by tall panels filled with lights and gauges, and most important of all: switches. All of the building's systems are computer controlled, but Cameron knows what people are like. You go into any office, big or small, and even if they're rocking the most cutting-edge accounting and cost efficiency software, they'll still have a folder full of receipts tucked at the back of a cupboard just in case the auditor comes knocking. You don't pull all the switches out of your walls just because you can turn the lights on from your phone.

There's a table to one side, and when Cameron puts her laptop down it raises enough dust to make Ray start coughing. 'You think this counts as archeology?' he asks, slapping himself on the chest to clear it.

'Close enough.' Cameron finds the power for the building's elevators and turns them all to off, flicking the switches up as she counts them off in her head. The last is marked *EXECUTIVE SUITE*, and she leaves that one alone.

'So what's your plan for getting us out of here?'

'Try to shut the building down,' she says. 'Lights, elevators, computers, everything. Once I get rid of all that, they'll be as blind as we are.'

'So we'll all be fumbling in the dark.'

'Country of the blind,' Cameron says. 'It's not a great plan, but it'll buy us some time.' She stands back from the board and folds her arms. 'What do you think, Ray? Turn them all off, or hit the master switch?'

Ray doesn't get a chance to answer. There's a burst of radio static from the corridor, and Cameron feels her blood freeze.

'Fuck,' Ray says, looking towards the door. He's holding his gun in both hands now, ready to bring it up into line. 'You think they know we're here?'

Cameron thinks of the chip in her arm. 'Yeah. Wherever I go, they'll know.'

Ray nods once, a crisp, nervous motion. 'Okay,' he says. 'Okay. So we have a three-man team coming, yeah?'

'Most likely.'

Ray nods at the panel. 'So we pull out a few pipes, fill this place with steam, kill the lights. Make a fight of it. We can still get out of here.'

It feels tough to swallow, to find her voice. 'There's something else, Ray.'

'What?'

'They put another implant in me. A modified pacemaker. They can give me a shock with it. I brought us down here to get as much cement between me and a kill signal as I could.'

'A shock. Like a smack on the wrist?'

'A bad one,' Cameron says. 'You'd have to wheel me out of here on a gurney.'

Ray's face falls, all of the fight dropping right out of him. 'Shit,' he says. Out in the corridor, there's a faint ringing sound as something metal is kicked aside, clattering along the floor ahead of the security team that has come down several flights of stairs to reach them. They're out of options, and out of time.

The memory card in Cameron's pocket feels like a lead weight. Her fingers have already found it, got hold of it before she could even think that far ahead.

'Hey, Perada,' she says, and the sound of his last name brings his head up like he's coming to attention. Cameron holds up the card to show him. 'We're not beat yet.'

Chapter 30

Cameron heads out of the control room with Ray in her wake. She isn't sure where they're going, but away from a dead end feels like the right call to make. She needs to find somewhere with a lot of cover to hide behind. She just has to hope that Nate's virus can infect the system before they get close enough to activate the implant and drop her.

The air cools perceptibly, and Cameron notices the density of pipes and vents increasing towards their destination. It puts her in mind of every spaceship she's seen in movies or on TV. Nothing is hidden: every pipe and lever, every button and switch is immediate and accessible.

There's a plastic-sheet curtain across a doorway up ahead, thick opaque strips glowing nebulous from the harsh lighting beyond it. Cameron pushes through, and shudders as the temperature beyond drops so much it's like walking into a wall. Her breath plumes in the air in front of her as she surveys the emptiness beyond.

No cover. The room is circular, about forty paces across, the floor tilted on a few degrees of slope so that anything spilled runs down into the drain in the center. It is almost completely empty, save for a tall metal tank marked *DANGER: CRYOGENIC FLUID*. It's mounted on four metal legs that lift it up past waist height and give access to the five connecting heads that are fused into its base.

Cameron looks at the tank, turns and looks back at the plastic sheet doorway they've come through, trying to judge the angles between them. 'Ray,' she says.

'You got a plan?'

'You won't like it.'

'Didn't get where I am today by following plans I liked the sound of.'

She waves her hand towards the far wall. 'See if you can find any hose or connectors for this tank. Failing that, something big and heavy.'

'Got you,' Ray says. 'What are you going to do?'

Cameron holds up the memory card. 'I'm gonna give Nate his wish.'

'Is that wise?'

She shrugs. 'Didn't get where I am today by—'

'Yeah, yeah,' Ray waves it away as he heads off across the room.

Cameron opens up her laptop and breathes a sigh of relief to see that it's still connected to the network. She doesn't have access to the cameras, the signal is so weak, but it's unlikely to matter. Whatever Nate's backers have cooked up is probably sophisticated enough to make use of any signal it can get. She comes close to putting the memory card in, and pauses.

For a brief, beautiful moment, Cameron imagines a different world, one where she cracks the memory card in two and goes to work for Miller and his friends. With Carrington's tracking system and their manpower at her back, hunting down Nate would be simple. And as a special thank-you for all that he has done for her, she would get to pull his spinal cord out through his asshole.

And everyone else would lose. Carrington would develop their surveillance net until it covered the state, the country, the world; and Miller would have it all at his fingertips. He'd have Cameron and whoever else they could recruit acting as enforcers, assassins. The corporate will made manifest. Manipulation, intimidation, and fear would be their choice of tools, and they would circle the world with a constant, controlling gaze. A hostile takeover, except Carrington wouldn't be gaining control of another company. They'd be in a position to run the country.

She puts the memory card into the laptop, and it immediately goes to work. The screen stutters, static flickering across it, and Cameron can almost feel the suite of intrusion tools unfold and launch themselves at Carrington's network, slamming into the system's internal security like a stag locking horns at the rut, pressing to seek out the vulnerabilities that will give it a route inside.

The lights overhead flicker, and Cameron's laptop screen goes dark. She can still hear it working, but as far as she is concerned it's a dead weight. She closes it and runs over to the wall, putting it up out of the way, as high as she can reach.

'Did it work?' Ray asks.

She lifts her left arm and presses gently at the lump under the skin on her side, down near the floating ribs, as though she could somehow tell by touching it that the implant has been disabled. 'I guess we'll find out. Did you find any hose?'

She turns to find Ray holding the biggest wrench she's ever seen.

'Couldn't see any,' he says. 'I got this, though.'

Cameron takes the wrench, and hefts it two-handed. It's even heavier than she thought. 'That'll do nicely.'

'What now?'

'We need this,' Cameron points at the liquid nitrogen tank, 'pointing there.' She pivots, pointing past Ray's shoulder to the door they came through. He frowns and looks at the base of the tank.

'I don't see any wheels on that thing.'

'No,' Cameron says. 'I'm going to have to push it over.'

'You mean we,' Ray says. 'There's no way you can—'

'I need you to buy us some time,' Cameron says. 'If they've lost their tracking signal, they'll be in a hurry. I need them to not be in a hurry.'

Ray shakes his head. 'This isn't going to work.'

'Ray, even if they can't zap me, there are still three of them. There's no cover here. Please.'

'Look,' Ray says, 'I'll go take a look. Maybe if this virus has worked, they'll be pulling back.' He goes out through the plastic curtain and then with a whoop of surprise comes barreling back through. There's a shouted command – stop, halt, freeze, a monosyllabic bark that could be any or all three at the same time – and the report of a gunshot. Ray pulls the pistol he is armed with and points it out through the plastic curtain to fire blind along the corridor towards wherever the challenge came from. It might have bought them a minute, maybe a little less.

Cameron puts the wrench down and stands very, very still,

reaching down inside herself to try and find a spot of absolute calm, a point she can use to focus. She's never trained for this. Never prepared. Her recovery has been limited to the weights they brought her, and a handful of physiotherapy exercises. She's never been tested like this, not even in the ring, and has never felt less ready for it.

From somewhere above, the dull crump of an explosion interrupts her train of thought. The concussion reverberates down through the building, and makes concrete dust fall in a fine shower from the ceiling.

Cameron realizes that the virus has found its way in, and has shut down the building's security systems. Every lock opened, every door breached, no automatic defenses. Perfect conditions for an assault team to carry out an insertion and take everything that isn't nailed down. With the computer system compromised, whatever arm of the military Nate works for will be facing only the lightest resistance. It's just a matter of time before they get their hands on the server, and on Miller.

She takes a deep breath and sizes up the tank again. *You can do this*, she thinks. Up on those stilts, the tank has to be top-heavy. They don't look like they were built to handle anything but weight coming straight down on them, either. All she needs to do is get high enough, and push. Cameron can feel the scar running down her arm like it's dragging at her every second she waits, sapping her strength.

She takes a run up, past the tank and up the wall, one high step and a jump up and round, turning back the way she came, arms reaching up to catch the top edge of the tank. She catches a bolt with her left hand, her right not so lucky but still holding on to the metal collar as the rest of her body touches the metal side of the tank. Even insulated, the tank is very cold to the touch, and Cameron can feels the cold burning from her forearms all the way down to her thighs.

Cameron hears a pistol shot, Ray trading her a bullet for a few more seconds, and she kicks off the tank with one foot, reaching for the wall behind her. Her heel finds it with a jolt, striking against steel with a deep ringing sound, and she turns, putting her back to the tank and her feet flat against the wall, sitting on nothing. Her knees have a ninety-degree bend in them, and she bears down into the brace, feeling the tension build in her thigh muscles.

She takes a final glance back to check she's got the angle right, but can't see anything past the bulk of the tank. Even if she is in the wrong place, there's no time to do anything about it. *Here goes nothing*. She rolls her shoulders once, feels her shoulder blades grind against the cold metal of the tank. She puts her chin down and pushes as hard as she can.

Cameron pushes so hard it's beyond any feeling she has ever experienced. No leg press, no deadlift, no workout has ever been this hard on her. Her jaw is clenched so tight, it feels as though her back teeth are going to force themselves up into her skull. The tendons in her neck are painfully tight, as though they are about to pull free of her collarbone. Her back pops with the strain, an uncomfortable shift of vertebrae as they realign themselves and settle against the unnaturally flat surface of the tank. Her ankles feel as though they're being ground to a paste, and her thigh muscles, for all the work she ever put into them, shiver with the effort of trying to push the tank over.

You can do this. She says it even though she knows she can't, that all that weight is just too much for her to move. *If you don't, Nate wins.* Cameron roars with the effort and leans into the push again, driving deep into it.

There is a crack, a thunderous release of energy, and Cameron half suspects that it is the sound of her thigh muscles tearing, the fibers detaching themselves to roll up the length of her upper leg like a roller blind snapping open. Instead, the legs on the far side of the tank have popped their welds, and the whole thing starts to shift. Cameron scrambles for purchase as her feet come away from the wall, but there is none and she puts her palms flat on the side of the tank and pushes off in the hope she'll fall clear.

Timber.

Chapter 31

The tank lands with a deep, concussive ringing sound that fills the room and kills all other noise. Cameron can feel it shudder through her even as she lands hard, trying to roll through it like she's just walked into the worst throw in history. The skin on her back feels like it's on fire, and her legs are shaking with every step, but she makes it to the wrench before Ray can get over to her.

'You okay?' He yells it, and yet to Cameron it sounds like he's shouting through an inch of bulletproof glass. She nods, not because it's true but because it gets him off her case, and drags the wrench back to the fallen liquid nitrogen tank. The angle it's landed at isn't perfect, but it's good enough: the row of valves are pointing roughly towards the plastic hanging over the door, and there's going to be a lot of spray when Cameron pops it. She puts the head of the wrench just behind where the valve is attached, a seam of gold against silver.

'Ray!' He's standing in the line of fire, holding his pistol like he's been trained to: barrel down, finger off the trigger. There's a team coming down the corridor and they're not shy about dropping automatic fire, and yet here he is trying not to escalate the situation by keeping his weapon down. Trapped, surrounded, about to get shot full of holes: his first instinct is hope. Cameron loves him for it. If she had any doubts about him before, she's got none now. 'Get out of the fucking way!'

Cameron visualizes the breach team setting up outside, the whisper of cloth on cloth as they communicate through gestures, getting ready to move in. She gets up on the balls of her feet, bounces some life back into her legs. She's going to have to be quick once this valve breaks. *If it breaks at all.*

A noise cuts through the buzz of the tank falling, something sharp and metallic, like a metal clip snapping shut. They're readying a grenade. A flashbang, like the team upstairs used on Ray. They're working off the same playbook, their tactics a to-do list that they tick off one by one. Cameron counts in her head, just like he will be doing.

Three. She looks down at the valve and tries to picture the pressure it must be under. *Hit it right, it'll break.*

Two. She takes a step back, clearing her swing as she lifts the wrench up over her head and brings it down two-handed, an executioner's axe aimed not at the neck it's going to cut through, but the block on the other side.

One. The valve cracks clean across the seam, and as Cameron turns to run it explodes with a sound like a cannon firing. A wall of cold washes up from the breach, the water in the air hissing as it turns to mist. Spray from the tank catches Cameron's left arm and leg as she sprints for the back of the room, the fluid sticking her clothes to her like water, burning so cold that she stumbles and screams, pulling at her sweatpants in a panic as it bites into her skin.

Ray grabs her, grunts as he half-carries, half-drags her and

Cameron wants to kill him because it's still burning her and she needs to get free of the clothing. It's only after he puts her down that she realizes the floor is awash with liquid nitrogen, and he had saved her from being covered in it. He's pulled her all the way back into one of the access corridors: a draft of warm air from the freight elevator is holding back the cold, the mist it makes as it hits the cold air a curtain that shifts like liquid. She tries to stop herself from screaming, the burning already beginning to fade, and realizes that she isn't screaming at all. The sound is coming from someone else.

It takes a minute for the mist to clear enough that Cameron feels safe walking into it. The screaming dies away long before she takes her first, hesitant step back into the room, and she and Ray make their way across the cambered floor in silence. The air is freezing cold – breathing it is an effort – and although the floor is dry again, the drain in the center of the floor has given way, collapsing under its own weight, and a white cloud of water vapor is pouring out of it, filling the room past knee height and slowing their steps. The plastic sheet curtain is almost entirely gone, frozen solid and shattered by the force of the blast hitting it, and only shards of it remain hanging in the frame. The walls have survived undamaged save for a grey-white discoloration where the liquid nitrogen caught them directly. Cameron doesn't touch it as she passes, but suspects the concrete would crumble beneath her fingertips.

Out in the corridor, there is carnage. Two of the three men are down: one is curled tight against the wall in a fetal ball, clutching his right arm and keening in pain. The other is flat on his back, with the third man trying to perform chest compressions on him. Cameron can see that it's a lost cause.

Most of the dead man's face and neck are gone, and his chest has collapsed inward on one side. He must have stuck half his upper body round the door frame to get a good swing on the flashbang, and caught the liquid nitrogen full-on.

Cameron reaches out to put a hand on the man's shoulder, and stops when she sees that he still has his gun slung across his chest. 'Ray?'

Ray nods as he passes her, lifting his gun a fraction higher as he comes, not quite pointing at the last man standing but close enough that he can beat any attempt at a draw. He cocks the gun, the sharp, distinct click enough to gain the man's full attention. He sits straight up off the last compression and doesn't move.

'Hands,' Ray says, no room for argument in the way he says it. The man complies immediately, arms coming up on each side, palms forward, fingers spread. 'Cameron, take his gun and sidearm. The same for the others.'

Cameron does as Ray asks, unclipping the guns from where they hang across each man's chest, the pistols from their hip holsters. The guns from the dead man have got an odd look to them, like they've been splattered with whitewash, and she doesn't trust either of them not to fall apart or misfire. She slides them back into the room, where they vanish into the fog.

While she does it, Ray talks the uninjured man through removing his tactical vest and having his wrists cuffed. Cameron keeps an eye on them, but realizes there'll be no trouble. All he can do is stare at the fallen point man, the ruin that the liquid nitrogen has made of him. Cameron doesn't share the same urge. She's trying not to look at the dead body, trying not to close the circle of cause and effect that started with her swinging a wrench at a valve and ended with a man being killed in the worst way she can think of. Ice crunches underfoot, and when she looks the sole of her shoe is red and pink. They're walking around in what once was his face.

'Oh fuck me,' Cameron says. 'Fuck this bullshit.'

'Cameron,' Ray says, a warning in his voice.

It's too late. Her reaction sets the other guy off. He struggles against his cuffs, tries to get to his feet. 'Fuck you! You killed him.' He looks from Ray to Cameron, his face wild with fear and hatred. 'He had a family. A family.'

Cameron can't find words, can't find the strength to reply. It's Ray that answers.

'Hey! We all got family.' He nods his head towards the guns that Cameron has taken. 'You sure as shit weren't thinking about what my mom would say when you were putting rounds past my ear.' He steps closer, his voice falling. 'You knew the risks when you took the job. You knew the risks coming down here.'

He shakes his head, not looking at Ray. 'I never—'

Ray doesn't give him the space. 'Hey.' He pushes out, bumps the other man's chest, makes him look up. 'Someone told you this would be easy? This would be a walk in the park? They lied to you.' He points at the corpse. 'Did he call the shots?'

The man sniffs, red-eyed, and nods.

'Yeah,' Ray says. 'He walked his team blind into an ambush. You heard the fucking tank go over, right?'

'We heard it.'

'You know what it was?'

'No, sir.'

'Then you should've backed off.' Ray shakes his head. 'You made the wrong call. Get your man on his feet, and get the fuck out of here.'

Cameron watches as the man scrambles to comply, waiting for Ray to chew her out, too. When he does turn, his face is drawn, ashen, like he hasn't slept in a week. All of the cold, parade-ground fury has drained out of him, and she realizes it wasn't for the other man's benefit that he turned it on. He did it because it put him in control, and that control was what kept him from falling apart. He looks down at the dead man, shakes his head. 'This isn't your fault, Cameron.'

Cameron tries to take that in, but can't. All she can hear is her own heartbeat, heavy in her chest, the sound climbing up through her neck and into her head until it is roaring, smothering every other sensation. The point man is dead, and she killed him. It is her fault, no matter what Ray says. She let Nate get into her head. She never once stopped to think that he was playing her. Had always been playing her.

'FUCK!' Cameron's yell is like an explosion. She turns on the ball of her foot and slams both fists into the wall behind her. She doesn't notice the damage, doesn't care what it does to her hands. She staggers back until she hits the opposite wall, bouncing off the pipework, a ragged edge catching one of the cold burns and sending a deep spike of pain through her. As suddenly as it came, all of the rage just drains out of her, like a valve has opened somewhere and it all floods out, leaving her completely empty. 'Look what you've done to me.' She knows that Nate can't hear her. That even if he could, he wouldn't listen. That is the worst of it. He never cared at all.

'Cam.' Ray isn't holding his gun anymore. He's there at her elbow, not touching her at all but *there*, warm and human and alive. He speaks with a calm, steady voice, not talking her down but talking *to* her. 'You can't blame yourself for this,' he says. 'He made a choice. Just like the guy in the garage did.'

'I didn't have to kill him, Ray. It's not the same.'

Ray looks as though he's about to disagree, then thinks better of it. Cameron wonders how many cops he's talked to after a bust went wrong and someone died. She wonders who talked to him, the first time. 'Maybe,' he says. 'And I ain't gonna lie to you. You won't ever stop thinking that.'

Cameron looks down at the dead point man. She can't imagine what it would have been like for him. *Was it over in an instant? Or did he have to stare up at the ceiling as his body fell apart?* Something shifts inside of her at the sight of the corpse, at the realization that whatever happened, there's no one left in there to think about it. She clenches both hands into fists, tight enough that it feels as though they'll start bleeding.

'We're getting out of this,' she says. 'We're getting out of this and I am going to find my brother. And when I find him, I'm going to kick his ass clean off the planet.'

Chapter 32

Ray goes through the pile of gear he stripped from the men seeing what he can find, what he thinks he will need. All three of them were carrying way too much for the job they'd been given, and even once the stuff that's been damaged by the liquid nitrogen has been put aside, it still looks like he's been handed the keys to an armory.

He feels oddly conspicuous shouldering his way into a bulletproof vest in his shirt and suit pants. There's a ritual to gearing up. The all-black outfit, the heavy boots and the helmet are part of it. The rest is that the whole team changes together, the conversation giving way to operational silence. It's how you put your conscience to one side and become part of the thin blue line. Without it, Ray feels exposed, unready; the bulletproof vest sits loose on his chest and no amount of fiddling with the straps is going to fix it.

They have automatic weapons but Ray sticks with his pistol. He's got more than enough ammunition for it and he's not planning on ventilating anyone as a first choice. He takes their flashbangs, though. Every. Single. One. The radios are silent: he's guessing the panic has caused security to switch channels at some point, and not even Cameron's knowledge of the facility can come up with the code to find it.

A pull at his side makes Ray look up to find Cameron taking the stack of cable ties off of him and clipping them to a loop of cord she's using as a makeshift bandolier. She's holding an extendable baton in her other hand, a collapsible steel tube with lead shot weighting the tip. She swings it experimentally, flicking the tube open and holding it vertical to let it fall shut, and Ray knows from experience what she's finding out from doing it – the lead shot puts the balance point further up the baton's length than you'd think. It's not the sort of thing you twirl around and look fancy doing it: it's built for short, brutal arcs, each one capable of breaking a bone.

Cameron throws it upwards, giving it a flick so it tumbles in the air, and catches it without looking.

'Is that all you're taking with you?' Ray asks.

'I've had enough of guns,' Cameron says.

'Easy to say,' Ray says, 'but they might not be done with you.'

Cameron nods. 'I'm not running into the crossfire,' she says. 'There's only one fight I'm looking for.'

Ray doesn't doubt it. He saw the way she climbed that tank, put everything she had into a plan that he wouldn't have thought possible. She put it over like she was knocking a glass of milk off the table, and walked off a handful of burns like they were nothing. If anything, he's not convinced she even needs the baton. Part of him doesn't want to know what she's going to do, but he still has to ask. Even without his badge, he still has a duty.

'What are we going to do, Cameron?'

She looks up at the ceiling. Through the ceiling. 'You heard that explosion, right?'

'Yeah.' Ray remembers the tremor, a God-hand punch to one side of the building. 'A big-ass breaching charge, or something like it.'

'The virus my brother gave us shut down the security system. I think they coordinated a physical attack with you coming in here.'

'So we've got a bunch of CIA dudes running around upstairs?'

'I thought military. Special Forces, maybe.'

'They're here to pull out everything Nate couldn't give them himself,' Ray says, and Cameron nods.

'High-value targets,' she says. 'They want physical access to the server and the staff. Team leaders, researchers, anyone with expertise that can help them replicate Carrington's work.'

'They've got some balls coming to grab them here,' Ray says. 'US citizens, US soil? That's free tickets to life in prison for everyone if word gets out.'

'To them, it's worth the risk.' Cameron flicks the baton open with a snap. 'If they get their hands on this tracking system that Carrington have built, they'll be able to roll it out nationwide. Call it an immunization drive, make up a scare that means everybody gets a chip. Total surveillance. Total control. We have to stop them.'

Ray feels like spitting. His arm feels hot with the memory of what was burned out of him. He knows Cameron has more than one in her, chips bound to the pins running all the way down her scarred arm. They've buried it in her bones, and that means she likely won't ever be rid of it. It's in so deep no amount of burning or cutting will be able to dig it out. Somehow, she's dealing with it better than he did with his. 'Your brother put all this together, yeah?'

She nods. 'Yeah, he did.'

'That is some fucked-up kind of family you have.'

'Tell me about it.'

Ray looks down at the gun he's holding, the vest hanging awkwardly off of him. He looks back up at Cameron. He knows why she has to do this. If she doesn't, the chip in her arm is a leash that will follow her the rest of her life. Destroying the thing that can access it is the only way she can be free. But her baton and his pistol aren't enough to take down Carrington, let alone Carrington and a government assault team. 'How are we gonna do this? You think I'm going to arrest them all?'

Cameron shrugs. 'You're a cop,' she says. 'Call nine-one-one, get some back-up.'

Ray shakes his head. 'Cops are on board,' he says. 'Carrington bought a lot of loyalty, and they'll sure as shit cave if any of the agencies lean on them.' He laughs at how stupid it is. 'I couldn't even get a squad car out to help your friends.'

'Shit.' She paces back and forth across the corridor in front of Ray, tapping her leg with the baton. 'We're gonna have to try and stop them ourselves.'

'I was just thinking that,' Ray says. 'I mean, we're stuck in the basement, I've got a pistol, you've got a stick, and there's a good chance one or both of us is going to get shot. Not getting the fuck out of here is the obvious choice.'

She ignores the sarcasm. 'The server room is on the ground floor. We need to destroy it, or any part of it they try to take out of the building.'

'Or get shot,' Ray says, in spite of himself. 'Anything else on that list?'

'Head of the snake,' she says. 'Top floor, executive suite. They want Miller.' Ray sees something shift in Cameron's expression, like for a moment the mask of calm has fallen away and he can see how much cold rage is driving her.

Miller. *Silicon Valley*. Ray wants to ask how she plans on keeping Miller out of their hands, but doesn't want to hear the answer. Instead, he steps carefully round it. 'How are we going to get up there?'

'There's an executive lift.' Cameron worries at her lip. 'The keycode I have might not work for it.'

'Are there stairs?'

She thinks about that for a second. 'That's like ten flights, Ray.'

'We're both gonna catch a bullet, you're worried about some cardio?'

'Worried I'll be too busy puking my guts up.'

'Doubling over makes you a smaller target.' Ray grins at her. 'See? I'm helping you out.'

Cameron doesn't look encouraged. 'We'll hit the server room, see where that gets us.' Ray takes a breath and she keeps talking. 'Aside from a trip out of here on a gurney.'

'Now you're talking,' Ray says. 'We can take the elevator up to the server, though, right?'

'Might not be the best idea to go up that way.' Cameron points in the opposite direction to the way they came.

'Maintenance stairwell. It runs up one corner of the building. Right to the roof.'

Ray gestures towards the pile of gear they'll be leaving behind. 'You sure you don't want a gun?'

Cameron crouches by the pile, and for a moment Ray thinks she's going to take one. Instead, she picks up two of the radios. 'I'll try and find an emergency band,' she says. 'If there's a news channel eavesdropping, it might force the cops to show their face.' She holds out one of the radios to him. 'If we get split up, I'm on channel two.'

Ray takes the radio. 'If this goes south on us . . .'

'Then we get the fuck out of here.' Cameron looks straight at him, and he knows she doesn't mean it. She's not leaving until this is done. Even trying to joke about it, Ray can feel the cold forming in the pit of his stomach. *You could die here, and no one would ever know the truth of it.* He swallows that thought down and buries it deep. That's the job. You wear a shield, you make the choice to accept the risks it brings with it. You could get shot by a perp on your first shift. *Hell, you could get hit by a fucking bus directing traffic.* Ray had always known it was part of the job, what you accepted if you wanted to make the world a better place.

He offers Cameron his hand. 'I'd say good luck, but . . .'

'Break a leg?' she offers, taking his hand.

Ray smiles at that. 'We're gonna break all their fucking legs.'

Chapter 33

Cameron takes the stairs two at a time, her steps as light as she can make them. Ray falls behind on the first flight, weighed down by the vest, and it is a relief to leave him behind. The look on his face after she broke the tank was something like awe, as though he couldn't believe she was still standing.

Cameron can barely believe it herself. The burn from the liquid nitrogen on her back is wet, like a scald, and she can feel the vest she is wearing sticking to it, the rest moving freely about that fixed point. The one on her leg is throbbing with every step, and she suspects that it's the tight fit of her sweatpants that is keeping her thigh in one piece. The effort of springing up the stairs is painful: she can feel it spiking in her calves, the hammer-blow beat of her heart, but there's no way left but forward. She's been forced right into a corner and all she can do is put her head down and charge, hope there's a way out on the far side of it.

The ascent is terrifying. There's no real telling what she'll find on each landing before she hits the turn. Looking up the height of the railings might let her spot someone looking down, but that would let them see her too. Setting up an ambush would be as simple as aiming down the stairs. She's light on her feet, but nobody alive is light enough to dodge a bullet.

The first person she sees is up on the ground floor. He's not dressed for an assault; he's dressed for bomb disposal. Full body armor with an armor-plated apron that hangs down to his knees, a high-angled neck cuff that obscures half his face, and enough helmet that she can barely see the man inside the suit; he's on his way out to the stairwell through an access door from the main corridor. Incongruous against the suit, he has a submachine gun slung across his chest, and as his head comes round Cameron grits her teeth and accelerates, flinging herself up the last few steps with a grunt before he can get his hands to it.

When he sees her he realizes she's too close, and tries to backpedal the way he came. Cameron flings her hand out and gets a grip on his right arm, the padding soft under her fingers, and yanks him forward into the stairwell. The door swings shut with a bang as he staggers, taking two long steps to recover, pulling his arm from her grip and fumbling for the sidearm at his hip. Cameron is already there, though, stepping in close to keep him from turning the barrel on her, flicking the baton open in her left hand. As he twists round, she takes his gun arm by the wrist, jerks it straight, and swings the baton as hard as she can into the gap in his armor over his elbow. With the leverage on his wrist and the swing combined, there's enough force in the blow that something snaps in his forearm. He makes a noise like he's just burned his hand, drawing in a huge, shocked gasp of air, and as he does Cameron throws him, the body armor just giving him more momentum as he goes over her hip, the impact with the ground knocking all that air back out of him before he can cry out for help.

He's not Carrington. Cameron takes the gun and does a quick check for identification. No rank, no numbers, no insignia. Through the visor, she can make out the expression on his face as he looks at her. Recognition. *He knows who I am*.

'Who are you?' she asks. He doesn't answer. Instead, he makes a move with his good hand for the push-button mic clipped to his chest armor. He isn't fast, not with the pain of a broken arm to deal with, and Cameron gets there first, pulling it free and tossing it down the stairwell. 'Special forces? CIA?' It gets no reaction.

She searches him as best she can for weapons and finds nothing more than the submachine gun and the pistol. Once they are safely away she hustles him to his feet and forces him to the railing by the scruff of his neck. He bangs his broken arm on the way, making a noise that lands halfway between a groan and a whine, and Cameron sees his eyes go wild with panic. 'You've got to give me something,' she says. 'Seeing as there's not a lot of space between the railings.' She leans him forward, making him look. 'Three flights, give or take. If I was to push you over, I reckon you'd hit every single one of them on the way down.' She makes a show of looking herself, clicks her teeth. 'All that body armor, a few bounces to slow you down? You'll survive. Won't be worse than, say, a car crash. Took me two years to get full use of my arm again.'

'Homeland.' It comes out thick, and he swallows hard after saying it.

'You work for Homeland Security?'

'ICE. I'm with the intervention team.'

Cameron frowns. 'Well isn't that something?'

'Cameron?' Ray is at the landing, looking up towards her.

'They're not Army,' Cameron calls down to him. 'They're Homeland Security.'

Ray stomps up the stairs, breathing heavily. He probably picked up the pace when he heard the fight. 'You sound surprised.'

'I thought they were . . . you know.'

'Glorified customs? Border patrol?'

'Something like that.'

'Biggest police force in the country.' Ray looks the man she's holding up and down once, as though to confirm his suspicions. 'No oversight, virtually no jurisdictional limits. Twenty billion dollars in funding.'

Cameron lets out a low whistle. 'Twenty. Billion. Dollars.'

Ray raises an eyebrow. 'To keep us all safe,' he says, sarcasm dripping from every word. 'What's with the bomb squad? There something we need to know?'

Cameron gives the Homeland agent a shake. 'You heard the man.'

'Fuck you.'

'Ah.' Either he's found a fresh stash of balls somewhere inside his armor, or he's worked out that Cameron has no intention of throwing him down the stairwell. She presses the Homeland agent down on to his knees, and pulls a cable tie free from the bundle. 'If you know about me,' she says, 'then you know about my brother. And if you know about my brother, you will know that he is a straight-up son of a bitch.'

He doesn't answer. Cameron sighs and holds the cable tie

up so he can see it. 'We're going to leave you here without your radio. There's no two ways about that part of the deal, but I am going to give you a choice. You can tell us why you're dressed up for Halloween and I put this on your good wrist, or you can keep quiet and discover exactly how painful that broken arm of yours can get.'

There's a mist forming on the inside of the man's visor, sweat and breath trapped inside an outfit that must be sitting north of one hundred and ten degrees inside. He's staring Cameron out, like he's daring her. *Bring it on.*

Ray draws level with Cameron's shoulder and slowly pushes her to the side, out of the Homeland agent's field of view.

'I know what you're thinking,' Ray says. He speaks with a low, even tone. 'You're thinking you'd rather die a hero than live out the rest of your days thinking you sold your buddies out.'

The agent shudders, and Cameron can just make out his face twisting, angry at being confronted. 'You don't know a thing about me.'

'I will always place the mission first.' Ray says it like a mantra. 'I will never accept defeat. I will never quit.'

'Hey,' Cameron says, resisting the urge to elbow him. 'Are you trying to fuck us?'

'I will never leave a fallen comrade.' The agent finishes for him.

'Your mission has changed,' Ray says. 'Is any of this what you signed up for? Taking on American citizens on American soil?'

'My orders—'

'Your orders are bullshit,' Ray says, his voice suddenly full of venom. 'You think this operation is on the books? You think there's going to be a medal and a parade? This whole thing is bullshit, and you and I are buried in it up to our necks.' He plucks the cable tie from Cameron's hand, throws it out into the stairwell. 'What's it going to be, soldier? Do you even remember the oath you swore?'

Cameron watches as the agent straightens, turns to face Ray, and for a moment she thinks he's going to try and rush him. Instead, he sighs, the armor settling awkwardly as he slumps inside of it.

'There's a bomb in the server room,' he says. 'Wired up to all the computers. If we try to take anything out, it'll blow. We've got a team inside trying to disarm it now.'

'And if it goes off?' Ray asks.

The agent swallows. 'The walls are load-bearing. If it goes off, it will level the building.'

'Fuck.'

'What about Miller?' Cameron asks. 'What about the executives?'

It takes a moment for the agent to reply, like he's embarrassed to talk about it. 'We had a team insert from the roof,' he says. 'We . . . lost contact with them shortly after. Orders were to take the server, then after extraction to . . . detonate the bomb remotely.'

Ray snorts, disgusted. 'So much for never leaving a fallen comrade.'

'Sir, I—'

'Don't tell me,' Ray says. 'Your orders.'

'Yes, sir.'

Cameron takes his good hand and binds him by the wrist to the railing with another cable tie. She crouches, gets hold of his opposite ankle and does the same to it. 'Look,' she says. 'Here's the deal. You get out of these as fast as you can, and you get the fuck out of here. Understand?'

'Yes, ma'am.'

Cameron stands. 'Second time I've been called that,' she says. 'Not sure it fits me.' She grabs hold of his neck armor, pulls his visor round to face her. 'You see anyone else on your way, you tell them to get the fuck out, too. If all that's true, I can't promise you this building will stay upright. You get me?'

'Yes, ma'am.'

'Good.' She stands back, and checks that the baton will close. The blow that broke his arm has put a bend in it, but it's slight enough that it still collapses down into the handle.

'You sure that's enough to hold him?' Ray asks.

'I don't want him dead,' Cameron says. 'Speaking of which, we need to move. Come on.'

She's at the door when the agent speaks.

'Wait,' he says. 'There's an eight-man team in there. You can't take them on.'

Cameron doesn't look back at him, feels an old pride burning up inside of her at the challenge. 'You bet your ass I can,' she says.

Chapter 34

Ray follows Cameron's lead through the ground floor of the Carrington building. The lobby could probably win awards for interior design: it's all glass and exposed steel, with a mezzanine deck branching across the space overhead. At least it would have done before the gunfight that destroyed it had taken place. There are at least twenty security personnel laid about the room, and all of them are dead. Ray goes to check one man that might not have lost all the blood in his body; Cameron just shakes her head and moves on. The skin of the guard's neck is cold under Ray's fingers. No pulse.

In spite of the thought that a bomb big enough to take the building out is being messed with, Ray makes the rounds to check as many as he can. All of them are Carrington, from their uniforms and weaponry. It feels odd that they are the only ones that got killed until Ray starts paying attention. There are other blood pools, mostly close to the doors, and long drag marks where bodies have been removed. The Homeland team are making sure that no one is left behind. Surrounded by dead bodies, it feels less like a code of honor and more like a cover-up in progress.

'I thought these guys were private military,' Ray says.

Cameron doesn't look at him. She's bobbing her head left and right, looking straight ahead, like an owl sizing up a distant field mouse. 'They were,' she says, as though answering him is an afterthought.

'Seems a little one-sided for private contractors,' Ray says. Even adding up all the drag marks, he still counts a loss of fewer than ten on the Homeland side. 'They were torn to pieces.'

'Carrington use a lot of surveillance tech,' Cameron says. She climbs past a body to get an angle on a set of double doors ahead and cranes her neck to try and see through the thin windows set high in them. 'I guess they were depending on it.'

Ray doesn't need to guess. He can see it. The Carrington security team, stripped of their eyes and ears when the security system failed, panicked and fell back to what they thought was a defensive position in the heart of the building. With all the locks disabled, the single path to their location had turned into multiple paths, and they found themselves engaged from three different directions, one of them being overhead. The crutch they had been leaning on was kicked out from under them, and they had been annihilated. 'No substitute for real training, I guess,' he says.

Cameron looks at him like he's just grown horns. 'We did this,' she says.

Ray takes a deep breath in and feels the weight of that settling on him. The air is heavy, thick with the smell of blood and spent brass. There's just too much for the air conditioning to clear. He can picture exactly how it went down. They had fought a cursory rearguard down the main corridor, enough to make it feel like they were worth chasing, and set up in a loose arc behind every available inch of cover to focus their fire on that entrance. The Homeland team had worked their way round to the sides, and up to the mezzanine deck. From the pattern of fire on the floor and the broken glass above he can see they had managed to spread out on the mezzanine, looking down on to the waiting Carrington crew. All they would have had to do was call for weapons down, drop a couple of stun grenades. Instead, they had turned the room into a killzone. No mercy, save for the bullet. He blows out a sigh and looks at Cameron. 'We opened the door,' he says, 'but this isn't on us. They could have taken them without casualties.'

'Maybe.' Her answer is a long time coming, and Ray can tell she doesn't believe it. Hell, he barely believes it himself. All those lives ended by a memory card no bigger than a fingernail. The only thing he can take from that is a real need to see the people who did this paying for it. An eight-man team.

Ray's hands are tight on the grip of the pistol, and it's an effort for him to ease them free. 'So these are the people who are bankrolling your brother?'

'Looks like it.' Cameron is looking at the far doors, towards the server. She's keen to move.

'You think he's here?'

She shakes her head. 'He won't be. He wants to be the one pulling the strings, not the one dancing along.'

'Shame.' Ray snorts, trying to clear his head of the smell. 'When we find him, I'll wait until you finish kicking him down a flight of stairs before I arrest him.'

Cameron jerks her chin forward, directing his attention to the doors ahead. 'Don't get ahead of yourself,' she says. 'We have to get through the rest of them first.'

'The server is that way?'

'Yeah,' Cameron says. 'It's that way.'

Ray looks at the double doors. 'We got any room to maneuver?'

'I think so.' Cameron shrugs. 'How would you set them up?'

Ray thinks back to his training, to the tactical exercises they played out at the academy. There's no exact model for it, but he can make a guess. 'If they're defusing a bomb, two of them will be in the room. Point man and someone to assist. The rest will be set up to keep them from being interrupted. Either four close and two roaming the perimeter, or a three-three split.'

Cameron makes a face. 'Let's hope for four and two,' she says.

Ray is surprised. 'You got a plan or something?'

'They know something is happening,' she says. 'But they haven't come looking for their man. We should expect them to be on high alert.'

'You're reaching for that four and two, aren't you?'

'It'd make my life a hell of a lot easier,' she says.

'Make my life easier if you told me what the plan is,' Ray says.

Cameron takes a quick breath, as though she's going to say something and thinks better of it at the last second. 'You'll see,' she says, and ducks to begin searching the first body her hands reach. 'Come on. We need to see if any of the Carrington security have keys or tools.'

Ray sighs and points across the room. 'You want that guy,' he says.

Cameron gives him a look, but goes anyway. She's barely crouched down before she holds up a bundle of keys. 'Bingo. How'd you figure he had them?'

'I'm a cop,' Ray says. 'Better quality uniform, more body armor. He's the leader.'

Cameron looks around, judging the distances. 'He was in the middle of the fight when he died,' she says. 'Would have put the boss in the back.'

'Yeah.' Ray can see the dead man from where he's standing. He was tall and athletic, but by no means a young man. His hair is grey and cropped short. Ex-military, maybe. The sort of guy who takes a security detail because another tour might see his luck run dry. 'My best guess? He did the best he could for his team.'

'Wasn't enough, though.'

'No, it wasn't.' Ray can't stop looking at him. All he can think is that the poor bastard had probably never heard the name Carrington until he saw they were hiring. He just picked the wrong people to sign up with. 'What are you planning, Cameron?'

'Call it restorative justice,' Cameron says. She's going through the keys at speed, looking closely at the bow on each one as she goes. 'Homeland cut the security system, used the building against them.' She peers intently at one of the bunch, holds it up in triumph. 'We're going to give them a taste of their own medicine.'

Chapter 35

Cameron moves as quickly as she can from corridor to corridor, trying to get as much information as she can before making her move. Ray pings her on the radio twice before she is forced to acknowledge that she's already seen everything worth seeing, and the real reason she's still circling the perimeter is that she really, really doesn't want to go any further.

They've done a great job of digging in. With the electronic locks disabled, they have barricaded most of the routes leading to the server room with furniture, enough that anyone clearing it is going to make a hell of a noise in the process. The route that they've left is basically a shooting gallery, a section of lobby with a door at one end and enough distance to cover that even surviving the first three seconds of an engagement would be nigh-on impossible.

They know Cameron is there. She tried to draw them out of cover by kicking a blockade until it drew fire, but couldn't make out if it was two or three men covering the server room. They haven't sent anyone to investigate, and she hopes that's because they don't have a man to spare rather than the fact that they hold the superior position and there's no need for them to give it up.

Eight men, at least three positioned defensively, all of them armed with automatic weapons. She weighs the baton in her hand and wonders if she shouldn't have opted for a gun after all. Leaving them untouched had felt like the right thing to do. She'd left a man dead, killed in the heat of the moment, and she'd promised herself that she'd do everything in her power not to repeat that mistake.

Eight, though, is too many for her to think about holding back over. When you pull a punch, you don't have your mind on the fight: you're thinking about how not to hurt the other person, and that slows you down, leaves you open. It's part of the reason why fixed fights are always so hard to spot: all you have to do is think about losing and it'll happen.

Cameron crouches behind the door, making sure she doesn't touch it. It would be a hell of a shame if one of them fired at a twitch of movement and killed her before she could even get started. She pulls out the baton, eases it out to its full length, then brings out her radio and keys the mic.

'Ray?'

There's a long pause before he replies. With the volume way down, his voice is tiny. 'Here, and ready. You need to let me know when you finish speaking. Over.'

'I'll bear that in mind. Give me a three count, then go for it.' She waits for a second, then remembers. 'Uh, I have finished speaking.'

'Acknowledged,' Ray says. As he speaks Cameron puts the radio on the floor and braces herself, like a runner getting ready to come out of the starting blocks. 'Going in three, two, one . . .'

She doesn't speak for the go signal. Instead she rams the baton through the door handles and puts every ounce of strength she has into bending it. The metal resists for a second, a long strip of pain peeling horizontally across her shoulder blades as she pushes, and with a creak of metal fatigue gives way, the slight bend becoming a tight curve.

Carrington don't have sprinklers anywhere near their server room. Spraying water over their central asset would be as bad as letting it burn. Instead, they use inert gas suppression, a mix of argon, nitrogen, and carbon dioxide that is pumped rapidly into every room to starve the fire of oxygen and heat and leave all of the delicate electrical components untouched. It's expensive and tricky to manage: if the oxygen gets too low, people start to faint; if the carbon dioxide gets too high, the air becomes toxic; if they pump too much gas into the room the barometric pressure can burst everyone's eardrums. When Cameron counted down, Ray was at the control box shorting the fuses on the feedback control for all three gases and before setting the system off. In the server room and the lobby beyond, all eight Homeland agents will have found themselves surrounded by jets of gas so cold that they freeze all the moisture in the air, the vast white plumes dropping from the ceiling like eager hands reaching out to grab them. The overpressure of the gas pumped into the room bangs the doors hard against the baton holding them closed, and Cameron ducks in case the noise is really panic fire chasing her down the corridor. An alarm is blaring, a pair of discordant klaxons so loud the noise is physically uncomfortable. If Cameron could have had Ray cut the lights, she would have, but deaf, half-blind, choking and confused will have to do.

Cameron counts to ten, forcing herself to space each number out. There's a sweet spot in the chaos she's created, a point where their concentration breaks. They'll be expecting an assault: they'll hold fast until the last second, and by the time they realize the air is no good to breathe, they'll panic. She hyperventilates, cycling as much oxygen as she can into her system before she goes in there. They looked for an oxygen mask near the control box, but there was nothing to be found. Whatever she can hold in the tank will have to do. She takes one last gasp, heaving in as much air as her lungs can hold, and starts back down the corridor towards the doors.

Cameron has the baton out from the handles and is through the door as fast as her legs will carry her. She doesn't have time to duck low or look for cover. Instead, she just runs flat-out at the first person she sees. He's got an assault rifle pointed straight at her, but he's not paying attention to the door at all. Instead he's staring straight up at the ceiling, and it gives Cameron the seconds she needs to cross the distance to him without him opening fire. She goes right, not willing to risk taking the gun straight on, and as she runs past lashes out with the remains of the baton left-handed, catching him hard across the visor. He goes down with a yelp, his finger pulling the trigger as he falls, and the sound of his gun firing is a staccato rattle over the sound of the alarms.

Shit.

The next one is standing behind the cover of an upturned desk, and his confusion evaporates when the gunfire starts. He's caught half-standing, his mouth opening as he witnesses

Cameron knocking his teammate to the ground, and she's covered half the distance to him when he changes his mind about shouting and decides to fire at her instead. His gun comes up, and even though he's molasses-slow in all his armor, Cameron knows that she isn't going to make it. She has to clear twelve feet of space, while all he has to do is shift the barrel of his gun a few more degrees.

She throws what's left of the baton, little more than the handle, sending it flying end-over-end straight at him far faster than she can sprint. He flinches, his reactions good enough that even in body armor he dodges it, and in the fraction of a second it buys her Cameron vaults the desk and launches herself two-footed into him, her full weight catching him mid-chest and bearing him to the ground. He lands badly, no hand thrown out to catch his weight, and his helmeted head smacks off of the floor with a sickening crack. Cameron gets on to one knee, but thinks better of getting up when bullets tear through the desk just next to where her head is.

Shit.

Five must have stayed in the server room, not six like she hoped. One to go, and he knows where she is. Cameron scrambles on her hands and knees to get away from the desk, heading for a column that will offer a lot more protection. The gunfire starts again, chasing her, and she goes full-out, rolling to the side as she clears the column. The space where she'd been a moment before hisses as bullets pass through it.

Shit shit shit.

More fire opens up on either side of the column, the stop-start rhythm of suppressive fire, not aimed to kill but to keep her pinned in place while the gunman moves to get a better angle on her. The fire suppression system is still pumping out gas: she can feel the chill of it and the weight of the pressure building up. Cameron closes her eyes and tries not to think about words like *oxygen debt* or *asphyxiation*.

The klaxon is still blaring at full volume, and Cameron can hear the Homeland agent gasping for breath over it. He's close. She keeps her eyes shut focusing all her attention on listening to him struggle for oxygen. A yelp of pain, probably at a burst eardrum, and more gasping. She ignores the tension building in her chest, the horror of what will happen to her if she tries to get her breath back by filling her lungs with air you can't breathe. *Like drowning on dry land.* Gunfire peppers the column she's hiding behind, one last defiant burst, and then footsteps as he turns and makes for the door, giving in to the need for fresh air.

Cameron breaks cover at a run. All of her limbs feel as though they are burning, the weight of them suddenly working against her, pulling all the momentum out of every step she takes. The last man standing is out of cover, his gun swaying this way and that as he staggers for the door that Cameron came in through. If he turned, he'd have a clear shot at her, but his focus is escape: she cuts across the width of the lobby space without a shot fired.

He knows she's coming. He doesn't look back, but there's a desperation in the way he moves that puts Cameron in mind of every horror movie she's ever seen. *And that makes you the monster.* She doubles down on the pace, ignores the spikes of pain that are climbing her shins and forearms. She knows what they are. It doesn't matter how stubborn a fighter you are, but when you get that feeling, when the edges of your vision turn blood-red, you better tap out. They reach your head or your heart, it won't be the hospital they take you to. It'll be the morgue.

The klaxon cuts out leaving a silence that's almost as painful as the noise itself, and the aircon shudders into life, fans rumbling like an earthquake as they try to cope with the overpressure in the room. Cameron doesn't dare breathe. Not yet.

The Homeland agent is at the door now, his helmet gone, black hair plastered flat against his skull with sweat. He's clean-shaven, square-jawed, and looks like he's in his mid-twenties, if that. Cameron takes this all in along with the fact that he's made it to the doorway. The drag from the air conditioning has pulled both doors open, breaking the gas seal, and he's sucking down one lungful after another of oxygen-rich, hypoallergenic, server-safe air. Cameron tries to put some power into her legs, to make one final spring at him, but their roles have been switched. He lifts his gun to make sure of his aim, and Cameron stares down the mouth of a barrel that suddenly looks wide enough that it could swallow her whole.

Three shots ring out, and Cameron falls forward, the anticipation of impact making her trip over her own feet. She catches herself awkwardly, arms braced, and as the rush of air washes over her face, finally takes a breath.

In front of her, the third Homeland agent falls, dropping through a fine red mist that used to be part of him to land face first on the floor. He's missing an eye, and as Cameron looks up past him she sees Ray standing in the corridor beyond, feet wide in a classic shooter's stance, shoulders square, arms straight, hands doubled over the grip. His aim has followed the agent to the ground, and it doesn't waver when he calls to her.

'Did we get them all?'

Cameron nods, swallowing hard, trying to find her voice between breaths. 'We got them,' she says. 'No one came out of the server room.'

Ray lowers his weapon and steps forward into the doorway. 'How many outside?'

'Three.' Cameron wants to get up, but is willing to give it a moment rather than try to push her weight upon leaden arms.

Ray lets out a low whistle. 'You took out two of them by yourself?'

Cameron doesn't reply, and coughs both to clear her throat and to cover the silence. One on three, and she'd come damn close to getting herself killed. Dumb-ass plans that work are still dumb-ass plans, and Ray's admiration sits uncomfortable on her.

'Wouldn't have been able to if they'd stuck with sprinklers. Thank whatever asshole architect got a free pass on his budget for this place.' She coughs again and spits out what comes up. The gases aren't meant to be harmful, but the mouthful she spits out has an unsettling metallic edge to it. She waves Ray inside. 'Thanks for the save.'

He steps over the body as he walks into the room. He doesn't even look down, his eyes fixed on a point somewhere a hundred yards past the back of the room, and his face looks as though it has been cut out of rock. Cameron knows what it is. It's what you do before a fight, when you're alone in the dressing room. You cut out the part of yourself that feels fear, sympathy, compassion. You take all the friendships you share in the business, all the goodness you have in you and you push it down into a box and you lock it up tight. You do it before you go in the ring so that you can win. Ray's doing it to survive. He didn't want to kill that man, to pump a near-lethal mix of gas into a room to disable seven more, but he knows that right now he has to, because hesitation will get him killed. What happens after, when he unlocks that box, Cameron doesn't want to think about. Just making it out will be enough.

Chapter 36

The server room is at the far end of the lobby. There's no sound save for the whir and tick of the computers running, no lights except the electric-blue glow of LEDs flickering on and off, streams of data chasing one another between the banks of machinery. Cameron lets Ray go first, gun ready, and she limps in his wake trying to stop herself from wheezing. Her chest feels tight, like she can't breathe deep enough to get all the air she needs, and only the thought of Miller's smug-ass face keeps her anchored. He would love for her to panic, to run, to let him go without a fight. She can't give him that victory, and her determination is the tether that holds fast against the waves of panic that crash into her every time she takes a breath.

Ray edges the server room door open, and leans back once he takes a look inside. 'Nothing,' he says.

'No one at all?'

'Looks like it.' He holsters the pistol and hauls the door open. The dull throb of the server room gets louder, the neat racks of computers humming away, completely undisturbed by the gunfire or the fire suppression system. Cameron feels something like dread stealing over her at the sight of how clean it all is. She expected them to be piled up against the door, half conscious from a lack of oxygen.

Between the blue lighting, the black racks of computers linked with cables that glow like they're under a blacklight, and the last wisps of mist from the lobby that chase after Cameron as she walks in, the server room feels like walking into a music video from the late nineties. All it needs is a shirtless dude in leather pants to swagger in and the image will be complete. Instead, she gets Ray Perada ducking past her.

'You see a bomb anywhere?' Cameron asks. 'I'm not exactly sure what I'm looking for.'

'If it's built in, we might not be able to see it at all,' Ray says. 'I'll go look.' He walks down the length of the first rack, ducking his head to check between the computers as he goes. When he gets to the end he turns back to give Cameron a shrug before heading on. She taps her foot, impatient. Miller is up there somewhere. She can almost feel him waiting.

'Hey, Cameron,' Ray's voice rings off the metal panels, giving it a weird, distant feel. 'You should come see this,' he says.

The remaining members of the Homeland team are laid out in a rough arc near the back corner of the server room. They're all dead, but it isn't from asphyxiation. They've been shot, the spiderweb cracks caused by a bullet passing through their visors masking what's left of their faces.

'What the fuck?' Cameron picks her way past the bodies, stepping round a blood pool that looks black under the lights, to where Ray is standing.

'They're not the only problem,' Ray says. He points up at

a display that is screwed into one of the racks at head height, the numbers on it presented in a stark white that stands out clearly against the flickering blue background.

9:38

9:37

9:36

'Ray, what did you press?' Cameron asks. He holds his hands up, innocent.

'It was like this when I got here, I swear,' he says. 'They must have triggered it when the shooting started.'

Cameron remembers the sound of the klaxons, too loud and too discordant to ignore. *It wasn't a fire alarm. It was an evacuation warning.* There's something about the bodies that doesn't add up, and even though the timer is counting down to a detonation, she finds herself standing over them.

'We should get out of here,' Ray says.

'Ray,' Cameron says. 'What's wrong with this picture?'

Ray joins her and tilts his head, looking down at the dead Homeland agents. 'They're all facing the same way,' he says, then lowers his voice. 'Someone else killed them.'

'Someone with an oxygen mask,' Cameron says. 'They wouldn't have been able to breathe otherwise.'

Ray's eyes go wide as she says it. 'Nate,' he says. 'Nate has an oxygen tank.'

Cameron almost slips on the blood pool, she turns so fast. *Nate is here.* He must have snuck round the other side of the room when they came inside. She hits the turn so fast she bounces off of one of the server racks and sprints for the door.

'Nate!'

When Cameron pushes through the door, Nate freezes. He's halfway across the room, his back to her. He's wearing a suit – no demolition armor or tactical gear – and in one hand he's got a small oxygen cylinder. In the other, a gun. He's hunched over, like walking is a labor, and Cameron is struck by how gaunt he is. Like a skeleton walking.

'Nate.' She doesn't shout. She knows he can hear her just fine. 'Look at me.' Nate straightens up, and slowly turns to face her. When Cameron sees his face, it feels as though someone has stabbed her just below her heart. He's so ill. The skin under his eyes is so dark it looks bruised. His lips are blue. He barely looks like her brother anymore.

He coughs once, a thick, pitiful sound, and looks down at the gun in his hand. At Cameron's side, Ray cocks his own gun.

'Don't even think about it, man,' Ray says.

Cameron can't stop herself. She pushes Ray's gun down out of line. 'Ray, don't,' she says. Ten paces away, Nate makes a sound that could almost pass for a laugh.

'You should just let him shoot me, Cam,' Nate says. 'It'd be quicker.'

'What are you doing here, Nate?' she asks.

Nate lifts his chin. 'Pulling out,' he says. 'Homeland have ditched the mission. Burned it.' He shakes his head, like he can't believe what's happening to him. 'I should have known you'd find a way to fuck me over.'

'Fuck you over?' Cameron can barely find words, she's so angry. After a few moments, they come. 'You fucking crashed a car with me in it. You ended my career. You almost killed me!'

'Almost,' Nate says, nodding grimly. 'I tried my best, though. Miller was too chickenshit to hold up on his end of the bargain. You both fucked me.'

'What the fuck are you talking about, Nate?' Cameron is yelling now, ready to start slapping it out of him, gun or no gun.

'He's dying,' Ray says, and it's like a needle piercing the bubble of Cameron's anger. She can feel it draining out of her, and the hollow feeling it leaves in its wake. 'He can't breathe. He wanted you here, because you're the one that can cure him.'

Chronic organ dysfunction. That was what the doctor called it. She'd looked it up, asked her own doctors about the outcomes. Total systemic collapse had been the most likely prognosis, with every major organ failing one after the other. He'd seemed almost healthy when the car went over, but now Nate looks like he's about to collapse. 'There's a cure?'

'He needs a transplant,' Ray says. 'Lungs, at least. My guess is you're a match.'

Nate coughs again, his face twisting with anger. He always hated being caught out. 'You're the only one that is,' he says. 'Thank Mom and Dad for their unique genetic markers.' He waves the gun he's holding at the servers. 'Carrington checked. I went to them because they had access to medical files in every developed country. Over two billion people on their books, and only you were a match.' He laughs at that, and the effort sets him to coughing, a wet, heavy sound that cuts deep. When he recovers he looks straight at her. 'Look at you. Healthy as a goddamn horse.' His jaw works for a moment and he spits a lump of phlegm to one side. 'You don't deserve it.'

Cameron feels lightheaded, like a balloon with a cut string. She can feel the hate coming off him like a heat haze. She just about manages to shake her head. 'That's not how it works, Nate. You don't get to decide.'

'The fuck I don't. Do you know what it's like to be shown a chart that tells you how little time you have left to live?' Nate asks. 'I do. Do you know what it feels like to have that timer running in your head?'

'I might have,' Cameron says. 'You could have talked to me.'

Nate ignores her. 'And all the time I get to watch you piss your life away. Punching people for a living. Every time I saw you fight, all I could think was, "what a waste". I used to dream you'd get hurt, end up in a coma.'

A flicker of anger, deep in Cameron's gut. *I used to dream you'd get hurt.* 'But I won.'

'You won.' Nate nods. 'Again and again, you won.'

'So you took matters into your own hands.' The words feel cold in her mouth as she says them.

'I did what I had to do. I told Carrington they could have their precious project if they got me what I needed.'

It feels like a light going on. Carrington played him, like they tried to play her. Crashing the car hadn't been a test of his loyalty. He'd planned it. 'And Miller strung you along.'

'The crash didn't work out. They were meant to take you, too. Keep you stable until I was ready for surgery,' Nate says. 'They told me it was too risky, that they needed more time. I could feel myself dying, and all he could say to me was, "wait".'

'So you went to Homeland.'

Nate looks up at that. 'I went to Homeland. And they told me if I could get them exclusive access to the server, then I would get what I want.'

'Me on a slab,' Cameron says.

Nate nods so fast he starts shaking. 'Couldn't wait around for someone with a matching set to just fall off their motorbike,' he says. 'You know twenty people die every day, waiting for that to happen? Wishing that someone out there will die in just the right circumstances to help them out? I couldn't do that, Cam.'

Cameron bristles. 'You don't get to call me that, Nate. Not anymore.'

Nate sags, looking down at the gun in his hand. He's so thin, it looks as though his arm is about to snap under the weight of it. 'I don't want to die, Cameron.'

'I can't think of anyone who does,' Cameron says. She wanted to beat him to a pulp, but all she can do is stand there, held fast by the weight of knowing what her brother had tried to do. He'd crashed a car trying to create the conditions for a perfect donor. He'd built the whole system for Carrington thinking they'd come and get her when it was done. And when they hadn't come through on the deal, he'd cut a deal with Homeland that made them dance to his tune, brought her all this way himself, engineering one last-ditch attempt to save his own life. 'Why didn't you just ask?'

'What?'

'What, you needed a lung off me?' Cameron's voice rises, hot with anger. 'You think I wouldn't have given it to you? Is that what you thought?'

Nate's head comes up, and she can see the old Nate still in there, his eyes fixed on some far point. Always looking ahead. So fucking clever, but just like her dad had said, not an ounce of sense in him. 'You wouldn't have thrown away your career,' he says.

'Bullshit,' Cameron says. 'You were there for me. I would have dropped it in a heartbeat.' She laughs, and feels a bitter spike of pain shoot down her scarred left arm. 'Hell, I started a whole new one just to find you.'

'Mom and Dad wouldn't have let you,' Nate says, and he's floundering, casting about for an excuse. 'They wouldn't have—'

'FUCK you, Nate.' Cameron yells it over him. 'Don't even try to lie to me. What's the real reason? Why the fuck would you do this?'

Nate drops his head, and Cameron watches as he takes a long breath, gathering himself. When he looks up, it's like a mask has fallen away. He hates her. And the anger on his face is a mirror to her own. 'You win, Cam,' he says. 'Just like you always did.' He peels the nasal tube from his face, and drops the oxygen bottle at his feet. 'Always first. For Mom. For Dad. You got everything you ever wanted.' The gun follows, hitting the gas bottle with a hollow, ringing noise. 'And I got to watch.'

'Nate, you know that's not true.' Saying it breaks her heart, because she knows it won't reach him. For the first time, she can see how deep that hate goes. She can't think how long he must have been holding on to it for it to turn out this way.

'I put all this together,' Nate says. 'I broke every rule, burned every bridge. I killed people, Cam. I did all of it, just to take you down.' When he breathes in, there's a crackling sound that makes Cameron wince. 'Just this once, I wanted to see you lose.' He shakes his head. 'Why couldn't you just lose?'

Cameron's voice comes thick, when she finds it. 'I couldn't lose,' she says. 'Because if I did, I'd be losing my big brother.'

Nate's mouth works as he takes that in, but he doesn't answer. All he does is turn, a painful half-circle, and start to walk away.

'Nate!' Cameron calls after him. 'You can't walk away from this.'

Nate doesn't even look back. 'Watch me.'

If he'd just fucking told her. There might have been something. A lung would have been the end of her career, it might even have killed her, but it would have meant his life in return. He'd been too proud to say it, too stubborn – driven by the same bone-deep pride that had kept her moving all these years – and it had twisted him into a monster.

Cameron knows only one thing for certain. She has never in her life wanted to punch someone more than she does right now.

Ray clears his throat. 'Six minutes, Cameron. We have to go.'

'He can't just walk away.' Cameron isn't sure who she's trying to convince. 'Someone has to pay for this.'

'If he lasts six months, I'll be surprised,' Ray says. 'Besides, he's not the only one.'

Cameron nods. Miller is still up in the executive suite. On the top floor. He has to be. She knows he won't leave until the last moment. 'You should get out of here,' she says.

Ray takes a moment to figure out that she means to go after Miller alone. 'Are you sure you want to go up there?'

The executive elevator isn't far from here. Cameron can imagine what it would be like to be trapped inside as it falls. She reckons there's enough time to get up to the top floor. It's unlikely that she'll come back down, though. The need to dish out some pain over this shit is under her skin, itching away. There's only one way she can think of to scratch it. *Miller*. The server will be gone, but it's Miller's dream. If he gets away, Carrington will just start again and there's no promise that anyone will be there to stop them.

Total surveillance. Total control. Three hundred million people shackled with a tracer in their arm; three hundred million points of data waiting to be harvested by Carrington. The population of the United States, turned into a corporate asset.

'I have to go,' she says. Cameron can think of at least three ways Ray can get out of here. Even if he has to clear a barricade, he should be able to get clear. 'When you get outside, stick to your new-hire cover story. Maybe they'll let you go.'

He stands for a long time looking down at the pistol in his hands. The moment only lasts a few seconds, but Cameron knows how long seconds can be when you're holding on for the bell to ring to mark the end of a round. 'Getting out of here would be the sensible thing to do,' he says. He pops the clip, and racks the slide to eject the bullet that was waiting to be fired. He stands there weighing the mag in his hand. 'You remember when I tried to arrest you, and you kicked me in the head?'

Cameron nods. 'Yeah, I remember.'

Chapter 37

Ray watches as Cameron punches a four-digit code into the keypad by the elevator door. There's a long silence filled with the dread of trying to take ten flights of stairs in eight minutes or less before the elevator kicks into life and starts its descent.

'Your code worked?' he asks.

Cameron shakes her head, looking up at the ceiling as though she can somehow see through concrete and watch the elevator coming down. 'I don't think so.'

'They know we're coming, don't they?'

'They know someone is.'

Ray backs off. He doesn't like the idea of standing square on to an elevator door that has the potential to open with a bullet. 'I'll just be standing over here while we wait,' he says.

Cameron doesn't move. 'If they want to kill us they could just drop a grenade on top of the elevator. Or fire down the shaft. Or riddle it with bullets once we're up there.'

Ray knows what concentrated automatic fire does to targets. He tries not to think what the same kind of firepower would be like in a closed metal box. *People soup with ricochet croutons.* 'You know, it's your cheerful outlook on life that really makes you fun to be around,' he says. He hears the elevator stopping and draws his pistol, leaning slightly to aim past Cameron's right shoulder.

The doors slide open to reveal an empty elevator.

Not quite empty. Ray can't see it directly, but Cameron reacts to something on the floor. She steps inside and lifts it. A business card, folded once across its width to make it stand up. It's a note, left for her to find.

'What does it say?' Ray asks.

Cameron is frowning as she half-turns, leaning to the side so he can see the writing. 'It says, "COME UP".'

'Now I really am suspicious,' Ray says, shaking his head. 'Dude with a gun, fine. I can handle that. Half-pound of plastic explosive with a bunch of wires sticking out of it? I get it. It'd be messy, but I'd get it, you know? This? This is some bullshit.'

Cameron laughs, a short, dry sound. 'They didn't need to send down a guy with a gun, Ray. Sounds like they just kicked your ass with a business card and a marker pen.'

Ray gets into the lift. It takes him a moment to swallow down that bitter pill of truth she's just served him, and he spends it looking at his own reflection in the mirrored back wall of the elevator. His face looks strange, stress and fatigue hidden behind a mask made of sweat and dust. He looks as though he's been just been rescued from a cave-in at a mine after three days of digging. 'I deserved that,' he says.

'No,' Cameron says. 'You're right. They wouldn't send down an invite unless there was a world of shit waiting for us at the top.' Compared to Ray, Cameron looks as if she's just getting warmed up. Her clothes are in a shit state, and her hair is almost flat to her skull with sweat, but her expression is wide awake. She catches Ray looking at her in the mirror and rolls her shoulders, like a prizefighter itching at the mark. 'Best not keep them waiting. They might change their mind about that grenade.' There is a single button set in a panel at chest height on the left-hand side of the elevator. Cameron presses it, and the plastic strip around it lights up blue. The doors close behind them.

Ray's reflection swallows hard, adjusts its grip on the gun in its hand as though holding it that little bit tighter is going to make a difference. He's put himself on Cameron's right shoulder so he can shoot the instant the doors open. *And push her to the side if you need to.* He thinks about offering her the vest, but before the question can even get past the thinking stage he knows she will decline. He knows she's psyching herself up for a fight, and this is the long walk to the ring. You don't take anything with you.

A speaker pops somewhere in the elevator ceiling, making Ray jump. Cameron doesn't move, save to look up in curiosity. After a moment, music begins to play. Guitar, double bass . . . and a saxophone. Ray bursts into laughter as he recognizes the song: 'On Days Like These.'

'What the fuck is that?' Cameron asks.

Ray raises his eyebrows at her. 'You don't recognize it?'

'Am I supposed to?' She frowns. 'Sounds like shit off an infomercial.'

'It's Quincy Jones. He used to score films in the sixties.'

'So about twenty years before you were born?'

Ray grins. 'I pulled the short straw on stakeout duty about ten months back. You see a lot of old movies at three in the morning.'

'Huh,' Cameron offers before lapsing into silence. Ray can tell she's not done. After five more seconds of it, she shifts her weight from one foot to the other and points upwards. 'Do you think you could shoot that speaker out?'

Ray feels the lift slowing. 'Sorry,' he says. 'Heads up.' He sets his feet as the lift comes to a halt, giving himself a stable base. It's what you do at the range, it's what you do in real life. It's not just good practice. It's what takes your mind off the fact that you've voluntarily gone up ten stories to the top of a building that is very shortly going to be demolished, and that the only comfort to be found in that decision is that you're more than likely going to get shot long before the floor falls out from under you.

The doors slide open to reveal the penthouse office, and Ray is relieved to discover that they aren't immediately shot.

The reason they aren't is because every person holding a gun is dead. The office is a wide open, airy space, with long windows that sit entirely in opposition to the rest of the building's concrete slab aesthetic. On two sides, the windows have been smashed completely, shards scattered on the floor about the open frames. Ray can guess at what happened to them. The incursion team came down from the roof, abseiling in on either side, using small charges to blow out the windows. What happened to the incursion team is less clear. There is gear all over the floor: webbing, ropes, harness. There are at least eight men stacked like firewood, leaning against a console that is covered in monitors, all showing security cameras still active inside the building. There aren't many of them live. *I shot a few*, Ray thinks, *Nate's virus blinded the rest*. The monitors are undamaged, as is the rest of the computer equipment that makes up the bulk of the room's furniture. If there was a firefight, it was a short one.

Silicon fucking Valley is standing dead center, about twenty-five feet away, looking straight at Cameron with a shit-eating grin on his face. In front of him, just to the right, is Bullet Head. He's not looking his best – his skin is so pale he's practically glowing, and his bad eye is covered by a bandage that is soaked through with blood – and yet he still looks like bad news. Neither Bullet Head nor Silicon Valley have a scratch on them. It isn't a big deductive leap for Ray to work out why Silicon Valley let them come up. He knows what Bullet Head is capable of, and yet the same guy lost an eye fighting Cameron. He wants to see them fight. He wants to see how she did it.

Fuck that, Ray thinks. Fucker probably has a vest on, but even a straight hit to a vest is going to wipe that smile off of his face. He takes aim – rear sight and front sight aligned over the center of mass – and Cameron's hand comes out, pressing the barrel of his gun downwards, spoiling his shot.

'Ray,' she says. 'Put the gun away.'

Ray looks at Cameron like she's gone mad, then realizes what he missed when the doors opened. There's a green box on the floor in front of them, standing on four thin legs. On the curved surface he can make out the words *FRONT TOWARDS ENEMY*. It's an M18 Claymore mine. Inside, there are several hundred steel balls and a wad of explosive capable of turning every single one of them into a bullet. If it fires, what's left of him and Cameron will drip out of the colander that was the elevator long before the building comes down. Suddenly he knows how the entire assault team died and why every single window is gone.

'Toss it.' Silicon Valley gestures with the detonator he's holding. Ray puts the safety on and tosses the gun forward and away, over to one side of the room. 'Thank you. Now, shall we get started?'

Chapter 38

There are ten paces between Cameron and Miller. Five if she runs it. It would only take two tenths of a second for him to detonate the mine and kill both her and Ray. As much as she wants to put her fist through Miller's head, there's no point in trying.

Miller rubs his hands together with the kind of oil-slick, uninhibited glee that is the sole preserve of fight promoters adding up pay-per-view revenues and casino pit bosses the moment a whale goes under at the high rollers' table. 'It is not often that I am surprised,' he says.

Cameron doesn't say anything. She can't find the stomach for it. Not with Samson there. His one good eye is fixed on her, and he looks furious. All he has to do is take the detonator off of Miller and press the switch to kill her. She's amazed that he hasn't already.

Miller keeps talking, like she somehow gives a shit. 'I was expecting to see your brother when those doors opened.' He gestures towards the mine pointed at the lift doors. 'As you can see, I was all ready for a reunion. I have to ask, did you kill your own brother?'

'Fuck you, Miller,' Cameron says. She looks at Samson. 'How's the eye, asshole?'

Samson's cheek twitches, but he stays put. Miller glances up at the back of his head, and says something that Cameron doesn't catch. It's short and terse – a warning – and she suddenly realizes that Miller himself is the source of Samson's new-found self-control.

'This building is coming down,' Cameron says.

Miller shrugs. 'It was always a possibility that we would have to activate the contingency plan,' he says. 'As my father always said, don't put all your eggs in one basket.'

Ray pipes up next to Cameron. 'Your daddy used really common sayings? That's a fucking revelation, man. You want to talk surprises, you should see your boys downstairs. Homeland spanked them without breaking a sweat.'

That gives Miller pause. Samson glances back at him, and Cameron can guess the question: *do you want me to deal with it?* Miller is vulnerable without him, and Cameron knows what his answer will be long before he gives a tiny head shake, *no*.

'You brought this on yourself,' Cameron says.

'I rather think your brother brought it on all of us,' Miller answers. 'He betrayed you, and us, and in the process betrayed you again. And yet, you let him use you.' He nods carefully. 'Yes. I know the virus came from you. It wouldn't have done the damage it did unless you let it out.'

'You know why I let it out, right?'

'You wanted to create an opportunity for yourself,' Miller says. 'A way out.'

Cameron is only half paying attention to what Miller says. Her mind is racing. There's no way Miller would have someone like Samson around if he didn't have a leash on him. An ex-soldier with nothing to show for his service, he's bitter and impulsive. Cameron pushed his buttons with a single kick; Miller would have needed an implant to control him, to let him know who the boss is. Cameron looks from Miller to Samson and back again. *He has a pacemaker implant, and he thinks Miller can still zap him with it.*

'. . . that it matters.' Miller is still talking, oblivious to the fact that Cameron is ignoring him. 'You were doubtless coming up here to silence me, maybe force me to authorize a complete system wipe?'

Cameron came up here to beat his ass like a drum, but she's not going to tell him that. There's no guarantee Miller won't press the detonator the instant she says it. If she can get past the mine and keep him busy there's a chance that Ray can make it out of this. Cameron looks past the two men, trying to pick out details. Every hold has a counter. There has to be an escape route. Miller wouldn't have stayed if there wasn't a way out. 'That was the plan.'

'Then you weren't paying attention. The central control program started a full system wipe the instant the virus went to work. Even if any code remains, it will be too fragmented to salvage.' Miller smiles thinly. 'You should have run.'

There's a roof view visible on one of the security cameras. Cameron can just make it out on one of the monitors. In the corner of the picture, a black bar is flickering. Cameron realizes that it's a rotor, and that there's a helicopter up there. A way out. 'I had to come,' she says, 'because I have something to say.'

Miller scoffs. 'What could you possibly say to me that—'

'Not to you, dick.' Cameron looks straight into Samson's one good eye. 'Him.'

Samson lifts his chin, and speaks in a thick voice. 'What is it?'

'I let the virus loose so Miller couldn't shock me anymore,' Cameron says. 'I bet you any money he can't shock you, either.' Samson's eyes widen, and Cameron's question is answered. He'd been bearing the weight of an implant so long that just the threat of it had been enough. And now Cameron was calling Miller's bluff.

Miller tries to grin, but Cameron can see it doesn't reach his eyes. 'That's not going to change a—'

Samson turns with a roar and catches Miller by the shirt front. Miller starts to shriek as his feet leave the floor, but it is cut off when Samson heaves him up past head height before throwing him back down on to the floor. The impact flings his arm out wide, and Cameron takes a deep breath as the detonator flies out of Miller's hand. Ray almost runs for it, but it bounces once and is gone, skittering through the broken glass from a window and falling out of sight. Miller isn't conscious when Samson lifts a booted foot and brings it down on him heel first and he's probably no longer breathing for the second, third, or fourth time, but Samson doesn't seem to care. He beats Miller's corpse until it's no longer recognizable as Miller, then stamps a triumphant foot in the bloody mess that's left.

Samson turns back to face Cameron and Ray, his face half-obscured by the blood on it, a trickle of red-black gore dripping from his right fist. He looks feral, and Cameron has a sinking feeling that killing Miller isn't going to be enough for him.

'Bet you've been wanting to do that for a long time,' she says.

'Since I met him.'

The floor shudders underfoot, and one of the surviving panes of glass on the far side of the room shatters with a crash. Ray jumps and yells out, thinking it's the claymore going off. The mine sits inert between them, and Cameron edges into the room, out of its arc of fire. Another tremor ripples up through the floor, and Cameron feels the shift that comes in its wake, like a wrecking ball dropping loose from its moorings. A moment after, a dull rumble far below their feet makes the room shake. Something – a ceiling, a stairwell – is collapsing down there. Ray's face goes blank. He knows what an earth-quake feels like, knows what it can do. There's no faking that fear. 'So we all friends here or what?' he asks. 'I mean, this building is coming down on us, so now would be a good time to decide.'

Samson lifts his bloody fist and extends a finger to point straight at Cameron. 'We have some business to settle.'

'Okay,' Ray says. 'So it's "or what". Just glad to see where we stand on that. Cameron?'

Cameron doesn't look at him. 'There's a helicopter on the roof. Get up there, get on it, get the fuck out of here.'

'What, and leave you with fucking . . . Prom Night Carrie over there?'

'He's going to be busy. Now get out of here.'

The floor moves underneath all of them. It's probably only a few inches at ground level, but here on the top floor it's closer to six feet of sway. Behind them, the elevator lets out a screech as the shaft warps around it. Ray puts his hand on Cameron's forearm. 'Cameron, if you don't make it out—'

'Ray, there isn't time for this.'

'There has to be another way,' he says.

There probably is, but they're out of time. 'If you think of it,' Cameron says, 'let me know.'

On the last word she launches herself at Samson, going from standing to sprinting as fast as her aching muscles will let her. It's not impressive, but it does get his attention. He grins, opening his arms as though welcoming her, and Cameron can see blood on his teeth. *Just hold him off until Ray is clear.* She promises herself that's all she needs to do. Even though it sends a spike of pain through her side, she puts her foot flat in front of her and changes direction, moving sideways so she's going round on Samson's blind side.

Samson lunges, the movement fast but inaccurate – his hands grabbing the air where Cameron was instead of where she is – and Cameron darts past his shoulder to end up behind him. She squares off to his back and kicks up between his legs, a hard, quick blow that connects with enough force to make her foot hurt.

Samson doesn't even flinch. He turns, the same grin spreading wider on his face at her having tried. He takes a step forward, and Cameron tries to convince herself that he's a little slower on his feet for having just been kicked in the balls.

No such luck. Samson comes at her, fast, and she bolts to get away from him, his fist slamming into the drone console as she scrambles up and over it, landing hard and rolling on the far side.

A gun fires, and Samson ducks faster than Cameron ever thought a person could move. Ray fires again, emptying his magazine as Samson takes cover behind the console.

'Cameron, come on!' He's yelling at her, but all she can think is how easy it would be for Samson to get over the console and run them both down if she tried to run now.

Cameron puts her hand out to push herself up on to her feet and finds a stick lying on the floor. It's a nightstick, two feet of black polymer with a handle sticking out at right angles down by one end. She picks it up and climbs to her feet as Samson comes round the side of the drone console.

'Is that it?' Cameron rolls her left shoulder as she brings her baton up in a guard, feeling out for gaps in her range of motion. 'That all you got?' The burn on her back has opened completely, and she can feel her vest sticking to the wound. Her right arm has a numb patch running from the peak of her elbow to her right pinkie, and she tries to put the thought of it giving out on her out of her head as she circles around the room, drawing Samson away from Ray.

Samson follows, his fists held up in a ragged guard, and starts swinging.

Cameron only ever took up stick fighting for the novelty of it. Timing and distance are everything in the ring – they're the difference between a clean takedown or walking face first into a right hook – and any excuse to break up the routine with something that helped you focus on it was welcome in her book. She was never great at it, but she has training enough to know that Samson is missing chances left and right to close on her and do some damage. He's throwing punches that would finish her if any of them landed, but every time she blocks him there's an opening that he isn't taking. It takes five of them for Cameron to realize what's happening.

He's afraid of her.

He's already lost an eye when she grappled with him, and that's the reason he's not comfortable closing. If she gets a hand to his other eye, she can blind him. It shouldn't matter – the floor is shaking under them like it's a drum skin instead of concrete – but in a fight fears aren't rational. They come from the gut. And if Samson is afraid of her, it doesn't matter how strong or fast he is. Cameron can beat him.

Fuck this guy. I'm gonna win. Cameron steps into the next blow when she should step out, angling herself into Samson's blind side, and when he veers away from her, trying to make some distance, she kicks away his lead foot and sends him stumbling backwards. She can feel her whole body surge with a kind of excitement, the fighter's pride waking, every wound and ache forgotten as she warms up to the challenge. She steps back for a beat and looks around, and sees that Ray has vanished out of the room. *Good.*

She dodges to the side on sheer instinct, and a chunk of metal torn from the drone console goes past her nose so close that for a fraction of a second she can see every line and curve in it like she's looking at it through a microscope. Samson charges after it, and instead of trying to dodge, Cameron stands her ground, lunging forward with the nightstick held straight out, a blunt spear for him to run himself on to. Samson jerks to the side to avoid it, off-balance, and Cameron grabs hold of him as he goes past, turning her body in time with his to throw him cleanly over her hip. She puts every ounce of strength she has into it, and Samson goes over like a whip being cracked, landing with a thump that makes the floor shake. Something in Cameron's back goes tight, and instead of following him down to crack his head open, she is forced to limp in a circle, trying to walk it off.

Samson gets to his feet, but doesn't attack. The building sways again, and he and Cameron both stare at the long, lightning-strike crack that is forming across the floor between them. Cameron grimaces as the pain in her back spikes, then eases, and lifts the nightstick up into a guard. She couldn't bring herself to punch her brother, but this guy will do just fine instead.

'Let's finish this.'

Chapter 39

Ray finds a set of metal steps leading up to the roof at the far corner of the room, and takes them on legs that are shaking so hard they feel ready to collapse under him. He took a clear shot at a target standing side-on to him, and missed. Too keen to take Bullet Head out, he couldn't calm down enough to line up the sights and ended up shooting high. Bullet Head didn't even look pissed about it, either, just crouched out of the fucking way and let Ray empty his mag into the console he ducked behind like some kind of idiot. Cameron was not impressed, and he'd beat feet out of there to keep from being a distraction. Get to the roof, secure the helicopter, make sure they both get an exit before the building falls out from under them. Simple.

Ray takes a deep breath as he hits the top step. *Get your shit locked down. You can do this.*

He comes out on to the roof through a maintenance door that is so flimsy it warps when he pushes it open. There isn't a lot of wind, but without any railings on a flat roof, it feels like a lot more than Ray is entirely comfortable with. The door is close to a corner, and his first steps take him straight for the center of the roof.

The drones are sitting docked in a nest that fills the center point, the nest a dark hump of black plastic and pipework that sits almost ten feet square and comes up to chest height on Ray. There's a canopy over it of corrugated plastic sprayed silver, a deliberately shoddy roof that hides the drone site from aerial and satellite view. On the far side of the nest, a helicopter perches on the roof like a giant insect, a touch of iridescence to the sky-blue airframe putting Ray in mind of a dragonfly. It's a Super Huey, loaned or appropriated from the Marine Corps, and Ray is only slightly relieved to see that there isn't a door gunner sitting waiting to open fire on him. Its rotors are turning, beating the air with the characteristic overpressure *whomp* that feels loud even with the wind noise. Ray can't see into the cockpit from this angle, but it doesn't look like it's getting ready to take off. It's making a hell of a noise, but if he was asked to guess, the helicopter is the equivalent of a getaway car left running outside the bank.

Ray ducks into the cover the drone nest offers and works his way round it to try and get a better angle on the cockpit. If he can work out where the pilot is, it gives him the best chance of getting across the open roof and into the helicopter before he can take off. *Or return fire*, Ray thinks. *Because pilots, especially Marine Corps ones, carry sidearms.*

There's the scuff of a footstep behind him, and Ray manages a quarter turn before he hears the hammer being pulled back on a pistol. 'Don't even try it, son.' The voice is even, measured, but far from calm. It's the voice of an experienced soldier standing in a world of shit. 'Two fingers only, pistol at arm's length, and drop it. Once that's done, put your ~~hands behind~~ your head.'

Ray does as he is told. The pilot must have been behind the flimsy structure where the door comes out on to the roof, standing with his heels over a sheer drop. He must have stayed there even when the bomb went off and the whole building started to shift. Ray can tell this isn't someone he can fuck with.

'Identify yourself.'

'Officer Ray Perada, SFPD.'

'You got a badge?'

Ray jerks his head towards the helicopter. 'Your helo's registration numbers are sprayed over and you want me to pull a badge? We're all off the books here, marine.'

There's a pause before the pilot snorts in agreement. 'You got that right. Turn around, Officer Perada.' Ray turns, and finds himself looking at a silhouette with the sun at his back. It takes a moment for his eyes to adjust, and in that time the pilot lowers his sidearm. He's not a young man, and his mouth is set in a thin, serious line that Ray suspects is a permanent fixture. He wears no rank or insignia, but from his age and demeanor Ray can tell he's in a command position. 'You can put your hands down,' he says. 'What's the word on those Homeland boys I brought in?'

Ray doesn't sugar-coat it. 'All dead.'

'Damn it.' He works his mouth for a moment, as though trying to build up the spit to get rid of a sour taste. 'I take it their insertion went to shit?'

'You could say that. They walked straight into an ambush.'

'Well, that's a peach,' the pilot says. 'How'd you get past it?'

Ray isn't that great a liar, but he knows all about talking round the truth. 'The foundations are compromised. This building is coming down.'

The pilot gives him a long, considering look. 'And everyone is running from it.'

'Everyone that can,' Ray says. 'Look, Major—'

'Major?' The pilot sounds offended.

'Wow,' Ray says. 'Too low?'

'Just an inch.' The pilot shrugs. 'How'd you call it?'

'Forgive me for saying it, but you aren't exactly a spring chicken and the armed forces aren't in the habit of keeping second lieutenants on to retirement.'

The pilot nods. 'No, they are not.'

'This is how I think it went down,' Ray says. 'ICE turn up at your base demanding an unmarked helo and a pilot to deliver ten men to a civilian building under radar and assist in the extraction of a valuable asset. It stinks to high heaven, especially when the crew turns up looking like they're inserting into Afghanistan. You try to pull the plug, but the call comes down to make it happen. So you take the helo yourself, because you know that no matter how the mission ends it's going to be a long walk off a short plank and you sure as hell aren't going to do that to anyone in your command.'

The pilot grins suddenly. 'I like you, Officer Perada,' he says. 'You got some good insight. And while I can't imagine how or why you managed to walk through a paramilitary black op without a scratch to show for it, I feel it is my duty to offer you a lift off of this building before it falls out from under us.'

'Colonel, that sounds like a great offer, but I've got one request to add to it.'

Chapter 40

Samson comes at Cameron with his fists high, taking a long step forward and lashing out with a jab that moves like lightning. There's no way to dodge it but to go backwards, and Cameron deliberately shortens the step and brings up the nightstick, bracing the length of it against her forearm and letting his punch hit it.

His punch is like a sledgehammer, and the force of it is enough to send Cameron stumbling back, taking long steps to keep herself from falling. If she'd blocked it with her arm alone, it probably would have broken something. The hardened polymer of the nightstick is strong enough to take it, and as Cameron recovers she sees Samson frowning at his hand, his fist opening and closing like he's testing it. *Probably broke a metacarpal.* It's a common fighter's injury: part of the reason why you strap your hands up and put on the biggest gloves you can get away with. It's hard to keep fighting when every punch you land makes the damage worse. Strong and quick aren't the same as smart, and if she's lucky he'll punch his own hand to pulp.

Samson shifts his stance, puts his other hand forward, and gestures for Cameron to come and get him. He's not that stupid. She knows she can't turn her back on him, can't run for the roof while he's still able to run her down. And she can't stay put. The building is collapsing. She can feel it going, the cement floor shuddering beneath her feet as more and more walls give way. The explosion wasn't big enough to take it all down in one go, but the building is, bit by bit, falling out from under them. Cameron doesn't have the time to string this out. She is going to have to go to him.

She takes a step closer, and another, the stick ready, her stance loose, ready to dodge out of the way. Samson waits her out. Cameron is wheezing in spite of herself, her chest still tight from the fight downstairs, and it pisses her off that he can see how tired she is. Already her legs are burning, the lactic acid making them feel they're pressed hard against the very edge of failure. Like if she stops now, even for a moment, they're going to fail her.

You won't win this by dodging, Cameron tells herself. *He's afraid of you getting close. Use it. You can beat him.*

With a grimace, she gets up on the balls of her feet and starts moving laterally, back into Samson's blind side. He turns awkwardly, nervous of losing her, and she lashes out at his lead arm with the nightstick.

He takes a step back.

He's still got that speed. He takes the step so quickly that Cameron is half-convinced he slides back like he's on skates, and she isn't nearly quick enough to capitalize on it. Still, his reaction is to retreat, when he could have just pulled his arm back, and Cameron reckons she's got at least one more before he realizes it, too.

She moves in again, working on the blind side, waiting for him to lift his lead foot to follow her round. Some fights you win without ever taking a hit. Cameron knows they exist, but she's never seen one close up. She knows what she's going to have to do to beat Samson. *You're dead anyway. Get on with it.*

Samson's lead foot comes up and Cameron throws the nightstick up into his face, ducking and slipping past his blind side as he reacts on instinct, stepping back and slamming into the drone console. Cameron gets a hand to Samson's shoulder, a foot up on the console and kicks off to get as much height as she can to leap on to his back. The instant she's up, Cameron snakes her right arm around Samson's tree-trunk neck and catches hold of her left bicep to apply the oldest and simplest hold she knows: a rear naked choke.

Samson responds by going insane. He charges in circles, flailing his arms up and over, hands trying to grab her, but she brings her free hand up to his face and it drives him into a panic. Cameron bears down on the choke, the bone in her forearm a hard edge across his throat, and his bald head turns brick-red as he hisses and grunts, trying to suck in a breath through the windpipe she's holding shut.

The floor goes from underneath them. One whole half of the room drops a clear foot lower than the other, and Samson loses his footing, stumbling once and falling backwards like a tree being felled. Cameron has to let go of him before he crushes her, and as she hits the floor a big chunk of the ceiling cuts loose and drops, forcing her to roll away as it smashes the drone console into scrap metal.

The floor is tilting underneath Cameron as she tries to get to her feet. She doesn't know where the roof access is from where she is right now. She doesn't even know if it exists anymore. *This building is going to fall, and you're going with it.* Her entire right side feels cramped with pain, and she takes a faltering step away from the pile of rubble, hoping it's in the right direction.

It's instinct that makes her duck more than anything else. A chunk of concrete the size of her fist whips through the space where her head was a fraction of a second before, and she turns back to face Samson. His face is crimson, a sheet of blood washing down his cheek where the bandage has been torn aside, his ruined eye bleeding freely. He's up on one knee, and as Cameron watches he drags his other leg out from the rubble as he climbs back to standing.

'You think we're done here?' he asks.

'Yeah,' Cameron says. 'I'd say so.'

'I'm going to kill you, bitch.' He says it slowly, like he's taking an oath. 'I'm gonna kill your family. I'll kill everyone you ever dared call a friend.'

Cameron knows he means it. Samson's good eye is shining with the kind of madness that would drive someone to fight even after a roof fell in on them, give them the will to survive the whole building falling down.

She takes a deep breath, feels every muscle sparking with pain as she does it. 'No,' she says, and lifts her hands up into a guard. 'You're going to try.'

Samson charges at her, coming up and over the rubble like a linebacker charging the quarterback, all fear and hesitation gone. There's nothing left in him but rage. Cameron watches him come, sees the hitch in his gait that wasn't there before, and makes her decision. She drops low into her stance and breaks into a run, kicking off the concrete to head straight for him.

The physics of a collision are simple enough that even a fighter can understand them. Two objects coming together at speed will collide with a force determined by the sum of their speeds. Even though she ducks down at the last moment, sliding under his arms to try and tangle up his legs, running into Samson's midriff is like headbutting an anvil. As he goes over, Cameron's head snaps back and to the side, and her vision is filled with purple-black bursts. Samson's momentum keeps him going, falling past her, and Cameron brings her legs up and over, years of practice turning it into muscle memory more than intent, tangling round Samson's right leg to trap the thigh and calf. As he bounces off of the concrete, Cameron's hands close around his foot.

There's no quarter here. No rules. There's fighting, and then there's survival.

The ankle lock is meant to be a submission move, but Cameron knows Samson isn't going to tap out and shake hands. He may be bigger and stronger, but Cameron has the advantage of biomechanics and a lifetime of training. With her whole body leaning into it, she turns his ankle the wrong way, the foot bending back at an impossible angle. She feels the tendons shudder, and there's a pop deep within the joint as Samson's ankle gives way. Something warm spills over her hands, soaking into her chest, and Cameron looks down to see a shard of bone has broken the skin, and he's bleeding all over her.

Samson roars with rage and pain, jerks his foot loose of her grip with a titanic effort, and pushes himself up and round on to one side to punch down the length of his body at Cameron, the blow catching her clean in the midriff. The force of it sends Cameron flying sideways, skin and clothes tearing on the concrete, her gut spasming with the shock of the blow. She lands on the gap in the concrete floor, bounces hard against the sheared ends of the steel rods that were buried inside it, and there's a terrifying flush of fear as she feels the back of her neck go cold, the sensation of all that air underneath her.

Samson is on her before she can get her bearings, looming over her, fist raised, his face twisted in fury, and Cameron rolls away from him as his fist smashes into the floor where her head was. He's screaming, bellowing at the top of his voice, and she rolls again as more blows land, showering her in dust and making the floor shake under them both. There's no way out. Cameron feels like she's standing to one side, watching it happen to someone else.

He's going to beat you to death, and all you can do is sit there letting it happen. Cameron can almost feel Ludo's disappointment that it's come to this. She can hear his voice, somewhere over to her left telling her to breathe. That this is easy. That all Samson's got is that hammer-blow punch of his, and without it, he's done.

Samson swings another punch and Cameron rolls, but instead of away she rolls inside it, feels it whip past her head as she rolls into his supporting arm and pulls it out from under him. He's still yelling on the way down, and only stops when his face smacks into the concrete with an audible crack. Cameron turns, the movement automatic as she controls Samson's wrist with one hand, wraps her other arm around

321

the back of his elbow and closes the lock by grabbing her own wrist. He groans as Cameron levers his arm back against its natural rotation, and she can feel him straining to hold her off. She leans hard into the hold and feels the man's shoulder giving way, the rotator cuff tearing under the strain. He's screaming now, helpless to stop her, but Cameron presses on until she feels the elbow separate: tendons tearing, cartilage shorn free of the bone. When Cameron lets him go, his arm is destroyed.

She rolls away from him and gets to her feet. Samson is still down, clutching at his useless arm, eyes closed, spine straight, every cord and tendon in his neck standing out, the fight forgotten.

'You walked away with one good eye last time,' Cameron says. Her voice is shaky, but she can keep it together long enough to let Samson know he's lost. 'You got one good leg and one good arm left. You come after me again, I'll take the rest.' The floor shudders underneath her and Cameron steps away from him, from the crack that's starting to widen. 'Enjoy the express elevator.'

She isn't sure that Samson can hear her, but Cameron knows he'll understand. There's no surgery, no steroid in the world that will fix that arm. If he even survives the building coming down, he'll struggle to lift a bowl of soup, let alone punch anyone.

She walks in a circle, trying to get her bearings. She knows that the building is coming down, that she has to get to the roof, but now that the fight is over it feels like someone has put a blanket over her head. Every part of her hurts. The building is going to fall, and part of her is tempted to just let that happen. Only the anger, the stubborn *fuck you* that still burns white-hot in the very center of her chest, is holding her upright. *You die, and even in Hell Miller can still call this a win.*

'Cameron!' She can hear Ray's voice, but the sound doesn't connect in her brain. Ray is long gone. 'Cameron! Come on!'

She can barely see, and the sound of Ray shouting is difficult to hear. She shuffles left and right, head cocked, trying to listen past the thrumming beat that fills her head.

The sound isn't in her head. It's a helicopter. It's flying lined up with the broken windows on the uphill side of the building, the broad side door fully open. Hanging out of it on a tether is Ray Perada. His face splits into a grin when he sees her looking at him. 'Come on, Cam! You got a fucking death wish?'

Cameron breaks into a run, stumbling at first and gaining speed as her stride lengthens. For the first time since waking up strapped to a table in Carrington's basement, she can feel a spark of something other than anger ignite inside of her. *Hope.*

As she runs, the building goes down.

It's the other half of the room that goes first. The floor jumps like a sheet snapping in the wind as the far side of the room tears free and drops, the noise a screaming wind that pulls at Cameron as she runs for the open window. Ray's eyes are so wide she can see a perfect circle of white around the pupil, and that is all Cameron can think of as she takes the last long step and launches herself out into thin air. Whoever is flying it knows their stuff, and as she stretches out her arms knowing that she will never be able to reach, the helicopter sways up and sideways, tilting the landing skid towards her.

Cameron catches it with both hands, and there's a stomach-dropping lurch as her weight on the skid pulls the helicopter off-balance and over towards the falling building. The engines scream, and Cameron swears she can see the rotors bending when they dive down and past the top three floors as they fall. The helicopter peels away from the building, and she gets her legs up and wraps them around the skid with the firm intent of never letting it go. A loop of rope is lowered past her face and bumps against her shoulder. Looking up, she sees Ray hanging over her, his hand braced against the winch.

'I'd offer you a hand up,' he says, 'but you have to promise not to break it first.'

Cameron stares at him for a long moment before she reaches for the loop of rope. 'Has anyone ever told you your sense of humor sucks?'

'Yeah, I've heard that,' he says. 'Here.' Ray reaches down and grips her wrist, holding her in place while she gets the loop under both her arms. Once she's safe, he lets go and uses the winch to pull her up into the crew space. 'I think it's the stress, you know?'

Cameron looks back as they fly towards the city. The Carrington facility is gone, the rubble obscured by a cloud of grey dust that is spilling out across the flat landscape that surrounds it. Something is burning in there, the orange-red flicker of flames like a heart beating in the middle of the cloud. On the highway, four police cruisers and a fire truck are speeding towards the scene, slowing to turn on to the access road. She turns away from the sight. They're not going to find anything there. Not now.

'Let's get the fuck out of here,' she says.

Chapter 41

One week later

The diner isn't doing a fast trade. It's the sort of place that has been around forever, sporting the same red and cream upholstery and the same gingham check tablecloths since the day it opened. It's a place that lives off its regulars, people who've been coming through the door every day at the same time for most of their professional lives, stopping off for pancakes or eggs and a straight gallon of coffee before they have to clock in.

Ray walks the length of the counter, a nod to the waitress as he goes, and slides into a booth on the far side, taking a seat across from its sole occupant.

'Bet you never had lunch with a dead man before,' he says. Across from him, Nate King's eyes go wide and he comes damn close to spitting his coffee straight back into the mug. He takes his time swallowing, hands fidgeting on the table like he's wondering if he can get one down into his lap without Ray noticing. 'Maybe just keep your hands on the table, keep this whole thing civil.'

'Are you here to arrest me?'

Ray gives the waitress a wave, and she signals back: *one*

minute. 'I'm not here to arrest you, Nate.'

Nate shifts uncomfortably in his seat, palms flat on the table. The waitress comes while he's squirming.

'What'll it be, hon?'

Ray gives her his best public relations smile. 'Pancakes would be fantastic, thank you.'

'You want butter with them?'

'You got syrup?'

'Sure thing.'

'I'll have syrup. And some of that coffee too?'

'Coming right up for you.'

'Thank you, ma'am.'

Nate leans forward the instant she steps away, his voice low and urgent. 'So why are you here? And how did you find me?'

Ray twirls a finger in the air. 'We'll take those in reverse order. Firstly, I didn't find you. Cameron did.'

'She's alive?'

'Your sister is definitely alive,' Ray says, 'and boy is she pissed with you.'

Ray watches Nate's face change, twisting into something like hatred. 'Figures,' he says. 'Fucking golden child. Drops a building on herself and walks out without a scratch.' Ray had hoped for some remorse, some kind of contrition from him, but all he can see is Nate's bitterness.

'You still holding that grudge?'

'You have any idea—' Nate says, a cough overtaking him. It goes on for a long time, and Ray watches him swallow before he speaks again. 'You have any idea what damage a chest infection can do to a growing boy?'

Ray looks at Nate's thin frame, his hollow cheeks. That

heavy cough. 'I can probably guess,' Ray says. 'You blaming that on Cameron?'

Nate spreads his hands. 'She's the one who made me like this. Hating her is all I have left.' Ray sees the tremor in his hands, and Nate quickly clasps them to cover it. 'Where is she now?'

'Not here,' Ray says. 'And she isn't coming. Considering what you did to her, you should consider yourself lucky.'

'I don't get what you mean.' Nate's face pales, then goes red like he's having a hot flash. He knows he's being played, but he can't work out how, and that's making him nervous.

'You didn't let me finish telling you why I came here.'

Ray's coffee arrives. He nods at the waitress but doesn't touch it.

'I came to bear witness,' he says. 'I came to let you know that if there was anything you wanted to say, I'm willing to hear it.'

The silence lies heavy across the table as Nate takes that in. Ray watches as he works his mouth, his chin jerking as the internal dialogue plays its course. He knows as well as Ray does that there's no way out. All he has to do now is come to terms with it.

'Homeland?' Nate asks.

Ray says nothing. Standard cop procedure.

'I can still be useful to them.' He can't hide the edge of desperation in his voice.

'No, you can't,' Ray says. 'You sold it to them as a quick, quiet snatch and grab with minimal resistance. What they got was a dozen men killed, another dozen injured, an official complaint from the Marine Corps about requisition of resources, and the uncontrolled demolition of a building on the edge of the city that put every emergency service on terror alert for two days straight. You're not useful, Nate. You're persona non grata.' Ray lifts his coffee and thinks better of it, setting it back down perfectly on the pale coffee-circle mark it had left on the table. 'That's Latin for a fuck-up.'

Nate's expression twists into one of disgust. He's brick-red in the face now, and he works a finger into his shirt collar, trying to ease it loose. 'So fucking proud of yourself. You think you'll come away clean from all this?'

'I don't think,' Ray says. 'I know I will. They did a sweep through the precinct, interviews for everyone who might have seen or heard something about what happened out at Carrington. I mentioned your name and all doors were opened. I cut a deal: help them find you, and everything goes away. My family get to go home, and I can go back to work with a clean sheet.'

'They won't let you go that easily.'

Ray shrugs. 'See, I thought that too, but they really, really want this to disappear, and as far as my part in this is concerned, sending me back to my captain with a vague but glowing commendation was their preferred outcome.' He leans forward.

The waitress comes with Ray's pancakes, and she looks down at Ray's full cup. 'Something wrong with the coffee, hon?'

'Not at all.' Ray keeps his eyes on Nate as he talks. 'I just wanted to check with you to make sure I'm not getting poisoned into the bargain.'

The waitress sighs. 'We're the FBI, not the CIA.'

Across from Ray, Nate splutters and jumps in his seat. The waitress has a gun in his face before he can do anything else, and three more guns appear seconds later, all trained on him.

'Nathan King,' the waitress says. 'You are under arrest for the murder of Sam Gorton.' She steps aside as one of the men pulls Nate out of the booth, and instead of standing he simply falls sideways out of the booth and on to the floor with a crash. None of the other diners react. As the man kneels on Nate's back to cuff him, they stay on their marks, going through the motions of a normal morning routine of eggs and coffee and idle conversation.

Ray doesn't move from where he's sitting. He stares straight ahead, picking out the tiny cracks in the upholstery as he listens to the waitress read Nate King his rights, feeling the weight of the badge in his pocket. Homeland washed their hands of the whole thing. Carrington Medical's stock took a hit at the news of a terror attack, but their global brand had bounced back stronger for it. Nate's arrest is the best he could get, and for all the satisfaction it gives him, Ray can't help but feel like he's been thrown the smallest fish in the sack to keep him quiet. He sighs and picks up his fork, digging into the first of the pancakes. 'Never knew the FBI did breakfast,' he says.

'That's eight ninety-five,' the waitress says.

He stops digging with the fork and looks up at her. 'You're shitting me.'

'Plus tip.' She's probably been in that get-up since seven a.m. to keep the pretense up, and looks like she wouldn't be above calling in the CIA to poison Ray for stiffing her on the bill.

'I didn't bring any cash,' he says. 'You take cards?'

The waitress turns and looks back at the counter. Ray follows her gaze to where a large cardboard sign proclaims *CASH ONLY*. She turns back and shakes her head at him.

'The dishes are in the back, Officer Perada,' she says.

Ray sighs, nods, and steps out of the booth, rolling up his sleeves as he heads for the back.

and orange as though his crucifixion burns like the sun. One of the murals catches her eye – an angel kneeling before Mary, one hand pointing to heaven, the other holding a flower between them. The angel's face and chest are delicate, as frail as they are human. The rest of it is not. Its legs are vast, hidden to Mary by the folds of its robes; its wings stand proud behind it, half-obscured by the angel itself, reaching far beyond the limits of the frame. Clouds roil around it, surrounding its feet, framing it as something wholly other than the human face it shows to the world.

Cameron closes and opens her left hand, feeling the tendons shifting beneath her skin. The chip Carrington put in her – the tracer – will never come out. All she can do is hope that all the data on how to access it was destroyed along with Carrington's server. Carrington Medical still exist as a company, but their brush with Homeland has blunted their ambition. Their stock rallied in the wave of support that followed the 'attack' on their building, but it doesn't look like they're going to rebuild anytime soon.

Sometimes when she sleeps, Cameron imagines that she's still stuck in that basement, with Miller's grinning face hanging over her as he presses the button on a remote control over and over, the paralysis creeping across her chest, suffocating her. She has nightmares about being caught in the collapse, Samson's weight holding her fast as his fist comes down on her hard enough that it drops the building around them. Tracking down Nate was hard work, even with the FBI's help, but it gave her something to do when she couldn't sleep anymore. Cameron looks up at the storm clouds that surround the angel's head, and wonders if maybe they're not his wrath at all. Maybe they're haunting him. Mary's face is enigmatic, making no promise of sanctuary. Or forgiveness.

She hears Ray coming, his footsteps unmistakable on the flagstones, and Cameron lets him walk all the way up to her before turning to acknowledge him. He's got a bag from a bakery in one hand, and coffee in a disposable cup in the other.

'I don't think you're meant to have those in here,' she says.

'That's the joy of confession,' Ray says. 'God forgives everything, even the little things.'

'Does he?' Cameron looks up at the angel standing over Mary again, and feels nothing but a coldness, as though the peace they both offer isn't intended for her.

'More than man, at any rate.'

'They picked up Nate?'

'This morning.'

'What's going to happen to him?' she asks. She could have let Nate go. It wouldn't have been impossible. Here at the altar, that thought feels like a lead weight on her soul. Even though he'd come close to killing her, she still feels guilty.

'Twenty to life in supermax,' Ray says.

'He won't last five,' Cameron says.

'You ask me, he still lucked out.'

'How'd you figure?'

'Between you, me, and this bag of Danish?' Ray leans closer, his voice dropping. 'Homeland wanted him gone. Erased. Boston PD would have found a partial skeleton near where your car crashed. Bleached, broken, covered in tooth marks from scavengers, but they'd have been able to identify them. Coroner would have ruled that he was thrown from the car and killed instantly, that the snow prevented the search

333

from finding him.' He stands straight again. 'Spend the rest of his days on a bed in an infirmary watching daytime TV? He got off light.'

Cameron can feel tears prickling at the corner of her vision. They're unexpected, but not unwelcome. She can imagine the relief her family would have felt if that had happened. Grief is easier to recover from than betrayal.

Ray waits until she recovers before offering her the pastry and the coffee. 'I thought you might need these,' he says.

Cameron laughs and wipes at her eyes. 'Thanks, Ray.'

'So what are you going to do now?' he asks.

'I could go home.' Cameron says it, just for the feel of it. She misses her friends. She misses the training, the life she had. She even misses the physiotherapy, God help her.

'You could stay here.' Ray says it simply, a statement of fact. A possibility.

'I could do that.' Cameron takes a deep, shuddering breath. She feels lost, like every tether that had held her life in place has been torn loose.

'Split the difference,' Ray says. 'Buy a field in the middle of nowhere. Build a ranch miles from the nearest phone line and raise cattle.'

'Make a good show of staying out of things, you mean?'

'It's just one idea.' Ray looks at her. Neither of them says it, but she knows that someone from Homeland or the FBI has been shadowing her. There's one of them in the church right now, sitting at the back, incongruous with his close-cropped hair and designer peacoat.

'Can you imagine them allocating satellite time to a patch of nowhere? Keep me pinned in the dirt like a bug mounted for show.' Cameron goes to take a swig of the coffee but the figure of Christ catches her eye and she lowers the cup, feeling guilty for trying. 'No thank you.'

'You planning on disappearing, Cam?' Ray says it softly, as though Cameron's shadow can hear him.

'I was thinking about that,' she says. 'But nobody can disappear forever. Nothing gets lost that can't be found again.'

'So what's the plan?'

'It's Saturday,' Cameron says. She sees Ray's confusion and throws him a wink. 'It's fight night.'

It's tough work getting past all of the layers of security that keep fans and creeps clear behind the scenes, but where Cameron's name falls short Ray's badge picks up the slack. There's a final hurdle as Ophelia's team try not to let her past the door of the locker room she's using, but Ophelia herself deals with that by hauling them out of the way and dragging Cameron inside.

'Cameron King,' Ophelia says. She's not started her warm-up yet, still dressed in loose sweatpants and a top with her own name plastered across it. Her hands are taped up, ready for the gloves. 'Look at you. You look like you got a building dropped on you.'

'You say that . . .'

Ophelia's eyes widen. 'You didn't.' She walks Cameron away from her entourage, her voice dropping low. 'That shit with the building going down? That was you?'

'It was the people who shot up your house,' Cameron says, 'but I was there.'

335

'You kicked their asses, right?' Ophelia nods, a smile breaking wide on her face. 'Right? You kicked their asses, didn't you?'

Cameron shrugs, feels suddenly shy in the face of her friend's enthusiasm. 'Yeah, Ophelia. I did.'

'YES!' She runs to the far wall, and hammers on the broad white tiles with her fist. 'Pickaxe! Hey! Can you hear me through there?' She waits, listening carefully, and a faint voice answers with something that sounds like '*What is it?*'

Ophelia pounds on the wall again. 'Cam's here!'

'*WHAT?*'

There's a lot of noise from the corridor, and then Sophia barrels in through the door, trailing a handful of outraged officials, to cross the room and haul Cameron off of her feet and crush her with a hug.

'Hey,' Ophelia says, 'be careful with her sling.' Cameron tries to agree, but all she can manage is a groan. It's like being crushed by a hydraulic press of affection.

'Fuck the sling,' Sophia answers before putting Cameron down and grinning at her like the devil herself. 'Which one of us are you walking down to the ring, Cam?'

Cameron looks from one fighter to the other. Both of them are smiling expectantly at her. *Shit.* She holds up her good hand, backing out of the stand-off. 'Look, I just wanted to come by and say good luck—'

'You should hand over the belt!' Sophia says, almost shouting in her excitement. 'It's here in the building! We can get you down in the ring and make a whole thing of it.' Cameron never lost to either of them, and when the crash took her out of the business she still held it undefeated.

Handing it over won't mean anything officially, but it's a great piece of theatre. Cameron isn't keen, but if it goes viral, then both women will likely see a better payday off of the back of it.

'I do owe you a new door.'

Sophia nods. 'Damn right you do. You need a change of clothes?'

The walk down to the ring is chaos. Ophelia okayed it with the fight promoter, but they agreed not to tell the announcer that Cameron was coming out to the ring. The instant she clears the doorway she can hear him yelling into his mic – '*Ladies and gentlemen, it's the champion herself, it's Cameron "The Hunter" King*' – and the crowd starts cheering and whistling like she's never heard before in her life.

By the time she gets to the cage doors, Cameron is dizzy with the sound of it, the noise giving way to stamping feet and a chant of her name – '*King, King, King, King*' – over and over, filling the arena to the roof.

She's got the belt over one shoulder, and when she gets to the center of the ring she knows what she is meant to do: lay it on the mat and step back from it, leaving it for Sophia and Ophelia to fight over. Both of them are standing watching her, warm now for the fight, skin shining with sweat, bobbing light on their feet and itching to go. Sophia grins, her mouthguard a wedge of blue smiling at her, and Cameron looks the other way to see Ophelia sporting the same in red.

You pair of bitches. They knew what bringing her down here would do to the crowd, and what it would do to her. It's fight night, and she can feel the excitement of it like adrenaline

337

coursing through her. She motions for a microphone, and the ref brings it to her.

'You want this?' Cameron asks the question, looking from one woman to the other. They both nod, as keen as she is. For the first time since the building came down, Cameron knows who she is. Who she has always been. She's a fighter.

Cameron drops the belt off her shoulder, slipping free of the sling to catch and heft it in her right hand. 'Then come and get it.'

Acknowledgements

It takes a lot of time and effort to make a book happen, and a great deal of that is provided by other people. First among all of them is my agent, Juliet Mushens. I signed as her client hoping to develop a strong professional partnership. Instead, I gained an amazing friend who has worked tirelessly to champion my writing to everyone who will hear it. None of this would have been possible without her.

A massive thank-you is due to my editor, Toby Jones, whose boundless enthusiasm has made working with Headline a genuine joy. Thanks also to the rest of the Headline team for both their warm welcome and for putting their collective shoulders to the wheel to turn out an amazing book.

Thank you to Jen Williams, my writing BFF, for always being there when I need a hand shoveling in the salt mines.

Special thanks go to Alasdair Stuart and Den Patrick for being relentlessly upbeat and always ready to enable my wildest ideas, and to the rest of Team CaskieMushens for being the greatest support network and hype team an author could ever hope for.

A huge thank-you to my brother, Alistair Reid, for being a

razor-sharp alpha reader, an endless idea generator, and a literal lifesaver. Thank you to my beta readers, Emma Maree and Rob for taking the time to read an early version of the book and drop some truth on me about it.

Thanks to my parents for all of their support, and for putting up with my childhood habit of buying every withdrawn library book I could find, and to Eva-Britt and Toshihiro for all of their patience with a son-in-law who spends most of his time staring at a notebook.

Finally, thank you to my children, Aoife and Eilidh, for reminding me that there is always more than just the book, and to my wife Lisa, for telling me to stop talking about the idea of a book and try writing one instead.

THRILLINGLY GOOD BOOKS
FROM CRIMINALLY
GOOD WRITERS

CRIME FILES BRINGS YOU THE LATEST RELEASES FROM
TOP CRIME AND THRILLER AUTHORS.

GN UP ONLINE FOR OUR MONTHLY NEWSLETTER AND BE THE FIRST
TO KNOW ABOUT OUR COMPETITIONS, NEW BOOKS AND MORE.

VISIT OUR WEBSITE: WWW.CRIMEFILES.CO.UK
LIKE US ON FACEBOOK: FACEBOOK.COM/CRIMEFILES
FOLLOW US ON TWITTER: @CRIMEFILESBOOKS